Honoring America

> **For Americans, the flag has always had a special meaning. It is a symbol of our nation's freedom and democracy.**

Flag Etiquette

Over the years, Americans have developed rules and customs concerning the use and display of the flag. One of the most important things every American should remember is to treat the flag with respect.

- The flag should be raised and lowered by hand and displayed only from sunrise to sunset. On special occasions, the flag may be displayed at night, but it should be illuminated.

- The flag may be displayed on all days, weather permitting, particularly on national and state holidays and on historic and special occasions.

- No flag may be flown above the American flag or to the right of it at the same height.

- The flag should never touch the ground or floor beneath it.

- The flag may be flown at half-staff by order of the president, usually to mourn the death of a public official.

- The flag may be flown upside down only to signal distress.

- The flag should never be carried flat or horizontally, but always carried aloft and free.

- When the flag becomes old and tattered, it should be destroyed by burning. According to an approved custom, the Union (stars on blue field) is first cut from the flag; then the two pieces, which no longer form a flag, are burned.

★ ★ ★ ★ ★ ★ ★ ★

The American's Creed

I believe in the United States of America as a Government of the people, by the people, for the people, whose just powers are derived from the consent of the governed; a democracy in a republic; a sovereign Nation of many sovereign States; a perfect union, one and inseparable; established upon those principles of freedom, equality, justice, and humanity for which American patriots sacrificed their lives and fortunes.

I therefore believe it is my duty to my Country to love it; to support its Constitution; to obey its laws; to respect its flag, and to defend it against all enemies.

The Pledge of Allegiance

I pledge allegiance to the Flag of the United States of America and to the Republic for which it stands, one Nation under God, indivisible, with liberty and justice for all.

The Star-Spangled Banner

O! say, can you see, by the dawn's early light,
What so proudly we hail'd at the twilight's last gleaming?
Whose broad stripes and bright stars, thro' the perilous fight,
O'er the ramparts we watched were so gallantly streaming?
And the rockets' red glare, the bombs bursting in air,
Gave proof thro' the night, that our flag was still there.
O! say, does that Star-Spangled Banner yet wave
O'er the land of the free and the home of the brave?

On the shore, dimly seen thro' the mist of the deep,
Where the foe's haughty host in dread silence reposes,
What is that which the breeze, o'er the towering steep,
As it fitfully blows, half conceals, half discloses?
Now it catches the gleam of the morning's first beam,
In full glory reflected now shines on the stream.
'Tis the Star-Spangled Banner. O long may it wave
O'er the land of the free and the home of the brave.

And where is that band who so vauntingly swore,
That the havoc of war and the battle's confusion
A home and a country should leave us no more?
Their blood has wash'd out their foul footstep's pollution.
No refuge could save the hireling and slave
From the terror of flight or the gloom of the grave,
And the Star-Spangled Banner in triumph doth wave
O'er the land of the free and the home of the brave.

O thus be it e'er when free men shall stand
Between their lov'd home and war's desolation,
Blest with vict'ry and peace, may the Heav'n-rescued land
Praise the pow'r that hath made and preserv'd us a nation.
Then conquer we must, when our cause it is just,
And this be our motto, "In God is our Trust."
And the Star-Spangled Banner in triumph shall wave
O'er the land of the free and the home of the brave.

Civics Today

Citizenship, Economics, & You

Richard C. Remy, Ph.D.

John J. Patrick, Ph.D.

David C. Saffell, Ph.D.

Gary E. Clayton, Ph.D.

**Glencoe
McGraw-Hill**

New York, New York   Columbus, Ohio   Chicago, Illinois   Peoria, Illinois   Woodland Hills, California

Richard C. Remy, Ph.D., is Professor Emeritus in the College of Education, The Ohio State University, and Senior Consultant on Civic Education with the Mershon Center for International Security and Public Policy at Ohio State. He received his Ph.D. in political science from Northwestern University. His books include: *United States Government: Democracy in Action, Building Civic Education for Democracy in Poland, American Government and National Security,* and *Lessons on the Constitution.* In the 1990s Dr. Remy created and codirected a long-term project with the Polish Ministry of National Education and the Center for Citizenship Education, Warsaw to develop new civic education programs for Polish students, teachers, and teacher educators.

John J. Patrick, Ph.D., is a professor in the School of Education at Indiana University, Bloomington, where he also is Director of the Social Studies Development Center and Director of the ERIC Clearinghouse for Social Studies/Social Science Education. He is the author or coauthor of many publications about civics and government, such as *The Oxford Guide to the United States Government* and *The Supreme Court of the United States: A Student Companion* (published by Oxford University Press in 2001).

David C. Saffell, Ph.D., received his Ph.D. in political science from the University of Minnesota. He has taught at Ohio Northern University since 1972, serving as chair of the Social Science Division for 15 years. Professor Saffell is coauthor of *State of Local Government: Politics and Public*

Policies, 7th edition, published by McGraw-Hill. He has authored and edited several other books dealing with American government.

Gary E. Clayton, Ph.D., currently teaches economics at Northern Kentucky University. He received his Ph.D. in economics from the University of Utah, has taught economics and finance at several universities, and has authored a number of books and articles in professional journals. Dr. Clayton appeared on numerous radio and television programs and was a guest commentator for Marketplace for American Public Radio. Dr. Clayton has a long-standing interest in economic education. He has participated in numerous economic education workshops, is a National Council on Economic Education Kazanjian award winner, and is former vice president of the Kentucky Council on Economic Education. Dr. Clayton most recently received a year 2000 Leavey Award for Excellence in Private Enterprise Education from the Freedoms Foundation at Valley Forge.

Contributing Author

Gordon P. Whitaker, Ph.D., is widely recognized as an authority on local government and on civic education. Dr. Whitaker received his Ph.D. at Indiana University and has taught at the University of North Carolina at Chapel Hill since 1973. He is professor of public administration and government in UNC's School of Government. He is also the author of a textbook supplement, *Local Government in North Carolina.*

Glencoe/McGraw-Hill

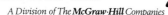

A Division of The **McGraw·Hill** Companies

TIME Reports and TIME Teens in Action © Time Inc. Prepared by TIME Learning Ventures in collaboration with Glencoe/McGraw-Hill. TIME and the red border design are trademarks of Time Inc. used under license.

Street Law™ The Law and You © Street Law, Inc. Prepared by Street Law, Inc. in collaboration with Glencoe/McGraw-Hill.

Send all inquiries to:

Glencoe/McGraw-Hill, 8787 Orion Place, Columbus, Ohio 43240-4027

ISBN 0-07-825989-4 (Student Edition), ISBN 0-07-825990-8 (Teacher Wraparound Edition)

Printed in the United States of America.

7 8 9 10 058/043 08 07 06 05 04

Academic Consultants

Dr. Godwin C. Duru
Associate Professor of Economics
Ohio Dominican College
Columbus, Ohio

Dr. Sanford D. Gordon
Adjunct Professor of Economics
University of South Florida
Sarasota, Florida

Dr. Robert L. Hardgrave
Temple Professor Emeritus of the
  Humanities
University of Texas at Austin
Austin, Texas

Dr. Leslie Horowitz
Assistant Professor of History
Hobart and William Smith Colleges
Geneva, New York

Dr. William E. Nelson, Jr.
Research Professor of Black Studies
  and Professor of Political Science
The Ohio State University
Columbus, Ohio

Dr. Charles E. Walcott
Professor of Political Science
Virginia Polytechnic Institute and State
  University
Blacksburg, Virginia

Bluma Zuckerbrot-Finkelstein
Consultant/Instructor, Middle Eastern
  and International Affairs
University of Memphis
Memphis, Tennessee

FOLDABLES Dinah Zike
Educational Consultant
Dinah-Might Activities, Inc.
San Antonio, Texas

Consultant/Reviewer

The North Carolina City and County Management Association
Raleigh, North Carolina

Teacher Reviewers

Michael Bremer
Social Studies Department Chair
Sandusky Middle School
Lynchburg, Virginia

Virginia L. Corbett
Teacher
Crestwood Middle School
Chesapeake, Virginia

Ashlee L. Dixon
Social Studies Department Chair
Centennial Campus Middle School
Raleigh, North Carolina

Robert Garland
History Teacher
Selma Middle School
Selma, North Carolina

Carol Catoe Hinson
Language Arts and Social Studies
  Teacher
Brawley Middle School
Mooresville, North Carolina

Sue Hollifield
Teacher
Bessemer City Middle School
Bessemer City, North Carolina

Colin W. Lowry
Assistant Principal
Dillard Drive Middle School
Raleigh, North Carolina

Denny Schillings
Instructor
Homewood-Flossmoor High School
Flossmoor, Illinois

Alan C. Willard
Teacher
Belgrade High School
Belgrade, Montana

Melissa Wood
Teacher
F.J. Carnage GT Magnet Middle School
Raleigh, North Carolina

TABLE OF CONTENTS

Jefferson Memorial in
Washington, D.C.

A crowd looks out at the Statue of Liberty.

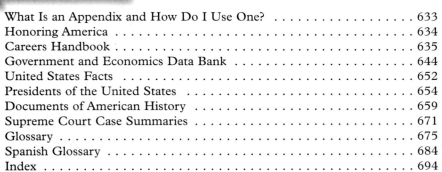

★ APPENDIX

FEATURES

TIME

Proudly displaying American flags

Fact Fiction Folklore

STREET LAW™ The Law and You

American ★ Biographies

César E. Chávez

SKILLBUILDER

Issues to Debate

Students wearing school uniforms

Illuminated manuscript, Middle Ages

$ Economics and You

DOCUMENTS OF AMERICAN HISTORY

Landmark Supreme Court Case Studies

The Tinkers show their armbands.

CHARTS, GRAPHS, AND MAPS

Charts and Graphs

UNIT 6 ⭐

UNIT 7 ⭐

UNIT 8 ⭐

Maps

UNIT 1 ⭐

UNIT 2 ⭐

UNIT 4 ⭐

UNIT 6 ⭐

UNIT 7 ⭐

UNIT 8 ⭐

REFERENCE ATLAS

NATIONAL GEOGRAPHIC

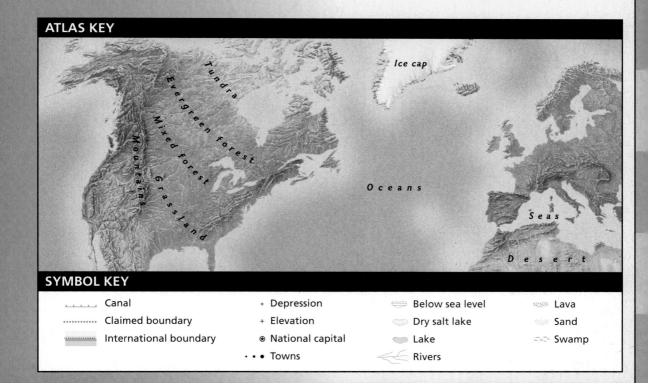

ATLAS KEY

Ice cap

Tundra

Evergreen forest

Mixed forest

Mountains

Grassland

Oceans

Seas

Desert

SYMBOL KEY

⊥⊥⊥⊥ Canal	∘ Depression	⬭ Below sea level	⬳ Lava	
·········· Claimed boundary	+ Elevation	⬭ Dry salt lake	⬳ Sand	
▓▓▓ International boundary	⊛ National capital	⬭ Lake	⋯⊃ Swamp	
	• • • Towns	⬱ Rivers		

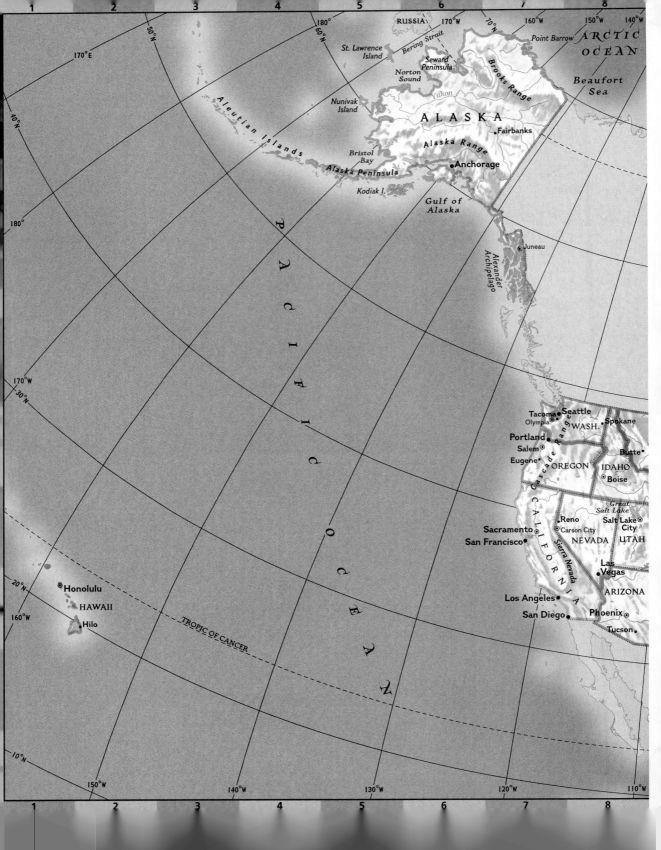

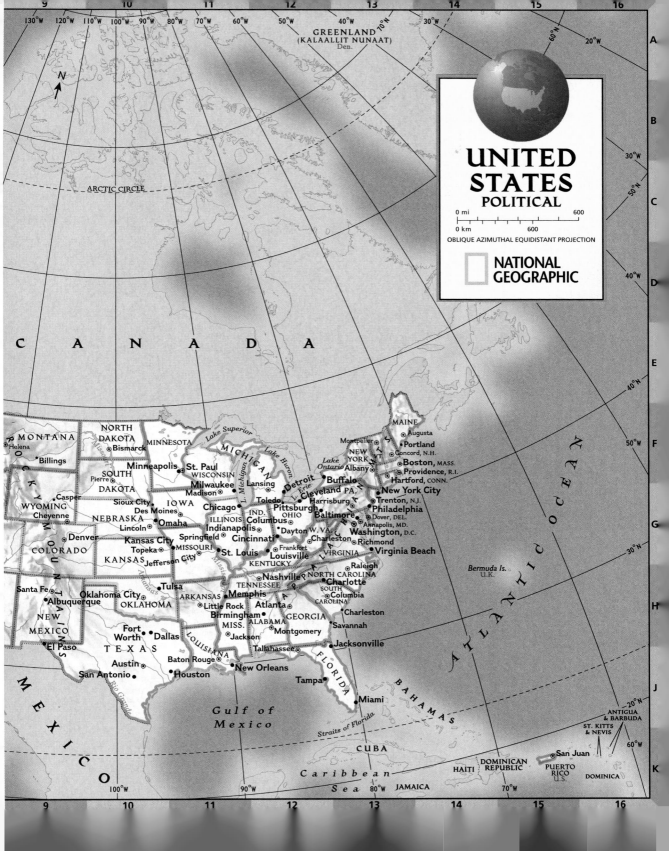

UNITED STATES POLITICAL

OBLIQUE AZIMUTHAL EQUIDISTANT PROJECTION

NATIONAL GEOGRAPHIC

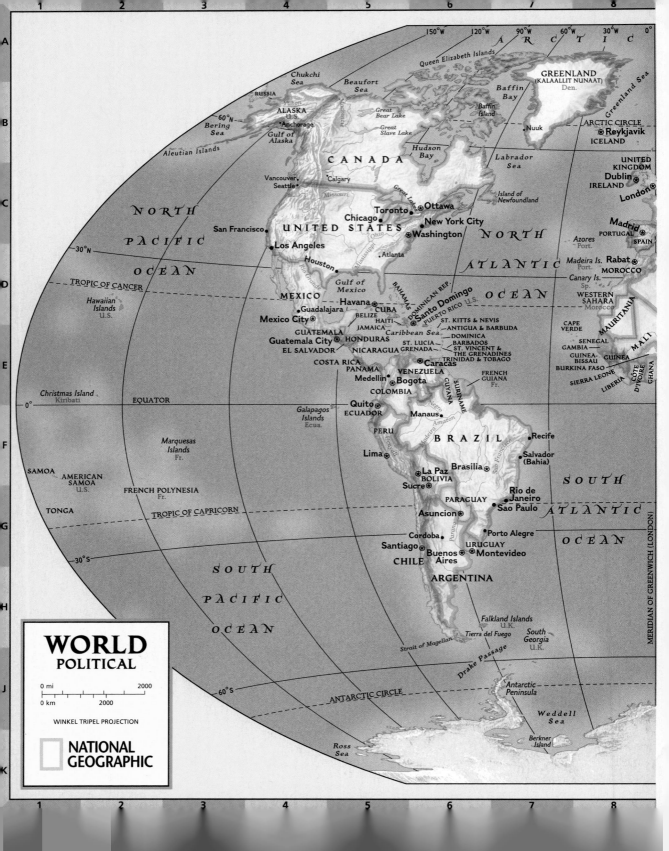

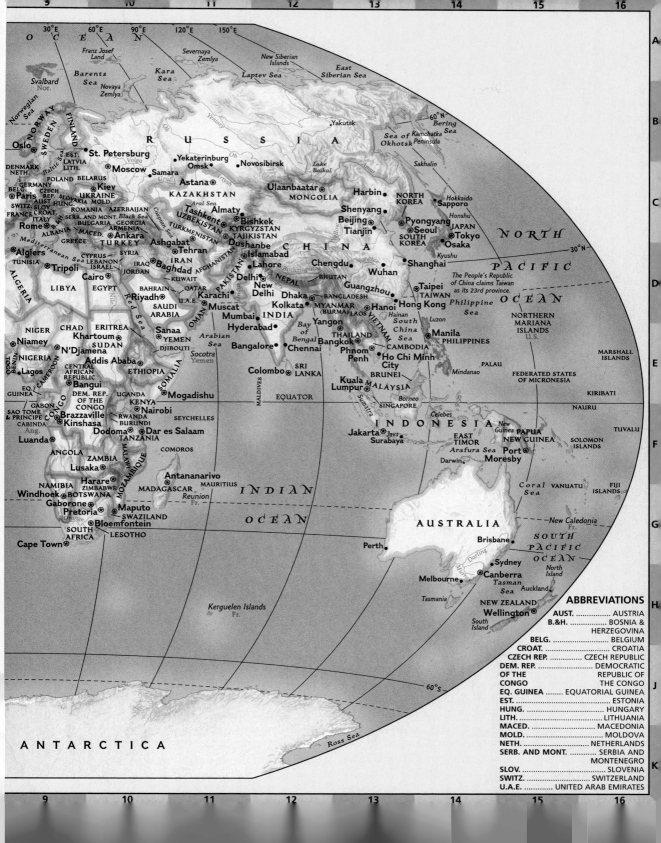

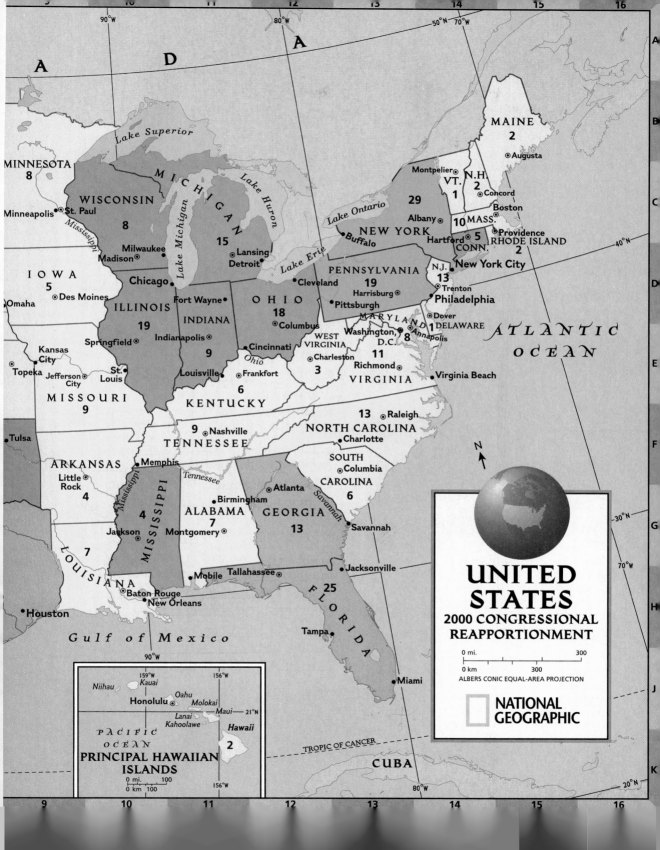

Be an Active Reader

Think about your textbook as a tool that helps you learn more about the world around you. It is an example of nonfiction writing—it describes real-life events, people, ideas, and places. Here is a menu of reading strategies that will help you become a better textbook reader. As you come to passages in your textbook that you don't understand, refer to these reading strategies for help.

✓ Before You Read

Set a purpose
- Why are you reading the textbook?
- How does the subject relate to your life?
- How might you be able to use what you learn in your own life?

Preview
- Read the chapter title to find what the topic will be.
- Read the subtitles to see what you will learn about the topic.
- Skim the photos, charts, graphs, or maps. How do they support the topic?
- Look for vocabulary words that are boldfaced. How are they defined?

Draw From Your Own Background
- What have you read or heard concerning new information on the topic?
- How is the new information different from what you already know?
- How will the information that you already know help you understand the new information?

Question

- What is the main idea?
- How do the photos, charts, graphs, and maps support the main idea?

Connect

- Think about people, places, and events in your own life. Are there any similarities with those in your textbook?
- Can you relate the textbook information to other areas of your life?

Predict

- Predict events or outcomes by using clues and information that you already know.
- Change your predictions as you read and gather new information.

Visualize

- Pay careful attention to details and descriptions.
- Create graphic organizers to show relationships that you find in the information.

α Clues : Pistas   α gather : Recolectar

Look For Clues As You Read

Comparisons and Contrast Sentences

- Look for clue words and phrases that signal comparison, such as *similarly, just as, both, in common, also,* and *too.*
- Look for clue words and phrases that signal contrast, such as *on the other hand, in contrast to, however, different, instead of, rather than, but,* and *unlike.*

Cause-and-Effect Sentences

- Look for clue words and phrases such as *because, as a result, therefore, that is why, since, so, for this reason,* and *consequently.*

Chronological Sentences

- Look for clue words and phrases such as *after, before, first, next, last, during, finally, earlier, later, since,* and *then.*

α rather than : Más bien que   α Unlike : Diferente a

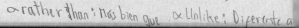

After You Read

Summarize

- Describe the main idea and how the details support it.
- Use your own words to explain what you have read.

Assess

- What was the main idea?
- Did the text clearly support the main idea?
- Did you learn anything new from the material?
- Can you use this new information in other school subjects or at home?
- What other sources could you use to find more information about the topic?

α Assess : Evaluar

BE AN ACTIVE
★ CITIZEN ★

As American citizens, we have certain rights, such as the right to freely express our opinions and the right to practice our religion. As American citizens, we also have certain duties. We are required to obey our nation's laws, serve on juries, pay taxes, and defend our nation whenever necessary. However, good citizenship does not depend on each of us doing *only* what we are required by law to do. The American ideal of citizenship has always stressed each citizen's responsibility to participate in the community and in the different levels of government.

a Stressed: Experiencing mental α Duties: Deberes.
or emotional strain or tension.

What is Good Citizenship?

A key part of being a good citizen is taking an active and engaged role in your community. You make a difference by engaging in community service where your efforts are needed, valued, and respected. Service learning is one way you can help your community. As you read, think about these questions:

- What exactly is service learning?
- Why should I participate?
- How do I get involved?

What exactly is service learning?

Performing important tasks that meet real community needs forms the basis of service learning. Service learning projects are organized as a partnership between your school and your community. Examples of these projects are refurbishing parks, teaching younger children to read, and sharing your time with nursing home residents. Service learning

α Refurbishing : Remodelation -

requires an investment of your time as well as your talents. You and your team play an active role in planning the project and deciding how to use your skills and talents to complete your tasks.

Why should I participate?

Service learning is challenging, but you can make a difference. You share your knowledge and skills to help others in your school and your community. At the same time, you develop new skills and cultivate new knowledge. A well-planned project also gives you opportunities to practice your rights and responsibilities as a citizen. You take part in setting the goals of the project. You decide what you will do and how you will do it. An effective service learning project also provides time to share your thoughts about the service experience with others.

Volunteer Opportunities

✔ Read to an elderly person
✔ Collect litter in your school yard
✔ Recycle at home
✔ Circulate a petition
✔ Put up a poster announcing Earth Day
✔ Bring groceries to a shut-in

How do I get involved?

Many students are already taking part in service learning. Many more are looking for ways to serve. National organizations such as AmeriCorps, Learn and Serve America, and the National Senior Service are always looking for volunteers. Look for local chapters of these organizations to investigate opportunities to participate. The USA Freedom Corps provides an easy-to-use Web site that helps you find local opportunities with a service organization. By exploring the needs of your community, you can plan and organize your own service learning project.

Why Study Civics?

President *Abraham Lincoln* once said that we have a government "*of the people, by the people, and for the people.*" What does this mean to you? This means that the United States government and the society it governs—you, your family, your friends, your fellow Americans—relies on the knowledge and skills of that society to operate and to operate well. The United States government is a democracy, which means that the ultimate power of the government rests with the people—you and me.

Democracies cannot simply exist; they require the participation of citizens.

As an American, you fill many roles. For example, you are a citizen and a consumer. The study of civics will help you play these roles well. Understanding how the government operates and how you can participate in it will help you become a responsible and informed citizen. Understanding the basic economic principles of the American market system will help you learn how to make wise economic decisions.

Civics National Content Standards

*The **Center for Civic Education** is a nonprofit, nonpartisan organization that seeks to educate Americans so they can become responsible and active citizens. Since our American democracy needs responsible and informed citizens to survive, the Center for Civic Education has identified five standards that describe what you should know after studying civics.*

I. What Are Civic Life, Politics, and Government? Your involvement with your local community, state, and nation is your civic life. This is a different part of your life than the time you spend on private and personal interests. Politics is a process by which a group of people with different interests and opinions reach decisions, which are then enforced. Government includes the people and institutions in a society that have the authority to create, carry out, and enforce laws, as well as settle disputes over laws.

II. What Are the Foundations of the American Political System? Our system of government is based on the U.S. Constitution, a document that is more than 200 years old. Our government, though, must rely on our knowledge and commitment to the values and principles found in the Constitution to fulfill its purposes—to protect the inalienable rights of the individual to life, liberty, and property and to promote the common good.

III. How Does the Government Established by the Constitution Embody the Purposes, Values, and Principles of American Democracy? All Americans live under three levels of government—local, state, and national governments. All of these governments have powers and responsibilities that are divided and shared among different branches and agencies. All of these governments affect your life every day; however, you also have the power to influence all of these governments.

IV. What Is the Relationship of the United States to Other Nations and to World Affairs? The world is divided into nation-states. Each nation-state claims authority over a defined territory and the people within that territory. The United States, the nation-state in which you live, interacts with other nation-states. How our country interacts and handles disputes with other nation-states affects our government and our lives.

V. What Are the Roles of the Citizen in American Democracy? Every citizen is an equal member of our American system of democracy. This means that we have certain rights and responsibilities. We must all protect individual rights and promote the common good. We must also make certain that our government serves the purposes for which it was created.

× Nonpartisan: No partidista
× Seek: Buscar
× Carry out: Realizar

× Settle: Asentarse
× Affairs: Asuntos
× Handles: Manejas.

Foundations
of American
Citizenship

Why It Matters

As citizens, we enjoy the rewards of our system of government, but we also have certain responsibilities. By participating in your government, you can help ensure that our system will continue to provide the blessings of life, liberty, and the pursuit of happiness. In Unit 1, you will learn about the citizens of the United States and how our democratic system of government developed.

 Use the **American History Primary Source Document Library CD-ROM** to find primary sources about Americans and the foundations of their citizenship.

Blessings: Bendiciones

 BE AN ACTIVE CITIZEN

Find out the purposes of your government firsthand. Contact a government leader, such as a state representative, a city council member, or a school board member, and ask how the government he or she represents serves American citizens.

Leader: Líder   *School board member: Miembro de la junta escolar.*

A ticker tape parade
in New York City

Citizenship and Government in a Democracy

★ CITIZENSHIP AND YOU ★

Our government protects our rights and provides us with benefits. Our responsibilities include knowing how our government works and how it affects our lives. Contact the offices of your local government to find out what issues officials are dealing with now and how they affect you.

To learn more about the roles government plays in our lives, view the **Democracy in Action** video lesson 1: Government and Our Lives.

FOLDABLES™ Study Organizer

Organizing Information Study Foldable *Make the following foldable to help you organize what you learn about citizenship and government in a democracy.*

Step 1 *Collect 2 sheets of paper and place them about 1 inch apart.*

Keep the edges straight.

Step 2 *Fold up the bottom edges of the paper to form 4 tabs.*

This makes all tabs the same size.

Reading and Writing *As you read the chapter, write the main ideas presented in each of the three sections of the chapter under the tabs of your foldable.*

Step 3 *When all the tabs are the same size, crease the paper to hold the tabs in place and staple the sheets together. Label each tab as shown.*

Staple together along the fold.

Citizenship & Government

Government of the People
Path to Citizenship
Diversity of Americans

∝ Edges 38 Bordes
∝ Straight 8 Rectos

A father and daughter at the swearing-in ceremony for U.S. citizenship ▶

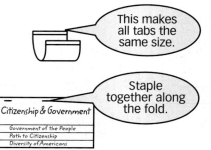

CIVICS Online

Chapter Overview Visit the *Civics Today* Web site at civ.glencoe.com and click on **Chapter Overviews—Chapter 1** to preview chapter information.

Government of the People, by the People, for the People

GUIDE TO READING

Main Idea
Democratic governments perform necessary functions so citizens can live together peacefully.

Key Terms
civics, citizen, government, public policy, budget, dictatorship, democracy, direct democracy, representative democracy, majority rule

Reading Strategy
Organizing Information Create a chart like the one below. Then list the levels of government, a function of each, and an example of the level and function in the correct columns.

Level	Function	Example

Read to Learn
- Why do people need governments?
- What purposes do governments serve?

★ ★ ★ ★

Americans in Action

When Americans vote or serve on a jury, their actions are based on ideas that people had in the fourth century B.C. In examining how people act, Aristotle wrote these words: "If liberty and equality, as is thought by some, are chiefly to be found in democracy, they will be best attained when all persons alike share in the government to the utmost."

Aristotle teaches

Chiefly: Principally, mainly, mostly   Alike: Equal, same, like
attained: Achieve, get, reach
utmost: higher, major, bigger

What Is Civics?

Civics is the study of the rights and duties of citizens. The concept of citizenship dates back more than 2,500 years to ancient Greece and Rome. In those days, only a few people—men with property—could be citizens. This elite group helped govern the city and enjoyed other privileges that the common people did not share.

Today gender and wealth are no longer requirements for citizenship. Indeed, most people are citizens of the country in which they live. **Citizens** have certain rights and duties. They are community members who owe loyalty to the government and are entitled to protection from it. However, being a citizen means much more than just living in a country. American citizens who live abroad are still citizens of the United States. Citizens are a part of a country. They may share a common history, common customs, or common values. They agree to follow a set of rules and to accept the government's authority.

Reading Check **Explaining** As a citizen, what do you agree to do?

Duties: Deberes
Indeed: Por supuesto
Duties: deber
Owe: Must, owe, job
loyalty: Allegiance, devotion
customs: Costumbre, comun

The Need for Government

A **government** is the ruling authority for a community. Any organization that has the power to make and enforce laws and decisions for its members acts as a government.

For hundreds of years, people have formed governments. Thomas Hobbes, an English political thinker during the 1600s, believed that without government life would be "solitary, poor, nasty, brutish, and short." Hobbes claimed that human beings naturally compete for territory, resources, and power. If each of us could do just as we pleased, fighting would be common, and survival would depend on strength and cunning.

Think about trying to play basketball with no rules or referees. How would players know what to do and what not to do? How would the winner be determined? The game would probably be a chaotic free-for-all. Similarly, if there were no government to make and enforce laws, we would live in a state of confusion, violence, and fear. We would also struggle to meet our needs entirely on our own. Fortunately, government can make it possible for people to live together peacefully and productively.

✓ Reading Check

Summarizing Why did Hobbes believe people needed governments?

The Functions of Government

Governments serve many purposes and offer citizens many benefits. They help keep order, settle conflicts, and protect the community.

They provide services that individuals could not supply independently. They also guide the community and plan for its future by setting policies, making budgets, and interacting with other communities.

Keeping Order and Providing Security

Conflicts are unavoidable when people live together in a community. Citizens may disagree on all sorts of matters—their choice of leaders, the best way to raise or spend money, the rightful owner of certain property, and so on. Governments make laws to help prevent conflicts and to settle those conflicts that do arise.

Governments have the power to enforce the laws. For example, to make sure that drivers obey traffic regulations,

Civic Participation Apple Valley High School students in Minnesota recite the Pledge of Allegiance. **How do you think reciting the pledge reflects citizenship?**

Chapter 1 Citizenship and Government in a Democracy **7**

police officers are empowered to ticket or arrest violators. Courts decide whether those accused of crimes are guilty and how they should be punished if found guilty.

Along with the need for law and order come concerns about community security—defending citizens and their land from enemies. Arrangements must be made to fight off possible threats. For this reason, governments set up armed forces and agencies that watch for likely sources of trouble.

Providing Public Services

Governments provide many services that would not be available without cooperation and coordination. Governments create and manage libraries, schools, hospitals, parks, and recreation centers. They develop systems to provide mass transit and supply water to our homes and businesses. Government workers build and repair streets, erect bridges, collect garbage, and deliver the mail.

Many government services are aimed at keeping the public healthy and safe. Local communities set up fire departments and ambulance services, for example. States license drivers and doctors. Other government agencies protect us from dangerous drugs or spoiled food. Government inspectors check for safety problems in everything from factories to day care centers to amusement park rides.

Governments also give help to needy people. For example, in each of the 50 states, poor families and people who are out of work can receive food aid or cash. Government agencies also supply affordable housing, health care, job training, and special programs for people with disabilities.

A banner created by American students after the terrorist attacks of September 2001

Functions of Government

KEEP ORDER	PROVIDE SERVICES
⭐ Pass and enforce traffic laws ⭐ Establish courts	⭐ Provide libraries, schools, hospitals, parks, water, utilities
PROVIDE SECURITY	**GUIDE THE COMMUNITY**
⭐ Prevent crime ⭐ Protect citizens from foreign attacks	⭐ Manage the economy ⭐ Conduct foreign relations

Evaluating Charts

Governments perform four major functions, as shown by the examples here. How do courts help keep order?

TIME

Political Cartoons

GET OFF MY BACK.

VOTER Demands Gov't

GOV'T.

and it seems to be diverted toward money and _ne_. Making the world a more convenient | Schneider, two men with little hope, of regaining the company's revenue. While the wage was | to be diverted tim

Analyzing Visuals Since our nation's earliest days, citizens have sought to balance the need for government services with the desire to be left alone. What statement is the voter making with his words? How do the voter's actions contradict his speech?

Guiding the Community

Another function of government is to formulate **public policy,** or a course of government action to achieve community goals. When government leaders decide they want to protect consumers, for example, or strengthen national security, they are setting public policy goals. When they pass laws or develop guidelines to reach these goals, they are making public policy.

Most public policy decisions involve some financial planning as well. Governments have limited amounts of money, and they must be careful to use it wisely. Creating a **budget,** or a plan for collecting and spending money, is key to the success of the community.

Another part of guiding the community is developing relations with the community's neighbors and other outsiders. Governments often take responsibility for communicating and cooperating with other governments for the benefit of their citizens. International trade, travel, and military pacts, or agreements—all part of

public policy—would be impossible if national governments did not concern themselves with foreign relations.

Reading Check **Concluding** Why is planning a budget important to a government's success?

Levels of Government

Within a single country, many levels of government may exist. Each exercises authority over a different group of people. The highest level in the United States is the national government, centered in the nation's capital, Washington, D.C. The national government makes and enforces laws for the entire country. Each of our 50 states has its own government as well, which decides matters for the people in that state. The level of government closest to Americans is local government. Local governments include counties, cities, and towns. Your school may have a student government, and if you choose to belong to a

club like Girl Scouts or 4-H, you respect that organization's governing body, too.

When people speak of "the government," they usually mean the national government. State and local governments, as well as governments of organizations, cannot take actions that go against the laws and authority of the national government.

Reading Check **Comparing** How do the general duties of the national government differ from those of state governments?

Democratic Government

In some parts of the world, governmental power lies in the hands of just a small group or even a single person. For example, the government of Cuba is a dictatorship. A **dictatorship** is a government controlled by one person or a small group of people. In the United States, all citizens share in governing and being governed. This kind of government, in which the people rule, is called a **democracy.**

The foundations of democracy are more than 2,500 years old. Democracy began in ancient Greece, most famously in the city of Athens. Every citizen of Athens had the right and responsibility to participate in the city's government, and all citizens had an equal voice. This was a **direct democracy**—all the citizens met to debate government matters and vote firsthand. Direct democracy is not practical for most countries today because of their large sizes and large populations. Many countries have **representative democracies** instead. The citizens choose a smaller group to represent them, make laws, and govern on their behalf, but the people remain the source of the government's authority.

The United States is the oldest representative democracy in the world. For more than 225 years, Americans have elected presidents, members of Congress, and other leaders to speak for them. Citizens express their views in person, over the phone, by e-mail and regular "snail" mail, and through public opinion polls and political groups. In later chapters you will read more about how you can participate in government and about your rights and responsibilities as a citizen.

Principles of American Democracy

Abraham Lincoln, America's sixteenth president, described our democracy as a "government of the people, by the people, for the people." His words make three important points. First, the power of the government comes from the citizens. Second, Americans themselves, acting through their representatives, run their government. Third, the purpose of the government is to make the United States a better place for those who live here.

Because democratic governments exist by the people, all genuine democracies have free, fair, and competitive elections. Through free elections, people have the chance to choose their leaders and voice their opinions on various issues.

What makes an election fair and free? First, everyone's vote must carry the same weight. This principle is often expressed in the phrase "one person, one vote." Second, all candidates have the right to express their views freely to the public. Citizens are free to support candidates or issues. The legal requirements for voting must be kept to a minimum. For example, our voting laws center on age, residence, and citizenship, while other factors like race and ethnic and religious background cannot be used to restrict voting. Finally, citizens may vote freely by secret ballot, without fearing punishment for their voting decisions.

Competitive elections and competing political parties are an important element in democracies. (A political party is a group of individuals with broad, common interests who organize to support candidates for office and determine public policy.) Competing political parties give voters a choice among candidates. Also, the parties out of power help make those in power more responsible to the needs of the people.

In a democracy, individuals are free to develop their own capacities. This means that the government works to promote equality, and all people have an equal opportunity to develop their talents.

Of course, you can't please all the people all the time. Another principle of our democracy is **majority rule.** Citizens agree that when differences of opinion arise, we will abide by what most people want. At the same time, we insist on respect for the rights of those in the minority.

A town meeting in Warren, Vermont

Fundamental Principles of American Democracy

RULE OF LAW

★ All people, including those who govern, are bound by the law.

LIMITED GOVERNMENT

★ Government is not all-powerful—it may do only those things that people have given it the power to do.

CONSENT OF THE GOVERNED

★ American citizens are the source of all governmental power.

INDIVIDUAL RIGHTS

★ In the American democracy, individual rights are protected by government.

REPRESENTATIVE GOVERNMENT

★ People elect government leaders to make the laws and govern on their behalf.

Evaluating Charts

Our American democracy is built on these fundamental principles. Who is the source of power in direct democracies and representative democracies?

Respect for minority rights is sometimes difficult to maintain, though, especially if society is under a great deal of stress. For example, the United States government imprisoned in excess of 100,000 Japanese Americans in relocation camps during World War II. Government leaders feared that these Americans would be disloyal. This relocation program caused severe hardships for many Japanese Americans and deprived them of basic liberties. In 1988 Congress recognized the "grave injustice" of the relocation camps and offered payments of $20,000 to those Japanese Americans still living who had been relocated.

After the terrorist attacks of 2001, President George W. Bush realized that many people might turn their anger against Muslims in the United States, so he visited the Islamic Center in Washington, D.C., soon after the attacks. He explained that Islam is a peaceful religion and urged Americans to treat Muslim Americans fairly.

Reading Check **Comparing** What is the difference between a dictatorship and a democracy?

SECTION 1 ASSESSMENT

Checking for Understanding

1. **Key Terms** Use the following terms in complete sentences that demonstrate the meaning of each term: civics, citizen, government, public policy, budget, dictatorship, democracy, direct democracy, representative democracy, majority rule.

Reviewing Main Ideas

2. **Compare** What is the difference between a direct democracy and a representative democracy?

3. **Identify** What three levels of government exist in the United States?

Critical Thinking

4. **Making Predictions** What do you think would happen if there were no governments anywhere in the world? Describe such a situation, and then explain why governments are necessary.

5. **Organizing Information** On a web diagram like the one below, write as many benefits of government as you can.

Benefits of Government

Analyzing Visuals

6. **Conclude** Review the fundamental principles of American democracy on page 11. How does the American government carry out the principle of consent of the governed?

★ **BE AN ACTIVE CITIZEN** ★

7. **Analyze Primary Sources** Find news articles that report on government performing the three functions explained in this section. Identify which function and level of government each article describes.

Issues to Debate

Should the Government Be Allowed to Use Electronic Surveillance?

In an effort to track down terrorists, government intelligence—the secret agents charged with protecting the nation's security—jumped into cyberspace. On October 26, 2001, President George W. Bush signed the Provide Appropriate Tools Required to Intercept and Obstruct Terrorism Act. Known as the PATRIOT Act, this anti-terrorist law armed the FBI and Central Intelligence Agency (CIA) with broad new powers. One provision included the use of electronic surveillance—government searches of the Internet, including e-mail sent from home computers. Critics charged that electronic surveillance violated the rights of Americans. Supporters claimed that it protected them from harm.

Is the government monitoring her?

Yes

The despicable acts of September 11 have taught us that the terrorists now targeting the United States are both resourceful and capable of evading standard investigative techniques. While being mindful to protect our civil liberties, we must act now to fight terrorism by giving our law enforcement and intelligence communities the tools they need to find and eliminate terrorists wherever they might hide. . . .

This bill, I believe, strikes an appropriate balance between the protection of our civil liberties and putting some teeth into the nation's antiterrorism laws.

—Mike Simpson, Republican
representative, Idaho, 2001

No

The House Republican Leadership today gave Americans, and the members of Congress that represent them, a false choice—stop terrorism or sacrifice fundamental civil liberties. . . .

The bill . . . would allow wholesale use of covert [secret] searches for any criminal investigation, allowing the government to enter your home or office and conduct a search, take photographs and download your computer files without notifying you until later. . . .

We must strengthen our nation's ability to destroy the threat of terrorism—but we must not destroy our constitutional rights and freedoms in the process.

—Michael M. Honda, Democratic
representative, California, 2001

Debating the Issue

1. What arguments does Simpson use to support the use of electronic surveillance?
2. Why does Honda oppose it?

3. What do you think about the use of electronic surveillance? When, if ever, should it be used?

The Path to Citizenship

GUIDE TO READING

Main Idea
A person not born in the United States can become a citizen through the process of naturalization. Some residents of the United States are not citizens.

Key Terms
naturalization, alien, immigrant, deport

Reading Strategy
Sequencing Information
As you read, complete a chart like the one below to list the steps in the naturalization process.

Naturalization Process					
Step 1	Step 2	Step 3	Step 4	Step 5	Step 6

Read to Learn
• How can people become citizens of the United States?
• How are both legal and illegal aliens able to live in the United States?

Americans in Action

He thought he was an American citizen. He was drafted in 1969 and served two years in the U.S. Army during the Vietnam War; but when Tom Castillo carried out some research on his family tree, he made a discovery. He had been born in Mexico. When Castillo was about five, he, his mother, and two siblings moved from Mexico to Texas. His mother kept his birthplace a secret, wanting him to grow up American. Now, at age 52, Castillo has become a naturalized citizen of the United States. It was a natural step for Castillo, who says, "I've always considered myself an American first."

American soldier during the Vietnam War

Who Are America's Citizens?

In Section 1 you learned that citizens are people with certain rights and duties under a government and who owe allegiance to that government. Although Tom Castillo thought and acted like an American citizen, he wasn't technically an American citizen until later. Every country has rules about how people gain citizenship. In the United States, the Fourteenth Amendment defines a U.S. citizen as anyone "born or naturalized in the United States." Therefore, the U.S. Constitution establishes two ways to become a citizen: by birth and, for foreigners who choose to become citizens, by a legal process called **naturalization.**

Citizenship by Birth

If you were born in any of the 50 states or the District of Columbia, you automatically became an American citizen at birth. The same is true if you were born outside the country but in American territory, such as Puerto Rico or Guam or on a U.S. military base overseas. Even if you were born elsewhere, you could still claim ... parents are both ... who has actually ...

Children bor... U.S. citizens also ... birth. An excepti... children born to ... government repr... United States. Su... zenship of their p...

Under some ... may hold dual cit... they enjoy rights ... in another countr... example, a child b... parents may be both a U.S. citizen and a citizen of the country of his or her birth.

The Naturalization Process

Several million noncitizens, or **aliens,** live in the United States. Some come to study, to work, or to visit relatives for a while. They remain citizens of their own countries and eventually return home. Other aliens, however, plan to settle here and become naturalized citizens. More than half a million **immigrants**—people who move permanently to a new country—gain American citizenship each year.

Aliens who want to become United States citizens must first sign a statement saying just that. This Declaration of Intention is then filed with the Immigration and Naturalization Service (INS), an agency of the national government. For most aliens, the next step comes after living in the United States at least five years. (Aliens who are married to citizens wait only three years.) During this time, many immigrants take special classes to prepare for citizenship. At this time, if they are at least 18 years old and have lived for at least three months in the state where they seek naturalization, they may file an application for citizenship.

INS
<Immigration
and Naturalization
Services

ATH OF ALLEGIANCE TO THE UNITED STATES

... declare, on oath, that I absolutely ... rely renounce and abjure [reject] ... ance and fidelity to any foreign ... otentate, state, or sovereignty, to ... which I have heretofore been a ... r citizen; that I will support and ... e Constitution and laws of the ... ates of America against all ... foreign and domestic; that I will ... faith and allegiance to the same; ... bear arms on behalf of the ... tes when required by law; that ... rm noncombatant service in ... forces of the United States ... required by law; that I will perform work of national importance under civilian direction when required by law; and that I take this obligation freely without any mental reservation or purpose of evasion; so help me God.

Becoming an American Citizen All citizenship applicants must take the citizenship oath. **What step in the naturalization process comes just before taking the citizenship oath?**

After the paperwork is checked, the alien has an interview with an INS official. Agency officials want to be sure the alien meets the necessary requirements and is of good moral character. The applicant must also take a citizenship exam that consists of questions about reading, writing, and speaking English and basic facts about the history and government of the United States. Afterward, the INS makes its decision.

If the application is granted, the final step in naturalization is attending a ceremony and pledging an oath of allegiance. The alien swears to be loyal to this country above all others, to obey the Constitution and other laws, and to perform military or other duties if needed. Then the person signs a document and is declared a citizen of the United States.

If he or she has children under 18, they automatically become naturalized citizens, too.

Reading Check **Comparing** What is the first step an alien takes to become a citizen?

A Lifelong Privilege

Whether they are naturalized or native-born, most Americans keep their citizenship forever. Only the federal government can both grant citizenship and take it away. Although state governments can deny a convicted criminal some of the privileges of citizenship, such as voting, they do not have the power to deny citizenship itself. The government may strip naturalized citizens of their citizenship if it was improperly obtained. However, in most cases, the only way to lose U.S. citizenship is to voluntarily give it up. This must be done in a foreign country, with a formal oath signed before an appropriate American official.

There is no going back for those who take this step. They cannot later change their minds and regain citizenship. They also remain liable for old debts and any crimes they may have committed in the United States.

Emma Lazarus
(1849–1887)

Emma Lazarus wrote the poem that today captures the meaning of the Statue of Liberty. Lines from "The New Colossus," written in 1883, appear at the statue's base. In words now famous, Lazarus declared:

*Give me your tired, your poor,
Your huddled masses yearning to
breathe free.*

Lazarus, the fourth of seven children, grew up in one of the oldest and most respected Jewish families in New York City. She published her first book at age 17 and by age 25 was a well-known writer.

All around her, Lazarus saw a city alive with immigration. New York more than doubled in size as millions of immigrants came to the United States in the late 1800s. Lazarus felt strong ties with Jews driven from Russia because of their religion. She started classes in English and helped Russian Jews find housing.

To Lazarus, the United States was the "golden door" to freedom. She hoped that the Statue of Liberty, erected in 1886, would serve as a beacon of liberty to the entire world.

Aliens in America

The United States restricts the number of immigrants who can enter the country. Millions apply, but only about 675,000 are accepted each year. Traditionally, the relatives of U.S. citizens and people with needed job skills received the highest priority. Family members still get special consideration, but because of the Immigration Act of 1990, emphasis has shifted toward welcoming "those who want to work and produce and contribute," as one member of Congress put it. The new policy benefits people with particular skills, talents, or the money to invest in our economy.

Illegal Aliens

Despite immigration limits, approximately 5 to 6 million aliens are living in the United States illegally. Some were refused permission to immigrate; others never applied for permission because they feared a long, slow process or being turned down.

Illegal aliens come to the United States in a variety of ways. A few enter the country as temporary visitors but never leave. Others risk capture and arrest by illegally crossing our borders with Mexico and Canada. Other illegal aliens are foreigners who have stayed in the United States after their legal permits have expired.

Whatever the method, the reason is usually the same. "I came for work and for a better life," explained one Mexican immigrant; yet illegal aliens often have a difficult time in the United States. Many have no friends or family here, no place to live, and no sure way to earn money. It is against the law to hire illegal aliens, and those who do find work usually receive little pay and no benefits. Every day they live with the fear that government officials will discover and **deport** them—send them back to their own country.

The United States Border Patrol is the law-enforcement unit of the INS. Its primary responsibility is to detect and prevent the illegal entry of aliens into the United States. The Border Patrol patrols the 6,000 miles of Mexican and Canadian international land borders and 2,000 miles of coastal waters surrounding the Florida Peninsula and the island of Puerto Rico.

Legal Aliens

Aliens who have entered the United States legally lead lives much like those of American citizens. Aliens—both legal and illegal—may hold jobs, own property, attend public schools, and receive other government services. They pay taxes and are entitled to legal protection.

Aliens do not have full political rights, however. They may not vote in elections or run for office. They may not serve on juries or work in most government jobs. In addition, unlike U.S. citizens, aliens must carry identification cards at all times.

✓**Reading Check** **Explaining** Why do you think aliens come to the United States?

SECTION 2 ASSESSMENT

Checking for Understanding

1. **Key Terms** Define each of the following terms and explain how it relates to citizenship in the United States: naturalization, alien, immigrant, deport.

Reviewing Main Ideas

2. **Explain** What is dual citizenship? How can an American obtain dual citizenship?

3. **Describe** What is the most common way that a person loses American citizenship? Explain the process by which this happens.

Critical Thinking

4. **Synthesizing Information** If you were a government official, how would you prevent illegal aliens from entering the United States?

5. **Comparing and Contrasting** On a chart like the one below, compare the rights of legal aliens to the rights of citizens of the United States.

Aliens	Both	Citizens

Analyzing Visuals

6. **Explain** Reread the Oath of Allegiance to the United States on page 15. What must naturalized citizens publicly renounce or give up?

★**BE AN ACTIVE CITIZEN**★

7. **Write** Interview an American who became a citizen through the naturalization process. What reasons brought him or her to the United States? Why did he or she want to become an American citizen?

Identifying the Main Idea

Why Learn This Skill?

When you read a sports or fashion article, you usually remember the highlights about the topic described. These highlights are main ideas. Identifying main ideas is a useful skill when you read textbooks, news reports, or reference materials. It will help you remember information for a test and become an informed citizen.

Learning the Skill

To identify the main ideas in a passage, follow these steps:

- Determine the topic discussed in the paragraph or other selection you are reading. There may be a title or bold heading to help you. You might also skim the selection to find the topic.
- Read to learn what the selection says about the topic. Ask yourself: What is the purpose of this information?
- Identify important details that support the topic being discussed.
- Identify the main idea. The main idea may be found in a topic sentence at the beginning or end of a passage. The main idea may also be described in several sentences. Sometimes, however, the main idea may be implied, or stated indirectly.
- After reading the selection, look away. Mentally restate the main idea in your own words.

Practicing the Skill

Read the passage below and answer the following questions.

A person who has dual citizenship claims citizenship in two countries. He or she is obliged to obey the legal requirements of citizenship of both countries. To avoid problems, a person who is or plans to become a dual citizen needs to know the laws of both countries. In some cases, the person may automatically lose citizenship in one country upon becoming a citizen of the other. The dual citizen will likely need separate passports for entering or leaving each country. Both countries may require the dual citizen to pay taxes or to serve in the military.

1 Which sentence states the main idea of the passage?
2 What details support the main idea?
3 Restate the main idea in your own words.

A new citizen examines her passport.

Applying the Skill

Read the paragraphs under the heading "A Lifelong Privilege" of your textbook on page 16. Identify the main idea and restate it in your own words.

GO TO

Practice key skills with Glencoe's
**Skillbuilder Interactive Workbook
CD-ROM, Level 1.**

The Diversity of Americans

GUIDE TO READING

Main Idea
In addition to its common values and civic unity, the United States benefits from its rich diversity.

Key Terms
migration, patriotism, terrorism

Reading Strategy
Identifying Information
As you read, create a web diagram like the one shown here, in which you list as many examples of diversity in the United States as you can.

Diversity in the United States

Read to Learn
• How and why do Americans represent diverse cultures?
• What are the common values and civic unity that hold together Americans from diverse racial, ethnic, and religious backgrounds?

Americans in Action

The diversity of the United States has been, and still is, a great strength. In 1888 Henry Cabot Lodge, a member of the U.S. Congress, urged Americans to actively accept immigrants: "Let every man honor and love the land of his birth and the race from which he springs and keep their memory green. It is a pious and honorable duty. But let us have done with British-Americans and Irish-Americans and German-Americans, and so on, and all be Americans. . . . If a man is going to be an American at all let him be so without any qualifying adjectives; and if he is going to be something else, let him drop the word *American* from his personal description."

Immigrants entering the United States at Ellis Island, New York, in the late 1800s

A Nation of Immigrants

On the back of every American coin, you'll find the Latin words *E pluribus unum,* meaning "Out of many, one." This phrase reminds us that the many diverse citizens of the United States have joined together to create a single, strong nation. For all our differences, we are linked by shared values and experiences. More than 281 million people live in the United States today. All of us are descended from families that immigrated at one time or another. Most scholars believe that the first Native Americans arrived here thousands of years ago by crossing over a "land bridge" that once connected Asia and North America.

European Settlers

Until the mid-1900s, most immigrants came from Europe. The first Europeans to settle permanently in North America arrived from Spain during the 1500s. They occupied territory in

Online
UPDATE
Visit civ.glencoe.com and click on *Textbook Updates– Chapter 1* for an update of the data.

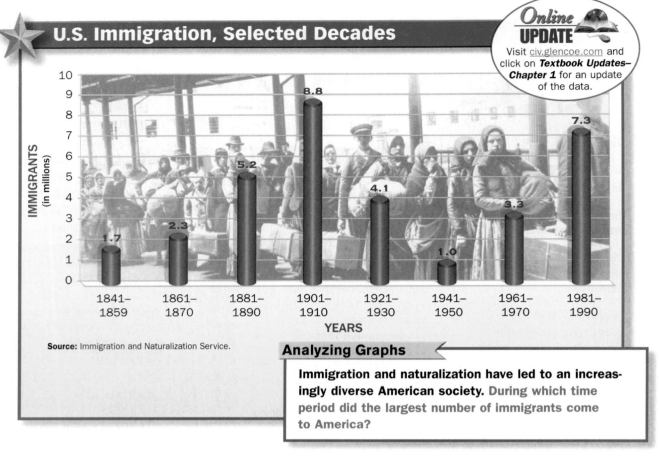

IMMIGRANTS (in millions)

10
9
8   8.8
7   7.3
6
5   5.2
4   4.1
3   3.3
2   2.3
1   1.7   1.0
0

1841– | 1861– | 1881– | 1901– | 1921– | 1941– | 1961– | 1981–
1859 | 1870 | 1890 | 1910 | 1930 | 1950 | 1970 | 1990

YEARS

Source: Immigration and Naturalization Service.

Analyzing Graphs

Immigration and naturalization have led to an increasingly diverse American society. During which time period did the largest number of immigrants come to America?

what is now Florida, California, and the Southwest, where their influence still lingers.

Beginning in the 1600s, people from France and England came to North America. The French settled primarily in Canada, but they also clustered around the Mississippi River. English immigrants settled mainly along the east coast of North America, creating the 13 colonies that became the United States. During the late 1600s and the 1700s, immigrants from Germany, the Netherlands, Ireland, Scotland, and Sweden joined these English settlers.

After the United States gained its independence, it became known throughout Europe as a land of promise. The number of immigrants grew from 600,000 in the 1830s to more than 2 million by the 1850s. Between 1860 and 1890, more than 10 million Europeans—many of them from

Denmark, Norway, and Sweden—streamed into this country.

Another flood of immigrants—about 22 million—reached our shores between 1890 and 1924. Most of them came from southern and eastern Europe, from countries such as Italy, Greece, Poland, and Russia.

Out of Many, One All American coins carry the Latin phrase *E pluribus unum.* How does this phrase reflect the population of the United States?

During the past 50 years, immigration from Europe to the United States has lagged far behind immigration from the rest of the world. Latin America now accounts for the largest share of foreign newcomers, followed by Asia.

African Immigrants

Among the early immigrants to America were some who did not come willingly. Western and central Africans were taken by force from their homes, shipped across the Atlantic Ocean, and sold as slaves in the Caribbean Islands and North and South America. Between 1619 and 1808, before it became illegal to bring enslaved persons into the United States, some 500,000 were brought to the country in this way. Most African Americans today are descendants of enslaved persons. Others are immigrants from various countries in Africa and the Caribbean region.

Reading Check **Summarizing** When did the largest group of European immigrants come to the United States?

A Diverse Population

The American population is extraordinarily diverse in terms of ethnic backgrounds. Many Americans today do not identify themselves as members of a single ethnic group. However, whites of European descent number more than 211 million. There are about 35 million African Americans, nearly 11 million Asians and Pacific Islanders, and almost 2.5 million Native Americans. Another 35 million people are Hispanics—people of any race who trace their ancestry to the Spanish-speaking countries of the Western Hemisphere.

Our ethnic diversity is matched by religious diversity. Christians are in the majority, with more than 158 million practicing

some form of Christianity. Jews, Muslims, Buddhists, and many other religious groups also worship freely; and those who don't practice any religion are equally at home here.

Displaying Patriotism Three New York City firefighters raise the American flag amid the rubble of the World Trade Center. Students at Yale Headstart Center in Mississippi show their support for America. **In what ways do Americans display their patriotism?**

As people with different beliefs and backgrounds have made lives for themselves in the United States, many of their "old country" traditions have become part of the American culture. The American culture is a rich blend of varied influences.

✓Reading Check **Concluding** How would you describe today's American culture?

A Growing and Changing Population

The growth of America's population is not due entirely to immigration. It also increased naturally as a result of Americans having many children. For example, between 1830 and 1930, the nation's population grew from about 12 million people to about 120 million people. Fewer than 40 million of those new Americans were immigrants.

Over the years, the American population has changed in many ways. In the mid-1800s, for example, people began moving from rural areas to cities. They started working in factories rather than on farms. In the past few decades, manufacturing has lost ground to what we call "the service economy." More and more Americans now earn a living by providing services—practicing law or medicine, clerking in stores, programming computers, teaching, and so forth. In addition, there are more women and at-home workers in the labor force than ever before.

The places where we live are changing too. For example, shortly after the Civil War, African Americans, freed from slavery, headed for the cities seeking jobs and a new way of life. The result was a **migration,** or the mass movement, of African Americans from the South to the North. For much of our history, the Northeast was the most populous part of the country. Today, the South claims that distinction, and the population there and in the West is growing faster than in any other region.

The population is changing in other ways as well. For example, the average age of citizens is climbing upward as people live longer and have fewer children. Record numbers of Americans are now earning college and graduate degrees.

Hispanic Americans are the fastest-growing ethnic group. Indeed, if current patterns continue, Hispanics and other minority groups, taken as a whole, will soon be in the majority.

✓Reading Check **Summarizing** In what ways is the American population changing?

Unity Among Citizens

There are various sources of American unity. One very important source of American unity is a common civic and political heritage based upon the country's founding documents, such as the Declaration of Independence, the U.S. Constitution of 1787, and the Bill of Rights of 1791. American ideals of individual rights to "life, liberty, and the pursuit of happiness" are in these founding documents. So are such values as popular sovereignty (government by consent of the governed), equal justice under law, and majority rule through the people's representatives in government. These representatives are accountable to the people through fair, free, and regular elections in which citizens have the right to participate. There is majority rule in government, but the majority is limited by the higher law of the people's Constitution to protect equally the rights of everyone as individuals in the political system.

A second significant source is a single language, English, which generally is accepted as the primary means of communication in education, government, and business. Americans are free to speak any language. However, the community of citizens in the United States is strengthened by the common and public use of one language, which can be used by diverse groups of Americans to communicate freely with one another.

As Americans, we demonstrate our **patriotism**—love for one's country—in many ways. We fly the flag proudly, sing the national anthem, and recite the Pledge of Allegiance. We follow the nation's laws and participate in civic life. We stand together and fight bravely in times of trouble.

Consider the events of September 11, 2001. On that day, suicide hijackers launched devastating attacks on New York City and Washington, D.C. These were acts of **terrorism**—the use of violence by groups against civilians to achieve a political goal. Americans, however, responded with courage and unity. We joined together to help people in need, repair the damage, and reaffirm our commitment to freedom.

✓**Reading Check** **Summarizing** What are two sources of American unity?

SECTION 3 ASSESSMENT

Checking for Understanding

1. **Key Terms** In a paragraph compare the terms patriotism and terrorism. Explain how they relate to each other.

Reviewing Main Ideas

2. **Identify** Who were the first immigrants to what is now the United States?

3. **Describe** What immigrants did not come willingly to the United States?

Critical Thinking

4. **Evaluating Information** What do you think is the most important source of American unity? Explain your answer.

5. **Sequencing Information** On a time line similar to the one below, show when various ethnic groups immigrated to the United States.

```
Pre-  1500    1700    1900
1500    1600    1800    2000
```

Analyzing Visuals

6. **Identify** Review the graph on page 20 that shows immigration to the United States. About how many immigrants came to the United States between 1981 and 1990?

★**BE AN ACTIVE CITIZEN**★
7. **Research** Choose an ethnic or religious group in your community. Using newspapers, TV, or other sources of information, list examples of the group's contribution to life in your community.

Assessment & Activities

Review to Learn

Section 1

- People need governments to make and enforce laws and to help us meet our needs.
- Three main levels of government exist in the United States.

Section 2

- According to the U.S. Constitution, people can become American citizens by birth and through nationalization.
- Millions of illegal aliens live in the United States. Legal aliens have entered the country legally.

Section 3

- The United States is a land of immigrants.
- Americans have a common civic and political heritage, and a single language.

FOLDABLES™
Study Organizer

Using Your Foldables Study Organizer
Review what you have learned by noting the main ideas you have written on your foldable. Next to each main idea, write some supporting facts and your opinions.

Reviewing Key Terms

Write the chapter key term that matches each definition below.

1. a display of love for one's country
2. the study of the rights and duties of citizens
3. a plan for making and spending money
4. noncitizens living in a nation
5. people who move permanently to a new country
6. a government in which citizens choose a smaller group to govern on their behalf
7. a legal process to obtain citizenship
8. to send an alien or immigrant back to his or her own country
9. the use of violence against civilians to achieve a political goal
10. the course of government action to achieve community goals

Reviewing Main Ideas

11. What three levels of government exist in the United States, and which is the highest?
12. What are the primary functions of government?
13. In what ways can a person become a citizen of the United States?
14. What political rights do legal aliens in the United States *not* have?
15. After whites of European descent, what are the two largest ethnic groups in the United States?
16. How did most African American immigrants differ from other racial or ethnic groups who came to the United States before 1808?
17. What is the INS? What is the role of the INS during the naturalization process?
18. What does it mean to say the United States has a "service economy"? In what other ways has the American labor force changed?

Critical Thinking

19. Making Predictions What do you think would happen to the United States if all immigration stopped?

20. Categorizing Information On a chart like the one below, write as many examples of the functions of government as possible.

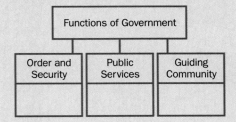

Functions of Government

Order and Security | Public Services | Guiding Community

Practicing Skills

21. Identifying the Main Idea Read the text under the main head "A Diverse Population" on pages 21 and 22. Identify the main idea of the paragraphs.

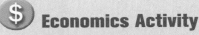 **Economics Activity**

22. The South and the West are the fastest-growing areas in the United States. What economic effect does that have on other parts of the United States?

Analyzing Visuals

23. Study the political cartoon below. What are these wealthy American citizens saying to newly arrived immigrants? How do you suppose these wealthy men came to be Americans?

Self-Check Quiz Visit the *Civics Today* Web site at civ.glencoe.com and click on **Self-Check Quizzes— Chapter 1** to prepare for the chapter test.

★ CITIZENSHIP COOPERATIVE ACTIVITY ★

24. Form a group of three to four students and research your community's ethnic, racial, and religious makeup. Create circle graphs that show the ethnic distribution and the religious distribution in your community.

 Technology Activity

25. Log on to the Internet and go to www.ins.gov for the home page of the INS. Find the "Naturalization Self-Test." Answer at least 20 questions on the self-test and check your answers. How did you do?

 The Princeton Review

Standardized Test Practice

Directions: Choose the *best* answer to complete the following statement.

A person may become a citizen of the United States by all of the following ways EXCEPT

A through naturalization.

B by being born in the United States.

C by being born in American territory outside the United States.

D by being born to a foreign diplomat working in the United States.

Test-Taking Tip

Read the question carefully. You are looking for the answer choice that does NOT fit with the question.

Roots of American Democracy

★ CITIZENSHIP AND YOU ★

When our nation's Founders met, they drew inspiration from ancient Greece and Rome and Great Britain. Contact a local historical society to learn more about your community's founders and history.

To learn more about the roots of American democracy, view the **Democracy in Action** electronic field trip 1: Independence Hall.

FOLDABLES
Study Organizer

Sequencing Events Study Foldable *Make this foldable to help you sequence the events that led to the creation of our American democratic system.*

Step 1 *Fold two sheets of paper in half from top to bottom.*

Step 2 *Turn the papers and cut each in half.*

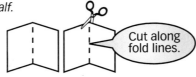

Cut along fold lines.

Step 3 *Fold the four pieces in half from top to bottom.*

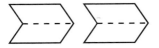

Step 4 *Tape the ends of the pieces together (overlapping the edges very slightly) to make an accordion time line.*

Pieces of tape

Reading and Writing *As you read the chapter, sequence the events that led to the writing of the Declaration of Independence and the formation of America's first government by writing a date and event on each part of the time line.*

Mount Rushmore in South Dakota ▶

CIVICS Online

Chapter Overview Visit the *Civics Today* Web site at civ.glencoe.com and click on **Chapter Overviews— Chapter 2** to preview chapter information.

Our English Heritage

Americans in Action

While framing the Articles of Confederation, the delegates used all that they knew to create a document that could and would be approved by the states. Despite his desire to be free from the laws of Great Britain, John Dickinson recognized the value of those laws. In praise of Britain's laws, he wrote that "no nation has existed that ever so perfectly united those distant extremes, private security of life, liberty, and property, with exertion of public force . . . or so happily blended together arms, arts, science, commerce, and agriculture." Dickinson later urged his fellow delegates, in the spirit of moderation, to ratify the Constitution even if it wasn't perfect.

John Dickinson

Influences From England's Early Government

Many of the rights that American citizens enjoy today can be traced back to the political and legal traditions of England. When English people began settling here in the 1600s, they brought with them a history of limited and representative government.

For centuries before the first English people arrived in America, England was ruled by a **monarch**—a king or queen. However, noble families also had considerable power. The monarch gave them ownership and control of vast lands in exchange for their loyalty, tax payments, and promises of military support.

The Magna Carta

King John, who inherited the throne in 1199, treated the nobles harshly. They rebelled in 1215 and forced the king to sign an agreement called the **Magna Carta** (Latin for "Great Charter"). This document protected the nobles' privileges and upheld their authority. It also granted certain rights to all landholders—rights that eventually came to apply to all English people. These rights included equal treatment under the law and trial by one's peers.

The Magna Carta was a contract that limited the power of the monarch by guaranteeing that no one would be above the law, not even the king or queen. 📖 See the Appendix to read this document.

Parliament

Henry III, the king who followed John, met fairly regularly with a group of nobles and church officials, who advised the king and helped govern the realm. Over the years, the group grew in size and power, expanding to include representatives of the common people. By the late 1300s, the group had developed into a **legislature**—a lawmaking body—known as **Parliament.**

For the next few centuries, the English monarch cooperated with Parliament. In the mid-1600s, however, serious power struggles began. Eventually, in 1688, Parliament removed King James II from the throne and invited his daughter Mary and her husband William to rule instead. In doing so, Parliament demonstrated that it was now stronger than the monarch.

This peaceful transfer of power, known as the Glorious Revolution, changed the idea of government in England. From that time on, no ruler would have more power than the legislature.

To clarify the new relationship, Parliament drew up the English Bill of Rights in 1689. This document stated that the monarch could not suspend Parliament's laws; the monarch also could not create special

Seal of William and Mary

Magna Carta The English nobles forced King John to sign the Magna Carta. **Why did the nobles draw up the Magna Carta?**

courts, impose taxes, or raise an army without Parliament's consent. The Bill of Rights also declared that members of Parliament would be freely elected and be guaranteed free speech during meetings, that every citizen would have the right to a fair trial by jury in court cases, and that cruel and unusual punishments would be banned.

Common Law

In its earliest days, England had no written laws. People developed rules to live by, however, and these customs came to have the force of law. In addition, as a system of courts arose, the courts' decisions became the basis of a body of law. When judges were asked to decide a case, they would look for a **precedent,** or a ruling in an earlier case that was similar. If someone were accused of trespassing, for example, the judge would see if anyone had ever faced a similar charge and what the outcome had been. The judge would then make a consistent ruling.

This system of law, based on precedent and customs, is known as **common law.** It rests on court decisions rather than regulations written by lawmakers.

England's system of common law came about without being planned. Because it worked well, this system of law has remained in place to this day. Our own laws about property, contracts, and personal injury are based on English common law.

Reading Check **Evaluating** Why was the English Bill of Rights important to English citizens?

Sources of American Law

COMMON LAW

⭐ Made by judges in the process of resolving cases, this law is sometimes called case law. It was brought to America from English courts.

EQUITY LAW

⭐ This law is a system of rules that resolves disputes on the basis of fairness. It was developed in the king's courts in England and merged with common law in America.

CONSTITUTIONAL LAW

⭐ America's fundamental and most important source of law was written in 1787 and has been changed by 27 amendments.

STATUTORY LAW

⭐ This law is made by legislatures at the national, state, and local levels. It is based on the Roman practice of writing down the laws of their senate.

Evaluating Charts

There are many kinds of law. This chart describes four sources of American law. Of these four bodies of law, which do you think is growing fastest today?

Bringing the English Heritage to America

In the 1600s and 1700s, England was busy establishing colonies in America. A **colony** is a group of people in one place who are ruled by a parent country elsewhere.

Although the early colonists made their lives far from home, they remained loyal subjects of England, with a strong sense of English political traditions. They accepted common law and believed that the ruler was not above the law. They also expected to have a voice in government and other basic rights.

The Virginia House of Burgesses

The first permanent English settlement in North America was Jamestown, in what is now the state of Virginia. Jamestown was founded in 1607 by the Virginia Company, a group of merchants from London, with a charter from King James I. A **charter** is a written document granting land and the authority to set up colonial governments. The Virginia Company's charter also promised the colonists "all liberties . . . as if they had been abiding and born within this our Realm of England."

At first the Jamestown colony was managed by a governor and council appointed by the Virginia Company. In 1619, however, the colonists chose two representatives from each county to meet with the governor and his council. These 22 men were called burgesses, and they formed the House of Burgesses, the first representative assembly, or legislature, in the English colonies. The House of Burgesses had little power, but it marked the beginning of self-government in colonial America.

In 1624 King Charles I canceled the Virginia Company's charter and made Virginia a "royal colony," a colony that would be controlled by the crown. The king

House of Burgesses Representatives of the people of Jamestown met as the House of Burgesses to deal with problems like hunger, disease, and attacks by Native Americans. **Why was the House of Burgesses important in American history?**

appointed a new governor, but he allowed the House of Burgesses to continue as an elected legislature.

The Mayflower Compact

In 1620, shortly after the House of Burgesses was formed, a new group of colonists, known as the Pilgrims, arrived in America. They built a settlement called Plymouth hundreds of miles north of Virginia. Today this area is in the state of Massachusetts, a part of New England.

Even before their ship, the *Mayflower*, reached America, the Plymouth colonists realized they needed rules to govern themselves if they were to survive in a new land. They drew up a written plan for government. Forty-one of the men aboard signed the **Mayflower Compact.** 📖 See the Appendix to read this document.

A compact is an agreement, or contract, among a group of people. The Mayflower Compact stated that the government would make "just and equal laws . . . for the general good of the colony." The signers pledged to obey those laws. The compact set up a direct democracy, in which all men would vote, and the majority would rule. (As was common at this time, only adult males were permitted to vote.)

The Mayflower Compact established a tradition of direct democracy that you can still see in New England today. Throughout the colonial period—and in New England today—citizens met at town meetings to discuss and vote on important issues.

✓ Reading Check **Explaining** How was the Mayflower Compact an example of direct democracy?

Early Colonial Governments

The success of the Jamestown and Plymouth colonies led to the formation of other settlements in America. By 1733, 13 English colonies stretched from Massachusetts in the north to Georgia in the south. Following the examples of the House of Burgesses and the Mayflower Compact, each new colony set up its own government.

Although there were differences among them, there were many similarities as well. Each colony had a governor, who was either elected by the colonists or appointed by the

Mayflower Compact
Tompkins H. Matteson painted *Signing the Compact on Board the Mayflower.* Colonists on board the *Mayflower* signed the agreement to set up a civil government and obey its laws. **Why do you think the colonists felt they needed to draw up the Mayflower Compact?**

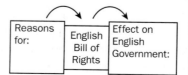

Colonial-era quill pen

English king. Each colony also had a legislature, with representatives elected by the free adult males. Many of the colonial legislatures were modeled after the English Parliament.

As years passed, the colonial governments took on more power and responsibility while the king and Parliament were preoccupied with matters at home in Great Britain (the country was renamed in 1707 when England unified with Scotland). The colonists in America soon grew used to making their own decisions. They built towns and roads. They organized their own churches, schools, hospitals, and fire departments. They built a thriving economy and felt comfortable solving problems without help from Britain.

✓ Reading Check **Concluding** Why did the American colonists grow used to making their own decisions?

SECTION 1 ASSESSMENT

Checking for Understanding

1. **Key Terms** Using all of the following terms, write complete sentences that relate to England's political legacy to the United States: monarch, legislature, Parliament, precedent, common law, colony, charter, compact.

Reviewing Main Ideas

2. **Explain** What is the historical significance of Virginia's House of Burgesses?

3. **Summarize** What did the Mayflower Compact do?

Critical Thinking

4. **Drawing Conclusions** Explain the significance of the Glorious Revolution.

5. **Determining Cause and Effect** Explain the reasons for and the effects of the English Bill of Rights by completing a graphic organizer like the one below.

```
Reasons     English      Effect on
for:        Bill of      English
            Rights       Government:
```

Analyzing Visuals

6. **Identify** Review the four sources of American law in the chart on page 30. What is equity law and where did it come from?

★ **BE AN ACTIVE CITIZEN** ★
7. **Use Primary Sources** Read the Mayflower Compact. How many men signed it? When and where did they sign it? What ideas do you see in the compact that also exist in the government of the United States?

The Birth of a Democratic Nation

GUIDE TO READING

Main Idea
When Great Britain attempted to exert tighter control over the American colonies, the colonists, who were used to running their own affairs, resisted and eventually declared independence.

Key Terms
mercantilism, boycott, repeal, delegate, independence

Reading Strategy
Cause and Effect As you read, complete a chart like the one below by explaining how the colonists responded to British actions.

British Actions	Colonists' Responses

Read to Learn
- How did the British government try to tighten control over its American colonies?
- How did American colonists resist and reject the British crackdown?

Americans in Action

Some people in Pennsylvania did not want Charles Thomson to be a delegate to the First Continental Congress. Thomson had actively and publicly resisted Britain's attempts to control the North American colonies. On the first day of assembly, however, the Congress unanimously elected Thomson as secretary. He served in that post through the duration of the Continental Congresses—from 1774 through 1789. Thomson is the little-known designer of the Great Seal of the United States.

Charles Thomson

Colonial Resistance and Rebellion

The First Continental Congress assembled because Americans began to demand more rights. Why did Americans demand more rights? Separated from Great Britain by more than 3,000 miles (5,556 km) of vast ocean and left largely to their own devices, the American colonists gained valuable experience in self-government. They took on more power and responsibility. They learned how to manage their own affairs, and they liked having local control. By the mid-1700s, however, the British government began to tighten its grasp on the American colonies.

After 1760, when George III took the throne, the British adopted a policy called mercantilism in which they tried to squeeze as much wealth as possible out of the British colonies in America and from other colonies around the world. Mercantilism is the theory that a country should sell more goods to other countries than it buys. For mercantilism to be successful, Great Britain needed the colonies to be a source of cheap, raw materials. Parliament required the American colonies to sell raw materials, such as cotton and lumber, to Great Britain at low prices. The colonists also had to buy British products at high prices. As a result, colonial businesses suffered.

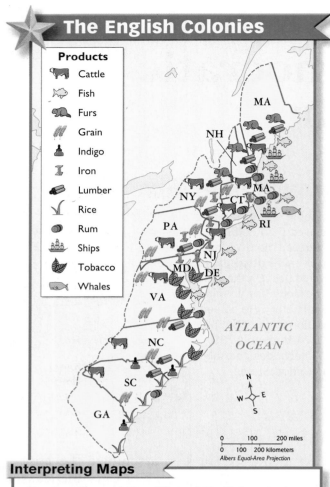

The English Colonies

Products
- Cattle
- Fish
- Furs
- Grain
- Indigo
- Iron
- Lumber
- Rice
- Rum
- Ships
- Tobacco
- Whales

MA
NH
MA
NY
CT
RI
PA
NJ
MD
DE
VA
ATLANTIC OCEAN
NC
SC
GA

N
W E
S

0   100   200 miles
0   100   200 kilometers
Albers Equal-Area Projection

Interpreting Maps

The locations of the different English colonies influenced the way of life in each colony. Whereas the economy of the New England Colonies depended on fishing and shipbuilding, the Southern Colonies grew rice and tobacco.
What were the 13 English colonies and what were their main products?

The situation worsened after 1763. Great Britain had fought a long, costly war against France—the French and Indian War—winning French territory in North America. To cover the costs of ruling these new lands and to pay off its heavy war debts, Britain placed steep taxes on the American colonies. In 1765, for example, Parliament passed the Stamp Act, which required colonists to attach expensive tax stamps to all newspapers and legal documents.

The colonists resented the British taxes. Because they had no representatives in Parliament, as people living in Great Britain did, the colonists believed that Parliament had no right to tax them. They summed up their feelings with the slogan "No taxation without representation!"

In protest, many colonists decided to **boycott,** or refuse to buy, British goods. Rebellious colonists began using homespun cloth and drinking coffee instead of British tea. The boycott had its intended effect; Parliament agreed to **repeal,** or cancel, the Stamp Act and other taxes.

Parliament, however, soon passed new tax laws to replace the Stamp Act. The same day it repealed the Stamp Act, Parliament passed the Declaratory Act of 1766, which stated that Parliament had the right to tax and make decisions for the American colonies "in all cases." Then, in 1767, Parliament passed a set of laws that came to be known as the Townshend Acts. These laws levied new taxes on goods imported to the colonies. The taxed goods included basic items, like glass, tea, paper, and lead, that the colonists needed because they did not produce them. These new laws further angered the colonists. The colonists responded by bringing back the boycott that they had used against the Stamp Act.

Relations between Great Britain and the colonists worsened. In 1773 Parliament passed another measure. The Tea Act gave the British East India Company the right to ship tea to the colonies without paying most of the taxes usually placed on tea. The act also allowed the company to bypass colonial merchants and sell tea directly to shopkeepers at low prices. This made the East India Company tea cheaper than any other tea in the colonies, giving the British company a very favorable advantage over colonial merchants.

Independence Day

Although we celebrate American independence on July 4th, the official vote actually took place on July 2, 1776. After much discussion, on July 4, the Congress voted to accept the final version of the Declaration. Not every representative signed the document. Many didn't sign until August 2, and some never signed the document at all.

Colonists immediately condemned the act as just another attempt to crush their liberty. Colonists blocked all East India Company ships from colonial ports, with the exception of the ships that arrived at the Boston port.

In 1773 a group of colonists dressed as Native Americans dumped 342 chests of British tea into Boston Harbor. The colonists did this to protest further taxes on tea. In reaction to this protest, known as the Boston Tea Party, Parliament passed the Coercive Acts, which Americans called the Intolerable Acts. These laws restricted the colonists' rights, including the right to trial by jury. The Intolerable Acts also allowed British soldiers to search, and even move into, colonists' homes.

Movement Toward Independence

The colonial governments banded together to fight the Intolerable Acts. In September 1774, 12 of the colonies sent **delegates,** or representatives, to Philadelphia to discuss their concerns. These representatives—from every colony except Georgia—wanted to establish a political body to represent American interests and challenge British control.

The First Continental Congress

The meeting in Philadelphia, known as the First Continental Congress, lasted seven weeks. During that time, the delegates sent a document to King George III demanding

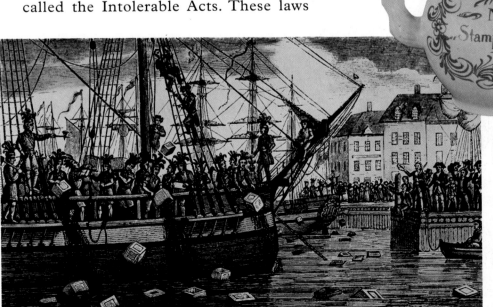

No Stamp Act.

Boston Tea Party Protestors in Boston destroy a ship's cargo of East Indian tea. **What do you think was the purpose of the Boston Tea Party?**

that the rights of the colonists be restored. They also made plans to extend the boycott of British goods. When the Congress ended, the delegates vowed to hold another meeting if their demands were not met by the following year.

King George responded with force. In April 1775, two battles between British and colonial soldiers took place in Massachusetts at Lexington and Concord. These became the first battles of the Revolutionary War. Until this time, most colonists still thought of themselves as loyal subjects of Great Britain. Now, with British soldiers shooting at Americans, many colonists began to question their attachment to Britain. People began talking about **independence,** or self-reliance and freedom from outside control.

Thinking About Independence Thomas Paine's *Common Sense* persuaded many colonists to break away from Great Britain. **How did Paine refer to King George III in his pamphlet? Why do you think he did this?**

The Second Continental Congress

In May 1775, colonial leaders convened the Second Continental Congress in Philadelphia. Not every member of the Congress favored independence. Some believed the colonists could never win a war against Great Britain. Others were still loyal to their home country. The Congress spent many months debating over the best course of action.

Meanwhile, support for independence grew. In January of 1776, an American colonist named Thomas Paine inspired many other colonists by publishing a pamphlet titled *Common Sense.* In it Paine called for complete independence from Britain. He argued that it was simply "common sense" to stop following the "royal brute," King George III. Paine called the colonists' actions a struggle for freedom.

See the **American History Primary Source Document Library CD-ROM** for the complete document.

By 1776 more than half of the delegates of the Second Continental Congress agreed with Paine that the colonies must break away from Britain.

Reading Check **Explaining** Why did colonists gather at the Second Continental Congress?

The Declaration of Independence

The Congress, acting now as a government for the colonies, appointed a committee to write a document that would officially announce the independence of the United States. Thomas Jefferson, however, did almost all the work. His draft of the Declaration of Independence explained why the United States of America should be a free nation.

The Declaration argued that the British government did not look after the interests of the colonists. The authors included a long list of abuses by King George III and called him a "Tyrant . . . unfit to be the Ruler of a free People." The document was much more than a list of complaints, though.

Democratic Ideals

The second paragraph of the Declaration of Independence set forth the colonists' beliefs about the rights of individuals. It said:

> 66 **We hold these truths to be self-evident, that all men are created equal, that they are endowed by their Creator with certain unalienable Rights, that among these are Life, Liberty, and the pursuit of Happiness.** 99

The paragraph went on to say:

> 66 **That to secure these rights, Governments are instituted among Men, deriving their just powers from the consent of the governed, that whenever any Form of Government becomes destructive of these ends, it is the Right of the People to alter or abolish it, and to institute new Government. . . .** 99

See the **American History Primary Source Document Library CD-ROM** for the complete document.

In other words, the purpose of government is to protect the rights of the people. Moreover, government is based on the consent of the people. The people are entitled to change or overthrow a government if it disregards their rights or their will.

These ideas were not new. The thinking of Thomas Jefferson and his fellow Americans was particularly influenced by John Locke, a seventeenth-century English philosopher. In his *Second Treatise of*

Government, published in 1690, Locke wrote that good government is based on a social contract between the people and the rulers. The people agree to give up some of their freedom and abide by the decisions of their government. In return, the government promises to protect the lives, property, and liberty of the people. If the government misuses its power, the people

TIME
Political Cartoons

JOIN, or DIE.

and it seems to be diverted toward money and
... Making the world a more convenient

Schneider, two men with little hope, of regaining the company's re...... While the wage was

to be diverte
tim

Analyzing Visuals This image was created in the 1750s by Benjamin Franklin, who is considered the father of political cartooning in America. Why do you think Franklin chose to depict the snake in several pieces instead of as a connected whole?

should rebel. Locke also wrote that all people should equally enjoy the rights to life, liberty, and property. •

An Uncertain Future

The Second Continental Congress approved the Declaration of Independence, with a few changes, on July 4, 1776. The American colonies were now independent states—at least in theory. True freedom, though, would not come until the war ended and Great Britain officially recognized the United States as a rightfully independent nation.

✓ Reading Check **Summarizing** According to the Declaration of Independence, what is the purpose of government?

SECTION 2 ASSESSMENT

Checking for Understanding

1. **Key Terms** Write complete sentences that include each pair of terms below.
   boycott, repeal;
   delegates, independence

Reviewing Main Ideas

2. **Explain** Why did Great Britain raise taxes on the American colonists after 1763? What effect did this have on the colonists?

3. **Identify** What British legislation prompted colonists to hold the First Continental Congress?

Critical Thinking

4. **Making Inferences** Assume the role of a British government official in 1774, and write a press release explaining why the Coercive Acts were necessary.

5. **Categorizing Information** In a web diagram like the one below, list the ideas of government found in the Declaration of Independence.

   Ideas in Declaration of Independence

Analyzing Visuals

6. **Interpret** Reexamine the political cartoon on this page. What do the labels or initials represent?

★ **BE AN ACTIVE CITIZEN** ★

7. **Use Primary Sources** Read the Declaration of Natural Rights in the Declaration of Independence (second, third, and fourth paragraphs on page 44). Select what you think is the single most important idea and explain how that idea affects your life today.

The Nation's First Governments

GUIDE TO READING

Main Idea

In 1777, the Second Continental Congress drafted the Articles of Confederation, thereby creating a weak national government. By 1780, all 13 of the original states had written constitutions.

Key Terms

constitution, bicameral, confederation, ratify, amend

Reading Strategy

Comparing and Contrasting Information As you read, create and complete a chart similar to the one below, listing features of state constitutions and the Articles of Confederation.

State Constitutions	Articles of Confederation

Read to Learn

- How did the original states fashion their constitutions?
- Why were the Articles of Confederation ineffective?

Americans in Action

Josiah Martin, the royal governor, ruled the colony of North Carolina with authority granted to him by the British king. However, Martin grew more and more nervous as the American colonists discussed independence and protested against what they called corrupt colonial government. On July 15, 1775, the colonists took action, and Martin was forced to flee with his family. He made it to safety aboard the British warship *Cruizer.* Martin was to be the last royal governor of North Carolina.

Coat of arms for king of England

Early State Constitutions

Even before the Declaration of Independence was signed, American colonists discussed the possibility of independence, and American leaders began preparing new state constitutions to replace the old colonial charters. As royal governors like Josiah Martin worried about their futures, some Americans saw the need for a central government that would unify and strengthen the 13 states.

In January 1776, New Hampshire became the first colony to organize as a state and craft a detailed, written plan for government, or **constitution.** By 1780 the other former colonies had followed suit.

The new state constitutions set up similar systems of government. Each state had a legislature to create laws, and most of these legislatures were **bicameral,** like the English Parliament; that is, they were divided into two parts, or houses. The members of each house of state legislatures were chosen by different methods. Each state also had a governor, who was elected either by the legislature or by the citizens. The governor's job was to carry out the laws. Finally, each state had judges and courts to interpret the laws—to decide what the laws meant and how they applied to each new situation.

Most state constitutions included a bill of rights, guaranteeing certain basic freedoms and legal protections to the state's citizens. Some of these rights, such as trial by jury and protection of personal property, can be traced back to the Magna Carta and the English Bill of Rights.

The Massachusetts Constitution

In 1780 Massachusetts became the last of the original 13 states to draw up its constitution. The document, the only one still in effect today, was unusual in three notable ways.

First, instead of making the legislature supreme, as most of the other states did, Massachusetts distributed power more evenly among the legislature, the governor's office, and the courts. Second, the governor and the courts were given the authority to check the legislature. Third, the Massachusetts constitution was created not by the legislature but through a special convention of delegates elected for that purpose. The document was then approved by a vote of the state's citizens.

The Massachusetts constitution would later become an important model for the U.S. Constitution, our country's framework for government. At the time, however, the states had loosely unified under a different framework of government called the Articles of Confederation.

Reading Check **Describing** What were the basic characteristics of governments that most states created?

Five-shilling note from Massachusetts, 1782

The Articles of Confederation

Although each state was well prepared and eager to govern itself when independence was declared, a state could not do some things on its own. It could not raise and maintain a large army, for example, and Americans realized that 13 small, separate forces would be no match for the mighty British army. Americans realized that if they wanted to win the war with Great Britain, they needed a single, strong army under central control.

For this and other reasons, the Second Continental Congress made plans for a union of the states. In 1777 the Congress detailed these plans in a document called the **Articles of Confederation,** the first constitution of the United States of America.

A confederation is a group of individuals—or, in this instance, individual state governments—who band together for a common purpose. The Articles of Confederation established a system for cooperation, or "league of friendship," among independent states.

The Articles set up a one-house legislature in which each state had one vote. This Congress was the only government body with control over the army and authority to deal with foreign countries on behalf of the states. These central powers were quite limited, though.

Student Web Activity Visit civ.glencoe.com and click on **Student Web Activities— Chapter 2** to learn more about our nation's first government.

As a result of their bad experiences with the British government, the 13 states refused to give the Congress two important powers. It had no power to enforce its laws and no power to tax. The Articles allowed the Congress to ask the states for money but not to demand it. The Congress could not, in fact, require the states to do anything.

Weaknesses of the Articles

By 1781 all 13 states had **ratified,** or approved, the Articles of Confederation. Within the next few years, however, it became clear that the Articles had some serious problems.

To begin with, the Congress could not pass a law unless 9 states voted in favor of it. Any attempt to **amend,** or change, the Articles required a unanimous vote of all 13 states. These strict voting requirements made it difficult for the Congress to accomplish anything.

Even when the Congress managed to pass laws, it could not enforce them. Unlike the state constitutions, the Articles did not provide for a governor or for courts. If a state decided to ignore a law, the Congress could do nothing about it.

A Shaky National Government

Despite its weaknesses, the Confederation Congress was able to win the Revolutionary War. A peace agreement with Great Britain, called the Treaty of Paris, was signed in 1783.

Independence, however, did not put an end to America's struggles. For one thing, the country faced serious financial troubles. Unable to collect taxes, the

Congress had borrowed money to pay for the Revolutionary War against Great Britain. It had run up a debt that would take years to repay.

The state governments had also fallen into deep debt. They taxed their citizens heavily as a result, driving many farmers out of business and sparking widespread resentment. The states also taxed goods from other states and foreign countries, hurting trade. The Confederation Congress had no power to remedy these problems.

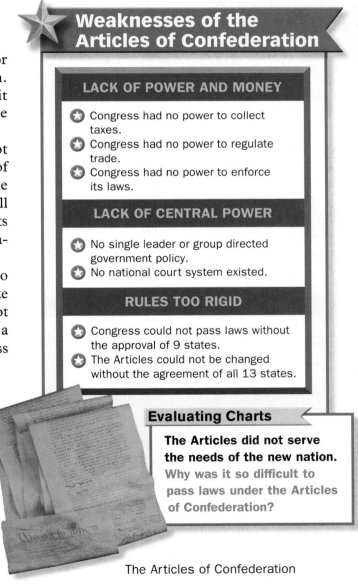

Weaknesses of the Articles of Confederation

LACK OF POWER AND MONEY

- ⭐ Congress had no power to collect taxes.
- ⭐ Congress had no power to regulate trade.
- ⭐ Congress had no power to enforce its laws.

LACK OF CENTRAL POWER

- ⭐ No single leader or group directed government policy.
- ⭐ No national court system existed.

RULES TOO RIGID

- ⭐ Congress could not pass laws without the approval of 9 states.
- ⭐ The Articles could not be changed without the agreement of all 13 states.

Evaluating Charts

The Articles did not serve the needs of the new nation. Why was it so difficult to pass laws under the Articles of Confederation?

The Articles of Confederation

Shays's Rebellion
Daniel Shays led a rebellion against high taxes that forced farmers into debt. **What need did the rebellion make clear to the states?**

taxes, led one of the most alarming disturbances. When Massachusetts courts threatened to take his farm away as payment for his debts, Shays felt the state had no right to punish him for a problem the state had created. Many other people agreed. Shays led an armed uprising of about 1,200 Massachusetts farmers on a federal arsenal. Although the rebellion, known as Shays's Rebellion, was quickly stopped, it sent a wake-up call through the country.

Many political leaders, merchants, and others were already arguing for a stronger national government. As George Washington wrote,

> **❝ I do not conceive we can exist long as a nation without having lodged somewhere a power, which will pervade the whole Union. ❞**

In 1787, 12 of the states sent delegates to a meeting in Philadelphia to revise the Articles of Confederation.

Even worse, it could do nothing about the public's insecurity. Americans feared that the government could not protect their safety or their property. During 1786 and 1787, riots broke out in several states. Daniel Shays, a farmer who like many Americans had fallen into debt because of heavy state

✓ **Reading Check** **Explaining** Why did Americans decide to revise the Articles of Confederation?

SECTION 3 ASSESSMENT

Checking for Understanding

1. Key Terms Write a paragraph related to early governments in the United States using all of the terms listed below.
constitution, bicameral, confederation, ratify, amend

Reviewing Main Ideas

2. Identify What was the first written constitution of the United States?

3. Contrast How did the Massachusetts state constitution (1780) differ from most of the other state constitutions?

Critical Thinking

4. Drawing Conclusions Why do you think most early state constitutions made the legislature supreme?

5. Categorizing Information On a graphic organizer like the one below, list the needs for the Articles of Confederation as well as its weaknesses.

Articles of Confederation	
Need for Articles:	Weaknesses of Articles:

Analyzing Visuals

6. Infer Review the weaknesses of the Articles on page 41. Why did Congress have to borrow money to pay federal expenses, thereby going into debt?

★ **BE AN ACTIVE CITIZEN** ★

7. Research Search your local newspaper for an article about federal taxes or regulations. How might this story be different if the U.S. government still operated under the Articles?

SKILLBUILDER

Analyzing Primary Sources

Why Learn This Skill?

You missed the school basketball game last week and want to know how well the team played. How will you find out? You probably would ask a schoolmate who went to the game. You might also ask a student from the opposing team's school. Their accounts would be on-the-scene, eyewitness accounts known as primary sources, but they may differ. Primary sources provide different perspectives about an event or issue.

Learning the Skill

To analyze primary sources, follow these steps:
- First determine if the information at hand is a primary or a secondary source. On-the-scene and eyewitness accounts are primary sources. Accounts prepared by persons who may have researched an event at a later time are secondary sources.
- Determine the identity of the person giving the account.
- Identify the person's purpose for creating the account.
- Look for information that may be based on the author's opinion rather than factual evidence.
- Draw conclusions about the reliability of the source material.

Continental currency

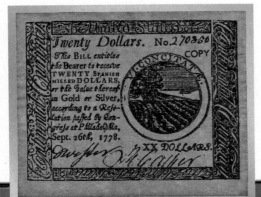

Practicing the Skill

In December 1777, during the Revolutionary War, General George Washington wrote a letter from his camp at Valley Forge to the Continental Congress. Read the excerpt below and answer the following questions.

Yesterday afternoon . . . I order'd the troops to be in readiness, . . . but . . . the men were unable to stir on [account] of provision, . . . Soap, vinegar and other articles allowed by Congress we see none of . . . the first indeed we now have little [use for due to] few men having more than one shirt, many only a [portion] of one, and some none at all . . . men now in camp [are] unfit for duty because they are bare foot and otherwise naked . . . numbers are [made unfit] on [account of scarce] blankets, being obliged to set up all night by fires, instead of taking comfortable rest in a natural way . . . I much doubt the practicability of holding the army together much longer.

❶ Why did Washington write to the Continental Congress?
❷ Is Washington's letter a primary or secondary source?
❸ How do you think the letter might have influenced the Continental Congress?

Applying the Skill

Select a primary source account from a printed news article. Use the steps you have learned to analyze it. Bring the article to class to share your conclusions with your classmates.

Practice key skills with Glencoe's **Skillbuilder Interactive Workbook CD-ROM, Level 1.**

The Declaration of Independence

In Congress, July 4, 1776. The unanimous Declaration of the thirteen united States of America,

[Preamble]

When in the Course of human events, it becomes necessary for one people to dissolve the political bands which have connected them with another, and to assume among the Powers of the earth, the separate and equal station to which the Laws of Nature and of Nature's God entitle them, a decent respect to the opinions of mankind requires that they should declare the causes which **impel** them to the separation.

[Declaration of Natural Rights]

We hold these truths to be self-evident, that all men are created equal, that they are **endowed** by their Creator with certain unalienable Rights, that among these are Life, Liberty, and the pursuit of Happiness.

That to secure these rights, Governments are instituted among Men, deriving their just powers from the consent of the governed,

That whenever any Form of Government becomes destructive of these ends, it is the Right of the People to alter or to abolish it, and to institute new Government, laying its foundation on such principles and organizing its powers in such form, as to them shall seem most likely to effect their Safety and Happiness. Prudence, indeed, will dictate that Governments long established should not be changed for light and transient causes; and accordingly all experience hath shown, that mankind are more disposed to suffer, while evils are sufferable, than to right themselves by abolishing the forms to which they are accustomed. But when a long train of abuses and usurpations, pursuing invariably the same Object evinces a design to reduce them under absolute **Despotism,** it is their right, it is their duty, to throw off such Government, and to provide new Guards for their future security.

[List of Grievances]

Such has been the patient sufferance of these Colonies; and such is now the necessity which constrains them to alter their former Systems of Government. The history of the present King of Great Britain is a history of repeated injuries and **usurpations,** all having

---

What It Means

The Preamble The Declaration of Independence has four parts. The Preamble explains why the Continental Congress drew up the Declaration.

impel *force*

What It Means

Natural Rights The second part, the Declaration of Natural Rights, lists the rights of the citizens. It goes on to explain that, in a republic, people form a government to protect their rights.

endowed *provided*

despotism *unlimited power*

What It Means

List of Grievances The third part of the Declaration lists the colonists' complaints against the British government. Notice that King George III is singled out for blame.

usurpations *unjust uses of power*

44

in direct object the establishment of an absolute Tyranny over these States. To prove this, let Facts be submitted to a candid world.

He has refused his Assent to Laws, the most wholesome and necessary for the public good.

He has forbidden his Governors to pass Laws of immediate and pressing importance, unless suspended in their operation till his Assent should be obtained; and when so suspended, he has utterly neglected to attend to them.

He has refused to pass other Laws for the accommodation of large districts of people, unless those people would **relinquish** the right of Representation in the Legislature, a right **inestimable** to them and formidable to tyrants only.

relinquish *give up*
inestimable *priceless*

He has called together legislative bodies at places unusual, uncomfortable, and distant from the depository of their Public Records, for the sole purpose of fatiguing them into compliance with his measures.

He has dissolved Representative Houses repeatedly, for opposing with manly firmness his invasions on the rights of the people.

He has refused for a long time, after such dissolutions, to cause others to be elected; whereby the Legislative Powers, incapable of **Annihilation,** have returned to the People at large for their exercise; the State remaining in the mean time exposed to all the dangers of invasion from without, and **convulsions** within.

annihilation *destruction*

convulsions *violent disturbances*

He has endeavoured to prevent the population of these States; for that purpose obstructing the Laws for **Naturalization of Foreigners;** refusing to pass others to encourage their migrations hither, and raising the conditions of new Appropriations of Lands.

Naturalization of Foreigners *process by which foreign-born persons become citizens*

He has obstructed the Administration of Justice, by refusing his Assent to Laws for establishing Judiciary Powers.

He has made Judges dependent on his Will alone, for the **tenure** of their offices, and the amount and payment of their salaries.

tenure *term*

He has erected a multitude of New Offices, and sent hither swarms of Officers to harass our people, and eat out their substance.

quartering *lodging*

He has kept among us, in times of peace, Standing Armies without the Consent of our legislature.

He has affected to render the Military independent of and superior to the Civil Power.

He has combined with others to subject us to a jurisdiction foreign to our constitution, and unacknowledged by our laws; giving his Assent to their acts of pretended legislation:

For **quartering** large bodies of troops among us:

For protecting them, by a mock Trial, from Punishment for any Murders which they should commit on the Inhabitants of these States:

For cutting off our Trade with all parts of the world:

For imposing taxes on us without our Consent:

For depriving us in many cases, of the benefits of Trial by Jury:

For transporting us beyond Seas to be tried for pretended offences:

render *make*

For abolishing the free System of English Laws in a neighbouring Province, establishing therein an Arbitrary government, and enlarging its Boundaries so as to **render** it at once an example and fit instrument for introducing the same absolute rule into these Colonies:

For taking away our Charters, abolishing our most valuable Laws, and altering fundamentally the Forms of our Governments:

For suspending our own Legislature, and declaring themselves invested with Power to legislate for us in all cases whatsoever.

abdicated *given up*

He has **abdicated** Government here, by declaring us out of his Protection and waging War against us.

He has plundered our seas, ravaged our Coasts, burnt our towns, and destroyed the lives of our people.

He is at this time transporting large armies of foreign mercenaries to compleat the works of death, desolation and tyranny, already begun with circumstances of Cruelty & **perfidy** scarcely paralleled in the most barbarous ages, and totally unworthy the Head of a civilized nation.

perfidy *violation of trust*

He has constrained our fellow Citizens taken Captive on the high Seas to bear Arms against their Country, to become the executioners of their friends and Brethren, or to fall themselves by their Hands.

insurrections *rebellions*

He has excited domestic **insurrections** amongst us, and has endeavoured to bring on the inhabitants of our frontiers, the merciless Indian Savages, whose known rule of warfare, is an undistinguished destruction of all ages, sexes and conditions.

petitioned for redress *asked formally for a correction of wrongs*

In every stage of these Oppressions We have **Petitioned for Redress** in the most humble terms: Our repeated Petitions have been answered only by repeated injury. A Prince, whose character is thus marked by every act which may define a Tyrant, is unfit to be the ruler of a free People.

unwarrantable jurisdiction *unjustified authority*

Nor have We been wanting in attention to our British brethren. We have warned them from time to time of attempts by their legislature to extend an **unwarrantable jurisdiction** over us. We have reminded them of the circumstances of our emigration and settlement here. We have appealed to their native justice and magnanimity, and we have conjured them by the ties of our common kindred to disavow these usurpations, which, would inevitably interrupt our connections and correspondence. They too have been deaf to the voice of justice and of **consanguinity**. We must, therefore, acquiesce in the necessity, which denounces our Separation, and hold them, as we hold the rest of mankind, Enemies in War, in Peace Friends.

consanguinity *originating from the same ancestor*

[Resolution of Independence by the United States]

We, therefore, the Representatives of the united States of America, in General Congress, Assembled, appealing to the Supreme Judge of the world for the **rectitude** of our intentions, do, in the Name, and by Authority of the good People of these Colonies, solemnly publish and declare, That these United Colonies are, and of Right ought to be Free and Independent States; that they are Absolved from all Allegiance to the British Crown, and that all political connection between them and the State of Great Britain, is and ought to be totally dissolved; and that as Free and Independent States, they have full Power to levy War, conclude Peace, contract Alliances, establish Commerce, and to do all other Acts and Things which Independent States may of right do.

And for the support of this Declaration, with a firm reliance on the Protection of Divine Providence, we mutually pledge to each other our Lives, our Fortunes and our sacred Honor.

John Hancock
    President from
    Massachusetts

Georgia
Button Gwinnett
Lyman Hall
George Walton

North Carolina
William Hooper
Joseph Hewes
John Penn

South Carolina
Edward Rutledge
Thomas Heyward, Jr.
Thomas Lynch, Jr.
Arthur Middleton

Maryland
Samuel Chase
William Paca
Thomas Stone
Charles Carroll
    of Carrollton

Virginia
George Wythe
Richard Henry Lee
Thomas Jefferson
Benjamin Harrison
Thomas Nelson, Jr.
Francis Lightfoot Lee
Carter Braxton

Pennsylvania
Robert Morris
Benjamin Rush
Benjamin Franklin
John Morton
George Clymer
James Smith
George Taylor
James Wilson
George Ross

Delaware
Caesar Rodney
George Read
Thomas McKean

New York
William Floyd
Philip Livingston
Francis Lewis
Lewis Morris

New Jersey
Richard Stockton
John Witherspoon
Francis Hopkinson
John Hart
Abraham Clark

New Hampshire
Josiah Bartlett
William Whipple
Matthew Thornton

Massachusetts
Samuel Adams
John Adams
Robert Treat Paine
Elbridge Gerry

Rhode Island
Stephen Hopkins
William Ellery

Connecticut
Samuel Huntington
William Williams
Oliver Wolcott
Roger Sherman

What It Means

Resolution of Independence The final section declares that the colonies are "Free and Independent States" with the full power to make war, to form alliances, and to trade with other countries.

rectitude *rightness*

What It Means

Signers of the Declaration The signers, as representatives of the American people, declared the colonies independent from Great Britain. Most members signed the document on August 2, 1776.

Assessment & Activities

Review to Learn

Section 1
- The Magna Carta limited the power of the monarch.
- By the late 1300s, Parliament had grown into the lawmaking body of England.

Section 2
- Although American colonists had learned to manage their own affairs, the British government tightened its control over the colonies in the mid-1700s.

- Great Britain did this by enforcing steep taxes on the colonists, which the colonists protested.

Section 3
- The first constitutions of the American states set up a legislature, a governor, and court systems. Most included a bill of rights.

- By 1781 all 13 states had ratified the Articles of Confederation. The first government of the United States, set up by the Articles of Confederation, had limited powers.

FOLDABLES™
Study Organizer

Using Your Foldables Study Organizer
Create a matching quiz of about 10 questions using your foldable. Trade quizzes with a classmate and see how you do on your classmate's quiz.

Reviewing Key Terms

Write the chapter term that matches each definition below.

1. the refusal to purchase certain goods
2. a written plan of government signed by the colonists of Plymouth, Massachusetts
3. a legislature consisting of two parts, or houses
4. the English legislature
5. the document that explained why the United States should be a free nation
6. the agreement that King John of England was forced to sign in 1215, which limited the power of the monarch
7. to change
8. a court ruling in an earlier case
9. to cancel
10. the first written constitution of the United States

Reviewing Main Ideas

11. What principle of English government did the Glorious Revolution establish?
12. What is a system of law based on precedent and customs called?
13. What is historically significant about Virginia's House of Burgesses?
14. What changed the relationship between Great Britain and the American colonies after 1763?
15. How did colonists react to the Stamp Act in 1765?
16. What were the Intolerable Acts and how did colonists react to them?
17. How did the first Massachusetts state constitution differ from most other state constitutions of the time?
18. Why were the Articles of Confederation important? What were the primary weaknesses of the Articles of Confederation?

Critical Thinking

19. Analyzing Information The Articles of Confederation denied Congress the power to collect taxes. Could a government survive today without this power? Why or why not?

20. Determining Cause and Effect Analyze the effects of British actions against the colonists by completing a graphic organizer like the one below.

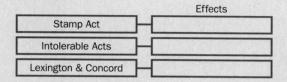

	Effects
Stamp Act	
Intolerable Acts	
Lexington & Concord	

Practicing Skills

21. Analyzing Primary Sources Read the Declaration of Independence on pages 44–47. State the main idea of the document. Then list at least five details that support the main idea.

 **Economics Activity**

22. One response of the colonists to the Stamp Act was a boycott of certain British goods. Boycotts can be an effective economic weapon when used by groups to influence government policy. Find an example of a twentieth-century boycott. What were the goals of the organizers? How successful was the boycott?

Analyzing Visuals

23. This painting from the 1770s uses symbols to represent the nation. What does the woman represent? What is she stepping on? What do all the symbols represent?

★ CITIZENSHIP COOPERATIVE ACTIVITY ★

24. The United States was born out of a protest movement against the British government. Research recent protest movements with a classmate. Compare the tactics of the colonists to the tactics used by recent protestors.

 Technology Activity

25. Use the Internet to research the constitutions of the original 13 states. Create and fill out a table in a word processing document with five columns labeled State, Date of First Constitution, Date of Current Constitution, Number of Constitutions, and Number of Amendments.

 Standardized Test Practice

The Princeton Review

Directions: Choose the *best* answer to the following question.

Many of the early state constitutions included a bill of rights. What was the purpose of these bills of rights?

F to set up three branches of government

G to guarantee certain basic freedoms and rights to citizens

H to guarantee the power of the legislature

J to declare independence from Great Britain

Test-Taking Tip

Read the question carefully. If you do not immediately recognize the correct answer, then eliminate answers that you know are incorrect and narrow your choices.

CHAPTER 3

The Constitution

★ CITIZENSHIP AND YOU ★

The Constitution is the nation's most important document. Written in 1787, it set up a system of government that has flourished for more than 200 years. Realizing that changes would be needed from time to time, the writers of the Constitution set up a process to add amendments. It is this ability to adapt, while preserving the basic form of American government, that is the Constitution's priceless heritage. Contact the National Archives in Washington, D.C., to learn more about the Constitution. Prepare a brief report that describes what you find.

To learn more about the drafting of the Constitution, view the *Democracy in Action* video lesson 2: The Creation of the Federal Government.

 FOLDABLES TM
Study Organizer

Summarizing Information Study Foldable *Make and use this study guide to record the main ideas of the chapter and information on the United States Constitution.*

Step 1 *Fold a sheet of paper in half from top to bottom.*

Step 2 *Fold the paper in half again from side to side.*

Reading and Writing *As you read the chapter, record events that led to the formation, ratification, and implementation of the United States Constitution.*

Step 3 *Label your foldable as shown.*

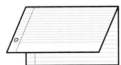

Journal on the U.S. Constitution

The Constitution on display ▶

CIVICS
Online

Chapter Overview Visit the *Civics Today* Web site at civ.glencoe.com and click on **Chapter Overviews— Chapter 3** to preview chapter information.

The Road to the Constitution

GUIDE TO READING

Main Idea

In 1787 a remarkable group of American leaders from all but one state gathered in Philadelphia to address the weaknesses of the Articles of Confederation, but they soon decided that a new constitution was needed.

Key Terms

Constitutional Convention

Reading Strategy

Identifying Information As you read, list prominent leaders and characteristics of delegates to the Constitutional Convention in a web diagram like the one below.

Delegates to the Constitutional Convention

Read to Learn

- Who attended the Constitutional Convention?
- What rules did the delegates adopt to conduct their business?

Americans in Action

Charles Pinckney was so intent on impressing his colleagues—the other delegates to the Constitutional Convention—that he lied about his age. Pinckney's vanity led him to boast that he was only 24, allowing him to claim distinction as the youngest delegate. He was, in fact, 30 years old. In spite of certain personal qualities, Pinckney distinguished himself in the process of creating an improved plan of government for the United States.

Charles Pinckney

A Distinguished Gathering

By early 1787, it was clear that the national government had to be strengthened. The Congress agreed there were serious problems with the Articles of Confederation. Each state was asked to send delegates to a convention in Philadelphia to fix the flaws. (This was to become the Constitutional Convention.) Only Rhode Island chose not to take part because its leaders opposed a stronger central government.

The convention began in Philadelphia's Independence Hall on May 25, 1787. Rain fell heavily during the opening week, leaving the roads to the city choked with mud. Many delegates had to travel long distances and arrived late. Once all were assembled, however, they were an extraordinary group.

Most of the 55 men present were well-educated lawyers, merchants, college presidents, physicians, generals, governors, and planters with considerable political experience. Eight of the delegates had signed the Declaration of Independence. Seven had been governors of their states, and forty-one were or had been members of the Continental Congress. Native Americans, African Americans, and women were not considered part of the political process, so none attended.

Benjamin Franklin of Pennsylvania, 81, was the oldest delegate. He was famous as a diplomat, writer, inventor, and scientist. Most delegates, however, were still young men in their thirties or forties with great careers ahead of them. Two delegates, George Washington and James Madison, would go on to become presidents of the United States. Nineteen would become U.S. senators, and thirteen served in the House of Representatives. Four men would become federal judges, and four others would become Supreme Court justices.

A few notable leaders were not at the convention. Thomas Jefferson and John Adams were both in Europe as representatives of the American government—Jefferson in Paris and Adams in London. Patrick Henry, a prominent Virginian, was also missing. Although elected as a delegate, he was against the convention and did not attend.

Reading Check **Generalizing** How would you describe the delegates to the Constitutional Convention?

Early Decisions

The delegates agreed unanimously that George Washington should preside over the convention. Widely respected for his leadership during the American Revolution, Washington would now call on speakers and make sure that the meetings ran in an orderly, efficient manner. At the start, he reminded the delegates of the importance of their task. He warned that if they could not come up with an acceptable plan of government, "perhaps another dreadful conflict is to be sustained."

Operating Procedures

One of Washington's first actions was to appoint a committee to set rules for conducting the convention. The committee decided that meetings could not be held unless delegates from at least seven states were present. Decisions were to be made by a majority vote of the states, with each state having only one vote. That meant that the delegates from each state would decide by majority rule how to cast their single ballot.

The participants at the convention also agreed to keep all discussions secret. The public was not allowed to attend meetings, the doors were guarded, and the windows were kept tightly shut despite the summer heat. Each delegate promised not to tell outsiders what was going on inside.

This secrecy rule enabled the delegates to speak freely, without worrying about the public's reaction. That made it easier for them to bargain with one another and to

Independence Hall The Pennsylvania State House, later known as Independence Hall, hosted the Declaration of Independence signing and the Constitutional Convention. It is now a museum. **What was the delegates' goal when they gathered at the convention?**

The Constitutional Convention Delegates to the convention had to make many compromises before working out a plan for a government acceptable to all. **What were the rules for conducting the convention?**

change their minds on the many issues debated. However, the secrecy policy also meant that no formal records of the convention were kept. Most of the details we know come from a notebook of daily events written by James Madison.

The Need for a New Constitution

The Congress had given delegates the job of revising the Articles of Confederation. They quickly agreed, however, that changing the Articles was not enough. They decided instead to discard the Articles and write a new constitution. All of the delegates set out to strengthen the national government by creating a new plan of government. Thus the meeting in Philadelphia came to be known as the **Constitutional Convention.**

✓**Reading Check** **Explaining** Why were no formal records kept at the Constitutional Convention?

SECTION 1 ASSESSMENT

Checking for Understanding

1. **Key Terms** Write a sentence using the term below that explains the purpose of the gathering in Philadelphia.
   Constitutional Convention

Reviewing Main Ideas

2. **Explain** Why did Rhode Island refuse to send a delegate to the Constitutional Convention? What did the delegates have in common?

3. **Describe** How were decisions made by the Constitutional Convention? What other decisions about operating procedures did the delegates make?

Critical Thinking

4. **Drawing Conclusions** If you had been a delegate to the Constitutional Convention, would you have voted for the secrecy rule? Why or why not?

5. **Categorizing Information** Organize information about the early decisions of the Constitutional Convention by completing a graphic organizer like the one below.

```
        Early Decisions of the
        Constitutional Convention
    ┌───┬───┬───┬───┬───┐
    │   │   │   │   │   │
    └───┴───┴───┴───┴───┘
```

Analyzing Visuals

6. **Infer** Examine the painting of the Constitutional Convention on this page. Who is shown leading the Convention? Why did the delegates choose him?

★**BE AN ACTIVE CITIZEN**★

7. **Research** Find out about your city council and state legislature. What are the secrecy rules for those bodies? Can they meet in secret like the Constitutional Convention did? Under what circumstances can they meet without having the public present? Report your findings to the class.

Creating and Ratifying the Constitution

GUIDE TO READING

Main Idea

Delegates to the Constitutional Convention arrived with varying ideas and plans of government, which meant that compromise would be necessary to reach agreement.

Key Terms

legislative branch, executive branch, judicial branch, Great Compromise, Three-Fifths Compromise, Electoral College, Federalists, federalism, Anti-Federalists

Reading Strategy

Comparing and Contrasting As you read, compare the Virginia Plan to the New Jersey Plan by completing a Venn diagram like the one below.

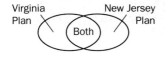

Virginia Plan   New Jersey Plan

Both

Read to Learn

• What plans of government did delegates offer at the Constitutional Convention?

• What compromises were agreed upon by the delegates?

Americans in Action

Credit for the Great Compromise goes to Roger Sherman, whose name most Americans have never heard. As a boy, he was apprenticed to a shoemaker. Sherman's thirst for knowledge led him to learn on his own, even resorting to reading while sitting at his cobbler's bench. When Sherman was 19, his father died, and Sherman became the head of the household. Even as he struggled to support his mother and siblings, he read and acquired knowledge. In time, a self-educated Sherman became a practicing attorney. From there, appointments as justice of the peace, as a delegate to the colonial assembly, and as judge of the court of common pleas led him further into a life of public service.

Roger Sherman

Two Opposing Plans

The delegates to the Constitutional Convention, like Roger Sherman, were determined to create a framework of government that all states could accept. Everyone knew that failure could mean disaster. Elbridge Gerry of Massachusetts spoke for most when he said,

> **❝I would bury my bones in this city rather than [leave] . . . the convention without anything being done.❞**

On May 29, 1787, shortly after the convention began, the Virginia delegates proposed a plan for the new government. James Madison had designed what became known as the Virginia Plan.

Under the Articles of Confederation, the national government had consisted of only a legislative branch with a one-house Congress. The Virginia Plan, by contrast, called for a government with three branches. In addition to the **legislative branch** (the lawmakers), there would be an **executive branch** to carry out the laws and a **judicial branch**—a system of courts—to interpret and apply the laws. The legislature, moreover, would be divided into two houses. In each house, states would be represented on the basis of their population. Large states would have more votes than smaller states.

The Virginia Plan appealed to delegates from Massachusetts, Pennsylvania, and New York, as well as Virginia. The small states, however, feared that a government dominated by the large states would ignore their interests.

After two weeks of angry discussion, William Paterson of New Jersey presented an alternative proposal. The New Jersey Plan, as it is known, also called for three branches of government. However, the legislature would have only one house and each state would get one vote, as under the Articles of Confederation. Delegates from Delaware, New Jersey, and Maryland approved of this plan. It made their states equal in power to the big states. Of course, the large states would not accept this plan. They thought larger states should have more power than smaller states.

Reading Check **Contrasting** How did the Virginia Plan differ from the New Jersey Plan?

Constitutional Compromises

For six weeks the delegates debated the merits of the two plans. Neither side wanted to give in. Some delegates even threatened to leave the convention; yet all the delegates shared the goal of creating a new constitution, so they kept working.

The Great Compromise

A committee headed by Roger Sherman of Connecticut finally came up with an answer. The committee proposed that Congress have two houses—a Senate and a House of Representatives. Each state would have equal representation in the Senate, which would please the small states. In the House, representation would be based on population, which would please the big states. (See Chapter 6 for more information.)

After much discussion, the delegates decided to accept Sherman's plan. No group was completely happy, but this was a solution

Biographies

Sam Ervin (1896–1995)

Sam J. Ervin, Jr., described himself as nothing but an "old country lawyer." However, members of the U.S. Senate, where he served for 20 years, knew otherwise. Whenever Ervin, the crusty senator from North Carolina, arched his eyebrows, they braced themselves for a lecture in constitutional law. "Senator Sam," as he came to be known, believed the Constitution should be followed to the letter.

Born in Morganton, North Carolina, Ervin gained his love of the Constitution from his father, a fiery, self-taught lawyer. He defended the Constitution on the battlefields of World War I and upheld it in the North Carolina state legislature and on the North Carolina state supreme court.

In the U.S. Senate, Ervin helped break the power of Senator Joseph McCarthy, who had falsely charged hundreds of Americans in the 1950s with communist activities. In 1974 he headed the committee charged with investigating wrongdoings by President Richard Nixon (known as the Watergate investigation). Ervin believed the Constitution was "the wisest instrument the earth has ever known." He spent his life ensuring that elected officials upheld it.

with which all could live. Historians call Sherman's plan the Connecticut Compromise or the **Great Compromise.** (A compromise is a way of resolving disagreements in which each side gives up something but gains something else.)

The Three-Fifths Compromise

Although the Great Compromise settled the structure of Congress, questions remained about how to calculate the population for purposes of representation. At the time of the Constitutional Convention more than 550,000 African Americans, mostly in the South, were enslaved. The Southern states wanted to count these people as part of their populations to increase their voting power in the House of Representatives. The Northern states, which had few enslaved persons, opposed the idea. They argued that because enslaved persons were not allowed to vote or otherwise participate in government, they should not be used to give Southern states a stronger voice in Congress.

In the **Three-Fifths Compromise,** delegates agreed that every five enslaved persons would count as three free persons. Thus three-fifths of the slave population in each state would be used in determining representation in Congress. That number would also be used in figuring taxes.

Other Compromises

Northern and Southern delegates to the convention compromised on trade matters, too. The Northern states felt that Congress should be able to regulate both foreign commerce and trade between the states. The Southern states, however, feared that Congress would use this power to tax exports—goods sold to other countries. If this happened, the Southern economy would suffer because it depended heavily on exports of tobacco, rice, and other products.

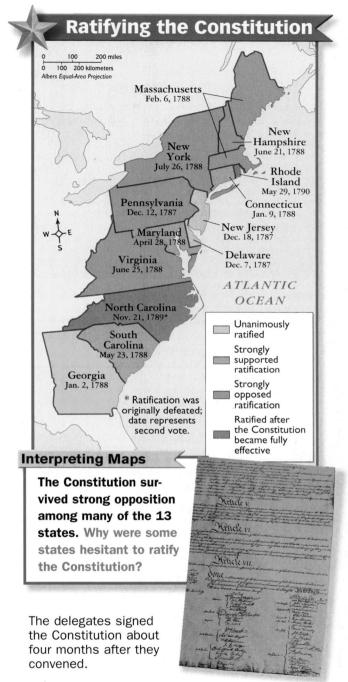

Ratifying the Constitution

Massachusetts
Feb. 6, 1788

New Hampshire
June 21, 1788

New York
July 26, 1788

Rhode Island
May 29, 1790

Pennsylvania
Dec. 12, 1787

Connecticut
Jan. 9, 1788

Maryland
April 28, 1788

New Jersey
Dec. 18, 1787

Virginia
June 25, 1788

Delaware
Dec. 7, 1787

ATLANTIC OCEAN

North Carolina
Nov. 21, 1789*

South Carolina
May 23, 1788

Georgia
Jan. 2, 1788

* Ratification was originally defeated; date represents second vote.

Unanimously ratified

Strongly supported ratification

Strongly opposed ratification

Ratified after the Constitution became fully effective

Interpreting Maps

The Constitution survived strong opposition among many of the 13 states. Why were some states hesitant to ratify the Constitution?

The delegates signed the Constitution about four months after they convened.

Southerners also feared that Congress might stop slave traders from bringing enslaved people into the United States. Again, Southern delegates objected because Southern plantations depended on the labor of slaves. Again a compromise among the delegates would settle the issue.

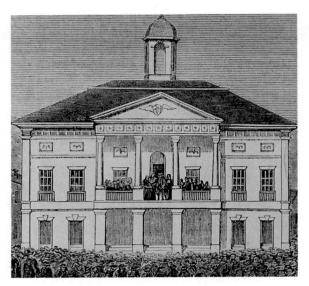

Federal Hall New York City became the nation's temporary capital. George Washington was elected president, and Congress met for the first time in 1789 in Federal Hall. **The Constitution took effect after which state ratified it?**

After some discussion, the Southern states agreed that Congress could regulate trade between the states, as well as with other countries. In exchange, the North agreed that Congress could not tax exports, nor could it interfere with the slave trade before 1808.

The delegates compromised on various other disagreements about their new government. Some delegates, for example, thought members of Congress should choose the president; others believed that the people should vote to decide the presidency. The solution was the **Electoral College,** a group of people who would be named by each state legislature to select the president and vice president. The Electoral College system is still used today, but the voters in each state, not the legislatures, now choose electors.

Reading Check **Cause and Effect** What two arguments resulted in the Electoral College compromise?

Approving the Constitution

All summer, the delegates to the Constitutional Convention hammered out the details of the new government. As their work drew to an end, some delegates headed home, but 42 remained. On September 17, 1787, they gathered for the last time. A committee, headed by Gouverneur Morris, had put their ideas in writing, and the Constitution was ready to be signed. All but three delegates signed their names at the bottom.

The next step was to win ratification, or approval, of the Constitution. The delegates had decided that each state would set up a ratifying convention to vote "yes" or "no." When at least 9 of the 13 states had ratified it, the Constitution would become the supreme law of the land.

A Divided Public

Americans reacted to the proposed Constitution in different ways. Supporters of the document called themselves **Federalists.** They chose this name to emphasize that the Constitution would create a system of **federalism,** a form of government in which power is divided between the federal, or national, government and the states.

To win support, the Federalists reminded Americans of the flaws in the Articles of Confederation. They argued that the United States would not survive without a strong national government. In a series of essays known as *The Federalist,* Alexander Hamilton, James Madison, and John Jay defended the Constitution. Madison argued in *The Federalist,* No. 10:

  ❝A republic, by which I mean a government in which the scheme of representation takes place . . . promises the cure for which we are seeking. . . .❞

TIME

Political Cartoons

"Hey, the Constitution isn't engraved in stone."

and it seems to be diverted toward money and | Schneider, two men with little b
time. Making the world a more convenient | ing the company's reven

Analyzing Visuals The writers of the Constitution looked to the future in many ways—including their decision to allow amendments to the document they created. What is the setting for this cartoon? What do you imagine prompted the speaker to make the statement he did?

Those who opposed the Constitution, the **Anti-Federalists,** felt that it gave too much power to the national government and took too much away from the states. The Anti-Federalists also objected to the absence of a bill of rights. They thought the Constitution failed to provide protection for certain individual liberties, such as the freedoms of speech and religion.

Reaching Agreement

The Federalists eventually agreed with the Anti-Federalists that a bill of rights was a good idea. They promised that if the Constitution was adopted, the new government would add a bill of rights to it.

That promise helped turn the tide. Several states had already voted for ratification. On June 21, 1788, New Hampshire became the ninth state to do so, and the Constitution took effect. In time, the four remaining states ratified the Constitution, ending with Rhode Island in 1790. The 13 independent states were now one nation, the United States of America.

✓ Reading Check **Identifying** What promise helped get the Constitution ratified?

SECTION 2 ASSESSMENT

Checking for Understanding

1. **Key Terms** Write short paragraphs about the Constitutional Convention using the group of terms below: Federalists, federalism, Anti-Federalists, Great Compromise.

Reviewing Main Ideas

2. **Identify** With what issue did the Three-Fifths Compromise deal? How did it resolve this issue?

3. **Explain** What was the purpose of *The Federalist*? Why did the Anti-Federalists object to the Constitution?

Critical Thinking

4. **Drawing Conclusions** Why were Southerners at the Constitutional Convention fearful of government control of trade?

5. **Comparing and Contrasting** On a graphic organizer like the one below, compare the views of the Federalists and the Anti-Federalists.

Federalists	Anti-Federalists

Analyzing Visuals

6. **Interpret** Examine the map on page 57. Which states ratified the Constitution after it took effect?

★ **BE AN ACTIVE CITIZEN** ★

7. **Survey** Conduct a survey of at least 10 adults in which you ask them whether they favor continuing the Electoral College or amending the Constitution to have the presidency determined by the popular vote. Ask respondents to explain their answers.

The Constitution of the United States

The Constitution of the United States is truly a remarkable document. It was one of the first written constitutions in modern history. The Framers wanted to devise a plan for a strong central government that would unify the country, as well as preserve the ideals of the Declaration of Independence. The document they wrote created a representative legislature, the office of president, a system of courts, and a process for adding amendments. For over 200 years, the flexibility and strength of the Constitution has guided the nation's political leaders. The document has become a symbol of pride and a force for national unity.

The entire text of the Constitution and its amendments follows. For easier study, those passages that have been set aside or changed by the adoption of amendments are printed in blue. Also included are explanatory notes that will help clarify the meaning of each article and section.

James Madison, author of the Constitution

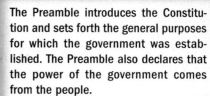

Preamble

We the People of the United States, in Order to form a more perfect Union, establish Justice, insure domestic Tranquility, provide for the common defence, promote the general Welfare, and secure the Blessings of Liberty to ourselves and our Posterity, do ordain and establish this Constitution for the United States of America.

Article I

Section 1

All legislative Powers herein granted shall be vested in a Congress of the United States, which shall consist of a Senate and House of Representatives.

Section 2

[1.] The House of Representatives shall be composed of Members chosen every second Year by the People of the several States, and the Electors in each State shall have the Qualifications requisite for Electors of the most numerous Branch of the State Legislature.

[2.] No person shall be a Representative who shall not have attained to the Age of twenty five Years, and been seven Years a Citizen of the United States, and who shall not, when elected, be an Inhabitant of that State in which he shall be chosen.

[3.] Representatives and direct Taxes shall be apportioned among the several States which may be included within this Union, according to their respective Numbers, which shall be determined by adding to the whole Number of free Persons, including those bound to Service for a Term of Years, and excluding Indians not taxed, three fifths of all other Persons. The actual Enumeration shall be made within three Years after the first Meeting of the Congress of the United States, and within every subsequent Term of ten Years, in such Manner as they shall by Law direct. The Number of Representatives shall not exceed one for every thirty Thousand, but each State shall have at Least one Representative; and until such enumeration shall be made, the State of New Hampshire shall be entitled to chuse three; Massachusetts eight, Rhode-Island and Providence Plantations one, Connecticut five, New-York six, New Jersey four, Pennsylvania eight, Delaware one, Maryland six, Virginia ten, North Carolina five, South Carolina five, and Georgia three.

[4.] When vacancies happen in the Representation from any State, the Executive Authority thereof shall issue Writs of Election to fill such Vacancies.

[5.] The House of Representatives shall chuse their Speaker and other Officers; and shall have the sole Power of Impeachment.

What It Means

The Preamble introduces the Constitution and sets forth the general purposes for which the government was established. The Preamble also declares that the power of the government comes from the people.

The printed text of the document shows the spelling and punctuation of the parchment original.

What It Means

Article I. The Legislative Branch The Constitution contains seven divisions called articles. Each article covers a general topic. For example, Articles I, II, and III create the three branches of the national government—the legislative, executive, and judicial branches. Most of the articles are divided into sections.

What It Means

Representation The number of representatives from each state is based on the size of the state's population. Each state is entitled to at least one representative. *What are the qualifications for members of the House of Representatives?*

Vocabulary

preamble: *introduction*
constitution: *principles and laws of a nation*
enumeration: *census or population count*
impeachment: *bringing charges against an official*

61

What It Means

Electing Senators Originally, senators were chosen by the state legislators of their own states. The Seventeenth Amendment changed this, so that senators are now elected by the people. There are 100 senators, 2 from each state. The vice president serves as president of the Senate.

John Adams, the first vice president

What It Means

Impeachment One of Congress's powers is the power to impeach—to accuse government officials of wrongdoing, put them on trial, and if necessary remove them from office. *Which body has the power to decide the official's guilt or innocence?*

Vocabulary

president pro tempore: *presiding officer of Senate who serves when the vice president is absent*
indictment: *charging a person with an offense*
quorum: *minimum number of members that must be present to conduct sessions*
adjourn: *to suspend a session*
immunity privilege: *members cannot be sued or prosecuted for anything they say in Congress*
emoluments: *salaries*
bill: *draft of a proposed law*
revenue: *income raised by government*

Section 3

[1.] The Senate of the United States shall be composed of two Senators from each State, chosen by the Legislature thereof, for six Years; and each Senator shall have one Vote.

[2.] Immediately after they shall be assembled in Consequence of the first Election, they shall be divided as equally as may be into three Classes. The Seats of the Senators of the first Class shall be vacated at the Expiration of the second Year, of the second Class at the Expiration of the fourth Year, and of the third Class at the Expiration of the sixth Year, so that one third may be chosen every second Year; and if Vacancies happen by Resignation, or otherwise, during the Recess of the Legislature of any State, the Executive thereof may make temporary Appointments until the next Meeting of the Legislature, which shall then fill such Vacancies.

[3.] No Person shall be a Senator who shall not have attained to the Age of thirty Years, and been nine Years a Citizen of the United States, and who shall not, when elected, be an Inhabitant of that State for which he shall be chosen.

[4.] The Vice President of the United States shall be President of the Senate, but shall have no Vote, unless they be equally divided.

[5.] The Senate shall chuse their other Officers, and also a President pro tempore, in the Absence of the Vice President, or when he shall exercise the Office of the President of the United States.

[6.] The Senate shall have the sole Power to try all Impeachments. When sitting for that Purpose, they shall be on Oath or Affirmation. When the President of the United States is tried, the Chief Justice shall preside: And no Person shall be convicted without the Concurrence of two thirds of the Members present.

[7.] Judgment in Cases of Impeachment shall not extend further than to removal from Office, and disqualification to hold and enjoy any Office of honor, Trust or Profit under the United States: but the Party convicted shall nevertheless be liable and subject to Indictment, Trial, Judgment and Punishment, according to Law.

Section 4

[1.] The Times, Places and Manner of holding Elections for Senators and Representatives, shall be prescribed in each State by the Legislature thereof; but the Congress may at any time by Law make or alter such Regulations, except as to the Places of chusing Senators.

[2.] The Congress shall assemble at least once in every Year, and such Meeting shall be on the first Monday in December, unless they shall by Law appoint a different Day.

Section 5

[1.] Each House shall be the Judge of the Elections, Returns and Qualifications of its own Members, and a Majority of each shall constitute a Quorum to do Business; but a smaller Number may adjourn from day to day, and may be authorized to compel the Attendance of absent Members, in such Manner, and under such Penalties as each House may provide.

[2.] Each House may determine the Rules of its Proceedings, punish its Members for disorderly Behaviour, and, with the Concurrence of two thirds, expel a Member.

[3.] Each House shall keep a Journal of its Proceedings, and from time to time publish the same, excepting such Parts as may in their Judgment require Secrecy; and the Yeas and Nays of the Members of either House on any question shall, at the Desire of one fifth of those Present, be entered on the Journal.

[4.] Neither House, during the Session of Congress, shall, without the Consent of the other, adjourn for more than three days, nor to any other Place than that in which the two Houses shall be sitting.

Section 6

[1.] The Senators and Representatives shall receive a Compensation for their Services, to be ascertained by Law, and paid out of the Treasury of the United States. They shall in all Cases, except Treason, Felony and Breach of the Peace, be privileged from Arrest during their Attendance at the Session of their respective Houses, and in going to and returning from the same; and for any Speech or Debate in either House, they shall not be questioned in any other Place.

[2.] No Senator or Representative shall, during the Time for which he was elected, be appointed to any civil Office under the Authority of the United States, which shall have been created, or the Emoluments whereof shall have been encreased during such time; and no Person holding any Office under the United States, shall be a Member of either House during his Continuance in Office.

Section 7

[1.] All Bills for raising Revenue shall originate in the House of Representatives; but the Senate may propose or concur with Amendments as on other Bills.

[2.] Every Bill which shall have passed the House of Representatives and the Senate, shall, before it become a Law, be presented to the President of the United States; If he approve he shall sign it, but if not he shall return it, with his Objections to that House in which it shall have originated, who shall enter the Objections at large on their Journal, and proceed to reconsider it. If after such Reconsideration two thirds of that House shall agree to pass the Bill, it shall be sent, together with the Objections, to the other House, by

Senate gavel

What It Means
Congressional Salaries To strengthen the federal government, the Founders set congressional salaries to be paid by the United States Treasury rather than by members' respective states. Originally, members were paid $6 per day. In 2001, all members of Congress received a base salary of $145,100.

What It Means
Where Tax Laws Begin All tax laws must originate in the House of Representatives. This ensures that the branch of Congress that is elected by the people every two years has the major role in determining taxes.

What It Means
How Bills Become Laws A bill may become a law only by passing both houses of Congress and by being signed by the president. The president can check Congress by rejecting—vetoing—its legislation. *How can Congress override the president's veto?*

which it shall likewise be reconsidered, and if approved by two thirds of that House, it shall become a Law. But in all such Cases the Votes of both Houses shall be determined by yeas and Nays, and the Names of the Persons voting for and against the Bill shall be entered on the Journal of each House respectively. If any Bill shall not be returned by the President within ten Days (Sundays excepted) after it shall have been presented to him, the Same shall be a Law, in like Manner as if he had signed it, unless the Congress by their Adjournment prevent its Return, in which Case it shall not be a Law.

[3.] Every Order, Resolution, or Vote to which the Concurrence of the Senate and House of Representatives may be necessary (except on a question of Adjournment) shall be presented to the President of the United States; and before the Same shall take Effect, shall be approved by him, or being disapproved by him, shall be repassed by two thirds of the Senate and House of Representatives, according to the Rules and Limitations prescribed in the Case of a Bill.

Section 8

[1.] The Congress shall have the Power To lay and collect Taxes, Duties, Imposts and Excises, to pay the Debts and provide for the common Defence and general Welfare of the United States; but all Duties, Imposts and Excises shall be uniform throughout the United States;

[2.] To borrow Money on the credit of the United States;

[3.] To regulate Commerce with foreign Nations, and among the several States, and with the Indian Tribes;

[4.] To establish an uniform Rule of Naturalization, and uniform Laws on the subject of Bankruptcies throughout the United States;

[5.] To coin Money, regulate the Value thereof, and of foreign Coin, and fix the Standard of Weights and Measures;

[6.] To provide for the Punishment of counterfeiting the Securities and current Coin of the United States;

[7.] To establish Post Offices and post Roads;

[8.] To promote the Progress of Science and useful Arts, by securing for limited Times to Authors and Inventors the exclusive Right to their respective Writings and Discoveries;

[9.] To constitute Tribunals inferior to the supreme Court;

[10.] To define and punish Piracies and Felonies committed on the high Seas, and Offences against the Law of Nations;

[11.] To declare War, grant Letters of Marque and Reprisal, and make Rules concerning Captures on Land and Water;

[12.] To raise and support Armies, but no Appropriation of Money to that Use shall be for a longer Term than two Years;

[13.] To provide and maintain a Navy;

[14.] To make Rules for the Government and Regulation of the land and naval Forces;

[15.] To provide for calling forth the Militia to execute the Laws of the Union, suppress Insurrections and repel Invasions;

Civil War money

Vocabulary

resolution: *legislature's formal expression of opinion*

naturalization: *procedure by which a citizen of a foreign nation becomes a citizen of the United States.*

tribunal: *a court*

letter of marque: *authority given to a citizen to outfit an armed ship and use it to attack enemy ships in time of war*

reprisal: *taking by force property or territory belonging to another country or to its citizens*

insurrection: *rebellion*

[16.] To provide for organizing, arming, and disciplining, the Militia, and for governing such Part of them as may be employed in the Service of the United States, reserving to the States respectively, the Appointment of the Officers, and the Authority of training the Militia according to the discipline prescribed by Congress;

[17.] To exercise exclusive Legislation in all Cases whatsoever, over such District (not exceeding ten Miles square) as may, by Cession of particular States, and the Acceptance of Congress, become the Seat of Government of the United States, and to exercise like Authority over all Places purchased by the Consent of the Legislature of the State in which the Same shall be, for the Erection of Forts, Magazines, Arsenals, dock-Yards, and other needful Buildings, —And

[18.] To make all Laws which shall be necessary and proper for carrying into Execution the foregoing Powers, and all other Powers vested by this Constitution in the Government of the United States, or in any Department or Officer thereof.

Section 9

[1.] The Migration or Importation of such Persons as any of the States now existing shall think proper to admit, shall not be prohibited by the Congress prior to the Year one thousand eight hundred and eight, but a Tax or duty may be imposed on such Importation, not exceeding ten dollars for each Person.

[2.] The Privilege of the Writ of Habeas Corpus shall not be suspended, unless when in Cases of Rebellion or Invasion the public Safety may require it.

[3.] No Bill of Attainder or ex post facto Law shall be passed.

[4.] No Capitation, or other direct, Tax shall be laid, unless in Proportion to the Census or Enumeration herein before directed to be taken.

[5.] No Tax or Duty shall be laid on Articles exported from any State.

[6.] No Preference shall be given by any Regulation of Commerce or Revenue to the Ports of one State over those of another: nor shall Vessels bound to, or from, one State, be obliged to enter, clear, or pay Duties in another.

[7.] No Money shall be drawn from the Treasury, but in Consequence of Appropriations made by Law; and a regular Statement and Account of the Receipts and Expenditures of all public Money shall be published from time to time.

[8.] No Title of Nobility shall be granted by the United States: And no Person holding any Office of Profit or Trust under them, shall, without the Consent of the Congress, accept of any present, Emolument, Office, or Title, of any kind whatever, from any King, Prince, or foreign State.

What It Means

Elastic Clause The final enumerated power is often called the "elastic clause." This clause gives Congress the right to make all laws "necessary and proper" to carry out the powers expressed in the other clauses of Article I. It is called the elastic clause because it lets Congress "stretch" its powers to meet situations the Founders could never have anticipated.

What does the phrase "necessary and proper" in the elastic clause mean? Almost from the beginning, this phrase was a subject of dispute. The issue was whether a strict or a broad interpretation of the Constitution should be applied. The dispute was first addressed in 1819, in the case of *McCulloch* v. *Maryland*, when the Supreme Court ruled in favor of a broad interpretation.

What It Means

Habeas Corpus A writ of habeas corpus issued by a judge requires a law official to bring a prisoner to court and show cause for holding the prisoner. A bill of attainder is a bill that punished a person without a jury trial. An "ex post facto" law is one that makes an act a crime after the act has been committed. *What does the Constitution say about bills of attainder?*

United States coins

Vocabulary

appropriations: *funds set aside for a specific use*
emolument: *payment*
impost: *tax*
duty: *tax*

Section 10

[1.] No State shall enter into any Treaty, Alliance, or Confederation; grant Letters of Marque and Reprisal; coin Money; emit Bills of Credit; make any Thing but gold and silver Coin a Tender in Payment of Debts; pass any Bill of Attainder, ex post facto Law, or Law impairing the Obligation of Contracts, or grant any Title of Nobility.

[2.] No State shall, without the Consent of the Congress, lay any Imposts or Duties on Imports or Exports, except what may be absolutely necessary for executing it's inspection Laws: and the net Produce of all Duties and Imposts, laid by any State on Imports and Exports, shall be for the Use of the Treasury of the United States; and all such Laws shall be subject to the Revision and Controul of the Congress.

[3.] No State shall, without the Consent of Congress, lay any Duty of Tonnage, keep Troops, or Ships of War in time of Peace, enter into any Agreement or Compact with another State, or with a foreign Power, or engage in War, unless actually invaded, or in such imminent Danger as will not admit of delay.

Article II

Section 1

[1.] The executive Power shall be vested in a President of the United States of America. He shall hold his Office during the Term of four Years, and, together with the Vice President, chosen for the same Term, be elected, as follows

[2.] Each State shall appoint, in such Manner as the Legislature thereof may direct, a Number of Electors, equal to the whole Number of Senators and Representatives to which the State may be entitled in the Congress: but no Senator or Representative, or Person holding an Office of Trust or Profit under the United States, shall be appointed an Elector.

[3.] The Electors shall meet in their respective States, and vote by Ballot for two Persons, of whom one at least shall not be an Inhabitant of the same State with themselves. And they shall make a List of all the Persons voted for, and of the Number of Votes for each; which List they shall sign and certify, and transmit sealed to the Seat of the Government of the United States, directed to the President of the Senate. The President of the Senate shall, in the Presence of the Senate and House of Representatives, open all the Certificates, and the Votes shall then be counted. The Person having the greatest Number of Votes shall be the President, if such Number be a Majority of the whole Number of Electors appointed; and if there be more than one who have such Majority, and have an equal Number of Votes, then the House of Representatives shall immediately chuse by Ballot one of them for President; and if no person have a Majority, then from the five highest on the List the said House shall in like Manner chuse the President. But in chusing the President, the Votes shall be taken by States, the Representation from each State having one Vote; A quorum for this Purpose shall consist of a Member or Members from two thirds of the States, and a Majority of all the States shall be necessary to a Choice. In every Case, after the Choice of the President, the Person having the greatest Number of Votes of the Electors shall be the Vice President. But if there should remain two or more who have equal Votes, the Senate shall chuse from them by Ballot the Vice President.

[4.] The Congress may determine the Time of chusing the Electors, and the Day on which they shall give their Votes; which Day shall be the same throughout the United States.

[5.] No Person except a natural born Citizen, or a Citizen of the United States, at the time of the Adoption of this Constitution, shall be eligible to the Office of President; neither shall any Person be eligible to that Office who shall not have attained to the Age of thirty five Years, and been fourteen Years a Resident within the United States.

[6.] In Case of the Removal of the President from Office, or of his Death, Resignation, or Inability to discharge the Powers and Duties of the said Office, the Same shall devolve on the Vice President, and the Congress may by Law provide for the Case of Removal, Death, Resignation or Inability, both of the President and Vice President, declaring what Officer shall then act as President, and such Officer shall act accordingly, until the Disability be removed, or a President shall be elected.

[7.] The President shall, at stated Times, receive for his Services, a Compensation, which shall neither be encreased nor diminished during the Period for which he shall have been elected, and he shall not receive within that Period any other Emolument from the United States, or any of them.

[8.] Before he enter on the Execution of his Office, he shall take the following Oath or Affirmation:—"I do solemnly swear (or affirm) that I will faithfully execute the Office of President of the United States, and will to the best of my Ability, preserve, protect and defend the Constitution of the United States."

Section 2

[1.] The President shall be Commander in Chief of the Army and Navy of the United States, and of the Militia of the several States, when called into the actual Service of the United States; he may require the Opinion, in writing, of the principal Officer in each of the executive Departments, upon any Subject relating to the Duties of their respective Offices, and he shall have Power to grant Reprieves and Pardons for Offences against the United States, except in Cases of Impeachment.

What It Means
Previous Elections The Twelfth Amendment, added in 1804, changed the method of electing the president stated in Article II, Section 3. The Twelfth Amendment requires that the electors cast separate ballots for president and vice president.

What It Means
Qualifications The president must be a citizen of the United States by birth, at least 35 years of age, and a resident of the United States for 14 years.

What It Means
Vacancies If the president dies, resigns, is removed from office by impeachment, or is unable to carry out the duties of the office, the vice president becomes president. The Twenty-fifth Amendment sets procedures for presidential succession.

What It Means
Salary Originally, the president's salary was $25,000 per year. The president's current salary is $400,000 plus a $50,000 nontaxable expense account per year. The president also receives living accommodations in two residences—the White House and Camp David.

What It Means
The Cabinet Mention of "the principal officer in each of the executive departments" is the only suggestion of the president's cabinet to be found in the Constitution. The cabinet is an advisory body, and its power depends on the president. Section 2, Clause 1 also makes the president—a civilian—the head of the armed services. This established the principle of civilian control of the military.

Impeachment ticket

[2.] He shall have Power, by and with the Advice and Consent of the Senate, to make Treaties, provided two thirds of the Senators present concur; and he shall nominate, and by and with the Advice and Consent of the Senate, shall appoint Ambassadors, other public Ministers and Consuls, Judges of the supreme Court, and all other Officers of the United States, whose Appointments are not herein otherwise provided for, and which shall be established by Law: but the Congress may by Law vest the Appointment of such inferior Officers, as they think proper, in the President alone, in the Courts of Law, or in the Heads of Departments.

[3.] The President shall have Power to fill up all Vacancies that may happen during the Recess of the Senate, by granting Commissions which shall expire at the End of their next Session.

Section 3

He shall from time to time give to the Congress Information of the State of the Union, and recommend to their Consideration such Measures as he shall judge necessary and expedient; he may, on extraordinary Occasions, convene both Houses, or either of them, and in Case of Disagreement between them, with Respect to the Time of Adjournment, he may adjourn them to such Time as he shall think proper; he shall receive Ambassadors and other public Ministers; he shall take Care that the Laws be faithfully executed, and shall Commission all the Officers of the United States.

Section 4

The President, Vice President and all civil Officers of the United States, shall be removed from Office on Impeachment for, and Conviction of, Treason, Bribery, or other high Crimes and Misdemeanors.

Article III
Section 1

The judicial Power of the United States, shall be vested in one supreme Court, and in such inferior Courts as the Congress may from time to time ordain and establish. The Judges, both of the supreme and inferior Courts, shall hold their Offices during good Behaviour, and shall, at stated Times, receive for their Services, a Compensation, which shall not be diminished during their Continuance in Office.

Section 2

[1.] The judicial Power shall extend to all Cases, in Law and Equity, arising under this Constitution, the Laws of the United States, and Treaties made, or which shall be made, under their Authority;—to all Cases affecting Ambassadors, other public Ministers and Consuls;—to all Cases of admiralty and maritime Jurisdiction;—to Controversies to which the United States shall be a Party;—to Controversies between two or more States;—between a State and Citizens of another State;—between Citizens of different States,—between Citizens of the same State claiming Lands under Grants of different States, and between a State, or the Citizens thereof, and foreign States, Citizens or Subjects.

[2.] In all Cases affecting Ambassadors, other public Ministers and Consuls, and those in which a State shall be Party, the supreme Court shall have original Jurisdiction. In all the other Cases before mentioned, the supreme Court shall have appellate Jurisdiction, both as to Law and Fact, with such Exceptions, and under such Regulations as the Congress shall make.

[3.] The Trial of all Crimes, except in Cases of Impeachment, shall be by Jury; and such Trial shall be held in the State where the said Crimes shall have been committed; but when not committed within any State, the Trial shall be at such Place or Places as the Congress may by Law have directed.

Section 3

[1.] Treason against the United States, shall consist only in levying War against them, or in adhering to their Enemies, giving them Aid and Comfort. No Person shall be convicted of Treason unless on the Testimony of two Witnesses to the same overt Act, or on Confession in open Court.

[2.] The Congress shall have Power to declare the Punishment of Treason, but no Attainder of Treason shall work Corruption of Blood, or Forfeiture except during the Life of the Person attainted.

Article IV
Section 1

Full Faith and Credit shall be given in each State to the public Acts, Records, and judicial Proceedings of every other State. And the Congress may by general Laws prescribe the Manner in which such Acts, Records and Proceedings shall be proved, and the Effect thereof.

Section 2

[1.] The Citizens of each State shall be entitled to all Privileges and Immunities of Citizens in the several States.

[2.] A Person charged in any State with Treason, Felony, or other Crime, who shall flee from Justice, and be found in another State, shall on Demand of the executive Authority of the State from which he fled, be delivered up, to be removed to the State having Jurisdiction of the Crime.

What It Means
The Supreme Court A Court with "original jurisdiction" has the authority to be the first court to hear a case. The Supreme Court has "appellate jurisdiction" and mostly hears cases appealed from lower courts.

What It Means
Article IV. Relations Among the States Article IV explains the relationship of the states to one another and to the national government. This article requires each state to give citizens of other states the same rights as its own citizens, addresses admitting new states, and guarantees that the national government will protect the states.

Vocabulary

original jurisdiction: *authority to be the first court to hear a case*
appellate jurisdiction: *authority to hear cases that have been appealed from lower courts*
treason: *violation of the allegiance owed by a person to his or her own country, for example, by aiding an enemy*

What It Means

New States Congress has the power to admit new states. It also determines the basic guidelines for applying for statehood. Two states, Maine and West Virginia, were created within the boundaries of another state. In the case of West Virginia, President Lincoln recognized the West Virginia government as the legal government of Virginia during the Civil War. This allowed West Virginia to secede from Virginia without obtaining approval from the Virginia legislature.

What It Means

Republic Government can be classified in many different ways. The ancient Greek Philosopher Aristotle classified government based on the question: Who governs? According to Aristotle, all governments belong to one of three major groups: (1) autocracy—rule by one person; (2) oligarchy—rule by a few persons; or (3) democracy—rule by many persons. A republic is a form of democracy in which the people elect representatives to make the laws and conduct government.

What It Means

Article V. The Amendment Process Article V spells out the ways that the Constitution can be amended, or changed. All of the 27 amendments were proposed by a two-thirds vote of both houses of Congress. Only the Twenty-first Amendment was ratified by constitutional conventions of the states. All other amendments have been ratified by state legislatures. *What is an amendment?*

Vocabulary

extradition: *surrender of a criminal to another authority*
amendment: *a change to the Constitution*
ratification: *process by which an amendment is approved*

[3.] No Person held to Service of Labour in one State, under the Laws thereof, escaping into another, shall, in Consequence of any Law or Regulation therein, be discharged from such Service or Labour, but shall be delivered up on Claim of the Party to whom such Service or Labour may be due.

Section 3

[1.] New States may be admitted by the Congress into this Union; but no new State shall be formed or erected within the Jurisdiction of any other State; nor any State be formed by the Junction of two or more States, or Parts of States, without the Consent of the Legislatures of the States concerned as well as of the Congress.

[2.] The Congress shall have Power to dispose of and make all needful Rules and Regulations respecting the Territory or other Property belonging to the United States; and nothing in this Constitution shall be so construed as to Prejudice any Claims of the United States, or of any particular State.

Section 4

The United States shall guarantee to every State in this Union a Republican Form of Government, and shall protect each of them against Invasion; and on Application of the Legislature, or of the Executive (when the Legislature cannot be convened) against domestic Violence.

Article V

The Congress, whenever two thirds of both Houses shall deem it necessary, shall propose Amendments to this Constitution, or, on the Application of the Legislatures of two thirds of the several States, shall call a Convention for proposing Amendments, which, in either Case, shall be valid to all Intents and Purposes, as Part of this Constitution, when ratified by the Legislatures of three fourths of the several States, or by Conventions in three fourths thereof, as the one or the other Mode of Ratification may be proposed by the Congress; Provided that no Amendment which may be made prior to the Year One thousand eight hundred and eight shall in any Manner affect the first and fourth Clauses in the Ninth Section of the first Article; and that no State, without its Consent, shall be deprived of its equal Suffrage in the Senate.

Article VI

[1.] All Debts contracted and Engagements entered into, before the Adoption of this Constitution, shall be as valid against the United States under this Constitution, as under the Confederation.

[2.] This Constitution, and the Laws of the United States which shall be made in Pursuance thereof; and all Treaties made, or which shall be made, under the Authority of the United States, shall be the supreme Law of the Land; and the Judges in every State shall be bound thereby, any Thing in the Constitution or Laws of any State to the Contrary notwithstanding.

[3.] The Senators and Representatives before mentioned, and the Members of the several State Legislatures, and all executive and judicial Officers, both of the United States and of the several States, shall be bound by Oath or Affirmation, to support this Constitution; but no religious Test shall ever be required as a Qualification to any Office or public Trust under the United States.

Article VII

The Ratification of the Conventions of nine States, shall be sufficient for the Establishment of this Constitution between the States so ratifying the Same.

Done in Convention by the Unanimous Consent of the States present the Seventeenth Day of September in the Year of our Lord one thousand seven hundred and Eighty seven and of the Independence of the United States of America the Twelfth. In witness whereof We have hereunto subscribed our Names,

> **What It Means**
> **Article VI. National Supremacy** Article VI contains the "supremacy clause." This clause establishes that the Constitution, laws passed by Congress, and treaties of the United States "shall be the supreme Law of the Land." The "supremacy clause" recognized the Constitution and federal laws as supreme when in conflict with those of the states.

> **What It Means**
> **Article VII. Ratification** Article VII addresses ratification and declares that the Constitution would take effect after it was ratified by nine states.

Signers
*George Washington, **President and Deputy from Virginia***

New Hampshire
John Langdon
Nicholas Gilman

Massachusetts
Nathaniel Gorham
Rufus King

Connecticut
William Samuel Johnson
Roger Sherman

New York
Alexander Hamilton

New Jersey
William Livingston
David Brearley
William Paterson
Jonathan Dayton

Pennsylvania
Benjamin Franklin
Thomas Mifflin
Robert Morris
George Clymer
Thomas FitzSimons
Jared Ingersoll
James Wilson
Gouverneur Morris

Delaware
George Read
Gunning Bedford, Jr.
John Dickinson
Richard Bassett
Jacob Broom

Maryland
James McHenry
Daniel of St. Thomas Jenifer
Daniel Carroll

Virginia
John Blair
James Madison, Jr.

North Carolina
William Blount
Richard Dobbs Spaight
Hugh Williamson

South Carolina
John Rutledge
Charles Cotesworth Pinckney
Charles Pinckney
Pierce Butler

Georgia
William Few
Abraham Baldwin

Attest: William Jackson,
Secretary

What It Means

The Amendments This part of the Constitution consists of amendments, or changes. The Constitution has been amended 27 times throughout the nation's history.

What It Means

Bill of Rights The first 10 amendments are known as the Bill of Rights (1791). These amendments limit the powers of government. The First Amendment protects the civil liberties of individuals in the United States. The amendment freedoms are not absolute, however. They are limited by the rights of other individuals. *What freedoms does the First Amendment protect?*

What It Means

Rights of the Accused This amendment contains important protections for people accused of crimes. One of the protections is that government may not deprive any person of life, liberty, or property without due process of law. This means that the government must follow proper constitutional procedures in trials and in other actions it takes against individuals. *According to Amendment V, what is the function of a grand jury?*

What It Means

Rights to a Speedy, Fair Trial A basic protection is the right to a speedy, public trial. The jury must hear witnesses and evidence on both sides before deciding the guilt or innocence of a person charged with a crime. This amendment also provides that legal counsel must be provided to a defendant. In 1963, the Supreme Court ruled, in *Gideon* v. *Wainwright*, that if a defendant cannot afford a lawyer, the government must provide one to defend him or her. *Why is the right to a "speedy" trial important?*

Amendment I

Congress shall make no law respecting an establishment of religion, or prohibiting the free exercise thereof; or abridging the freedom of speech, or of the press; or the right of the people peaceably to assemble, and to petition the Government for a redress of grievances.

Amendment II

A well regulated Militia, being necessary to the security of a free State, the right of the people to keep and bear Arms, shall not be infringed.

Amendment III

No Soldier shall, in time of peace be quartered in any house, without the consent of the Owner, nor in time of war, but in a manner to be prescribed by law.

Amendment IV

The right of the people to be secure in their persons, houses, papers, and effects, against unreasonable searches and seizures, shall not be violated, and no Warrants shall issue, but upon probable cause, supported by Oath or affirmation, and particularly describing the place to be searched, and the persons or things to be seized.

Amendment V

No person shall be held to answer for a capital, or otherwise infamous crime, unless on a presentment or indictment of a Grand Jury, except in cases arising in the land or naval forces, or in the Militia, when in actual service in time of War or public danger; nor shall any person be subject for the same offence to be twice put in jeopardy of life or limb; nor shall be compelled in any criminal case to be a witness against himself, nor be deprived of life, liberty, or property, without due process of law; nor shall private property be taken for public use without just compensation.

Amendment VI

In all criminal prosecutions, the accused shall enjoy the right to a speedy and public trial, by an impartial jury of the State and district wherein the crime shall have been committed, which district shall have been previously ascertained by law, and to be informed of the nature and cause of the accusation; to be confronted with the witnesses against him; to have compulsory process for obtaining Witnesses in his favor, and to have the assistance of counsel for his defence.

Amendment VII

In Suits at common law, where the value in controversy shall exceed twenty dollars, the right of trial by jury shall be preserved, and no fact tried by a jury, shall be otherwise reexamined in any Court of the United States, than according to the rules of common law.

Amendment VIII

Excessive bail shall not be required, nor excessive fines imposed, nor cruel and unusual punishments inflicted.

Amendment IX

The enumeration in the Constitution, of certain rights, shall not be construed to deny or disparage others retained by the people.

What It Means
Powers of the People This amendment prevents government from claiming that the only rights people have are those listed in the Bill of Rights.

Amendment X

The powers not delegated to the United States by the Constitution, nor prohibited by it to the States, are reserved to the States respectively, or to the people.

What It Means
Powers of the States The final amendment of the Bill of Rights protects the states and the people from an all-powerful federal government. It establishes that powers not given to the national government—or denied to the states—by the Constitution belong to the states or to the people.

Amendment XI

The Judicial power of the United States shall not be construed to extend to any suit in law or equity, commenced or prosecuted against one of the United States by Citizens of another State, or by Citizens or Subjects of any Foreign State.

What It Means
Suits Against States The Eleventh Amendment (1795) limits the jurisdiction of the federal courts. The Supreme Court had ruled that a federal court could try a lawsuit brought by citizens of South Carolina against a citizen of Georgia. This case, *Chisholm* v. *Georgia*, decided in 1793, raised a storm of protest, leading to passage of the Eleventh Amendment.

Amendment XII

The electors shall meet in their respective states and vote by ballot for President and Vice-President, one of whom, at least, shall not be an inhabitant of the same state with themselves; they shall name in their ballots the person voted for as President, and in distinct ballots the person voted for as Vice-President, and they shall make distinct lists of all persons voted for as President, and of all persons voted for as Vice-President, and of the number of votes for each, which lists they shall sign and certify, and transmit sealed to the seat of the government of the United States, directed to the President of the Senate;—The President of the Senate shall, in the presence of the Senate and House of Representatives, open all the certificates and the votes shall then be counted;—The person having the greatest number of votes for President, shall be the President, if such number be a majority of the whole number of Electors appointed; and if no person have such

Vocabulary

quarter: *to provide living accommodations*
probable cause: *police must have a reasonable basis to believe a person is linked to a crime*
warrant: *document that gives police particular rights or powers*
common law: *law established by previous court decisions*
bail: *money that an accused person provides to the court as a guarantee that he or she will be present for a trial*

majority, then from the persons having the highest numbers not exceeding three on the list of those voted for as President, the House of Representatives shall choose immediately, by ballot, the President. But in choosing the President, the votes shall be taken by states, the representation from each state having one vote; a quorum for this purpose shall consist of a member or members from two-thirds of the states, and a majority of all the states shall be necessary to a choice. And if the House of Representatives shall not choose a President whenever the right of choice shall devolve upon them, before the fourth day of March next following, then the Vice-President shall act as President, as in the case of the death or other constitutional disability of the President. The person having the greatest number of votes as Vice-President, shall be the Vice-President, if such number be a majority of the whole number of Electors appointed, and if no person have a majority, then from the two highest numbers on the list, the Senate shall choose the Vice-President; a quorum for the purpose shall consist of two-thirds of the whole number of Senators, and a majority of the whole number shall be necessary to a choice. But no person constitutionally ineligible to the office of President shall be eligible to that of Vice-President of the United States.

Amendment XIII

Section 1

Neither slavery nor involuntary servitude, except as a punishment for crime whereof the party shall have been duly convicted, shall exist within the United States, or any place subject to their jurisdiction.

Section 2

Congress shall have power to enforce this article by appropriate legislation.

Amendment XIV

Section 1

All persons born or naturalized in the United States, and subject to the jurisdiction thereof, are citizens of the United States and of the State wherein they reside. No State shall make or enforce any law which shall abridge the privileges or immunities of citizens of the United States; nor shall any State deprive any person of life, liberty, or property, without due process of law; nor deny to any person within its jurisdiction the equal protection of the laws.

Section 2

Representatives shall be apportioned among the several States according to their respective numbers, counting the whole number of persons in each State, excluding Indians not taxed. But when the right to vote at any election for the choice of electors for President and Vice President of the United States, Representatives in Congress, the Executive and Judicial officers of a State, or the members of the Legislature thereof, is denied to any of the male inhabitants of such State, being twenty-one years of age, and citizens of the United States, or in any way abridged, except for participation in rebellion, or other crime, the basis of representation therein shall be reduced in the proportion which the number of such male citizens shall bear to the whole number of male citizens twenty-one years of age in such State.

Section 3

No person shall be a Senator or Representative in Congress, or elector of President and Vice President, or hold any office, civil or military, under the United States, or under any State, who, having previously taken an oath, as a member of Congress, or as an officer of the United States, or as a member of any State legislature, or as an executive or judicial officer of any State, to support the Constitution of the United States, shall have engaged in insurrection or rebellion against the same, or given aid or comfort to the enemies thereof. But Congress may by a vote of two-thirds of each House, remove such disability.

Section 4

The validity of the public debt of the United States, authorized by law, including debts incurred for payment of pensions and bounties for service in suppressing insurrection or rebellion, shall not be questioned. But neither the United States nor any State shall assume or pay any debt or obligation incurred in aid of insurrection or rebellion against the United States, or any claim for the loss or emancipation of any slave; but all such debts, obligations and claims shall be held illegal and void.

Section 5

The Congress shall have power to enforce, by appropriate legislation, the provisions of this article.

Amendment XV

Section 1

The right of citizens of the United States to vote shall not be denied or abridged by the United States or by any

What It Means

Representation in Congress This section reduced the number of members a state had in the House of Representatives if it denied its citizens the right to vote. Later civil rights laws and the Twenty-fourth Amendment guaranteed the vote to African Americans.

What It Means

Penalty The leaders of the Confederacy were barred from state or federal offices unless Congress agreed to remove this ban. By the end of Reconstruction all but a few Confederate leaders were allowed to return to public life.

What It Means

Public Debt The public debt acquired by the federal government during the Civil War was valid and could not be questioned by the South. However, the debts of the Confederacy were declared to be illegal. *Could former slaveholders collect payment for the loss of their slaves?*

What It Means

Right to Vote The Fifteenth Amendment (1870) prohibits the government from denying a person's right to vote on the basis of race. Despite the law, many states denied African Americans the right to vote by such means as poll taxes, literacy tests, and white primaries. During the 1950s and 1960s, Congress passed successively stronger laws to end racial discrimination in voting rights.

Internal Revenue Service

State on account of race, color, or previous condition of servitude.

Section 2
The Congress shall have power to enforce this article by appropriate legislation.

Amendment XVI
The Congress shall have power to lay and collect taxes on incomes, from whatever source derived, without apportionment among the several States and without regard to any census or enumeration.

Amendment XVII
Section 1
The Senate of the United States shall be composed of two Senators from each State, elected by the people thereof, for six years; and each Senator shall have one vote. The electors in each State shall have the qualifications requisite for electors of the most numerous branch of the State legislatures.

Section 2
When vacancies happen in the representation of any State in the Senate, the executive authority of such State shall issue writs of election to fill such vacancies: *Provided,* That the legislature of any State may empower the executive thereof to make temporary appointments until the people fill the vacancies by election as the legislature may direct.

Section 3
This amendment shall not be so construed as to affect the election or term of any Senator chosen before it becomes valid as part of the Constitution.

Amendment XVIII
Section 1
After one year from ratification of this article, the manufacture, sale, or transportation of intoxicating liquors within, the importation thereof into, or the exportation thereof from the United States and all territory subject to the jurisdiction thereof for beverage purposes is hereby prohibited.

Section 2
The Congress and the several States shall have concurrent power to enforce this article by appropriate legislation.

What It Means
Election of Senators The Seventeenth Amendment (1913) states that the people, instead of state legislatures, elect United States senators. *How many years are in a Senate term?*

What It Means
Prohibition The Eighteenth Amendment (1919) prohibited the production, sale, or transportation of alcoholic beverages in the United States. Prohibition proved to be difficult to enforce. This amendment was later repealed by the Twenty-first Amendment.

Vocabulary
apportionment: *distribution of seats in House based on population*
vacancy: *an office or position that is unfilled or unoccupied*

Section 3

This article shall be inoperative unless it shall have been ratified as an amendment to the Constitution by the legislatures of the several States, as provided in the Constitution, within seven years from the date of the submission hereof to the States by the Congress.

Amendment XIX

Section 1

The right of citizens of the United States to vote shall not be denied or abridged by the United States or by any State on account of sex.

Section 2

Congress shall have power by appropriate legislation to enforce the provisions of this article.

What It Means

Woman Suffrage The Nineteenth Amendment (1920) guaranteed women the right to vote. By then women had already won the right to vote in many state elections, but the amendment put their right to vote in all state and national elections on a constitutional basis.

Amendment XX

Section 1

The terms of the President and Vice President shall end at noon on the 20th day of January, and the terms of the Senators and Representatives at noon on the 3d day of January, of the years in which such terms would have ended if this article had not been ratified; and the terms of their successors shall then begin.

Section 2

The Congress shall assemble at least once in every year, and such meeting shall begin at noon on the 3d day of January, unless they shall by law appoint a different day.

Section 3

If, at the time fixed for the beginning of the term of the President, the President elect shall have died, the Vice President elect shall become President. If a President shall not have been chosen before the time fixed for the beginning of his term, or if the President elect shall have failed to qualify, then the Vice President elect shall act as President until a President shall have qualified; and the Congress may by law provide for the case wherein neither a President elect nor a Vice President elect shall have qualified, declaring who shall then act as President, or the manner in which one who is to act shall be selected, and such person shall act accordingly until a President or Vice President shall have qualified.

What It Means

"Lame-Duck" Amendments The Twentieth Amendment (1933) sets new dates for Congress to begin its term and for the inauguration of the president and vice president. Under the original Constitution, elected officials who retired or who had been defeated remained in office for several months. For the outgoing president, this period ran from November until March. Such outgoing officials had little influence and accomplished little, and they were called lame ducks because they were so inactive. *What date was fixed as Inauguration Day?*

What It Means

Succession This section provides that if the president-elect dies before taking office, the vice president-elect becomes president.

John Tyler was the first vice president to become president when a chief executive died.

What It Means

Repeal of Prohibition The Twenty-first Amendment (1933) repeals the Eighteenth Amendment. It is the only amendment ever passed to overturn an earlier amendment. It is also the only amendment ratified by special state conventions instead of state legislatures.

What It Means

Term Limit The Twenty-second Amendment (1951) limits presidents to a maximum of two elected terms. It was passed largely as a reaction to Franklin D. Roosevelt's election to four terms between 1933 and 1945.

Vocabulary

president-elect: *individual who is elected president but has not yet begun serving his or her term*

District of Columbia: *site of nation's capital, occupying an area between Maryland and Virginia*

Section 4

The Congress may by law provide for the case of the death of any of the persons from whom the House of Representatives may choose a President whenever the right of choice shall have devolved upon them, and for the case of the death of any of the persons from whom the Senate may choose a Vice President whenever the right of choice shall have devolved upon them.

Section 5

Sections 1 and 2 shall take effect on the 15th day of October following the ratification of this article.

Section 6

This article shall be inoperative unless it shall have been ratified as an amendment to the Constitution by the legislatures of three-fourths of the several States within seven years from the date of its submission.

Amendment XXI

Section 1

The eighteenth article of amendment to the Constitution of the United States is hereby repealed.

Section 2

The transportation or importation into any State, Territory, or possession of the United States for delivery or use therein of intoxicating liquors, in violation of the laws thereof, is hereby prohibited.

Section 3

This article shall be inoperative unless it shall have been ratified as an amendment to the Constitution by conventions in the several States, as provided in the Constitution, within seven years from the date of the submission hereof to the States by the Congress.

Amendment XXII

Section 1

No person shall be elected to the office of the President more than twice, and no person who had held the office of President, or acted as President, for more than two years of a term to which some other person was elected President shall be elected to the office of the President more than once. But this Article shall not apply to any person holding the office of President when this Article was proposed by the Congress, and shall not prevent any person who may be holding the office of President, or acting as President, during the term within which this Article becomes operative from holding the office of President or acting as President during the remainder of such term.

Section 2
This article shall be inoperative unless it shall have been ratified as an amendment to the Constitution by the legislatures of three-fourths of the several States within seven years from the date of its submission to the States by the Congress.

Presidential campaign buttons

Amendment XXIII
Section 1
The District constituting the seat of Government of the United States shall appoint in such manner as the Congress may direct:

A number of electors of President and Vice President equal to the whole number of Senators and Representatives in Congress to which the District would be entitled if it were a State, but in no event more than the least populous State; they shall be in addition to those appointed by the States, but they shall be considered, for the purposes of the election of President and Vice President, to be electors appointed by a State; and they shall meet in the District and perform such duties as provided by the twelfth article of amendment.

Section 2
The Congress shall have power to enforce this article by appropriate legislation.

What It Means
Electors for the District of Columbia The Twenty-third Amendment (1961) allows citizens living in Washington, D.C., to vote for president and vice president, a right previously denied residents of the nation's capital. The District of Columbia now has three presidential electors, the number to which it would be entitled if it were a state.

Amendment XXIV
Section 1
The right of citizens of the United States to vote in any primary or other election for President or Vice President, for electors for President or Vice President, or for Senator or Representative in Congress, shall not be denied or abridged by the United States or any State by reason of failure to pay any poll tax or other tax.

Section 2
The Congress shall have power to enforce this article by appropriate legislation.

What It Means
Abolition of Poll Tax The Twenty-fourth Amendment (1964) prohibits poll taxes in federal elections. Prior to the passage of this amendment, some states had used such taxes to keep low-income African Americans from voting. In 1966 the Supreme Court banned poll taxes in state elections as well.

What It Means

The Vice President The Twenty-fifth Amendment (1967) established a process for the vice president to take over leadership of the nation when a president is disabled. It also set procedures for filling a vacancy in the office of vice president.

This amendment was used in 1973, when Vice President Spiro Agnew resigned from office after being charged with accepting bribes. President Richard Nixon then appointed Gerald R. Ford as vice president in accordance with the provisions of the 25th Amendment. A year later, President Nixon resigned during the Watergate scandal and Ford became president. President Ford then had to fill the vice presidency, which he had left vacant upon assuming the presidency. He named Nelson A. Rockefeller as vice president. Thus individuals who had not been elected held both the presidency and the vice presidency. *Whom does the president inform if he or she cannot carry out the duties of the office?*

President Gerald Ford

Amendment XXV

Section 1

In case of the removal of the President from office or his death or resignation, the Vice President shall become President.

Section 2

Whenever there is a vacancy in the office of the Vice President, the President shall nominate a Vice President who shall take the office upon confirmation by a majority vote of both Houses of Congress.

Section 3

Whenever the President transmits to the President pro tempore of the Senate and the Speaker of the House of Representatives his written declaration that he is unable to discharge the powers and duties of his office, and until he transmits to them a written declaration to the contrary, such powers and duties shall be discharged by the Vice President as Acting President.

Section 4

Whenever the Vice President and a majority of either the principal officers of the executive departments or of such other body as Congress may by law provide, transmit to the President pro tempore of the Senate and the Speaker of the House of Representatives their written declaration that the President is unable to discharge the powers and duties of his office, the Vice President shall immediately assume the power and duties of the office of Acting President.

Thereafter, when the President transmits to the President pro tempore of the Senate and the Speaker of the House of Representatives his written declaration that no inability exists, he shall resume the powers and duties of his office unless the Vice President and a majority of either the principal officers of the executive department or of such other body as Congress may by law provide, transmit within four days to the President pro tempore of the Senate and the Speaker of the House of Representatives their written declaration that the President is unable to discharge the powers and duties of his office. Thereupon Congress shall decide the issue, assembling within forty-eight hours for that purpose if not in session. If the Congress, within twenty-one days after receipt of the latter written declaration, or, if Congress is not in session, within twenty-one days after Congress is required to assemble, determines by two-thirds vote of both Houses that the President is unable to discharge the powers and duties of his office, the Vice

President shall continue to discharge the same as Acting President; otherwise, the President shall resume the power and duties of his office.

Amendment XXVI

Section 1

The right of citizens of the United States, who are eighteen years of age or older, to vote shall not be denied or abridged by the United States or by any State on account of age.

Section 2

The Congress shall have power to enforce this article by appropriate legislation.

Amendment XXVII

No law, varying the compensation for the services of Senators and Representatives, shall take effect, until an election of representatives shall have intervened.

What It Means
Voting Age The Twenty-sixth Amendment (1971) lowered the voting age in both federal and state elections to 18.

What It Means
Congressional Pay Raises The Twenty-seventh Amendment (1992) makes congressional pay raises effective during the term following their passage. James Madison offered the amendment in 1789, but it was never adopted. In 1982 Gregory Watson, then a student at the University of Texas, discovered the forgotten amendment while doing research for a school paper. Watson made the amendment's passage his crusade.

Joint meeting of Congress

The Structure of the Constitution

GUIDE TO READING

Main Idea
The Constitution is a remarkable document, which serves as an adaptable blueprint for governing the United States.

Key Terms
Preamble, amendment, Bill of Rights, income tax

Reading Strategy
Categorizing Information As you read, create and complete a chart like the one below by listing important features of the U.S. Constitution.

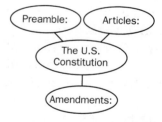

Read to Learn
- How is the Constitution organized?
- What do the three parts of the Constitution accomplish?

Americans in Action

Throughout his remarkable career, Patrick Henry stood out as a supporter of the colonists and their rights. At the First Continental Congress in 1774, he energetically spoke for measures that assumed the unity of the colonies. At the same time, he was against a strong central government. Though selected to be a delegate, he refused to attend sessions in 1787 and 1788, while the Constitution was being drafted. Henry was perhaps the most famous Anti-Federalist to speak against ratification of the Constitution. With the addition of the Bill of Rights, however, Henry embraced the Constitution. As a Federalist, Henry won a seat in the Virginia legislature. He died before he could assume his post, though.

Patrick Henry

The Constitution and Its Parts

Men with strong but often opposing ideas about the role of government shaped the Constitution. When you read the Constitution, you discover how remarkable it is. In the words of Harry S Truman, our thirty-third president, "It's a plan, but not a straitjacket, flexible and short." In very few pages, it manages to provide an adaptable framework for government that has held up for more than 200 years.

Although the main purpose of the Constitution is to provide a framework for the U.S. government, it does much more than that. It is the highest authority in the nation. It is the basic law of the United States. The powers of all the branches of government come from the Constitution. Like the American flag, the Constitution is a symbol of our nation. It represents our system of government and our basic beliefs and ideals, such as liberty and freedom.

The Constitution has three main parts. First is the Preamble, an introduction that states the goals and purposes of the government. Next are seven articles that describe the structure of the government. Third are 27 amendments, or additions and changes, to the Constitution.

The Preamble

The opening section of the Constitution, the Preamble, tells why the Constitution was written. It consists of a single, concise sentence that begins and ends as follows:

> **We the People of the United States . . . do ordain and establish this Constitution for the United States of America.**

These carefully chosen words make clear that the power of government comes from the people. The government depends on the people for its power and exists to serve them.

The middle part of the Preamble states six purposes of the government:

- "To form a more perfect Union"—to unite the states more effectively so they can operate as a single nation, for the good of all

- "To establish Justice"—to create a system of fair laws and courts and make certain that all citizens are treated equally

- "To insure domestic Tranquility"—to maintain peace and order, keeping citizens and their property safe from harm

- "To provide for the common defense"—to be ready militarily to protect the country and its citizens from outside attacks

- "To promote the general Welfare"—to help people live healthy, happy, and prosperous lives

- "To secure the Blessings of Liberty to ourselves and our Posterity"—to guarantee the freedom and basic rights of all Americans, including future generations (posterity)

The Articles

The seven articles that follow the Preamble explain how the government is to work. The first three articles describe the powers and responsibilities of each branch of government in turn. The remaining articles address more general matters.

Article I: The Legislative Branch It is no accident that the first article deals with the legislative branch. The Framers of the Constitution intended the legislature to take the leading role in government.

Article I says that a Congress made of two houses—the Senate and the House of Representatives—will have all lawmaking

The Oath of Office Every American president takes an oath to "preserve, protect, and defend the Constitution of the United States." George Washington and George W. Bush were sworn in as the first and forty-third presidents. **What is the president really pledging to protect?**

CONSTITUTION

Legislature

Senate, with states represented equally, and House of Representatives, apportioned according to population, have power to:

- ⭐ Pass laws by majority vote
- ⭐ Declare war
- ⭐ Coin and borrow money
- ⭐ Approve treaties
- ⭐ Amend Constitution by 2/3 vote in both houses and approval by 3/4 of states
- ⭐ Tax
- ⭐ Regulate commerce
- ⭐ Confirm presidential appointments

Executive

President chosen by electors has power to:

- ⭐ Enforce laws
- ⭐ Make treaties
- ⭐ Command armed forces

Judiciary

Supreme Court and lower federal courts have power to:

- ⭐ Interpret laws
- ⭐ Settle disputes between states

ARTICLES OF CONFEDERATION

Congress of one house with equal representation of 13 states has power to:

- ⭐ Pass laws by vote of 9 states
- ⭐ Declare war
- ⭐ Coin and borrow money
- ⭐ Make treaties
- ⭐ Amend Articles if all 13 states agree

No executive branch

No judicial branch

Evaluating Charts

The Constitution replaced a weak central government with a strong one. Which branches of government did the Constitution add?

authority. The article then describes how members of each house will be chosen and what rules they must follow in making laws. For example, a majority of both senators and representatives must vote for a bill before it can become a law.

Article I also lists specific powers that Congress does and does not have. For example, Congress may collect taxes, regulate foreign and interstate trade, coin money, and declare war. It may not tax exports, however, or favor one state over another. You will learn more about Congress in Chapter 6.

Article II: The Executive Branch

Article II provides for an executive, or law-enforcing, branch of government headed by a president and vice president. Article II explains how these leaders are to be elected and how they can be removed from office. The article also describes some of the president's powers and duties. As you will learn in Chapter 7, these include commanding the armed forces, dealing with the leaders of other countries, and appointing certain government officials.

Article III: The Judicial Branch The judicial branch is the part of government that interprets the laws and sees that they are fairly applied. Article III calls for "one Supreme Court" and such lower courts as Congress deems appropriate.

Article III then lists the powers of the federal courts and describes the kinds of cases they may hear. These include cases involving the Constitution, federal laws and treaties, and disputes between states. Read about our federal judiciary in Chapter 8.

Articles IV–VII In Article IV of the Constitution, the Framers shifted their focus to the states. The article says that all states must respect each other's laws, court decisions, and records. Article IV also explains the process for creating new states, and it promises that the federal government will protect and defend the states.

Article V reveals the foresight of the Framers. They realized that in a changing world, the Constitution might need modification over time. Thus they specified how amendments are to be made.

Article VI contains a key statement declaring the Constitution the "supreme Law of the Land." It adds that if state laws or court decisions conflict with federal law, the federal law shall prevail.

In Article VII, the Framers dealt with practical matters. The Constitution would take effect, they wrote, when nine states had ratified it.

✓ Reading Check **Describing** What is the main purpose of the U.S. Constitution?

Amending the Constitution

Since the Constitution was signed in 1787, it has been amended 27 times. (Any change in the Constitution is called an amendment.) The first 10 amendments, known as the **Bill of Rights,** were added in 1791. Chapter 4 discusses the Bill of Rights, along with other amendments that safeguard individual rights and liberties.

A number of amendments address entirely different matters, such as improving the way our government works. For example, the Sixteenth Amendment was passed in 1913 to allow Congress to collect an **income tax**—a tax on people's earnings. This is now an important source of money for the government, helping it pay for services.

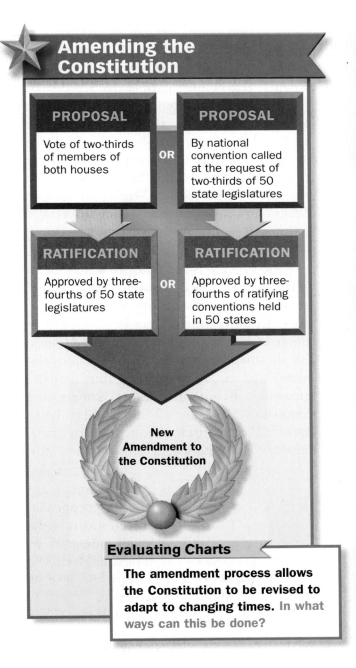

Amending the Constitution

PROPOSAL
Vote of two-thirds of members of both houses

OR

PROPOSAL
By national convention called at the request of two-thirds of 50 state legislatures

RATIFICATION
Approved by three-fourths of 50 state legislatures

OR

RATIFICATION
Approved by three-fourths of ratifying conventions held in 50 states

New Amendment to the Constitution

Evaluating Charts

The amendment process allows the Constitution to be revised to adapt to changing times. In what ways can this be done?

The Amendment Process

Would it surprise you to know that thousands of amendments to the Constitution have been considered over the years? Only 27 have become law because the Framers deliberately made the amendment process difficult. After months of debate and compromise, they knew how delicately balanced the Constitution was. Changing even one small detail could have dramatic effects throughout the government. Therefore, the Framers made sure the Constitution could not be altered without the overwhelming support of the people.

At the same time, the ability to amend the Constitution is necessary. Constitutional amendments safeguard many of our freedoms. For example, the abolition of slavery and the right of women to vote were added in amendments. If the Constitution could not have been amended to protect the rights of African Americans, women, and other oppressed groups, it—and our government—might not have survived.

The process for making an amendment to the Constitution, as outlined in Article V, involves two steps: proposal and ratification. An amendment may be proposed in either of two ways. The first method—used for all amendments so far—is by congressional action. A vote of two-thirds of the members of both houses of Congress is required. The second method is by a national convention requested by two-thirds of the state legislatures.

Once a national amendment has been proposed, three-fourths of the states must ratify it. The states have two ways to do this: by a vote of either the state legislature or a special state convention. Only one amendment, the Twenty-first Amendment, has been ratified by means of state conventions. Congress proposed and the state legislatures ratified all others.

Reading Check **Inferring** Why are amendments to the Constitution necessary?

Interpreting the Constitution

Although the Constitution has been amended only 27 times, there have been many other changes to it. These changes have taken place through interpretation. The Framers of the Constitution wrote a general document, so many matters are left open to interpretation.

The Necessary and Proper Clause

Article I lists the powers of Congress. In this article, the Constitution gives Congress the power "to make all Laws which shall be necessary and proper" to carry out its duties. This necessary and proper clause allows Congress to exercise powers that are not specifically listed in the Constitution. These powers are known as "implied powers."

Americans, though, do not agree about which laws are "necessary and proper." Some people feel Congress should be allowed to make any laws the Constitution does not specifically forbid. These people believe in a loose interpretation of the Constitution. Others believe in a strict interpretation. They feel Congress should make only the kinds of laws mentioned by the Constitution.

Interpretation Through Court Decisions

The Supreme Court has the final authority on interpreting the Constitution. Over the years, the Supreme Court has interpreted the

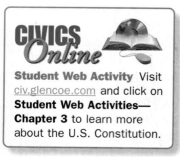

CIVICS Online

Student Web Activity Visit civ.glencoe.com and click on **Student Web Activities— Chapter 3** to learn more about the U.S. Constitution.

Constitution in different ways—sometimes strictly, sometimes loosely. With each new interpretation, our government changes.

Interpretation Through Congressional and Presidential Actions

Actions taken by Congress and the president have also caused new interpretations of the Constitution. The Constitution allows the House of Representatives to impeach, or accuse, federal officials, while the Senate determines the person's guilt or innocence. Congress has investigated more than 60 people on impeachment charges.

How has the president interpreted the Constitution? In 1841 William Henry Harrison became the first president to die in office. Vice President John Tyler assumed the powers of the president according to the Constitution. The Constitution, however, was unclear on this matter. Did Tyler automatically become president, or was he merely acting as president until the next election? Tyler went ahead and took the presidential oath. Not until 1967, when the Twenty-fifth Amendment was ratified, was Tyler's action officially part of the Constitution.

Presidents interpret the Constitution in other ways, too. Not only does the president make agreements with other countries without congressional approval, the president also requests legislation from Congress. The Constitution does not direct the president to take these actions.

Interpretation Through Custom

The interpretation of the Constitution has also changed through customs that have developed. For example, although the Constitution does not mention political parties, they are a very important part of today's political system. Today, parties help organize the government and conduct elections.

The government under the Constitution today is very different from the government set up by the Constitution in 1787. It will probably go through many more changes, too. However, the basic structure and principles of our government—a delicate balance between three branches—will no doubt remain.

✓ **Reading Check** **Identifying** What type of powers does the necessary and proper clause give to Congress?

SECTION 3 ASSESSMENT

Checking for Understanding

1. **Key Terms** Write a paragraph about the Constitution in which you use all of the following terms: Preamble, amendment, Bill of Rights, income tax.

Reviewing Main Ideas

2. **Identify** What is the purpose of the Preamble to the U.S. Constitution?

3. **Describe** In what two ways can an amendment to the U.S. Constitution be ratified? How are the states involved in these processes?

Critical Thinking

4. **Evaluating Information** Which part of the Constitution do you think is the most important? Explain your answer.

5. **Summarizing Information** In a chart like the one below, describe the features of Articles I, II, and III of the Constitution.

Article I	Article II	Article III

Analyzing Visuals

6. **Compare and Contrast** Review the chart that compares the Articles of Confederation and the U.S. Constitution on page 84. How did Congress differ under both forms of government?

★ *BE AN ACTIVE CITIZEN* ★

7. **Organize** Read a section of your state's constitution. Find one similarity and one difference from the U.S. Constitution.

Critical Thinking
SKILLBUILDER

Understanding the Parts of a Map

Why Learn This Skill?

Students and adult citizens need to acquire many different kinds of information. You gain knowledge through a variety of activities, such as observing, listening, and reading. Maps can present a great deal of information in brief and interesting formats. Maps can direct you down the street, across the country, or around the world. To make the most of map reading, you need to understand the parts of a map.

Learning the Skill

Follow these steps to read a map:

- Read the title to discover the subject of the map. The title may include a date, location, or special concept.
- Locate the map key, often found in a corner of the map. Identify the key's symbols, including colors and lines.
- Find the scale, which is often located in the key. The scale tells you what distance on the earth is represented by the measurement on the scale bar. For example, 1 inch (2.54 cm) on the map may represent 100 miles (160.9 km) on the earth.
- Note the compass, which shows directions on the map.
- Use the labels on the map, which identify physical and political features.

Practicing the Skill

Look at the parts of the map on this page and answer the following questions.

1. What is the subject of the map?
2. What color are the 13 states?
3. What is the name of the large western territory unclaimed by any states?
4. Along which of the Great Lakes did the British hold forts?
5. What other countries claimed land near the United States?

Land Area of the United States, 1787

Applying the Skill

List five types of information found on a map in your history or geography textbook. Describe this information to the class.

Practice key skills with Glencoe's **Skillbuilder Interactive Workbook CD-ROM, Level 1.**

Principles Underlying the Constitution

GUIDE TO READING

Main Idea
The Framers of the Constitution designed a government that incorporated the principles of popular sovereignty, rule of law, separation of powers, checks and balances, and federalism.

Key Terms
popular sovereignty, rule of law, separation of powers, checks and balances, expressed powers, reserved powers, concurrent powers

Reading Strategy
Summarizing Information As you read, complete a graphic organizer like the one below to describe the five principles included in the U.S. Constitution.

- U.S. Constitution
  - Popular Sovereignty:
  - Rule of Law:
  - Separation of Powers:
  - Checks and Balances:
  - Federalism:

Read to Learn
- How is power distributed in the U.S. government?
- What principles of government are contained in the U.S. Constitution?

Americans in Action

As Benjamin Franklin was leaving the last session of the Constitutional Congress, a woman asked, "What kind of government have you given us, Dr. Franklin? A republic or a monarchy?" Franklin answered, "A republic, Madam, if you can keep it." Franklin's response indicated that a republic—a system of government in which the people elect representatives to exercise power for them—requires citizens to take an active role.

Benjamin Franklin

Popular Sovereignty

In designing their plan for government, the delegates to the Constitutional Convention disagreed on many details. They had a common vision, however, of how the government should operate. It should be representative of the people and limited in scope. In addition, power should be divided among different levels rather than concentrated in a single, central authority.

To achieve these ends, the Framers embraced five fundamental principles: popular sovereignty, the rule of law, separation of powers, checks and balances, and federalism. These principles are the backbone of the Constitution.

In Article IV, the Constitution guarantees the American people "a Republican Form of Government." Today the word "republic" can mean any representative government headed by a president or similar leader rather than a king or queen who inherits the position. To the Framers of the Constitution, though, a republic was a representative democracy. In a traditional republic, supreme power belongs to the people, who express their will through elected representatives. This idea was important to the English colonists who came to America.

The notion that power lies with the people is called **popular sovereignty.** ("Sovereignty" means the right to rule; "popular," in this case, means the population or public.) The Declaration of Independence expresses strong support for popular sovereignty, saying that governments should draw their powers "from the consent of the governed." The Constitution echoes this idea in its opening statement that "We the People . . . establish this Constitution."

Further, the Constitution includes several provisions that ensure the sovereignty of the people. Of special importance are provisions about the right of citizens to vote. It is through elections that the people exercise their power most clearly. By a majority vote, citizens decide who will represent them in Congress. Through the Electoral College, they also choose the president and vice president. Elected officials are always accountable to the people. Elections are regularly scheduled, and voters can reject and replace representatives who serve them poorly.

Reading Check **Defining** What is a republic?

Rule of Law

The Framers firmly believed that the government should be strong, but not too strong. As James Madison put it,

> " You must first enable the government to control the governed, and in the next place oblige it to control itself. "

To limit the power of both the federal government and the states, the Constitution specifies what they may and may not do. Article I, for example, forbids the spending of government funds without the approval of Congress.

Under the Constitution, the government is also limited by the **rule of law.** This means that the law applies to everyone, even those who govern. No one may break the law or escape its reach.

Foundations of Our Rights and Freedoms

RIGHTS AND FREEDOMS	Magna Carta (1215)	English Bill of Rights (1689)	Virginia Declaration of Rights (1776)	Bill of Rights (1791)
Trial by jury	★	★	★	★
Due process	★	★	★	★
Private property	★		★	★
No unreasonable searches or seizures	★		★	★
No cruel punishment		★	★	★
No excessive bail or fines	★	★	★	★
Right to bear arms		★		★
Right to petition		★		★
Freedom of speech				★
Freedom of the press				★
Freedom of religion			★	★

Evaluating Charts

The ideas for the rights and freedoms we enjoy today came from various documents. These rights and freedoms, though, have not always applied equally to all Americans. Which rights or freedoms were included in all four documents?

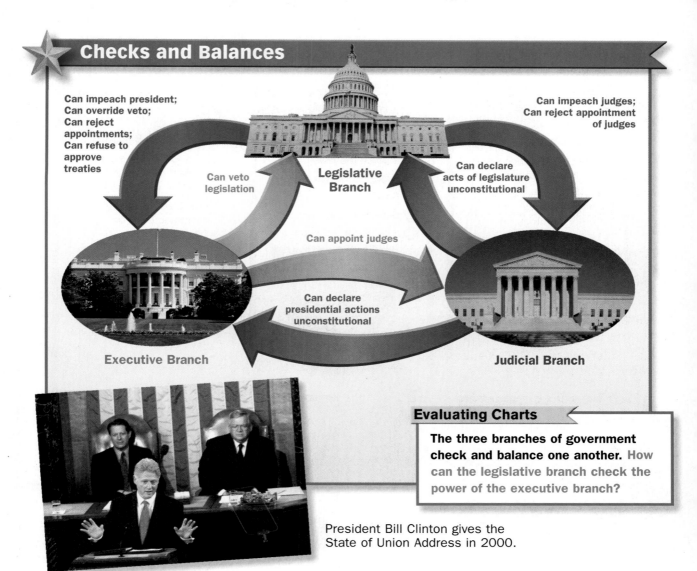

Checks and Balances

Can impeach president;
Can override veto;
Can reject appointments;
Can refuse to approve treaties

Can veto legislation

Legislative Branch

Can declare acts of legislature unconstitutional

Can impeach judges;
Can reject appointment of judges

Can appoint judges

Can declare presidential actions unconstitutional

Executive Branch

Judicial Branch

Evaluating Charts

The three branches of government check and balance one another. How can the legislative branch check the power of the executive branch?

President Bill Clinton gives the State of Union Address in 2000.

Separation of Powers

To further protect against abuse of power and the possibility of one person or group gaining too much power, the Framers divided the government into three branches, each with different functions. The Framers were influenced by the ideas of French philosopher Baron de Montesquieu, who believed that the best way to protect the liberty of the people was to clearly separate the legislative, executive, and judicial functions of government and assign each to a separate governmental branch. This split of authority among the legislative, executive, and judicial branches is called separation of powers.

Checks and Balances

To keep any one branch from becoming too powerful, the Constitution also includes a system of checks and balances. Each branch of government is able to check, or restrain, the power of the others. The president, for example, can veto laws proposed by Congress and name federal judges. Congress can block presidential appointments and treaties, control spending by the

Federal and State Powers

ENUMERATED POWERS (Powers given to the federal government)	CONCURRENT POWERS (Powers shared by state and federal governments)	RESERVED POWERS (Powers given to state governments)
⭐ Pass all laws necessary and proper to carry out its powers ⭐ Regulate trade with other countries and among the states ⭐ Conduct foreign affairs ⭐ Raise and support an army ⭐ Coin and print money ⭐ Establish a postal system ⭐ Govern U.S. territories, admit new states, and regulate immigration	⭐ Enforce the laws ⭐ Establish courts ⭐ Collect taxes ⭐ Borrow money ⭐ Provide for the general welfare	⭐ Provide for the public safety, health, and welfare within the state ⭐ Regulate trade and commerce within the state ⭐ Establish local governments ⭐ Conduct elections, determine qualifications of voters ⭐ Establish a public school system

Evaluating Charts

The Constitution is very clear about the expressed powers of government. What are three powers that state and federal governments share?

executive branch, and, in cases of serious wrongdoing, remove the president from office. Congress can also reject judicial appointments and remove judges through the impeachment process. The Supreme Court can overturn laws and executive policies that it finds contrary to the Constitution.

Reading Check **Explaining** Why did the Framers divide the government into three branches?

Federalism

Further limits on government arise from our federal system. Under federalism, as you read in Section 3, power is shared by the national government and the states. Each level of government—national and state—has independent authority over people at the same time. Americans must obey both federal and state laws.

Dividing Power

In outlining our federal system, the Constitution gives the national government certain exclusive powers. For example, Article I says that only the national government may coin money and make treaties with other nations. None of the 50 state governments may do these things.

The powers specifically granted to the national government are called the enumerated or **expressed powers.** You will read more about them in Chapter 6. Powers that the Constitution does not give to the national government are kept by the states. These **reserved powers,** as they are called, include regulating trade within state borders, establishing schools, and making rules for marriage and divorce.

In some areas, the authority of the states and the national government overlaps. Powers that both levels of government can exercise are called **concurrent powers.** Examples include the power to collect taxes, borrow money, and set up courts and prisons.

The Supremacy of the Constitution

In a federal system, the laws of a state and the laws of the nation may conflict. To deal with this possibility, the Framers included the supremacy clause in Article VI of the Constitution. As you read earlier, Article VI declares that the Constitution and other laws and treaties made by the national government "shall be the supreme Law of the Land."

Because the Constitution is the highest law, the national government is not supposed to act in violation of it. Likewise, states may do nothing that goes against either the Constitution or federal law.

Thomas Jefferson admired the Constitution. He wrote,

> 66 **I am persuaded no Constitution was ever before so well calculated as ours for . . . self-government.** 99

The Constitution is both durable and adaptable. It expresses our commitment to democracy, individual liberty, and equal justice under the law. The principles that underpin it—popular sovereignty, the rule of law, separation of powers, checks and balances, and federalism—ensure government restraint as well as power. The Constitution gives our chosen representatives enough power to defend our country's freedom, keep order, and protect individuals' rights. At the same time, it sets limits so that Americans need never fear tyranny. The United States Constitution stands as a powerful symbol of American values and a source of pride and unity.

Reading Check **Concluding** If a state law conflicts with a federal law, which law should you follow?

SECTION 4 ASSESSMENT

Checking for Understanding

1. **Key Terms** Use the group of words below to write a paragraph about the U.S. Constitution.
   separation of powers
   popular sovereignty
   rule of law
   checks and balances

Reviewing Main Ideas

2. **Analyze** How are the principles of separation of powers and checks and balances related?

3. **Evaluate** What are the five principles of government embodied in the United States Constitution?

Critical Thinking

4. **Drawing Conclusions** Why do you think the Framers of the Constitution thought the supremacy clause was necessary?

5. **Categorizing Information** Classify information about the way the Constitution divides powers by completing a graphic organizer like the one below.

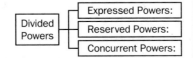

Divided Powers
- Expressed Powers:
- Reserved Powers:
- Concurrent Powers:

Analyzing Visuals

6. **Contrast** Review the chart on page 90. Compare the Virginia Declaration of Rights to the Bill of Rights. How do the two documents differ?

★ **BE AN ACTIVE CITIZEN** ★

7. **Analyze** Read your local or national newspaper for a week. Find at least one example of each of the five principles of government embodied in the Constitution. Share your examples with the class.

Assessment & Activities

Review to Learn

Section 1

- In 1787, 55 men met at what would become known as the Constitutional Convention.
- The convention delegates agreed on several operating procedures.

Section 2

- Two major plans were offered at the Constitutional Convention.
- The Great Compromise settled the dispute over the two plans.

Section 3

- The Constitution is divided into three parts.

Section 4

- The Constitution ensures that the government's power comes from the people and is limited.
- The federal system further limits the U.S. government.

FOLDABLES™
Study Organizer

Using Your Foldables Study Organizer
Use the foldable journal you have created to answer the following essay question: What led to the creation of the U.S. Constitution, and when and how was it ratified?

Reviewing Key Terms

Choose the italicized term that best completes each of the following sentences.

1. The idea of popular sovereignty is represented by *separation of powers/the right to vote.*
2. *Federalists/Anti-Federalists* favored ratification of the new Constitution.
3. *The Three-Fifths Compromise/Great Compromise* settled the question of whether the Virginia Plan or the New Jersey Plan would be adopted.
4. The first 10 amendments to the Constitution are called the *supremacy clause/Bill of Rights.*
5. The issue of how to count enslaved Americans for the purpose of representation in Congress was settled by the *Great Compromise/Three-Fifths Compromise.*
6. The idea of dividing power among different levels of government is found in the principle of *federalism/separation of powers.*
7. Those who opposed the Constitution because it gave too much power to the national government were called *Federalists/Anti-Federalists.*
8. No state law can conflict with the U.S. Constitution because of the *supremacy clause/separation of powers.*
9. Checks and balances are most closely associated with the principle of *popular sovereignty/separation of powers.*
10. The notion that governments draw their powers from the consent of the governed is *federalism/popular sovereignty.*

Reviewing Main Ideas

11. For what purpose did the delegates to the Constitutional Convention originally meet?
12. Why did convention delegates decide to keep the proceedings secret?
13. What two competing plans did delegates to the Constitutional Convention debate?
14. Explain the Three-Fifths Compromise.

15. What do the first three articles of the Constitution do?

16. What are the first 10 amendments to the Constitution called and what do they do?

17. What five fundamental principles are embodied by the U.S. Constitution?

18. Explain the difference among expressed, reserved, and concurrent powers.

Critical Thinking

19. Predicting What might happen if amendments were easier to propose and ratify?

20. Cause and Effect In a chart like the one below, explain the causes and effects of the major debate that occurred at the Constitutional Convention.

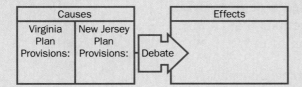

Causes		Effects
Virginia Plan Provisions:	New Jersey Plan Provisions:	Debate

Practicing Skills

21. Understanding the Parts of a Map Study the map on page 57. Which states unanimously ratified the Constitution? How many states strongly opposed ratification?

$ Economics Activity

22. One of the concurrent powers in the Constitution is the power to collect taxes. The main source of tax revenue for the national government is personal and corporate income tax. Investigate your state tax structure. What taxes comprise the largest sources of revenue in your state?

Analyzing Visuals

23. Study the chart on page 91. How does the judicial branch check the Congress? How can the Congress check the president? Do you think the system works? Explain.

★ CITIZENSHIP COOPERATIVE ACTIVITY ★

24. With a partner, search your local newspaper for articles that deal with constitutional issues. Select an issue from one of the articles and write a letter to your senator or representative expressing your opinion about the issue.

Technology Activity

25. Do an Internet search to find a Supreme Court case. Use the information you find to write a brief report and describe the constitutional issues raised by the case.

The Princeton Review
Standardized Test Practice

Directions: Choose the *best* answer to the following question.

In what way are the Articles of Confederation and the U.S. Constitution similar?

A Under both plans, the national government could impose taxes.

B Under both structures, the national government could declare war.

C The national government could take all necessary actions to run the government.

D Both documents set up a judicial system.

Test-Taking Tip

Review what you know about these two documents and note all the areas in which the two structures of government were alike.

The Bill of Rights

★ CITIZENSHIP AND YOU ★

The Bill of Rights—the first 10 amendments to the U.S. Constitution—guarantees certain basic rights to all Americans. Among the most important is freedom of speech. This right allows Americans to speak out on issues and make their feelings known. Contact a local organization concerned with civil liberties. Ask about incidents in your community that threatened the free speech of an individual or group. Create a proposal that lists actions that can be taken to protect free speech in your community.

 To learn more about the rights that the Constitution guarantees, view the **Democracy in Action** video lesson 3: The Constitution—A Living Document.

FOLDABLES™
Study Organizer

Evaluating Information Study Foldable *Make this foldable to write questions and answers as you study the Bill of Rights.*

Step 1 *Write a summary of the Bill of Rights on one side of a sheet of paper.*

Step 2 *Fold the sheet of paper into thirds from top to bottom.*

Step 3 *Unfold, turn the paper over (to the clean side), and label as shown.*

What is the Bill of Rights?

The Bill of Rights and You

Extending the Bill of Rights

Reading and Writing *As you read about the Bill of Rights, write down three main questions under each heading. Then write an answer to each question.*

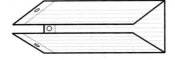

Americans express their views at the Lincoln Memorial. ▶

CIVICS Online

Chapter Overview Visit the *Civics Today* Web site at civ.glencoe.com and click on **Chapter Overviews— Chapter 4** to preview chapter information.

IN THIS TEMPLE
AS IN THE HEARTS OF THE PEOPLE
FOR WHOM HE SAVED THE UNION
THE MEMORY OF ABRAHAM LINCOLN
IS ENSHRINED FOREVER

EQUAL RIGHTS
FOR ALL SPECIES
SAVE THE RAINFOREST
EARTH FIRST!

The First Amendment

GUIDE TO READING

Main Idea

Soon after ratification of the Constitution, the First Amendment was added to guarantee basic freedoms essential to American democracy.

Key Terms

civil liberties, censorship, petition, slander, libel

Reading Strategy

Analyzing Information As you read, list in a chart like the one below the freedoms guaranteed by the First Amendment, along with the limitations to those freedoms.

First Amendment	
Freedoms	Limitations

Read to Learn

- How does the First Amendment protect five basic freedoms?
- What are the limits to First Amendment freedoms?

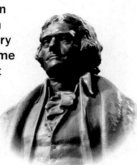

Americans in Action

Thomas Jefferson was an outspoken supporter of Americans' personal freedoms. In a letter to Colonel Edward Carrington, dated January 16, 1787, Jefferson wrote: ". . . [W]ere it left to me to decide whether we should have a government without newspapers, or newspapers without a government, I should not hesitate a moment to prefer the latter." In his lifetime, Jefferson took full advantage of the freedom of the press. He wrote and published dozens of articles and papers to express his views and to encourage his fellow citizens to think and act according to their beliefs.

Thomas Jefferson

First Amendment Freedoms

The Founders of the United States believed that protecting individual rights and providing for the safety and well-being of citizens were important purposes of government. The Constitution might not have been ratified had the Bill of Rights not been promised. Added in 1791, the 10 amendments in the Bill of Rights place strict limits on how the national government can use its power over the people. The Bill of Rights protects our civil liberties—the freedoms we have to think and act without government interference or fear of unfair treatment.

The First Amendment to the Constitution protects five basic freedoms: freedom of religion, freedom of speech, freedom of the press, freedom of assembly, and freedom to petition the government.

These civil liberties are the cornerstone of our democracy. They ensure that each of us can develop our own beliefs, express ourselves freely, meet openly with others, and have our views on public matters heard by those who govern.

Freedom of Religion

Intolerance of different beliefs in their homelands forced many colonists to come to America in the first place. To safeguard religious freedom, the First Amendment prohibits Congress from establishing an official religion in the United States. It protects the freedom of Americans to practice their faith as they wish. The government may not favor one religion over another or treat people differently because of their personal beliefs.

Freedom of Speech

In some countries, people can be jailed for criticizing the government or voicing unpopular ideas, even if they do so only in private conversations. In the United States, however, the First Amendment guarantees that we can say what is on our minds, in public or in private, without fear of punishment by the government.

Face-to-face discussions, telephone conversations, lectures, and radio and TV broadcasts are covered by the guarantee of free speech; so are other forms of expression besides the spoken word. As interpreted by the Supreme Court, "speech" can mean Internet communication, art, music, or even clothing.

In 1965, for example, 13-year-old Mary Beth Tinker and two other students wore black armbands to school to mourn those who died in the Vietnam War. School authorities suspended them for wearing the armbands, and the teens eventually took their case to the Supreme Court. In its

landmark 1969 decision, the Court ruled that the armbands were a form of speech protected by the First Amendment. See Landmark Supreme Court Case Studies on page 108.

Freedom of the Press

The First Amendment allows Americans to express themselves in print as well as in speech. When the Bill of Rights was written, "the press" referred to printed publications such as books, newspapers, and magazines. Today the press includes many other sources of media, such as radio, television, and computer networks.

Freedom of the press ensures that the American people are exposed to a wide variety of viewpoints. The government cannot practice **censorship**; that is, it cannot ban printed materials or films merely

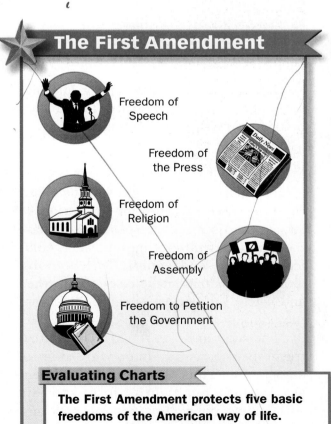

The First Amendment

Freedom of Speech

Freedom of the Press

Freedom of Religion

Freedom of Assembly

Freedom to Petition the Government

Evaluating Charts

The First Amendment protects five basic freedoms of the American way of life.
Which freedoms protect your right to demonstrate against a government policy?

Freedom of Religion Many early colonists and immigrants throughout history came to the United States so they could freely practice religion. **How does the First Amendment protect religious freedom?**

because they contain alarming or offensive ideas, and it also cannot censor information before it is published or broadcast.

Freedom of Assembly

The First Amendment protects our right to gather in groups for any reason, so long as the assemblies are peaceful. We have the right to attend meetings, parades, political rallies, and public celebrations. Governments may make rules about when and where such activities can be held, but they cannot ban them.

The Supreme Court has decided that freedom of assembly implies freedom of association. Thus the First Amendment also protects our right to form and join social clubs, political parties, labor unions, and other organizations. Even if we never assemble with fellow members, we have the right to belong to such groups.

Freedom to Petition

Finally, the First Amendment guarantees all Americans the right to petition the government. A **petition** is simply a formal request. Often we use the word to refer to a specific kind of document—a brief, written statement signed by hundreds or thousands of people. Even a simple letter or e-mail written by an individual, however, could be considered a petition.

The right to petition means the right to express one's ideas to the government. If you want to complain about overcrowded schools, for example, or suggest that a skating park be built in your community, you can write to your elected representatives. If enough people express similar views, government leaders may take action.

✓ Reading Check **Summarizing** What freedoms does the First Amendment protect?

Limits to First Amendment Freedoms

The Supreme Court has decided that compelling public interests—the safety and security of Americans—may justify limitations on our First Amendment freedoms. Freedom of speech, for example, does not include the right to endanger our government or other Americans. You do not have freedom to provoke a riot or other violent behavior. You are not free to speak or write in a way that immediately leads to criminal activities or efforts to overthrow the government by force.

Citizens should use their civil liberties responsibly, which means they should not interfere with the rights of others. For example, you are free to talk with your friends in the street, but you must not block traffic. You may campaign for causes, but you may not disturb your neighbors with blaring loudspeaker broadcasts. You may criticize government officials, but you may not spread lies that harm a person's reputation. Spreading such lies is a crime called **slander** if the lies are spoken and **libel** if they are printed.

The First Amendment was never intended to allow Americans to do whatever they please. Unlimited freedom is not possible in a society of many people. The rights of one individual must be balanced against the rights of others and against the rights of the community. When there is a conflict, the rights of the community often come first. Otherwise, the society would break apart.

Reading Check **Explaining** Why are your First Amendment rights limited?

Fact Fiction Folklore

203 years to pass . . .

The 27th amendment states that no change in congressional pay can go into effect until after the next general election. Originally, it was the second of 12 separate articles that became the Bill of Rights in 1791. In the 1980s, it was rediscovered. By 1992 the required 38 states had ratified it, putting it at last into the Constitution—203 years after it was proposed!

SECTION 1 ASSESSMENT

Checking for Understanding

1. **Key Terms** Define the following terms and use them in sentences related to the First Amendment: civil liberties, censorship, petition, slander, libel.

Reviewing Main Ideas

2. **Infer** Besides the spoken word, "speech" refers to what other forms of expression?

3. **Identify** What are the limits to First Amendment freedoms? Give an example of a limit to a First Amendment right.

Critical Thinking

4. **Drawing Conclusions** Which First Amendment right do you think is the most important?

5. **Cause-and-Effect** In a graphic organizer like the one below, explain the effects of Mary Beth Tinker's antiwar protest.

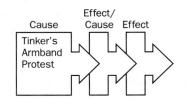

Cause — Tinker's Armband Protest — Effect/Cause — Effect

Analyzing Visuals

6. **Describe** Reexamine the photos on page 100. How do these images reflect First Amendment rights?

★ **BE AN ACTIVE CITIZEN** ★

7. **Use Primary Sources** Read your local newspaper for a week. Note all of the examples of people exercising First Amendment rights that you can find. Report your findings to the class.

Taking Notes

Why Learn This Skill?

Reading and listening are a part of your student life. You read your textbook, library books, and Web pages. You listen to your teachers and to television broadcasts. Whatever your purpose, it helps to know how to take notes. Taking notes helps you organize and learn information and makes studying easier.

Learning the Skill

To take good notes, follow these steps:
- Record the date and identity of your source.
- Define the purpose of your note taking, and stay focused on it.
- Watch for proper names, dates, events, or headings in the selection you use. Include this type of information in your notes.
- Write down short phrases that summarize the main ideas of the selection. Use complete sentences sparingly.
- Use your own words as much as possible. Try to develop your own system of abbreviations and symbols. Arrows, for instance, can be a quick way to show relationships between two or more points.

- Leave space to come back and write further information about important ideas. This is helpful when you use two or more sources.

Practicing the Skill

Read the passage below and follow the steps to create notes for it.

Censorship and Cyberspace

Can the Internet and the First Amendment coexist? Congress acted early to outlaw inappropriate cyber contact between adults and children. In the mid-1990s, it reached further. Congress first considered holding online providers to standards similar to those used by mainstream TV and radio networks. Owners of these "airway" communications chose their own programs and so could control content. The Communications Decency Act finally passed by Congress in 1996 had fewer limits. This law simply outlawed "indecent" and "offensive" materials. The Supreme Court found the law a "heavy burden" on freedom of speech, and struck it down.

Studying and taking notes

Applying the Skill

Scan a local newspaper for a short editorial or article about a constitutional issue. Take notes on the article. Summarize the article using only your notes.

GO TO

Practice key skills with Glencoe's
**Skillbuilder Interactive Workbook
CD-ROM, Level 1.**

Other Guarantees in the Bill of Rights

GUIDE TO READING

Main Idea

In addition to the important civil liberties protected by the First Amendment, the other nine amendments in the Bill of Rights guarantee the right to fair legal treatment, as well as other freedoms.

Key Terms

search warrant, indictment, grand jury, double jeopardy, due process, eminent domain, bail

Reading Strategy

Categorizing Information As you read, list the rights guaranteed by Amendments 2–10 of the Bill of Rights in a web diagram like the one below.

Amendments 2–10

Read to Learn

• How does the Bill of Rights protect the rights of the accused?

• What other rights and freedoms are guaranteed by the Bill of Rights?

Americans in Action

The Fourth Amendment is an important safeguard against "unreasonable searches and seizures." This amendment protects Americans from unlawful searches by the police. However, you, as a student, are not protected in the same way. In the case of *New Jersey* v. *T.L.O.,* the Supreme Court ruled that the Fourth Amendment's "warrant requirement . . . is unsuited to the school environment." The Constitution includes other amendments that protect the rights of Americans accused of crimes.

Are school lockers private?

Protecting the Rights of the Accused

The First Amendment freedoms you have just read about are among our most important civil liberties. Equally precious, however, is the right to fair legal treatment. This is the subject of several amendments in the Bill of Rights.

Suppose someone accuses you of committing a crime. In some countries, government agents might ransack your home, drag you off to jail, beat you, and hold a trial without even letting you respond to the charges. In the United States, the Fourth, Fifth, Sixth, and Eighth Amendments help prevent such a scenario from occurring.

The Fourth Amendment

The Fourth Amendment protects Americans "against unreasonable searches and seizures." No soldier, government agent, or police officer can search your home or take your property without good cause.

However, if law enforcement officers believe you have committed a crime, they can ask a judge to issue a search warrant. This is a court order allowing law enforcement officers to search a suspect's home or business and take specific items as evidence.

Judges do not give out search warrants readily. They must be convinced that a search will probably turn up evidence of criminal activity. If warrants were issued frivolously, the Fourth Amendment would give us little sense of security. Any time of the day or night, the police could invade our privacy and confiscate our possessions.

The Fifth Amendment

The Fifth Amendment protects the rights of people accused of crimes. It states that no one can be put on trial for a serious federal crime without an indictment—a formal charge by a group of citizens called a grand jury, who review the evidence against the accused.

A person who is indicted is not necessarily guilty of a crime. An indictment simply indicates the grand jury's belief that an individual *may* have committed a crime. This provision protects people from being brought to trial hastily and perhaps needlessly.

The Fifth Amendment also protects people from double jeopardy. This means that people who are accused of a crime and judged not guilty may not be put on trial again for the same crime.

In addition, the Fifth Amendment protects an accused person's right to remain silent. Throughout history, innocent people have been threatened, tortured, or bullied into confessing to crimes they did not commit. To prevent this, the Fifth Amendment states that people cannot be forced to testify against themselves. This is called protection against self-incrimination.

The Fifth Amendment goes on to say that no one may be denied life, liberty, or property "without due process of law." Due process means following established legal procedures. It also includes the idea that the laws themselves must be reasonable.

Finally, the Fifth Amendment protects citizens' property rights by limiting the government's power of eminent domain.

★ Rights of the Accused

FIFTH AMENDMENT

- ★ No trial may be held unless a person is formally charged, or indicted by a grand jury.
- ★ A person found not guilty may not be put on trial again for the same crime.
- ★ Accused persons may not be forced to testify against themselves.
- ★ Every person is entitled to due process of law.
- ★ No one may be deprived of their property by the government without compensation.

SIXTH AMENDMENT

- ★ The accused must be informed of the nature of the charges.
- ★ The accused must be allowed a speedy and public trial by an impartial jury.
- ★ If possible, the trial must be held in the area where the crime took place.
- ★ The accused must be permitted to hear and question all witnesses.
- ★ The accused is entitled to a lawyer and to call witnesses for his or her defense.

Evaluating Charts

The Fifth and Sixth Amendments contain important protections for people accused of committing crimes. Which amendment guarantees that if you are arrested, you will be informed of the charges against you?

Eminent domain is the right of the government to take private property—usually land—for public use. For example, if your home lies in the path of a proposed highway, the government may legally take the land and destroy your house. Under the Fifth Amendment, however, the government must pay you a fair price for the property.

The Sixth Amendment

The Sixth Amendment gives additional due process rights to people accused of crimes. It requires that they be told the exact nature of the charges against them. It also guarantees them a trial by jury, although they may ask to be tried by only a judge instead.

If an accused person requests a jury trial, the trial must be speedy and public, and jurors must be impartial. If possible, the trial should be held in the same district where the crime took place.

Accused individuals have the right to hear and question all witnesses against them. They must also be permitted to call witnesses in their own defense. Finally, they are entitled to have a lawyer. Since the Sixth Amendment was written, the Supreme Court has ruled that if an accused person cannot afford a lawyer, the government must provide one and pay his or her fees.

The Eighth Amendment

Although the Sixth Amendment guarantees a speedy trial, sometimes months go by before a case can be heard. During that time, the accused may have two choices: stay in jail or remain free by paying bail. Bail is a sum of money used as a security deposit. If the accused person comes to court for the trial, the bail is returned. If the person fails to appear, though, the bail is forfeited.

The judge decides how much bail a person must pay. Judges consider various

American Biographies

James Madison (1751–1836)

Even in his day, James Madison, the nation's fourth president, was known as the "Father of the Constitution." Madison protested: "You give me credit to which I have no claim. . . . It ought to be regarded as the work of many heads and many hands."

However, when it came to creating a constitution, Madison had few equals. He not only played a leading role in shaping the Constitution, he wrote many of the *Federalist* papers defending it. Madison, though, at first opposed the addition of a bill of rights. He felt the Constitution gave the people the power to protect their own rights through the election of officials. The Constitution also limited the powers of government by such means as separation of powers and checks and balances. He feared that future governments might honor only those rights listed in the bill.

When some leaders threatened to call a second constitutional convention, Madison agreed to a list of rights. To make sure the amendments did not weaken the new government, he helped write them himself. Then, as the U.S. representative from Virginia, Madison pushed the amendments through Congress, fulfilling the Constitution's promise to create a "more perfect union."

factors, including the type of crime committed, the record of the accused person, the likelihood that he or she will appear in court, and what he or she can afford. The Eighth Amendment, however, forbids "excessive" bail—that is, an amount that is much too high.

TIME

Political Cartoons

and it seems to be diverted toward money and time. Making the world a more convenient place to live was a collaboration among several

Analyzing Visuals The Bill of Rights extended the protections of the Constitution by granting freedom of the press, due process, and other important rights to Americans. **What details reveal the cartoonist's view of the Bill of Rights?**

The Eighth Amendment also forbids excessive fines for people convicted of crimes. In addition, it forbids "cruel and unusual punishments." For many years, Americans have debated what kinds of punishment are cruel and unusual. It is generally agreed that punishment should be in proportion to the crime committed. For example, a sentence of life imprisonment for stealing a loaf of bread would be too harsh. People disagree strongly, however, about whether the death penalty for very serious crimes is cruel and unusual punishment.

Reading Check **Identifying** Which amendment protects a person accused of a crime from double jeopardy?

Protecting Other Rights

In addition to the First Amendment freedoms and due process guarantees, the Bill of Rights includes other protections for American citizens.

The Second Amendment

There is much debate over what rights, exactly, are guaranteed by the Second Amendment. Some argue that it provides only for each state to maintain "a well regulated militia" by allowing the members of those militias to carry arms. When the Second Amendment was written, a militia was a small, local army made up of volunteer soldiers. These militias helped to win America's independence from Great Britain. Later, they helped defend the states and their communities.

Other people hold that the Second Amendment guarantees the right of all individual citizens to "keep and bear arms" without the interference of the government. The courts have generally ruled that the government can pass laws to control, but not prevent, the possession of weapons. For example, federal and state laws determine who can be licensed to own firearms.

Lawmakers continue to discuss the extent of our right to bear arms today. They also debate the kinds of gun regulations that may be necessary for public safety.

The Third Amendment

One cause of the American Revolution was the colonists' resentment of the law requiring them to house and feed British soldiers. The Third Amendment makes it unlikely that Americans will ever be forced to shelter the military again. The amendment says that, in peacetime, soldiers may not move into private homes without the consent of the homeowner. In times of war, the practice must be authorized by Congress.

The Seventh Amendment

The Fifth, Sixth, and Eighth Amendments deal with people's rights in criminal cases. The Seventh Amendment concerns civil cases—lawsuits that involve disagreements between people rather than crimes. If you were disputing a contract, for example, or claiming that a doctor had not treated you properly, you could initiate a civil suit.

The Seventh Amendment guarantees the right to a jury trial in civil cases if the amount of money involved is more than $20. The amendment does not, however, require a jury trial. Both sides may decide to have their dispute settled by a judge instead.

The Ninth Amendment

The people who wrote the Bill of Rights realized that they could not spell out every right of the American people. The Ninth Amendment makes it clear that citizens have other rights beyond those listed in the Constitution. These unwritten rights are just as valuable and may not be taken away.

The right to privacy, for example, is not mentioned in the Constitution. However, the Supreme Court has drawn on the First, Fourth, Fifth, and Ninth Amendments to uphold this right. We thus enjoy privacy in our homes, confidentiality in our medical and financial records, and freedom from government interference in our personal choices regarding friends, families, and careers.

The Tenth Amendment

The Constitution discusses certain powers of the national and state governments. Many other powers of government—such as the authority to set up schools and license lawyers—are not mentioned at all.

Under the Tenth Amendment, any powers the Constitution does not specifically give to the national government are reserved to the states or to the people. (This amendment is the source of the reserved powers you learned about in the Chapter 3 discussion of federalism.) In this way, the Tenth Amendment prevents Congress and the president from becoming too strong. The government of the United States can have only the powers the people give it.

Reading Check **Describing** What is the purpose of the Tenth Amendment?

SECTION 2 ASSESSMENT

Checking for Understanding

1. **Key Terms** Use the following terms in sentences related to the Bill of Rights: search warrant, indictment, grand jury, double jeopardy, due process, eminent domain, bail.

Reviewing Main Ideas

2. **Explain** When can law enforcement officers search a suspect's house?

3. **Identify** What current controversial issue is tied to the Eighth Amendment's prohibition of cruel and unusual punishment?

Critical Thinking

4. **Drawing Conclusions** Which of the first 10 amendments do you think is the most important? Why?

5. **Organizing Information** In a similar chart, describe how the rights of the accused are protected by each amendment.

Amendment	Rights Protected
4	
5	
6	
8	

Analyzing Visuals

6. **Conclude** Review the chart that lists the rights of persons accused of crimes on page 104. What is the role of a grand jury in the trial process?

★ **BE AN ACTIVE CITIZEN** ★

7. **Write** Select an issue related to the amendments in this section, such as the death penalty or gun control. Write a letter to the editor of your local newspaper expressing your views on the issue.

Landmark Supreme Court
Case Studies

Tinker v. Des Moines Independent Community School District

The Tinkers show their armbands.

Public school officials set standards of behavior that students are expected to follow. Does this arrangement leave students with any rights? Sometimes the Supreme Court must decide.

The Decision

On February 24, 1969, the United States Supreme Court in a 7–2 decision declared the school suspensions unconstitutional. Justice Abe Fortas, who wrote the majority opinion, first established that the students' action was "akin to pure speech." Even though their protest involved no speaking, it deserved "protection under the First Amendment." Then he wrote:

> It can hardly be argued that either students or teachers shed their constitutional rights to freedom of speech or expression at the schoolhouse gate.

Background of the Case

Division over the war in Vietnam racked the nation during the 1960s. Millions of Americans agreed with the war, while other millions disagreed. Protests occurred frequently. One night in December 1965, a group of public school students, led by high-school sophomores Christopher Eckhardt and John Tinker and eighth-grader Mary Beth Tinker, planned their own protest. They decided to wear black armbands to school as silent expressions of mourning for deaths on both sides in the war. As other students joined the armband protest, principals and members of the school board met the growing protest with a ban on armbands—to prevent "disturbing influences."

On December 16, 1965, Christopher, John, and Mary Beth were suspended for wearing their armbands to school. Their parents protested the suspensions in federal courts. They contended the students' First Amendment free speech rights had been violated.

Why It Matters

Supporters saluted the decision. Critics predicted harmful consequences. Dissenter Justice Hugo Black suggested that the Court's decision was "the beginning of a new revolutionary era of permissiveness in this country fostered by the judiciary." He argued that no one has a complete right to freedom of speech and expression.

Analyzing the Court Decision

1. How did Justice Fortas's concept of "pure speech" extend First Amendment free speech rights?

2. What arguments might you use to support or oppose the viewpoints of Justice Fortas and Justice Black?

Extending the Bill of Rights

GUIDE TO READING

Main Idea

The amendments adopted after the Bill of Rights extended liberties and voting rights to African Americans, women, and other minority groups.

Key Terms

suffrage, poll tax

Reading Strategy

Explaining Information
As you read, complete a graphic organizer like the one below to explain the Civil War amendments.

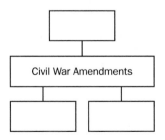

Read to Learn

- **How were the Civil War amendments intended to extend civil liberties to African Americans?**
- **How did the Seventeenth, Nineteenth, Twenty-third, Twenty-fourth, and Twenty-sixth Amendments extend voting rights in the United States?**

Americans in Action

Even as a teenager, William Lloyd Garrison's dedication to the abolition of slavery was apparent. As a newspaper apprentice, and later as the owner of his own newspapers, ending slavery was nearly his sole concern. In the first edition of *The Liberator,* published in 1831, Garrison promised his readers, "I am in earnest—I will not equivocate—I will not excuse—I will not retreat a single inch—AND I WILL BE HEARD." Thirty-four years later came proof that Garrison's words had been heard when the Thirteenth Amendment was passed.

William Lloyd Garrison

Protecting All Americans

The Bill of Rights was passed to safeguard individual liberties. However, the rights guaranteed to all Americans have not always been applied equally and fairly. The Bill of Rights was intended originally to restrain only the national government. For many years, local and state governments were not bound by its terms. As a result, states sometimes used their reserved powers to pass laws that violated civil liberties. In most parts of the country, for example, women and African Americans could not vote to elect representatives in government. Before 1865, many states had laws that sanctioned the enslavement of African Americans, who were treated as property and had almost no rights at all.

Gradually, however, the Bill of Rights came to cover all Americans equally and to limit government power at all levels. Additional amendments to the Constitution and court rulings both played a part in this process.

Three amendments were passed after the Civil War to extend civil liberties to African Americans. The promise of these Civil War amendments, as they are known, was not fulfilled, however, for almost 100 years. Many states were slow to change their customs; some actively resisted. The federal government, including the Supreme Court, often seemed indifferent. Nonetheless, the Civil War amendments signaled a move toward greater equality.

The Thirteenth Amendment (1865)

The Thirteenth Amendment officially outlawed slavery in the United States and thus freed thousands of African Americans. It also outlawed any sort of forced labor, except as punishment for a crime.

The Fourteenth Amendment (1868)

Although the Thirteenth Amendment ensured the freedom of African Americans, it did not guarantee them full rights. After the Civil War, many Southern states passed "black codes" that kept African Americans

Constitutional Amendments 11–27

AMEND-MENTS	DATE	PURPOSE
11	1795	Removed cases in which a state was sued without its consent from the jurisdiction of the federal courts
12	1804	Required presidential electors to vote separately for president and vice president
13	1865	Abolished slavery and authorized Congress to pass legislation implementing its abolition
14	1868	Granted citizenship to all persons born or naturalized in the United States; banned states from denying any person life, liberty, or property without due process of law; and banned states from denying any person equal protection under the laws
15	1870	Guaranteed voting rights to African Americans by outlawing denial of the right to vote on the basis of race, color, or previous condition of servitude
16	1913	Empowered Congress to levy an income tax
17	1913	Provided for the election of U.S. senators by direct popular vote instead of by the state legislatures
18	1919	Authorized Congress to prohibit the manufacture, sale, and transportation of liquor
19	1920	Guaranteed the right to vote to women
20	1933	Shortened the time between a presidential election and inauguration by designating January 20 as Inauguration Day; set January 3 as the date for the opening of a new Congress
21	1933	Repealed the Eighteenth Amendment and empowered Congress to regulate the liquor industry
22	1951	Limited presidents to two full terms in office
23	1961	Granted voters in the District of Columbia the right to vote for president and vice president
24	1964	Forbade requiring the payment of a poll tax to vote in a federal election
25	1967	Provided for succession to the office of president in the event of death or incapacity and for filling vacancies in the office of the vice president
26	1971	Guaranteed the right to vote to 18-year-olds
27	1992	Banned Congress from increasing its members' salaries until after the next election

- Amendments changing the powers of the national and state governments
- Amendments changing the government structure or function
- Amendments extending the suffrage and powers of voters

Evaluating Charts

One of the strengths of the Constitution is its ability to respond to changes in society. The amendment process contributes to that flexibility. Which amendment establishes the process by which the vice president takes over when the president is disabled?

from holding certain jobs, limited their property rights, and restricted them in other ways.

To remedy this situation, the Fourteenth Amendment was enacted in 1868. It defined a United States citizen as anyone "born or naturalized in the United States," a definition that included most African Americans. The amendment also required every state to grant its citizens "equal protection of the laws." This clause has been extremely important. In recent years, it has been used to benefit women, people with disabilities, and other groups whose rights have not always been protected fairly.

Another element of the Fourteenth Amendment forbids state governments from interfering with the "privileges or immunities of citizens of the United States." Further, state governments may not take an individual's "life, liberty, or property, without due process of law." The intent of these provisions was to make the Bill of Rights binding for state governments as well as the federal government. This is called the nationalization of the Bill of Rights.

For many years, however, the Supreme Court ignored this interpretation of the Fourteenth Amendment. Then, in 1925, in *Gitlow* v. *New York,* the Court ruled that the Fourteenth Amendment could safeguard free speech and a free press "from impairment by the states."

Since the *Gitlow* case, the Supreme Court has used the Fourteenth Amendment to apply other rights in the Bill of Rights to the states. This "incorporation" of the Bill of Rights by the Fourteenth Amendment's due process clause means that U.S. citizens in every part of the country have the same basic rights. A string of later cases further extended the reach of the Bill of Rights. By the end of the 1960s, most protections in the Bill of Rights were considered to apply at the state level.

The Fifteenth Amendment (1870)

The last of the Civil War amendments, the Fifteenth, says that no state may take away a person's voting rights on the basis of race, color, or previous enslavement. The amendment clearly aimed to guarantee suffrage—the right to vote—to African Americans. Still, many states found ways to keep African Americans away from the polls.

The Fifteenth Amendment protected only men in practice. The various states had the power to decide whether women could vote. Women, regardless of their race, could not vote in most federal or state elections.

The Seventeenth Amendment (1913)

According to Article I of the Constitution, the people were to elect members of the House of Representatives, but the state legislatures were to choose members of the Senate. The Seventeenth Amendment was passed in order to allow voters to elect their senators directly. This change in the election process gave Americans a greater voice in their government.

The Nineteenth Amendment (1920)

Although the Constitution did not guarantee women the right to vote, it did not explicitly deny them suffrage. As a result, states made their own laws on the matter, using the powers reserved to them under the Tenth Amendment. The territory of Wyoming permitted women to vote in 1869, and several other territories and states did so as well in the years that followed.

However, national support for woman suffrage was slow in coming. Leaders like Susan B. Anthony and Elizabeth Cady Stanton had insisted as early as 1848 that women belonged at the polls. It was only in 1920, however, that the Nineteenth Amendment protected the right of women to vote in all national and state elections.

The Twenty-Third Amendment (1961)

African Americans and women were not the only citizens who were denied voting rights for many years. Residents of our nation's capital, Washington, D.C., also fell into this group.

"D.C.," as you may know, stands for the District of Columbia, an area between Maryland and Virginia. Because the District is not a state, the people who lived there were not initially allowed to vote in national elections. The Twenty-third Amendment changed that in 1961. The amendment says that residents of the District of Columbia may vote for the president and vice president, just as other Americans do.

The Twenty-Fourth Amendment (1964)

Although the Fifteenth Amendment gave African Americans the right to vote, many had trouble exercising this right. One reason was that several Southern states had poll taxes. In other words, they required voters to pay a sum of money before casting a ballot. Because many African Americans could not afford the tax, they could not vote. Poor whites were in the same situation.

In 1964, the Twenty-fourth Amendment made poll taxes illegal in national elections. Two years later, the Supreme Court ruled that poll taxes were illegal in state elections as well.

The Twenty-Sixth Amendment (1971)

Throughout our nation's history, people still in their teens have bravely fought for our country. By law, however, they were not old enough to vote for the leaders who sent them into battle. Although the Constitution did not specify a minimum age for voters, most states set the minimum at 21.

That standard finally changed in 1971, a year when many young Americans were fighting in the Vietnam War. The Twenty-sixth Amendment guaranteed the right to vote to citizens 18 and older for all national and state elections. As a result, millions more Americans could now exercise their right to vote.

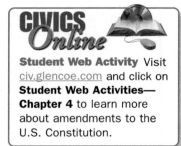

CIVICS Online

Student Web Activity Visit civ.glencoe.com and click on **Student Web Activities— Chapter 4** to learn more about amendments to the U.S. Constitution.

Reading Check **Explaining** How did the Nineteenth Amendment expand suffrage?

SECTION 3 ASSESSMENT

Checking for Understanding

1. **Key Terms** Define the following terms and use them in sentences related to voting rights: suffrage, poll tax.

Reviewing Main Ideas

2. **Explain** How was the promise of the Civil War amendments fulfilled in the mid-twentieth century?

3. **Describe** How did the Twenty-fourth Amendment expand voting rights?

Critical Thinking

4. **Concluding** Which of the voting rights amendments (17, 19, 23, 23, 24, 26) do you think was the most important? Why?

5. **Cause-and-Effect** In a graphic organizer like the one below, explain the effects of poll taxes in the South.

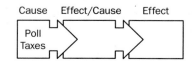

Cause   Effect/Cause   Effect

Poll Taxes

Analyzing Visuals

6. **Infer** Review the chart on page 110. Which amendment limited presidents to two terms in office?

★ **BE AN ACTIVE CITIZEN** ★

7. **Write** Because many 18- to 21-year-olds do not vote, some believe the 26th Amendment should be repealed. Write your representatives in Congress to get their views on this issue.

The Civil Rights Struggle

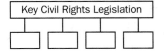 **Americans in Action**

On August 23, 1963, more than 200,000 people marched in Washington, D.C., for their rights. On that day, they heard Reverend Martin Luther King, Jr., utter these words: "I have a dream that one day this nation will rise up and live out the true meaning of its creed: 'We hold these truths to be self-evident; that all men are created equal'. . . . I have a dream that my four little children will one day live in a nation where they will not be judged by the color of their skin but by the content of their character. . . ."

Martin Luther King, Jr., leads a march in Mississippi.

Background of the Struggle

Despite the advances made after the Civil War, African Americans routinely faced **discrimination,** or unfair treatment based on prejudice against a certain group. Southern states, for example, passed so-called "Jim Crow" laws requiring African Americans and whites to be separated in most public places, such as schools. Later, African Americans had to ride in the back of buses, and sit in separate sections of restaurants and theaters. They even had to use separate public restrooms. The social separation of the races was known as **segregation.** African Americans in the North fared better. They could vote freely, and segregation was less noticeable. Even so, prejudice restricted opportunities for many. It would take more than 100 years for African Americans to secure their **civil rights**—the rights of full citizenship and equality under the law.

From an early time, many Americans objected to the treatment of African Americans as "second-class citizens." In 1909 a group of African Americans and whites founded the National Association for the Advancement of Colored People (NAACP). The association worked mainly through the courts to challenge laws and customs that denied African Americans their constitutional rights.

In 1910 other concerned citizens formed the National Urban League. The Urban League aided the growing numbers of African

Landmark Acts of the Civil Rights Movement

BROWN v. BOARD OF EDUCATION OF TOPEKA, KANSAS, 1954

⭐ Supreme Court rules segregated schools unconstitutional

CIVIL RIGHTS ACT OF 1957

⭐ Congress sets up commission on civil rights and creates a division of civil rights in Justice Department

EQUAL PAY ACT OF 1963

⭐ Bans wage discrimination based on race, gender, religion, or national origin

CIVIL RIGHTS ACT OF 1964

⭐ Strengthens Fourteenth Amendment protections; bans discrimination in employment, voting, and public accommodations

VOTING RIGHTS ACT OF 1965

⭐ Empowers federal government to intervene in voter registration discrimination

OPEN HOUSING ACT OF 1968

⭐ Prevents people selling or renting homes from using certain forms of discrimination

EQUAL EMPLOYMENT OPPORTUNITY ACT OF 1972

⭐ Provides that businesses receiving federal funds must have affirmative action programs to increase number of female and minority employees

AMERICANS WITH DISABILITIES ACT OF 1990

⭐ Bans discrimination in employment, transportation, public accommodations, and telecommunications against persons with physical or mental disabilities

WE DEMAND EQUALITY NOW N.A.A.C.P.

Evaluating Charts

It was not until 1964 with the passage of the Civil Rights Act that racial segregation in public places became illegal. What legislation banned wage discrimination?

Americans in cities, helping them find jobs and improve their opportunities to get ahead.

Gradually, these organizations and other groups and individuals built a civil rights movement supported by millions. An important gain came in 1948, when President Harry Truman ordered an end to segregation in the nation's armed forces. A bigger victory was the Supreme Court's decision in *Brown* v. *Board of Education of Topeka, Kansas* (1954). In that landmark case, NAACP lawyers successfully argued that racial segregation in the public schools was unconstitutional. Segregation violated the Fourteenth Amendment's principle of equal protection under the law.

In the 1950s, Dr. Martin Luther King, Jr., became one of the main leaders of the civil rights movement. A Baptist minister and stirring speaker, King believed in non-violent resistance—the peaceful protest of unfair laws. He helped organize marches, boycotts, and demonstrations that opened many people's eyes to the need for change.

African American students began staging "sit-ins" at lunch counters that served only whites. White and African American "Freedom Riders" traveled together on buses to protest segregation. In his 1963 "I Have a Dream" speech, King inspired thousands with his hopes for racial equality and harmony. As the civil rights movement gained strength, however, some whites opposed it with violence.

In response to the growing demand for government action, Congress passed the Civil Rights Act of 1964. This far-reaching law prohibited discrimination in public facilities, employment, education, and voter registration. It also banned discrimination not only by race and color, but also by gender, religion, and national origin.

Earlier that same year, the Twenty-fourth Amendment had outlawed poll taxes. The Voting Rights Act of 1965 took further steps to protect the free access of minorities to the polls.

Ongoing Challenges

The civil rights laws of the 1960s certainly opened more doors for minorities. African Americans, Hispanic Americans, and other minorities have made striking gains in educational achievement. They increasingly hold professional and managerial jobs and serve in government, yet whites still tend to have more opportunities.

In the 1970s, the federal government began **affirmative action** programs to try to make up for past discrimination. These programs encouraged the hiring and promoting of minorities and women in fields that were traditionally closed to them. Colleges, too, practiced affirmative action to help minority students gain admission.

As planned, affirmative action was supposed to be a short-term policy to make up for past discrimination. From the start, affirmative action was controversial. Critics complained that giving preferential treatment to women and minorities amounted to discrimination against men and whites. Recent court decisions and state laws have curtailed many affirmative action programs.

The struggle for equal rights continues. Each year, the federal government receives more than 75,000 complaints of workplace discrimination. Many Americans and others are sometimes subject to **racial profiling** by law enforcement officers—being singled out as suspects because of the way they look. Some Americans even become the victims of hate crimes—acts of violence based on a person's race, color, national origin, gender, or disability.

Reading Check **Describing** How did Martin Luther King, Jr., hope to change unfair laws?

SECTION 4 ASSESSMENT

Checking for Understanding

1. Key Terms Use the following terms in a paragraph that summarizes the civil rights movement: discrimination, segregation, civil rights, affirmative action, racial profiling.

Reviewing Main Ideas

2. Identify List examples of the discrimination that African Americans faced after the Civil War.

3. Define What was the purpose of the Civil Rights Act of 1964?

Critical Thinking

4. Drawing Conclusions Why was the civil rights movement started?

5. Explaining Information Use the graphic organizer below to list Martin Luther King, Jr.'s tactics in the civil rights movement.

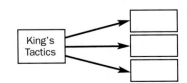

Analyzing Visuals

6. Conclude Reexamine the chart on page 114 that lists some landmark acts achieved by civil rights activists. What was the purpose of the Americans with Disabilities Act?

★ **BE AN ACTIVE CITIZEN** ★
7. Write Do you think that affirmative action laws are a fair way to change past discrimination? Write your opinion in a letter to the editor.

Assessment & Activities

Review to Learn

Section 1
- The First Amendment to the Constitution protects five basic freedoms of Americans.
- There are limits to our First Amendment rights.

Section 2
- The Fifth, Sixth, and Eighth Amendments protect the rights of persons accused of crimes.
- The Bill of Rights also protects other rights and important liberties.

Section 3
- The Civil War amendments ended slavery, defined American citizenship to include African Americans, and guaranteed suffrage to African Americans.

Section 4
- Groups of African Americans joined together to fight for equality in a struggle called the civil rights movement.

FOLDABLES
Study Organizer

Using Your Foldables Study Organizer
Find a classroom partner and take turns asking each other the three questions you each have written on your foldable. Can you answer each other's questions correctly?

Reviewing Key Terms

Write the chapter key term that matches each definition below.

1. a formal accusation of a crime issued by a grand jury
2. the criminal act of verbally lying about another person to harm that person's reputation
3. procedures established by law and guaranteed by the Constitution
4. a formal request for government action
5. the right of the government to take private property for public use
6. a sum of money paid in exchange for the right to vote
7. banning printed materials because they contain alarming or offensive ideas
8. the criminal act of printing lies about other people
9. money paid to the court by an accused person to guarantee that she or he will appear for trial
10. the right to vote

Reviewing Main Ideas

11. What five basic freedoms does the First Amendment protect?
12. What was the significance of the *Brown* v. *Board of Education of Topeka, Kansas* decision?
13. What practice led to the inclusion of the Third Amendment in the Bill of Rights?
14. Why is protection from "double jeopardy" important?
15. What was the impact of the Supreme Court's decision in *Gitlow* v. *New York* (1925)?
16. Explain the significance of the Fourteenth Amendment.
17. What was the purpose of the NAACP and the National Urban League?
18. What does the "incorporation" of the Bill of Rights mean?

Critical Thinking

19. **Predicting Consequences** The Twenty-fourth Amendment to the U.S. Constitution made poll taxes illegal in national elections. What do you think would have happened if the Twenty-fourth Amendment had not been ratified?

20. **Making Judgments** In a chart like the one below, reorder the 27 amendments to the U.S. Constitution in their order of importance. Explain your choice for most important and least important.

Order	Number of Amendment
First in importance:	
Second in importance:	
Third in importance:	

Practicing Skills

Taking Notes **Turn to the Supreme Court Case Summaries in the Appendix. Read the following cases: *Gideon* v. *Wainwright* and *Miranda* v. *Arizona*. Take notes as you read and answer the following questions using only your notes.**

21. Which amendments to the Constitution were involved in these cases?

22. What was the Court's ruling in each case?

23. Do you agree or disagree with these rulings? Explain your answers.

 **Economics Activity**

24. Contact a lawyer in your community who handles criminal cases. Conduct an interview to find out what costs are involved in defending a criminal charge.

Analyzing Visuals

25. Study the chart that lists Amendments 11–27 on page 110. Which amendment spells out the procedure for replacing a president who leaves office? Which amendment repeals an earlier amendment?

★ **CITIZENSHIP COOPERATIVE ACTIVITY** ★

26. The First Amendment guarantees freedom of assembly. Work with a partner to contact a local government to find out its rules about holding assemblies, such as political rallies, meetings, or parades. Find out what restrictions apply to where and when the assemblies take place. Report your findings to the class.

 Technology Activity

27. Use the Internet to research current debates over Americans' First Amendment rights. For example, you might research the proposed amendment to protect the American flag or the separation of church and state. Summarize the issue and share your opinion about it in a brief presentation.

 The Princeton Review
Standardized Test Practice

DIRECTIONS: Choose the *best* answer to complete the statement.

The right to express yourself in an editorial letter to your local newspaper is protected by

F the First Amendment.
G the Second Amendment.
H the Third Amendment.
J the Fourth Amendment.

Test-Taking Tip
Although you may not immediately recall the answer, start by eliminating answer choices that you know are incorrect.

The Citizen and the Community

★ CITIZENSHIP AND YOU ★

It is the combination of rights, responsibilities, and duties that characterizes what it means to be a citizen of a free, democratic society. As citizens, we are free to exercise our rights. In return we are expected to fulfill certain duties and responsibilities. Contact a volunteer organization in your community to learn what services it provides to area residents. Volunteer to work at the organization.

To learn more about the responsibilities of American citizenship, view the *Democracy in Action* video lesson 14: Citizenship in the United States.

Comparing Information Study Foldable *Make this foldable to help you compare and contrast responsibilities of the citizen and the community.*

Step 1 *Fold one sheet of paper in half from side to side.*

Step 2 *Turn the paper and fold it into thirds.*

Step 3 *Unfold and draw two overlapping ovals and label them as shown.*

Make the ovals overlap in the middle section.

Step 4 *Cut the top layer only along both fold lines.*

This will make three tabs.

Reading and Writing *As you read, write the responsibilities the citizen has to the community and the responsibilities that the community has to the citizen under the appropriate tabs of your foldable. Be sure to fill out the "Both" area, too.*

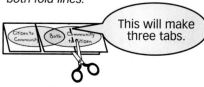

A volunteer at Earth Day plants a tree in Long Beach, California. ▶

CIVICS Online

Chapter Overview Visit the *Civics Today* Web site at civ.glencoe.com and click on **Chapter Overviews— Chapter 5** to preview chapter information.

The Duties and Responsibilities of Citizenship

GUIDE TO READING

Main Idea
The privilege of U.S. citizenship brings with it certain responsibilities. Some are legal, such as obeying laws and paying taxes, and some are voluntary, such as participating in the political process and being informed.

Key Terms
responsibility, duty, draft, tolerance

Reading Strategy
Summarizing Information As you read, on a web diagram like the one below list the legal responsibilities of U.S. citizens.

Legal Responsibilities of U.S. Citizens

Read to Learn
- What legal duties come with U.S. citizenship?
- What voluntary responsibilities of citizenship help the United States fulfill its democratic goals?

Americans in Action

On September 11, 2001, terrorist acts killed thousands of Americans. President George W. Bush led the nation during this troubled time and in 2002 proclaimed: ". . . [A]fter America was attacked, it was as if our entire country looked into a mirror and saw our better selves. We were reminded that we are citizens, with obligations to each other, to our country, and to history. We began to think less of the goods we can accumulate and more about the good we can do. . . . In the sacrifice of soldiers, the fierce brotherhood of firefighters, and the bravery and generosity of ordinary citizens, we have glimpsed what a new culture of responsibility could look like. We want to be a nation that serves goals larger than self. We have been offered a unique opportunity, and we must not let this moment pass."

Proud Americans

A Citizen's Legal Duties

When you think of your community, do you think of your neighborhood or perhaps your town? Actually, each of us belongs to many communities—our school or workplace; our church, synagogue, or mosque; our state; and our country. On the broadest level, we are also members of the global community, more connected than ever before to people around the world.

We all have a stake in making our communities safe and successful. Thus we all have certain responsibilities to fulfill. **Responsibilities** are things we should do; they are obligations that we fulfill voluntarily. As American citizens, we also have legal duties that we are required to perform. **Duties** are things that we must do.

National, state, and local governments require Americans to perform certain duties established by laws. If we fail to perform them, we are subject to legal penalties, such as fines or imprisonment. By accepting all of these responsibilities and duties, we strengthen our communities and help secure our rights. Some countries require their citizens to perform many duties, such as serving a certain number of years in the military. Although the U.S. government asks less of its citizens, it does require that they fulfill the following duties.

Obey Laws

Following the law is a citizen's most important duty. Our laws are designed for specific purposes—to help people get along, to prevent accidents, to see that resources are used fairly, and so on. If we do not obey the law, then governments cannot maintain order or protect our health, safety, and property.

Pay Taxes

Taxes pay for the government's activities. Without them, the federal government could not pay its employees, maintain armed forces to defend the country, and help those in need. Your local government could not hire police officers or firefighters, and your state could not pave roads or maintain prisons.

Citizens pay taxes in several ways. The federal government and some states and cities collect income taxes—a percentage of what people earn. Most states and some cities collect taxes on the sale of goods and services. Most local governments collect taxes on the residential and commercial property within school districts.

Defend the Nation

In the United States, all men aged 18 through 25 are required to register with the government in case the country needs to **draft,** or call up, men for military service. Since the end of the Vietnam War, there has been no draft, and America's military has been made up of volunteers. Nevertheless, the government has the authority to use the draft if the country should suddenly have to go to war.

Serve in Court

In criminal cases and most civil matters, the Constitution guarantees the right to a trial by jury. To ensure this, every adult citizen must be prepared to serve on a jury. People can be excused from jury duty if they have a good reason, but service is usually rewarding. People involved in court cases depend on their fellow citizens to reach a fair verdict. Another duty of citizens is to serve as witnesses at a trial if called to do so.

Attend School

Most states require young people to attend school until age 16. This benefits both you and the government because you need knowledge and skills to make wise decisions, and our democratic system of government needs informed citizens to operate well. In school you not only gain an understanding of history, government, and other important subjects, but you also learn to think through problems, form opinions, and express your views clearly.

Reading Check **Explaining** Why do we pay taxes?

Economics and You

Nonrenewable Resources

When nonrenewable resources are used up, they cannot be replaced. Some of the most important industrial resources—mineral ores, petroleum, and natural gas—fall into this category. Think about what your community might do to conserve a nonrenewable resource such as oil. Then devise a plan and put your plan into action.

Civic Responsibilities

Several responsibilities of citizenship are voluntary obligations rather than legal duties. If you ignore these, you won't be arrested or punished. If you fulfill them, however, you help our democracy flourish and reap personal benefits as well.

Be Informed

Every day government leaders make decisions that affect your life. The state legislature, for example, might pass a law changing the rate of sales tax you pay. Your school board might vote to start the school day earlier. Your town council might set aside funds for a new recreation center. As a citizen, you have a responsibility to know what the government is doing so that you can voice your opinions on matters you feel strongly about.

To learn about issues and leaders, you can read books, newspapers, and magazines. You can listen to the news on radio and television and talk with your teachers, family, and friends. You can also find useful information on the Internet.

Being informed includes knowing your rights. For example, people accused of crimes have the right to be represented by a lawyer. If people were unaware of that right, they might not receive fair trials.

Speak Up and Vote

The Founders of our nation set up a government based upon the principle of popular sovereignty, or "consent of the governed." People are the source of any and all governmental power; that is, government exists to serve you. You must make your concerns known, however, if you expect public officials to act in your interests. Call, write, or send e-mail to your elected representatives. Join a political party or a group working for a particular cause. Above all, vote.

Voting is one of a citizen's most important rights and responsibilities. By electing political leaders and voting for or against proposed measures, Americans give their consent to the government. As former President Franklin D. Roosevelt said,

> **"The ultimate rulers of our democracy are not a president and senators and congressmen and government officials but the voters of this country."**

Thoughtful voters study the candidates and issues carefully before marking their ballots. They also regularly check on what

Citizens' Duties and Responsibilities

RIGHTS

- Security—protection by government
- Equality—equal treatment under the law
- Liberty—rights guaranteed under the Constitution

DUTIES

- Obey the law
- Pay taxes
- Defend the nation
- Serve in court
- Attend school

RESPONSIBILITIES

- Be informed and vote
- Participate in your community and government
- Respect the rights and property of others
- Respect different opinions and ways of life

Evaluating Charts

American citizens have responsibilities as well as rights. Is paying taxes a duty or responsibility?

elected leaders are doing. If an official's performance falls short, it is up to the voters to choose someone else in the next election. Voting responsibly ensures that leadership is changed in a peaceful and orderly manner.

Respect Others' Rights

To enjoy your rights to the fullest, you must be prepared to respect other people's rights as well. For example, if you own a dog, you have an obligation to keep it from becoming a nuisance to your neighbors. If you're in the library, you should not interfere with anyone's right to work quietly.

Citizens also have a responsibility to show respect for public property and for the property of others. Some people might claim that "no one gets hurt" when they litter in a park or paint graffiti on a school wall, yet such public property belongs to us all, and we all pay if it is damaged.

Vandalism and littering are actually more than disrespectful acts; they are crimes. Indeed, many of our laws have been enacted to encourage people to respect others' rights. If you have a party that gets out of hand, for example, you could be arrested for disturbing the peace.

Respect Diversity

In a democratic society like ours, with such a diverse population, it is especially important to respect the civil liberties of others. Although you may disagree with people or disapprove of their lifestyles, they have an equal right to their beliefs and practices. Respecting and accepting others, regardless of their beliefs, practices, or differences, is called **tolerance.** Treating others politely and respectfully is thus part of being a good citizen. One of America's strengths has always been the diversity of its people.

Immigrants have brought a variety of religions, traditions, and lifestyles to this country, and they continue to do so. As

Celebrate Our Diversity As Americans we have a responsibility to respect the practices and traditions of others. Thai Americans celebrate the Thai New Year during a Songkran Festival in New York City in April. **What is the difference between a responsibility and a duty?**

citizens, we have a responsibility to respect the practices and traditions of others when they are different from our own, just as we expect them to respect our differences. There are no degrees of citizenship in the United States. All citizens are equal and entitled to be treated the same.

Contribute to the Common Good

Responsible citizens care about others as well as themselves. They are willing to contribute time, effort, and money to help other people and to improve community life for everyone.

Think about what your community would be like if no one donated to charities, volunteered in after-school programs, or lent a hand at the local health clinic. What if no one even spoke out about community problems? Communities and governments need people to participate. All American citizens must be active participants and not just idle bystanders if we want our communities to thrive.

Reading Check **Explaining** Why is voting such an important civic responsibility?

SECTION 1 ASSESSMENT

Checking for Understanding

1. **Key Terms** Define draft and tolerance and use them in sentences related to U.S. citizenship.

Reviewing Main Ideas

2. **Identify** When was the last time the United States instituted a military draft?

3. **Explain** Why is it important for citizens of the United States to be informed about issues and about their political leaders? How can you become informed?

Critical Thinking

4. **Drawing Conclusions** What do you think is the most important responsibility of citizens? Explain.

5. **Making Comparisons** Compare the legal with the voluntary responsibilities of citizenship in a chart like the one below.

Responsibilities of Citizens	
Legal	Voluntary

Analyzing Visuals

6. **Review** Look at the chart that lists the rights, duties, and responsibilities of citizens on page 122. What are the three categories of Americans' rights?

★ **BE AN ACTIVE CITIZEN** ★

7. **Research** Contact your local board of elections. Find out what percentage of citizens of voting age is registered to vote in your community. Then find out how many of those registered voted in the last three elections. Share your findings with the class.

Volunteering in Your Community

GUIDE TO READING

Main Idea
Every year in the United States, millions of people donate their time, effort, and money to help make their communities and their country a better place to live.

Key Terms
community, bureaucracy, welfare, volunteerism

Reading Strategy
Organizing Information
As you read, complete a graphic organizer like the one below in which you list ways that people volunteer.

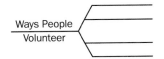

Ways People Volunteer

Read to Learn
- Why does our country need people to volunteer?
- What are the various ways in which people volunteer?

Americans in Action

Without Korczak Ziolkowski, there would be no Crazy Horse Memorial. Ziolkowski, born of Polish descent in Boston, became famous as a mountain carver, but it is his life and dedication that have inspired the people who learn about him. Ziolkowski assisted Gutzon Borglum at Mount Rushmore and then dedicated the rest of his life to sculpting the Crazy Horse Memorial. Crazy Horse was a Native American leader who bravely defended his people and their way of life. Ziolkowski carved Crazy Horse as a memorial to the leader's spirit. Ziolkowski worked on the memorial—the world's largest sculpture—for 36 years, until his death in 1982, refusing to be paid for his work. Ziolkowski's wife and family continue his work on the Crazy Horse Memorial.

Honoring Crazy Horse

The Need for Citizens' Involvement

Why did Korczak Ziolkowski do so much work and not accept payment? He was a volunteer. Another volunteer, John Gatus, a retired steamfitter, who volunteers in an antigang neighborhood patrol, tries to explain: "Volunteer work brings real change, change you can be a part of, change you can see with your own eyes. You don't need politicians or police to tell you things are better. You can see it and feel it for yourself and know you were a part of it. . . . There's a real pride involved. We're part of a community."

Every year more than half of all Americans do volunteer work to help make their communities better places to live. (A community is a group of people who share the same interests and concerns.) These volunteers include more than 14 million students in grades 6 through 12. Without the efforts of so many private citizens, many pressing social needs simply would not be met.

In the United States, as you read in Chapter 1, governments provide a wealth of services. We rely on government for everything from local police protection to national defense,

Political Cartoons

"DEMOCRACY"

EDWARDS

and it seems to be diverted toward money and ... ne. Making the world a more convenient ... | Schneider, two men with little hope, of regain-ing the company's ... While the wage was ... | to be divert... tim...

Analyzing Visuals Democracy is often depicted as a chorus of voices—sometimes singing in harmony, other times singing clashing melodies that reflect citizens' contrasting demands. What "song" are the figures in this cartoon singing? How could volunteerism balance this image?

from collecting household trash to ensuring clean water and air nationwide. Citizens, though, also share responsibility for meeting community needs.

The government, after all, has limited resources. In addition, governments are bureaucracies—complex systems with many departments, many rules, and many people in the chain of command. Because of this, government cannot always respond quickly or efficiently to social problems. In many cases, the best solutions come from private citizens. Good citizens are concerned about the welfare—the health, prosperity, and happiness—of all members of the community.

In 1961 President John F. Kennedy issued his famous challenge, "Ask not what your country can do for you; ask what you can do for your country." In 2001 President George W. Bush called for a renewed commitment to community service. He noted that we can show "the world the true values of America through the gathering momentum of a million acts of responsibility and decency and service."

Donating Time and Money

People contribute to their communities in countless ways, working independently or as part of volunteer groups both large and small. You probably know a mom or dad who is active in the PTA (Parent Teacher Association) or leads a Scout troop. Neighbors might spend a Saturday afternoon cleaning up a vacant lot or preparing holiday baskets for needy families. Retirees mentor schoolchildren, record books on audiotapes and CD-ROMs for the blind, and lead museum tours. You or your fellow students might visit nursing home patients, volunteer in an animal shelter, or collect canned goods for a local food pantry.

Contributing your time to work on community projects is the heart of volunteerism—the practice of offering your time and services to others without payment. However, Americans may also support worthy causes by contributing money. In 2000, individual Americans gave more than $152 billion to charity. Much of this money came from small donations by average citizens. The typical American donates about 2 percent of his or her income to charity.

Many companies, too, believe in giving something back to the community. Small businesses may sponsor a recreational sports team or donate prizes for a charity's fund-raiser. Large companies often contribute thousands of dollars to community projects, like building a new public swimming pool or putting on a free concert. They frequently match the charitable donations of their employees, chipping in a dollar of corporate funds for every dollar that a worker gives to charity.

Many companies make a special commitment to investing in young people. They may offer college scholarships to students or give their employees time off to volunteer in the schools.

Reading Check **Inferring** Why is volunteerism so important?

Volunteers in Action

Community involvement tends to be rooted in individual action and informal groups. People are more likely to participate when they feel a personal connection to a cause or know others involved. Thus they join their Neighborhood Watch or become active at their child's school. They reach out to the community through their religious congregations or service clubs like the Lions and Kiwanis. Some people, however, volunteer through more formal channels.

Charitable Organizations

More than one million charities are officially registered with the federal government. Many are small and locally based. They often work on one or two projects, such as helping the victims of domestic abuse or preserving historic landmarks.

Other organizations, such as the United Way, the Boys and Girls Clubs of America, and Big Brothers Big Sisters, are large, national bodies with varied activities serving millions of people.

All of these groups depend on ordinary people who give their time freely. Most, however, also have some paid staff who help set organizational goals, manage the budget, and oversee operations.

American Biographies

Justin Dart, Jr. (1930–)

Justin Dart, Jr., has a message to deliver: "People with disabilities are fully equal." To spread that message, he has traveled to all 50 states at least four times and to nations around the world. Stricken with polio at age 18, Dart uses a wheelchair and knows personally the hurdles people with disabilities must overcome. He has worked to tear down these hurdles by launching, along with his wife Yoshiko Saji Dart, the disability rights movement.

Dart has advised governors, presidents, and the U.S. Congress on the subject of disabilities. However, he relies on grassroots support—the support of ordinary people—to bring about change. "Get into politics as if your life depended on it," he told one audience.

In 1990 Dart's grassroots army won passage of the Americans with Disabilities Act. The act prohibits discrimination against people with disabilities. In 1998 Dart received the Presidential Medal of Freedom, the nation's highest civilian award. As the 2000s opened, Dart announced a new goal—to carry the disability rights movement worldwide.

School-Based Programs

Across the country, more than half of all schools now arrange community service for students in grades 6 through 12. Several hundred school districts even require it. In Atlanta, Chicago, and the entire state of Maryland, for example, high school students must volunteer a set number of hours to earn a diploma.

Some people believe that community service is less meaningful when it is obligatory. According to one school official in Atlanta, however, the "students think it's a neat idea, and for many of them it is nothing new." Many have already been active volunteers in the community.

National Service Programs

Over the years, the federal government has created various national programs to encourage volunteerism. In 1961, for example, the Peace Corps was launched to help people in the poorest corners of the world. The Peace Corps has sent tens of thousands of Americans to 135 countries, where they advise farmers, teach children, dig wells, help start small businesses, and fight the spread of AIDS and other serious diseases. Here in the United States, the government provides community service opportunities through AmeriCorps and the Senior Corps.

More than 50,000 Americans participate each year in AmeriCorps. Most work through local and national organizations to meet community needs. Under the guidance of the American Red Cross, for example, volunteers help victims of floods, fires, earthquakes, and other disasters. Working with other groups, they might clean up polluted rivers, immunize children, or assist people with disabilities. In return for a year of full-time service, AmeriCorps volunteers receive an allowance to live on and money to help pay for college.

The Senior Corps provides volunteer opportunities to Americans aged 55 or older. These senior citizens take part in three main programs. Foster Grandparents work one on one with children with special needs. Senior Companions help other seniors meet their daily needs while living in their own homes. The Retired and Senior Volunteer Program

Working Together in Emergencies Workers formed a human chain to transport supplies to boats, which carried them to Manhattan to help recovery efforts at the World Trade Center in 2001. **Why do you think the government encourages volunteerism?**

President Bush proposes the Freedom Corps.

American Volunteers in Action

PERCENTAGE OF ADULTS ACTIVE IN VOLUNTEER WORK

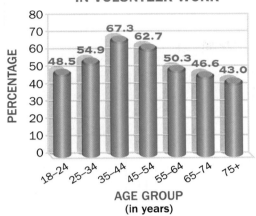

Source: *Statistical Abstract of the United States, 2000.*

VALUE OF U.S. VOLUNTEERS, 1987–1998
(Total Value of Volunteer Time)

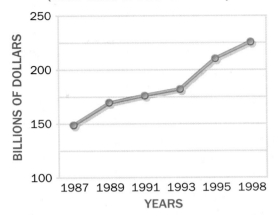

Source: www.childstats.gov

HOW CAN YOU VOLUNTEER?

Places to Volunteer

- Homeless shelters
- Food banks
- Hospices and hospitals
- Special Olympics
- Habitat for Humanity
- State and local parks
- City parks
- Schools or after-school programs
- Libraries
- Senior citizen centers
- Animal shelters
- Environmental organizations
- Political campaigns
- Red Cross and Salvation Army
- Local charities and organizations
- Your school or community government

Sample Volunteer Activities

- Prepare and distribute meals
- Help organize a food drive
- Talk with families and kids
- Help raise funds or lead activities
- Help build a house
- Clean up trails or pick up trash
- Assist with recreational activities
- Tutor a child or new immigrant
- Read to children or reshelve books
- Deliver meals to homebound seniors
- Take care of animals
- Lead hikes or lobby for a cause
- Lend a hand at the campaign office or join a letter-writing campaign
- Help out in an emergency
- Create a Web site
- Hold an elective office, attend a city council or school board meeting or public hearing and voice your opinion

WHY SHOULD YOU VOLUNTEER?

- To help others
- To learn something new about an activity or organization
- To meet people and make friends
- To beat boredom
- To better deal with a loss you have experienced (such as the death of a loved one)
- To learn something new about life
- To explore careers

Analyzing Graphs

There are many volunteering opportunities in your local community. All volunteers are valuable resources to their communities. Which age group of Americans has the highest percentage of people volunteering?

(RSVP) links volunteers to service opportunities right in their backyards. For example, they might deliver hot meals with Meals on Wheels, help plant and tend a neighborhood garden, or teach English to immigrants.

On January 29, 2002, in his annual State of the Union Address, President Bush asked Americans to join together and help, saying, "If you aren't sure how to help, I've got a good place to start." Bush went on to describe a new program, called USA Freedom Corps. The program brought together the Peace Corps, AmeriCorps, and Senior Corps. Bush added another component called "Citizen Corps." He stated that the purpose of Freedom Corps was a focus on three "areas of need: responding in case of crisis at home, rebuilding our communities, and extending American compassion throughout the world." Bush appealed to Americans to serve their neighbors and their nation.

The Benefits of Volunteering

The United States has always been a nation of volunteers. When Alexis de Tocqueville, a French political writer, visited America in the 1830s, he was amazed to see citizens pitching in to solve community problems rather than relying on the government. He explained it as "self-interest rightly understood." In other words, by banding together to serve the community, we also serve ourselves.

By volunteering we make our communities better places to live and gain new opportunities to learn, make friends, and improve our teamwork, leadership, and problem-solving skills. It is satisfying to know that you can make a difference in someone else's life.

Reading Check **Inferring** How does volunteering serve self-interests?

SECTION 2 ASSESSMENT

Checking for Understanding

1. **Key Terms** Define bureaucracy, community, and welfare and use them in sentences related to volunteerism.

Reviewing Main Ideas

2. **Explain** Why does our government need people to volunteer in their communities?

3. **Identify** What program was launched in the early 1960s to assist people in the poorest parts of the world? What types of activities do volunteers with this organization perform? How do these activities help people in other countries?

Critical Thinking

4. **Making Judgments** Do you think that community service projects should be required of all students? Explain.

5. **Summarizing Information** In a chart like the one below, give examples of the following types of volunteerism.

Types of Volunteerism	Examples
Charitable Organizations	
School-Based Programs	
National Service Programs	

Analyzing Visuals

6. **Review** Examine the chart that lists reasons to volunteer on page 129, then answer this question: Why is volunteering a worthwhile activity?

★ **BE AN ACTIVE CITIZEN** ★

7. **Research** Contact a local volunteer organization that has been mentioned in this chapter. Find out what projects or problems they are working on in your community and how they use volunteers. Report your findings to the class.

SKILLBUILDER

Reading a Diagram

Why Learn This Skill?

What is the best way to show a complicated idea? Sometimes the answer is a diagram. A diagram is a drawing with labels and symbols. Developing the skill of reading a diagram can help you acquire a great deal of information quickly. Reading a written description of the same information could take much longer. The visual images offered in the diagram also make the information easier to remember.

THE RECYCLING PROCESS

Citizen decides to recycle.

Processors make new products.

Items picked up for recycling plant.

Recycling plant sorts recyclable items.

Learning the Skill

There are certain steps to follow as you interpret a diagram.

- Read the title. The title describes the information found in the diagram. A diagram may also contain a key that shows what the symbols and colors on the diagram represent.
- Read all the labels on the diagram carefully to clearly determine their meanings.
- If there is a legend, identify symbols and colors used in the diagram.
- Look for numbers indicating a sequence of steps or arrows showing movement.
- Define how the diagram is organized. What types of divisions are shown? How are processes or events described? How do the separate parts of the diagram relate to one another?
- Summarize the information found in the diagram in one or two sentences.

Practicing the Skill

Answer the following questions using the diagram on this page.

1. What concept does this diagram present?
2. How many steps are involved?
3. What is the individual's role in the recycling process?
4. Write a sentence summarizing information shown in the diagram.

——Applying the Skill——

Create a diagram showing how you bake a cake or wash a car. Label your diagram clearly.

Practice key skills with Glencoe's **Skillbuilder Interactive Workbook CD-ROM, Level 1.**

Assessment & Activities

Review to Learn

Section 1

- The legal duties of Americans include obeying laws, paying taxes, defending the nation, serving in court, and attending school.
- To help the nation flourish, Americans should be informed, vote, respect the rights of others, and contribute to the common good.

Section 2

- Our government provides many services; however, its resources are limited. Therefore our nation needs people to volunteer so that communities can meet the needs of the people.

- People volunteer by donating their time and money. Volunteers may work through charitable organizations, school-based programs, or national service programs.

FOLDABLES™
Study Organizer

Using Your Foldables Study Organizer
Use your completed foldable to explain the interdependence, or the relationship, that exists between a citizen and his or her community. Your explanation may take the form of an essay or a brief oral presentation.

Reviewing Key Terms

Choose the term from the chapter that best matches each clue below.

1. complex systems with many departments, many rules, and many people in the chain of command
2. the requirement of registering with the government for military service
3. the obligations that we fulfill voluntarily
4. the things we are legally required to do
5. the health, happiness, and prosperity of a community
6. respecting and accepting others regardless of their beliefs, practices, or differences
7. offering your time and services to others without payment
8. a group of people who share the same interests and concerns
9. this program will combine the AmeriCorps, Peace Corps, and Senior Corps

Reviewing Main Ideas

10. What types of projects do charitable organizations usually perform?
11. Name three duties of U.S. citizens.
12. Why do people have a responsibility to respect the rights of others?
13. Why is it important for U.S. citizens to be informed?
14. Name three services provided by the government.
15. What are two ways people can volunteer to help their community?
16. To what "areas of need" does the Freedom Corps hope to respond?
17. Give at least two examples of useful services provided by volunteer groups and organizations in a community.
18. How has the U.S. government encouraged volunteerism?

Critical Thinking

19. **Evaluating Information** Why are citizens' responsibilities to their communities such an important part of our democratic system?

20. **Classifying Information** Complete a chart similar to the one below by listing examples under each category.

Government Service	Legal Duty	Voluntary Action

Practicing Skills

Reading a Diagram Examine the diagram on page 131. Using your own words, outline the steps involved in the recycling process. Then answer the following questions.

21. What do the arrows in the diagram represent?

22. How could you show the information in a different way?

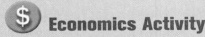

Economics Activity

23. Most cities and towns have a chamber of commerce or business association that promotes the welfare of its members and the community. A typical chamber may sponsor everything from tourist centers to cleanup campaigns to support of favorable business laws. Contact your local chamber—or a chamber in a nearby city—to learn about some of its activities. Summarize its activities in a brief report or chart.

Analyzing Visuals

24. Examine the line graph on page 129. About how much money was volunteer time worth in the United States in 1998? How has the value of volunteer time changed since 1987?

Self-Check Quiz Visit the *Civics Today* Web site at civ.glencoe.com and click on **Self-Check Quizzes— Chapter 5** to prepare for the chapter test.

★ CITIZENSHIP COOPERATIVE ACTIVITY ★

25. Form groups of four. Then choose an election in your community. Find out how you could volunteer for one of the candidates in the election. Interview a current campaign volunteer to see why he or she is working for this person or issue and how he or she is involved in the election process. Summarize your findings in a brief report.

Technology Activity

26. Use the Internet to find the names and addresses of local not-for-profit agencies that need volunteers. E-mail or send a letter to one of these agencies to ask about their volunteer needs. Ask what volunteers do and whether they are currently needed. Share your findings with the class.

The Princeton Review

Standardized Test Practice

Directions: Choose the *best* answer to the following question.

Which of the following is a legal duty of citizenship?

A register and vote

B hold elective office

C keep informed about issues

D obey laws

Test-Taking Tip

To answer this question correctly, you must determine the difference between a civic duty and a responsibility. Which is required?

The National Government

Why It Matters

In our federal government, the executive, legislative, and judicial branches share the responsibility of governing the nation. They derive their powers from the American people. We have a responsibility to learn about the officials who represent us and to express our views through voting.

Use the **American History Primary Source Document Library CD-ROM** to find primary sources about the federal government.

★ BE AN ACTIVE CITIZEN ★

As you study the national government, pay attention to primary sources around you, such as the important national issues discussed in the media. Consider how you would deal with them if you were a member of Congress. With a partner, prepare a speech outlining your proposal about a specific issue.

The United States Capitol

Congress

 CITIZENSHIP AND YOU

Congress represents the American people. When citizens express their views to members of Congress, they participate in the lawmaking process. Find out what legislation is pending in Congress and your representatives' positions on the issues. Investigate an issue and decide your position on it. Do you agree with your representatives?

 To learn more about Congress, view the **Democracy in Action** video lesson 7: Congress at Work.

FOLDABLES™
Study Organizer

Summarizing Information Study Foldable *Make the following foldable to help you organize and summarize what you learn about the U.S. Congress.*

Step 1 *Fold a sheet of paper in half from side to side.*

Step 2 *Turn the paper and fold it into fourths.*

Fold in half, then fold in half again.

Step 3 *Unfold and cut up along the three fold lines, cutting through just the top layer.*

Make four tabs.

Step 4 *Label your foldable as shown.*

Organi-zation of Congress | Powers of Congress | Repre-senting Americans | From Bill to Law

Reading and Writing *As you read the chapter, write down what you learn about Congress under each appropriate tab. Focus on writing main ideas and supporting details you find in the chapter.*

The U.S. Capitol ▶

CIVICS Online

Chapter Overview Visit the *Civics Today* Web site at civ.glencoe.com and click on **Chapter Overviews— Chapter 6** to preview chapter information.

How Congress Is Organized

Americans in Action

Senator Jon Kyl represents the people of the state of Arizona. Kyl, though, does much of his work for the people of Arizona miles and miles away in the nation's capital. How does Kyl know what the people he represents want? One way is through Kyl's official Web site. Arizonans and other interested people can contact Kyl through e-mail and learn about current legislation, college internships, casework, and tours. Check it out at www.senate.gov/~kyl/services.htm

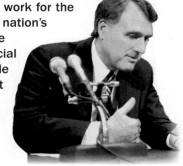

Senator Jon Kyl

Terms of Congress

Every year, inside the U.S. Capitol in Washington, D.C., 535 of our fellow citizens gather to make new laws and address countless issues facing our country. These are our elected representatives, the members of Congress.

The Framers of the U.S. Constitution intended to make the legislative branch of government more powerful than any other branch. In fact, Congress is described in the first part of the Constitution, Article I. As James Madison said, Congress is "the First Branch of this Government."

Each term of Congress starts on January 3 of odd-numbered years (unless a different day is appointed) and lasts for two years. Each "new" Congress is given a number to identify its two-year term. For example, the first Congress met in 1789, and the 107th Congress began meeting in 2001.

Each term of Congress is divided into two sessions, or meetings. A typical session of Congress today lasts from January until November or December. Congress may also meet in times of crisis during special sessions. A joint session occurs when the House and Senate meet together. This usually occurs when the Congress gathers to hear the president's State of the Union address.

Reading Check **Identifying** Which article of the Constitution describes Congress?

A Bicameral Legislature

As you'll recall from Chapter 3, one of the major conflicts at the Constitutional Convention in 1787 concerned state representation in Congress. While delegates from the smaller states wanted equal representation, delegates from the larger states wanted representation to be based on population. The resulting Great Compromise established Congress as a two-part, or **bicameral,** body, consisting of the House of Representatives and the Senate.

The House of Representatives

The House of Representatives, the larger body of Congress, has 435 voting members, allotted to the states according to population. According to the Constitution, each state is entitled to at least one seat in the House, no matter how small its population. After each 10-year **census,** or population count taken by the Census Bureau, Congress adjusts the number of representatives given to each state.

Each state is divided into one or more congressional districts, or areas, with one representative elected from each district. State legislatures must draw the boundaries so that the districts include roughly the same number of **constituents,** or people represented. Sometimes states abuse this process by gerrymandering. A **gerrymander** is an oddly shaped district designed to increase the voting strength of a particular group. For example, if most of a state's representatives are Republican, they might draw the lines so that as many districts as possible have more Republican than Democratic voters.

Representatives serve two-year terms and may not be well known outside their districts. They usually focus on concerns in their districts, rather than the concerns of the state as a whole. This is as the Framers of the Constitution intended. They designed Congress so that members of the House would be closer to the people than would members of the Senate.

The Senate

The Senate has 100 members—2 from each of the 50 states. Each senator represents his or her entire state rather than a particular district.

Senators serve six-year terms, but elections are staggered so that no more than one-third of the senators are up for

TIME

Political Cartoons

and it seems to be diverted toward money and time. Making the world a more convenient place to live was a collaboration among several | Schnei inn t

Analyzing Visuals In 1812 Governor Elbridge Gerry created a new voting district in Andover, Massachusetts. In response, artist Gilbert Stuart drew the outline of the district and added a head, claws, and wings. A newspaper editor named the fictional beast, which resembled a salamander, a "Gerrymander." What comment was Stuart making about the shape of the voting district that Governor Gerry created?

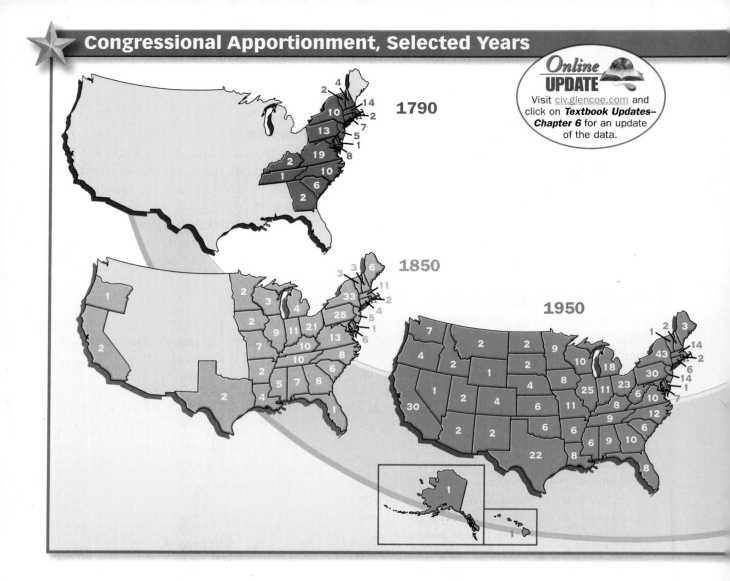

Online UPDATE

Visit civ.glencoe.com and click on **Textbook Updates–Chapter 6** for an update of the data.

1790

1850

1950

reelection at any one time. This ensures a certain amount of stability and continuity.

Reading Check **Comparing** Which is the larger body of Congress?

Congressional Leaders

In both the House and the Senate, the political party to which more than half the members belong is known as the majority party. The other party is called the minority party. At the beginning of each term, the party members in each house choose leaders to direct their activities.

The Constitution states that the House "shall choose their Speaker and other officers." Members of the majority party of the House choose the Speaker at a caucus, or closed meeting. The entire membership of the House then approves the choice of Speaker of the House.

The **Speaker of the House** is the most powerful leader within the House of Representatives. Always an experienced member of the majority party, the Speaker steers legislation through the House, is in charge of floor debates (those in which all representatives may participate), and influences most other House business. If

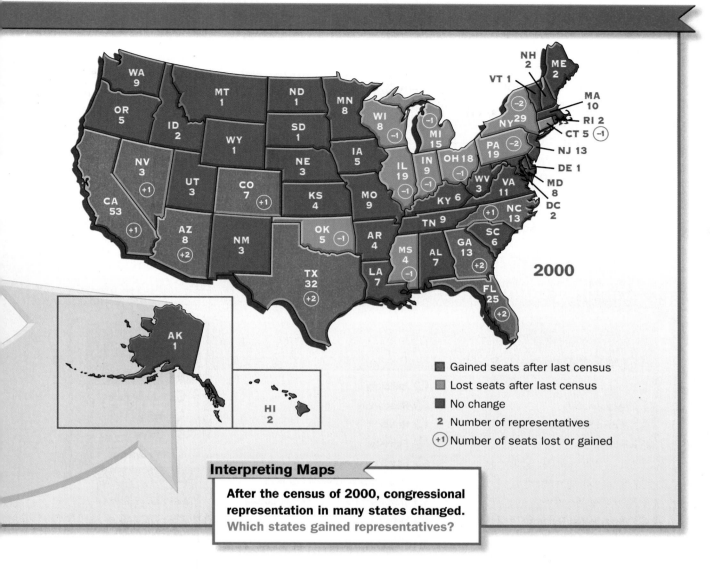

WA 9
OR 5
ID 2
MT 1
ND 1
MN 8
WI 8
MI 15 (-1)
NY 29 (-2)
VT 1
NH 2
ME 2
MA 10
RI 2
CT 5 (-1)
NJ 13
DE 1
MD 8
DC 2
SD 1
WY 1
NE 3
IA 5
IL 19 (-1)
IN 9 (-1)
OH 18 (-1)
PA 19 (-2)
WV 3
VA 11
NV 3 (+1)
UT 3
CO 7 (+1)
KS 4
MO 9
KY 6
CA 53 (+1)
AZ 8 (+2)
NM 3
OK 5 (-1)
AR 4
TN 9
NC 13 (+1)
SC 6
TX 32 (+2)
LA 7
MS 4 (-1)
AL 7
GA 13 (+2)
FL 25 (+2)

AK 1

HI 2

2000

- ■ Gained seats after last census
- ■ Lost seats after last census
- ■ No change
- **2** Number of representatives
- (+1) Number of seats lost or gained

Interpreting Maps

After the census of 2000, congressional representation in many states changed. Which states gained representatives?

anything happens to the president and vice president, the Speaker is next in line to become president, provided he or she is legally qualified.

Speakers today rely on their powers of persuasion as much as their formal powers to exercise influence. On a typical day, the Speaker may talk with dozens of members of Congress. Often the Speaker does this just to listen to requests for a favor. Former Speaker of the House Thomas P. "Tip" O'Neill once stated: "The world is full of little things you can do for people." The Speaker, though, expects something in return—the representatives' support on important issues.

The Senate has no leader with comparable power. The presiding officer is technically the vice president of the United States, called the president of the Senate. However, the vice president rarely attends Senate debates and votes only in case of a tie. The person who usually acts as chairperson of the Senate is the **president pro tempore** (or pro tem, for short). "Pro tempore" means "for the time being." This position is typically filled by someone from the majority party and is more ceremonial than influential.

The real leaders in the Senate, and the most powerful players in the House of Representatives, aside from the Speaker, are the floor leaders. Floor leaders try to make sure that the laws Congress passes are in the best interest of their own political party. The majority and minority floor leaders in each house speak for their parties on the issues, push bills along, and try to sway votes. Party "whips" help the floor leaders. They keep track of where party members stand on proposed legislation and round up their colleagues for key votes.

Reading Check **Describing** What do floor leaders do?

Committees: Little Legislatures

The detailed work of lawmaking is done in committee rather than on the House or Senate floor. So many bills are introduced each year that few of them would be considered if the work were not divided among smaller groups of legislators.

Types of Committees

Each house of Congress has both well-established, ongoing committees and those set up for a specific short-term purpose.

Standing Committees

HOUSE OF REPRESENTATIVES
Standing Committees

- Agriculture
- Appropriations
- Armed Services
- Budget
- Education and the Workforce
- Energy and Commerce
- Financial Services
- Government Reform
- House Administration
- International Relations
- Judiciary
- Resources
- Rules
- Science
- Small Business
- Standards of Official Conduct
- Transportation and Infrastructure
- Veterans Affairs
- Ways and Means

SENATE
Standing Committees

- Agriculture, Nutrition, and Forestry
- Appropriations
- Armed Services
- Banking, Housing, and Urban Affairs
- Budget
- Commerce, Science, and Transportation
- Energy and Natural Resources
- Environment and Public Works
- Finance
- Foreign Relations
- Governmental Affairs
- Health, Education, Labor, and Pensions
- Indian Affairs
- Judiciary
- Rules and Administration
- Small Business and Entrepreneurship
- Veterans Affairs

Select and Special Committees

- Intelligence
- Aging
- Ethics
- Intelligence

Joint Committees

- Economic
- Printing
- Taxation
- Library

- House Committee
- Senate Committee
- Joint Committee

Evaluating Charts

Most of the legislative work of Congress is done in committees. Which Senate committee deals with appointments of judges to the federal courts?

The permanent committees that continue their work from session to session are called **standing committees.** The Senate has 17 standing committees and the House has 19, covering areas such as education, veterans affairs, and commerce.

Most standing committees are divided into smaller subcommittees that deal with more specialized issues. For example, the Senate Armed Services Committee has subcommittees on military readiness, personnel, and armament. Some subcommittees are very powerful. Others are not.

In addition to standing committees, both houses of Congress also have **select committees** that are created to do a special job for a limited period. In 1976, for example, the House formed the Select Committee on Assassinations to investigate the deaths of President John F. Kennedy and Dr. Martin Luther King, Jr. Like all select committees, the House Assassinations Committee disbanded when it finished its work.

The House and Senate have also formed four **joint committees,** which include members of both houses. The Joint Economic Committee reviews economic conditions and recommends improvements in economic policy. Other joint committees focus on federal tax policy, the Library of Congress, and the Government Printing Office.

A fourth type of committee is a temporary committee, the **conference committee,** which helps the House and Senate agree on the details of a proposed law. You will learn more about conference committees later in this chapter.

This 2001 coin commemorates the first meeting of Congress in the Capitol in 1800.

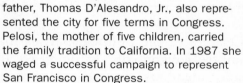

American Biographies

Nancy Pelosi (1940–)

Nancy Pelosi made history in 2002 when Democrats in the House of Representatives elected her as minority leader. In winning the position, Pelosi claimed the highest post ever held by a woman in Congress.

Politics runs in Pelosi's family. Both her father and brother served as the mayor of Baltimore, Maryland. Her father, Thomas D'Alesandro, Jr., also represented the city for five terms in Congress. Pelosi, the mother of five children, carried the family tradition to California. In 1987 she waged a successful campaign to represent San Francisco in Congress.

When Pelosi traveled to Washington, D.C., only 12 Democratic women sat in the House of Representatives. They lacked the numbers and the seniority to make their voices heard. By 2001, however, the number of Democratic female representatives had grown to 42. Their vote, plus Pelosi's considerable experience on important committees, changed the face of politics. Her election meant not only that women's issues would be heard by the Democrats but that women could win top leadership posts in government.

★ ★ ★ ★

Committee Assignments

When senators and representatives first come to Congress, they try to get assigned to important committees that affect the people who elected them. For example, members of Congress from farm areas might want to serve on agriculture committees. Those with many factories in their districts might be interested in serving on labor committees.

Senate Leaders Senate majority leader Tom Daschle, Democrat (left), and minority leader Trent Lott, Republican, are the most important officers in the Senate. **How does leadership in the House and Senate differ?**

Leaders of the political parties make committee assignments. In doing so, they consider members' preferences, expertise, and loyalty to the party. Another key factor is **seniority,** or years of service. The senators and representatives who have been in Congress longest usually get the preferred committee spots. The longest-serving committee member from the majority party traditionally becomes chairperson. Chairpersons of standing committees are the most powerful members of Congress. These members decide when and if a committee will meet, what bills will be studied, and who will serve on which subcommittees.

Some people think the seniority system is a good idea. They say it prevents fights over committee jobs and ensures that chairpersons will have experience. Other people complain that talented people may be overlooked in favor of those who have simply been around for a while. There has been so much criticism of the seniority system over the years that both political parties have moved slightly away from it. The senior majority party member on a committee still usually wins the role of chairperson, but it is no longer guaranteed.

✓ Reading Check **Explaining** What is the difference between a standing committee and a select committee?

SECTION 1 ASSESSMENT

Checking for Understanding

1. Key Terms Write sentences or short paragraphs in which you use the following terms: bicameral, census, constituent, gerrymander, majority party, minority party, standing committee, seniority.

Reviewing Main Ideas

2. Describe How many members does the Senate have? How does the U.S. Constitution provide for stability and continuity in the Senate?

3. Explain Why is so much of the business of Congress conducted in committees? How are senators and representatives assigned to committees?

Critical Thinking

4. Drawing Conclusions Do you think that the seniority system in Congress is an effective way to select leaders and assign committee members? Why or why not?

5. Comparing Information On a chart like the one below, compare the roles of each kind of congressional committee.

Committee	Role
Standing	
Select	
Joint	
Conference	

Analyzing Visuals

6. Interpret Review the maps on pages 140–141. How many representatives did New Jersey have in 1790? In 1950? In 2000? What does this tell you about how New Jersey's population has changed?

★**BE AN ACTIVE CITIZEN**★

7. Write Choose a representative from your state. Check the House or Senate Web site (www.house. gov or www.senate.gov) to find out on what committees that person serves. Write a letter to that person about an issue related to that committee.

Making Comparisons

Why Learn This Skill?

How do you decide which pair of jeans to buy? How will you decide which college to attend or which candidates to vote for in an election? Making comparisons is a part of decision making. It also helps you understand and remember different types of information.

Learning the Skill

To make comparisons, follow these steps:

- Decide which subjects or concepts you will compare. Decide which characteristics of the subjects you will compare.
- Identify similarities and differences in the characteristics.
- Look for relationships and patterns among the items you have analyzed.

Practicing the Skill

On a separate sheet of paper, answer the following questions about the passages on this page.

1 How is the British Parliament like the Congress of the United States?

2 What differences are there between the British and American heads of state?

3 How does the British constitution differ from the U.S. Constitution?

Government in the United States

The Constitution, written in 1787, forms the basis of democracy in the United States. It provides for a president—the head of state and head of government. The president is elected by the Electoral College system and is charged with enforcing the nation's laws. The president serves a four-year term in office and may be reelected to another term.

The two-house Congress proposes and passes laws. Voters from each state elect the 435 members of the House of Representatives every two years. Each state also elects two senators to the 100-member Senate every six years.

Government in Great Britain

The British form of government is a constitutional monarchy. The hereditary king or queen is the head of state but exercises no actual power. Legal traditions make up the unwritten constitution.

Parliament, as the legislature is called, is the seat of real power. It consists of the House of Lords and the House of Commons. The approximately 700 lords in the House of Lords may inherit or be appointed to membership. Some lords give advice, vote, and act as the highest British court. However, the lords do not control final legislation.

The 650 members of the House of Commons hold real power. They are elected by British voters at least once every five years. They propose and pass laws for the nation that cannot be challenged in courts. The prime minister, the actual head of government, is the chief officer of the Parliament.

——Applying the Skill——

Learn about Mexico's form of government. Write a paragraph comparing it with the government of the United States.

 GO TO

Practice key skills with Glencoe's **Skillbuilder Interactive Workbook CD-ROM, Level 1.**

The Powers of Congress

GUIDE TO READING

Main Idea

While the Constitution limits the powers of Congress, it also gives Congress the powers it needs to conduct its business and accomplish its goals.

Key Terms

expressed powers, implied powers, elastic clause, impeach, writ of habeas corpus, bill of attainder, ex post facto law

Reading Strategy

Comparing Information
As you read, complete a chart similar to the one below to compare Congress's legislative powers to its nonlegislative powers.

Legislative Powers	Nonlegislative Powers

Read to Learn

- What powers did the Constitution give to Congress?
- What powers did the Constitution deny to Congress?

Americans in Action

In 1998 the House of Representatives impeached President Bill Clinton. Then it was up to the Senate to convict or acquit him. Would you believe that 210 years earlier the Framers of the U.S. Constitution had discussed this very type of situation? They had decided that the Senate should hold impeachment trials because, as Alexander Hamilton put it, it would be the only "tribunal sufficiently dignified [and] sufficiently independent . . . to preserve, unawed and uninfluenced, the necessary impartiality between an individual accused and the representatives of the people, his accusers."

Supporting Clinton

Legislative Powers

The Founders knew that they could not foresee every situation Congress might face. They gave that body broad powers. The U.S. Constitution spells out the major powers of Congress in Article I, Section 8. The first 17 clauses list specific or **expressed powers.** Clause 12, for example, says, "The Congress shall have the Power . . . To raise and support Armies."

The last clause of Section 8—Clause 18—gives Congress the authority to do whatever is "necessary and proper" to carry out the expressed powers. The powers that Congress has because of Clause 18 are called **implied powers** because they are not stated explicitly in the Constitution. Clause 18 is often called the **elastic clause** because it has allowed Congress to stretch its powers to meet new needs. For instance, you won't find the power to create an air force written in the Constitution. However, the elastic clause has allowed Congress to do so as part of its expressed powers to support armies.

Most of Congress's powers are related to making laws. Congress can pass laws governing all federal property, including our national parks and military bases. Congress can also enact laws to establish post offices and federal courts. Some of the most important legislative powers involve raising and spending money, regulating commerce, and dealing with foreign countries.

Taxing and Spending

To pay for the government and the many services it provides, Congress has the power to collect taxes. All tax bills and other measures to raise money must start in the House of Representatives because the Framers believed that the members of Congress closest to the people should be the ones to propose taxes. The Senate must approve such bills, though.

Bills to spend money must also begin in the House. Each year, Congress spends money by means of a two-step process. **Authorization bills** create projects like the space shuttle program and establish how much money can be spent on them. **Appropriations bills** actually provide the money for each program or activity. No government agency can spend money without approval from Congress.

Regulating Commerce

Article I, Section 8, Clause 3, of the Constitution gives Congress the power to regulate foreign and interstate commerce. Interstate commerce includes trade and other economic activities among the states. This commerce clause, as it is called, is the basis for many of the most important powers of Congress. Laws dealing with air traffic, railroads, trucking, radio, television, air pollution, and the stock market are all based on this clause.

Foreign Relations and Treaties

Along with the president, Congress has important responsibilities regarding foreign policy and national defense. Only Congress can declare war. Congress also has the power to create, maintain, and oversee an army and navy. The Senate must approve any treaties the president makes with other countries. Regulating commerce with other countries is another power granted to Congress.

✓Reading Check **Explaining** Where must all tax bills start? Why?

U.S. Military in Action U.S. soldiers keep watch while crossing Afghanistan by air on a U.S. Army Special Forces Chinook helicopter. **How does the elastic clause of the Constitution relate to the U.S. Air Force?**

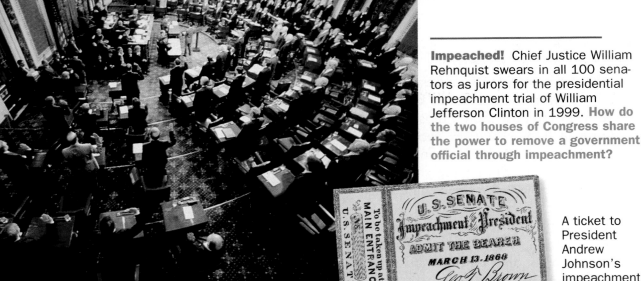

Impeached! Chief Justice William Rehnquist swears in all 100 senators as jurors for the presidential impeachment trial of William Jefferson Clinton in 1999. **How do the two houses of Congress share the power to remove a government official through impeachment?**

A ticket to President Andrew Johnson's impeachment trial

Nonlegislative Powers

Congress enjoys a number of powers that do not relate to making laws. For example, the Constitution allows Congress to propose constitutional amendments by a two-thirds vote of both houses. Congress is also in charge of counting electoral votes in presidential elections. If no candidate receives a majority, the House picks the president from among the three top vote getters; the Senate chooses the vice president. Congress can also settle problems that might arise if a presidential or vice presidential candidate dies or if an elected president dies, resigns, or is too ill to serve.

Among Congress's most important nonlegislative powers are those it uses to check the other branches of government. Some of these are set forth in the Constitution; others have developed over time.

The Power of Approval and Removal

The Senate has the power to approve or reject the president's nominees for various high-ranking officials, including Supreme Court justices, federal judges, and ambassadors. It takes this duty seriously and regularly rejects nominees.

The Constitution also allows Congress to remove from office any federal official who has committed serious wrongdoing. The House has the sole authority to impeach, or to accuse officials of misconduct in office. If a majority of the House votes to impeach a public official, the Senate acts as jury and decides by a two-thirds vote whether to convict and remove the person from office.

The House uses its impeachment power sparingly, most often with federal judges. Only two presidents have been impeached: Andrew Johnson in 1868 and Bill Clinton in 1998. Both presidents were tried by the Senate and acquitted (they were not removed from office).

Oversight and Investigation

Although the Constitution does not explicitly grant Congress any watchdog authority, overseeing government activities is another role it has taken on. Standing committees routinely review how well the executive branch puts into practice the many laws Congress has passed. For example, the House Committee on Agriculture might monitor the effectiveness of federal programs designed to help America's farmers.

Congress also began conducting special investigations as early as 1792. Today television brings such probes right into our homes. We have watched witnesses testify under oath about organized crime, communism, the 1986 Iran-Contra affair, and campaign fund-raising, for example.

Sometimes investigations lead to new laws aimed at dealing with a problem. At other times they may result in criminal charges against people. In 1973–74, the Senate's investigation of the Watergate scandal prompted President Richard Nixon to resign.

Reading Check **Describing** How can congressional standing committees check the powers of the executive branch?

Powers of Congress

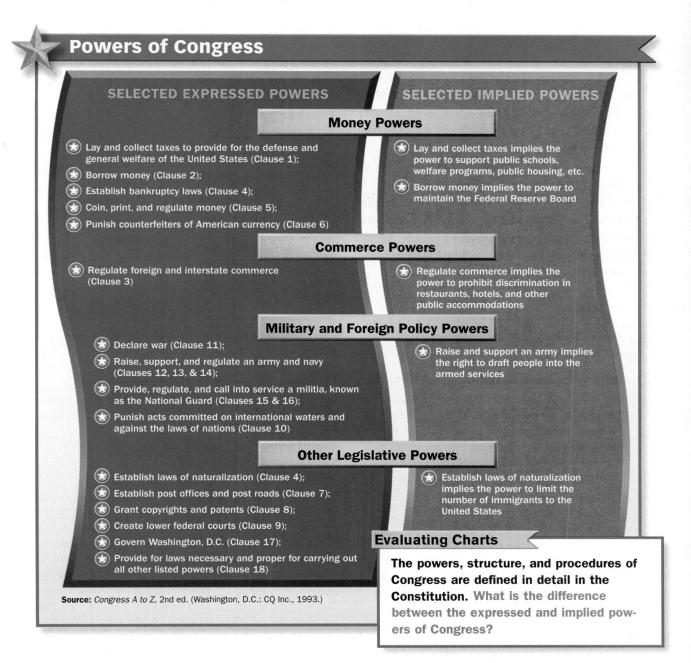

SELECTED EXPRESSED POWERS

Money Powers
- ★ Lay and collect taxes to provide for the defense and general welfare of the United States (Clause 1);
- ★ Borrow money (Clause 2);
- ★ Establish bankruptcy laws (Clause 4);
- ★ Coin, print, and regulate money (Clause 5);
- ★ Punish counterfeiters of American currency (Clause 6)

Commerce Powers
- ★ Regulate foreign and interstate commerce (Clause 3)

Military and Foreign Policy Powers
- ★ Declare war (Clause 11);
- ★ Raise, support, and regulate an army and navy (Clauses 12, 13, & 14);
- ★ Provide, regulate, and call into service a militia, known as the National Guard (Clauses 15 & 16);
- ★ Punish acts committed on international waters and against the laws of nations (Clause 10)

Other Legislative Powers
- ★ Establish laws of naturalization (Clause 4);
- ★ Establish post offices and post roads (Clause 7);
- ★ Grant copyrights and patents (Clause 8);
- ★ Create lower federal courts (Clause 9);
- ★ Govern Washington, D.C. (Clause 17);
- ★ Provide for laws necessary and proper for carrying out all other listed powers (Clause 18)

SELECTED IMPLIED POWERS

Money Powers
- ★ Lay and collect taxes implies the power to support public schools, welfare programs, public housing, etc.
- ★ Borrow money implies the power to maintain the Federal Reserve Board

Commerce Powers
- ★ Regulate commerce implies the power to prohibit discrimination in restaurants, hotels, and other public accommodations

Military and Foreign Policy Powers
- ★ Raise and support an army implies the right to draft people into the armed services

Other Legislative Powers
- ★ Establish laws of naturalization implies the power to limit the number of immigrants to the United States

Source: *Congress A to Z,* 2nd ed. (Washington, D.C.: CQ Inc., 1993.)

Evaluating Charts
The powers, structure, and procedures of Congress are defined in detail in the Constitution. What is the difference between the expressed and implied powers of Congress?

Limits on Power

Our Constitution explains not only what Congress may do but also what it may *not* do. Some limitations are imposed by the Bill of Rights. For example, Congress may not pass laws that ban freedom of speech or religion.

According to Article I of the Constitution, Congress may not favor one state over another, tax interstate commerce, or tax exports. In addition, Congress cannot suspend the **writ of habeas corpus.** This is a court order that requires police to bring a prisoner to court to explain why they are holding the person. Congress is also prohibited from passing **bills of attainder,** or laws that punish a person without a jury trial. Further, Congress may not pass **ex post facto laws.** These are laws that make an act a crime after the act has been committed.

The Constitution also reserves many powers for the states. Congress cannot interfere with these powers, such as the right to regulate public school systems and establish local governments.

U.S. Space Program Congress's taxing and spending power is extremely important because a government agency, like NASA, cannot spend money without congressional authorization. **What are authorization bills?**

Other restrictions come from the Constitution's system of checks and balances, whereby each branch of government exercises some control over the others. The Supreme Court can declare laws established by Congress unconstitutional. The president can veto bills passed by Congress before they become laws. If both houses of Congress can muster a two-thirds vote, they can override the president's action.

✓Reading Check **Concluding** How does the Bill of Rights limit Congress's powers?

SECTION 2 ASSESSMENT

Checking for Understanding

1. Key Terms Explain how each of the following terms relates to Congress: expressed powers, implied powers, elastic clause, impeach, writ of habeas corpus, bill of attainder, ex post facto law.

Reviewing Main Ideas

2. Compare What do writs of habeas corpus, bills of attainder, and ex post facto laws have in common?

3. Contrast What is the difference between authorization bills and appropriation bills? Where do bills to spend money begin?

Critical Thinking

4. Making Predictions What problems might have arisen in our government if the elastic clause had not been included in the Constitution?

5. Categorizing Information In a chart similar to the one below, categorize the powers of Congress as well as the powers denied to Congress.

U.S. Congress		
Legislative Powers	Nonlegislative Powers	Powers Denied

Analyzing Visuals

6. Interpret Reexamine the powers of Congress on page 149. What implied power is based on Congress's power to regulate foreign and interstate commerce?

★BE AN ACTIVE CITIZEN★

7. Write Find news articles (newspaper, magazine, online news) that report on Congress exercising legislative and nonlegislative powers. Underline the portions of the articles that describe the powers. Create a chart showing examples of each type of power.

Representing the People

GUIDE TO READING

Main Idea
The work of Congress is so complex that in addition to elected representatives, Congress employs many staffers who help with the workload.

Key Terms
franking privilege, lobbyist, casework, pork-barrel project

Reading Strategy
Analyzing Information On a web diagram like the one below, write as many examples of congressional support personnel as you can.

Congressional Staff/Agencies

Read to Learn
- What benefits do members of Congress enjoy?
- What are the duties of congressional support staff members?

Americans in Action

On December 7, 1829, nine-year-old Grafton Hanson took his place as the first Senate page. Hanson served in various positions in the Senate throughout his life. He left it only in the 1840s to fight in the Mexican War, for which he was decorated for bravery. Pages in the nineteenth century were expected to fill inkwells, light gas lamps, and keep the woodstoves burning. Once a week they were given a ticket entitling them to bathe in the big marble bathtubs located in the Capitol basement.

The U.S. Capitol in the 1800s

Requirements and Benefits of Congress

Congress is more than an institution with formal rules and powers. It consists of people, like congressional pages. Thousands of people work full-time for Congress, keeping the wheels of government turning.

The legal qualifications for members of Congress are simple. According to the Constitution, to run for senator you must be at least 30 years old, live in the state you plan to represent, and have been a U.S. citizen for at least nine years before being elected. Members of the House of Representatives must be at least 25 years old, live in the state they represent, and have been a U.S. citizen for at least seven years before being elected. Although not required, representatives traditionally live in the district they represent.

Senators and representatives have more in common than legal qualifications. Nearly half are lawyers. Almost all have college degrees. They also tend to be "joiners." Members of Congress are more likely than the average citizen to be active in community organizations like the Rotary Club. In addition, most have held elected offices at the state or local level.

Members of Congress receive an annual salary, currently $150,000 for both senators and representatives. Further, they receive free office space, parking, and trips to their home states. Senators and representatives can send job-related mail without paying postage. This is called the **franking privilege.** The Constitution also grants senators and representatives immunity, or legal protection, in certain situations. This allows them to say and do what they believe is right without fear of interference from outsiders. The guarantee of immunity does not mean that members of Congress are free to break the law, though.

Members of Congress also have low-cost life insurance and the use of a gymnasium, special restaurants, and a medical clinic.

✓ Reading Check **Explaining** Why are members of Congress granted immunity?

Congressional Staff: Behind-the-Scenes Helpers

During our country's early history, Congress met only a few months each year. Today serving in Congress is a full-time job. To get help with their workload, members of Congress hire a staff of clerks, secretaries, and special assistants.

Personal Staff

The personal staff of members of Congress run an office in Washington, D.C., as well as one or more offices in the congressional member's home district. Why are personal staffs needed? These workers gather information on new bills and issues that are to be discussed in Congress. They arrange for meetings and write speeches. They handle requests for help from voters. They deal with news reporters and **lobbyists**—people hired by private groups to influence government decision makers. They also work for the reelection of the congressional member, even though the law requires them to do this on their own time.

In addition to professional staffers, many members of Congress hire students from their home states or districts to serve as interns and pages. Interns typically help with research and office duties; pages deliver messages and run other errands. This experience gives young people a first-hand look at the political process. One former congressional intern commented, "I felt like I had a backstage pass to the greatest show in the world."

The Oath of Office Speaker of the House Dennis Hastert administers the oath of office to Representative Mary Bono of California in 1999 as her children watch. **What are the qualifications to become a member of the House?**

Committee Staff

Congressional committees also need staff. Every committee and subcommittee in Congress has staff members who work for that committee. Many of these people have expert knowledge about special topics such as taxes, military defense, and health care. Committee staff members view their jobs as working for the committee rather than for any individual lawmaker.

Committee staff members do many of the various day-to-day lawmaking chores of Congress. They draft bills, gather information, organize committee hearings, and negotiate with lobbyists. In short, they keep the complex lawmaking process moving.

Support Services

Congress has created several agencies to support its work. The Library of Congress is one of the largest libraries in the world. Did you know that one copy of every book published in the United States is kept there? The Library of Congress is an important source of information for members of Congress and their staff. The Congressional Research Service (CRS) is part of the Library of Congress. It looks up facts and spells out arguments for and against proposed bills. CRS also uses computers to keep track of every major bill before Congress.

The General Accounting Office (GAO) is the investigative arm of Congress in financial issues. It reviews the spending activities of federal agencies, studies federal programs, and it recommends ways to improve the financial performance of the government. The staff of the GAO prepares hundreds of reports

Congress's Interns President George W. Bush thanks congressional interns as he shakes their hands in 2001. **What are the typical duties of a congressional intern?**

each month, issues legal opinions, and testifies before congressional committees to make sure that taxpayers' dollars are spent wisely.

The Congressional Budget Office (CBO) provides Congress with information and analysis for making budgetary decisions. It makes no policy recommendations but rather estimates the costs and possible economic effects of programs. It also helps Congress come up with—and stick to—a budget plan.

✓ **Reading Check** **Describing** What is the purpose of the CRS?

Members of Congress at Work

Congress does its work in regular time periods, or sessions, that begin each January 3 and continue through most of the year. The basic job of senators and representatives is to represent the people of their state or district. In carrying out that responsibility, members of Congress perform three major jobs.

Born in southern India, Diana Bhaktul has always been interested in global affairs, but she never felt connected to American politics until last year, when she landed an internship with Congressman Jim Davis, a Florida Democrat.

"It used to be that I would rather watch world news than a Social Security debate," Bhaktul, 18, told TIME. "I didn't think it was relevant to me, even though I grew up in this country. But after working in Congress and watching these issues play out, I saw that [domestic politics] is something you can get into as well."

What's more, Bhaktul says, interning for Congressman Davis gave her a bird's-eye view of how the government actually works. All her negative preconceptions were swept away.

Bhaktul's internship came through a high school political science class. Day to day, she would open the mail, organize databases, and clip newspapers, among other tasks. She also got to sit in on congressional hearings, district conferences, and staff meetings. Plus, she learned a lot about negotiation—how to balance the sometimes conflicting demands of constituents, the nation, and one's personal opinion.

Would you like to intern on Capitol Hill? Contact the local office of your state senator or representative (go to www.house.gov or www.senate.gov for a complete listing).

Diana Bhaktul from Virginia

Lawmaking

Making laws is perhaps the best known task of Congress. Members write and introduce bills, take part in committee work, listen to the input of people for and against a bill, and then vote on the floor of the House or Senate. You will learn more about this process in the next section of this chapter.

Casework

Do you know people who have asked their representative or senator to help them with a problem? Members of Congress spend a lot of time acting as troubleshooters for people from their home district or state who request help in dealing with the federal government. This help is called **casework.** Most requests come by letter or e-mail. Congress gets 80,000 e-mails each day. Over the course of a year, some congressional offices receive as many as 10,000 requests for information or services.

Why do people seek help from members of Congress? One congressional aide put it this way: "Usually, it's a problem of some sort with the bureaucracy. A Social Security check doesn't come. Or a veteran's claim is held up. Maybe it's a slipup by a computer . . . but getting action . . . is tough for the average person."

Most requests for help are handled by the senator's or representative's office staff. They contact the appropriate federal agencies to gather information and request action. If a staffer can't get results, the senator or representative usually steps in. Former senator Jacob Javits of New York once said,

❝**My staff handles problems until the moment of truth. Then I'm called in to push a button, so to speak, to make a phone call at a crucial moment.**❞

Helping the District or State

Another part of a representative's or senator's job is to protect the interests of his or her district or state. Congress appropriates billions of dollars each year for a variety of local projects. These projects might include things like post offices, dams, military bases, veterans' hospitals, and mass transit system projects. Congress members from Florida, for example, might try to limit offshore oil drilling that could harm the state's beaches and tourism. Senators and representatives from states with strong timber industries might seek to influence federal policies on logging.

All members of Congress also work to give their constituents a share in the trillion or so dollars the national government spends every year. A contract to make army uniforms, for example, might mean lots of money for a local business. A new dam or highway would create new jobs for workers. Government projects and grants that primarily benefit the home district or state are

Economics and You

Tax Credits

Congress frequently uses tax credits, or credits that reduce taxes, to encourage certain types of economic activity by individuals or businesses. For example, Congress gave tax credits to homeowners who insulated their homes, an activity intended to reduce U.S. dependence on foreign oil. Find out what tax credits are currently in effect by sending an e-mail or letter to your U.S. representative or senator.

known as **pork-barrel projects.** To understand why this term is used, think of a member of Congress dipping into the "pork barrel" (the federal treasury) and pulling out a piece of "fat" (a federal project for his or her district).

✓**Reading Check** **Inferring** Why do members of Congress try to get pork-barrel projects?

SECTION 3 ASSESSMENT

Checking for Understanding

1. **Key Terms** Write a true and false statement for each term below. Beside each false statement, explain why it is false.
   franking privilege, lobbyist, casework, pork-barrel project

Reviewing Main Ideas

2. **Contrast** Explain the difference between a congressional committee staff member and a member of the personal staff of a representative or senator.

3. **Summarize** Describe the role of the General Accounting Office (GAO). What does the Congressional Budget Office (CBO) do?

Critical Thinking

4. **Drawing Conclusions** Why do you think congressional committees need permanent, full-time staff members?

5. **Summarizing Information** On a graphic organizer like the one below, write the three major jobs or functions of members of Congress. Give an example of each job.

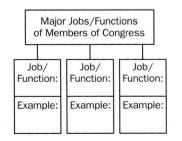

Major Jobs/Functions of Members of Congress		
Job/Function:	Job/Function:	Job/Function:
Example:	Example:	Example:

Analyzing Visuals

6. **Conclude** Reexamine the photograph of Representative Mary Bono taking the oath of office on page 152. Why do you think the Speaker administers the oath?

★**BE AN ACTIVE CITIZEN**★

7. **Interview** Contact the local office of your representative or senator. Ask for an aide to explain his or her role in the office. How does that role differ from staff members in the Washington, D.C., office? Report your findings in a brief presentation to the class.

Issues to Debate

Should There Be Term Limits for Members of Congress?

How long can members of Congress serve in office? Right now, the answer is as long as voters elect them. In 2002 Strom Thurmond of South Carolina held the Senate record of more than 7 consecutive 6-year terms, while John Dingell of Michigan held the House record of 24 consecutive 2-year terms.

Not everyone agrees that U.S. officials should serve so long. In the 1990s, some newly elected members to Congress promised to limit their terms voluntarily, and a number of states passed term-limit laws. In 1995, however, the Supreme Court narrowly ruled that states could not set term limits for Congress. Then, in 1997, a term-limit amendment failed to pass Congress. Are term limits for Congress a good idea?

The Senate and House of Representatives meet in a joint session to hear President Bill Clinton's State of the Union address.

Yes

I think our Founding Fathers intended political office to be a service, not a career. . . . With term limits I don't have the luxury of thinking in terms of a career that spans decades. I have very specific goals and time lines. . . . With term limits, maybe congressmen would be emboldened enough to do their own work and fire some of these self-important staffers!

—*Matt Salmon, Republican representative from Arizona, 1999*

No

As our nation hurtles forward into an ever more complicated world, how self-destructive is it to jettison [throw out] our most capable leaders, when we need their wisdom and judgment so much. To adopt term limits is to play Russian roulette with the future. . . . If the consent of the governed means anything to you—then . . . defend it. Trust the people.

—*Henry Hyde, Republican representative from Illinois, 1997*

Debating the Issue

1. Why does Representative Salmon favor term limits?
2. Why does Representative Hyde oppose term limits?
3. Form groups of three to four. Your group will create a presentation supporting one side of the issue.
4. To prepare for your group presentation, list additional arguments in favor of each point of view. Then decide which viewpoint your group supports.
5. Do additional research to find evidence to support your position. Organize your presentation around your strongest arguments. Include examples and expert opinions.
6. Make your presentations. Then hold a class vote to see what position is supported by a majority of the class members.

How a Bill Becomes a Law

 **Americans in Action**

"I have never seen a better example of Members standing together, working together, swallowing our legalistic desires and our budgetary restraint feelings. These are difficult times. We have got to act decisively. The American people expect it of us, and they will accept nothing less. We are doing that. We are moving today to provide humanitarian funds to assist in the cleanup, disaster assistance, and military action that is necessary."

—Senate Majority Leader Trent Lott, September 14, 2001, in the process of passing legislation in response to the terrorist attacks of September 11, 2001

Members of Congress honor the memory of victims of the 2001 terrorist attacks.

Types of Bills

It is Congress's job to pass laws that the nation needs. However, have you heard people say there are two things you should never watch being made—sausages and laws? Strange elements may go into the final product, and the process requires patience. One scholar has compared lawmaking to running an obstacle course. More than 10,000 bills are often introduced during each term of Congress, yet only several hundred pass all the hurdles and become law.

Bills generally fall into two categories. **Private bills** concern individual people or places. They usually deal with people's claims against the government. **Public bills** apply to the entire nation and involve general matters like taxation, civil rights, or terrorism. They may be debated for months and get much media coverage.

Along with bills, Congress considers different kinds of resolutions, or formal statements expressing lawmakers' opinions or decisions. Many resolutions, such as those creating a new congressional committee or permitting a ceremony in the Capitol, do not have the force of law. **Joint resolutions**, however, which are passed by both houses of Congress, do become laws if signed by the president. Congress uses joint resolutions to propose constitutional amendments, to designate money for a special purpose, and to correct errors in bills already passed.

✓ Reading Check **Concluding** Why might public bills take months to debate?

From Bill to Law

Every bill starts with an idea. Some of these ideas come from members of Congress or private citizens. Many more ideas begin in the White House. Other bills are suggested by **special-interest groups,** or organizations made up of people with some common interest who try to influence government decisions.

Whatever their source, bills can be introduced in Congress only by senators and representatives. Any bill that involves money must start in the House. Every bill is given a title and a number when it is submitted. For example, during the first session of Congress, the first bill introduced is called S.1 in the Senate and H.R.1 in the House. The bill is then sent to the standing committee that seems most qualified to handle it.

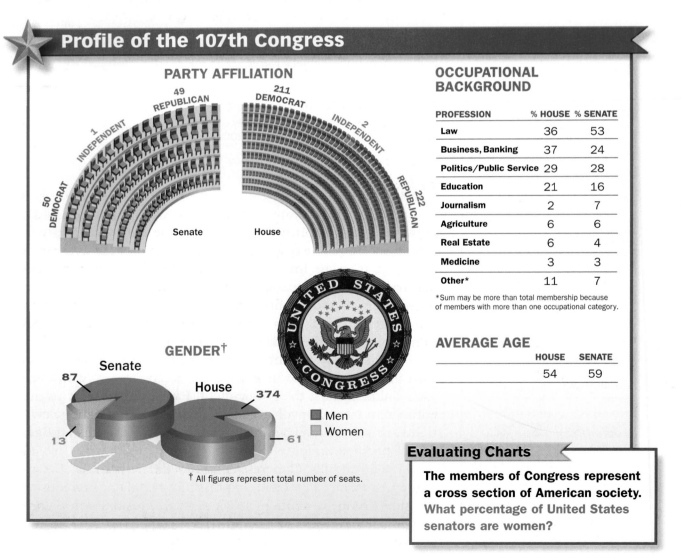

Profile of the 107th Congress

PARTY AFFILIATION

Senate: 49 REPUBLICAN, 1 INDEPENDENT, 50 DEMOCRAT

House: 211 DEMOCRAT, 2 INDEPENDENT, 222 REPUBLICAN

OCCUPATIONAL BACKGROUND

PROFESSION	% HOUSE	% SENATE
Law	36	53
Business, Banking	37	24
Politics/Public Service	29	28
Education	21	16
Journalism	2	7
Agriculture	6	6
Real Estate	6	4
Medicine	3	3
Other*	11	7

*Sum may be more than total membership because of members with more than one occupational category.

AVERAGE AGE

	HOUSE	SENATE
	54	59

GENDER†

Senate: 87, 13
House: 374, 61

■ Men
■ Women

† All figures represent total number of seats.

Evaluating Charts

The members of Congress represent a cross section of American society. What percentage of United States senators are women?

Public Hearing Senator Kent Conrad, a Democrat from North Dakota, speaks during a hearing on the president's 2002 budget before the Senate budget committee. **Why are public hearings of bills held?**

Committee Action

Committees receive far more bills than they can process. The chairperson is the main person to decide which bills get ignored and which get studied. Those that merit attention are often researched and reported on by a subcommittee. Public hearings may be held to allow experts and concerned citizens to voice their opinions. People may also submit written statements for or against the bill.

Standing committees have life-and-death power over bills. The committee can (1) pass the bill without changes, (2) mark up a bill with changes and suggest that it be passed, (3) replace the original bill with a new alternative, (4) ignore the bill and let it die (which is called "pigeonholing" the bill), or (5) kill the bill outright by majority vote. The full House or Senate can overrule the decisions of its committees, but this rarely happens. When a committee is against a bill, it almost never becomes a law.

Floor Debate

Bills approved in committee are ready for consideration by the full House or Senate. The bills are put on calendars, or schedules, in chronological order as they come out of committees. The Senate usually takes up bills in the order listed. The House schedule, however, is controlled by the powerful Rules Committee. This "traffic cop" can give priority to the bills that are most important. It can also kill a bill by not letting it get to the floor.

When bills do reach the floor of the House or Senate, the members argue their pros and cons. Amendments may be discussed as well. The House accepts only amendments relevant to the bill. The Senate, however, allows **riders**—completely unrelated amendments—to be tacked onto the bill. Senators include riders to bills that are likely to pass. Sometimes they attach these riders to benefit their constituents.

In the House, the Rules Committee sets the terms for debate. It usually puts time limits on the discussion, for example, to speed up action. The Senate, because it is smaller, has fewer rules. Senators can speak as long as they wish, and they are not even required to address the topic at hand. Now and then they take advantage of this custom to **filibuster,** or talk a bill to death. One member can hold the floor for hour after hour, delaying a vote until the bill's sponsor gives up and withdraws the measure.

The Senate can end a filibuster if three-fifths of the members vote for **cloture.** Under this procedure, no one may speak for more than one hour. Senators rarely resort to cloture, though. In 1964, during debate on the Civil Rights Act, the Senate waited out a 74-day filibuster by senators opposed to the legislation.

How a Bill Becomes Law

HOUSE

1. Representative hands bill to clerk or drops it in hopper.
2. Bill given *HR* number.

SENATE

1. Senator announces bill on the floor.
2. Bill given *S* number.

Committee Action

HOUSE
1. Referred to House standing committee.
2. Referred to House subcommittee.
3. Reported by standing committee.
4. Rules Committee sets rules for debate and amendments.

Bill is placed on committee calendar.

Bill sent to subcommittee for hearings and revisions.

Standing committee may recommend passage or kill the bill.

SENATE
1. Referred to Senate standing committee.
2. Referred to Senate subcommittee.
3. Reported by standing committee.

Floor Action

HOUSE
1. House debates, votes on passage.
2. Bill passes; goes to Senate for approval.
   OR
   A different version passes; goes to conference committee.

SENATE
1. Senate debates, votes on passage.
2. Bill passes; goes to House for approval.
   OR
   A different version passes; goes to conference committee.

Conference Action

★ Conference committee works out differences and sends identical compromise bill to both chambers for final approval.

★ House votes on compromise bill.   ★ Senate votes on compromise bill.

Passage

★ President signs bill or allows bill to become law without signing.*

OR

★ President vetoes bill.

★ Congress can override a veto by a 2/3 majority in both chambers. If either fails to override, the bill dies.

> **Evaluating Charts**
>
> **The process by which all bills become law is complex.** Who can introduce bills in Congress?

* President can keep bill for 10 days and bill becomes law. If Congress adjourns before the 10 days (Sundays excluded) then it does not become law.

Source: *Congress A to Z*, 2nd ed. (Washington D.C.: CQ Inc., 1993).

Voting on a Bill

When members of Congress are ready to vote on a proposed law, they may do so in several ways. In the House and Senate, the simplest is a **voice vote,** in which those in favor say "Yea" and those against say "No." In a **standing vote,** those in favor of a bill stand to be counted, and then those against it stand to be counted. Today the House uses a computerized voting system to produce a permanent record of each representative's vote. In the more tradition-bound Senate, members voice their votes in turn as an official records them in a **roll-call vote.**

A simple majority of all members that are present is needed to pass a bill. If a bill passes in one house, it is sent to the other. If either the Senate or the House rejects a bill, it dies.

The Constitution requires that the Senate and House pass a bill in identical form before it becomes law. If either house of Congress makes changes in a bill after receiving it from the other house, a conference committee is formed with members from both houses. They meet privately to work out differences between the two versions of the bill. Once they have a revised bill, the House and Senate must either accept it without amendments or completely reject it.

Presidential Action

After a bill is approved by both houses of Congress, it goes to the president. One of four things may then happen. The president may sign the bill and declare it a new law. The president may **veto,** or refuse to sign, the bill. The president may also do nothing for 10 days. At that point, if Congress is in session, the bill becomes law without the president's signature. If Congress had adjourned, the bill dies. Killing legislation in this way is called a **pocket veto.**

If the president vetoes a bill, Congress has one last chance to save it. As you read earlier, Congress can override the veto with a two-thirds vote of each house. This is not an easy task, though. In recent decades, Congress has managed to overturn only about one in five regular vetoes.

✓ Reading Check **Defining** What happens when a bill is pigeonholed?

SECTION 4 ASSESSMENT

Checking for Understanding

1. **Key Terms** Use the following terms in sentences that relate to the lawmaking process: joint resolution, special-interest group, rider, filibuster, cloture, voice vote, roll-call vote, veto, pocket veto.

Reviewing Main Ideas

2. **Contrast** What is the difference between public and private bills? What are resolutions?

3. **Summarize** Describe what can happen to a bill once it passes Congress and reaches the president's desk.

Critical Thinking

4. **Making Inferences** Why do you think members of the House of Representatives consider assignment to the Rules Committee an important appointment?

5. **Determining Cause** On a web diagram like the one below, write all the points in the lawmaking process at which a bill can be stopped or killed.

Stopping or Killing a Bill

Analyzing Visuals

6. **Conclude** Review the steps that a bill must go through to become a law on page 160. What do you think is the step in which the bill is most closely examined by Congress?

★ **BE AN ACTIVE CITIZEN** ★

7. **Organize** Review what you have learned about the characteristics of the two houses of Congress. Create a chart that compares and contrasts the basic characteristics of each body. Present your chart to the class.

Assessment & Activities

Review to Learn

Section 1
- Congress is organized into two bodies.
- Leadership powers include committee selection, bill monitoring, and leading sessions.

Section 2
- Congress has broad powers dealing with defense, finance, and lawmaking.
- Congressional support staffs research bills, deal with public inquiries, and arrange appointments.

Section 3
- Members of Congress receive a salary, plus benefits.
- The support staff of Congress helps with the workload.

Section 4
- Bills are introduced in either the House or the Senate, travel through a committee approval process, and then are voted on.

Study Organizer

Using Your Foldables Study Organizer
After you have read the chapter and completed your foldable, close the four tabs. Then write one more fact under each heading on the tabs. Check the facts you have written against your text. Are they correct? Are they different from the information you wrote under the tab?

Reviewing Key Terms

Write the chapter key term that matches each definition below.

1. president's power to kill a bill, if Congress is not in session, by not signing it for 10 days
2. government projects and grants that benefit the home district of a member of Congress
3. system that gives most desirable committee assignments to members of Congress who have served the longest
4. dividing a state into odd-shaped election districts to benefit a particular party or group
5. the part of the Constitution that gives Congress the authority to do whatever is necessary and proper to carry out its expressed powers
6. people from a legislative district
7. permanent committee of Congress that focuses on a particular topic
8. court order guaranteeing a person who is arrested the right to appear before a judge in a court of law
9. tactic for defeating a bill in the Senate by talking until the bill's sponsor withdraws it
10. person who tries to persuade government officials to support a particular group or position

Reviewing Main Ideas

11. Between the Speaker of the House and the president pro tempore of the Senate, which position has more power? Explain.
12. How are committee assignments made and leadership positions filled in Congress?
13. Describe two nonlegislative powers of Congress.
14. Describe three powers denied to Congress.
15. What are the three major jobs of Congress?
16. What are the qualifications for members of the House of Representatives and the Senate?

17. What four things can happen after a bill has been approved by both houses of Congress and goes to the president?

18. Explain why the Rules Committee is such an important committee in the House.

Critical Thinking

19. **Analyzing Information** What is the relationship between the census and gerrymandering?

20. **Categorizing Information** Create a web diagram for this chapter. On each strand write as many details as possible.

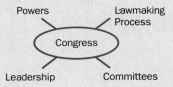

Powers

Lawmaking Process

Congress

Leadership

Committees

Practicing Skills

Making Comparisons Reread the paragraphs under "Congressional Leaders" on pages 140–142. Then answer the following questions.

21. Which party—majority or minority—holds the most power in Congress? Why?

22. How do the duties of majority and minority floor leaders and party whips differ?

 Economics Activity

23. Congress has the power to pass tax legislation. Explain how Congress might use its power to tax to influence our economy.

★ *CITIZENSHIP COOPERATIVE ACTIVITY* ★

24. With a partner, research in the library or on the Internet how a bill becomes a law in your state legislature. Compare the steps in the state lawmaking process to the steps in Congress. Create a chart that shows the similarities and differences.

Self-Check Quiz Visit the *Civics Today* Web site at civ.glencoe.com and click on **Self-Check Quizzes— Chapter 6** to prepare for the chapter test.

Analyzing Visuals

25. Study the map on pages 140–141. It shows changes in the House of Representatives following the 2000 census. Which states gained representatives? Which states lost representatives? Did any particular region of the country gain or lose seats? Explain.

 Technology Activity

26. Log on to the Internet and choose either www.house.gov or www.senate.gov. Choose one of the representatives or senators who represents your community. Make a record of how your representative or senator voted on roll-call votes for the past week or two. Select a particular bill in which you have an interest and write a letter to your representative or senator, either agreeing or disagreeing with the vote. Explain why you agree or disagree.

The Princeton Review

Standardized Test Practice

Directions: Choose the *best* answer to the following question.

Which of the following is a cause that could prevent a bill from becoming a law in Congress?

F A bill is given a title and a number.
G A bill is put on the calendar.
H A senator filibusters a bill.
J The Senate votes for a cloture.

Test-Taking Tip

Read the question carefully. It is asking you to mark the choice that leads to the rejection of a bill.

The President and the Executive Branch

★ CITIZENSHIP AND YOU ★

The Constitution says very little about what a president is expected to do. The nation's first president, George Washington, established many traditions that shaped the presidency. Contact a federal information center to learn about the various divisions of the Executive Office of the President. Create a brochure to present what you find.

 To learn more about the presidency, view the **Democracy in Action** video lesson 8: The Presidency.

FOLDABLES™
Study Organizer

Know-Want-Learn Study Foldable *Make this foldable to determine what you already know, what you want to know, and what you learn about the executive branch of government.*

Step 1 *Fold a sheet of paper into thirds from top to bottom.*

Step 2 *Turn the paper horizontally, unfold, and label the three columns as shown.*

Reading and Writing *Before you read, write down what you already know and what you want to know under each heading. As you read the chapter, record what you learn.*

President George W. Bush and Vice President Dick Cheney get ready to go to a government ceremony. ▶

CIVICS *Online*

Chapter Overview Visit the *Civics Today* Web site at civ.glencoe.com and click on **Chapter Overviews— Chapter 7** to preview chapter information.

The President and Vice President

GUIDE TO READING

Main Idea

Every four years, electors selected by popular vote cast their ballots for president and vice president, whose terms of office are established in the United States Constitution.

Key Terms

Electoral College, elector

Reading Strategy

Categorizing Information As you read, categorize information by completing a chart like the one below with information about the U.S. presidency.

U.S. Presidency		
Qualifications	Background	Term of Office
Election	Salary & Benefits	

Read to Learn

- What qualifications are needed to be president?
- How are presidents elected?
- What are the rules of presidential succession?

Americans in Action

"The presidency of the United States carries with it a responsibility so personal as to be without parallel. . . . No one can make decisions for him. . . . Even those closest to him . . . never know all the reasons why he does certain things and why he comes to certain conclusions. To be President of the United States is to be lonely, very lonely at times of great decisions."

—Harry S Truman

President Truman

Qualifications for President

Harry S Truman was the thirty-third president of the United States, serving from 1945 to 1953. The president heads the executive branch of the United States government. The presidency is the top political job in the country. Because of the power and global influence of the United States, the president is generally considered to hold the most important job in the world. Our country's first president was George Washington. Just as the nation has grown tremendously since that time, so has the office of the presidency.

The constitutional requirements for the presidency remain the same as they did when George Washington was president. The U.S. Constitution lists only three rules about who can become president of the United States. A person must be (1) at least 35 years old, (2) a native-born American citizen, and (3) a resident of the United States for at least 14 years. By law, anyone who meets these qualifications can become president. Of course, someone who hopes to become president must have many more qualifications than those three.

So far, every American president has been a white male. All but one have been Protestant Christians. Most have won elections before. Most have had a college education. Many have been lawyers. Most came from states with large populations.

Only in the past few decades has the presidency become a possibility for a wider group of Americans. John F. Kennedy became the first Catholic president in 1960. In 1984 the

Democratic Party nominated Geraldine Ferraro as its first female vice-presidential candidate. Four years later Jesse Jackson, an African American, ran a close second in the race to become the Democratic candidate for president. In 2000 the Democrats nominated Connecticut senator Joseph Lieberman as the first Jewish candidate for vice president.

Electing a President

Presidential elections take place every four years in years evenly divisible by the number 4—for example, 1996, 2000, and 2004. The Constitution does not provide for direct popular election of the president. Instead, it set up an indirect method of election called the **Electoral College.** The Constitution says that each state "shall appoint" **electors,** who then vote for one of the major candidates. Although the ballot will show the names of the presidential candidates, when you vote for a candidate, you are actually voting for a list of presidential electors pledged to that candidate.

Each state has as many electoral votes as the total of its U.S. senators and representatives. The Electoral College includes 538 electors. (Washington, D.C., has three electoral votes.) This means that the states with large populations have many more electoral votes than less populated states. In almost every state, the Electoral College is a "winner-take-all" system. Even if a candidate wins the popular vote by just a tiny majority, that candidate usually gets all of the state's electoral votes. Candidates thus pay much more attention to these states

John F. Kennedy won the presidency in 1960.

during election campaigns. Even so, the electoral votes of a few small states can decide the outcome of a close election.

To be elected president or vice president, a candidate must win at least 270 of the 538 electoral votes. The winner-take-all system makes it difficult for third-party candidates—candidates not from the two major parties—to win electoral votes.

Although the winning presidential candidate is usually announced on the same evening as the popular election, the formal election by the Electoral College doesn't take place until December, when the electors meet in each state capital to cast their ballots. Congress counts the electoral votes and declares the winner as the next president. You will read more about the Electoral College system in Chapter 10.

Reading Check **Defining** What is a presidential elector?

Term of Office

Presidents serve four-year terms. Originally the Constitution placed no limits on how many terms a president could serve. The nation's first president, George Washington, served for eight years, then refused to run for a third term. Presidents followed Washington's example and no president served more than two terms until 1940, when Franklin D. Roosevelt ran for and won a third term. In 1944 Roosevelt won a fourth term. The Twenty-second Amendment, ratified in 1951, limits each president to two elected terms in office, or a maximum of 10 years if the presidency began during another president's term.

Salary and Benefits

The president receives a salary of $400,000 per year, plus money for expenses and travel. The president lives and works

Presidential Succession

- ⭐ Vice President
- ⭐ Speaker of the House
- ⭐ President Pro Tempore of the Senate
- ⭐ Secretary of State
- ⭐ Secretary of the Treasury
- ⭐ Secretary of Defense
- ⭐ Attorney General
- ⭐ Secretary of Homeland Security
- ⭐ Secretary of the Interior
- ⭐ Secretary of Agriculture
- ⭐ Secretary of Commerce
- ⭐ Secretary of Labor
- ⭐ Secretary of Health and Human Services
- ⭐ Secretary of Housing and Urban Development
- ⭐ Secretary of Transportation
- ⭐ Secretary of Energy
- ⭐ Secretary of Education
- ⭐ Secretary of Veterans Affairs

Source: Nelson, Ed. *The Presidency A to Z,* 2nd ed. (Washington, D.C.: CQ Inc., 1994).

Evaluating Charts

In 1947 Congress passed a law on the order of succession to the presidency. **Who follows the Speaker of the House in succession?**

and airplanes. For long trips, the president uses *Air Force One,* a specially equipped jet.

Reading Check **Identifying** What is the maximum number of years that a U.S. president can serve in office?

The Vice President

The vice president is elected with the president through the Electoral College system. The qualifications for the office are the same as those for the presidency. The Constitution gives little authority to the vice president. Article I states that the vice president shall preside over the Senate and vote in that body in case of a tie.

Vice presidents are usually not very visible to the public. Their activities rarely receive front-page newspaper coverage. Yet, if the president dies, is removed from office, becomes seriously ill, or resigns, the vice president becomes president. Nine vice presidents have become president due to the death or resignation of a president. John Adams, our nation's first vice president, described the situation well. He said,

❝ I am Vice President. In this I am nothing, but I may become everything. ❞

Presidential Succession

Eight presidents have died while in office. The original wording of the Constitution states that if the president dies or leaves office during his term, the vice president takes on the "powers and duties" of the presidency. Early government officials were not sure what that meant. Should the vice president become president, or should he remain vice president while doing the president's job?

in the White House, which contains a private movie theater, a small gym, a bowling alley, and a heated pool. A White House domestic staff of more than 80 people takes care of the president's family.

In addition, the president has the use of Camp David, a beautiful estate in the Catoctin Mountains of Maryland, about 60 miles north of Washington, D.C. It serves as a retreat and as a place to host foreign leaders. When presidents need to travel, they command a fleet of special cars, helicopters,

In 1841 Vice President John Tyler settled the question when William Henry Harrison became the first president to die in office. Tyler declared himself president, took the oath of office, moved into the White House, and served out the remainder of Harrison's term.

In 1947 Congress passed the Presidential Succession Act, which indicates the line of succession after the vice president. According to this law, if both the president and vice president die or leave office, the Speaker of the House becomes president. Next in line is the president pro tempore of the Senate, then the secretary of state and other members of the cabinet.

Twenty-Fifth Amendment

Twenty years later, remaining questions about presidential succession were answered with the adoption of a constitutional amendment. The Twenty-fifth Amendment says that if the president dies or leaves office, the vice president becomes president. The new president then chooses another vice president. Both the Senate and House of Representatives must approve the choice. This amendment also gives the vice president a role in determining whether a president is disabled and unable to do the job. Should that occur, the vice president would serve as acting president until the president is able to go back to work.

The Twenty-fifth Amendment has been used only three times. In 1973 Vice President Spiro Agnew resigned, and President Richard Nixon replaced him with Gerald Ford, a representative from Michigan. When Nixon resigned from the presidency in 1974, Ford became the new president and chose Nelson A. Rockefeller to be his vice president. In 1985 President Ronald Reagan informed Congress that he would need to undergo surgery and be unable to carry out his presidential duties. As a result, Vice President George H.W. Bush served as acting president for about eight hours.

✓ Reading Check **Defining** What was the purpose of the Twenty-fifth Amendment?

SECTION 1 ASSESSMENT

Checking for Understanding

1. Key Terms Write complete sentences about the United States presidency using each of the following terms: Electoral College, elector.

Reviewing Main Ideas

2. Describe What three qualifications for the U.S. presidency are listed in the Constitution of the United States?

3. Identify What are the constitutional duties of the vice president of the United States?

Critical Thinking

4. Making Inferences What did John Adams mean by saying, "I may become everything"?

5. Sequencing Information In a graphic organizer like the one below, explain the order of presidential succession.

Who replaces the president in order of succession?

| President Dies or Leaves Office | | | | | → |

Analyzing Visuals

6. Identify Examine the chart— Presidential Succession—on page 168. Who is fifth in line to become president of the United States?

★ BE AN ACTIVE CITIZEN ★

7. Research In the library or on the Internet, research the gubernatorial succession in your state. What is the line of succession if the governor dies or leaves office?

Reading an Election Map

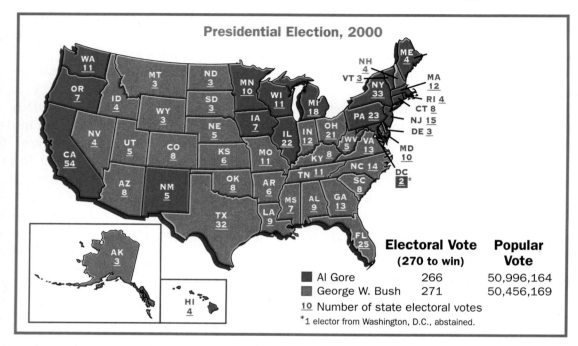

Presidential Election, 2000

| Electoral Vote | Popular |
| (270 to win) | Vote |

Al Gore — 266 — 50,996,164
George W. Bush — 271 — 50,456,169

10 Number of state electoral votes
*1 elector from Washington, D.C., abstained.

Why Learn This Skill?

Knowing how to read and understand an election map helps you understand an election clearly. It can also help you understand past elections.

Learning the Skill

To read an election map, follow these steps:
- Check the year of the election, most likely noted in the title or the key.
- Study the key. See how the different candidates are represented on the map.
- Note the number of electoral votes each state has. Remember that each state's total number of senators and representatives determines its electoral votes. Its popular vote count is the number of actual voters.
- Study the entire map. Determine voting patterns and trends.

Practicing the Skill

On a separate sheet of paper, answer the following questions about the map on this page.

1. How many electoral votes did the state of California have? The state of Texas?
2. Which candidate won the election? How many total electoral votes did he win?
3. Which candidate won the popular vote?

—— Applying the Skill ——

In a history book or encyclopedia, find an election map for the election of 1860. Compare it to the map for the election of 2000. Describe two ways in which the elections were alike and one way in which they were different.

Practice key skills with Glencoe's
**Skillbuilder Interactive Workbook
CD-ROM, Level 1.**

The President's Job

GUIDE TO READING

Main Idea

In addition to the powers of the office described in the Constitution, the president fills other roles that are important to the functioning of the United States government.

Key Terms

executive order, pardon, reprieve, amnesty

Reading Strategy

Summarizing Information As you read, in a graphic organizer like the one below, list the powers of the president and give an example of each.

Powers of President

Read to Learn

- What are the powers assigned to the president by the Constitution?
- What are the various roles filled by the president?

Americans in Action

Fewer than 50 men have been able to say what it feels like to be president of the United States. Some former presidents' thoughts are revealing.

"Frankly, being President is rather an unattractive business unless one relishes the exercise of power. That is a thing which has never greatly appealed to me."
—Warren Harding, 1921

"You know, the President of the United States is not a magician who can wave a wand or sign a paper that will instantly end a war, cure a recession, or make a bureaucracy disappear."
—Gerald Ford, 1976

President Warren Harding shakes hands with Babe Ruth.

Constitutional Powers

The president is the most powerful public official in the United States. The U.S. Constitution is the basis of the president's power. Article II says "Executive Power shall be invested in a President . . ." Thus, the president's main job is to execute, or carry out, the laws passed by Congress.

The Constitution also gives the president the power to

- veto, or reject, bills passed in Congress.
- call Congress into special session.
- serve as commander in chief of the armed forces.
- receive leaders and other officials of foreign countries.
- make treaties with other countries (with Senate approval).
- appoint heads of executive agencies, federal court judges, ambassadors, and other top government officials (also subject to Senate approval).
- pardon or reduce the penalties against people convicted of federal crimes.

Because the Constitution requires the president to give Congress information about the "state of the union," the president gives several speeches to Congress each year. The most important is the State of the Union address every year. In this speech the president comes before a gathering of all members of Congress to discuss the most important issues facing the nation and describe the new program of legislation he would like Congress to take up.

Roles of the President

The president fills a number of different roles. Some of these roles come directly from the Constitution; others are not established in the Constitution but have developed over the years.

Chief Executive

The most important role of the president is carrying out the laws passed by Congress. To do this, the president is in charge of 15 cabinet departments and the approximately 3 million civilians who work for the federal government. The president appoints the heads of the cabinet departments and of other large government agencies, with the Senate's approval.

One of the president's most important tools for carrying out the laws is the power to issue executive orders. An **executive order** is a rule or command that has the force of law. Only Congress has the authority to make laws. Issuing executive orders, however, is generally considered to fall under the president's constitutional duty to "take care that the laws are faithfully executed."

Many executive orders deal with simple administrative problems. Some, however, have had a great impact. President Harry S Truman, for instance, used an executive order in 1948 to integrate the armed forces. This gave Americans of all races the opportunity to serve in the armed forces equally.

The Constitution gives the president the power to appoint judges to the Supreme Court and other federal courts. This is an important power because the Supreme Court has the final authority to determine whether a law is acceptable under the Constitution. This power to interpret laws greatly influences life in the United States. Most presidents try to appoint Supreme Court justices who share views similar to their own.

The Constitution also gives the president the power to grant pardons. A **pardon** is a declaration of forgiveness and freedom from punishment. The president may also issue a **reprieve,** an order to delay a person's punishment until a higher court can hear the case, or grant **amnesty,** a pardon toward a group of people.

Powers and Duties of the President

Commander in Chief

Party Leader

Chief Diplomat

Legislative Leader

Chief Executive

Economic Leader

Head of State

Evaluating Charts

These symbols show the many roles of the president of the United States. Which is the president's most important role?

Chief Diplomat

The president directs the foreign policy of the United States, making key decisions about how the United States acts toward other countries in the world.

Commander in Chief

The Constitution makes the president commander in chief of the nation's armed forces. This role gives presidents the ability to back up their foreign policy decisions with force, if necessary. The president is in charge of the army, navy, air force, marines, and coast guard. The top commanders of all these branches of service are subordinate to the president.

Congress and the president share the power to make war. The Constitution gives Congress the power to declare war, but only the president can order American soldiers into battle. Congress has declared war only five times: the War of 1812, the Mexican War, the Spanish-American War, World War I, and World War II. Presidents, however, have sent troops into action overseas more than 150 times since 1789. These situations may threaten the system of checks and balances. For example, although Congress never declared war in Korea or in Vietnam, American troops were involved in conflicts in those countries because they were sent there by U.S. presidents. In 1973, after the Vietnam War, Congress passed the War Powers Resolution. According to this law, the president must notify Congress within 48 hours when troops are sent into battle. These troops must be brought home after 60 days unless Congress gives its approval for them to remain longer or it declares war.

Legislative Leader

Most of the bills Congress considers each year come from the executive branch. Only members of Congress have the power to introduce bills for consideration, but in practice Congress expects the executive branch to propose the legislation it would like to see enacted.

Every president has a legislative program. These are new laws that he wants Congress to pass. The president makes speeches to build support for this program and meets with key senators and representatives to try to persuade them to support the proposed laws. In addition, the president appoints several staff members to work closely with members of Congress on new laws. The president may also influence legislation by appealing directly to the American people.

The president and Congress have often disagreed over what new laws Congress should adopt. One reason for this is that presidents represent the entire United States, while members of Congress represent only the people of their state or district.

The difference in the length of time that presidents and members of Congress can hold office also contributes to this conflict. While presidents can serve no more than two elected terms, members of Congress can be elected over and over again for decades. Therefore, many members of Congress may not want to move as quickly on programs as the president does.

Head of State

The president is the living symbol of the nation. In this role, the president aids diplomacy by greeting visiting kings and queens, prime ministers, and other foreign leaders. The president also carries out ceremonial functions for Americans, such as lighting the national Christmas tree and giving medals to the country's heroes.

Economic Leader

Every president tries to help the country's economy prosper. Voters expect the president to deal with such problems as unemployment, rising prices, or high taxes.

TIME

Political Cartoons

THIS IS ONE RABBIT THAT NEVER FAILED ME!

SPENDING

OLD RELIABLE!

and it seems to be diverted toward money and ... Making the world a more convenient | Schneider, two men with little hope, of regaining the company's ... While the wage was | to be diverted ... tim

Analyzing Visuals During the Great Depression, President Franklin D. Roosevelt transformed the role of the federal government by spending money on new programs to improve the lives of ordinary people. What does the rabbit symbolize in this cartoon? What comment is the cartoonist making about the impact of government spending?

One key task the president must accomplish each year as economic leader is to plan the federal government's budget.

Party Leader

The president is generally regarded as the leader of his or her political party. Members of the president's party work hard to elect the president. In turn, the president gives speeches to help fellow party members who are running for office as members of Congress, governors, and mayors. The president also helps the party raise money.

Reading Check **Defining** What is a president's legislative program?

SECTION 2 ASSESSMENT

Checking for Understanding

1. Key Terms Define the following terms and use them in complete sentences related to the presidency: executive order, pardon, reprieve, amnesty.

Reviewing Main Ideas

2. Identify What duties does the president carry out as commander in chief?

3. Describe What power does the president have that carries the force of law and assists the president in enforcing laws passed by Congress?

Critical Thinking

4. Drawing Conclusions Which of the roles of the president do you think is the most important? Least important? Why?

5. Organizing Information In a web diagram like the one below, classify the roles filled by the president and give an example of each.

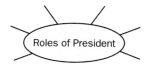

Roles of President

Analyzing Visuals

6. Contrast Review the chart on page 172. How does the role of head of state differ from that of chief diplomat?

★**BE AN ACTIVE CITIZEN**★

7. Use Primary Sources Just as the president delivers a State of the Union address, most governors give a state of the state speech. Read a copy of your governor's last address and list the roles your governor carries out.

Making Foreign Policy

GUIDE TO READING

Main Idea

In attempting to achieve the nation's foreign policy goals, both the president and Congress have important roles to play.

Key Terms

foreign policy, national security, treaty, executive agreement, ambassador, trade sanction, embargo

Reading Strategy

Comparing and Contrasting As you read, complete a chart like the one below to compare the role of Congress in foreign policy to that of the president.

U.S. Foreign Policy	
Congress	President

Read to Learn

• What are the goals of U.S. foreign policy?

• What are the roles of Congress and the president in conducting foreign policy?

Americans in Action

World events sometimes dictate the nature of the United States's foreign policies. At the same time, the president's views play a role in shaping his administration's approach to foreign affairs. In 1946, President Harry S Truman summed up his foreign policy with these words: "We must have a policy to guide our relations with every country in every part of the world. No country is so remote from us that it may not someday be involved in a matter that threatens the peace. . . . Who knows what may happen in the future? Our foreign policy must be universal."

Protecting American interests abroad

The President and Foreign Policy

A nation's overall plan for dealing with other nations is called its **foreign policy.** The basic goal of American foreign policy is **national security,** the ability to keep the country safe from attack or harm. This goal is essential. No government can effectively meet other important goals, such as better health care or cleaning up the environment, if the nation is under attack.

Another key goal is international trade. In today's global economy, trade with other nations is vital to economic prosperity. Trade can create markets for American products and jobs for American workers.

A third goal is promoting world peace. Even a war far from the United States can disrupt trade and endanger U.S. national security. When other nations are at peace, the United States runs no risk of being drawn into a foreign war.

A fourth goal of foreign policy is to promote democracy around the world. Promoting democracy and basic human rights in other countries encourages peace and thus helps protect our own national security.

"I make American foreign policy," President Harry S Truman declared in 1948. The president is indeed a very important foreign-policy decision maker. Americans and others in the world look to the president to strongly represent our country in foreign affairs.

The president and various White House assistants work with a large foreign-policy bureaucracy in the executive branch. This bureaucracy includes the State Department, the Defense Department, the Central Intelligence Agency, and the National Security Council. These agencies have helped make the president very powerful in foreign affairs. They give the president valuable information. They can carry out presidential decisions around the world. At the same time, presidents must often choose among conflicting advice from these agencies. President Lyndon Johnson complained,

> **The State Department wants to solve everything with words, and the generals, with guns.**

The Constitution divides the power to conduct foreign and military affairs between the president and Congress. The president is chief diplomat and commander in chief, but Congress has the power to declare war, to prohibit certain military actions, and to spend—or withhold—money for defense. The Constitution does not clearly spell out how the legislative and the executive branches can use their powers. As a result, there has always been competition between Congress and the president over who controls foreign policy.

In this struggle, one branch or the other has dominated at various times. After World War II, Congress lost much of its control over foreign policy to the president. Then, in the late 1960s and early 1970s, widespread dislike of the Vietnam War led Congress to try to regain some of its war powers. In starting the American war on global terrorism in 2001, President George W. Bush tipped the balance back toward the presidency.

Tools of Foreign Policy

The president and Congress have several methods they can use to influence other nations and carry out American foreign

The President in Action President Bush comforted a New York City Fire Department member (at right) in September 2001 after a terrorist attack on the World Trade Center. The president greeted military troops at the West Virginia National Headquarters in Charleston. **What executive agencies help President Bush carry out foreign policy?**

policy. These methods include creating treaties; appointing ambassadors; and directing foreign aid, international trade, and military forces.

Creating Treaties and Executive Agreements Formal agreements between the governments of two or more countries are called treaties. Some treaties are based on defense: nations that become allies agree to support each other in case of attack. One of the most important treaties for the United States is the North Atlantic Treaty Organization (NATO). This is a mutual defense treaty between the United States, Canada, and the nations of Europe.

The Senate must approve a treaty by a two-thirds vote. However, the president can bypass the Senate by making an executive agreement. This is an agreement between the president and the leader of another country. Most such agreements deal with fairly routine matters.

Appointing Ambassadors An official representative of a country's government is an ambassador. The president appoints about 150 ambassadors, who must be approved by the Senate. Ambassadors are sent only to those countries where the United States recognizes, or accepts, the legal existence of the government. If the government of a certain country is thought to hold power illegally, the president can refuse to recognize that government. In that case, no American ambassador will be sent to that country, and that country will not be allowed to send an ambassador to the United States.

Foreign Aid This is money, food, military assistance, or other supplies given to help other countries. One of this nation's greatest foreign aid triumphs was the Marshall Plan, a program created to help Western Europe rebuild after World War II.

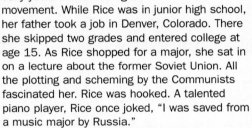

American Biographies

Condoleezza Rice (1954–)

Condoleezza Rice juggles numbers of missiles and tanks as confidently as any general. An expert on Russia and arms control, Rice launched her foreign policy career while only a teenager.

Born in Birmingham, Alabama, Rice lived through the early years of the civil rights movement. While Rice was in junior high school, her father took a job in Denver, Colorado. There she skipped two grades and entered college at age 15. As Rice shopped for a major, she sat in on a lecture about the former Soviet Union. All the plotting and scheming by the Communists fascinated her. Rice was hooked. A talented piano player, Rice once joked, "I was saved from a music major by Russia."

Rice went on to earn a Ph.D. and by her late 20s was teaching political science at Stanford University in California. The White House asked Rice to serve on the National Security Council from 1989 to 1991, years when the Soviet Union crumbled apart. In 2001 Rice returned to the National Security Council, this time as the first woman to head the entire agency.

International Trade As the leader of a great economic power, the president can make agreements with other nations about what products may be traded and the rules for such trading. Sometimes trade measures include trade sanctions, or efforts to punish another nation by imposing trade barriers. Another punishing tool is the embargo, which is an agreement among a group of nations that prohibits them all from trading

Protecting American Interests A bronze model of the Statue of Liberty and a statue depicting an American taken hostage in 1979 stand outside the U.S. embassy in Iran. **How might a president withdraw formal recognition from a country's government?**

with a target nation. Congress takes the lead in other areas, such as tariffs—taxes on imported goods—and membership in international trade groups, such as the North American Free Trade Agreement (NAFTA) and the World Trade Organization (WTO).

Military Force As commander in chief of the armed forces, presidents may use the military to carry out some foreign-policy decisions. This is a powerful tool of foreign policy, but one that must be used with great care. Presidents throughout history have made use of this power. President George Washington summoned troops to put down the Whiskey Rebellion in 1794. President Bill Clinton ordered cruise missiles to be launched at terrorist facilities in Afghanistan and Sudan in 1998. In 2001 President George W. Bush committed the American armed forces to a long-term global struggle against terrorism.

Reading Check **Concluding** What foreign policy tools does the president have to deal with international terrorism?

SECTION 3 ASSESSMENT

Checking for Understanding

1. **Key Terms** Define the following terms and use them in sentences related to U.S. foreign policy: foreign policy, national security, treaty, executive agreement, ambassador, trade sanction, embargo.

Reviewing Main Ideas

2. **Describe** In what way can trade sanctions and embargoes be used in conducting foreign policy?

3. **Define** What is NATO and how does it fit into United States foreign policy? What is NAFTA and how does it fit into U.S. foreign policy?

Critical Thinking

4. **Making Judgments** Should Congress or the president have more power in conducting foreign affairs? Explain your answer.

5. **Organizing Information** Categorize the tools available to Congress and the president in carrying out foreign policy by completing a graphic organizer like the one below.

Foreign Policy Tools

Analyzing Visuals

6. **Infer** Review the photograph of the United States embassy in Iran on this page. What sort of impression do you think this building gives to people in Iran?

★ **BE AN ACTIVE CITIZEN** ★
7. **Survey** Interview several adults, all of whom have different jobs, about the North American Free Trade Agreement (NAFTA). Find out why they think it is good or bad foreign policy. Share your results with the class.

Presidential Advisers and Executive Agencies

GUIDE TO READING

Main Idea
Thousands of employees and advisers help the president.

Key Terms
cabinet, federal bureaucracy, independent agency, government corporation, political appointee, civil service worker, civil service system, spoils system, merit system

Reading Strategy
Categorizing Information
As you read, complete a chart similar to the one below to categorize functions of the president's executive office.

President's Executive Office	
White House Office	Role:
OMB	Role:
NSC	Role:
Homeland Security Council	Role:
CEA	Role:

Read to Learn
- How does the EOP help presidents perform their duties?
- What are the duties of the federal bureaucracy?

Americans in Action

Early presidents governed the nation with the help of just a small circle of advisers. Over time, presidents' cabinets have grown to meet the increasing demands of governing a vast and diverse nation. On November 25, 2002, President George W. Bush signed the Homeland Security Act of 2002 into law. The act established a new Department of Homeland Security, whose primary mission President Bush noted "will be to help prevent, protect against, and respond to acts of terrorism on our soil." Former Pennsylvania Governor Tom Ridge, who had coordinated antiterrorism efforts since the September 11 attacks, said the new department will unify efforts to protect "American citizens and their way of life."

Tom Ridge

Executive Office of the President

In 1801 President Thomas Jefferson did his job with the help of a few advisers, a messenger, and a part-time secretary. Today thousands of highly trained specialists like Tom Ridge, secretaries, and clerks assist the president. Most of these people work in the Executive Office of the President (EOP). These people are often referred to as a president's administration.

Franklin D. Roosevelt's administration created the EOP in 1939 to help the president do his job. The office has been growing ever since. Currently it has about 2,000 employees and a budget of more than $100 million. The men and women in the EOP do a variety of things. They prepare reports for the president on special topics, such as new taxes that might be needed. They help write bills for the president to send to Congress. They check on the work of the many different agencies of the executive branch.

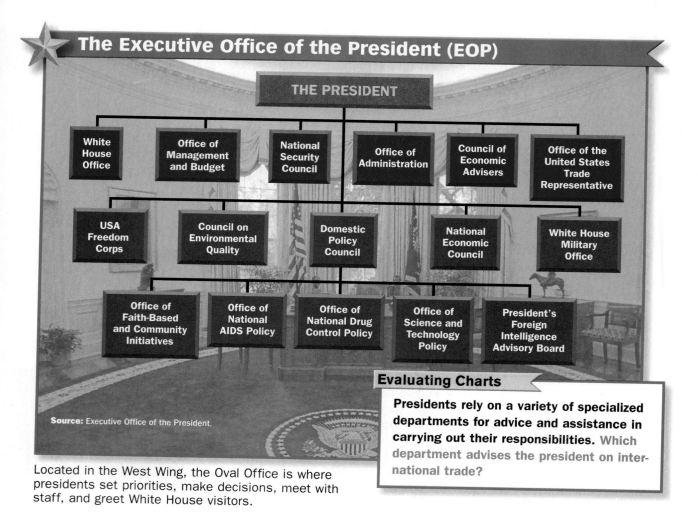

The Executive Office of the President (EOP)

THE PRESIDENT

- White House Office
- Office of Management and Budget
- National Security Council
- Office of Administration
- Council of Economic Advisers
- Office of the United States Trade Representative

- USA Freedom Corps
- Council on Environmental Quality
- Domestic Policy Council
- National Economic Council
- White House Military Office

- Office of Faith-Based and Community Initiatives
- Office of National AIDS Policy
- Office of National Drug Control Policy
- Office of Science and Technology Policy
- President's Foreign Intelligence Advisory Board

Source: Executive Office of the President.

Evaluating Charts

Presidents rely on a variety of specialized departments for advice and assistance in carrying out their responsibilities. Which department advises the president on international trade?

Located in the West Wing, the Oval Office is where presidents set priorities, make decisions, meet with staff, and greet White House visitors.

The most important parts of the EOP include the following: the White House Office, the Office of Management and Budget, the National Security Council, the Office of Administration, and the Council of Economic Advisers.

White House Office

This unit consists of about 500 people who work directly for the president. Among them are 10 to 12 people who serve as the president's closest political advisers. The most powerful among this group is the chief of staff. Other top advisers are the deputy chief of staff, the assistant for domestic affairs, the counsel (lawyer) to the president, the appointments secretary, the assistant for public relations, the assistant for legislative affairs, and the press secretary. (The press secretary provides the public with news about and statements from the president.) As a group, such advisers make up the White House staff.

The White House staff screens the flow of information and people trying to reach the president. Presidents cannot possibly meet with everyone who wants to see them; nor can they read all the reports, memos, and letters sent to them. The White House staff largely decides who and what gets through to the president. As a result, this group of advisers has a lot of political power. Lawmakers and others know that to influence, or sometimes even to speak with, the president, they must go through the White House staff.

Office of Management and Budget (OMB)

This agency prepares the federal budget and monitors spending in hundreds of government agencies. The director of the OMB reports directly to and works closely with the president. The federal budget is the clearest statement of the administration's plans and goals for the coming year.

National Security Council (NSC)

This group helps the president coordinate United States military and foreign policy. It deals with matters affecting the safety and security of the United States. Its members include the vice president, the secretaries of state and defense, and the chairman of the Joint Chiefs of Staff, a group made up of the top commander from each of the armed services. The president may also invite others to be a part of the NSC. The national security adviser heads the NSC staff. The NSC also supervises the Central Intelligence Agency (CIA), which gathers information about the governments of other countries.

Office of Administration

The Office of Administration provides administrative services to all of the executive offices of the president. The Office also responds to individuals who are seeking records under the Freedom of Information Act.

Council of Economic Advisers (CEA)

This group helps the president carry out the role of economic leader. The president names the CEA's three members, and the Senate must approve them. The CEA's primary duty involves giving the president advice about complex economic matters such as employment, tax policy, inflation, and foreign trade.

Reading Check Identifying What are the duties of a president's chief of staff?

Cabinet

The **cabinet** is a group of presidential advisers that includes the heads of the 15 top-level executive departments. The head of the Department of Justice is called the attorney general; all the other department heads are called secretaries. The president may also ask the vice president and other top officials to join the cabinet.

Department of Homeland Security

On November 25, 2002, President Bush signed the Homeland Security Act of 2002 into law. In forming the new Department of Homeland Security, the act created a federal department to consolidate the nation's defenses against terrorist attack and better coordinate counterterrorism intelligence. It is the first new department established since the Department of Veterans Affairs was established in 1989.

Cabinet Responsibilities

As cabinet members, the secretaries advise the president on issues related to their departments. The secretary of agriculture, for instance, might keep the president and White House staff informed about problems of concern to American farmers. Cabinet secretaries often make important policy decisions.

No mention of the cabinet appears in the Constitution. Instead, this body developed over the years through custom and usage. The cabinet started when George Washington began to meet regularly with the heads of the first four executive departments. These were the attorney general and the secretaries of state, war, and the treasury.

The cabinet meets whenever the president determines that it is necessary. This may be as often as once a week or hardly at all.

The Law and You

How Much Power Does the President Have During a Crisis?

Imagine the following scenario. Terrorists have just attacked the United States, killing thousands of Americans. Country X has supported these terrorists.

The president plans to issue an executive order because he fears more attacks and wants to find the terrorists and those who aided them. Assume that you and your classmates are legal advisers to the president. Decide which of the following provisions should be included in the executive order. Use the amendments to the Constitution (pages 72–81) to help you decide if the provisions are constitutional.

- Five thousand people from Country X who are in the country but are not yet U.S. citizens are called in for questioning. Those "suspected of being terrorists" can be kept secretly in jail for up to 180 days, without seeing family, friends, or a lawyer.
- All people with last names like those found in Country X are stopped at airports for extra questioning and searches of their luggage and handbags.
- Newspapers, radio, and television stations are told not to print or air any criticism of the president in the war against terrorism. Violations will result in fines of up to $1,000.
- No one is allowed to give money to a charity for Country X until the U.S. government decides it is not working with the terrorist group.
- All e-mail exchanged between the United States and Country X will be subject to monitoring by U.S. government officials.

★BE AN ACTIVE CITIZEN★

Do you think that this type of executive order—that suspends constitutional rights—is justified? Explain your reasons.

Many presidents have not relied heavily on their cabinet and have felt free to ignore cabinet advice. As heads of executive agencies, these department secretaries must spend most of their time coordinating those departments' activities. Department heads of the cabinet must be approved by the Senate.

✔ Reading Check **Recalling** When does the cabinet meet?

The Vice President and the First Lady

Most presidents have delegated little authority to their vice presidents. Recently, however, some have tried to give their vice presidents more responsibility. Vice President Al Gore, for example, served as a close adviser to President Bill Clinton on environmental issues, and Vice President Dick Cheney advised President George W. Bush closely on foreign policy issues.

The Constitution does not mention the spouse of a president. Many First Ladies, though, have served the country. Eleanor Roosevelt worked tirelessly for the young and the disadvantaged. Nancy Reagan spoke out for drug abuse prevention, Hillary Clinton worked to improve health care for all Americans, and Laura Bush promoted education and reading. Today First Ladies have an office in the White House as well as a staff that includes a chief of staff and a press spokesperson.

The Federal Bureaucracy

Below the cabinet departments are hundreds of agencies that deal with everything from setting standards for the hot dogs you eat to running the space shuttle program. About 3 million civilians work in these many departments and agencies. Taken together, the agencies and employees of the executive branch are often called the **federal bureaucracy.** The people who work for these organizations are called bureaucrats, or civil servants.

What Does the Federal Bureaucracy Do?

The executive branch of government must carry out the many programs that Congress has created to serve the American people. Executive departments and agencies do this by performing three basic jobs. First, they turn new laws into action by deciding how to apply the laws to daily life. When Congress writes new laws, it often uses very general language. Federal agencies then must develop specific rules and procedures to put the laws into practice.

Second, departments and agencies administer the day-to-day operations of the federal government. Agencies deliver the mail, collect taxes, send out Social Security checks, patrol the borders, run national parks, and perform thousands of other services.

Third, with authority from Congress, federal agencies regulate various activities. They regulate, or police, the activities of broadcasting companies, labor unions, banks, airlines, nuclear power plants, and many other enterprises and organizations.

In doing these jobs, federal agencies help shape government policy. By deciding how

Cabinet Departments

 Department of State (1789)
Plans and carries out the nation's foreign policies

 Department of the Treasury (1789)
Collects, borrows, spends, and prints money

 Department of Defense (1789 as War Department; renamed in 1949)
Manages the armed forces

 Department of Justice (1870)
Has responsibility for all aspects of law enforcement

 Department of the Interior (1849)
Manages and protects the nation's public lands and natural resources

 Department of Agriculture (1889)
Assists farmers and consumers of farm products

 Department of Commerce (1903)
Supervises trade, promotes U.S. tourism and business

 Department of Labor (1913)
Is concerned with the working conditions and wages of U.S. workers

 Department of Health and Human Services (1953)
Works for the health and well-being of all Americans

 Department of Housing and Urban Development (1965)
Deals with the special needs and problems of cities

 Department of Transportation (1966)
Manages the nation's highways, railroads, airlines, and sea traffic

 Department of Energy (1977)
Directs an overall energy plan for the nation

 Department of Education (1979)
Provides advice and funding for schools

 Department of Veterans Affairs (1989)
Directs services for veterans

 Department of Homeland Security (2002)
Oversees America's defenses against terrorist attack

Evaluating Charts

The heads of the 15 executive departments are members of the cabinet. Which department manages public lands?

U.S. Secretary of State Colin Powell and his Thai counterpart talk at an economic forum in China in 2001.

It's not every kid who has attended a presidential inauguration. Then again, Haamid Johnson is hardly "every kid." At 17, Johnson has already been elected Youth Mayor of Chicago and had an internship at City Hall. He has organized a school political science club, been twice elected class president, worked briefly for the Democratic Party, and logged some 50 hours passing out flyers and making phone calls for then-candidate George W. Bush.

"Even though Bush did lose Illinois," says Johnson, "I feel I did contribute something. I guess that's the important part: Participating is the main thing."

Johnson's political passion stems from a teacher. "I just saw this guy and I said 'wow!'" Johnson recalls. "He motivated me to speak and to write. We just hit it off. He said I should start a political science club. Then, he encouraged me to run for freshman class president. I was thinking about running for treasurer. But he said, 'No, go for the big one.'"

Haamid Johnson from Illinois

to run a government program or what to do in a certain situation, federal agencies often determine what government policy will be.

Independent Agencies

The executive branch includes hundreds of independent agencies. They are called independent because they are not part of the cabinet. They are not, however, independent of the president. The president appoints the directors of these agencies, with the approval of the Senate. In general, however, they can be divided into three types: executive agencies, government corporations, and regulatory commissions.

Executive Agencies These are independent agencies responsible for dealing with certain specialized areas within the government. The National Aeronautics and Space Administration (NASA) is an example. It operates the United States space program.

Government Corporations More than 50 independent agencies are government corporations. These are like private businesses, except that the government rather than individuals owns and operates them. With Senate approval, the president chooses a board of directors and a general manager to run each corporation. Like private businesses, they charge fees for their services and products, but they are not supposed to make a profit. The United States Postal Service, for example, is a government corporation.

Regulatory Boards and Commissions These units differ from other independent agencies. They do not have to report to the president, who appoints the members but cannot fire them. Only Congress can remove them, through impeachment.

Regulatory commissions are supposed to protect the public. They make and enforce rules for certain industries or groups. For instance, the Federal Communications Commission (FCC) makes broadcasting rules for the nation's television and radio stations. Other regulatory commissions place limits on how companies can operate in order to promote honesty and fair competition.

Government Workers

A former cabinet secretary once said, "A Cabinet member does not run a Cabinet department [alone]." Indeed, each department has thousands of employees. The top leadership jobs generally go to **political appointees**—people whom the president has chosen because they have proven executive ability or were important supporters of the president's election campaign. Their employment usually ends when the president leaves office.

About 90 percent of all national government employees are **civil service workers.** Unlike political appointees, civil service workers usually have permanent employment. These career government employees develop much experience on the job. These are people, ranging from clerks to doctors and lawyers, employed by the federal government through the **civil service system**—the practice of hiring government workers on the basis of open, competitive examinations and merit.

Before 1883 a great many federal jobs fell under the **spoils system.** In this system, government jobs went to people as a reward for their political support. Each newly elected president would sweep out most of the old federal workers and replace them with his own political supporters and friends. The idea was "To the victor belong the spoils [jobs]." Public dissatisfaction with abuses of the spoils system, and public outrage over the assassination of President James Garfield in 1881 by a man who was refused a job under the system, led Congress to pass the Pendleton Act.

This law, also known as the Civil Service Reform Act of 1883, placed limits on the number of jobs a new president could hand out to friends and backers, and it created the civil service system. The Office of Personnel Management (OPM) directs the civil service system today. It sets standards for federal jobs, and it gives demanding written tests to people who want those jobs. The civil service system is a **merit system.** Government officials hire new workers from lists of people who have passed the tests or otherwise met civil service standards.

Reading Check **Describing** What is the purpose of regulatory commissions?

SECTION 4 ASSESSMENT

Checking for Understanding

1. Key Terms Define the following terms and use them in complete sentences related to the presidency: federal bureaucracy, independent agency, government corporation, political appointee.

Reviewing Main Ideas

2. Describe What does the Constitution say about the role of the First Lady in our government?

3. Contrast What is the difference between a private and a government corporation?

Critical Thinking

4. Making Inferences What part of the EOP do you think is the most important? Why?

5. Analyzing Information Organize the roles of people who assist the president by completing a graphic organizer like the one below.

People and agencies who assist the president

Analyzing Visuals

6. Infer Review the cabinet departments of the executive branch on page 183. Why are there so many cabinet departments under the president of the United States?

★ **BE AN ACTIVE CITIZEN** ★

7. Research Find out about your governor's staff. How many people work as assistants and advisers to the governor? How are they similar to the president's staff?

Assessment & Activities

Review to Learn

Section 1
- There are constitutional and informal requirements for the U.S. presidency.
- Presidents are elected through an indirect method called the Electoral College.

Section 2
- According to the Constitution, the president's main job is to carry out the laws passed by Congress.

Section 3
- The basic goal of American foreign policy is national defense.

Section 4
- The EOP is the president's administration.

FOLDABLES™
Study Organizer

Using Your Foldables Study Organizer
Exchange completed foldables with a classmate. On your classmate's foldable, find what he or she "wanted to know." Then use this information to ask your classmate a few questions. Did your classmate find out what he or she wanted to know?

Reviewing Key Terms
Write the key term from the chapter that fits each definition below.

1. a rule issued by the president that has the force of law
2. people chosen by the president to fill a certain post because they were important supporters of the president's election campaign
3. a pardon toward a group of people
4. secretaries of the executive departments, the vice president, and other top officials who help the president make decisions and policy
5. members of a party chosen in each state to formally elect the president and vice president
6. a government's plan for dealing with other nations
7. the practice of victorious politicians rewarding their followers with government jobs
8. an agreement prohibiting trade
9. a business owned and operated by the government to provide services to the public
10. the practice of government employment based upon competitive examination and merit

Reviewing Main Ideas
11. How is the number of each state's electoral votes determined?
12. Who would assume the presidency if both the president and vice president died?
13. To whom does the Constitution give the power to officially declare war?
14. What role do presidents play when they help someone campaign for a Senate seat?
15. What president created the EOP?
16. What agency has the most responsibility for preparing the federal budget?
17. How are directors of independent agencies appointed?
18. What event spurred passage of the Civil Service Reform Act of 1883?

Critical Thinking

19. **Analyzing Information** Why do you think an EOP was not needed prior to 1939? How did previous presidents manage without this office?

20. **Cause and Effect** What effect does the civil service system have on the work of the federal bureaucracy? Explain this relationship using a graphic organizer like the one below.

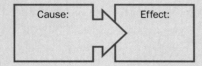

Practicing Skills

Reading an Election Map Refer to the presidential election map on page 170. Then answer the following questions.

21. How many electoral votes does your state have? Which 2000 presidential candidate did your state support?

 Economics Activity

22. The president's annual budget is a plan for managing the nation's economy. Like any blueprint, it states overall goals and the strategies for achieving them. Design an economic blueprint for a small business that you might start. Take into account spending, earning, and investment goals.

 Technology Activity

23. One of the services provided by an executive department of the government is travel warnings for U.S. citizens who are thinking about foreign travel. Search the Internet for the United States Department of State Web site. Find a country for which there is a travel warning and summarize the warning.

Self-Check Quiz Visit the *Civics Today* Web site at civ.glencoe.com and click on **Self-Check Quizzes—Chapter 7** to prepare for the chapter test.

★ CITIZENSHIP COOPERATIVE ACTIVITY ★

24. Divide into groups and write a letter to the president expressing your views on a current issue. Share any response you receive with the class.

Analyzing Visuals

Study the political cartoon on page 174 and answer the following question.

25. This cartoon shows President Roosevelt acting as president. Which roles of the presidency is he filling in the cartoon? Explain your choices.

 Standardized Test Practice

Directions: Choose the *best* answer to the following question.

Which of the following statements is a description of the winner-take-all system of electing the president of the United States?

A American citizens elect the president directly through popular vote.

B If a candidate wins the popular vote, that candidate usually gets all of the state's electoral votes.

C The electoral votes a candidate receives are proportional to the popular votes that candidate received.

D Large states have more electoral votes than small states.

Test-Taking Tip

Before reviewing the answer choices, jot down an answer to the question in your own words.

T HE WHITE HOUSE—ONCE described by Gerald Ford as "the best public housing in the world" and by Harry Truman as a "glamorous prison"—turns 203 in 2003. On a typical morning it is a village of 6,000 busy souls: the president and First Lady, gardeners, journalists, clerks, cooks, cops, economists, guests, and tourists operating in harmony on 18 acres.

This intricate model of the presidential mansion, built on a scale of 1 inch to 1 foot, was begun in 1962 by John and Jan Zweifel of Orlando, Florida. Except for the location of the library, which was pushed forward for show purposes, the Zweifels' White House is a faithful recreation of the original, down to TVs , furniture, and paintings. The Zweifels contact the White House every few weeks to find out if anything has changed. The 60-foot by 20-foot, 10-ton model, which includes the East and West wings (not shown), took more than 500,000 hours to construct and cost more than $1 million.

1 SITTING ROOM Generally claimed by the First Lady, this room was allocated one of the building's first water closets in 1801.

2 MASTER BEDROOM Nancy Reagan decorated this room in hand-painted paper from China.

3 PRESIDENT'S STUDY F.D.R. used this room as a bedroom; the Reagans liked to have quiet dinners here in front of the TV.

4 YELLOW OVAL ROOM One of the most historic rooms in the house, it took on the color yellow during the tenure of Dolley Madison.

5 TREATY ROOM Originally a large bedroom, it served as Bill Clinton's office in the residence.

6 LINCOLN BEDROOM Lincoln signed the Emancipation Proclamation here.

7 LINCOLN SITTING ROOM McKinley's war room during the Spanish-American War.

8 STATE DINING ROOM Gilbert Stuart's portrait of George Washington hung here when the British torched the mansion in 1814.

THE WHITE HOUSE

STEVEN P WIDOFF FOR TIME

9 RED ROOM
John Adams's breakfast room was where Rutherford B. Hayes took the oath of office in 1877.

10 BLUE ROOM
Where Grover Cleveland married Frances Folsom, in 1886.

11 GREEN ROOM
Thomas Jefferson's dining room is now used for receptions.

12 EAST ROOM
The largest room in the mansion, it was used by Abigail Adams to dry the family wash.

13 LIBRARY
Placed here by the replica designers, the library is actually located behind the Vermeil Room.

14 MAP ROOM
Decorated with Chippendale furniture, it was inspired by Churchill's World War II map room.

15 DIPLOMATIC RECEPTION ROOM Site from which F.D.R. broadcast his fireside chats (though the fireplace at that time was fake).

16 CHINA ROOM
Edith Wilson set aside this room to display china.

17 VERMEIL ROOM Once used as a billiard hall, it takes its name from a display of vermeil (gilded silver).

CHAPTER 8

The Judicial Branch

★ CITIZENSHIP AND YOU ★

The American judicial system is one of the nation's most important institutions. It is up to the courts that make up the judicial branch to see that our nation's laws are justly enforced. It is also up to the courts to interpret the laws and to preserve and protect the rights the Constitution guarantees. Find out the location of the nearest federal district court and court of appeals and the names of the judges in these courts. Prepare an informational directory.

To learn more about the judicial branch, view the *Democracy in Action* video lesson 11: The Federal Court System at Work.

Compare and Contrast Study Foldable *Make this foldable to help you determine similarities and differences between the federal courts and the Supreme Court of the United States.*

Step 1 *Fold one sheet of paper in half from top to bottom.*

Step 2 *Fold it in half again, from side to side.*

Step 3 *Unfold the paper once, label it, and cut up the fold of the top flap only.*

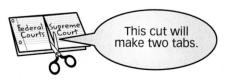

This cut will make two tabs.

Reading and Writing *As you read, write information under each appropriate tab to help you compare and contrast the purpose and organization of these courts.*

The Supreme Court building in Washington, D.C. ▶

CIVICS Online

Chapter Overview Visit the *Civics Today* Web site at civ.glencoe.com and click on **Chapter Overviews— Chapter 8** to preview chapter information.

The Federal Court System

Main Idea

Three levels of federal courts try to ensure that everyone in the United States receives equal justice under the law.

Key Terms

jurisdiction, exclusive jurisdiction, concurrent jurisdiction

Reading Strategy

Organizing Information As you read, complete a web diagram similar to the one below by listing the eight kinds of cases for which federal courts have exclusive jurisdiction.

U.S. Federal Courts

Read to Learn

• How did the federal court system originate?

• What kinds of cases are handled in federal courts?

Americans in Action

In 1942 the government dismissed Mitsuye Endo from her civil service job in California and ordered her to a relocation center. Although Endo was a U.S. citizen with a brother serving in the U.S. Army, she and other Japanese Americans were forced into relocation camps during World War II because the government questioned their loyalty. Endo took the matter to the Supreme Court and won her case. The Court ruled that Endo "should be given her liberty." Justice William O. Douglas proclaimed that "loyalty is a matter of the heart and mind, not of race, creed or color . . ."

Japanese Americans were locked up in internment camps during World War II.

Equal Justice for All

In the 1940s, the Supreme Court upheld an act of Congress that allowed the relocation of thousands of Japanese Americans to internment camps. The Supreme Court claimed such camps were constitutional. Later the United States government would acknowledge the injustice of the camps and apologize. Shortly after the Court made its decision in the *Ex parte Endo* case, many detained Japanese Americans were released and returned home.

Federal courts, like the Supreme Court, make up the third branch of the U.S. government. Courts use the law to settle civil disputes and to decide on the guilt or innocence of people accused of crimes.

Whether a civil dispute is between two private parties (people, companies, or organizations), between a private party and the government, or between the United States and a state or local government, both sides come before a court. Each side presents its position. The court then applies the law to the facts that have been presented and makes a decision in favor of one or the other. The courts also hold criminal trials in which witnesses present evidence and a jury or a judge delivers a verdict.

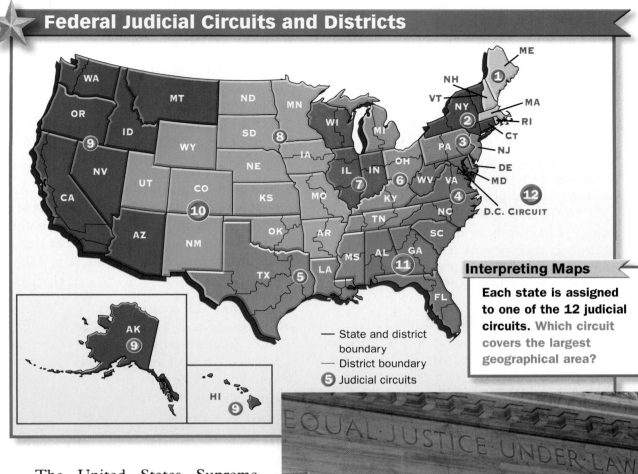

Federal Judicial Circuits and Districts

ME
NH
VT
NY
MA
RI
CT
NJ
DE
MD
D.C. CIRCUIT 12

WA
OR
ID 9
MT
ND
MN
WI
MI
SD 8
WY
NE
IA
IL 7
IN
OH
WV VA 4
PA 3
NY 2
1

NV
UT
CO 10
KS
MO
KY
TN
NC
SC

CA
AZ
NM
OK
AR
MS
AL
GA 11
LA
TX 5
FL

AK 9

HI 9

— State and district boundary
— District boundary
5 Judicial circuits

Interpreting Maps

Each state is assigned to one of the 12 judicial circuits. Which circuit covers the largest geographical area?

EQUAL JUSTICE UNDER LAW

The United States Supreme Court is at the top of the federal court system. If you visit the Court, you will see the words "Equal Justice Under Law" on the face of its marble building. Our legal system is based on this important ideal. The goal of the legal system is to treat every person the same. Under the Constitution, every person accused of breaking the law has the right to have a public trial and a lawyer. If an accused person cannot afford a lawyer, the court will appoint and pay for one. Each person is considered innocent until proven guilty and has the right to ask for a review of his or her case if, in that person's view, the courts have made a mistake.

The ideal of equal justice is difficult to achieve. Judges and juries are not free from personal prejudices or the prejudices of their communities. Poor people do not have the money to spend on the best available legal help, unlike wealthy citizens and large companies. Nonetheless, American courts try to uphold the ideal of equal justice.

Reading Check **Defining** What is the goal of the U.S. court system?

The Federal Court System

The Founders created the federal court system in Article III of the Constitution. This article established a national Supreme Court. It also gave Congress the power to establish lower federal courts.

Over the years, Congress has created two kinds of lower courts. In 1789 it passed the Judiciary Act, which established federal district courts and circuit courts of appeals. Much later, in 1891, Congress created a system of federal appeals courts. Thus, the federal court system has three levels—the district courts at the bottom, the appeals courts in the middle, and the Supreme Court at the top.

Our federal court system exists alongside 50 separate state court systems. Each state has its own laws and courts. The state courts get their powers from state constitutions and laws. You will read more about state courts in Chapter 12.

Cases Heard in Federal Courts

Jurisdiction is a court's authority to hear and decide cases. Article III of the Constitution gives the federal courts jurisdiction over eight kinds of cases.

Cases Involving the Constitution If the law in question applies to the U.S. Constitution, the case must be heard in a federal court. For example, if a person believes a constitutional right, such as freedom of speech, has been violated, that person has a right to be heard in a federal court.

A Federal Crime This U.S. Secret Service agent displays counterfeited Federal Reserve bonds. More than $2 trillion worth of fake bonds were seized in the Philippines in this incident in 2001. **What type of court—federal or state— would try this case?**

Violations of Federal Laws If the government accuses a person of a federal crime—for example, kidnapping, tax evasion, or counterfeiting—a federal court has jurisdiction. Disputes regarding the issues over which the Constitution gives the federal government control, such as patent rights or bankruptcy, also go to a federal court.

Controversies Between States Disagreements between state governments are resolved in federal courts. If Colorado and California, for example, disagree over rights to water in the Colorado River, it is a federal case.

Disputes Between Parties From Different States Lawsuits between citizens of different states also come under the federal courts. For example, Ms. Jones of Maine may bring suit in a federal court against Mr. Smith of Iowa for not fulfilling his part of a business agreement.

Suits Involving the Federal Government The U.S. government may sue someone. For example, the Defense Department might sue a company that contracted to build missile parts but did not complete the work on time. The suit would be heard in a federal court. Also, private parties can sue the government. For instance, if a mail truck hit you, you could sue the U.S. Postal Service for damages; or if the Department of Agriculture failed to pay your company for equipment it ordered, you could sue for your money.

Cases Involving Foreign Governments and Treaties Any dispute between a foreign government and either the U.S. government or an American private party is heard in a federal court. A treaty case might involve a dispute over the way the State Department interpreted a trade agreement.

Economics and You

Bankruptcy

Bankruptcy is a legal proceeding in which people or companies can be released from all or most of their debts. Because the Constitution gives Congress the right to establish bankruptcy laws, cases cannot be heard in state courts. Jurisdiction belongs exclusively to special federal bankruptcy courts. Invite a loan officer from a local bank to class to discuss the pros and cons of declaring bankruptcy.

Cases Based on Admiralty and Maritime Laws These laws concern accidents or crimes on the high seas. One recent case involved a dispute over the rights to millions of dollars in sunken treasure recovered from a shipwreck 160 miles off the coast of South Carolina.

Cases Involving U.S. Diplomats If, for example, an American diplomat working in the U.S. embassy in France is accused of breaking an American law, the case would go to a federal court.

Relation to State Courts

For most of the areas just described, federal courts have **exclusive jurisdiction,** which means that only these courts may hear and decide such cases. State courts have jurisdiction over all other matters. Most U.S. court cases involve state law and are tried in state courts.

In a few circumstances, however, a case can be heard in either a state or a federal court. In these instances, the state and federal courts have **concurrent jurisdiction,** meaning that they share jurisdiction. Either court may try crimes that violate both state and federal law. Concurrent jurisdiction also applies when citizens of different states are involved in a dispute concerning at least $50,000. In such a case, a person may sue in either a federal court or a state court. If the person being sued insists, however, the case must be tried in a federal court. Such appeals might eventually reach the United States Supreme Court.

Reading Check **Identifying** Which article of the Constitution lists the jurisdiction of federal courts?

SECTION 1 ASSESSMENT

Checking for Understanding

1. **Key Terms** Define jurisdiction. Then explain the difference between exclusive and concurrent jurisdiction.

Reviewing Main Ideas

2. **List** Name the three levels of federal courts. What is the relationship between the federal district court system and the state court system?

3. **Explain** Define what is meant by the words that are inscribed on the United States Supreme Court building: "Equal Justice Under Law."

Critical Thinking

4. **Making Inferences** Why do you think Congress established federal appeals courts in 1891?

5. **Organizing Information** On a chart like the one below, write the eight kinds of cases for which federal courts have jurisdiction and give an example of each kind of case.

Kinds of Cases								
Examples								

Analyzing Visuals

6. **Identify** Study the map of federal judicial circuits and districts on page 193. Which judicial circuit is your state in?

★ **BE AN ACTIVE CITIZEN** ★

7. **Research** Find the United States Supreme Court in the library or online. Select a famous case decided by the Supreme Court. Of the eight kinds of cases for which federal courts have jurisdiction, which kind does the case you found fall under?

How Federal Courts Are Organized

GUIDE TO READING

Main Idea

Three levels of federal courts—district courts, appeals courts, and the Supreme Court—handle a wide array of cases every year.

Key Terms

district courts, original jurisdiction, appeals courts, appellate jurisdiction, circuit, remand, opinion, precedent

Reading Strategy

Analyzing Information As you read, take notes on a graphic organizer like the one below. Why is a pyramid chart appropriate for the federal court system?

Read to Learn

• How do the three levels of federal courts differ?

• How are federal judges selected?

Americans in Action

Mary M. Schroeder used to be a judge for the Arizona Court of Appeals in Phoenix. Now she's the chief judge of the United States Court of Appeals for the Ninth Circuit. She is the first woman to serve in this post in the Ninth Circuit. This, the largest circuit, comprises the seven westernmost continental states, plus Alaska, Hawaii, and the islands of Guam and the Northern Marianas. Schroeder has come a long way from the days in the 1960s, when she was one of just six women in her law school class. Her role, and that of other female judges, says Schroeder, is "not to feminize the courts but to humanize them."

The Ninth U.S. Circuit Court of Appeals

U.S. District Courts

Judge Schroeder serves in a U.S. district court, which is part of the federal court system. The federal court system can be illustrated as a pyramid. The Supreme Court sits alone above a number of appeals courts, and has a broad base of district courts.

Most federal cases are handled in the 94 U.S. district courts. **District courts** are the federal courts where trials are held and lawsuits are begun. Every state has at least one district court, and some states have two, three, or four. All federal cases must begin in a district court, because district courts have **original jurisdiction,** the authority to hear cases for the first time. District courts are responsible for determining the facts of a case; they are the trial courts for both criminal and civil federal cases. Thus, in a criminal case, a district court will decide if a person is guilty or innocent based on the evidence presented. District courts are the only federal courts in which witnesses testify and juries hear cases and reach verdicts.

Reading Check **Explaining** What is the purpose of federal district courts?

U.S. Courts of Appeals

A large percentage of people who lose their cases in a district court appeal to the next highest level—a U.S. court of appeals. These courts are also referred to as federal appeals courts, circuit courts of appeals, or appellate courts.

The job of the appeals courts is to review decisions made in lower district courts. This is referred to as appellate jurisdiction, or the authority of a court to hear a case appealed from a lower court. Lawyers usually appeal when they think the judge in their case applied the law incorrectly, used the wrong procedures, or if new evidence turns up. Appeals courts may also review federal regulatory agency rulings, if the people or groups involved believe the agency acted unfairly.

There are 12 United States courts of appeals. Each one covers a particular geographic area called a circuit. In addition, a thirteenth appeals court, the Court of Appeals for the Federal Circuit, has nation-wide jurisdiction to hear special cases, such as those involving patent law or international trade.

Making a Decision

Appeals courts do not hold trials. Instead, these courts may decide an appeal in one of three ways: uphold the original decision, reverse that decision, or remand the case, that is, send the case back to the lower court to be tried again. A panel of three or more judges reviews the record of the case being appealed and listens to arguments from lawyers for each side. The judges then meet and make a decision by majority vote.

The judges do not decide the guilt or innocence of a defendant in a criminal case or which side should win in a civil lawsuit. They rule only on whether the defendant's rights have been protected and on whether he or she received a fair trial. In the majority of cases, the decision of the appeals court is final. In some cases, however, lawyers may appeal the decision to the U.S. Supreme Court.

Announcing the Decision

When an appeals court makes a decision, one judge writes an opinion for the court. The opinion offers a detailed explanation of the legal thinking behind the court's decision. The opinion sets a precedent for all courts and agencies within the district. A precedent gives guidance to other judges by offering a model upon

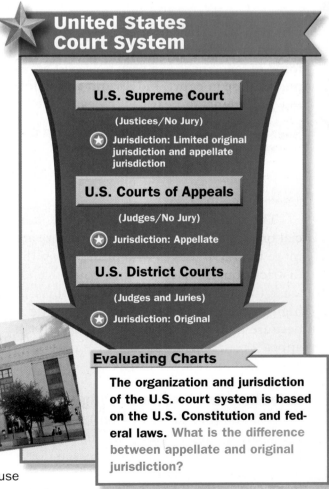

U.S. courthouse in Texas

United States Court System

U.S. Supreme Court

(Justices/No Jury)

★ Jurisdiction: Limited original jurisdiction and appellate jurisdiction

U.S. Courts of Appeals

(Judges/No Jury)

★ Jurisdiction: Appellate

U.S. District Courts

(Judges and Juries)

★ Jurisdiction: Original

Evaluating Charts

The organization and jurisdiction of the U.S. court system is based on the U.S. Constitution and federal laws. What is the difference between appellate and original jurisdiction?

John Ashcroft As attorney general, the head of the Department of Justice, and the chief law enforcement officer of the federal government, Ashcroft represents the United States in legal matters. **What court officials report to the attorney general?**

which to base their own decisions on similar cases. A precedent does not have the force of law, but it is a very powerful argument to use in court. Judges and courts follow precedents in nearly all cases.

Reading Check **Describing** What does it mean if the judge remands a case?

Federal Judges

The chief decision makers in the judicial branch are the federal judges. There are more than 550 judges who preside over the district courts. Each district court has at least two judges. Some district courts in high-population areas have more judges because there are more cases to hear. Each appeals court has from 6 to 27 judges. The Supreme Court has 9 justices.

Selection and Tenure of Judges

According to the U.S. Constitution, the president appoints judges, with the approval of the Senate. The Constitution sets forth no particular qualifications for federal judges. Presidents want to appoint judges

who share their ideas about politics and justice. Thus, they usually choose people who belong to their political party. Because judges are appointed for life, presidents view their judicial appointments as an opportunity to affect the country after they have left the White House.

When naming judges, presidents usually follow a practice called senatorial courtesy. Under this system, a president submits the name of a candidate for judicial appointment to the senators from the candidate's state before formally submitting it to the entire Senate for approval. If either or both senators object to the candidate, the president will usually withdraw the name and nominate another candidate. The practice of senatorial courtesy usually applies only to the selection of judges to the district courts and other trial courts, not to the selection of judges to courts of appeals or the Supreme Court.

Once appointed, federal judges may have their jobs for life. A judge can be removed from office only through the process of impeachment. The writers of the Constitution gave federal judges this sort of job security because they wanted judges to be able to decide cases free from public or political pressures. Federal judges know that their jobs are safe even if they make unpopular decisions.

Other Court Officials Judges do not work alone. They have help from clerks, secretaries, court reporters, probation officers, and other workers.

Each district court has magistrate judges. These officials take care of much of a judge's routine work. They issue court orders, like search and arrest warrants in federal cases. They hear preliminary evidence in a case to determine whether the case should be brought to trial. They also decide whether people who have been arrested should be held

Enforcing Laws A U.S. marshal in the West in the 1800s was often the only law enforcement officer in territories that had not yet become states. Today, marshals make sure the federal judiciary runs smoothly. **What are the duties of U.S. marshals today?**

in jail or released on bail. Magistrates may also hear minor cases.

Every federal judicial district also has a United States attorney and one or more deputies. The U.S. attorneys are government lawyers who prosecute people accused of breaking federal laws. They look into complaints of crime, prepare formal charges, and then present evidence in court. It is the U.S. attorney's job to represent the United States in civil cases in which the government is involved. U.S. attorneys are appointed to four-year terms by the president, with consent of the Senate. They report to the attorney general of the United States, who is the head of the Justice Department.

Each federal judicial district also has a United States marshal. Marshals and their staffs make arrests, collect fines, and take convicted persons to prison. They protect jurors, keep order in federal courts, and serve legal papers, including subpoenas. A subpoena is a court order requiring someone to appear in court. Marshals work for the Department of Justice. The president appoints U.S. marshals with Senate approval.

Reading Check **Defining** What is senatorial courtesy?

SECTION 2 ASSESSMENT

Checking for Understanding

1. Key Terms Use the following terms in sentences: district courts, original jurisdiction, appeals courts, appellate jurisdiction.

Reviewing Main Ideas

2. Describe What takes place in federal district courts that does not happen in federal appeals courts or in the Supreme Court?

3. Identify Explain the three rulings that are possible in a U.S. court of appeals case.

Critical Thinking

4. Making Judgments Do you agree with the practice of appointing federal judges for life? Explain your answer.

5. Making Comparisons On a Venn diagram like the one below, compare U.S. district courts to U.S. courts of appeals.

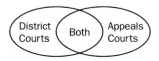

District Courts — Both — Appeals Courts

Analyzing Visuals

6. Identify Review the organization of U.S. courts on page 197. What type of jurisdiction do U.S. Courts of Appeals have? Explain what this means.

★ **BE AN ACTIVE CITIZEN** ★

7. Write Create a job description for a federal district judge. Include the qualifications you believe federal judges should have.

The United States Supreme Court

GUIDE TO READING

Main Idea
The Supreme Court's decisions have wide-ranging effects because court justices interpret the meaning of the U.S. Constitution.

Key Terms
constitutional, judicial review

Reading Strategy
Summarizing Information On a graphic organizer similar to the one below, describe the powers of the Supreme Court and give an example of each.

Read to Learn
- Who serves as Supreme Court justices?
- What are the powers of the Supreme Court?

Americans in Action

Stephen G. Breyer received President Bill Clinton's Supreme Court nomination on May 14, 1994. The Senate confirmed Breyer with an 87–9 vote. Breyer has summarized his view of the Court's role in the following way: "It is important that the public, trying to cope with the problems of the nation, state, and local community, understand that the Constitution does not resolve, and was not intended to resolve, society's problems. Rather, the Constitution provides a framework for the creation of democratically determined solutions, which protect each individual's basic liberties . . . , while securing a democratic form of government. We judges cannot insist that Americans participate in that government, but we can make clear that our Constitution depends upon it."

Justice Breyer

The Supreme Court Justices

As Justice Breyer implied, the Supreme Court exerts its influence all across the United States. The Court stands above all other courts. Its main job is to decide whether laws are allowable under the U.S. Constitution.

The Supreme Court has original jurisdiction in only two instances. It can preside over trials in cases that involve diplomats from foreign countries and in cases in which a state is involved. In all other instances, the Supreme Court hears cases that have come on appeal from lower district courts or from federal regulatory agencies. The Supreme Court is not required to hear all the cases presented to it. It carefully chooses the cases it hears. It has final authority in any case involving the Constitution, acts of Congress, and treaties with other nations. The decisions of the Court are binding on all lower courts. When the Court refuses to review a case, the decision of the lower court remains unchanged.

The Supreme Court is made of eight associate justices led by a chief justice. Congress sets this number and has the power to change it. The justices are important political decision makers. Their rulings often affect citizens as much as do presidential or congressional decisions.

The main duty of justices is to hear and rule on cases. They choose which cases to hear from among the thousands appealed to the Court each year, then decide the case itself and issue a written explanation for the decision, called the Court's opinion. The chief justice has additional duties, such as presiding over sessions and conferences at which cases are discussed.

Selection of Justices

The president appoints Supreme Court justices, with the consent of the Senate. Presidents are careful to choose nominees who are likely to be approved by the Senate. When selecting nominees, the president often gets help from the attorney general and other Justice Department officials. The president's decision may also be influenced by the American Bar Association, the largest national organization of attorneys; interest groups, such as labor and civil rights groups; and other Supreme Court justices, who may recommend or support certain candidates. Senators have usually felt that the president should have a fairly free hand in appointing new justices. Throughout history, though, the Senate has rejected many presidential nominees to the Supreme Court because of doubts about the qualifications or the legal philosophy of the persons nominated.

Background of the Justices

Supreme Court justices are always lawyers. They have had successful careers practicing or teaching law, serving as judges in lower courts, or holding other public positions prior to appointment.

Political support and agreement with the president's ideas are important factors in who gets appointed. Of course, once appointed, a justice may make rulings that the president does not like.

The first African American justice, Thurgood Marshall, joined the Court in 1967. The first female justice, Sandra Day O'Connor, was appointed in 1981.

Reading Check **Identifying** Who makes up the Supreme Court?

TIME

Political Cartoons

A Al Gore   B George W. Bush   C Supreme Court

Analyzing Visuals In 2000 Americans voted for the president on November 7, but because of an unprecedented dispute over the counting of ballots, the winner of the election was not declared until December 13. Why do you think the cartoonist picked these figures to depict in the cartoon? What does the seesaw represent?

American Biographies

John Marshall (1755–1835)

John Adams once said that his greatest act as president was "the gift of John Marshall to the people." Marshall, the fourth chief justice of the United States, hardly looked like the head of the judiciary. He often wore mismatched clothes and an old floppy hat. He rejected the gold-braided robes worn by justices at the time in favor of the simple black robes worn by justices today.

Marshall, the oldest of 15 children, grew up along the Virginia frontier. He never forgot the principles for which he fought during the American Revolution. As a soldier, he once sewed the words "Liberty or Death" onto his shirt before heading into battle. He upheld both the national government and the new Constitution.

During his 34 years as chief justice, Marshall put the judicial branch on an equal footing with the other two branches of government. He made sure the Court had the final say in all cases involving the Constitution. By overseeing more than 1,000 decisions, Marshall proved once and for all that the Constitution was the "supreme law of the land."

Powers of the Court

The powers of the Supreme Court have developed since its creation. Today the Supreme Court enjoys a great deal of power and prestige. The legislative and executive branches of government must follow the rulings of the Supreme Court. Because the Supreme Court is removed from politics and from the influences of special-interest groups, it is more likely that the parties involved in a case before the Court will get a fair hearing. The Court exercises political influence in several ways. The most important is through the use of judicial review. Additionally, the Court interprets the meaning of laws.

Judicial Review

A significant job of the Supreme Court is to decide whether laws or actions by government officials are allowed by the Constitution, or are constitutional. It does this through a process called judicial review. This is the power to say whether any federal, state, or local law or government action goes against the Constitution. If the Court decides a law is unconstitutional, it has the power to nullify, or cancel, that law or action. Former Chief Justice Charles Evans Hughes described the great power of judicial review when he said,

> ❝ We are under a constitution, but the Constitution is what the Supreme Court says it is. ❞

Marbury v. Madison The Constitution does not give the Supreme Court the power of judicial review. The Court claimed this power in 1803, when it decided the case of *Marbury* v. *Madison*. 📖 See Landmark Supreme Court Case Studies on page 211.

On his last night in office, President John Adams signed an order making William Marbury a justice of the peace. When Thomas Jefferson took office as president the next day, he told Secretary of State James Madison not to carry out Adams's order.

William Marbury took his case directly to the Supreme Court, under the provisions of the Judiciary Act of 1789. John Marshall, the chief justice, wrote an opinion stating that Marbury's claim was valid according to the Judiciary Act. However, Marshall also ruled that one part of the act gave the Court powers that it should not have and was therefore unconstitutional.

John Marshall's opinion set forth three principles of judicial review:
- The Constitution is the supreme law of the land.
- If there is a conflict between the Constitution and any other law, the Constitution rules.
- The judicial branch has a duty to uphold the Constitution. Thus, it must be able to determine when a law conflicts with the Constitution and to nullify, or cancel, unconstitutional laws.

Marbury v. *Madison* helped make the judicial branch equal in power to the executive and legislative branches. The power of judicial review is an important part of the system of checks and balances of the national government. By declaring acts of Congress or executive orders unconstitutional, the Supreme Court can check the actions of the legislative and executive branches of government. The final interpretation of the United States Constitution is reserved to the Supreme Court.

Interpreting Laws

The Court also exercises power when it interprets laws. Congress often uses very general language when it writes laws. For example, Congress passed a law that imposed a five-year prison sentence for anyone convicted of a violent crime in which he or she "uses" a gun. What does "uses" mean? What if a robber has a gun in his pocket but does not actually show it during the crime? In 1995 the Court ruled that "uses" means the person must show, fire, or at least say he has a gun.

Because a Supreme Court decision is the law of the land, a ruling like this affects police departments and courts all across the United States. Over the years the Court has interpreted many major laws.

Reading Check **Explaining** What important power did the *Marbury* case establish?

Limits on the Courts' Power

In the American system of checks and balances, there are limits on the power of the federal courts, including the Supreme Court. The Court depends on the executive branch as well as state and local officials,

The Justices Since 1869 the number of justices on the highest court in the land has been fixed at nine. They include (from left to right) Antonin Scalia, Ruth Bader Ginsburg, John Paul Stevens, David Souter, Chief Justice William Rehnquist, Clarence Thomas, Sandra Day O'Connor, Stephen Breyer, and Anthony Kennedy. **What factors might a president consider when selecting a justice?**

such as governors or police officers, to enforce its decisions. The executive branch usually follows Court rulings, but there have been exceptions. President Andrew Jackson refused to obey a Court ruling in the case of *Worcester* v. *Georgia,* in which Chief Justice John Marshall ordered the state of Georgia to stop violating federal land treaties with the Cherokee nation in 1832. The president is reported to have said: "John Marshall has made his decision; now let him carry it out."

The president did not choose to enforce this Court decision. Because most citizens agreed with President Jackson, there was no public pressure to force him to uphold the Court's decision.

Congress can get around a Court ruling by passing a new law or changing a law ruled unconstitutional by the Court. Congress and state legislatures can also try to undo Court rulings by adopting a new amendment and thus changing the Constitution. The system of checks and balances also includes the president's power to appoint justices and Congress's power to approve judicial appointments or to impeach and remove justices.

Another limit is the fact that the Court can only hear and make rulings on the cases that come to it. All cases submitted to the Court must be actual legal disputes. A person cannot simply ask the Court to decide whether a law is constitutional. The Court will not rule on a law or action that has not been challenged on appeal. The Court also accepts only cases that involve a federal question. Traditionally, the Court has refused to deal with political questions because it believes that these are issues the executive or legislative branch of the United States government should resolve. However, in the 2000 presidential election, the Supreme Court for the first time heard two cases involving the recounting of votes in the state of Florida.

Student Web Activity Visit civ.glencoe.com and click on **Student Web Activities— Chapter 8** to learn more about Supreme Court decisions.

Reading Check **Inferring** How can the president check the power of the Supreme Court?

SECTION 3 ASSESSMENT

Checking for Understanding

1. **Key Terms** Write a true statement *and* a false statement for the terms below. Beside each false statement explain why it is false.
   constitutional, judicial review

Reviewing Main Ideas

2. **Infer** The Supreme Court refuses to hear many more cases than it accepts. What happens in a case when the Supreme Court refuses to hear it?

3. **Describe** Explain how a person becomes a Supreme Court justice.

Critical Thinking

4. **Drawing Conclusions** Do you think the Supreme Court should have a police force with the power to enforce its decisions? Explain your answer.

5. **Organizing Information** On a graphic organizer like the one below, summarize the effects of the ruling in *Marbury* v. *Madison* on the judicial branch.

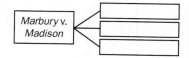

Analyzing Visuals

6. **Infer** Review the political cartoon on page 201. Explain the action the Supreme Court is taking in the cartoon. What does this mean?

★**BE AN ACTIVE CITIZEN**★

7. **Research** Log on to the Supreme Court Web site (www.supremecourtus.gov). Read the brief biographical sketches of the justices. Select one justice to read more about and write a report about the justice.

Reading a Bar Graph

Why Learn This Skill?

Reviewing long lists of statistics can involve a great deal of work. You would probably prefer to read a graph. A graph is a visual device that condenses a large body of data into a small space. You can use it to cite individual statistics quickly. You can also use it to make comparisons and spot overall trends. A commonly used type of graph is a bar graph.

Learning the Skill

To read a bar graph, follow these steps:
- Read the title of the graph. This will tell you the kind of information shown.
- Study the vertical and horizontal axes. The vertical axis runs from top to bottom along the left side of the graph. Read the names, numbers, or other labels along the vertical axis. This will identify the type of data sectioned off along the vertical axis. Do the same with the horizontal axis, which runs along the bottom of the graph.
- Study the key. Identify the meaning of colors or other symbols used in the graph.
- Note the length of individual bars to cite specific facts.
- Look at and compare the length of all the bars to identify trends or to draw conclusions.

Practicing the Skill

On a separate sheet of paper, answer the following questions about the graph on this page.

1. What information does this graph show?
2. What do the numbers on the vertical axis indicate?
3. What time period does the graph cover?
4. In which year did the Supreme Court issue the fewest opinions?
5. What change has occurred in the caseload of the Supreme Court?
6. In general, how does the number of cases appealed to the Supreme Court compare with the number it hears and decides?

SUPREME COURT CASELOAD

NUMBER OF CASES

Year	Number of cases appealed	Signed opinions
1945	1,460	134
1955	1,849	82
1965	3,256	97
1975	4,761	138
1985	5,158	146
1995	7,565	75
2000	8,965	87

YEARS

■ Number of cases appealed   ■ Signed opinions

Source: www.supremecourtus.gov

Applying the Skill

Find a bar graph in a recent newsmagazine. Cite two facts and one comparison you draw from the graph.

Practice key skills with Glencoe's
Skillbuilder Interactive Workbook CD-ROM, Level 1.

Deciding Cases at the Supreme Court

GUIDE TO READING

Main Idea

Supreme Court justices weigh many factors and go through several complex steps before making a decision.

Key Terms

docket, brief, majority opinion, dissenting opinion, concurring opinion, stare decisis

Reading Strategy

Sequencing Events As you read, on a graphic organizer similar to the one below, take notes on the steps involved in reaching a Supreme Court decision.

Steps in Court Decision

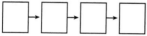

Read to Learn

• What are the steps in the Supreme Court's decision-making process?
• What factors influence Supreme Court decisions?

Americans in Action

Most Supreme Court justices are—or will be—remembered for certain issues about which they felt particularly strongly. Justice Louis Brandeis worked for social justice and democracy throughout his life, including during his 23 years of service (from 1916 until 1939) on the Supreme Court. He recognized the value of debate and dissent, as revealed by these words: "In the frank expression of conflicting opinions lies the greatest promise of wisdom in governmental action."

The scales of justice

How Cases Reach the Court

The Supreme Court decides the issues that affect all Americans. It conducts its business each year from October until the following June or July. Each month during this time, the justices spend two weeks listening to oral arguments on cases and then two weeks in recess. During recess the justices write opinions and study new cases. During the summer break they study applications for review, write opinions, and catch up on other legal work.

The Supreme Court is both a trial court and an appeals court. Two kinds of disputes have their original trials there: cases involving representatives of foreign governments and certain cases in which a state is a party.

Most cases, however, are appeals from a lower federal court or a state court. A person can ask the Court to review a lower court's decision. In addition, a lower court may sometimes ask the Court to make a ruling because it is not sure how to apply the law to a case.

Acceptance

From the many cases submitted to them, the justices make a list of cases they want to discuss more carefully. Once a week they meet to pick from this list the cases the Court will actually review. The Court will accept a case if four of the nine justices agree to do so. Accepted cases go on the Court **docket,** or calendar.

Landmark Decisions of the Supreme Court

FEDERAL POWER

- ⭐ *Marbury* v. *Madison* **(1803)** established the Supreme Court's power of judicial review

- ⭐ *McCulloch* v. *Maryland* **(1819)** ruled that in a conflict between national and state power, the national government is supreme

- ⭐ *Gibbons* v. *Ogden* **(1824)** established that Congress has sole authority to regulate interstate commerce

CIVIL LIBERTIES

- ⭐ *Brown* v. *Board of Education* **(1954)** overturned *Plessy* v. *Ferguson* **(1896),** which said African Americans could be provided "separate but equal" public facilities; began school integration

- ⭐ *Heart of Atlanta Motel, Inc.* v. *United States* **(1964)** upheld Civil Rights Act of 1964, which prohibits racial discrimination

- ⭐ *Reed* v. *Reed* **(1971)** held that a state law that discriminated against women was unconstitutional

- ⭐ *Roe* v. *Wade* **(1973)** legalized a woman's right to an abortion under certain circumstances

FIRST AMENDMENT RIGHTS

- ⭐ *Brandenburg* v. *Ohio* **(1969)** expanded the scope of political speech by protecting all political speech unless it is linked to immediate lawless behavior

- ⭐ *Near* v. *Minnesota* **(1931)** ruled against censorship of information, defining "prior restraint" of written material as unconstitutional

- ⭐ *DeJonge* v. *Oregon* **(1937)** reinforced peaceable assembly and association protection of the First Amendment

- ⭐ *Engle* v. *Vitale* **(1962)** held that a public school district's practice of starting the day with prayer violates the establishment clause

- ⭐ *United States* v. *Eichman* **(1990)** struck down Federal Flag Protection Act; held that flag burning is expressive speech

RIGHTS OF THE ACCUSED

- ⭐ *Gideon* v. *Wainwright* **(1963)** declared that a person accused of a major crime had the right to legal counsel during a trial

- ⭐ *Miranda* v. *Arizona* **(1966)** ruled that at the time of arrest suspects cannot be questioned until informed of their rights

Evaluating Charts

These decisions helped determine the rights of citizens. What earlier decision did *Brown* v. *Board of Education* overturn?

Official seal of the Supreme Court

Each year the Court gets more than 7,000 applications. Of these, it selects fewer than 200 cases to hear. The Court can review just about any kind of case. Usually the justices take cases that involve important constitutional issues, such as freedom of speech, equal protection of the laws, or civil liberties. They also tend to select cases that involve legal, rather than political, issues, as well as those that affect the entire country rather than just the individuals or groups directly involved.

Steps in Decision Making

Every case the Supreme Court accepts goes through a series of steps: written arguments, oral arguments, conference, opinion writing, and announcement.

Written Arguments

Once the Court takes a case, the lawyers for each side prepare a **brief.** This is a written document that explains one side's position on the case. The justices then study the briefs.

Oral Arguments

Next, lawyers for each side present oral arguments. Each side gets only 30 minutes to summarize its case. The justices often ask the lawyers very tough questions about the case.

Conference

On Fridays the justices get together to make their first decisions about the cases they have been studying. These meetings take place in secret; no audience is present and no meeting minutes are kept. The chief justice presides over the discussion of the case. A majority—at least five votes, when all nine justices are participating—decides a case. At least six justices must be present for a decision.

Opinion Writing

Once the Court has reached a decision on a case, one justice gets the job of writing the majority opinion. A **majority opinion** presents the views of the majority of the justices on a case. The opinion states the facts of the case, announces the ruling, and explains the Court's reasoning in reaching the decision. Written opinions are very important. They set a precedent for lower courts to follow in future cases, and they also communicate the Court's view to Congress, the president, interest groups, and the public. This is also an important step because there is still time for justices to change their minds. An opinion may influence a justice to change his or her vote.

Besides the majority opinion, the Court may issue four other types of opinions. In a unanimous opinion, all the justices vote the same way. A justice who disagrees with the majority's decision may write a **dissenting opinion.** Sometimes two, three, or even four justices write their own dissenting opinions. A justice who votes with the majority, but for different reasons, may write a **concurring opinion.**

Announcement

When the opinion writing is completed, the Court announces its decision. Printed copies of the opinion go to waiting news reporters, and the opinion is placed on the Court's Web site. The Supreme Court and other courts around the country use the written opinions to guide their decisions regarding new cases.

Reading Check **Concluding** Why must the Supreme Court print its opinions?

Reasons for Court Decisions

Many factors, such as precedents, the social atmosphere in the country, and the justice's own legal and personal views, influence justices when they decide a case that comes before the Court.

Fact **Fiction** Folklore

Do Supreme Court justices always get along?

In 1924 Justice James McReynolds refused to appear in the official Supreme Court photo with Justice Louis D. Brandeis. McReynolds disliked Brandeis so much that he would leave the room when Brandeis spoke! Chief Justice William Howard Taft considered McReynolds "a continual grouch."

Impact of the *Brown* Decision Segregated facilities, such as separate entrances at a movie theater in Belzoni, Mississippi, were declared unconstitutional in 1954. **Why must the Supreme Court react to changes in American values?**

Thurgood Marshall argued the *Brown* case before the Court.

The Law

The law is supposed to be the most important influence on a justice's decisions. Justices look at the Constitution when deciding a case. They consider how the language applies to the facts of the case. In doing this, they rely heavily on precedents, because our legal system places great importance on deciding cases consistently. A guiding principle for all judges is called stare decisis, a Latin term, which means "let the decision stand." By following precedent, courts make the law predictable.

At the same time, the law needs to be flexible to adapt to changing times. Social conditions, public attitudes, and technology change over the years. As the highest court in the land, the Supreme Court is in a position to overrule outdated precedents.

Social Conditions

Although the Supreme Court is somewhat protected from public and political pressures, the social situation can also influence Court decisions. When social conditions change, the Court may make new interpretations of the law. Justices, like all citizens, know what people around the country are thinking about important social issues.

In the 1890s, many restaurants, schools, and trains were segregated, which means that separate areas were marked for whites and African Americans. In Louisiana, Homer Plessy, an African American, decided to sit in a section of a train marked "For Whites Only." When Plessy refused to move, he was arrested and convicted of violating Louisiana's segregation law. When Plessy appealed his case to the Supreme Court, the Court upheld the Louisiana law as constitutional in *Plessy* v. *Ferguson*. The Court ruled that the equal protection clause of the Fourteenth Amendment permitted "separate but equal" facilities for whites and African Americans. This decision permitted governments across the nation to justify racial segregation.

However, by the 1950s, society's views on racial segregation were beginning to change. In 1954, in the case of *Brown* v. *Board of Education of Topeka, Kansas,* the Court overturned the precedent of "separate but equal." The justices ruled that racially separate schools are unequal simply because

TIME

Political Cartoons

and it seems to be diverted toward money and
time. Making the world a more convenient
place to live was a collaboration among several

Schnei
ing

Analyzing Visuals Fast-moving national and state governments often make decisions and policies that "bump up" against the slower-moving Supreme Court. What does the figure on the motorcycle represent? What is the overall message of the cartoon?

they are separate. The unanimous opinion of the Court found that segregation was a violation of the equal protection clause of the Fourteenth Amendment. 📖 See the **Supreme Court Case Summaries** in the Appendix.

Legal Views

Justices have varying views of the law and the proper role of the courts in our society. Some justices, for example, believe that the Court should be very active and hear many different kinds of cases. Others believe that the Court should hesitate to use the power of judicial review to promote new ideas or policies.

Personal Beliefs

Finally, justices are human beings. Each sees the world based on his or her own life experiences. Justice Benjamin Cardozo once said, "We may try to see things as objectively as we please. Nonetheless, we can never see them with any eyes except our own."

Reading Check **Summarizing** Why are precedents important in Supreme Court decision making?

SECTION 4 ASSESSMENT

Checking for Understanding

1. **Key Terms** Define the following terms and use them in sentences that relate to the Supreme Court: docket, brief, majority opinion, dissenting opinion, concurring opinion, stare decisis.

Reviewing Main Ideas

2. **Identify** Describe the steps that every Supreme Court case must follow.

3. **Recall** Most of the cases that reach the Supreme Court are what kinds of cases?

Critical Thinking

4. **Drawing Conclusions** Of all the factors that influence justices when they make a decision, which do you think is the most significant? Explain your answer.

5. **Categorizing Information** On a web diagram like the one below, categorize the factors that influence Supreme Court justices when making decisions.

Influences on Supreme Court Decisions

Analyzing Visuals

6. **Infer** Review the chart on page 207. Which ruling guarantees you the right to be informed of your rights if you are arrested?

★ **BE AN ACTIVE CITIZEN** ★

7. **Interview** Read more about *Brown* v. *Board of Education of Topeka, Kansas.* Summarize the facts in the case. Interview someone who was an adult in 1954 about how they think the *Brown* decision changed American society.

Landmark Supreme Court
Case Studies

Marbury v. Madison

President Adams spent his last night in office signing commissions.

Background of the Case

Democratic-Republican Thomas Jefferson won the presidential election of 1800. During the months before Jefferson was sworn into office, congressional supporters of outgoing Federalist president John Adams approved 58 new appointees to the federal courts. President Adams signed the commissions—official papers allowing the new judges to assume their positions—on his last night in office.

It was the duty of John Marshall, Adams's secretary of state, to deliver the 58 commissions, but he failed to deliver all of them. William Marbury and three other appointees who had not received their commissions petitioned the new secretary of state, James Madison, to deliver them. President Jefferson, who wanted to repeal all of Adams's last-minute judgeships, told Madison not to deliver the papers. The four waiting appointees then asked the Supreme Court to order Madison to deliver their commissions.

The Decision

If the Court agreed with Marbury, Jefferson would likely ignore the order. If the Court ruled for Madison, it would appear frightened of the

By the early 1800s, the role of the judiciary branch was unclear and its influence small. How did the Supreme Court achieve equal footing with the legislative and executive branches?

executive branch. Either choice would further weaken the judiciary. Chief Justice John Marshall issued the decision on February 24, 1803.

Marshall agreed that Marbury's rights had been violated and that he should receive his commission. For Marbury to receive his commission, a writ of mandamus, or a court order to perform a certain action, had to be issued. Although Congress gave the Court such authority in Section 13 of the Judiciary Act of 1789, Marshall wrote that the Court's "authority to issue writs of mandamus to public officers appears not to be warranted by the Constitution." He further asserted that it was the duty of the judicial branch "to say what the law is."

Why It Matters

The Supreme Court claimed its right to declare acts of the legislative and executive branches unconstitutional for the first time in *Marbury* v. *Madison*. By doing this, it defined its role as the final authority on what the Constitution means. Each year, the Supreme Court strikes down numerous state and local laws. It rarely strikes down congressional laws, though.

Analyzing the Court Decision

1. Why is *Marbury* v. *Madison* a landmark Court case?
2. Why did the Supreme Court refuse to issue writs of mandamus?

Assessment & Activities

Review to Learn

Section 1

- The Founders created the federal court system in Article III of the Constitution. This article establishes the Supreme Court.
- Over the years, Congress created the federal district courts and the appeals courts.

Section 2

- Most federal cases are held in U.S. district courts.
- People who lose in federal district courts may appeal to federal appeals courts.

Section 3

- The Supreme Court includes nine justices. All are appointed by presidents.
- An important job of the Supreme Court is to decide whether laws are permitted under the U.S. Constitution.

Section 4

- Every case the Supreme Court accepts goes through certain steps.

FOLDABLES™
Study Organizer

Using Your Foldables Study Organizer
Using your completed foldable, write at least five statements that compare or contrast the federal courts with the Supreme Court.

Reviewing Key Terms

Write the key term that matches each definition below.

1. an earlier model upon which judges may base decisions
2. the lowest level of courts of the federal judiciary
3. the power of the Supreme Court to say whether any federal, state, or local law is unconstitutional
4. a court's authority to hear and decide cases
5. the opinion written by a justice who votes with the majority but for different reasons
6. a Latin term, which means "let the decision stand"
7. a law that is allowed by the Constitution
8. the written document a lawyer who is arguing before the Supreme Court prepares
9. an order to send a case back to a lower court
10. the written opinion by a justice who disagrees with the majority's decision

Reviewing Main Ideas

11. Describe how the current federal court system originated.
12. Name at least four kinds of cases over which federal courts have jurisdiction.
13. How do federal district courts and federal appeals courts differ?
14. What three rulings can result from a case in a federal appeals court?
15. How does someone become a Supreme Court justice?
16. What is the significance of the case of *Marbury* v. *Madison?*
17. What two kinds of disputes have their original trials in the Supreme Court?
18. Describe the steps in the Supreme Court's decision-making process.

Critical Thinking

19. **Analyzing Information** How is *Plessy* v. *Ferguson* related to *Brown* v. *Board of Education of Topeka, Kansas?*

20. **Cause and Effect** On a chart like the one below, explain some of the factors that influence Supreme Court decisions.

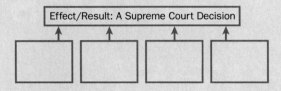

Effect/Result: A Supreme Court Decision

Practicing Skills

21. **Reading a Bar Graph** Look at the bar graph below. About how many laws did the Warren Court overturn? Which court overturned the most state and local laws?

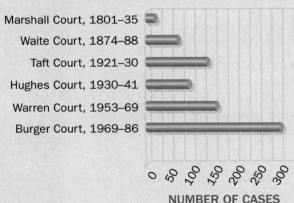

STATE AND LOCAL LAWS OVERTURNED BY SELECTED SUPREME COURTS

Marshall Court, 1801–35
Waite Court, 1874–88
Taft Court, 1921–30
Hughes Court, 1930–41
Warren Court, 1953–69
Burger Court, 1969–86

0 50 100 150 200 250 300
NUMBER OF CASES

$ Economics Activity

22. In the library or online, research the case of *Gibbons* v. *Ogden* (1824). In what ways do Americans feel the economic effect of that decision today?

Analyzing Visuals

23. Review the chart on page 207. Why was the *Brandenburg* case important?

★ CITIZENSHIP COOPERATIVE ACTIVITY ★

24. Jury duty is a responsibility of United States citizenship. Working with about two other students, find two or three people who have served on juries and interview them. Ask them to recall their impressions of the experience.

Technology Activity

25. Log on to the Internet and search for a Web site that has information about recent cases heard by the Supreme Court. Write a summary of the ruling. Do you agree with the ruling? Explain your opinion.

The Princeton Review

Standardized Test Practice

Directions: Choose the *best* answer to the following question.

Which court holds jurisdiction for the following court case?

The government of New York has sued a company in New Jersey for not following through on the terms and deadlines of a contract signed last year. The contract is worth more than $50,000.

F the U.S. Supreme Court
G a U.S. court of appeals
H a U.S. district court
J a special federal court

Test-Taking Tip

Read the question carefully. Recall that jurisdiction is a court's authority to hear and decide cases.

Political Parties and Interest Groups

Why It Matters

As American citizens, each of us has certain rights and responsibilities—to participate in political parties, vote, and express our opinions on government policies. To ensure the continuation of democracy in this country, Americans must constantly involve themselves in their government.

Use the **American History Primary Source Document Library CD-ROM** to find primary sources about political parties and interest groups.

★ BE AN ACTIVE CITIZEN ★

Participate in an ongoing activity that demonstrates your American citizenship. For example, volunteer to work in a nursing home on Saturdays, help out at a shelter for the homeless, or work with a peer counseling group. Give ongoing reports of your experiences to the class.

George W. Bush campaigns for the presidency in California.

9

Political Parties and Politics

★ CITIZENSHIP AND YOU ★

The Constitution does not mention political parties, but the first ones formed during the early days of our nation. Today the United States has several political parties. Find out how political parties in your state nominate candidates for office. Then interview neighbors who are active in a political party. Prepare a brochure using the information you find.

To learn more about American political parties, view the *Democracy in Action* video lesson 16: Political Parties.

FOLDABLES™
Study Organizer

Organizing Information Study Foldable *Make the following foldable to help you organize your thoughts and notes about political parties and politics.*

Step 1 *Fold a sheet of paper in half from side to side.*

Fold it so the left edge is about ½ inch from the right edge.

Step 2 *Turn the paper and fold it into thirds.*

Reading and Writing *As you read the chapter, write what you learn about the development, organization, and role of political parties today under the appropriate tabs.*

Step 3 *Unfold and cut the top layer only along both folds.*

This will make three tabs.

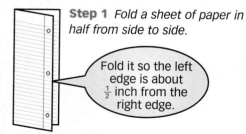

Step 4 *Label as shown.*

POLITICAL PARTIES

Development | Organization | Role Today

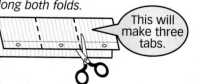

Students rally for presidential candidate Al Gore in Arkansas in 2000. ▶

CIVICS Online

Chapter Overview Visit the *Civics Today* Web site at civ.glencoe.com and click on **Chapter Overviews— Chapter 9** to preview chapter information.

Development of American Political Parties

GUIDE TO READING

Main Idea
Shortly after our nation's birth, political leaders formed parties in an attempt to gain control of decision making in the government.

Key Terms
political party, two-party system, third party, platform, plank

Reading Strategy
Organizing Information
As you read, complete a web diagram similar to the one below by writing in political parties that have developed in the United States. Also include the time period in which each party originated.

Political Parties in the United States

Read to Learn
• How have political parties formed throughout U.S. history?
• What are the differences between the two major parties?

Americans in Action

It was the hope of some Founders of our nation, George Washington in particular, that parties—or factions, as he thought of them—would not develop. During Washington's presidency, his secretary of state, Thomas Jefferson, and his secretary of the treasury, Alexander Hamilton, had some major differences. Those two men became, in essence, the founders of today's political parties. In May of 1792, President Washington wrote to Jefferson: "How unfortunate, and how much is it to be regretted then, that whilst we are encompassed on all sides with avowed enemies and insidious friends, that internal dissensions should be harrowing and tearing our vitals."

Gilbert Stuart's painting of Washington

The Two-Party System

Despite the wishes of our first president, political parties formed. A **political party** is an association of voters with broad, common interests who want to influence or control decision making in government by electing the party's candidates to public office. Party members usually share beliefs about politics and about the proper role of government. They pick candidates who agree with those beliefs. Then they try to persuade voters to support these candidates. In the United States anyone can join a political party. It is not necessary to pay dues, take a test, or even vote. It is only necessary to declare yourself a member of the party.

During most of American history there have been two major political parties. Other parties have sometimes run in elections, but they have seldom won. For these reasons, the United States is said to have a **two-party system.**

The Republican and Democratic Parties have been the two major parties for many years. Both parties have millions of supporters around the country. In fact, they have so much strength that since 1860 one or the other has always held the presidency. Together they have held most seats in Congress as well.

Roots of the Two-Party System

The U.S. Constitution says nothing about political parties. In fact, many delegates to the Constitutional Convention were against them. Despite Washington's warning, however, two rival political groups formed shortly after he became president. Secretary of State Thomas Jefferson led one group, and Secretary of the Treasury Alexander Hamilton led the other. They disagreed strongly about how the U.S. government should operate.

Hamilton, like Jefferson, favored protection for individual rights. Hamilton believed that individual rights were at risk if the government was too weak, so he favored a strong national government. He especially wanted the president to have more power. Jefferson wanted to limit the power of the national government. He argued for more power for state governments, which were closer to the citizens.

The Democratic Party At first Jefferson's group was called the Democratic-Republican Party. Then, in 1828, under the leadership of Andrew Jackson, the Democratic-Republican Party split and Jackson aligned with the **Democratic Party.** From 1800 to 1816 Jefferson's party grew stronger, while Hamilton's group, the **Federalist Party,** faded away. From 1816 to 1828 the Democratic-Republicans faced no serious challenges. In 1830 a new party, the **Whigs** (or National Republicans), rose to compete with the newly named Democrats. The Whigs and the Democrats remained the two major parties until the 1850s.

The Republican Party In 1854 a group of breakaway Democrats and Whigs, many of whom opposed slavery, formed the **Republican Party.** It soon replaced the Whig Party, which had lost most of its support during the growing national dispute over slavery. In 1860 Abraham Lincoln won election as the first Republican president. Since then, Republicans and Democrats have been the major parties in our system.

Reading Check **Explaining** Why did Washington not want political parties to form?

Third Parties

Throughout American history, third parties have arisen to influence politics. Because these parties almost always challenge the two major parties, they are called **third parties.** No third party has ever won a presidential election, and third parties rarely win other major elections, so these parties are also called minor parties. Third parties can, however, affect the outcome of elections, and they may influence government and social policy. Although third parties differ, they do share one thing: they believe that neither of the major parties is meeting certain needs.

Two third parties, the **Populists** and the **Progressives,** did have some impact on American politics. The members of the

Campaign bandanna for the Progressive, or Bull Moose, Party

Other Party Systems Members of India's multiparty legislature commemorate India's fiftieth anniversary of independence from Great Britain in 1997 (right), while Vietnam's legislators, representing the Communist Party, cast their votes for the country's most powerful post of party general secretary in 2001 (left). **What type of party system does Vietnam have?**

Populist Party of the 1890s included a combination of farmers and laborers. The Populists called for the direct election of senators and an eight-hour working day. Although they never won the presidency, the two major parties adopted many of their ideas.

The Progressive, or Bull Moose, Party split from the Republicans in 1912, when Theodore Roosevelt, a former Republican president, ran for president as a Progressive. Roosevelt took so many votes away from the Republican candidate, William Howard Taft, that the Democratic nominee, Woodrow Wilson, won the election. In this way Roosevelt and his Progressive Party played a "spoiler" role in the election.

Single-Issue Parties

Some third parties arise not to win elections but to promote a social, economic, or moral issue. For example, the Prohibitionist Party, formed in 1872, wanted to ban the sale of alcohol. The party's candidates did not expect to be elected. Instead, they used election campaigns to try to influence citizens to accept the party's ideas about drinking alcohol. They hoped to persuade legislators to pass laws against the sale of alcoholic beverages. A single-issue party usually doesn't last long. It may fade away when the issue is no longer important or if a major party adopts the issue.

Ideological Parties

Some third parties—called ideological parties—focus on changing society in major ways. For example, the Socialist Labor Party and the Communist Party USA support government ownership of factories, transportation, resources, farmland, and other businesses. The Libertarian Party wants to cut the size of the U.S. government in order to increase individual freedoms. The Green Party opposes the power of corporations and favors decision making at the grassroots level.

Independent Candidates

Sometimes third parties form around well-known individuals who cannot get support from one of the two major parties. Such parties usually do not survive beyond the defeat of their candidate.

In 1980 John Anderson, a member of Congress from Illinois, lost the Republican presidential nomination and ran as the candidate of a campaign organization he created called the Independent Party. In 1992 wealthy business leader H. Ross Perot challenged both major party candidates as an independent. Perot ran again in 1996, under the banner of the Reform Party.

Third parties rarely win major elections because of the United States's two-party tradition. While the names of the Republican and Democratic candidates are automatically placed on the ballot in many states, third-party candidates must obtain a large number of voter signatures in order to get on the ballot. Also, nearly all elected officials in the United States are selected by single-member districts. This means that only one candidate wins each district. Because most voters support the major parties, the winners are usually Democrats and Republicans. Third parties also often have trouble raising enough money to compete in campaigns against the major-party candidates.

✓**Reading Check** **Describing** Why do single-issue parties form?

Other Party Systems

Political parties are not unique to the United States. They exist in most countries. Two-party systems, however, are rare. The role that political parties play differs with each nation's political system.

Most democracies have multiparty systems. In these systems, three or more parties compete for control of the government. For example, Canada has 3 major parties, Germany has 5, and Israel has more than 20. In these countries, voters face many options on Election Day. The parties all represent different ideas about government. In multiparty systems, one party rarely wins enough support to control the government, so several parties often must work together. This is a situation that may easily break down and become politically unstable because of so many competing interests of the parties.

In a one-party system, the party and the government are nearly the same thing. In the People's Republic of China, for instance, only one party—the Communist Party—is allowed to exist, and only Communist candidates may run for office. As a result, only Communist Party members fill government positions, where they carry out the party's orders. Elections are an empty exercise since there are no rival candidates. One-party systems, obviously, are not democratic systems.

One-party systems also exist in some non-Communist nations. The government of Iran, for example, is dominated by religious

American Biographies

H. Ross Perot (1930–)
In 1992 H. Ross Perot sensed American anger over high unemployment and the huge national debt. Perot, a self-made billionaire from Texas, founded the Reform Party and promised to improve the economy. Perot, who made his fortune in computer technology, had the money to finance his campaign. He also had "name recognition." In 1969 Perot started a crusade to free American prisoners of war (POWs) in Vietnam. In 1978 he organized a commando raid to free two of his employees from an Iranian jail. When voters went to the polls in 1992, 19 percent cast their ballots for Perot. Because many Republicans voted for Perot, some people say he cost George H.W. Bush reelection as president.

leaders. Muslim leaders control the Islamic Republican Party. All major opposition parties have been outlawed or are inactive.

Today's Major Parties

Competing political parties are a necessary part of democratic government. They are a key link between citizens and their elected officials. They give voters a choice among candidates and ideas. They help make elections meaningful.

A basic difference between the major parties is their belief in how much the government should be involved in the lives of Americans. For example, the Democrats tend to believe that the federal government should be more directly involved in regulating the economy and in providing housing, income, education, and jobs for the poor. The Republicans tend to believe that if they help the nation's economy grow, poor people will have a better chance of finding jobs and meeting their needs on their own. They favor less government regulation of the economy as the best way to promote the growth of production.

Sometimes it can be difficult to tell the difference between the two parties. Both try to appeal to as many voters as possible because ignoring large numbers of voters may lead to defeat on Election Day. By adopting moderate and mainstream positions and avoiding extreme or radical positions, the major parties hope to attract the largest number of votes and win elections. The parties are also similar because the majority of American people generally agree about many political and social issues.

One way to find out how the parties differ is to read the political document, or platform, that each party writes at its presidential nominating convention, held every four years. The **platform** is a series of statements expressing the party's principles, beliefs, and positions on election issues. Each individual part of the platform is called a **plank.** The platform communicates to voters what the party claims it will do if it wins the White House.

✓ Reading Check **Explaining** Why do the two major parties seem so similar?

SECTION 1 ASSESSMENT

Checking for Understanding

1. **Key Terms** Write sentences or short paragraphs about political parties in which you use the following terms: political party, two-party system, third party, platform, plank.

Reviewing Main Ideas

2. **Contrast** Describe the basic differences between the views of Thomas Jefferson and Alexander Hamilton regarding how government should operate.

3. **Explain** In what way have third parties been influential in U.S. politics?

Critical Thinking

4. **Making Inferences** Which view of how government should operate—Jefferson's or Hamilton's—is most evident in the United States today? Explain.

5. **Making Comparisons** In a chart like the one below, describe the differences between the Democratic and Republican Parties.

Democratic Party	Republican Party

Analyzing Visuals

6. **Infer** Examine the campaign party artifact on page 219. What party does it represent? Which type of third party described in the text do you think this party was? Explain your answer.

★ **BE AN ACTIVE CITIZEN** ★

7. **Research** Make a list of major local and state government offices where you live. Name the people who hold each office along with their political party.

Organization of American Political Parties

GUIDE TO READING

Main Idea

Both the Republicans and the Democrats have highly organized political organizations at the local, state, and national levels.

Key Terms

national committee, national party chairperson, delegate, caucus, precinct, ward, county chairperson, political machine

Reading Strategy

Summarizing Information As you read, use a chart like the one below to help you take notes about the three levels of political party organizations.

National	State	Local

Read to Learn

• How are local, state, and national political party committees organized?

• How do political machines sometimes emerge?

Americans in Action

Gary Risley, a corporate lawyer, was 38 years old when he attended the Republican National Convention in 1996. It was his first time serving as a delegate. After working on his candidate's platform committee, Risley looked forward to convention week, when he could listen to good speeches and nominate "the next president of the United States." As a delegate, Risley also considered it his job to return home and "spread the message" about the issues and his chosen candidates.

The Republican National Convention of 1996

National Party Organization

Both major political parties today hold national conventions like the one Gary Risley attended. In fact, the Democratic and Republican Parties are organized at the local, state, and national levels. These different levels are only loosely tied together. There is no chain of command that lets the national organization control state or local party leaders. All the levels do, however, have roughly the same political beliefs, and they are united in their ultimate goal—to help the party win as many offices as possible.

Each party has a national committee made up of representatives from every state. This committee helps raise funds for presidential elections and organizes the party's national convention. A national party chairperson runs the committee. The chairperson's main job is to manage the office, direct the committee staff, and lead fund-raising efforts.

In recent years the national committees of both parties have become increasingly active. For example, they have created Web sites with information about candidates and positions. They recruit candidates, teach them effective campaign strategies, and give them some campaign funds. They also create television and radio advertisements.

Sandra Valasquez used to be on the shy side, but that was before she joined the Oregon Latino Voter Registration Education Project in 1998. These days, the 17-year-old high school junior from Salem, Oregon, is front and center as she pounds the pavement to get out the minority vote.

Whenever Valasquez has free time, she's out talking up the value of the democratic process. She canvasses the community for potential new voters—going to colleges and meeting centers with brochures and registration forms in hand.

"I think a lot of the time people don't think of voting as a positive thing," Valasquez says. "They always complain about the government, but most of those people aren't even registered. If you want to get your voice out there, you have to register and vote."

Evidently, that message is beginning to sink in: the Oregon Latino Voter Registration Education Project signed up 5,000 new Latino voters before the 2000 presidential election. If you would like to get involved in registering people to vote in your community, contact your local board of elections.

Sandra Valasquez from Oregon

A key job of the national committee is to hold the national convention every four years. At the convention, party **delegates** from all the states nominate candidates for president and vice president. Each party chooses its delegates through a combination of presidential primary elections and **caucuses,** or meetings, of state and local party organizations.

The delegates' first job is to write the platform. This task can cause conflict because each party includes members with a wide range of positions on key issues. In 1968, for example, Democratic delegates fought long and hard over a plank calling for an end to the Vietnam War.

Once the platform has been prepared and approved, delegates nominate the party's presidential candidate. There are speeches and demonstrations supporting the candidate. Historically, conventions were exciting and suspenseful events where delegates from around the country decided upon their presidential candidate. The conventions were a grand spectacle on television. Today the increasing use of early primary elections, where voters narrow down the list of candidates, has caused the nomination for president to be almost entirely decided by the time of the convention.

Both parties also have House and Senate campaign committees made up of members of Congress. These committees work to help elect and reelect party members as senators and representatives.

The congressional campaign committees have been growing more important because they have begun raising large amounts of money. The money—mostly from private sources—goes to the party's congressional candidates and to state and local party organizations.

State and Local Organization

Each party has 50 state committees or organizations. In some states the parties are well organized, have large staffs, and spend a lot of money each year. In others the organization is weak. State committees focus on electing party candidates to state offices—governor, attorney general, state legislators, and others. They also work to elect their party's candidates for national offices.

Local party organizations consist of thousands of city, town, and county committees across the country. These committees include people elected by their fellow party members.

Precinct Captains

Each city or county is divided into election districts or precincts. A **precinct** is a geographic area that contains a specific number of voters. A precinct may consist of an entire small town or, in a large city, a group of adjacent neighborhoods. All voters in a precinct cast their ballots at the same voting place.

For each precinct, the local party has a volunteer precinct captain, whose job is to organize other party volunteers during campaigns and encourage voters on Election Day. The volunteers distribute leaflets, register voters, and try to convince voters to support the party's candidates.

Several adjoining precincts make up a larger election unit called a **ward.** Party members in each ward typically elect a volunteer to represent the ward at the local party's next level of organization—the county committee.

County Committees

Counties are the largest political units in a state. There are more than 3,000 of them across the country. Both major parties have county committees. A **county chairperson,** who runs the committee, often has a great deal of political power in the county. If the county is large, state party leaders such as the governor or a U.S. senator may consult with the county chairperson about important appointments, such as judgeships.

Local party people are very important. Higher-level party leaders depend on precinct and ward leaders to build the party at the "grassroots," or neighborhood, level. These local leaders have to know what issues their neighbors are worried about and keep track of how local political sentiment is running. At election time they must "deliver

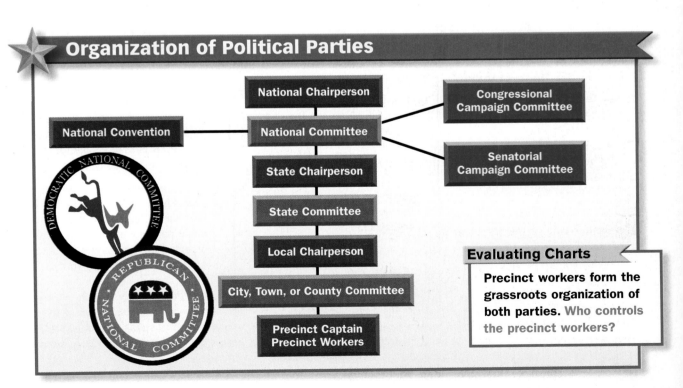

Organization of Political Parties

National Convention

National Chairperson

National Committee

Congressional Campaign Committee

Senatorial Campaign Committee

State Chairperson

State Committee

Local Chairperson

City, Town, or County Committee

Precinct Captain
Precinct Workers

Evaluating Charts

Precinct workers form the grassroots organization of both parties. Who controls the precinct workers?

the vote" for party candidates at every level of government, from school board member to president of the United States.

Political Machines

At times in the past some local party organizations became so powerful that, year after year, their candidates swept almost every election. Such a strong party organization is called a **political machine.** One of the most famous—and notorious—political machines was New York City's Tammany Hall. This organization ruled New York City in the late 1800s and early 1900s. Its leader, William Marcy "Boss" Tweed, and his friends grew rich from bribes and kickbacks given by building contractors seeking to do business with the city. Eventually, many members of the Tweed ring ended up in prison.

At a time in American history when no social service agencies existed to help poor people and immigrants, political machines often served a useful purpose, though. The machines provided needy citizens with jobs, food, fuel, and help with medical care

in return for their votes. Today most people think of political machines as harmful. When one party is in power for too long, it may become unresponsive to the needs of the community. Political leaders are less accountable to citizens when the leaders do not have to worry about getting reelected.

Joining a Political Party

You don't need to join a political party in the United States to vote. However, political parties offer every citizen a great way to get involved in politics. Political parties do everything they can to attract members, and they welcome whomever wishes to belong. Party membership involves no duties or obligations other than voting. If a member of a party chooses to do more, then he or she may contribute money, do volunteer work, or participate in other activities, especially during election campaigns. The parties depend on citizen involvement to accomplish their goals.

Reading Check **Concluding** Why is it important to build grassroots support for a party?

SECTION 2 ASSESSMENT

Checking for Understanding

1. **Key Terms** Explain the following terms by using each in a complete sentence: national committee, national party chairperson, delegate, caucus, precinct, ward, county chairperson, political machine.

Reviewing Main Ideas

2. **Describe** What is the first order of business for delegates at a national convention?

3. **Explain** What do congressional campaign committees do? Why have congressional campaign committees become more important in recent years?

Critical Thinking

4. **Drawing Conclusions** Why do you think citizens in the past allowed political machines to exist?

5. **Categorizing Information** On a web diagram like the one below, categorize the structure and functions of political party organizations at all levels.

Analyzing Visuals

6. **Describe** Review the organization of political parties on page 225. According to this diagram, what body is responsible for the party's national convention?

★ BE AN ACTIVE CITIZEN ★

7. **Interview** Choose one of the two major parties. Research its local organization. Who is the precinct, ward, or county chairperson? Set up an appointment to interview that person, or with your teacher's permission, invite the person to speak to your class.

Role of Political Parties Today

GUIDE TO READING

Main Idea
Although selecting candidates and running campaigns are the most important roles of political parties, they also serve other significant functions.

Key Terms
nomination, direct primary, closed primary, open primary, plurality, runoff primary, petition

Reading Strategy
Summarizing Information As you read, write the roles performed by political parties in a chart similar to the one below.

Roles of Political Parties					

Read to Learn
- How do political parties nominate and campaign for candidates?
- What other roles are performed by political parties?

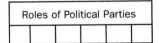 **Americans in Action**

It isn't only elected officials who make a career out of politics. Terry McAuliffe is certainly a career politician, even though he has never held an elected position. He has, however, held many appointed positions. In fact, he has worked for every Democratic presidential candidate since Jimmy Carter's reelection campaign in 1980. McAuliffe's personal business experience gives him special expertise in finance and business. As a result, he has served as finance director for the Democratic National Committee and for various individual presidential and congressional campaigns. As National Chair of the Democratic National Committee, McAuliffe plays a vital, although somewhat behind-the-scenes, role in national politics.

Terry McAuliffe

Nominating Candidates

The people who make up political parties, like Terry McAuliffe, play an important role in the American system of government. They select candidates for office. They keep people informed and interested in the issues and the candidates. They try to see that party members elected to office do a good job. They keep an eye on the opposition party, publicly criticizing many of its actions. They also act as a link between different branches and levels of government. The parties carry out these activities throughout the year. They are busiest, however, at election time. Political parties are the only organizations that select and offer candidates for public office. They do this through the nomination process.

Primary Elections

Today major parties in all states nominate candidates at all levels of government through direct primaries. The direct primary is an election in which voters choose candidates to represent each party in a general election. In recent years, these elections have been very competitive, and the winner of the most primaries is often nominated by his or her party. There

are two main forms of the direct primary: closed and open.

Most states hold a **closed primary.** This is an election in which only the declared members of a party are allowed to vote for that party's nominees. Thus, only Republicans can vote in the Republican Party's primary.

Rules for how voters declare their party affiliation vary by state. In some states you must declare your party when you register. In others, you do not have to declare your party preference until you actually vote.

A few states hold an **open primary,** in which voters do not need to declare their party preference in order to vote for the party's nominees. In most open-primary states, you choose a party in the privacy of the voting booth.

People who favor the closed primary claim that it helps keep the members of one party from crossing over into the other party's primary to try to promote weak candidates (who would then be easy to defeat). An argument against the closed primary is that it does not permit a truly secret ballot, since voters must first declare a party preference. It also prevents unaffiliated voters from taking part in primary elections in most states.

Sometimes a political office can have more than one vacancy, and thus each party can nominate more than one candidate. Most offices, however, are open to only one winner. In these cases, most states award the party's nomination to the candidate who receives a **plurality**—the most votes among all those running. In a few states, however, the winner must have a majority. (A majority is a number greater than half of the total.) If no candidate receives a majority, the party holds a **runoff primary** between the two

Leading Third-Party Presidential Candidates

DATE	CANDIDATE	PARTY	POPULAR VOTE (thousands)
1948	Strom Thurmond	States' Rights	1,176
1952	Vincent Hallinan	Progressive	104
1956	T. Coleman Andrews	States' Rights	111
1960	Eric Hass	Socialist Labor	48
1964	Eric Hass	Socialist Labor	45
1968	George Wallace	American Independent	9,906
1972	John Schmitz	American	1,099
1976	Eugene McCarthy	Independent	757
1980	John Anderson	Independent	5,720
1984	David Bergland	Libertarian	228
1988	Ron Paul	Libertarian	432
1992	H. Ross Perot	Independent	19,742
1996	H. Ross Perot	Reform	8,085
2000	Ralph Nader	Green	2,883

Evaluating Charts

This chart shows the significant third-party candidates in presidential elections for part of American history. Which of the candidates listed was most successful in gaining popular votes?

Source: Federal Election Commission and United States Census Bureau, 2000.

top vote getters. The winner then becomes the party's candidate in the general election.

Unaffiliated Candidates Candidates who are not affiliated with one of the two major parties can get on the ballot for the general election in most states by petition. If enough qualified voters sign papers declaring support for a candidate, he or she goes on the ballot for the general election.

Reading Check **Contrasting** What is the difference between an open and closed primary?

Other Party Roles

Nominating candidates for office is just one of many roles that political parties perform.

Campaigning for Candidates

Once a party has nominated its candidates for office, it begins to campaign for them in the general election. The parties raise money for the campaign. They also help candidates get across their ideas and views on public issues to voters. A key role for party volunteers is to make sure party supporters are registered to vote and to ensure that on Election Day these voters go to the polls.

Informing Citizens

The party's goal during the campaign is for its candidates to win office. However, running a campaign serves another important purpose in a democracy: it informs citizens about public issues and the way government works through informational pamphlets; speeches; and TV, radio, and newspaper advertisements.

Helping Manage Government

Things slow down for political parties once an election is over, but work does continue. In fact, parties are involved in one of

Watchdogs Ralph Nader, a third-party candidate in the 2000 presidential election, writes a weekly column called "In the Public Interest." In it, Nader closely examines and criticizes governmental actions. **What benefit might the public get from Nader's actions?**

the first tasks that comes up after an election—handing out government jobs.

Most government jobs are civil service jobs gained on the basis of open, competitive examinations and merit. However, the president, governors, and some mayors have the power to appoint their trusted supporters to many high-level jobs. These supporters will usually be party members who believe in their party's ideas and want the opportunity to serve in government. If a chief executive has jobs to fill but does not have enough high-level supporters to fill them, he or she often seeks recommendations from party leaders.

Linking the Different Levels of Government

Party ties are important in helping different levels of government and branches of government cooperate with each other. For example, suppose the mayor of Columbia, South Carolina, and the governor of South Carolina are both Democrats. They are likely to have similar goals and ideas. They may be personal friends. Perhaps they have worked together on election campaigns or

TIME

Political Cartoons

and it seems to be diverted toward money and time. Making the world a more convenient | Schneider, two men with little h ing the company's reve

Analyzing Visuals In many elections, more than half of all eligible voters fail to cast ballots. What do you think of the concept of a "nonvoters' party"? What course of action is the cartoonist supporting?

Acting as a Watchdog

Finally, parties play an important "watchdog" role after an election. The party that is out of power—the party that lost the election for president, governor, or Congress—watches the actions of the party in power for any mistakes or misuse of power. This opposition party may criticize the party in power and offer its own solutions to political problems. In this way, the opposition party hopes to attract voters to support it in future elections. Competition between parties forces the party in power to pay attention to the will of the people.

Reading Check **Explaining** Why do parties out of power act as watchdogs?

party business in the past. These connections may make it easier for them to join forces to tackle mutual problems. Likewise, when a majority of legislators belong to the same party as a chief executive, cooperation between the two branches is likely to be better than if they belong to opposing parties.

SECTION 3 ASSESSMENT

Checking for Understanding

1. **Key Terms** Write a paragraph that summarizes the key points of this section. Use all of the following terms: nomination, direct primary, closed primary, open primary, plurality, runoff primary, petition.

Reviewing Main Ideas

2. **Identify** When does a runoff primary occur? Where does the winner go from there?

3. **Describe** How does a candidate who is not affiliated with either major party get on the ballot?

Critical Thinking

4. **Drawing Conclusions** In your opinion, which is a better system, the open primary or the closed primary? Explain.

5. **Organizing Information** On a web diagram like the one below, write the roles that political parties play in our nation and give an example of each role.

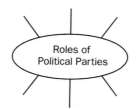

Roles of Political Parties

Analyzing Visuals

6. **Identify** Examine the chart on page 228. What party did George Wallace represent in 1968? How much of the popular vote did he receive?

★ **BE AN ACTIVE CITIZEN** ★

7. **Research** Contact the local Democratic and Republican Party offices. Find out what jobs are available for volunteers. Make a list of the jobs and categorize them according to the six roles of political parties.

Interpreting a Political Cartoon

Why Learn This Skill?

The First Amendment assures Americans the freedom to express their views on political matters. Political cartoonists use art to express political opinions. Their work appears in newspapers, magazines, and books, and on the Internet. Political cartoons are drawings that express an opinion. They usually focus on public figures, political events, or economic or social conditions. Reading a political cartoon can give you a summary of an event or circumstance and the artist's opinion in a quick and entertaining manner.

Learning the Skill

To interpret a political cartoon, follow the steps listed in the next column.

- Read the title, caption, or conversation balloons. Most cartoons will carry at least one of these elements. They help you identify the subject of the cartoon.
- Identify the characters. They may be caricatures, or unrealistic drawings that exaggerate the characters' physical features.
- Identify the symbols. Some caricatures may stand for something else. Commonly recognized symbols may not be labeled. Unusual symbolism will be labeled.
- Examine the actions in the cartoon to determine what is happening and why they are important.
- Identify the cartoonist's purpose. State the point the cartoonist makes about the actual situation. Decide if the cartoonist wants to persuade, criticize, or provoke thought.

Practicing the Skill

On a separate sheet of paper, answer the following questions about the political cartoon on this page.

1. Who are the main characters in the cartoon? What do they represent?
2. In what ways is the main character a caricature?
3. Describe the action in the drawing.
4. What is the cartoonist's comment on the situation represented?

"Someday, son, all this and more will be yours if you remember to always support the Republican party."

──Applying the Skill──

Use a current news source to locate two political cartoons. Write a brief summary of the cartoonist's message and purpose for each cartoon.

Practice key skills with Glencoe's **Skillbuilder Interactive Workbook CD-ROM, Level 1.**

Assessment & Activities

Review to Learn

Section 1

- Shortly after our nation began, two political parties formed.
- The basic difference between the two parties today is their belief in how much the government should be involved in Americans' lives.

Section 2

- Each party has a national committee and congressional campaign committees. Each party also has 50 state committees and many local party organizations.
- Some local party organizations became so powerful in the past that their candidates won almost every election. These were known as political machines.

Section 3

- Political parties nominate candidates through a nomination process of direct primaries.

- Political parties campaign for their candidates by raising money, informing voters, and getting people to vote.

FOLDABLES™
Study Organizer

Using Your Foldables Study Organizer
Use your completed foldable to create a time line that includes information to answer the following question: Why have political parties been important throughout American history?

Reviewing Key Terms

Write the term from the chapter that best matches the clues below.

1. the party system of the United States
2. they nominate the presidential candidate at the national convention
3. New York's Tammany Hall
4. helps prevent crossover voting
5. a party that is not a major party
6. the party system of China
7. advocates claim that it preserves the secret ballot
8. read this to find out what a party stands for
9. the smallest geographical unit of a party
10. part of a party's platform

Reviewing Main Ideas

11. What were the first two political parties in the United States, and who were their leaders?
12. Name three third parties that organized around independent candidates for president.
13. What party replaced the Federalists as the main challenger to the Democratic-Republicans in 1830?
14. What two mechanisms are used by parties to select delegates to the national convention?
15. What role do congressional campaign committees play in the political arena?
16. Prior to nominating the party's candidate for president and vice president, what is the main job of delegates at a national convention?
17. Even if a party's candidate for office loses, how has the party benefited the community?
18. In what way do political parties help manage the government?

Critical Thinking

19. **Analyzing Information** Why do you think there has never been a successful third-party candidate for president?

20. Making Comparisons In a chart like the one below, compare the basic beliefs of the major parties.

Democratic Party	Republican Party

Practicing Skills

Mr. Moore
∨

21. Interpreting a Political Cartoon Examine the political cartoon. In it, cartoonist Thomas Nast portrayed Boss Tweed of the political machine. How is Tweed's head portrayed? Why?

Analyzing Visuals

Study the circle graph below; then answer the following questions.

22. What percentage of the popular vote did the third-party candidate receive? How might the results have been different if there had been only two candidates?

2000 PRESIDENTIAL ELECTION
(POPULAR VOTE)

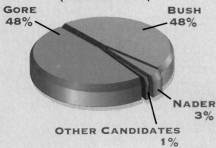

GORE 48%
BUSH 48%
NADER 3%
OTHER CANDIDATES 1%

★ CITIZENSHIP COOPERATIVE ACTIVITY ★

23. As a class, organize a poll to see how many plan to register and vote when they are of age. Discuss the results of your poll.

CIVICS Online

Self-Check Quiz Visit the *Civics Today* Web site at civ.glencoe.com and click on **Self-Check Quizzes— Chapter 9** to prepare for the chapter test.

$ Economics Activity

24. When politicians talk about political capital, they mean a special kind of property—the influence, prestige, and fame "owned" by a politician. Look up the term "capital," and explain its economic meaning. If you were a businessperson, how would you acquire capital? How would you acquire it as a politician?

Technology Activity

25. Search for both the Republican and Democratic platforms from the 2000 election on the Internet. Read through each platform. With which platform did you most agree? Why?

The Princeton Review Standardized Test Practice

Directions: Choose the answer that *best* completes the following statement.

All of the following are key roles that political parties play in the U.S. political process EXCEPT

A bring charges of misconduct against the presidency if necessary.

B nominate candidates for office.

C monitor the activities of government officials.

D educate the American public about campaign issues and candidates.

Test-Taking Tip

Remember, when a question contains the term *except,* you must find the answer choice that is not true.

Voting and Elections

★ CITIZENSHIP AND YOU ★

The right to vote is one of the fundamental rights of citizens in a democratic society. It is also a major responsibility of citizenship. Conduct a poll in your neighborhood to learn who is registered to vote.

 To learn more about elections and voting, view the **Democracy in Action** video lesson 17: Elections and Voting.

FOLDABLES™
Study Organizer

Analyzing Information Study Foldable *Make this foldable to help you answer questions about voting and elections.*

Step 1 *Mark the midpoint of a side edge of one sheet of paper. Then fold the outside edges in to touch the midpoint.*

Step 3 *Open and cut along the inside fold lines to form four tabs.*

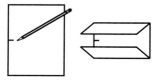

Cut along the fold lines on both sides.

Step 2 *Fold in half from side to side.*

Step 4 *Label as shown.*

Who can vote? | What are election campaigns? | When are elections held? | How are campaigns paid for?

Reading and Writing *As you read the chapter, ask yourself the questions labeled on the foldable. As you read each section, find the answer to each question. Record your answers under the appropriate tab.*

Supporters of George W. Bush during the disputed 2000 presidential election ▶

CIVICS Online

Chapter Overview Visit the *Civics Today* Web site at civ.glencoe.com and click on **Chapter Overviews— Chapter 10** to preview chapter information.

Who Can Vote?

Main Idea

After meeting the qualifications, people who want to vote must register before going to the polling place to cast their ballots.

Key Terms

polling place, precinct, ballot, absentee ballot, returns, exit poll, electorate, apathy

Reading Strategy

Sequencing Information As you read, complete a chart like the one below by listing the steps in the voting process.

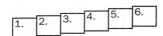

Read to Learn

• How has the right to vote expanded?

• How does the registration and voting process work?

Americans in Action

On the first Tuesday after the first Monday of every November, Mary Gettinger has a regular job. It lasts all day. Mary describes herself as "tired but satisfied" at the end of the day. Ever since she retired from her teaching job 17 years ago, Mary has worked as a poll worker. She puts in a long day at the elementary school in her community, where two precincts' worth of people vote on local, state, and national issues and candidates. Mary views her work as a poll worker as an important public service. "After voting myself," she says, "working the polls is the most important thing I do, because it helps other people vote."

Pointing the way to the polling place

Qualifying to Vote

Voting is an important right of American citizenship. Without it, citizens would not be able to choose the people who will run their government. Voting is also a major responsibility. Those who do not vote are failing to carry out a civic responsibility. They are also handing over their share of political power to voters whose views they may oppose. President Franklin D. Roosevelt reminded Americans of the importance of voting when he said, "Let us never forget that government is ourselves. The ultimate rulers of our democracy . . . are the voters of this country."

During our nation's early years, most voters were white, adult males, and property owners. The many people often barred from voting included white adult males who could not afford to buy property, women, African American males, Native American males, and people under 21 years of age. Today, however, property ownership is no longer a consideration, and the U.S. Constitution states that no state may deny the right to vote because of race, color, gender, or age—if the person is at least 18 years old. People who have been convicted of serious crimes are the most common exception to the general rules. Most states deny them the right to vote until they have served their prison sentences.

To be eligible to vote, you must be at least 18, a resident of the state for a specified period of time, and a citizen of the United States. In most states, you must also be registered to vote.

Voter Registration

People who meet the qualifications must register to vote before they can take part in an election. Most states require registration at least 25 days before an election. In a few states, however, the deadline is much later—10 or even fewer days before the election.

Registration requirements vary. Registration applications may be obtained from county offices. Some states make the process easier, permitting registration by mail or offering more convenient times and places for in-person registration such as allowing registration at public libraries or high schools. A federal law that took effect in 1995, the National Voter Registration Act, widely known as the Motor Voter Act, requires the states to allow people to register when they renew their drivers' licenses. Citizens may also mail in registrations or register at numerous state offices, welfare offices, and agencies that serve the disabled.

Registering to vote involves filling out some forms. These forms ask for your name, address, age, and often your party preference. You may register as a Democrat, a Republican, unaffiliated, or a member of some other party. If you register as a Democrat or Republican, you will be able to vote in primary elections where you can choose your party's candidates for the general election.

When you register for the first time, you must show proof of citizenship, address, and age by showing a driver's license or birth certificate. Once you have registered, you are assigned to an election district. On Election Day, election officials will use a list of voters registered in the district to verify that the people who vote are eligible and to prevent people from voting more than once.

Reading Check **Identifying** What requirements must you meet to qualify to vote?

Steps in Voting

On Election Day, voters go to the polling place in their precinct. A **polling place** is the location where voting is carried out, and a **precinct** is a voting district. Polling places are usually set up in town halls, schools, fire stations, community centers, and other public buildings.

At the Polls

Polling places are generally open from early morning until 7 or 8 P.M. When you first arrive, you can study a sample ballot posted on the wall at the entrance. A **ballot** is the list of candidates on which you cast your vote. Once inside, you go to the clerk's table. Here you write your name and address on an application form and usually sign it. The clerk reads your name aloud and passes the form to a challenger's table.

A challenger—there are challengers representing each party—looks up your registration form and compares the signature on it with the signature on your application. If the two do not appear to match, the challenger may ask you for additional identification. When the challenger is convinced that you are eligible to vote, he or she initials the application form and returns it to you.

Casting a Vote

You then go to the voting booth where you hand the application form to an election judge. Judges watch over the operation of the voting booths, making sure that everyone can vote in secret and helping voters who are physically challenged, elderly, or unable to read.

As Carl Jaramillo sees it, voter apathy is one of the country's biggest problems. "In [the 2000 presidential] election, we had barely over 50 percent turnout," says the 19-year-old Raleigh, North Carolina, native. "Compared to other western democracies, that's ridiculously low. People just aren't paying attention."

But Jaramillo is. He joined Kids Voting USA, a grassroots organization that gets young people involved in the voting process. With Jaramillo leading the way, the local chapter registered eligible high school seniors and hosted a mayoral debate, among other activities.

"Kids Voting is really a smart solution," Jaramillo tells TIME. "What they're working on is future voters, 20 years down the line. In the short term, it also has a trickle-up effect, because kids push their parents [to vote]."
For more information about Kids Voting USA, click on their Web site: www.kidsvotingusa. org

Carl Jaramillo from North Carolina

You will cast your ballot by using a voting machine. The two most common types are the punch-card machine and the lever machine. Whatever machine you use, you will usually use a ballot with the candidates' names listed according to their political party and the office they are seeking.

Because election methods are left to the states, the kinds of voting machines used vary widely. It is always important to read the ballot carefully. In the 2000 presidential election, many voters in Florida were confused by the "butterfly ballot," a paper ballot in which opposing candidates were listed across from each other instead of vertically. The 2000 election in Florida also proved that some machines were more reliable than others. Punch-card ballots, in which voters punched a hole next to the name of a candidate, were run through machines and misread much more often than computerized, scanned ballots. Since the 2000 election, many states are upgrading their voting machines.

All types of voting machines allow voters to cast a secret ballot. All also allow voters to vote for a straight ticket, which means voting for all the candidates in one political party. If you choose some candidates from one party and some from another, you are voting a split ticket. You may even decide to cast a write-in vote by writing in the name of someone who is not on the ballot.

Absentee Voting

Citizens who cannot get to the polls on Election Day can vote by **absentee ballot.** People who know they will be out of town that day, those who are too sick to get to the polls, and military personnel serving away from home often use absentee ballots. Voters must request an absentee ballot from their local election board sometime before Election Day. Then they mark this ballot and return it by mail. On Election Day, or shortly thereafter, election officials open and count the absentee ballots.

Counting the Vote

When the polls close, election workers count the votes at the polling place and take the ballots and the results—called **returns**—to the election board. The board then collects and counts the returns for the entire city or county. If the voting machines are not computerized, gathering all the returns and tallying the results can take several hours or longer. Then the board sends the returns to the state canvassing authority. A few days after the election, the state canvassing authority certifies the election of the winner.

In a major election, the news media and party workers try to predict winners as soon as possible. One way they do this is to ask a sample of voters leaving selected polling places how they voted. This is known as an **exit poll.** Through exit polling, specialists can often predict the winners long before all the votes have been officially counted.

Major television networks always devote the entire evening and night to covering the vote during presidential elections. They use computerized predictions based on the past voting history of key precincts in every state to "call" winners of Senate, House, and governors' seats, as well as the electoral vote in the race for president. In some cases the networks make these calls with as little as 10 percent of the vote counted. Their projections are usually correct, but some networks were embarrassed by an early and incorrect call on the presidential vote in the decisive state of Florida in the 2000 election.

Some political commentators have criticized these early calls. The predictions usually come when millions of Americans in the Western time zones have yet to vote and the polls there are still open. These observers charge that such early projections may persuade great numbers of Westerners not to bother going out to vote. This not only reduces overall voter turnout but also may affect the results of local, state, and congressional elections.

Reading Check Explaining What does it mean to vote a split ticket?

Why Your Vote Matters

The best way to prepare to vote is to stay informed about candidates and public issues. Newspapers, TV, radio, newsmagazines, and the Internet carry useful information. Other good sources include the *Voters' Information Bulletin,* published by the League of Women Voters; literature distributed by each political party; and information published by interest groups such as the American Conservative Union or the AFL-CIO Committee on Political Education. As you read about candidates and the issues they support, though, read carefully to separate facts from opinions. Everyone has different reasons for supporting particular candidates. As you read

Supporting Issues American citizens express their feelings about issues. The percentage of voters who participate in presidential elections is usually greater than the percentage who take part in state and local elections. **Why do you think this is so?**

about various candidates, answer the following questions to help you decide whom to support with your vote.

- Does the candidate stand for the things I think are important?
- Is the candidate reliable and honest?
- Does the candidate have relevant past experience?
- Will the candidate be effective in office?
- Does the candidate have a real chance of winning? Sometimes Americans vote for candidates, even though they do not have a real chance of winning the election, because they wish to show their support for a certain point of view.

All the people who are eligible to vote are called the **electorate.** Each person's vote counts. If you doubt it, consider this. The 2000 presidential election was decided by about 500 votes in the state of Florida. In fact, a very small percentage of the population determined the election's outcome.

Despite the fact that voting gives Americans a chance to participate in their government, not everyone in the electorate votes. Some citizens do not vote because they do not meet state voting requirements, or they have not reregistered after changing residences. Other Americans do not think that any of the candidates represent their feelings on issues, or they think that their vote will not make a difference. Another reason is **apathy,** or lack of interest.

The citizens who do vote share some characteristics. These citizens generally have positive attitudes toward government and citizenship. Usually the more education a citizen has, the more likely it is that he or she will be a regular voter. Middle-aged citizens have the highest voting turnout rate of all age groups. The higher a person's income, the more likely he or she is to vote.

There are important reasons to exercise your right to vote, though. Voting gives citizens a chance to choose their government leaders. It gives them an opportunity to voice their opinions on past performances of public officials. If voters are dissatisfied, they can elect new leaders. Voting also allows citizens to express their opinions on public issues.

Reading Check **Summarizing** What are two good reasons to exercise your right to vote?

SECTION 1 ASSESSMENT

Checking for Understanding

1. **Key Terms** Write a true statement *and* a false statement for each term below. Below each false statement explain why it is false. polling place, precinct, ballot, absentee ballot, returns, exit poll, electorate, apathy

Reviewing Main Ideas

2. **Explain** How did the Motor Voter Act affect voter registration in the United States?

3. **Identify** In the early days of our nation, what was the only group of people eligible to vote?

Critical Thinking

4. **Drawing Conclusions** Do you think the federal government should prohibit exit polls during presidential elections? Why or why not?

5. **Sequencing Information** On a graphic organizer like the one below, write all of the steps involved in voting.

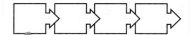

Analyzing Visuals

6. **Infer** Examine the photographs on page 239. Why would other Americans encourage you to vote?

★ **BE AN ACTIVE CITIZEN** ★

7. **Research** Contact your local board of elections. Find out the qualifications for people to work at the polls. Ask the board of elections officials to explain the duties of the poll workers or interview people who have been poll workers.

Election Campaigns

GUIDE TO READING

Main Idea

Every two years for Congress and every four years for the president, voters respond to political campaigns by going to the polls and casting their ballots.

Key Terms

initiative, proposition, referendum, recall, Electoral College, elector, winner-take-all. system

Reading Strategy

Organizing Information
As you read this section, complete a graphic organizer like the one below by listing features of the three types of elections.

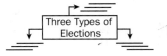

Three Types of Elections

Read to Learn

- What are the types of elections available to voters?
- What are the steps in the presidential election process?

Americans in Action

The Electoral College received more attention in the 2000 election year than it ever had before. And that's why Democratic Senator Richard Durbin of Illinois proposed a constitutional amendment to abolish the Electoral College. Durbin contends that presidential elections would be fairer if they were based solely on a popular vote. His only qualification is that if no candidate wins more than 40 percent of the popular vote, a runoff election be held between the two top vote getters. Durbin's proposal was referred to the Senate Judiciary Committee.

Senator Durbin

Types of Elections

The Electoral College is part of the process that Americans use to select their president. Americans also vote in various other elections. With about half a million elected officials in the United States, it seems as if someone, somewhere, is always running for office. In addition, Americans have many opportunities to vote on issues as well as candidates. Besides primary elections, there are three types of elections in the United States: general elections, elections on issues, and special elections.

General Elections

As you learned in Chapter 9, elections are a two-part process. The first part of the process is the nomination of candidates in a primary election. Primary races help to narrow the field of candidates. Then, in a general election, the voters choose candidates for various offices. General elections always take place on the first Tuesday after the first Monday in November. All seats in the U.S. House of Representatives and about one-third of the seats in the Senate are at stake in general elections every even-numbered year. Presidential elections occur every four years. In these elections the ballot also often includes candidates for governor, the state legislature, county government, and local offices. In some states, however, elections for mayor and other city offices take place in odd-numbered years.

For all races except the presidential race, the candidate who wins a majority of the popular vote is elected to office. If an election is very close, the loser has the right to demand a recount of the votes. Occasionally, a disputed election cannot be resolved through a recount and another election must be held. In the case of a national election, a dispute may be referred to Congress for settlement. If it is a presidential election and neither candidate wins a majority of electoral votes, the House of Representatives elects the president. This happened in the elections of 1800 and 1824.

Voting on Issues

In some state and local elections, voters may decide on issues as well as candidates. The initiative, for example, is a way that citizens can propose new laws or state constitutional amendments. Citizens who want a new law gather signatures of qualified voters on a petition. If enough people sign the petition, the proposed law, or proposition, is put on the ballot at the next general election.

The referendum is a way for citizens to approve or reject a state or local law. Citizens in more than half the states have the right to petition to have a law referred, or sent back, to the voters for their approval at the next general election.

Special Elections

From time to time, state or local governments also hold special elections. Runoff elections may be held when none of the candidates for a particular office wins a majority of the vote in the general election. The runoff is held to determine the winner.

The recall is another type of special election. In a recall, citizens can vote to remove a public official from office. Like the initiative, the recall starts with a petition. Voters may recall an official because they do not like his or her position on issues or because the official has been charged with wrongdoing.

Reading Check Comparing What is the difference between an initiative and a referendum?

TIME

Political Cartoons

DAVE GRANLUND © 2000 METROWEST DAILY NEWS www.davegranlund.com

and it seems to be diverted toward money and time. Making the world a more convenient | Schneider, two men with little b ing the company's reve

Analyzing Visuals In presidential elections, citizens do not vote directly for candidates; instead they vote for electors, who in turn cast their ballots for candidates on a state-by-state basis. What is the cartoonist's view of the Electoral College? What details support your answer?

Presidential Elections

Presidential elections have three major steps: (1) nomination of candidates, (2) the campaign, and (3) the vote.

Nomination

Presidential hopefuls start campaigning for their party's nomination a year or more before the election. In the past, both major parties held national conventions in the summer of the election year

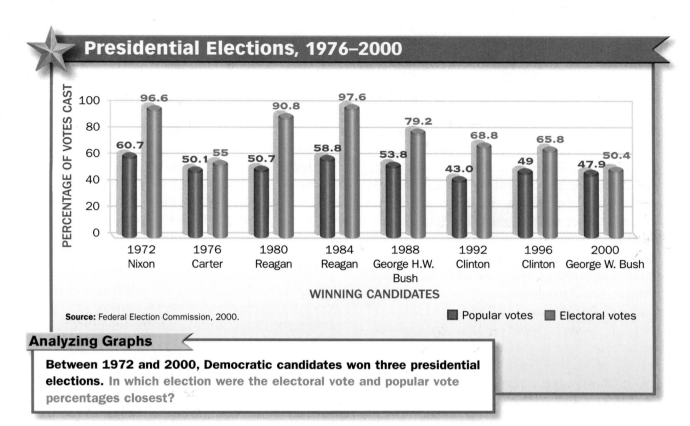

Presidential Elections, 1976–2000

Source: Federal Election Commission, 2000.

■ Popular votes ■ Electoral votes

Analyzing Graphs

Between 1972 and 2000, Democratic candidates won three presidential elections. In which election were the electoral vote and popular vote percentages closest?

to choose their candidate. Delegates came to these conventions from each state, the District of Columbia, and U.S. territories.

These conventions were dramatic events full of behind-the-scenes negotiations. Backers of various candidates would move around the convention floor, promising future political favors to state delegations in hopes of stealing their votes away from a rival. The political dealings would be interrupted for suspenseful and colorful state-by-state roll-call votes to see if any contender had rounded up enough support to win the nomination.

In recent years, however, the conventions have lost their main purpose—choosing the nominee. So much campaigning now goes on in the primary elections that by convention time one contender has already wrapped up the nomination. The parties use the conventions mainly to kick off the campaign and rally party members across the country for the work ahead.

Campaign

Presidential campaigns are usually in full swing by early September. Candidates travel across the country giving speeches, appearing on TV, and holding news conferences—even though there is seldom any real news to announce. They may face their opponents in televised debates. They meet with state and local political leaders, and they give pep talks to lower-level members of the party who are working for them.

The Vote and the Electoral College

We have already seen in Chapter 7 that presidents are not chosen by direct popular vote but by a body known as the **Electoral College.** In every state a slate, or list, of **electors** is pledged to each candidate. The purpose of the popular vote in each state is to choose one of these slates of electors. The candidate who wins the popular vote in a state usually receives all of the state's electoral votes. This is called the **winner-take-all system.**

The winning electors meet in their state capitals in December to cast the state's electoral votes for president and vice president. The electors send their votes to Congress, which counts them. Because every state has one elector for each of its U.S. senators and representatives, the total number of votes in the Electoral College is 538. (Washington, D.C., has three electoral votes.) The candidate who receives a majority of these votes—270 or more—wins the election.

The Electoral College system is as old as the U.S. Constitution. It was a compromise measure. Some of the Founders wanted the American people to have direct control over the new national government. Others strongly believed that the government must be able to function without having to give in to popular whims. The first group demanded a direct popular election of the president. Their opponents pushed to have Congress name the president. Their compromise was to have the legislatures in each state choose presidential electors. Now the voters in each state directly choose the electors.

Critics of the Electoral College charge that large states like California, which have many more electoral votes than small states, have too much influence in deciding the election. Others argue that by including votes for senators, the system gives unfair power to states with small populations. Under a truly proportional system the will of the people would be more fairly carried out in elections. Critics also point out that under the winner-take-all system, a candidate who loses the popular vote can still win the electoral vote and the presidency. This has happened four times in our history. Also, a third-party candidate could win enough electoral votes to prevent either major-party candidate from receiving a majority. The third-party candidate could then bargain to release electoral votes to a major-party candidate. The winner-take-all system also makes it extremely difficult for third-party candidates to be represented at all in the electoral vote.

Reading Check **Inferring** When you vote for the U.S. president, for whom are you actually voting?

SECTION 2 ASSESSMENT

Checking for Understanding

1. **Key Terms** Write a paragraph that summarizes the key points of this section. Use all of the following terms: initiative, proposition, referendum, recall, Electoral College, elector, winner-take-all system.

Reviewing Main Ideas

2. **Explain** Why have national political conventions lost the main purpose of choosing nominees?

3. **Summarize** How is the total of 538 Electoral College votes determined? What is the purpose of the popular vote in the Electoral College system?

Critical Thinking

4. **Making Judgments** Analyze the criticisms of the Electoral College. Do you think it should be eliminated or maintained? Explain your answer.

5. **Sequencing Information** List and explain the steps involved in presidential elections by completing a graphic organizer like the one below.

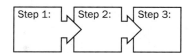

Analyzing Visuals

6. **Review** Look at the bar graph on page 243. Which president shown on the graph received the largest percentage of popular votes? Electoral votes?

⭐ **BE AN ACTIVE CITIZEN** ⭐
7. **Research** Using the library or Internet, research your state's election laws. Does your state allow the initiative? The referendum? Recall? If so, explain the last time they were used successfully.

Should the Electoral College Be Abolished?

Al Gore was the winner of the 2000 presidential election by a popular vote of about 333,000. He conceded the election to George W. Bush. Reports like this left people scratching their heads. As Senator Robert Torricelli of New Jersey remarked at the time, "Americans are about to engage in a great civics lesson." The subject was the Electoral College—the 538 delegates who elect the president and vice president based on each state's popular vote. Most states, except Maine and Nebraska, operate on the winner-take-all rule. The candidate who finishes first, even narrowly, gets all of the state's electoral votes. The Electoral College had decided elections before—three times in the 1800s. However, this was the first time it had happened in more than 100 years.

A vote cast for an elector

Until our recent national crash course in the federal election process, most Americans saw the Electoral College as a harmless anachronism [a person or thing out of place in time]. But 10 days ago, for the first time in over a century, the nation watched as the oath of office was administered to an elected president who failed to secure a plurality of the votes cast. . . . [W]e must also ask—as many of my constituents have—whether an electoral system that negates the votes of half a million citizens is compatible with democratic values. . . . If the Electoral College merely echoes the election results, then it is superfluous [not necessary]. If it contradicts the voting majority, then why tolerate it?

—*Representative William D. Delahunt from Massachusetts*

I believe that the current Electoral College system offers many advantages over a popular vote. In our republic, a citizen who resides in a state with low population deserves just as much representation as a citizen in a city. Though at first glance it may seem that a popular vote would grant an equal voice to each, in fact it would eliminate it. Population centers would grab nearly all the consideration, as the number of popular votes in the farmlands of the country is measly compared to someplace like Boston. Why would a candidate bother with states with low populations? . . . The Electoral College ensures that candidates campaign to the entire country and safeguards the importance of each state's voice, be it large or small.

—*Meredith Miller Hoar, Bowdoin College*

Debating the Issue

1. Why does Hoar support the Electoral College?
2. Why does Delahunt oppose the system?
3. Any change in the Electoral College system would require a constitutional amendment.

Should the Electoral College be kept, abolished, or reformed in some way? Phrase your views in a letter to the editor of your local newspaper.

Paying for Election Campaigns

GUIDE TO READING

Main Idea

Political campaigns in the United States require millions of dollars and, although regulations exist, parties find ways to raise and use soft money to fund their candidates.

Key Terms

propaganda, soft money, political action committee (PAC), incumbent

Reading Strategy

Comparing and Contrasting Information Use a chart like the one below to compare public and private campaign funding.

Public	Private

Read to Learn

- How are campaigns financed, both publicly and privately?
- What are possible reforms of the campaign finance system?

Americans in Action

Many legislators, discouraged by the fact that spending on political campaigns is rising while voter participation is decreasing, approved an act to reform the nation's campaign finance law in 2002. The bill bans the large unlimited contributions to national political parties known as soft money. The bill was the result of continued efforts by Senators John McCain and Russell Feingold. "This great center of democracy is truly tainted by money," Feingold explained. "Particularly after September 11, all of us in this chamber hope the public will look to the Capitol and to the Senate with reverence and pride, not with derision." If upheld by the courts, the new law will be the most far-reaching reform yet.

Cash for campaigns

Running for Office

Americans spend more than $3 billion on national, state, and local elections every four-year period. Former House Speaker Tip O'Neill once said, "There are four parts to any campaign. The candidate, the issues . . . , the campaign organization, and the money. Without money you can forget the other three."

It takes a great deal of money to run a successful campaign for a major office today. Once candidates are nominated, they spend weeks and even months campaigning for the election.

The purpose of campaigns is to convince the public to vote for a particular candidate. Each campaign has a campaign organization to help run the campaign. An organization for a local candidate may have only a few workers. Presidential campaigns, though, have thousands of workers. Campaign workers must acquaint voters with the candidate's name, face, and positions on issues, and convince voters to like and trust the candidate. Campaign workers use several techniques to accomplish their goals.

Canvassing

When candidates or campaign workers travel through neighborhoods asking for votes or taking public opinion polls, they are canvassing. At the local level, candidates often go door-to-door to solicit votes and hand out campaign literature. At the national level, campaign organizations conduct frequent polls to find out how their candidates are doing.

Endorsements

When a famous and popular person supports or campaigns for a candidate, it is an endorsement. The endorser may be a movie star, a famous athlete, a popular politician, or some other well-known individual. The idea behind endorsements is that if voters like the person making the endorsement, they may decide to vote for the candidate.

Endorsements are a kind of propaganda technique. Propaganda is an attempt to promote a particular person or idea. Candidates use propaganda techniques to try to persuade or influence voters to choose them over another candidate.

Advertising and Image Molding

Campaign workers spend much time and money to create the right image for a candidate. Much of that money goes for advertising. Political advertisements allow a party to present only its candidate's position or point of view. They also enable a candidate to attack an opponent without offering an opportunity to respond.

Candidates for a local election may use newspaper advertisements or posters, while state and national candidates spend a great deal of money advertising on television. Why? Television ads can present quick and dramatic images of a candidate and his or her ideas. Such television images tend to stay in the viewer's mind.

Campaign Expenses

Television commercials are a very effective way to win votes, but they cost tens of thousands of dollars per minute. Other campaign costs include airfare and other transportation, salaries of campaign staff members, and fees to professional campaign consultants, such as public opinion pollsters. There are also computer, telephone, postage, and printing costs.

A small-town mayoral race may cost only a few hundred or a few thousand dollars. A state legislative or congressional race may cost several hundred thousand dollars to several million dollars. In recent elections, spending for each seat in Congress has averaged out to about $1.5 million. Some congressional candidates spent $15 million or more. A presidential race can cost hundreds of millions of dollars.

Reading Check **Describing** What is the purpose of election propaganda?

Political TV Television commercials have become more popular than other advertising forms. TV ads help candidates create an image that appeals to the public. **Why are television commercials an effective way to campaign?**

Financing a Campaign

Until the 1970s, candidates relied on contributions from business organizations, labor unions, and individuals. This system of financing campaigns tended to give wealthy individuals and groups a better chance of winning elections and, therefore,

Carrie Chapman Catt (1859–1947)

"Everybody counts in a democracy," declared Carrie Chapman Catt during the battle over woman suffrage, or the right to vote. Catt felt that self-government would never be safe until "every responsible and law-abiding adult" possessed the vote.

Catt, born Carrie Clinton Lane, grew up along the Iowa frontier. She put herself through college by washing dishes, teaching, and working in the library. She went on to become one of the nation's first female school superintendents. In 1885 Lane married Leo Chapman and helped co-edit his newspaper. Widowed a year later, she joined the suffrage movement. When her second husband, George Catt, died in 1902, Carrie Chapman Catt went overseas to help spread the movement worldwide.

With the support of Susan B. Anthony, one of the founders of the suffrage movement, she led the campaign to add the Nineteenth Amendment to the Constitution when she returned to America. Victory came in 1920. To prepare some 20 million women for "political independence," Catt founded the League of Women Voters. Today the League honors its founder by educating all citizens on the importance of voting to a democracy.

more political power. The public also wondered if successful candidates then owed special favors to the people who contributed to their campaigns.

Starting in 1971 Congress tried to place some controls on campaign financing. The Federal Election Campaign Finance Act of 1971 (and its amendments in 1974, 1976, and 1979) established the main rules for campaign finance today. The law required public disclosure of each candidate's spending, established federal funding of presidential elections, and tried to limit how much individuals and groups could spend. For example, the law limited the amount of money that an individual may donate to a presidential candidate. It also created the Federal Election Commission (FEC)—an independent agency of the executive branch—to administer all federal election laws and monitor campaign spending. A 2002 bill loosened some of these restrictions while placing greater restrictions in other areas.

Public Funding

A major source of money is the Presidential Election Campaign Fund created by the 1971 law. This fund allows taxpayers, by checking a box on their federal income tax return, to designate $3 of their annual taxes to go to the fund. In general, major-party presidential candidates can qualify to get some of this money to campaign in primary elections if they have raised $100,000 on their own. After the national conventions, the two major-party candidates receive equal shares of money from the fund, so long as they agree not to accept any other direct contributions.

Third-party candidates can also qualify for this funding if their party received more than 5 percent of the popular vote in the previous presidential election. H. Ross Perot, a candidate of the Reform Party in the 1996 presidential race, received enough votes to qualify the Reform Party's candidate, Pat Buchanan, for federal funding in the 2000 election.

Private Funding

Most campaign funding does not come from public sources, however. Private sources provide campaign funds and include individual citizens, party organizations, and corporations. In addition, a wide variety of special-interest groups, such as labor unions, the National Rifle Association, and the American Medical Association donate funds to candidates.

After presidential candidates receive their federal funds and the modest amounts that individuals and groups may give them directly, their fund-raising is supposed to be finished. However, presidential as well as congressional candidates have found ways to get around the limits of the 1971 law. The two key ways are so-called soft money donations and contributions made through organizations known as political action committees (PACs).

Donations given to political parties and not designated for a particular candidate's election campaign are called soft money. By law, this money must be used for general purposes, such as voter registration drives or direct mailings or advertisements about political issues. A law proposed in 2002 banned unlimited amounts of soft money.

National political parties have figured out ways to use soft money to support their candidate's campaign without giving the money directly to the candidate. Instead, they spend the money on other activities that benefit the campaign. Most soft money goes for national TV ads for the parties' candidates. Soft money provides a way for wealthy people and groups to spend as much as they want in support of a party's candidates, especially the presidential candidate.

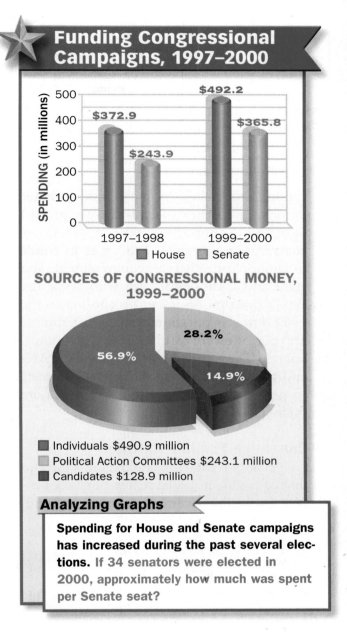

Funding Congressional Campaigns, 1997–2000

SPENDING (in millions)

	1997–1998	1999–2000
House	$372.9	$492.2
Senate	$243.9	$365.8

■ House   ■ Senate

SOURCES OF CONGRESSIONAL MONEY, 1999–2000

56.9%   28.2%   14.9%

■ Individuals $490.9 million
■ Political Action Committees $243.1 million
■ Candidates $128.9 million

Analyzing Graphs

Spending for House and Senate campaigns has increased during the past several elections. If 34 senators were elected in 2000, approximately how much was spent per Senate seat?

Candidates themselves do not hesitate to help their parties raise soft money. For example, during the 2000 election Republican candidate George W. Bush held a fundraising dinner where individuals and corporations donated $21 million for the party. Not long after, President Bill Clinton and Vice President Al Gore held a similar dinner for Democrats and raised $26 million. Before Election Day each party had raised more than $200 million in soft money.

The 1971 campaign finance law also led to the growth of political action committees (PACs). **Political action committees** are political organizations established by corporations, labor unions, and other special-interest groups designed to support political candidates by contributing money. A PAC uses its funds to support presidential, congressional, and state and local candidates who favor the PAC's position on issues. According to the 1971 law, corporations and labor unions are not allowed to give directly to campaigns. They can, however, set up PACs and give unlimited amounts of soft money to political parties. Today there are more than 4,700 PACs.

Campaign Finance Reforms

An important democratic value is the idea that government should represent all the people, including ordinary citizens without money or power. Critics of the current system argue that when groups and individuals are able to give huge amounts of money to support candidates, they may later receive special favors not available to average citizens. On the other hand, some people argue that trying to restrict how much people can donate to election campaigns is a limitation on free speech. In a 1976 decision, the Supreme Court ruled that it was a violation of free speech to limit how much a candidate could spend on his or her own election campaign. The effect of this ruling is that wealthy candidates can, and do, spend vast amounts of their own money to get elected—an outcome that some would call "buying" an election.

Congress discussed reforming campaign finance for many years. Reform, though, was difficult to achieve because PACs give most of their soft money to **incumbents**— politicians who have already been elected to office. As a result, many lawmakers were reluctant to change the rules in ways that could help their opponents in the next election and will challenge the 2002 law.

Reading Check **Identifying** What are the private sources of campaign funding?

SECTION 3 ASSESSMENT

Checking for Understanding

1. **Key Terms** Use the following terms in sentences related to campaign finance: propaganda, soft money, political action committee (PAC), incumbent.

Reviewing Main Ideas

2. **Identify** What federal agency administers election laws and monitors campaign spending?

3. **Describe** How do presidential candidates qualify for federal election funds? How do third-party candidates qualify for federal election funds?

Critical Thinking

4. **Making Judgments** Explain the two sides in the campaign spending reform issue. With which side do you agree? Explain your position.

5. **Summarizing Information** On a graphic organizer like the one below, list the effects resulting from the high costs of modern political campaigns.

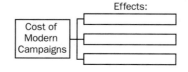

Effects:

Cost of Modern Campaigns

Analyzing Visuals

6. **Summarize** Review the graphs about funding the congressional campaigns from 1997 to 2000 on page 249. How much money was spent on congressional campaigning in 1999–2000?

★**BE AN ACTIVE CITIZEN**★

7. **Interview** Contact your local representative and your senators. Find out how much money they spent on their last campaigns. Who contributed the most to their campaigns?

Distinguishing Fact From Opinion

Why Learn This Skill?

A politician is behind the podium giving a campaign speech. The speaker probably offers some facts and some opinions. While you may value the speaker's opinion, you still want to know which is which so you can know whom to support. Distinguishing facts from opinions will help you make a more informed decision—the one that is right for you.

Learning the Skill

When learning about candidates, you must determine if they support the things you think are important. To distinguish facts from opinions in this circumstance and others, follow these steps:

- Identify statements that can be checked. Could you verify the information in a news or library source, for instance? If so, it is a fact.
- Identify statements that cannot be verified. These statements may be based on feelings or prejudices. They often make predictions or contain superlative words such as "best" or "worse." These kinds of statements are opinions.
- Look for "clue words." The speaker or writer may identify opinions with expressions such as "I think," "in my view," "we believe," and so on.

Practicing the Skill

On a separate sheet of paper, identify each of the newspaper editorial statements below as fact or opinion.

1. Mayor C.T. Hedd has more charisma than any mayor Park City has ever had.
2. During Mayor Hedd's first term, a total of 12 new corporations moved to the city.
3. The new jobs created by these corporations are the most important jobs ever offered to the Park City workforce.

Candidates for office publish many campaign materials.

4. City tax revenues have risen by 9.6 percent since Mayor Hedd took office.
5. It is the official view of this newspaper that Mayor Hedd's foresight and charm are directly responsible for Park City's growth.
6. Mayor Hedd deserves reelection.

Applying the Skill

Distinguish the facts from the opinions expressed in an editorial you find in a recent newspaper or magazine. Make a list of any clue words that identify opinions. Tell how you identified opinions that did not contain clue words.

Practice key skills with Glencoe's **Skillbuilder Interactive Workbook CD-ROM, Level 1.**

Assessment & Activities

Review to Learn

Section 1

- To vote, you must be registered first. On Election Day, you cast your vote at the polls usually by using some type of voting machine.

Section 2

- There are many types of elections.
- The presidential election process includes nomination, the campaign, and the vote.

Section 3

- Running for office costs money. Campaigns are funded privately and publicly.
- Many people are concerned about campaign spending.

FOLDABLES™
Study Organizer

Using Your Foldables Study Organizer
After completing your foldable, turn your desk to face a classmate. Take turns asking each other the questions labeled on the front of your foldables. See how many you can answer completely and correctly without looking under the tabs.

Reviewing Key Terms

Find the chapter term that matches each clue below.

1. the location where voting takes place
2. when a person votes for candidates from only one party
3. when citizens cast votes for a presidential candidate they are really voting for these people
4. donations to a political party that are supposedly not designated for a particular candidate
5. a way for citizens to vote on state or local laws
6. a voting district
7. a way for citizens to propose new laws or state constitutional amendments

Reviewing Main Ideas

8. In addition to primary elections, what three types of elections exist in the United States?
9. What group of citizens can be denied the right to vote even if they meet all the qualifications?
10. What was the purpose of the Federal Election Campaign Finance Act of 1971?
11. What law went into effect in 1995 that made voter registration more convenient?
12. Why are national party conventions less important than they used to be?
13. How can people vote if they are too sick or out of town on Election Day?
14. When do general elections take place?
15. What do third-party candidates for president have to do to qualify for federal campaign funds?

Critical Thinking

16. **Drawing Conclusions** What is your opinion of the use of soft money in campaign financing? Should the system be reformed? Defend your answer.

17. Cause and Effect Since the mid-1900s, television has become increasingly important in political campaigns. Show the effect this has had on politics in the United States by completing the graphic organizer below.

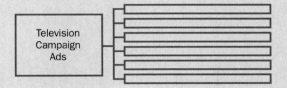

Television Campaign Ads

Practicing Skills

18. Distinguishing Fact From Opinion Label each statement below as a fact or opinion.

I believe money warps government decision-making in favor of special interests.

The way to "level the playing field" is to give all major candidates free or reduced-cost airtime on television and radio.

The election for city attorney cost the city $2 million, about $29 per ballot.

$ Economics Activity

19. Using the Internet or the library, find out what your representative or senator spent on the last campaign. Also determine the total number of votes cast in the election. What was the cost per ballot?

Analyzing Visuals

20. Study the political cartoon below. What statement is the cartoonist making about campaigning?

"According to our estimates, a campaign budget around six point two million is needed to successfully sing your praises."

★ CITIZENSHIP COOPERATIVE ACTIVITY ★

21. Form groups to investigate the political preferences of your community. Find out if the majority of registered voters are Democrats or Republicans. In the last three presidential elections, how did the majority of your community vote—Democratic or Republican?

Technology Activity

22. Using the Internet or library, find voter participation rates in the United States and two other countries and compare them in a spreadsheet.

The Princeton Review

Standardized Test Practice

Directions: Choose the *best* answer to the following question.

Which of the following statements best describes the Electoral College?

F The candidate who wins the popular vote in each state usually wins all that state's electoral votes too.

G This primary race helps narrow the field of candidates.

H It is a body of electors, pledged to each candidate, that casts a state's electoral votes after the popular vote is taken.

J It is a way that citizens can propose new constitutional amendments.

Test-Taking Tip

Eliminate answers one by one by crossing out answers you know are incorrect.

IT WAS 10 O'CLOCK ON ELECTION NIGHT 2000, and poll watchers in the small Georgia town of Dallas had a problem. The weather was humid and rainy. Now their vote-counting machine was rejecting thousands of punch-card ballots because the cardboard had warped. What to do? Break out the blow-dryers! "As weird as it sounds, it's standard procedure," says election superintendent Fran Watson. "We blow a hair dryer over them, and then they'll go through."

It's easy to demand reform of America's voting system—but the reality is that there is no national system. The Constitution left election procedures to the states. They in turn have passed the responsibility down to the counties and cities—some 3,000 of them—which choose their preferred methods and pay for them. "If your choice is between new voting machines and a road grader, it's no contest," explains Arkansas secretary of state Sharon Priest. Some experts have called for a uniform national voting technology, but for now, balloting around the country occurs through a patchwork of flawed and often antiquated methods.

STEVE KELLEY/COPLEY NEWS SERVICE

HOW AMERICANS VOTE: AN IMPERFECT SYSTEM

A look at the various methods used throughout the United States *

CHARLES BENNETT—AP

PUNCH CARD

■ **PERCENT WHO VOTE THIS WAY:** 34%

■ **HOW IT WORKS:** Voters insert blank cards into clipboard-size devices, then punch the hole opposite their choice. Ballots are read by a computer tabulator.

■ **PROS/CONS:** An economical method, but holes are often incompletely punched. The dangling bits of cardboard, known as "chads," lead to inaccurate tabulation of votes.

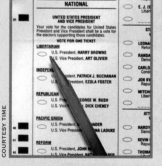

COURTESY TIME

OPTICAL SCAN

■ **PERCENT WHO VOTE THIS WAY:** 27%

■ **HOW IT WORKS:** Voters fill in rectangles, circles, ovals, or incomplete arrows next to their candidate. A computer selects the darkest mark as the choice.

■ **PROS/CONS:** Easy for voter to use, and double-marked ballots are immediately rejected. The equipment, however, is expensive and can have problems reading sloppily marked forms.

* NOTE: Figures are for the presidential election held in November 2000. Additional 9% is made up of voters in counties where more than one voting method is used. Sources: Election Data Services; Federal Election Commission.

VOTING METHODS IN THE U.S.

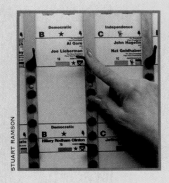

STUART RAMSON

LEVER MACHINE

- **PERCENT WHO VOTE THIS WAY:** **19%**

- **HOW IT WORKS:** Each candidate is assigned a lever, which voters push down to indicate their choices.

- **PROS/CONS:** Once the most popular form of voting, the machines are simple to use but heavy, old, and no longer manufactured. There is no paper trail if recounts are necessary.

CARLOS PUMA—THE PRESS-ENTERPRISE

ELECTRONIC

- **PERCENT WHO VOTE THIS WAY:** **9%**

- **HOW IT WORKS:** Voters directly enter choices into the machine using a touch screen or push buttons. Votes are stored via a memory cartridge.

- **PROS/CONS:** Though as easy as using an ATM, this new technology is still fairly expensive. There is no physical ballot in the event of a recount.

VINCENT LERZ—AP

PAPER BALLOT

- **PERCENT WHO VOTE THIS WAY:** **2%**

- **HOW IT WORKS:** Voters record their choices in private by marking the boxes next to the candidate and then drop ballots in a sealed box.

- **PROS/CONS:** An inexpensive and straightforward method that dates back to 1889. Counting and recounting can be very slow.

IS THERE A BETTER WAY OF BALLOTING AHEAD?

A UNIFORM BALLOT Some think there should be a single ballot design for all federal elections—same type, style, and size, with ballot marks in the same place.

MOVE ELECTION DAY Should it be a holiday or moved to the weekend so more people don't have to squeeze in their civic responsibility around work? It's a nice idea, but voters might just take a vacation.

VOTING BY MAIL Oregon tried it in 2000, with mixed success. If the kinks can be worked out, though, it could relieve the crowding on Election Day and boost turnout by giving people more time to vote.

COMPUTERIZED VOTING Some experts see elections being eventually held entirely over the Internet. Security problems have to be solved first, though. And what about voters who are not computer-literate?

COURTESY TIME

Influencing Government

★ *CITIZENSHIP AND YOU* ★

In America, many different groups of people hold many different viewpoints. Some groups form to try to persuade government officials to support their views. These groups are exercising the important rights of freedom of speech and assembly. Find out what issues are most important to local environmentalists. Investigate an issue and form your own opinion about it. Contact a group that supports your opinion to see how you can help.

 To learn more about interest groups and public opinion, view the *Democracy in Action* video lesson 18: Interest Groups and Public Opinion.

Summarizing Information Study Foldable *Make this foldable to help you take notes on groups, organizations, and institutions that influence our government.*

Step 1 *Fold a sheet of paper into thirds from top to bottom.*

Step 2 *Turn the paper horizontally, unfold, and label the three columns as shown.*

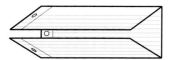

INFLUENCING GOVERNMENT

| Public Opinion | Mass Media | Interest Groups |

Reading and Writing *Take notes as you read the chapter. Place your notes under the heads of the appropriate columns.*

Americans voice their concerns at an Earth Day demonstration. ▶

CIVICS *Online*

Chapter Overview Visit the *Civics Today* Web site at civ.glencoe.com and click on **Chapter Overviews— Chapter 11** to preview chapter information.

SECTION 1

Public Opinion

GUIDE TO READING

Main Idea
Politicians and government officials at all levels pay close attention to public opinion because they know that public support is necessary to stay in office and achieve their goals.

Key Terms
public opinion, mass media, interest group, public opinion poll, pollster

Reading Strategy
Analyzing Information As you read, complete a graphic organizer like the one below by explaining the sources of public opinion.

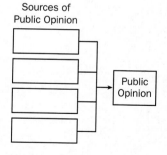

Sources of Public Opinion

Public Opinion

Read to Learn
- Why is public opinion important to politicians and government officials?
- How is pubic opinion formed?

Americans in Action

One man's legacy is to be remembered as an "American public opinion statistician." When George H. Gallup founded the American Institute of Public Opinion in 1935, he probably had little idea that his now-famous Gallup Poll would be so widely recognized in our culture. Today the Gallup Organization is the world's largest management consulting firm. However, the Gallup Poll is most closely associated with public opinion surveys, especially those associated with presidential elections. It is perhaps difficult to determine whether Gallup's polls measure public opinion or shape public opinion.

George Gallup

Forming Public Opinion

Public opinion includes the ideas and attitudes that most people hold about elected officials, candidates, government, and political issues. Public opinion plays a key role in a democracy.

For example, public opinion helps shape the decisions of every president. Presidents know they need the support of the public to carry out their programs. They also need the support of Congress. They are more likely to have this support if their public popularity is high.

Understanding public opinion can also help presidents time their decisions so they are most effective. Successful presidents have a good sense of when the public is ready for a new idea and when it is not. Franklin D. Roosevelt expressed this idea when he said, "I cannot go any faster than the people will let me."

The public opinion of Americans is not uniform, though. In fact, most Americans agree on very few issues. On any given issue, different groups of the "public" often hold different viewpoints. For example, some Americans support increasing the nation's military forces, while others strongly disagree and wish to decrease military spending. Between these two positions are many shades of opinions. Enough people must hold a particular opinion, however, to make government officials listen to them.

Where does public opinion come from? Why do people often hold widely differing opinions about a particular issue or government action?

Personal Background

People's backgrounds and life experiences have a major influence on their opinions. Age, gender, income, race, religion, occupation, and place of residence play important roles. For example, a young, wealthy person who lives in a big city may have very different opinions about the government's role in providing social services than might a poor and elderly person who lives in a small town.

The Mass Media

A medium is a mechanism of communication. (The plural form of the word is "media.") A letter you send to a friend, for example, is a private medium of communication between the two of you. Television, radio, newspapers, magazines, recordings, movies, and books are called the **mass media** because they communicate broadly to masses of people.

The mass media have a major influence on public opinion, providing powerful images and political information that directly affect people's attitudes. For example, broadcasts of a protest rally in the nation's capital or the aftermath of a terrorist bombing can help shape viewers' opinions. The issues and events that the media cover and the way they cover them play a strong part in affecting public opinion.

Public Officials

Political leaders and public officials may also strongly influence public opinion. When voters elect people to office, they are indicating that they trust those officials and rely on their opinions. Public officials state their views in speeches, news conferences, television appearances, and newspaper and magazine articles. In doing so, they hope to persuade as many people as possible to support their positions.

Interest Groups

People who share a point of view about an issue sometimes unite to promote their beliefs. They form what is called an **interest group**. Interest groups work at influencing public opinion by trying to persuade people—including public officials—toward their point of view. For instance,

Expressing Views In these demonstrations, groups of Americans express their views about animal rights Medicare people promot belief

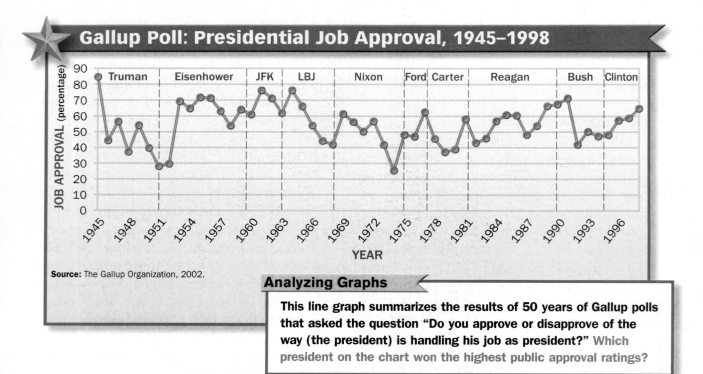

Gallup Poll: Presidential Job Approval, 1945–1998

JOB APPROVAL (percentage)

Truman Eisenhower JFK LBJ Nixon Ford Carter Reagan Bush Clinton

YEAR

Source: The Gallup Organization, 2002.

Analyzing Graphs

This line graph summarizes the results of 50 years of Gallup polls that asked the question "Do you approve or disapprove of the way (the president) is handling his job as president?" Which president on the chart won the highest public approval ratings?

---

groups that try to protect animals from harm make people aware of the treatment of animals used for laboratory testing and for making fur coats. Such groups hope to change people's attitudes about buying products tested on animals or wearing fur coats.

Reading Check **Describing** Why are government officials interested in public opinion?

Components of Public Opinion

Political scientists and public opinion experts often describe public opinion in terms of three features: direction, intensity, and stability. Here is what they mean.

̶n

̶ey question is whether public ̶ any given topic is positive or ̶ example, are people for or ̶ng more money on national ̶le support or oppose a cut ̶t topics, public opinion is

mixed, with some people expressing positive opinions, and other people holding negative opinions.

Intensity

This refers to the strength of opinion on a given issue. Generally, Americans do not have intense opinions about most political topics. When they do have strong feelings, however, many are often willing to act upon them by voting for or against a candidate, working in an election campaign, or even participating in demonstrations.

Stability

Experts explain that the stability of public opinion—meaning how firmly people hold their views—may differ greatly from issue to issue. People's opinions are less likely to change when they have a firm belief about a topic. For example, most people's opinions about civil rights are more stable than are their opinions about political candidates. In many campaigns, especially for president, voters change their minds many times before Election Day. Thus, public opinion on candidates is relatively unstable.

Reading Check **Explaining** Why is public opinion on political candidates considered unstable?

Measuring Public Opinion

How do political leaders, interest groups, and others find out what the public's opinion is on an issue? One way to measure public opinion is by looking at election results. If voters elect a particular candidate to office, presumably many of them agree with the candidate's ideas and proposals. Measuring public opinion by looking at election results is not always reliable, though. People vote for particular candidates for a variety of reasons. Perhaps they liked how a candidate looked, or they voted a straight ticket. Election results show only a broad measure of public opinion.

A more accurate measure is to ask individuals to answer questions in a survey, or a **public opinion poll.** Today hundreds of organizations conduct public opinion polls. Every major elected official uses polls to closely monitor public opinion. Most presidents, for example, have a specialist—a **pollster**—whose job is to conduct polls regularly. The pollster measures the president's popularity or public attitudes toward a White House proposal, such as a possible tax increase.

Random Samples

Modern polling organizations have made a science out of taking polls. Pollsters usually question a group of people selected at random from all over the United States. Such a sample, often of about 1,500 people, will usually include both men and women of nearly all races, incomes, ages,

and viewpoints. A well-constructed sample will reflect the characteristics of the entire population so that it can present a reasonably accurate picture of public opinion.

To find out what people really think, pollsters must be careful how they word their questions. By changing the wording of the questions, pollsters can manipulate the process to get nearly any answers they want. For example, the question "Do you

STREET LAW™

The Law and You

Commission on Violent Video Games

A video game called "Death" has just been released. It contains cutting-edge technology and popular music, and many stores have run out of copies to sell because it is in such high demand. Two groups of citizens have waged campaigns to ban violent video games like "Death." There are also two groups that do not want the government to make the sale of these games illegal. The issue has raised considerable public interest, and the government has established a commission to consider and decide how to deal with the issue. The following groups have been invited to give their input at a public meeting of the government commissioners: Group A: Concerned Parents, Group B: Women Against Violence, Group C: Artists for the First Amendment, Group D: Businesses Against Government Interference.

★ BE AN ACTIVE CITIZEN ★

Select five people in the class to be the government commissioners, who will decide how they will run the meeting. Divide the rest of the class into the four groups above. Each group should give a three-minute presentation to the commission. After the commissioners have heard all the arguments, they should take a vote and explain their decision.

favor cutting taxes?" might produce one kind of answer from a person. "Do you favor cutting taxes if it means letting poor people go hungry?" might make the same person respond differently. When they are considering poll results, thoughtful citizens, as well as legislators, should ask themselves whether the questions were fair and unbiased.

Polls and Democracy

Some people believe that public-opinion polling supports democracy. Polling, they argue, allows officeholders to keep in touch with citizens' changing ideas about issues. With polls, officials do not have to wait until the next election to see if the people approve or disapprove of government policies.

Critics of polling, however, claim it makes our elected officials more concerned with following the public rather than exercising political leadership. Many people also worry that polls are distorting elections. The media conduct polls constantly during campaigns so they can report who is

ahead. Critics argue that these polls treat an election like a horse race, ignoring the candidates' views on issues to concentrate on who is winning at the moment. Furthermore, polls may discourage people from voting. If they show one candidate far ahead of another, some people may decide not to bother voting because they think the election has already been won or lost.

The Framers of the Constitution sought to create a representative democracy that provided for popular rule, but also insulated government leaders from the shifting whims of public opinion. Research has shown that the Framers succeeded. Our government is responsive to public opinion—to the wishes of the people. However, public opinion is not the only influence on public policy. Interest groups, political parties, the mass media, other institutions of government, and individuals also shape public policy.

Reading Check **Explaining** Why is measuring public opinion by using election results considered unreliable?

SECTION 1 ASSESSMENT

Checking for Understanding

1. Key Terms Define the following terms and use them correctly in complete sentences: public opinion, mass media, interest group, public opinion poll, pollster.

Reviewing Main Ideas

2. Identify People who organize to influence public opinion about a particular issue have formed what?

3. Describe In polling, what are random samples? Why must pollsters carefully create the questions they ask?

Critical Thinking

4. Making Judgments Do you think political polling supports or distorts democracy? Explain your opinion.

5. Summarizing Information In a graphic organizer like the one below, describe the features or components of public opinion.

Components of Public Opinion

Analyzing Visuals

6. Compare Review the line graph on page 260. Which president enjoyed greater public approval, Truman or Eisenhower? Which president received the lowest approval ratings?

★**BE AN ACTIVE CITIZEN**★

7. Survey Select an issue of importance to you and develop four or five polling questions about it. Conduct a poll of your classmates using the questions that you developed. Tally the results.

Landmark Supreme Court
Case Studies

Hazelwood School District v. Kuhlmeier

A student holds up the Hazelwood school paper.

The Supreme Court's 1969 ruling in **Tinker** v. **Des Moines** *affirmed students' First Amendment rights to freedom of expression in public schools (see the* **Tinker** *decision in Chapter 4, page 108). How far did those rights extend?*

reversed this ruling. The Court did not overturn *Tinker.* Instead it drew a sharp line between individual expression—as in the wearing of armbands in *Tinker*—and the content of a school-sponsored newspaper. Justice Byron R. White wrote for the 6–3 majority:

> *A school must be able to set high standards for the student speech that is disseminated [distributed] under its [sponsorship] . . . and may refuse to disseminate student speech that does not meet those standards.*

Background of the Case

Hazelwood East High School near St. Louis, Missouri, sponsored a student newspaper as part of its journalism classes. Before each issue went to the printer, the journalism teacher submitted the pages to Principal Robert Reynolds for review.

Reynolds objected to two articles he read in the pages for an issue. One article discussed three pregnant students. The other described a certain student's experience with divorcing parents. Although actual names were not used, Reynolds felt readers could easily identify the featured individuals. Reynolds cancelled the two pages on which the articles appeared.

Kathy Kuhlmeier and two other students who worked on the newspaper sued the school. They claimed their First Amendment rights had been denied.

The Decision

Relying on the Supreme Court's earlier *Tinker* decision, a lower court upheld Kuhlmeier's claim. On January 8, 1988, however, the Supreme Court

Why It Matters

Although students still have some First Amendment protections, the *Hazelwood* decision brought on cries of censorship among advocates of free speech and student interest groups. The Student Press Law Center reports that a number of schools, fearing lawsuits, have done away with student newspapers. Schools have also applied the *Hazelwood* decision to prevent the publication of student yearbooks, stop stage performances, and censor the content of Internet Web pages.

Analyzing the Court Decision

1. What distinction did the Court draw between the free-speech issues in *Tinker* and *Hazelwood*?
2. How do you think *Hazelwood* could affect a school's responsibility to educate?

263

SECTION 2

The Mass Media

Main Idea
The mass media—both print and electronic—play a vital role in politics and government in the United States, linking the people to their elected officials.

Key Terms
print media, electronic media, public agenda, leak, prior restraint, libel

Reading Strategy
Organizing Information As you read, note the impact of the media on politics and government by completing a graphic organizer like the one below.

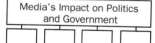

Media's Impact on Politics and Government

Read to Learn
- What are the types of mass media?
- How do the media influence politics and government?

★ ★ ★ ★

Americans in Action

"I purposely went to vote early in the day, before the news programs started telling me who was winning." Florida resident Lora Axtell was certain of her vote. Her husband Fred, on the other hand, was undecided and wanted to see how the returns were coming in. The Axtells live in one of Florida's nine counties that are in the central time zone. After hearing the network news anchors analyze the returns from polls in the eastern time zone, Fred went to vote. It seemed that Al Gore was running well ahead, so Fred cast his vote for Ralph Nader. Gore didn't seem to need his vote, and by voting for Nader, Fred felt he was making a statement. Fred was upset to discover, many hours later, that the networks had called the election prematurely. Perhaps Al Gore had really needed his vote after all.

Election 2000

Types of Media

In modern America the mass media play an important role in influencing politics and government. They also form a link between the people and elected officials.

Print media consist of newspapers, magazines, news-letters, and books. The **electronic media** are radio, television, and the Internet. In the United States, most media outlets are private businesses, run to make a profit. For that reason, media managers often decide what news to run based on what will attract the most viewers, listeners, or readers. The larger the audience, the more money the media can charge for advertising.

Television has become the most important medium for American politics at every level. Ninety-eight percent of American homes have a TV. People have come to rely on TV for news and political information.

More than 70 percent of adults read newspapers, spending an average of about three and a half hours a week on them. Newspapers—and weekly newsmagazines—provide far deeper coverage of current events than does television.

The Internet allows people to get their news and ideas electronically whenever they wish. Internet users can get much more information than is possible from brief radio and television reports.

✓Reading Check **Defining** What does the print media include?

The Media's Impact on Politics and Government

It is hard to imagine modern politics without the mass media. The media have a major impact on public opinion, on the public agenda, on campaigns and elections, and on how politicians perform.

Setting the Public Agenda

Countless problems and issues compete for the government's attention. The ones that receive the most time, money, and effort from government leaders make up what is often called the public agenda. The media have great influence on which problems governments consider important. When the media publicize a problem, such as pollution, people begin to worry about it and to expect that government officials will deal with the problem. The media have the power to define some issues as problems while others go unnoticed.

Candidates and Elections

The modern media, especially television, are making it possible for some people to run for office who might never have done so in an earlier time. Previously candidates

TV and Leaders The first televised presidential debates occurred in 1960. They pitted a campaign-weary Richard Nixon against a youthful and witty John F. Kennedy. Kennedy won the election. After the terrorist attacks in 2001, President Bush appeared on national TV and calmly reassured the public. **Why do you think a government leader's manner on TV is important to public opinion?**

From Star to Politician Former President Ronald Reagan (above) and Minnesota Governor Jesse Ventura (right) were movie and television celebrities before entering the world of politics. **How does TV help former celebrities during campaigns for elections?**

were usually experienced politicians who had spent many years working their way up through their political party. Today sports and show business celebrities with little or no political experience can quickly move into major political positions.

Elected Officials

Journalists and politicians have a complicated relationship. They need one another, yet they often clash. One presidential assistant explained it this way: "Politicians live—and sometimes die—by the press. The press lives by politicians."

Elected officials want the media to show them as hardworking and effective leaders. They also rely on the media to communicate information to the public about government activities and decisions. With the help of professional media assistants called press secretaries, they hold news conferences, give interviews, and stage media events such as a visit to a new housing project or to the site of a disaster.

Officials may also secretly pass on, or **leak,** information to friendly reporters about proposed actions. Leaks allow them to test

public reaction to a proposal without having to acknowledge that the government is considering it. If the public reacts favorably, the government might officially move ahead with the idea. If the public reaction is negative, they can quietly drop it. Politicians also use leaks to make competing officials look bad, to change public opinion on an issue, or to gain favor with a reporter. For example, officials may leak information to expose corruption or to get top government leaders and the media to pay attention to a problem.

Leaking information is part of political life. Many journalists go along with the practice because they benefit from being able to report "inside" information. When they can get hot news from politicians and "scoop" their rivals—break a story first—they become more successful as journalists. President Lyndon B. Johnson understood the game. He once told a reporter, "You help me and I'll help make you a big man in your profession."

Watchdog Role

The mass media play an important "watchdog" role over government activities. Journalists are eager to expose government waste or corruption. They know that stories about government misconduct will attract a large audience. Throughout American history the media have served both their own interests and the public interest by exposing corruption and warning of mistakes or misconduct in government.

A more recent trend in journalism, however, has been to erase the dividing line between politicians' official actions and their private lives. Throughout much of American history, newspapers reported freely on the official deeds and misdeeds of politicians but steered clear of anything personal. In the past few decades, however, the media have stopped honoring this distinction. Now, they often look eagerly for personal scandals not only regarding politicians, but even regarding their families. Some critics condemn the media for this practice and claim that it could drive good people out of politics.

Media and National Security

There is a tension between the American citizens' need for information and the need for the government to keep secrets to protect national security. These tensions are especially evident in foreign affairs in which intelligence information and military secrets are involved. The government can control information the media reports by classifying information as secret and limiting press coverage of military actions. For example, during the 1991 Persian Gulf War and the conflict in Afghanistan starting in 2001, the Defense Department limited the media's access to battlefields and knowledge of military maneuvers. Most reporters covering the events had to rely upon official briefings to gain information about military progress.

Reading Check **Explaining** Why would a government official leak information to the media?

FCC seal

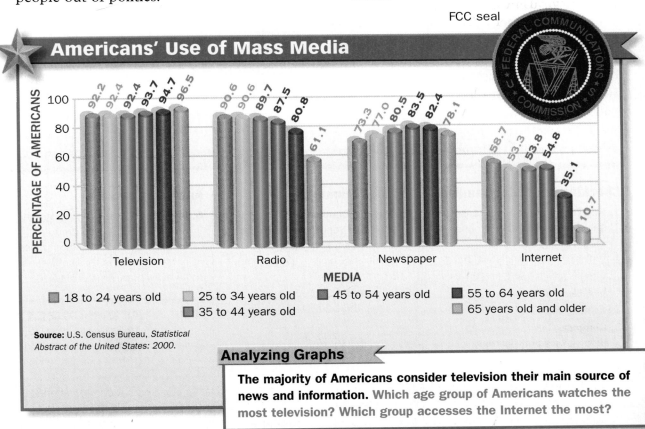

Americans' Use of Mass Media

PERCENTAGE OF AMERICANS

Television: 92.2, 92.4, 92.4, 93.7, 94.7, 96.5
Radio: 90.6, 90.6, 89.7, 87.5, 80.8, 61.1
Newspaper: 73.3, 77.0, 80.5, 83.5, 82.4, 78.1
Internet: 58.7, 53.3, 53.8, 54.8, 35.1, 10.7

MEDIA

■ 18 to 24 years old   ■ 25 to 34 years old   ■ 45 to 54 years old   ■ 55 to 64 years old
■ 35 to 44 years old   ■ 65 years old and older

Source: U.S. Census Bureau, *Statistical Abstract of the United States: 2000.*

Analyzing Graphs

The majority of Americans consider television their main source of news and information. Which age group of Americans watches the most television? Which group accesses the Internet the most?

Protecting the Media

Democracy requires a free flow of information and ideas. In the United States the government plays an important role in protecting the ability of the mass media to operate freely.

The First Amendment to the U.S. Constitution states, in part, "Congress shall make no law . . . abridging the freedom . . . of the press." Today, "press" in this usage refers not only to print media, but to radio, television, and the Internet as well.

The Supreme Court has ruled that the key to this First Amendment protection is freedom from **prior restraint,** or government censorship of material *before* it is published. Generally the government cannot tell the media what or what not to publish. This means that reporters and editors are free to decide what they will say, even if it is unpopular or embarrassing to the government or to individual politicians.

Freedom of the press is not, however, completely unlimited. For example, no one is free to publish false information that will harm someone's reputation. This is called **libel.** Anyone who believes a story has damaged him or her may sue for libel. Unlike ordinary people, however, government officials rarely win libel lawsuits. In 1964 the Supreme Court ruled that public officials must prove actual malice—meaning that the publisher either knew that the material was false or showed a reckless disregard for the truth.

The federal government does have some power to regulate the broadcast media. This is because the government decides who gets access to the limited number of airwaves available for radio and television broadcasting. One way the government regulates broadcasting is through the Federal Communications Commission (FCC). The FCC is a regulatory commission of the federal bureaucracy. The FCC cannot censor broadcasts, but it can penalize stations that violate its rules.

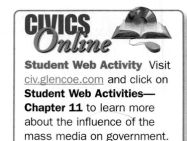

✓ **Reading Check** **Describing** How does the First Amendment protect the media?

SECTION 2 ASSESSMENT

Checking for Understanding

1. **Key Terms** Write a sentence or short paragraph about mass media using each of these terms: print media, electronic media, public agenda, leak, prior restraint, libel.

Reviewing Main Ideas

2. **Compare** Do more people get their news from electronic or print media?

3. **Explain** How does the Federal Communications Commission (FCC) regulate the broadcast media?

Critical Thinking

4. **Drawing Conclusions** Do you think that reporters should be prohibited from writing about a politician's private life or family? Why or why not?

5. **Summarizing Information** Explain how the media are protected in the United States by completing a graphic organizer like the one below.

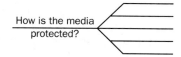

How is the media protected?

Analyzing Visuals

6. **Interpret** Review the bar graph on page 267. Which group of Americans reads the most newspapers? What is the most popular form of mass media?

★**BE AN ACTIVE CITIZEN**★

7. **Research** Interview or write to a local newspaper editor to find out what precautions the newspaper takes to prevent libel suits. Share the information you obtain with the class.

Citizenship SKILLBUILDER

Analyzing News Media

Why Learn This Skill?

Following the news is pretty easy in this high-tech media era. Click on the radio, TV, or the Internet. Pick up a newspaper or magazine. You can get your fill of current events on countless topics. However, you need to examine your sources of information. Some may have biases that blur the facts. Careful analysis can help you find the true facts and become a well-informed citizen.

Learning the Skill

To analyze the news media, follow these steps:

- Know the source and the author of the article. They should have solid credentials and reputations for accuracy.
- Be alert for nonfactual comments in news stories. A valid news story describes events without revealing the reporter's opinions or feelings about them.
- Identify opinion pieces. Writers on editorial pages in print media and many TV commentators are paid for their opinions, not necessarily for reporting facts. Ask yourself whether the news is presented in an even-handed and thorough way.

Practicing the Skill

On a separate sheet of paper, answer the following questions as you analyze the news report on this page.

1. What might be the source of this news report? Is this source generally acknowledged as trustworthy?
2. List two points of information from the story.
3. What opinion is expressed in the story?
4. Explain how you would rate the news value of this article.

People are increasingly spending more time online but not at the cost of family relationships or social activities, says a study to be released Thursday. . . . Jeffrey Cole, director of the UCLA Center for Communication Policy . . . conducted the survey. . . . Internet users watch 4.5 hours less of TV per week than non-Internet users. . . . More Americans than ever are now online, . . . according to the study. And contrary to early warnings sounded by some social scientists, the UCLA survey shows overwhelmingly that Internet usage does not take away from normal family activities. Some 97.3 percent of those surveyed said they spend about the same or more time with their family members since being connected to the Internet. . . .

Overall, online shopping [continues] strong. . . . All this is beneficial to both the public and the private sector, Cole says. . . . Those surveyed . . . said they would buy less if there's a sales tax allowed on Internet sales, a [thought] that lawmakers might want to know . . . as the issue is a subject of congressional deliberation. . . .

Applying the Skill

Read a newspaper editorial aimed at influencing the government. Give at least one example of how the writer weaves fact and opinion together.

GO TO

Practice key skills with Glencoe's **Skillbuilder Interactive CD-ROM, Level 1.**

Interest Groups

GUIDE TO READING

Main Idea

Citizens join together in various kinds of interest groups in order to pool their skills, knowledge, and resources to influence decisions made by politicians and government officials.

Key Terms

public interest group, public policy, political action committee (PAC), lobbyist

Reading Strategy

Organizing Information As you read, complete a graphic organizer similar to the one below by listing various types of interest groups and the kinds of decisions they attempt to influence.

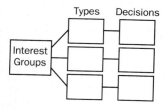

Types   Decisions

Interest Groups

Read to Learn

- What types of interest groups attempt to influence decision making?
- How do interest groups try to influence government?

Americans in Action

All special programs at Longwood Middle School were to be discontinued. Students' grades had fallen on the last standardized tests, and all resources were to be spent on hiring additional teachers to raise students' grades. Pat Vesper wanted her children to continue playing in the band and on a soccer team. Dozens of parents flooded the school board office with telephone calls and e-mails, expressing their anger. After a month, everyone was still angry, but nothing had been accomplished. Then Vesper and several other parents drafted a letter to the school board. In the letter, the parents requested an open meeting with the school board to discuss any possible alternatives. The school board granted the parents' request.

A school soccer team

Types of Interest Groups

Whereas Pat Vesper couldn't achieve much alone, when she worked within a united team, the school board listened. Vesper and those who joined her formed an interest group. As you recall from Section 1, interest groups are groups of people who share a point of view and unite to promote their viewpoints. By their very nature, interest groups are biased; that is, they support a particular viewpoint. To be biased is the opposite of being impartial—considering all viewpoints equally. Citizens join or support interest groups, also called special-interest groups, because they believe that by pooling their resources—time, money, and skills—they can increase their chances of influencing decision makers. An individual may belong to many different interest groups at the same time. For example, a person may belong to a labor union, the Gray Panthers—who protect the interests of older Americans—and also contribute to the National Wildlife Federation. The First Amendment protects your right to belong to interest groups by guaranteeing "the right of the people peaceably to assemble and to petition the government."

Economic Interest Groups

Some of the largest and most powerful interest groups in the United States are based on economic interests. The U.S. Chamber of Commerce, which promotes free enterprise, is one of the largest, with more than 200,000 members. Others represent specific types of businesses, such as the Tobacco Institute, which represents cigarette manufacturers. Such groups try to influence government decisions on issues that affect their industry, like taxes, new safety regulations, or the rules for winning government contracts.

Other interest groups, especially labor unions, work to promote the economic interests of workers. They are concerned with wages, working conditions, benefits such as pensions, and medical care for workers. The American Federation of Labor and Congress of Industrial Organizations (AFL-CIO), an alliance of labor unions, is the largest of these groups. Professionals such as lawyers, doctors, and accountants have their own interest groups. The American Medical Association, for instance, represents doctors.

Other Interest Groups

People have also organized to promote an ethnic group, age group, or gender. The National Association for the Advancement of Colored People (NAACP) and the Congress of Racial Equality work to improve the lives of African Americans. The National Organization for Women (NOW) and the National Women's Political Caucus represent women's interests. The American Association of Retired Persons (AARP) and the National Council of Senior Citizens promote the interests of older Americans.

Another category of interest groups covers those working for special causes. For example, the Sierra Club and the National Wildlife Federation are concerned with protecting nature and wildlife.

Public Interest Groups

All the interest groups described so far are considered private groups because they promote only the special interests of their own members. Some groups, however, work to benefit all, or at least most, of society. These are **public interest groups.** These groups support causes that affect the lives of Americans in general.

One example is Common Cause. This organization has 250,000 members and works to promote the common needs of all citizens. For example, it has fought for legislation to control pollution, to reform election campaign practices, and to protect consumers. The League of Women Voters is a nonpartisan, or impartial, group that promotes voting and educates voters about candidates and issues.

Reading Check **Comparing** What is the difference between private and public interest groups?

The NFL The National Football Players Association is an AFL-CIO union. **What is the AFL-CIO?**

Influencing Government

Interest groups are an important part of our democratic process because their primary goal is to influence **public policy,** which is the course of action the government takes in response to an issue or problem. To do this, interest groups focus their efforts on elections, the courts, and lawmakers.

Election Activities

Some groups use political resources to support certain candidates at election time. For example, the Sierra Club might back candidates who support laws to protect nature and oppose those who disagree with its beliefs.

Many interest groups, including most labor unions and a large number of corporations and trade associations, have formed **political action committees (PACs)**.

PACs collect money from the members of their groups and use it to support some candidates and oppose others. (Read more about how PACs influence elections in Chapter 10.)

Going to Court

Interest groups also try to influence public policy by bringing cases to court. For example, when a law—in the opinion of an interest group—is not being properly enforced, the group may sue the party who is breaking the law. A group may also use the courts to argue that a law or government policy is unconstitutional. For example, Public Citizen, Inc., a consumer group led by Ralph Nader, has brought suits against various companies for violating consumer protection laws.

Lobbying Lawmakers

Interest groups use lobbyists to help them influence government officials, especially national and state legislators. **Lobbyists** are representatives of interest groups who contact lawmakers or other government officials directly to influence their policy making. Lobbyists operate at all levels of government—local, state, and national. Lobbyists may be volunteers or paid employees whose job is to persuade government officials to support their interest group's policies.

The term "lobbyist" dates from the 1830s, when it was applied to people who waited in the lobbies of statehouses to ask politicians for favors. Today lobbyists use a variety of strategies to influence lawmakers. Lobbyists have a good understanding of how the government functions. They know where to go and whom to see. The federal government and each state government have hundreds of departments,

TIME

Political Cartoons

WHOEVER WINS...DON'T FORGET YOUR PROMISES TO ME

LOBBYI$T

GORE

BUSH

and it seems to be diverted toward money and time. Making the world a more convenient | Schneider, two men with little b ing the company's reve

Analyzing Visuals Lobbyists play an active role on Capitol Hill, where they attempt to persuade lawmakers to support the interests of specialized groups of voters. Is the cartoonist expressing a favorable or unfavorable opinion of lobbyists? How do you know?

offices, and agencies, but a good lobbyist knows which department to contact about a particular concern. They are also talented public relations agents who know how to make friends and talk persuasively.

Information is one of the lobbyist's most important resources. Lawmakers need up-to-date information about public issues. The most effective lobbyists are able to supply to lawmakers useful information that helps their own cases. They suggest solutions to problems and issues. Lobbyists sometimes prepare their own drafts of bills for lawmakers to consider and even testify in legislative hearings on bills. All of these activities provide lawmakers with a tremendous amount of information. This is important because lawmakers deal with thousands of bills each year.

The job of lobbyists does not end once a law is enacted. Their interest groups are also concerned with making sure the laws are carried out, enforced, and upheld in court. For example, if an oil exploration bill is approved, environmental groups are likely to watch the whole operation carefully. They want to make sure the oil companies observe any provisions aimed at protecting the environment. If not, lobbyists for the environmental groups will lobby various government departments or agencies to see that the law is enforced.

Reading Check **Concluding** Why might a lawmaker want to interact with a lobbyist?

American Biographies

Ethel Percy Andrus (1884–1967)

Ethel Percy Andrus spent her life as an educator, becoming the first female principal of a California high school at age 32. When she retired at age 60 in 1944, Andrus volunteered to direct California's Retired Teachers Association. What she discovered troubled her. Many retired teachers struggled to survive on small pensions, often with no health insurance.

Andrus decided to form retired teachers into an alliance that would force lawmakers to listen to them. In 1947 she founded the National Retired Teachers Association. In 1956 the organization won the first health insurance program for educators over age 65. Two years later, Andrus founded the American Association for Retired Persons, now know as the AARP.

Under the direction of Andrus, the AARP became a powerful lobby, focused on meeting the needs of all Americans over age 50. Today the AARP has more than 34 million members. The AARP advises governments on age-related issues and protects programs like Social Security. Staffed mostly by volunteers, the AARP tries to fulfill the motto given to it by Andrus: "To Serve; Not to be Served!"

Techniques of Interest Groups

All interest groups want to influence public opinion both to increase their memberships and to convince people of the importance of their causes. Many use direct-mail campaigns to recruit members. They target potential members by using subscriber or membership mailing lists from magazines or groups with a similar viewpoint.

Interest groups also advertise on television and radio, and in newspapers and magazines. Maybe you've seen the ads urging you to drink milk, buy American-made products, or eat pork. Trade associations sponsor these types of ads. Interest groups also stage protests and organize public events to get coverage in the media. Interest groups use propaganda techniques to promote a particular viewpoint or idea. To avoid being misled, citizens need to recognize the following types of propaganda:

- **Endorsements**
  The idea behind endorsements is that if people admire the person endorsing a candidate or product, they will support the candidate or product, too.

- **Stacked Cards**
  Card stacking is a technique that presents only one side of the issue, often by distorting the facts.

- **Name-Calling**
  Name-calling is an attempt to turn people against an opponent or an idea by using an unpleasant label or description for that person or idea.

- **Glittering Generality**
  A glittering generality is a statement that sounds good but is essentially meaningless.

- **Symbols**
  Political candidates and interest groups use and misuse symbols when appealing to the public.

- **Just Plain Folks**
  Political campaigns often use many photographs of candidates wearing hard hats, talking to factory workers, eating pizza or tacos, or even milking cows. The idea of the plain-folks appeal is to make people think that the candidate is just like them, with the same desires and concerns.

- **The Bandwagon**
  Getting on the bandwagon means convincing people that everyone else agrees with the interest group's viewpoint or that everyone is going to vote for a certain candidate. This technique tries to appeal to many people's desire to be on the winning team.

Types of Propaganda Techniques

NAME-CALLING

"Candidate A is a dangerous extremist."

ENDORSEMENT

Popular movie star says, "I'm voting for Candidate A and so should you."

GLITTERING GENERALITY

"Candidate A is the one who will bring us peace and prosperity."

THE BANDWAGON

"Polls show our candidate is pulling ahead, and we expect to win in a landslide."

JUST PLAIN FOLKS

"My parents were ordinary, hardworking people, and they taught me those values."

STACKED CARDS

"Candidate A has the best record on the environment."

SYMBOLS

"I pledge allegiance . . ."

Evaluating Charts

Interest groups and political parties use various techniques to promote their causes. How does name-calling differ from the other techniques?

Regulation of Interest Groups

Although the Constitution guarantees Americans the right to participate in interest groups, state and federal governments may pass laws regulating their activities. (In the past, lobbying was criticized because some lobbyists tried to win legislators' votes by providing them with fancy meals and gifts.) For example, the Federal Election Campaign Act of 1971 limits the amount of money PACs may contribute to candidates for national office. The Federal Regulation of Lobbying Act, passed in 1946, states that any person hired as a lobbyist to influence Congress must register with the Clerk of the House of Representatives and the Secretary of the Senate. Lobbyists are required to disclose who hired them, how much they are paid, and how they spend money related to their work. State governments have passed similar laws. These laws have not been very effective, though, because they apply only to people whose primary job is lobbying. People who claim that only a small part of their time is spent lobbying are not required to register. As a result, only about one-fifth to one-quarter of all lobbyists are registered. Also, the law does not provide any means of enforcement.

Federal and state laws also require a waiting period before former government officials can become lobbyists. The terms of these laws vary from state to state. A typical law might bar a former state legislator from lobbying the legislature for two years after leaving office. These laws are meant to prevent ex-public officials from taking unfair advantage of inside knowledge and friendships with former associates on behalf of interest groups. These laws have proved inadequate, especially at the federal level.

Some people argue that interest groups and lobbyists have too much say in government. Critics claim that campaign contributions give interest groups improper influence over officeholders. Others, however, point out that, by themselves, most citizens can have little effect on government officials, but as members of an effective interest group, with skilled lobbyists, citizens can increase their influence.

Reading Check **Explaining** Why has lobbying been criticized in the past?

SECTION 3 ASSESSMENT

Checking for Understanding

1. Key Terms Define the following terms and use them in sentences related to interest groups: public interest group, public policy, political action committee (PAC), lobbyist.

Reviewing Main Ideas

2. Explain What was the purpose of the Federal Election Campaign Act of 1971?

3. Conclude With what kind of issues would public interest groups be most likely concerned? Give an example.

Critical Thinking

4. Making Comparisons Compare and contrast the benefits and dangers of interest groups and lobbyists in our political system.

5. Summarizing Information Complete a web diagram like the one below to show how interest groups influence governmental decision making.

How Interest Groups Influence Government

Analyzing Visuals

6. Identify Review the chart on page 274. Which technique is a group using when it lists all the advantages of supporting its cause, but fails to list any disadvantages?

★ **BE AN ACTIVE CITIZEN** ★
7. Research Contact a large corporation that has a presence in your community. Find out how many lobbyists they employ and what kinds of issues they deal with.

Assessment & Activities

Review to Learn

Section 1

- Public opinion helps shape the decisions of government officials.
- A person's background, the mass media, public officials, and interest groups all play a role in shaping public opinion.

Section 2

- There are two types of mass media—print and electronic.
- The mass media help set the public agenda, publicize candidates, and present information to the public.
- The mass media also monitor government activities.

Section 3

- Economic interest groups, public interest groups, and private groups like the NAACP, AARP, and environmental groups all influence government decision making.

FOLDABLES
Study Organizer

Using Your Foldables Study Organizer
Form groups of about five students. Place your desks in a circle. Then each person in the circle, in turn, describes one way that the government is influenced, using the completed foldable.

Reviewing Key Terms

Write the chapter key term that matches each clue below.

1. often hired by interest groups to help them influence government officials
2. ideas and attitudes that most people hold about elected officials and political issues
3. government censorship of material before it is published
4. television, radio, newspapers, magazines, recordings, movies, and books
5. publishing false information that harms a person's reputation
6. actions taken by government leaders to resolve a problem or issue
7. people who share a point of view about an issue and join together
8. problems that government leaders consider most important and receive the most attention
9. surveys of individuals that ask questions about issues or candidates
10. organizations that collect money from members of their group and use it to support some candidates and oppose others

Reviewing Main Ideas

11. Why do people form interest groups?
12. Why do some people criticize public opinion polls?
13. What factors can influence a person's opinion on particular issues?
14. What impact do the mass media have on politics and government in the United States?
15. What role does the Federal Communications Commission (FCC) have in regulating the media?
16. What do political action committees (PACs) do?
17. What are the main tasks of lobbyists?
18. What are the provisions of the Federal Regulation of Lobbying Act of 1946?

Critical Thinking

19. **Analyzing Information** What role do you think public opinion polls should play in the political process? Explain.

20. **Cause and Effect** In a chart like the one below, determine the effect of constitutional protections as they relate to the media.

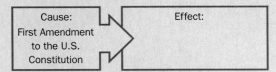

Cause: First Amendment to the U.S. Constitution → Effect:

Practicing Skills

Analyzing News Media **Find a report of a recent political opinion poll on the Internet or in a newsmagazine or newspaper and answer the following questions.**

21. What is the poll about and when was it conducted?

22. What specific questions were asked? Can you think of a way that these questions might be phrased that would be less biased?

23. Summarize the results of the poll in sentence form.

Analyzing Visuals

24. Examine the photograph that opens the chapter on page 257. What actions are taking place in the photo? What type of interest group is most likely sponsoring these actions? Why do you think these citizens are taking these actions? What do you think they hope to accomplish?

$ Economics Activity

25. On the Internet, go to www.opensecrets.org/lobbyists/. Look at the chart "Total Lobbyist Spending (in Millions)." In 1999 what industry spent the most on lobbying? Which spent the least? Why do you think industries spend such large amounts of money on lobbyists each year?

★ CITIZENSHIP COOPERATIVE ACTIVITY ★

26. Form groups of four or five and select an issue in your community. Assume the role of a lobbyist working for a group that supports your position on the issue. Develop a plan for lobbying. The plan should include a clear statement of your position, a list of officials you would lobby, and an outline of your presentation.

Technology Activity

27. Think about a political or social issue in which you are interested. Then do an Internet search to find an interest group related to the issue that you might want to join. Create a visual presentation about the group.

The Princeton Review
Standardized Test Practice

Directions: Choose the answer that *best* completes the following statement.

_____ influence public policy by identifying issues, making political contributions, and lobbying government officials.

A The mass media
B Interest groups
C Pollsters
D Random samples

Test-Taking Tip

Define each answer choice as best as you can before answering the question. Which definition best fits the statement?

State and Local Government

Why It Matters

The relationship between the American people and government is closest at the state and local levels. As citizens, one of our most important roles is to work with local leaders to improve our communities and solve problems affecting their well-being.

Use the **American History Primary Source Document Library CD-ROM** to find primary sources about state and local governments.

 BE AN ACTIVE CITIZEN

As you study Unit 4, participate in an ongoing activity to help your community. You might, for example, help clean up local highways or tutor younger students. Keep a journal describing your activities and then share your thoughts and experiences with the class at the end of the unit.

Old State House in
Little Rock, Arkansas

State Government

★ CITIZENSHIP AND YOU ★

When you make a purchase, you probably pay a state sales tax. Your state maintains many of the roads you ride on and funds the police forces that patrol those roads. Prepare a chart of your state government that shows major officials and their responsibilities. Contact a state official to express your opinion on a specific state policy.

 To learn more about state government, view the *Democracy in Action* video lesson 23: The State and You.

Organizing Information Study Foldable *Make this foldable table to help you organize what you learn about state government.*

Step 1 *Fold a sheet of paper into thirds from top to bottom.*

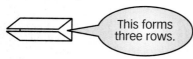

This forms three rows.

Step 2 *Open the paper and refold it into fourths from side to side.*

Fold it in half, then in half again.

This forms four columns.

Step 3 *Unfold, turn the paper, and draw lines along the folds.*

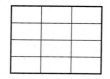

Step 4 *Label as shown.*

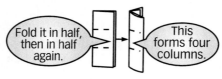

	Organization	Responsibilities
State Legislative Branch		
State Executive Branch		
State Judicial Branch		

Reading and Writing *Fill out your table foldable as you read the chapter. You will organize information about the three branches of state government.*

CIVICS *Online*

Chapter Overview Visit the *Civics Today* Web site at civ.glencoe.com and click on **Chapter Overviews— Chapter 12** to preview chapter information.

The Federal System

GUIDE TO READING

Main Idea
When the Framers of the U.S. Constitution created a federal system, they ensured that power would be shared between the national and state governments.

Key Terms
federal system, reserved powers, concurrent powers, grants-in-aid

Reading Strategy
Organizing Information As you read, use a graphic organizer like the one below to help you take notes about our federal system of government.

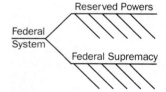

Federal System
Reserved Powers
Federal Supremacy

Read to Learn
- How does the federal system of government operate?
- How do state governments cooperate

Americans in Action

In 2001, before the Winter Olympics in Salt Lake City, Utah, were to begin, Deputy Attorney General Larry D. Thompson of the United States proclaimed: "[I]n August of 1999, the 2002 Olympics were designated as a National Special Security Event. Consistent with that designation, the [Department of Justice] as lead agency for crisis management is working closely with the Secret Service, FEMA, and other federal, state, and local law crisis management and consequent management agencies to plan not only for security and public safety at the Olympics but also for crisis response." Federal, state, and local agencies worked as a team to protect the more than 1,000 athletes and thousands of spectators at the Games.

The 2002 Olympics opening ceremony

The Constitution and Federalism

As you learned in Chapter 2, when the original 13 American colonies became states, they behaved like 13 individual nations. Each wrote its own constitution, set up its own government, and made its own laws. During the Revolutionary War, the first national government was established under the Articles of Confederation. This government was weak and ineffective, though, so less than 10 years later, national leaders gathered to develop a better system of government. This government was established by the United States Constitution, under which the states agreed to give up some of their independence.

One of the most important decisions the Framers of the Constitution made was to create a **federal system** of government. In a federal system, or federalism, the central government and the governments of the states share power. The sharing, however, is not equal. If a state law conflicts with a national law, the national law has supremacy and must be followed.

Federalism is a middle position between having an all-powerful central government and a system in which the states dominate. The writers of the Constitution wanted to place some limits on national power and yet not allow the states to be so strong—as under the Articles of Confederation—that the central government would be ineffective.

The Constitution protects states in several ways. For example, no state can be divided or merged with another state without its consent. States have the right to maintain a militia—a military force called the National Guard—under the control of each state's governor. The governor may call on the National Guard in local emergencies, such as civil unrest or natural disasters. In a national emergency, however, the president may federalize the National Guard, putting it under control of the U.S. armed forces.

Each state is largely free to govern itself the way its citizens consider best. The Constitution does not list the powers of state governments as it does for the national government. Instead it specifies what the state governments may *not* do. Article I of the Constitution forbids states to make treaties with foreign countries or declare war, keep an army in peacetime, issue their own money, or impose taxes on imports from other countries or states. In addition, several constitutional amendments prevent state governments from taking away civil liberties and rights granted by the federal government. The most important of these is the Fourteenth Amendment, which guarantees all Americans "equal protection of the laws."

Reserved Powers

The Tenth Amendment to the U.S. Constitution gives the states additional authority. It establishes that state governments may exercise all powers not given to the federal government or denied to the states. These powers are called **reserved powers** because they are reserved to the states. Among them are the powers to make marriage and divorce laws, to regulate education, and to hold elections.

In general, each state is responsible for the public health, safety, and welfare of its citizens. State governments often use their

Protecting States Members of the Montana National Guard trudge up a fire-scarred hill in Helena National Forest in 2000, after wildfires destroyed the area. Virginia State police demonstrate a robot, which is used to take over the dangerous task of finding and defusing bombs. **What government official controls a state's National Guard?**

Division of State and Federal Powers

National Government	**National and State Governments**	**State Governments**
(Expressed, Implied, and Inherent Powers)	*(Concurrent Powers)*	*(Reserved Powers)*
★ Regulate foreign and interstate commerce	★ Levy taxes	★ Regulate intrastate commerce
★ Coin money	★ Borrow money	★ Establish local government systems
★ Provide an army and a navy	★ Spend for general welfare	★ Administer elections
★ Declare war	★ Establish courts	★ Protect the public's health, welfare, and morals
★ Establish federal courts below the Supreme Court	★ Enact and enforce laws	
★ Conduct foreign relations		
★ Exercise powers implied from the expressed powers		

Evaluating Charts

These are the major constitutional functions of each level of government. At what level do you think most criminal trials take place?

---

reserved powers to meet this responsibility. They set up police forces and other law enforcement operations. They build roads and bridges. They regulate business and trade within the state. They set educational requirements and provide money to run the schools. They organize local governments for counties, cities, and towns. Your state government affects many of your daily activities.

Federal Supremacy

The Constitution grants some concurrent powers—those shared by state governments and the federal govern- ____ Both, for example, may impose ____ row money. If, however, ____ tween the states and the ____ nt over certain kinds of ____ eme Court decides the ____ the Constitution states ____ ongress makes shall be ____ f the land." This clause ____ macy clause.

In the landmark case *McCulloch* v. *Maryland* in 1819, the Supreme Court held that Maryland could not tax a branch of the Bank of the United States in Baltimore. This ruling was interpreted to mean that if a state's powers conflict with the powers of the federal government, federal powers take precedence. 📖 Read more about this **Landmark Supreme Court Case** on page 519.

States' Rights v. Nationalists

Throughout our history, Americans have argued over how federalism should operate. One view—the states' rights posi- tion—argues that because the states created the national government, all of the national government's powers should be limited. Those who favor states' rights believe that state governments are closer to the people and better reflect the people's wishes than the national government can. On the other hand, Americans who support the national- ist position argue that the people, not the states, created the national government and the states. Therefore, the powers granted to the national government should be expanded as needed to carry out the people's will. Supporters of this nationalist position argue that the "necessary and proper" clause of the Constitution means that Congress has the right to adopt any means it needs to carry out its delegated powers. Supporters of the nationalist position look to the national government to take the lead in solving major social and economic problems facing the nation.

The balance of powers between the national and state governments has shifted back and forth throughout American history. The national government's ability to wage war, regulate commerce, and levy taxes has increased the national government's authority. However, some people believe that state and local governments will always be very important because Americans identify more closely with their local communities and look to these communities to understand their needs.

Reading Check **Defining** What are reserved powers?

Governmental Cooperation

Since the 1930s, state governments and the federal government have increasingly cooperated to fund and administer a wide variety of programs. These include highways, education, and welfare. Usually the federal government provides **grants-in-aid**—awards of money—to the states to help them pay for some of their programs. States must contribute some of their own money, and they must obey rules set by Congress in order to receive these grants. For example, the federal government contributes 90 percent of the money to build interstate highways, but states must comply with a list of regulations, such as the width of driving lanes and the quality of building materials.

The federal government gives some grants-in-aid directly to cities and counties. In other cases federal grants "pass through" state governments to cities. Like the federal government, states award grants to cities and counties, with conditions attached.

The Constitution also helps ensure that states cooperate with each other. Article IV of the Constitution encourages interstate cooperation by requiring states to give "full faith and credit" to the public laws and court decisions of other states. This means, for example, that if people get married in one state, the legality of the marriage must be accepted in all other states.

Article IV of the U.S. Constitution also requires every state to have a "republican form of government." The federal government will defend these state governments if they are threatened. The federal government will protect each state against invasion and domestic violence. When a state or local police force cannot control violent incidents within a state, the governor may call for the assistance of federal troops. In 1967, for example, President Lyndon Johnson sent troops to Detroit to help control racial unrest and rioting when Michigan's governor declared that the Detroit police and the Michigan National Guard could not stop the widespread violence.

In return, states provide certain services to the federal government. For example, states conduct elections for federal offices, such as president and vice president of the United States. This is considere reserved powers of the st play a key role in the pro the Constitution. No ar added to the Constitut fourths of the states app

Reading Check **Expla** grants-in-aid work?

State Constitutions

State constitutions differ from state to state because every state has its own ideas about what makes a good government. All state constitutions, though, share certain characteristics.

Every state constitution provides for separation of powers among three branches of government—legislative, executive, and judicial. The state constitutions outline the organization of each branch, the powers and terms of various offices, and the method of election for state officials. States have also included their own bills of rights in their constitutions, which include all or most of the protections of the Bill of Rights in the U.S. Constitution. Often, they also include rights not provided in the national Constitution, such as workers' right to join unions and protections for the physically challenged.

State constitutions also establish different types of local governments, including counties, townships, municipalities, special districts, parishes, and boroughs. State constitutions usually define the powers and duties as well as the organization of these forms of local government.

State constitutions regulate the ways state and local governments can raise and spend money. In many states, for example, the state constitution limits the taxing power of local governments.

Finally, state constitutions establish independent state agencies, boards, and commissions, such as public utility commissions and state boards of education.

Just as the U.S. Constitution is the highest law in the nation, a state's constitution is the highest law in that state. State constitutions, however, cannot include provisions that clash with the U.S. Constitution.

The amendment process is an important part of every state constitution. While the procedure for changing the constitution varies from state to state, it is usually a two-step process similar to amending the U.S. Constitution. An amendment must first be proposed, generally by the legislature, then it must be ratified by the voters. As states' powers have grown and changed, state constitutions have been amended hundreds of times.

Reading Check **Comparing** What do all state constitutions have in common?

SECTION 1 ASSESSMENT

Checking for Understanding

1. Key Terms Define the following terms and use them in complete sentences related to the section: federal system, reserved powers, concurrent powers,

s in a federal
the United
conflicts

federal-
faith and

Critical Thinking

4. Making Comparisons How are reserved powers different from concurrent powers?

5. Categorizing Information On a web diagram like the one below, categorize the important features of the federal system of government.

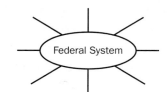

Federal System

Analyzing Visuals

6. Interpret Review the Venn diagram on page 284. How did the Constitution involve the states in national elections?

★ **BE AN ACTIVE CITIZEN** ★
7. Organize Look at both the state and federal government pages of your phone book. List the government agencies that reflect "reserved" and those that reflect "concurrent" powers.

State Government

The State Legislative Branch

GUIDE TO READING

Main Idea
State legislatures operate much like the U.S. Congress at the national level, but they also have the important task of apportioning election districts.

Key Terms
unicameral, apportion

Reading Strategy
Summarizing Information As you read, take notes by completing a web diagram like the one below by adding details under each of the three secondary heads.

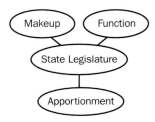

Read to Learn
• How do state legislatures compare to the U.S. Congress?
• How do state legislatures operate?

Americans in Action

Mary Fallin took over the Oklahoma state senate. This had never been done before. The event made the news, but it was really just part of Fallin's job. As Oklahoma's elected lieutenant governor, Fallin serves as the head of the state's senate. Under normal circumstances, the lieutenant governor rarely attends legislative sessions. In this case, though, Fallin asserted her leadership when state senators were making no headway on a right-to-work issue. As a result of Fallin's intervention, senators were able to come to some agreement and vote on the issue for the first time in 25 years. Fallin is Oklahoma's first female lieutenant governor.

Lieutenant Governor Fallin

Makeup of Legislatures

State lawmaking bodies vary in name and size. In some states the legislature is called the general assembly or the legislative assembly. Most states, however, simply call it the legislature. New Hampshire, one of the nation's smallest states in both area and population, has the largest legislature—more than 400 members. Nebraska has the smallest, with only 49 members.

Except for Nebraska's **unicameral,** or one-house, legislature, every state has an upper house, called the senate, and a lower house, usually called the house of representatives. Senators typically serve four-year terms, represe[...] year terms. Their salaries are the same. The h[...] two to four times as many members as the se[...]

Each state constitution lists the qualificat[...] of its legislature. Generally, members must [...] zens and live in the district they represent. [...] resentatives must be at least 18 years old, [...] age for senators ranges from 18 to 30.

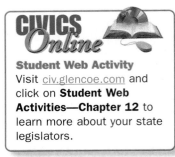
Originally, service in the state legislature required little of a member's time. Many legislatures met for only a few months every two years, and members received little more than token pay. As state governments have become burdened with ever-growing responsibilities, however, membership in the legislature has become a far more demanding job. Some legislatures meet year-round, and pay for members is becoming more suited to the level of work.

Reading Check **Identifying** What are state lawmaking bodies called?

How State Legislatures Function

State legislatures operate much like the U.S. Congress (see Chapter 6). Each house has a leader. A speaker of the house directs business in the house of representatives, and a president—the lieutenant governor in about half the states—does the same in the senate. The majority political party in the house selects the speaker, and in states where the lieutenant governor does not preside over the senate, the majority party picks the senate president. These leaders have a great deal of influence over what happens to proposed legislation.

Ideas for bills come from many sources, including the governor, the executive branch, interest groups, individuals, and the legislators themselves. State legislatures, like Congress, have various committees. The majority party in each house chooses committee chairpersons. After a member in either house introduces a bill, it goes to the appropriate committee of that house, such as the education or agriculture committee.

The committees study bills, hold hearings, and revise the bills if necessary. In many cases, bills die in committee, never making it to a vote. Otherwise, a committee may send a bill to the full house, with a recommendation that it be passed or rejected. If the two houses pass differing versions of the same bill, it goes to a conference committee, which works out agreeable language. Both houses must approve a bill and the governor must sign it before it becomes a law.

Reading Check **Identifying** Who are the leaders in state legislatures?

Official seal of the Vermont state legislature

State Legislators The Vermont state legislature holds a session in the State House in the capital, Montpelier. **What is the purpose of state legislatures?**

Teen Legislator
State Representative Derrick Seaver, at age 18, became the youngest resident elected to the Ohio state legislature in 2000. Seaver, a part-time student, spends more time than he ever imagined on legislative work. He says, "The idea of a 16- to 17-hour day in Columbus was new to me." **How has the job of state legislator changed from the past?**

Legislative Apportionment

The Census Bureau takes a national census, or population count, every 10 years. So every 10 years, state legislatures set up or reexamine congressional districts. Representatives to the U.S. Congress and the state legislature are elected from districts. In most states, legislatures draw the boundary lines for each congressional election district.

Each state legislature divides its state into many election districts. Generally, one set of districts is laid out for senators and another for representatives. For many years, senate districts were based roughly on land area, and house districts were **apportioned,** or divided into districts, based on population. Area-based districts often produced malapportionment, or unequal representation, in many state legislatures. For example, a city district and a rural district might each have had one senator, even though the city district had 10 times as many people. This happened because as the population grew, especially in cities and suburbs, powerful rural senators refused to allow districts to be redrawn more fairly.

This situation began to be corrected in 1962 after the U.S. Supreme Court ruled in *Baker* v. *Carr* that federal courts can hear suits to force state authorities to redraw electoral districts. Then in 1964, in *Reynolds* v. *Sims,* the Court held that both chambers of state legislatures must be apportioned on the basis of equal population. In the language of the Court, districts must be redrawn on the principle of "one man, one vote." As a result, many states had to change the apportionment of their legislatures.

Reading Check **Defining** What is malapportionment?

Problems Facing States

Americans have begun to and more from their state They demand better publi better schools, and bette ple who are disabled They also expect state g tect the environment, and reduce crime and

Lobbying for His Cause House Speaker Pro Tempore Sherman Copelin, Jr., of the Louisiana House of Representatives (left), speaks with a lobbyist. Recall from Chapter 11 that a lobbyist tries to persuade government offi-cals to support certain issues or groups. **What pressures do state legislators face when it comes to providing necessary services for their constituents?**

State governments, however, are finding it difficult if not impossible to pay for these services. Many legislators refuse to vote to raise taxes because such a vote may harm them in reelections. Also, whereas federal grants paid for many of these services in the past, the federal government has eliminated many of these grants because of its own budget concerns.

As a result, state legislators are faced with a difficult choice: Should they cut state programs or raise taxes to pay for them? Legislators fear they may be defeated in the next election if they raise taxes. They also do not wish to cut essential services. Cutting services at a time when crime, homelessness, and pollution are rising may be considered by many legislators and voters to be unwise and irresponsible. The Supreme Court's "one man, one vote" rule also increased the representation of city dwellers in state legis-latures. Since cities are where crime, drug abuse, and unemployment are often highest, today's state legislators face tremendous pressure in dealing with these issues.

Reading Check **Inferring** What issues face state legislators today?

SECTION 2 ASSESSMENT

Checking for Understanding

1. Key Terms Write complete sen-tences for each of the following terms related to state legisla-tures: unicameral, apportion.

Reviewing Main Ideas

2. Identify What problem did the ~~me~~ Court case ~~dress?~~
~~is meant by~~
~~e"? From~~
~~t ruling did~~
~~ow did it~~
~~es?~~

Critical Thinking

4. Making Judgments Originally most state legislatures required only part-time lawmakers. Today many state legislators work full time. Do you think this is a good development? Why or why not?

5. Cause and Effect On a graphic organizer similar to the one below, list the causes and effects of *Baker* v. *Carr* and *Reynolds* v. *Sims*.

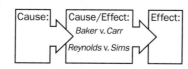

| Cause: | Cause/Effect: *Baker* v. *Carr* *Reynolds* v. *Sims* | Effect: |

Analyzing Visuals

6. Recall Review the photograph of Derrick Seaver, a young state legislator, on page 289. What are the qualifications for mem-bers of state legislatures? What is unique about Derrick Seaver?

★ **BE AN ACTIVE CITIZEN** ★

7. Write Choose one of your state representatives or senators to research. Write a brief biography of the person focusing on his or her legislative priorities.

State Government

Issues to Debate

Should Students Have to Wear School Uniforms?

There's no uniform thinking on the subject of school uniforms. Students, parents, teachers, and officials have debated the topic ever since President Bill Clinton gave uniforms a huge boost in his 1996 State of the Union address. "Too often, we learn that students resort to violence and theft to obtain designer clothes or fancy sneakers," Clinton declared.

Since that time, the U.S. Department of Education has sent its *Manual on School Uniforms* to every school district in the nation, and nearly one-quarter of all schools have adopted uniforms on a mandatory or voluntary basis. In early 2001, a federal appeals court in Louisiana became the first to uphold the policy, but the debate still goes on. Are school uniforms a good idea?

Wearing mandatory uniforms

Yes

I think the wearing of school uniforms improves the tone of a school, and helps young people put the focus on who they are and what they know and what they think, rather than on what they wear.

—*Carol Gresser, Board of, Education member, New York*

No

Before you make a decision on school uniforms, you should consider the First Amendment, which gives U.S. citizens the freedom of speech. Speech can be defined many ways. . . . Forcing students to wear the same thing infringes on their First Amendment rights. When little children ask their parents why everybody is not the same, most parents reply with a popular saying: "Variety is the spice of life."

—*Mary H., student, Gainesville, Florida*

Debating the Issue

1. What benefits does Carol see to wearing school uniforms?
2. What arguments does Mary use to oppose school uniforms?
3. What reasons did President Clinton give for mandatory uniforms?
4. Write down where you stand on the issue of school uniforms. Then defend the opposite position either in a brief essay or an oral presentation. This will help you understand the feelings of the other side—a good way to reduce conflict and build compromises.
5. Did writing the essay (called for in question 4) make you change your mind about the issue? In just one or two sentences, explain why it did or did not change your opinion about mandatory school uniforms.

The State Executive Branch

GUIDE TO READING

Main Idea

Much like the president at the national level, governors act as the chief executives of their states and carry out the laws passed by their legislatures.

Key Terms

line-item veto, commute, parole

Reading Strategy

Organizing Information As you read, take notes on the qualifications, powers, and duties of governors by completing a chart like the one below.

Governors	
Qualifications	
Powers	
Duties	

Read to Learn

- How are governors elected?
- What are the powers and duties of state governors?

Americans in Action

In 2001 California faced a summer of energy shortages that could have led to rolling blackouts. Governor Gray Davis launched a plan: "Our first priority must be providing reliable, reasonably priced energy to power our homes and businesses. Yes, we have a power shortage, but we are far from powerless. By reducing our electricity demand by even a small amount, we can reduce the price, avoid shortages and lower energy bills. And our long-range goal must be greater energy production within our borders." Meanwhile, Davis knew that how he dealt with the crisis would affect his reelection chances. One of his aides put it this way: "[W]hat people care about are two things: The lights stay on and bills don't go through the roof. Everything else is background noise."

Governor Davis

Office of Governor

As in the federal government, every state government has an executive branch consisting of a chief executive—the governor—and a number of departments and agencies that carry out the business of the state.

Each state constitution includes a set of qualifications for the office of governor. In most states a governor must be an American citizen, at least 30 years old, and a resident of the state for at least 5 years. Of course, serious candidates for the office of governor have many more qualifications. Most governors have previously been elected to other public offices or have been active in state politics. Many have had successful careers in law or business. Often, they are talented at public speaking and are able to "think on their feet"—meaning that they can give thoughtful and intelligent answers to challenging questions from reporters or from citizens in public forums.

The voters of each state elect their governor directly. There is no Electoral College in state elections. Other than that difference, candidates for governor are nominated and elected in much the same way as the president of the United States. First, an individual must gain the nomination of a major political party, usually by winning a party primary. Then that party nominee runs in the general election.

Most governors serve four-year terms. In nearly every state, a governor can be impeached and removed from office for committing a crime. In several states, the voters themselves can take steps to unseat their governor by demanding a special "recall" election.

In most states, governors and lieutenant governors run as a team in elections. In the past they ran separately, making it possible for a governor to have a lieutenant governor from another political party. Typically, the lieutenant governor moves up to the top position if the governor leaves office. In most states, the lieutenant governor has only a few official duties, such as presiding over the state senate.

Powers and Duties of the Governor

Like the president of the United States, a governor heads the executive branch of state government and fills many of the same kinds of roles. A governor's most important role is that of the state's chief executive. In this role the governor is responsible for carrying out the laws of the state. To help with this job, the governor issues executive orders to a large state bureaucracy. The governor appoints some of the top officials of the bureaucracy, usually with the approval of the state senate. In most states the governor is also responsible for preparing a budget and winning its approval from the legislature.

The governor is also the state's chief legislator. Although only the legislature has the power to adopt laws, the governor can play a part. He or she can suggest new bills and try to persuade the legislature to pass them, either by making speeches to the legislators or lobbying privately with leading members of the legislature.

All governors have the power to veto bills the legislature has passed. Indeed, most governors have greater veto power than the president of the United States has. Governors in many states have the power to veto specific parts of a bill—an action called a line-item veto—while the president of the United States must either sign a bill just as it is or veto it completely. State legislatures may override governors' vetoes. Usually, however, overrides require a two-thirds vote, and they rarely happen.

Massachusetts' Governor Lt. Governor Jane Swift accepted a ceremonial key to the governor's office in 2001 to become the first female governor of Massachusetts. **What are the qualifications to become a governor?**

Governors also have certain judicial powers. A governor may grant pardons to convicted criminals or commute—reduce—a

Powers and Duties of the Governor

Judicial Leader
Offers pardons and reprieves;
Grants parole

Ceremonial Leader
Greets important visitors;
Represents the state

Chief Executive
Carries out state laws;
Appoints officials;
Prepares a budget

Chief Legislator
Proposes legislation;
Approves or vetoes legislation

Commander in Chief
In charge of the National Guard
(state militia)

Party Leader
Leads the political party in the state

Evaluating Charts

A state governor has many of the same roles as the president of the United States. What does the role of chief legislator involve?

criminal's sentence. In states that permit capital punishment, for example, a governor may decide to commute a death sentence to life in prison. Governors also have the power to grant a prisoner a parole, an early release from prison, with certain restrictions.

Governors play other roles as well. Every governor is commander in chief of the state National Guard. The governor is the state leader of his or her political party. The governor also serves as ceremonial leader of the state, greeting important visitors.

Until recently nearly all governors were white males. Since the 1960s many states have elected female governors. Several Southwestern states have elected Hispanic American governors. Washington State has had an Asian American governor. Virginia has had the only African American governor in American history.

Reading Check **Recalling** What legislative powers does a governor have?

Executive Departments

Not every governor has a cabinet, but every state has a number of top officials who are in charge of executive departments and who advise the governor on important issues related to their area of responsibility. Governors appoint many of these officials. In most states, some of these officials are elected to office, however.

While the top officials vary from state to state, most states have a few in common. Usually a secretary of state manages elections and maintains the state's official records. An attorney general represents the state in lawsuits and gives legal advice to the governor, state agencies, and the legislature. A treasurer collects taxes and invests state funds. An auditor reviews the record keeping of state agencies to make certain that their money is used according to state law.

Political Cartoons

and it seems to be diverted toward money and _ne_. Making the world a more convenient | Schneider, two men with little hope, of regain-ing the company's revenue. While the wage was | to be diverted tim

Analyzing Visuals As part of the "welfare-reform" legislation in the 1990s, the federal government shifted significant responsibility for welfare programs to individual states. In the cartoonist's view, what is the impact of the federal government's decision to transfer responsibility for welfare to the states?

In addition, every state has a number of executive departments, agencies, boards, and commissions. Some, such as departments of justice, agriculture, and labor, are like their federal counterparts. Others exist only at the state level. Most states have a department or board of health, which runs programs in disease prevention and health education, and departments of public works and highways, which are responsible for building and maintaining roads, bridges, public buildings, and other state properties. Most states also have a state welfare board to help the unemployed and people living in poverty.

✓**Reading Check** **Describing** What does a state auditor do?

SECTION 3 ASSESSMENT

Checking for Understanding

1. Key Terms Use the following terms in a sentence or short paragraph related to state governors: line-item veto, commute, parole.

Reviewing Main Ideas

2. Identify What judicial powers do governors have?

3. Describe What role does an attorney general perform in state governments?

Critical Thinking

4. Drawing Conclusions Do you think a governor should have the power to pardon or commute the sentence of a person convicted of a crime? Why or why not?

5. Making Comparisons In a chart like the one below, compare the powers of a president and state governors.

President's Powers	Governors' Powers

Analyzing Visuals

6. Describe Study the chart that lists the powers and duties of the governor on page 294. What duties do governors fulfill as chief executive?

★**BE AN ACTIVE CITIZEN**★

7. Write Read a local newspaper for the next five days. Write a brief summary of all the articles related to your state's governor. For each article, indicate which power or duty of the governor is involved.

Using Library Resources

Why Learn This Skill?

Perhaps you have a report to write. Maybe you just want to know more about a topic. Either circumstance can send you to the library, looking for information. The success of your search depends on how skillfully you use the many resources the library offers.

Learning the Skill

To make efficient use of library resources, follow these steps:

- Define the topic and subtopics of your search.
- For current events, you might start with the newspaper and periodicals section. Use the *Readers' Guide to Periodical Literature* to locate magazine articles on your topic.
- Use almanacs and abstracts in the library's reference section for condensed facts and figures. The *World Almanac,* for instance, lists a wide variety of information, from cultural to political facts. The *Statistical Abstract of the United States* and the *Historical Abstract of the United States* provide political and economic data from colonial times to the present. Refer to atlases for geographical data.
- For general information, check an encyclopedia or the card catalog, which may be computerized. In the card catalog, you will find descriptions of books, videos, and other library resources related to your topic.
- If you need help, ask a reference librarian.

Practicing the Skill

On a separate sheet of paper, list the library resources you might use to find information on the following topics.

❶ Your governor's speech on raising state taxes
❷ Names of your state's representatives in the Senate and House of Representatives
❸ Biography of your favorite president
❹ Dollars your state spends on public education
❺ United States territories in 1850
❻ A book about the president

The Library of Congress in Washington, D.C., is the largest research library in the United States.

— Applying the Skill —

Write a one-sentence description of a state issue that interests you. Briefly summarize the information you find in the library on your topic. Below your summary, name the library resource or resources you used.

Practice key skills with Glencoe's
Skillbuilder Interactive Workbook CD-ROM, Level 1.

The State Judicial Branch

GUIDE TO READING

Main Idea

Most legal matters in a state are handled in a three-tiered state court system similar in structure to the federal judiciary.

Key Terms

justice of the peace, misdemeanor, magistrate court, plaintiff, defendant, felony

Reading Strategy

Summarizing Information As you read, use a graphic organizer similar to the one below to list features of state court systems.

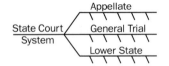

State Court System

- Appellate
- General Trial
- Lower State

Read to Learn

- How are state courts organized?
- How are state court judges selected?

Americans in Action

"We keep punishing the kids and we punish them and return them to the same environment that created the problem." Judge Yvette McGee Brown cites this cycle as the reason she has been supporting reform efforts for the sentencing and treatment of juvenile offenders. In 1992 McGee Brown won a seat on the Franklin County [Ohio] Common Pleas Court, Domestic Relations and Juvenile Division. At the time, she was Ohio's youngest elected judge and the first African American and only the second woman to be elected to this position in Franklin County. McGee Brown hopes to serve in her position long enough to improve the juvenile system in ways that will continue long after she's gone.

Court seal

Lower State Courts

The federal court system handles only a small portion of the nation's judicial business. Most of the legal matters that arise within a state fall under the state court system. State courts interpret and apply state and local laws.

In most states, courts are organized similarly to the federal court system. They have a three-tiered system that includes courts for minor law violations and lawsuits, courts for serious crimes and large-scale civil cases, and appeals courts.

In many rural areas and small towns, the local court is called a justice court, and the judge is called a **justice of the peace.** These courts almost always handle less serious crimes, which are known as **misdemeanors.** They operate without juries. Instead, a judge or justice of the peace hears and decides each case. In most communities the voters elect these judges.

Larger towns may have police courts or **magistrate courts.** These courts handle minor cases such as traffic violations or disturbing the peace. They may also hear civil cases involving small sums of money, usually less than $1,000. (Civil cases occur when a person or group takes legal action against another person or group.) Criminal defendants convicted in these courts usually receive a small fine or a short jail term.

State Judicial System

STATE SUPREME COURT
★ Panel of judges hears appeals from lower courts.

APPELLATE COURTS
★ Panel of judges hears appeals from lower courts.

GENERAL TRIAL COURTS
★ Judges or judge and jury hear criminal and civil cases.

LOWER COURTS
★ Justice Courts—rural and small towns
★ Magistrate Courts—larger towns, small cities
★ Municipal Courts: traffic, juvenile, misdemeanors—larger cities

Evaluating Charts

General trial courts handle criminal cases involving felonies. Which courts try criminal cases involving misdemeanors?

Large cities may have municipal courts that serve the same purpose. These are often divided into specialized areas, such as traffic, juvenile, and small claims courts. Small claims courts decide civil cases involving minor amounts of money; **plaintiffs** (people filing lawsuits) and **defendants** (people being sued) speak for themselves with no lawyers present for either side.

Reading Check Describing What kinds of cases do magistrate courts handle?

Higher State Courts

The second tier of state courts deals with more serious crimes, which are called **felonies,** and with civil cases involving large amounts of money. The third tier consists of courts that consider appeals of lower-court decisions.

General Trial Courts

Defendants charged with felonies— murder, armed robbery, drug trafficking, and other major crimes—go on trial in general trial courts. Depending on the state, such a court may be called a district court, county court, common pleas court, circuit court, or superior court.

Trials in these courts may be held before a jury. In such cases, the judge's job is to make sure the trial is conducted fairly and lawfully. The judge does this by ruling on whether certain evidence or testimony is permissible, ruling on objections by attorneys in the case, and guiding the jury on points of law. In many states, the judge also decides on the penalty in case of a guilty verdict.

Appellate Courts

Most states have a tier of intermediate appeals courts. They review decisions made by trial courts. Appeals courts do not have juries. Instead, a panel of judges decides cases by a majority vote. If the judges feel that the defendant did not have a fair trial, they can decide to overturn the lower court's decision.

$ Economics and You

Public Debt

The public debt is the total amount of money owed by the national, state, and local governments. Use the *World Almanac* or the *Statistical Abstract of the United States* to examine finances in your state. Find both the state debt and the per capita, or per person, debt. Figure out what percentage of the state debt belongs to you.

The court of last resort in most states is the state supreme court. It reviews decisions of appeals courts and is responsible for supervising all courts in the state. State supreme courts also interpret the state's constitution and laws. Supreme courts have from five to nine judges. A successful appeal at this level requires a majority vote of the judges hearing the case. Except for cases involving federal law or the United States Constitution, the decisions of the state supreme courts are final.

Reading Check **Explaining** Why do you think state supreme courts are called courts of last resort?

Selection of Judges

State judges are selected in different ways. Some are elected by popular vote; others are elected by the state legislature. In some states, the governor appoints judges, usually subject to the legislature's approval. Still other states select judges through a method called the Missouri Plan, which combines appointment by the governor and popular election. Under this plan, the governor appoints a judge from a list prepared by a commission. Then, in the next election, voters either reject or confirm the appointed judge.

Many people disagree with the practice of electing judges. These people argue that judges who must run election campaigns may be too concerned about the effect of their decisions on the public. These critics fear that judges may be more concerned with pleasing voters rather than administering the law impartially. Also, voters may know little or nothing about the candidates who are running for judicial posts. Other people argue that popular election of judges ensures a government "of the people, by the people, and for the people."

American Biographies

Judy Martz (1943–); Ruth Ann Minner (1935–)

Since the founding of the nation, only 19 women have served as state governors. However, it looks like the number of female governors may be on the rise. At the start of 2001, five of the nation's 50 governors were women. Two of these state executives included Judy Martz, the Republican governor of Montana, and Ruth Ann Minner, the Democratic governor of Delaware.

Martz, a former Olympic speed skater and small-business owner, got her start in politics by working for Republican candidates on the local, state, and national levels. The daughter of ranching parents, Martz spent nearly 10 years working for the Republican U.S. senator from Montana. In 1995 she resigned to become the state's first female lieutenant governor. Four years later, voters elected Martz as Montana's first female governor.

Ruth Ann Minner also worked her way up through the ranks. Raised on a farm, she left school at age 16 to help support her family. She later started her own family, only to be widowed at age 32. Left with three sons to raise, she worked two jobs, while earning a high school general equivalency diploma (GED) and then attending college.

Minner, who later remarried, got her start in government as a page for the Delaware house of representatives. She went on to win election to the house itself in 1974 and to the state senate in 1988. Minner successfully campaigned for lieutenant governor in 1992 and 1996. Then, in 2000, she became the first woman to claim the governorship of Delaware.

State Judiciaries This courthouse is located in Nevada City, California. **How are state judges selected?**

State judges usually have longer terms of office—6 to 12 years—than legislators or governors. In theory, the longer their terms, the more shielded they are from public opinion, and thus the more independent they can be.

Judges can be removed from office by impeachment. Impeachment, though, can be inefficient and time-consuming. Most states have created boards or commissions to investigate any complaints about judges. If the board finds that a judge has acted improperly, it makes a recommendation to the state supreme court. The court may then suspend or remove the judge.

Reading Check **Explaining** How can state judges be removed from office?

SECTION 4 ASSESSMENT

Checking for Understanding

1. Key Terms Using all of the following terms, write a paragraph that summarizes the main points of this section: justice of the peace, misdemeanor, magistrate court, plaintiff, defendant, felony.

Reviewing Main Ideas

2. Identify Of the three tiers of state courts, which one uses juries to decide guilt or innocence or to settle civil suits?

3. Conclude What kind of lower court would you most likely find in a large city?

Critical Thinking

4. Making Judgments In your opinion, should judges be elected, as they are at the state level, or appointed, as they are at the federal level? Explain.

5. Organizing Information On a web diagram like the one below, write the three tiers of state courts and at least two features of each tier.

State Courts

Analyzing Visuals

6. Identify Review the state judicial system as shown in the diagram on page 298. What body hears cases in general trial courts?

★ **BE AN ACTIVE CITIZEN** ★
7. Write Research your community government to discover the lowest level of court. Write to the judge or presiding officer and ask him or her to explain the types of cases handled in the court.

Landmark Supreme Court
Case Studies

Mapp v. Ohio

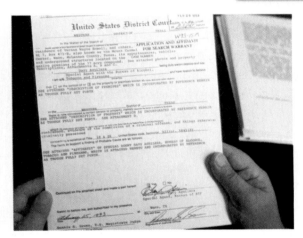

An official search warrant

The Fourth Amendment aims to protect citizens from unreasonable searches by requiring government officials to first obtain search warrants. In 1914 the Supreme Court declared that any evidence obtained without this protection cannot be used in federal court trials. How did this "exclusionary" rule find its way into state courts as well?

Background of the Case

In 1957 police officers arrived at the Cleveland, Ohio, apartment of Dollree Mapp. They were looking for evidence linking her with a gambling operation. Mapp asked to see a search warrant. The police flashed a piece of paper, but it never became clear whether the paper was actually a warrant. Although the police found no evidence of gambling, they did discover some pieces of alleged pornography. Ohio courts sentenced Mapp to prison for possession of illegal goods. They held that the pornography could be used against her in court even though the police were not searching for it under their supposed warrant.

The Decision

With Justice Tom C. Clark writing the 5–4 decision, the Supreme Court issued its ruling on June 19, 1961. Clark first called on the Fourteenth Amendment's protection against certain state actions. From there he argued:

Having once recognized that the right to privacy embodied in the Fourth Amendment is

enforceable against the States, and that the right to be secure against rude invasions of privacy by state officers is, therefore, constitutional . . . , we can no longer permit that right to remain an empty promise. . . . we can no longer permit it to be revocable [able to be cancelled] at the whim of any police officer who . . . chooses to suspend [it] . . .

The Court declared that the presentation of evidence obtained through improper police searches is unconstitutional in state criminal courts.

Why It Matters

The *Mapp* case marked a shift in the thinking of the Supreme Court. For decades, the Court had argued that the Bill of Rights governed only the actions of the federal government. During the 1960s, though, the Court included the states in more and more protections under the Bill of Rights as implied under the Fourteenth Amendment.

Analyzing the Court Decision

1. On what basis did Justice Clark establish citizens' right to privacy?
2. How might you answer the criticism that the *Mapp* decision could hamper law enforcement?

Assessment & Activities

Review to Learn

Section 1
• In a federal system, the central government and the state governments share power.
• Cooperation among the federal and state governments involves highways, education, and welfare.

Section 2
• State legislatures operate much like the U.S. Congress does.
• Proposed bills go through the committee system.

Section 3
• Voters of each state elect their governors directly.
• Governors are the states' chief executives.

Section 4
• State courts are organized in a three-tier system. State judges are elected, appointed, or selected.

FOLDABLES
Study Organizer

Using Your Foldables Study Organizer
Form groups of three. Each person in the groups will act as the "expert" about one branch of state government. Give each expert 3 to 5 minutes to explain the organization and responsibilities of a branch using only the foldable as notes.

Reviewing Key Terms

Write the chapter key term that matches each definition below.

1. a single or one-house legislature
2. powers shared by the national government and state governments
3. less serious crimes
4. basing legislative districts on population
5. a government in which the central government and state governments share power
6. people being sued
7. powers that only states have
8. serious crimes
9. to reduce a criminal's sentence
10. people filing lawsuits

Reviewing Main Ideas

11. Why did the Framers of the Constitution decide that the United States needed a new government?
12. What limits does the U.S. Constitution place on state governments?
13. In what way do most governors have greater veto power than the president?
14. In most states, how are the heads of most executive agencies chosen?
15. What are the leaders of houses of representatives in state legislatures called?
16. What resulted from the Supreme Court decisions in *Baker* v. *Carr* and *Reynolds* v. *Sims?*
17. What takes place in general trial courts?
18. What kind of cases would you most likely see in a justice court?

Critical Thinking

19. **Analyzing Information** Why do you think the Framers of the U.S. Constitution created a federal system in which federal law has supremacy over state laws?

20. Comparing Information In a graphic organizer like the one below, list the major powers of the governments.

 Economics Activity

21. Contact the municipal court nearest your community to find out its budget for a year. How many judges and courtrooms does the court have? What is the average cost per judge and per courtroom for a year?

Analyzing Visuals

Study the diagram below, and then answer the following question.

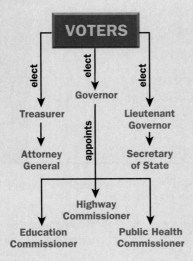

22. Which state officials are usually chosen by voters? What avenue of complaint might there be for people dissatisfied with a commissioner?

Practicing Skills

23. Using Library Resources In your local library, find an article in the local newspaper about a civil or criminal case. Skim the article

to determine its general subject. Look for the ideas that the article's details support. Identify the central issue.

★ CITIZENSHIP COOPERATIVE ACTIVITY ★

24. Working as a class, contact your local court system to find out all the courts that exist within your county's boundaries. Make a list of all the courts and describe the kinds of cases that appear in each one.

Technology Activity

25. Go to www.ncsconline.org. Under "Popular Links," click on "Court Statistics." Then, click on "Frequently Requested Information," then on "State Court Structure Charts." Compare your state's structure to three other states of your choice.

 Standardized Test Practice

Directions: Choose the *best* answer to the following question.

Which part of the U.S. Constitution grants the states reserved powers?

F the Preamble
G Article I
H the First Amendment
J the Tenth Amendment

Test-Taking Tip

Although you may not be able to define all the parts of the Constitution listed in the answer choices, you can narrow down the choices by eliminating the answers you know are wrong.

Local Government

★ CITIZENSHIP AND YOU ★

Within the 50 states, approximately 86,000 units of local governments serve the people. These units include 3,043 counties; nearly 20,000 cities; about 16,600 towns, townships, and villages; and almost 13,750 school districts. In addition, there are special districts that provide particular services. Choose an issue facing your local community. Draft a petition stating your ideas for dealing with the issue and have citizens sign it. Present your petition to your local government officials.

To learn more about local government, view the *Democracy in Action* video lesson 24: Local Government.

FOLDABLES ™
Study Organizer

Compare and Contrast Study Foldable *Make this foldable to help you compare and contrast three types of local government.*

Step 1 *Fold a sheet of paper in half from side to side.*

Fold it so the left edge lies about $\frac{1}{2}$ inch from the right edge.

Step 2 *Turn the paper and fold it into thirds.*

Step 3 *Unfold and cut the top layer only along both folds.*

This will make three tabs.

Step 4 *Label as shown.*

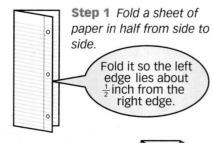

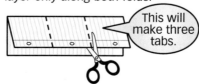

City | County | Town Township Village

LOCAL GOVERNMENT

Reading and Writing *As you read the chapter, write notes under each appropriate tab of your foldable. Keep in mind that you are trying to compare these forms of government.*

The skyline of Dallas, Texas ▶

CIVICS Online

Chapter Overview Visit the *Civics Today* Web site at civ.glencoe.com and click on **Chapter Overviews—Chapter 13** to preview chapter information.

City Government

GUIDE TO READING

Main Idea
Most people in the United States today live in cities that have a variety of governmental structures.

Key Terms
incorporate, city charter, home rule, ordinance, strong-mayor system, weak-mayor system, at-large elections, special district, metropolitan area

Reading Strategy
Organizing Information
As you read, complete a web diagram like the one below by listing services provided and problems faced by city governments.

City Services and Problems

Read to Learn
• What is a city?
• What are the various forms of city governments?

Americans in Action

Jeffrey J. Dunkel is an 18-year-old Democrat and student. He is also the mayor of Mount Carbon, Pennsylvania. How did that happen? Well, Dunkel had to attend town meetings for a class assignment. He continued to attend the meetings even after the assignment had ended. As Dunkel put it, "When I started asking questions, they told me I'm only 18, and there's a lot involved in local government, and if I think I can do a better job, then I should run for office." Dunkel thought that wasn't a bad idea. Dunkel claims that establishing a police force will be his first priority. As mayor, he'll earn $50 a month.

Jeffrey Dunkel

Created by the State

Although they are the closest units of government to the people, local governments, like the city government of Mount Carbon, have no legal independence. The U.S. Constitution does not even mention the existence of local governments. They are created by, and are entirely dependent upon, the state. The state may take control or even do away with them. For example, a state may take control of a local school district that is in financial trouble. State constitutions usually establish the powers and duties of local governments.

As you know, the United States has become a mostly urban nation over the past century. In 1900 only about one-third of the nation's 76 million people lived in urban areas. Today about three-fourths of the more than 280 million Americans do.

In legal terms, most states define a municipality as an incorporated place—a locality with an officially organized government that provides services to residents. A city is a municipal government. New cities are created every year as people living in urban communities incorporate. They do this by applying to the state legislature for a city charter, a document that grants power to a local government. Generally a community must meet certain requirements to obtain a charter. For example, the community may be required to have a

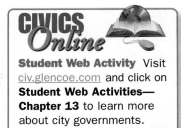
city charter is much like a constitution, describing the type of city government, its structure, and its powers. The state legislature still maintains control, however. It may change the powers granted to the city government at any time.

In recent years many state legislatures have begun to grant home rule to cities. Home rule allows cities to write their own charters, choose their own type of government, and manage their own affairs, although they still have to follow state laws.

Whether an urban community is called a city, a town, or a village depends on local preference or the charter specifications. Obviously, there are great differences in how government operates in a city of 10,000 people and in one of a million people. Regardless of population, however, most city governments provide the same basic services: law enforcement, fire protection, street repair, water and sewage systems, garbage pickup, and parks and recreation.

A city charter usually creates one of three forms of government: the mayor-council form, the council-manager form, or the commission form.

Reading Check **Summarizing** How are city governments created?

The Mayor-Council Form

Until early in the twentieth century, almost all American cities had a mayor-council form of government, and it remains a common form of government today. In this population of a certain minimum size and submit petitions signed by residents supporting the application for a charter. A

form of government, power is divided between separate legislative and executive branches. Voters elect a mayor and the members of the city council. The mayor is the chief executive of the city government and is responsible for overseeing the operation of administrative offices. Often the mayor appoints the heads of departments, such as public works, planning, police and fire protection, recreation, roads and buildings,

American Biographies

John Liu (1967–)

In the Flushing, Queens, section of New York City, voters made history in 2001. They elected John C. Liu to represent their district on the city council. Liu became the first Asian American to win elected office in New York City—or anyplace else in New York State. "We are in a new era," Liu declared in his victory speech.

Liu, who describes himself as a "Flushing boy," immigrated to Queens from Taiwan at age 5. He attended New York City public schools and state college before taking a job at a major accounting firm. Public service paved his way to the city council. Liu did volunteer work in junior high and high school. In college, he took part in student government. As an adult, Liu worked to improve Flushing by forming community action groups.

As a member of the city council, Liu faced the task of not only representing Flushing, but of uniting one of the city's most diverse districts. In a post-election pep talk, Liu told supporters, "The issues facing this district affect us all, and we will solve these issues together."

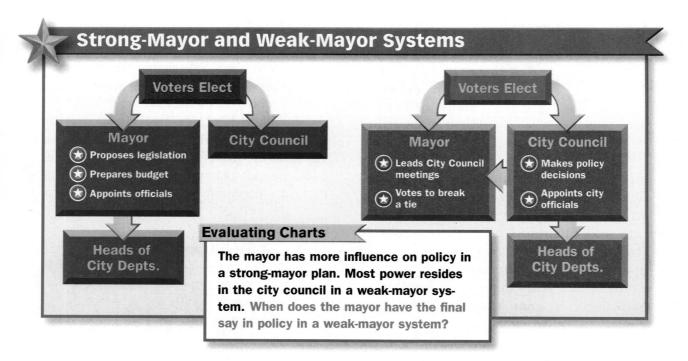

Strong-Mayor and Weak-Mayor Systems

Voters Elect

Mayor
- ★ Proposes legislation
- ★ Prepares budget
- ★ Appoints officials

City Council

Heads of City Depts.

Voters Elect

Mayor
- ★ Leads City Council meetings
- ★ Votes to break a tie

City Council
- ★ Makes policy decisions
- ★ Appoints city officials

Heads of City Depts.

Evaluating Charts

The mayor has more influence on policy in a strong-mayor plan. Most power resides in the city council in a weak-mayor system. When does the mayor have the final say in policy in a weak-mayor system?

health and welfare, and other matters. The council acts as the city's legislature, approving the city budget and passing city laws, which are generally known as ordinances. Most city councils have fewer than 10 members, who usually serve four-year terms. Larger cities have larger councils. In most cities, the residents of the city elect council members. Some cities are divided into voting districts called **wards.** Each ward elects a representative to the city council. In other cities, some or all of the council members are known as members-at-large. A **member-at-large** is elected by the entire city.

The powers of the mayor vary from city to city. Large cities usually have what is called a strong-mayor system. Under this arrangement, the mayor has strong executive powers, such as the power to veto ordinances the city council passes, appoint and remove numerous city officials, and put together the city budget. Strong mayors tend to dominate city government because membership on the city council, even in large cities, is usually a part-time job, and council members receive fairly small

salaries. Furthermore, in many cities, since council members are elected from districts within the city, they tend to focus on issues that are important to their part of town. By contrast, a strong mayor usually works full-time, has a staff of assistants, and represents the entire city.

Many smaller towns, and even a few big cities, have a weak-mayor system. In this type of government, the mayor's authority is limited. The council, not the mayor, appoints department heads and makes most policy decisions. The mayor usually presides over council meetings but votes only in case of a tie. The weak-mayor system dates from the nation's earliest days when former colonists, tired of the injustices they suffered at the hands of the British king and his government, were reluctant to grant any official too much power. By its very nature, such a government often suffers from relatively weak executive leadership.

Reading Check **Analyzing** Who makes up the executive and legislative branches of the mayor-council government?

The Council-Manager Form

The council-manager form of government is a popular form of city government today. When this form first appeared in 1912, it was seen as a way to reform corrupt or inefficient mayor-council governments. Under the council-manager form, the elected council or board and chief elected official (the mayor in many cases) are responsible for making policy. A professional administrator appointed by the council or board has full responsibility for the day-to-day operations of the government

The city council, as the legislative body, appoints the manager in much the same way that a company board of directors might appoint a new chief executive officer. The manager recommends a budget, oversees city departments, and deals with personnel matters. The manager reports to the council as a whole. The council can hire and remove the manager by a majority vote.

In many smaller cities with managers, council members are elected in at-large elections. This means they run in citywide elections rather than representing one district. Some people believe that this system forces members to consider the interests of the entire city instead of just looking out for the concerns of their own neighborhoods. This form of government allows professional city managers to bring a level of expertise to the daily job of running city departments. Most managers have advanced degrees in management and specialized training in areas such as budgeting, financial management, and planning.

In this form of government the line between making policy and carrying out policy may become blurred. Although councils set policy, managers often must make decisions in the course of applying those policy decisions that effectively clarify, limit, or expand the set policies. Managers serve at the pleasure of the elected body, though, so they strive to correctly interpret and apply the council's position on issues.

Reading Check **Contrasting** How does the council-manager government differ from the mayor-council government?

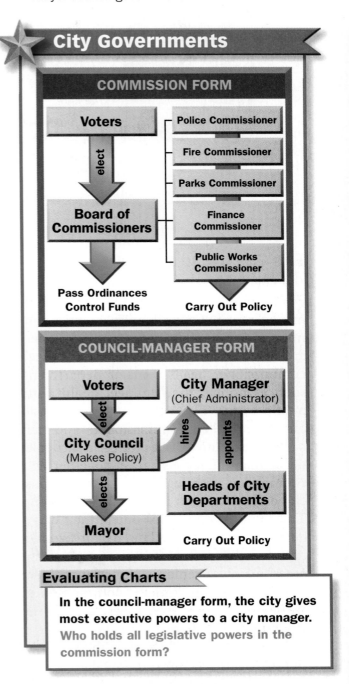

City Governments

COMMISSION FORM

Voters → elect → Board of Commissioners

Board of Commissioners → Pass Ordinances Control Funds

Police Commissioner
Fire Commissioner
Parks Commissioner
Finance Commissioner
Public Works Commissioner

→ Carry Out Policy

COUNCIL-MANAGER FORM

Voters → elect → City Council (Makes Policy)

City Manager (Chief Administrator)

City Council → hires → City Manager

City Manager → appoints → Heads of City Departments

City Council → elects → Mayor

Heads of City Departments → Carry Out Policy

Evaluating Charts

In the council-manager form, the city gives most executive powers to a city manager. Who holds all legislative powers in the commission form?

Analyzing Visuals Cities and towns are responsible for making their own laws to govern speed limits, parking regulations, and other transportation-related issues. Does the cartoonist support or oppose a ban on cell-phone usage by drivers? Do you share this view? Explain your answer.

The Commission Form

The commission form of government was invented a few years before the council-manager form. Only a handful of cities continue to use it. Usually five commissioners are selected in citywide elections. Each commissioner heads a major department, such as police, fire, finance, health, and public works. The heads of these departments are called commissioners and they perform executive duties for their particular department. They also meet together as a commission with legislative power to pass city ordinances and make policy decisions. The commissioners pick one of their members to act as mayor. This mayor presides over commission meetings and performs other, mainly ceremonial, functions. Under this form of government, commissioners are legislators *and* executives; there is no separation of powers.

Despite its initial success, the commission form of city government has several drawbacks. With a commission, no one person is in charge, making it difficult to pinpoint overall responsibility for how the city is run. In addition, newly elected commissioners may not know much about the departments they are responsible for managing, and when commissioners disagree, it may become very difficult to make decisions or establish policy. For these reasons, many cities that once used a commission system have switched to a council-manager or mayor-council form of government.

Reading Check **Explaining** What officials comprise the commission in the commission form of government?

Special Districts

The **special district** is a unit of government that deals with a specific function, such as education, water supply, or transportation. Special districts are the most numerous types of local government, because in some states several kinds of special districts overlap most cities. The local school district is the most common example of a special district. A board or commission, which may be elected or appointed, runs a special district. The board sometimes has the power to collect taxes from district residents to pay for the services it provides. Some boards charge user fees to raise money.

Metropolitan Areas

A **metropolitan area** is a central city and its surrounding suburbs. (Suburbs are communities near or around cities.) This area may also include small towns that lie beyond the suburbs. The U.S. Census Bureau has an official name for urban concentrations made up of a central city and suburbs with a combined population of 50,000 or more. These areas are called Metropolitan Statistical Areas. When the concentration includes more than one central city, such as San Francisco and Oakland, California, it is called a Consolidated Metropolitan Statistical Area.

A trend in the United States since the 1950s has been for suburbs to expand around central cities. As a result, oftentimes the suburban population has become much greater than that of the central city. For example, Detroit's population dropped from nearly 2 million in 1950 to just under 1 million in 2000, while its suburbs now have more than 3 million people.

The great growth in population and the expansion of business and industry in metropolitan areas have created many problems in transportation, pollution control, and law enforcement that cities acting alone cannot solve. Land-use management is an especially pressing problem because most metropolitan areas suffer from the negative impacts of urban sprawl. At or just beyond city limits, shopping malls, franchise restaurants, and superstores line major roads clogged with traffic.

Some large metropolitan areas have created a council of governments. In this body the central city joins with its suburbs to make areawide decisions about growth. It may also coordinate services such as mass transit. Often the council consists of elected members representing all communities in the region. In other cases, the local governments appoint representatives to the council.

✔**Reading Check** **Comparing** What is the difference between a city and a metropolitan area?

SECTION 1 ASSESSMENT

Checking for Understanding

1. **Key Terms** Define the following terms and use them in complete sentences related to city government: incorporate, city charter, strong-mayor system, weak-mayor system, special district.

Reviewing Main Ideas

2. **Describe** How do city governments obtain charters?

3. **Identify** What is the least used form of city government in the United States?

Critical Thinking

4. **Evaluating Information** If you were asked to create a city government, what form would you use and why?

5. **Comparing and Contrasting** Compare forms of city government by completing a graphic organizer like the one below.

Forms of City Government

Analyzing Visuals

6. **Compare** Review the charts on page 308. How do the duties of the mayor differ between the two systems?

★ *BE AN ACTIVE CITIZEN* ★

7. **Research** Investigate the government in your city or the city nearest to you. What form of government does it have? If it is a mayor-council form, is it a strong- or weak-mayor system?

County Governments

GUIDE TO READING

Main Idea

County governments in the United States range in area and population from very small to very large. Like other governmental structures, counties provide services necessary to their citizens.

Key Terms

county, county seat

Reading Strategy

Comparing and Contrasting Information
As you read, compare county and city governments on a chart like the one below.

County Governments	City Governments

Read to Learn

- What are the functions of county governments?
- Who are the elected officials of county governments?

Americans in Action

"A promise for change . . . a promise kept."
As a second-term county commissioner, Tom Balya of Westmoreland County, Pennsylvania, has had time to carry out a number of promises he made during his two successful campaigns for office. Based on his list of accomplishments, it does not look as if Balya is afraid of change. He gets credit for closing a money-losing energy plant and for cutting millions of dollars out of the county budget *each year.* He also figured out how to outsource [contract out] the management and health care services for the county's prisons.

Tom Balya

Counties

Tom Balya heads a county government. The county is normally the largest territorial and political subdivision of a state. All states except Connecticut and Rhode Island are divided into counties, each of which has its own government. There is great variety among American counties. Los Angeles County, California, for example, has about 10 million residents, while barely 100 people live in Loving County, Texas. San Bernardino County, California, has more land area than the entire states of Vermont and New Hampshire combined. Texas has 254 counties, and Delaware and Hawaii have 3 each. Alaska and Louisiana do not even use the word "county." In Alaska, counties are called boroughs; in Louisiana, parishes.

When many Midwestern and Southern states were mapping out counties in the nineteenth century, the idea was that residents living in the farthest corners of a county should be able to get to the county courthouse and back by horse and buggy in the same day. That is why states in these regions have so many relatively small counties. The county courthouse was the center of government, serving as a headquarters for law enforcement, record keeping, and road construction, as well as courts. The towns where the county courthouse is located are called county seats.

County Government Functions

With modern transportation and the growth of cities, the nature of county government has changed. In some areas, cities now provide many of the services that counties once handled. In other areas, however, county governments have grown in importance and assumed functions that city governments once handled. Many counties today provide water, sewer, and sanitation services. Many also operate large, modern hospitals, police departments, and mass transit systems. Counties also administer elections, offer public health, mental health, and social services, provide emergency medical care, and support volunteer EMS squads.

A board of three to five elected commissioners, or supervisors, governs most counties. Board members' terms vary, but most serve a four-year term. The board acts as a legislature, adopting ordinances and the annual budget, levying taxes, and administering and enforcing laws. County governments have a variety of organizational structures across the country. These include the commission-manager, commission-elected executive, and strong commission forms.

As governmental responsibilities have grown, especially in those counties with large urban populations, many counties have adopted a form of government in which the county board operates only as a legislature. In some cases, the board of commissioners appoints a county manager, who acts much like a city manager in running the county government (see the previous discussion of the council-manager form). In other cases, counties have created a new elective office, that of a chief administrative official. This person, often called the county executive, handles all executive responsibilities. Whether appointed or elected, the county manager or executive appoints top officials, manages the organi-

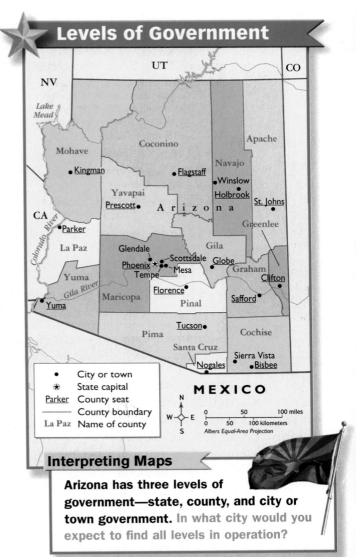

Levels of Government

Interpreting Maps

Arizona has three levels of government—state, county, and city or town government. In what city would you expect to find all levels in operation?

zation, and submits proposed policies to the legislature. The board of commissioners functions alongside this leader, but only as a legislative body.

Separately elected officials run some county administrative offices. The sheriff is the county's chief law enforcement officer. The sheriff's department, which usually includes deputies and jailers, enforces court orders and manages the county jail. In some counties, the sheriff's department shares law-enforcement duties with a separate police department. The district attorney (DA) is the county's prosecutor. The

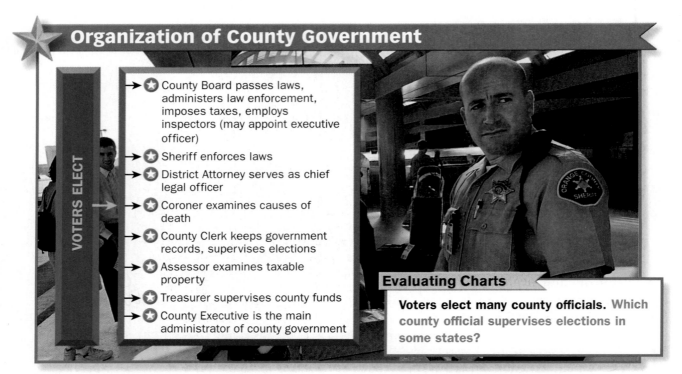

Organization of County Government

VOTERS ELECT

- ⭐ County Board passes laws, administers law enforcement, imposes taxes, employs inspectors (may appoint executive officer)
- ⭐ Sheriff enforces laws
- ⭐ District Attorney serves as chief legal officer
- ⭐ Coroner examines causes of death
- ⭐ County Clerk keeps government records, supervises elections
- ⭐ Assessor examines taxable property
- ⭐ Treasurer supervises county funds
- ⭐ County Executive is the main administrator of county government

Evaluating Charts

Voters elect many county officials. Which county official supervises elections in some states?

DA investigates crimes, brings charges against suspected lawbreakers, and prosecutes the cases in court. In many states, county judges are also elected.

Other county functions are led by officials who may be appointed or elected. The assessor examines all taxable property within the county and estimates how much it is worth. The county's property tax is based on the assessor's estimate. The county finance director or treasurer supervises the county's funds and makes payments from the treasury. An auditor makes sure that the county's money is spent within state and local law. A county clerk keeps official government records. A coroner works closely with the police department to establish the cause of unusual or suspicious deaths.

Reading Check **Identifying** What body governs most counties in the United States?

SECTION 2 ASSESSMENT

Checking for Understanding

1. Key Terms Define the following terms and use them in complete sentences related to county government: county, county seat.

Reviewing Main Ideas

2. Explain Why are counties relatively small in the South and Midwest?

3. Describe How does a county resident become a county commissioner?

Critical Thinking

4. Comparing and Contrasting What is a county? How does a county differ from a city?

5. Organizing Information In a graphic organizer like the one below, list and define the duties of county officials.

County Officials

Analyzing Visuals

6. Identify Reexamine the map on page 313. What levels of government are represented in Tucson, Arizona?

⭐ **BE AN ACTIVE CITIZEN** ⭐

7. Research Find out about your county government. What is its structure? What other services does your county provide?

Towns, Townships, and Villages

GUIDE TO READING

Main Idea

At the smallest level of local government, towns, townships, and villages address the everyday needs of American citizens.

Key Terms

town, town meeting, township

Reading Strategy

Identifying Information
As you read, name the different forms of government below the county level by completing a graphic organizer like the one below.

Forms of Government
Smaller Than
County Level

Read to Learn

• How are towns, townships, and villages structured?

• How do towns, townships, and villages differ?

Americans in Action

In 1654, six years after a large area of land was granted to the town of Sudbury, Massachusetts, a group of young men sat down together in a wood-and-thatch meetinghouse to discuss how to divide the land. They decided "to every man an equal portion to divvy up the land in quantity." The town has seen many changes since that day about 350 years ago, but some things haven't changed at all. Today men and women of Sudbury still sit down to discuss issues in town meetings.

Honoring
Sudbury's soldiers

Town Government

Just as most states are divided into counties, counties are often divided into smaller political units. In the New England states these units are called towns, like the town of Sudbury. In many other states, especially in the Midwest, they are called townships. Still smaller areas within towns or townships may be incorporated into villages. Town, township, and village governments, like those of cities and counties, receive their authority from the state.

The relationship between town or township governments and their surrounding counties varies. In New England, town governments handle the needs of most small communities, while counties are mainly judicial districts. In all other states that have townships, county and township governments share authority. In the South and the West, county governments tend to be more important and there may be no

In everyday speech, Americans use *to*
a small city—or even a large one. P
described New York City as a "wonderful t
"my kind of town." *Town*, however, also ha
as a particular type of local government.
government occurs in the New England sta

Speaking at a Town Meeting Artist Norman Rockwell painted typical American scenes like this New England town meeting (left). At a public meeting in west Philadelphia in 2001, citizen Ronald Johnson speaks out about proposed zoning changes. **How are town meetings an example of direct democracy?**

towns in these states consist of both an urban area and the surrounding rural area.

New England town government is one of the oldest forms of government in the United States. Within the New England Colonies, colonists met regularly to discuss issues that involved everyone in the majority. A majority vote settled any disagreements. Eventually, these "town meetings" became the colonists' form of local government. Citizens, rather than elected representatives, made all the important decisions. **Town meetings** are an exercise in direct democracy—as opposed to the representative dem‗‗‗‗‗‗‗ on throughout most of the ‗‗‗‗‗‗ lew England today, resi-‗‗‗‗‗‗ gether once a year at a ‗‗‗‗‗‗ ss what the town should ‗‗‗‗‗‗ te on local ordinances, ‗‗‗‗‗‗ et.

‗‗‗‗‗‗ meetings occur so rarely, ‗‗‗‗‗‗ ly for broad policymaking.

They cannot handle the everyday details of government. For this reason, each New England town elects a group of officials called "selectmen" to run local government. Selectman, a very old title, now applies to women as well as men. Towns may also elect executives such as a clerk, a treasurer, and a tax assessor.

Over the years, as New England towns grew and their governments became more complex, direct democracy became impractical. Some New England towns have replaced the traditional town meetings with representative town meetings. In these meetings, elected representatives make the decisions instead of the people as a whole. Other towns have eliminated the meetings altogether, and instead have a town council that runs the local government.

✓ Reading Check **Defining** What are town meetings?

Township Governments

The states of New York, New Jersey, and Pennsylvania were organized a bit differently than New England. Their counties are divided into **townships,** which are smaller than New England towns but have similar governments.

Townships in the Midwest have a different history. As the United States expanded westward in the early nineteenth century, it acquired new land where Americans had not yet settled. Congress divided the land into perfectly square blocks, usually six miles wide and six miles long—originally designed to be an hour's buggy ride to the township hall for any resident. As settlers moved in, they set up local governments, like those in the East, called civil townships. Midwestern townships kept the borders established by Congress, so today many appear perfectly square on a map.

Most townships elect a small body of officials known as a township committee, board of supervisors, or board of trustees. They have legislative responsibilities and oversee the administration of services.

Townships have declined in importance as cities have expanded their boundaries and county governments have taken on more functions. In some instances, county and township governments work together to provide local services. For example, county and township police forces may divide up law-enforcement duties.

Village Government

A village is the smallest unit of local government. Like cities, villages almost always lie within the boundaries of other local governments, such as townships or counties. When residents of a community find some particular reason to organize legally, they seek to incorporate a municipality, which may be called a village, city, or town. Residents may be dissatisfied with

The Law and You

Be a Public Policy Advocate

Advocacy is the art of persuading others. Most of us advocate every day and are not even aware that

we are doing it. For instance, have you ever tried to convince your parents to extend your curfew hour or raise your allowance? If so, then you have advocated. Advocacy skills provide effective ways for citizens to participate in making laws.

★ BE AN ACTIVE CITIZEN ★

Look around your community. Is there a problem you would like to change? Use the steps below and become a public policy advocate today.

- The problem that we want to address is:
- Statistics and research on our problem indicate the following about our issue:
- The law/public policy decision that should be changed is:
- The public policy solution we are proposing is:
- We have to influence the following decision makers and stakeholders that:
- Our campaign/media message is:
- Our advocacy plan for change includes:
- We will know we are successful when the following happens:

the services they are receiving from the township or county, or they may want to control their own police force, public library, or recreation facilities. These residents can then request permission from the state to set up a village government.

The government of most villages consists of a small board of trustees elected by the voters. Some villages also elect an executive. This official is known as the chief burgess, president of the board, or mayor. Large villages might hire a professional city manager.

The village board has the power to collect taxes and spend money on projects that benefit the community. Those projects include building and maintaining streets; providing water, sewer services, and public libraries; or setting up recreation facilities. The board may hire officials to supervise these projects and provide other services.

Becoming a village has both advantages and disadvantages. The main drawback is that residents often have to pay higher taxes to support the extra layer of government. In return, however, they usually receive better services. Becoming a village also tends to upgrade the community's status, making it more attractive to visitors and potential new residents and businesses.

Reading Check **Explaining** Why do people set up village governments?

SECTION 3 ASSESSMENT

Checking for Understanding

1. Key Terms Explain how the following terms differ: town, town meeting, township.

Reviewing Main Ideas

2. Identify In the United States, where are town meetings most prevalent?

3. Explain Why have township governments declined in importance over the years?

Critical Thinking

4. Evaluating If you lived in a small community, would you support the establishment of a village government? Why or why not?

5. Analyzing Explain why townships developed differently using a diagram similar to the one below.

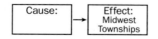

Analyzing Visuals

6. Conclude Examine the images of town meetings on page 316. How do they differ?

★ **BE AN ACTIVE CITIZEN** ★

7. Research Contact a town or village official. Ask: What are some of the issues facing the community? How are local officials trying to deal with those problems?

SKILLBUILDER

Making Inferences

Why Learn This Skill?

You hear a siren scream in the distance. You conclude there is a fire or an accident in the area. You see people file into the stadium and conclude there is a baseball game this afternoon. In each case, you make an inference— a decision based on your observations and knowledge. Your inference may or may not be correct. Making inferences, however, can prompt you to discover new information and improve your understanding. You make inferences every day as you study, read, watch TV, and observe the world around you.

Learning the Skill

To sharpen your skill of making inferences, follow these steps:

- Focus on the facts, or what you know to be true. The facts may be statements you read in print or any situation you observe.
- Recall information or facts you may have acquired from reading about related topics or observing similar situations.
- Pay close attention to details. They can indicate facts that are not stated.
- Decide what you know from the passage you read or the situation you observe. Then apply your prior knowledge. The conclusions you reach will be reasonable inferences.

Practicing the Skill

Use the following questions to help you draw inferences from the passage on this page. Write your answers on a separate sheet of paper.

1. What issue has aroused argument among residents of Forest City?
2. Has the argument just arisen or has it been around awhile?
3. What groups represent the opposing sides of the argument?

Forest City, U.S.A. . . .

Citizen opposition to the proposed widening of the intersection at Pine and Oak Streets continues to mount. Dozens of residents turned out to speak at last night's open council meeting.

Homeowners living south of Pine Street expressed concern over losing a portion of their neighborhood soccer park. Those west of Oak Street feared an enlarged intersection would invite even more traffic. They objected to the noise and pollution that would result.

The mayor and motorists, however, held to their position in favor of the proposal. Council members listened to both sides. Their final vote will not come until sometime next week.

4. What kind of traffic conditions might one expect to find at Pine and Oak Streets?
5. What form of city government does Forest City have?
6. Review your answers to questions 1–5. Place a check mark beside those that required you to make an inference.

Applying the Skill

Find a photograph of citizens in acti[on in a] local newspaper. Read the caption[. Make] one inference about the activity a[nd one] about the setting in which the act[ivity...]

GO TO

Practice key skills w[ith] **Skillbuilder Interac[tive]** **CD-ROM, Level 1.**

Assessment & Activities

Review to Learn

Section 1

- A city is an urban unit of government.
- City governments take several forms, including the mayor-council, council-manager, and commission forms.

Section 2

- County governments act as legislatures, decide on budgets, levy taxes, and plan for the health and safety of county residents. They also administer and enforce laws.
- The elected officials of county governments may include the sheriff, clerk of courts, treasurer, prosecutor, coroner, and, in some counties, judges.

Section 3

- In some states, town governments handle the needs of small communities. In some areas, towns are called townships.
- Villages are the smallest units of local governments and always lie within the boundaries of other local ̶governments.

LITTLEROCK

̶lables Study Organizer

̶eted foldable to answer
̶ essay questions: What
̶of government have in
̶do these forms of
̶er?

Reviewing Key Terms

Write the key term that matches each definition below.

1. a division of a county that has its own government
2. the power that allows a city to write its own charter
3. a town where the county courthouse is located
4. the designation for a city that has an officially organized government with a charter
5. a document that grants power to a municipal government
6. a unit of government set up to deal with a single issue or to provide a single service
7. voting for citywide candidates rather than district representatives
8. a local law
9. an urban concentration made up of a central city and suburbs with a combined population of 50,000 or more
10. a form of government that occurs in New England states and consists of both a community and the surrounding rural area

Reviewing Main Ideas

11. What are the advantages to a city of having home rule?
12. How does a weak-mayor system of city government differ from a strong-mayor system?
13. Why have regional governments grown since the 1950s?
14. Identify at least three needs for special districts.
15. Name an advantage and a disadvantage of establishing a village or city government.
16. What is the purpose of New England town meetings?
17. What is the purpose of a city charter?
18. What does a DA do?

Critical Thinking

19. Identifying Alternatives What do you think could be done to encourage cooperation among local governments in a region?

20. Classifying Information On a web diagram like the one below, identify the various forms of local government discussed in this chapter.

Forms of Local Government

Practicing Skills

Making Inferences **Read the passage below and then answer the following question.**

> The bells of ice cream trucks will jingle-jangle again for the first time in nearly 50 years in this Detroit suburb, thanks to a persistent 9-year-old. The Board of Trustees' unanimous vote Monday night to repeal the township's ban on "frozen confection vendors" was the payoff for five months of work by fourth-grader Josh Lipshaw.

21. What do you think Josh Lipshaw had to do with the board's vote?

Economics Activity

22. Funding for local government comes, in part, from licenses and permits. Local governments often charge fees for issuing and/or registering these documents. Suppose you wanted to build a house or open a business. Find out what licenses and permits would be needed for one of these activities and how much each would cost.

Analyzing Visuals

23. Study the flowcharts that depict the various forms of city government on pages 308 and 309. What are the three major forms of city government? What offices do voters elect in each form?

Self-Check Quiz Visit the *Civics Today* Web site at civ.glencoe.com and click on **Self-Check Quizzes— Chapter 13** to prepare for the chapter test.

★ CITIZENSHIP COOPERATIVE ACTIVITY ★

24. With a partner, contact your county government. Get a copy of the annual budget and show your county expenditures in a circle or bar graph.

Technology Activity

25. On the Internet, go to the U.S. Census Bureau home page, www.census.gov. Find your state and county. Compare your county's population and size to others. Has your county's population increased or decreased? Why do you think that has occurred?

The Princeton Review Standardized Test Practice

Directions: Choose the answer that *best* completes the following statement.

All of the following statements about local government are true EXCEPT

A local governments make ordinances for the community.

B the U.S. Constitution provides for local governments.

C the powers of local governments ar͏ limited by the state.

D the county is usually the l political subdivision of a

Test-Taking

Read the question care words like NOT or EXCEF a common error. You ar statement that is

Dealing With Community Issues

★ CITIZENSHIP AND YOU ★

The responsibilities of state and local governments have increased to respond to Americans' needs. Find out what your local government is doing to solve an issue. Then interview community members about the issue.

To learn more about community issues, view **Democracy in Action** video lesson 21: Social and Domestic Policies.

FOLDABLES™
Study Organizer

Cause-Effect Study Foldable *Make this foldable and use it to record the causes and effects of various issues that communities face.*

Step 1 *Fold one sheet of paper in half from side to side.*

Fold the sheet vertically.

Step 2 *Fold again, 1 inch from the top. (Tip: The middle knuckle of your index finger is about 1 inch long.)*

label as shown.

Draw lines along the fold lines.

Reading and Writing *As you read the chapter, write what you learn about the causes and effects of community issues under the appropriate columns of your foldable.*

Volunteering with Habitat for Humanity ▶

CIVICS Online

Chapter Overview Visit the *Civics Today* Web site at <u>civ.glencoe.com</u> and click on **Chapter Overviews— Chapter 14** to preview chapter information.

How a Community Handles Issues

GUIDE TO READING

Main Idea

When ideas for public policy come before a community, leaders must consider many factors, including infrastructure, priorities, resources, and financing.

Key Terms

public policy, infrastructure, priorities, resources, master plan

Reading Strategy

Analyzing Information As you read, list on a web diagram like the one below factors that must be considered by community leaders when making public policy.

Factors to Consider in Making Public Policy

Read to Learn

• How do community leaders make public policy?

• What factors must ...nity leaders ...n making

Americans in Action

Amy Sloan is a member of Licking County (Ohio) Citizens for a Safe Environment (LCCSE). Her membership has to do with chickens—or rather, with 7 million chickens. Sloan lives about a mile from these chickens, which are residents of the nation's fourth-largest egg-producing farm. "Sometimes the smell is so bad it makes your eyes water," says Sloan. After years of "pleading with government agencies," according to Sloan, the state's attorney general finally stepped in to get the huge farm to comply with environmental standards and to make life tolerable for Sloan and her neighbors.

The cause of the smell

Making Public Policy

Amy Sloan became involved in the process of making public policy. All organizations like schools; businesses; and national, state, and local governments have policies, or a set of rules or guidelines that they follow when making decisions and carrying out actions. Most businesses, for example, have policies about hiring, promoting, and firing employees. Schools have policies about student conduct, registration, and many other aspects of school activities. **Public policy** is a general agreement among government leaders about how to deal with issues or problems that affect the entire community. A public policy is not necessarily a law. It may not even be written down.

Ideas for public policy come from many different sources. They may originate from within the government. Party leaders or interest groups may propose them. Even members of the media may suggest them. One other important source of policy ideas, especially at the local level, is private citizens. Often a single person can have a great impact on government policies. In 1980, after a drunk driver killed her 13-year-old daughter Cari, a California real estate agent named Candy Lightner began a campaign to change government policy toward drunk driving. Lightner explained, "I promised myself on the day of Cari's death that I would fight to make this needless homicide count for something positive in the years ahead."

MADD Statistics

About 3 in every 10 Americans will be involved in an alcohol-related crash at some time in their lives. In 1999, there were nearly 2 alcohol-related traffic deaths per hour, 43 per day, and 303 per week. That is the equivalent of 2 jetliners crashing week after week.

Traffic crashes are the greatest single cause of death for every age from 6 through 33.

She founded Mothers Against Drunk Driving (MADD), and within five years she became the leader of a nationwide organization with more than 600 chapters in every state. Through intensive lobbying of legislators and frequent public appearances, Lightner helped MADD bring about the passage of more than 1,000 tough, new laws against drunk driving nationwide.

Changing a public policy is not often easy. It may take months or even years. Governments often do research and hold public hearings before making policy decisions. During that time disagreements may arise over what the policy should be. The policy that results may be a compromise.

Reading Check **Contrasting** What is the difference between school policy and public policy?

Planning for the Future

Many useful public policies try to foresee problems and prevent them. This requires looking at what is likely to happen in the future and planning for it now. A growing number of local governments have planning commissions to do this kind of work for land use in the community. A planning commission is an advisory group that may include government leaders, businesspeople, local residents, and professionals such as architects and traffic engineers.

Short-Term and Long-Term Plans

Local governments and their planning commissions make both short-term and long-term plans. A short-term plan is a policy meant to be carried out over the next few years. For example, granting a builder a permit to construct apartments is a short-term plan.

A long-term plan is a broader, less detailed policy meant to serve as a guide over the next 10, 20, or even 50 years. To make long-term plans, a planning commission must make educated guesses about a community's future needs. For example, it

Influencing Public Policy Members of MADD called attention to the 724 people killed in alcohol-related crashes in Florida in 1995 by laying 724 pairs of shoes in the state capitol. **How might this demonstration affect public policy?**

American Biographies

Juana Beatriz Gutierrez (1932–)

In 1984 Juana Gutierrez learned that the state of California planned to build a prison near her East Los Angeles home. Gutierrez—the mother of nine and Neighborhood Watch organizer—invited her Mexican American neighbors to a meeting at her house. There Gutierrez and six other women formed the Mothers of East Los Angeles Santa Isabel (MELASI).

MELASI not only blocked the prison, it won passage of a law declaring that no state prisons could be built in Los Angeles County. In the next few years, Gutierrez and other leaders of MELASI became environmental experts as they successfully fought off a toxic waste incinerator, a dumpsite, a chemical treatment plant, an oil pipeline, and more.

Today MELASI works to improve East Los Angeles as well as to protect it. A few of its many programs include water conservation projects, youth programs, free computer classes, scholarships, and a door-to-door campaign by students to end graffiti. When people ask Gutierrez, president of MELASI, what they should do to fight for a cause, she tells them, "Stay united, don't give up, and remember, it won't be easy."

plan for completely recon-
it believes will be the city's
eled streets so that they can
ed traffic from anticipated
ew subdivisions.

ays requires answering a
ult questions. Take a hypo-
small-town company that

has developed an important new device for airport security. The company suddenly becomes very busy as demand increases. As it expands, it builds several new buildings. The growing economy attracts other businesses to the town. New residents pour in to work for these companies.

A situation like this raises a number of questions for local government. Will increased traffic overload roads and highways? Should the town build new roads or promote public transportation? What other demands will the growing population put on the town's infrastructure—its system of roads, bridges, water, and sewers? If the infrastructure needs to be expanded, how will the town pay for the work?

Evaluating Priorities and Resources

Local governments and planning commissions around the country face such questions every year. The answers to these questions about planning usually depend upon two things—priorities and resources.

Priorities are the goals a community considers most important or most urgent. In setting priorities, a community must first decide what it values most. For example, is it more important to have thriving commerce or a peaceful place to live? While deciding about its values, a community must also determine its specific goals and rank them in order of importance. It may decide, for example, that its most important goal is to attract new businesses. Lesser goals may include improving services, preserving open spaces, upgrading the school system, and so on.

Once a community has set its priorities, it must determine what resources it has and how to use them. Resources are the money, people, and

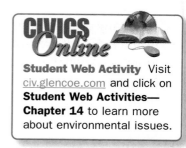

Student Web Activity Visit civ.glencoe.com and click on **Student Web Activities— Chapter 14** to learn more about environmental issues.

r 14   Dealing With Community Issues

materials available to accomplish the community's goals. Suppose, for example, that a community has decided to improve its public transportation system. Is there enough money to build and maintain a new fleet of large buses for busy routes, or would a system of minibuses on short routes fit the budget better?

Creating a Master Plan After setting priorities and calculating resources, a planning commission makes concrete decisions about the community's future. It usually spells these out in a document called a **master plan.** This plan states a set of goals and explains how the government will carry them out to meet changing needs over time.

A planning commission normally submits its plan to the government, which then decides whether to adopt it and use it as a guide. If the plan is accepted, it becomes public policy, and the government is then responsible for carrying it out. The city or town council must approve funds for any

Building Roads and Rails As the population of communities grows, changes in infrastructure, like roads, need to be made to accommodate the growth. The new Airtrain shuttle will improve access to Newark International Airport by reducing highway congestion. **Do you think road construction would be an example of a short- or long-term plan?**

projects outlined in the plan. The mayor's or manager's team writes rules and regulations to enforce the plan.

✓**Reading Check** **Explaining** Why must government leaders consider community resources before creating a master plan?

SECTION 1 ASSESSMENT

Checking for Understanding

1. Key Terms Define the following terms and use them in sentences related to public policy: infrastructure, priorities, resources, master plan.

Reviewing Main Ideas

2. Identify Where do ideas for public policy come from? What are the most useful public policies?

3. Explain Why have many local governments developed planning commissions? What do planning commissions do?

Critical Thinking

4. Making Judgments Which do you think is most important, long-term or short-term planning? Why?

5. Organizing Information In a graphic organizer like the one below, explain the steps leading to a master plan and what a typical master plan includes.

Master Plan	→

Analyzing Visuals

6. Inferring Reexamine the actions taking place in the photos on this page. Name some of the priorities and resources a pl[a]... commission might [need] this to happen.

★**BE AN ACT**...
7. Research Fin... munity has a ... Describe the ... plan. If there ... a local officia... are made in ...

Recognizing Bias

Why Learn This Skill?

Journalists, experts, and authorities are frequently the sources of information you depend upon. Sometimes you need to examine that information for bias. Often a writer or speaker will promote a particular point of view or personal prejudice in the account. Biased information is not necessarily bad information, but you should be able to recognize it and decide what it's worth to you.

Learning the Skill

To recognize bias, follow these steps:

• Identify the source of information. Ask yourself if the author or speaker is identified with a known cause or organization.

• Determine if your source has the facts straight. Watch for any attempts to distort or exaggerate the facts.

• Look for hidden clues, such as the use of descriptive and colorful language or emotionally charged words.

• Decide how the piece of information influences your own opinion.

Practicing the Skill

On a separate sheet of paper, list the numbers of the following statements that you think are biased. Beside each number, briefly describe the particular bias demonstrated.

❶ *School Board Member:* District 907 has added girls' basketball to its roster of varsity sports. Student interest in expanded sports activities has prompted the move. program is expected to involve about seventh- and eighth-grade girls in each in the district.

ol Coach: Demands on the use of nasium will increase next year. The uccessful boys' sports program

must now compete with a girls' program of questionable value. A much-needed expansion of the boys' program goes on hold.

❸ *A Parent in District 907:* Once again District 907 has demonstrated its praiseworthy commitment to physical education. At least another 150 students will have the opportunity to improve their skills and experience the thrill of competition.

❹ *Local Resident:* Taxpayers in District 907 can look forward to higher property taxes next spring. The School Board expects to hire at least three new coaches to handle the extra teaching needs of the frivolous girls' basketball teams. The sensible proposal to eliminate all school sports has not been discussed in at least five years.

── Applying the Skill ──

Read an editorial, commentary, or letter to the editor in your local newspaper. Write a brief summary of two examples of bias you identify.

GO TO

Practice key skills with Glencoe's
Skillbuilder Interactive Workbook CD-ROM, Level 1.

Education and Social Issues

GUIDE TO READING

Main Idea

Increasingly, local school boards must deal with a number of problems and challenges that include increased state and federal control, funding inadequacies, privatization, vouchers, charter schools, and mass testing. Governments also spend time and money on protecting the safety and welfare of Americans.

Key Terms

charter schools, tuition vouchers

Reading Strategy

Summarizing Information As you read, list challenges faced by local school districts on a web diagram like the one below.

School District Challenges

Read to Learn

• What are the challenges faced by local school districts?

• How does the government protect Americans' safety and welfare?

Americans in Action

How important is your education? Well, according to UNICEF (United Nations Children's Fund), "Nearly a billion people will enter the 21st century unable to read a book or sign their names and two-thirds of them are women. And they will live, as now, in more desperate poverty and poorer health than those who can." UNICEF views education ". . . as the single most vital element in combating poverty, empowering women, safeguarding children . . . promoting human rights and democracy, protecting the environment, and controlling population growth." Our government believes that education is important, too. That is why public education is a service provided by our government.

UNICEF poster

Public Education

The writers of the U.S. Constitution left the power over public education to the states. As far back as colonial times some local governments took the lead and began offering free public education to children. The practice spread until it became almost universal after the Civil War. Today about 55 million students attend the nation's public elementary and secondary schools. (Some 7 million other students go to private schools.)

As public education grew, along with it grew a tradition of local control of the schools. Local school districts raised most of the money for schools and determined how students would be taught. Then, in 1816, Indiana set up the first modern public school system. Today in most states, elementary and high school education remains a local responsibility under state guidelines. The basic administrative unit for public schools is the local school district.

The federal government, though, plays an important role in education, providing aid to local schools in several forms. Its share of the total funding is less than 10 percent, but it imposes certain rules on local schools. These include prohibiting gender discrimination in school activities, including sports, and spelling out how schools must meet the needs of disabled students.

In 2001 President George W. Bush signed a landmark education bill, known as the "No Child Left Behind Act." This law authorizes $26.5 billion in federal spending on education, but it also increased the rules that schools must follow. For example, all students in grades three through eight must take a series of state tests in reading and math starting in the 2004–2005 school year. A year later, tests in science will start. With this law, Bush hopes to establish a system of new accountability measures for schools that do not perform well. Bush claims that "[t]he fundamental principle of this bill is that every child can learn. We expect every child to learn, and you must show us whether or not every child is learning."

The biggest education issue facing state governments is how to provide high-quality schooling equally to all students. Currently there is a large spending gap between wealthy and poor school districts. The gap occurs because many districts depend heavily on property taxes to fund the schools, and property values vary greatly from one district to another. A community with a healthy, expanding tax base, for example, has far more to spend per student than a community that has not benefited from the same growth in property tax values.

Challenges to Schools and Teachers

Among the nonfinancial problems facing schools today are low test scores, high dropout rates, and crime and violence on school property. Dealing with dropout rates and violence requires a wide range of remedies, many of them necessarily occurring outside the schools. This is because those problems are rooted in broader social problems of poverty, broken families, drug abuse and alcoholism, and crime and violence in the streets.

Charter Schools To combat poor academic performance, more than 30 states now permit the creation of charter schools. These schools receive state funding, but they are excused from meeting many public school regulations. Some educators believe that this freedom will encourage charter

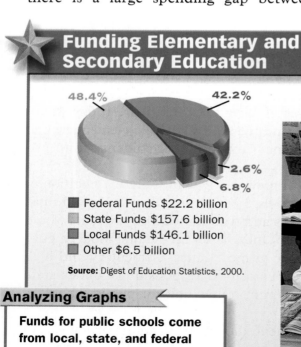

Funding Elementary and Secondary Education

48.4% 42.2% 2.6% 6.8%

■ Federal Funds $22.2 billion
State Funds $157.6 billion
■ Local Funds $146.1 billion
Other $6.5 billion

Source: Digest of Education Statistics, 2000.

Analyzing Graphs

Funds for public schools come from local, state, and federal sources. In this example, which source contributed the most?

Students at Live Oak Elementary School in California

schools to be more innovative than conventional public schools. Former public school teachers and community groups may establish and run charter schools.

Opponents of charter schools argue that they take away funds from public schools and that they are likely to enroll many of the better students, leaving "problem" students behind in the public schools. Supporters of charter schools, however, claim that charter schools are not necessarily more innovative than public schools, and there also seems to be no sign that they are luring away the best students from public schools.

The Voucher Controversy Another form of school choice is cities and states giving parents **tuition vouchers**—a kind of government money order. The parents can use these vouchers to pay for their children to attend private schools. Only a few places, such as Cleveland, Ohio; Milwaukee, Wisconsin; and the state of Vermont, have experimented with vouchers.

Teachers' unions oppose vouchers because they feel they funnel education funds out of the public school system and into private schools. Other opponents contend that vouchers violate the First Amendment because they can be used to pay tuition at religious schools. In Cleveland, about 95 percent of students participating in the voucher program attend religious schools. The Supreme Court has ruled that it is constitutional to use public money (vouchers) at religious schools.

Privatization A more extreme alternative to the traditional management of schools is for private companies to contract with local districts to run the schools. These corporations promise to improve the quality of education and do it more cheaply than public school administrations, while making a profit for themselves.

TIME

Political Cartoons

and it seems to be diverted toward money and time. Making the world a more convenient... | Schneider, two men with little h ing the company's reve

Analyzing Visuals In the aftermath of a wave of shootings on school grounds, citizens and lawmakers searched for ways to reduce the level of violence in U.S. society. What argument is the cartoonist making about television and its impact on society?

Only a few privatized schools exist, so it is difficult to judge their effectiveness. Opponents of privatization argue that companies will cut corners on education, putting profit ahead of what is best for students.

The Rise of Mass Testing As mentioned earlier, the 2001 federal education bill requires states to test all students in reading, math, and soon science, in grades three through eight. Some states also require students to pass competency tests in order to be promoted to the next grade or receive a high school diploma at the end of the 12th grade.

Supporters of competency testing claim that it holds schools and teachers to high levels of accountability, but many teachers' organizations oppose such testing. They claim that it forces teachers to

Community Policing

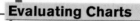

CITY POPULATION	PERCENT OF OFFICERS IN COMMUNITY POLICING PROGRAM	
	1997	**1999**
500,000 or more	1.4	24.1
150,000–499,000	4.7	14.4
50,000–149,000	4.8	16.9
10,000–49,999	4.6	18.4
less than 10,000	5.6	23.8

Evaluating Charts

Community policing addresses the causes of crime and seeks to prevent crime through problem solving and police-community partnerships. How did the percentage of personnel serving as community officers change between 1997 and 1999?

spend valuable classroom time teaching students how to pass tests instead of how to understand the subjects they are supposed to be learning.

✓Reading Check **Describing** Why are school vouchers controversial?

Crime

Many Americans fear that they will become victims of crime. The crime rate in the United States increased rapidly from 1960 to 1980 but began to level off and then decline in the 1980s and 1990s. Federal and state prisons hold more than 1 million inmates, and the ratio of prisoners per 100,000 population in the United States is among the highest in the world.

Crime rates are usually highest in large cities, where poverty and crime often go hand in hand. For poor people who have struggled with dead-end, minimum-wage jobs, robbery or drug dealing may seem like a better way to make a living. For others, having a normal job may not seem possible. Many of the poorest inner-city residents drop out of school early and spend much of their time on the streets. Crime is often the only way of life they know.

Police Forces

America's large cities have many more police officers than in all the nation's state, county, and small-town law-enforcement units combined. As a result, urban police are the main crime-fighting force in the United States. In addition, more than 3,000 county sheriffs and their deputies are the main law enforcement presence in rural areas. Every state has a law enforcement agency known as the highway patrol or state police. Its main responsibility is highway safety, but it often plays an important role in investigating crimes and capturing suspects.

A major function of the police is to enforce the law, but most of the daily work of uniformed police officers involves keeping the peace. This might include handling neighborhood disputes and providing services, such as directing traffic. Much of the credit for the recent drop in crime is given to the use of community policing. Under this program, police become a visible presence in neighborhoods, walking or riding bicycles and getting to know local residents. The program also works to get residents involved in neighborhood watch efforts.

✓Reading Check **Defining** What is community policing?

Social Programs

Our government tries to help Americans suffering from ill health, old age, poverty, and physical disabilities with welfare programs. Policymakers have long struggled over the two-pronged problem of how to reduce poverty and how to administer government financial aid to the best effect. Critics of welfare claim that it undermines self-respect among the poor and encourages dependency. Defenders of welfare assert that it is the only way poorly educated, unemployed female heads of households and their children can avoid homelessness and hunger.

After years of debate, in 1996 Congress passed an act called Temporary Assistance for Needy Families (TANF). It ended a 60-year-old federal program, Aid to Families with Dependent Children, and gave more power to the states to set the rules for future welfare eligibility. Under TANF, the federal government gives money to the states to pass on as welfare payments to poor people. Each state has considerable authority to decide who is eligible for welfare and how much money they get, but there are some federal rules attached. There is a five-year lifetime limit on receiving welfare, and states are required to develop job-training programs for the poor to help them leave the welfare rolls and become self-sufficient taxpayers.

The number of people on welfare dropped tremendously following passage of TANF. In 1995 about 14.2 million people received welfare benefits. By 2000 there were slightly more than 6 million recipients. In 11 states, welfare caseloads dropped by more than 60 percent.

Some critics of the law claim, however, that its successes are due mostly to the booming economy of the late 1990s. The labor shortage of the period made it relatively easy for unemployed welfare recipients to find work. Some observers fear that if the economy were to slump as it did in 2001, people being forced off the welfare rolls will be helpless—without jobs *and* without the so-called safety net of welfare to at least ensure them food and shelter.

Reading Check **Explaining** What do welfare programs do?

SECTION 2 ASSESSMENT

Checking for Understanding

1. **Key Terms** Define the following terms and use them in sentences related to public education: charter schools, tuition vouchers.

Reviewing Main Ideas

2. **Explain** Why is there a large spending gap between wealthy and poor school districts?
3. **Identify** How do charter schools differ from regular public schools? What are the arguments used by supporters and opponents of charter schools?

Critical Thinking

4. **Making Judgments** Do you support or oppose TANF? Explain your reasons.
5. **Making Comparisons** In a chart like the one below, compare the arguments for and against tuition vouchers.

Tuition Vouchers	
For	Against

Analyzing Visuals

6. **Compare** Review the chart on page 332. In what sized city did community policing increase the most? In what sized city did it increase the least?

★ BE AN ACTIVE CITIZEN ★

7. **Interview** Talk with at least two of your district's school board members. Ask them to list the three most serious problems facing your district and how they propose to address these problems.

Environmental Issues

GUIDE TO READING

Main Idea

Protecting the environment is an important issue that community leaders must deal with.

Key Terms

solid waste, recycling, conservation

Reading Strategy

Comparing and Contrasting As you read, use a diagram like the one below to compare and contrast the processes of recycling and conservation.

Recycling (Both) Conservation

Read to Learn

• What is environmentalism?

• How has the government tried to stop air and water pollution?

Americans in Action

Can you imagine managing the waste of 388,000 households? That's exactly what Thomas Buchanan does. Solid waste management has become a big business, especially for America's big cities. In Houston, Texas, Buchanan is the director of the Department of Solid Waste Management. His department manages basic trash services as well as a host of household recycling services, including general recyclables, hazardous waste, heavy trash, and yard waste. Following the Houston mayor's guiding principle of "neighborhood-oriented government," Buchanan looks for ways to provide efficient and useful waste management services to the people of Houston.

Solid waste

The Emergence of Environmentalism

We live in an industrialized society and we pay a high price for doing so. Every time we turn on a light, drive our car, or throw away trash, we may harm our environment. Environmentalism, or protecting our environment, is a national and worldwide concern, but most often it is up to local communities to deal with environmental problems.

Until the 1970s, state and local governments paid little attention to environmental problems. This changed in 1970 when Congress passed the Clean Air Act and established the Environmental Protection Agency (EPA).

While the EPA has taken the lead in setting goals and standards, the states and their environmental protection departments have implemented the programs by monitoring air and water quality and inspecting industrial facilities.

The management of solid waste—the technical name for garbage—is a huge problem for cities. Americans produce about 250 million tons of solid waste each year, and most places where it can be dumped, called landfills, are filling up fast. To make matters worse, some landfills have been closed because rainwater seeping through them has damaged underground water reservoirs and streams.

Complicating the search for new landfill sites is the fact that no one wants a garbage dump in their general area. Indeed, there is a name for this attitude—NIMBY, meaning "not in my backyard." Opposition from citizen groups makes it difficult for governments to find new sites.

Incineration

As an alternative to landfills, much solid waste is burned in huge incinerators. These, however, cause problems of their own: toxic, or poisonous, substances in the smoke from incineration can cause serious air pollution. Unfortunately, pollution-control devices on incinerator smokestacks are very expensive.

Recycling

A second alternative to landfills is recycling, which means reusing old materials to make new ones. Most communities across the United States have recycling programs. All of us are encouraged to recycle materials such as newspapers, printer and copier paper, metal cans, plastic and glass bottles, and plastic bags in our homes, schools, and workplaces.

Unfortunately, not all waste is recyclable. Furthermore, many people simply don't take the trouble to participate in such recycling efforts. Another problem is that the recycling industry sometimes suffers economic slowdowns. Local governments may then feel less incentive to spend money on curbside pickup programs because the recycling companies pay them less for materials.

Conservation

Many communities with active recycling programs also encourage residents to practice conservation. Conservation is the careful preservation and protection of our natural resources. For example, you may buy peanut butter in recyclable glass jars instead of throwaway plastic containers. Some stores offer customers a rebate if they return bags or use their own shopping bags. Businesses are encouraged, and sometimes required by law, to eliminate unnecessary packaging of products.

Reading Check **Comparing** What is the difference between recycling and conserving?

RECYCLE Give Your Trash a Second Chance

Recycling Waste A waste truck dumps refuse at a landfill site. Recycling is an alternative to landfills. **When does recycling fail as an alternative to landfills?**

It wasn't the bus ride to school that bothered then nine-year-old Brooke Crowther. It was all the garbage she saw when she looked out her window. Broken bottles, old newspapers, all kinds of trash—it was an offensive view that Crowther couldn't ignore. That's when the Reedville, Virginia, native decided to form Pollution Solution Kids—a children's group focused on protecting the environment. Their first project: a roadside cleanup.

Initially, Crowther says, only about five kids were interested in the new organization, but these days PSKids includes at least 40 active members. "It just spread by word of mouth," Crowther, 16, told TIME. "There are always people out there who are interested in the same things you are; it's just a matter of finding them."

These days, when she's not busy coordinating an event for PSKids, doing schoolwork, practicing gymnastics, hiking, or swimming, she serves as a youth adviser to Earth Force, an organization that helps identify and solve environmental problems in communities. If you'd like to get involved with Earth Force, e-mail earthforce@earth force.org

Brooke Crowther from Virginia

Threat of Hazardous Waste

Hazardous waste, much of it toxic or by-products of industry that can cause cancer, is a major environmental danger. Perhaps the most serious form is radioactive waste from our nuclear power plants. Hazardous waste also includes runoff from pesticides that farmers and gardeners spray on plants and residues from improperly discarded used motor oil, auto engine coolant, and batteries.

Some environmentalists estimate that only 10 percent of hazardous wastes is disposed of properly. Until the late 1960s, much of it was put in metal containers, which were then encased in concrete and dumped into the ocean. That policy ended in 1970. Without ocean dumping, land disposal is the only way to dispose of hazardous waste. Most current disposal facilities are nearly full. Unfortunately, at present there is no such thing as a completely safe method of disposing of hazardous waste. Sometimes entire communities are affected by a site. Communities such as Love Canal, near Niagara Falls, New York, and Times Beach, Missouri, had to be abandoned because residents had so many serious health problems due to exposure to toxic waste.

Protecting the Air and Water

Pollution of air and water is a nationwide problem. Cars and trucks produce fumes, and factory smokestacks belch out toxic gases. Even cigarettes pollute the air. Air pollution can cause many health problems. It can also harm animal and plant life.

Water pollution comes mainly from factories, which produce all sorts of chemical waste. For generations, some factories pumped this waste directly into rivers and streams. Others buried it, allowing it to seep into underground water supplies. Polluted water kills fish and other sea life. Eating fish from contaminated waters can make people dangerously ill.

The federal government, through the EPA, has done much to stop industrial pollution of air and water. Federal regulations limit the amounts and kinds of waste that factories may discharge. Unfortunately, budget limitations keep many of these regulations from being strictly enforced.

Pollution from factories, nevertheless, is far easier to regulate than pollution from the activities of individuals. In most cities, cars and trucks are the worst air polluters. To reduce the pollution they cause, the federal government mandated the removal of lead from gasoline. It also required the automobile industry to develop more efficient, cleaner-burning engines and equip cars with devices such as catalytic converters to remove pollutants from exhaust gases.

Another important way to reduce urban air pollution is to persuade people to drive less. Local governments are trying to do this in two ways. First, they are building or improving public transportation systems to get more people to use subways and buses instead of cars. Second, they are encouraging drivers to carpool. Many commuter highways now have separate, less congested carpool lanes for cars carrying two or more people.

Smoking is a far more serious threat to the health of individuals than to the natural environment, but it is a source of indoor air pollution. Many cities and counties have

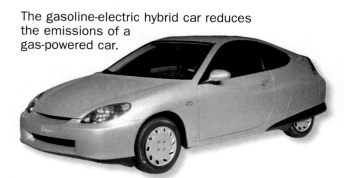
The gasoline-electric hybrid car reduces the emissions of a gas-powered car.

passed no-smoking ordinances, even though restaurant and bar owners strongly oppose them. In 1998 the California legislature approved a statewide ban on smoking inside all restaurants. This marked the strongest antismoking law up to that point.

Almost all states regulate smoking in public buildings, but antismoking groups want to prohibit smoking inside all buildings. Montgomery County in Maryland went so far as to try to outlaw smoking altogether—even in private homes and outdoors. The ban caused a local uproar, and the county executive refused to let it stand.

✓ **Reading Check** **Identifying** How are local governments trying to persuade Americans to drive less?

SECTION 3 ASSESSMENT

Checking for Understanding

1. Key Terms Define the following terms and use them in sentences related to social problems in American communities: solid waste, recycling, conservation.

Reviewing Main Ideas

2. Identify What is the EPA? What does the EPA have to do with environmentalism?

3. Explain What is meant by "NIMBY"? How does NIMBY affect the management of solid waste?

Critical Thinking

4. Making Inferences Why do you think some people do not recycle or conserve resources?

5. Problem Solving In a graphic organizer like the one below, describe environmental threats to communities and possible solutions.

Problem: Solution(s):	Problem: Solution(s):
Environmental Threats to Communities	
Problem: Solution(s):	Problem: Solution(s):

Analyzing Visuals

6. Explain Look again at the photo of the hybrid car on this page. How would you describe a hybrid car to someone who's never heard of one?

★ **BE AN ACTIVE CITIZEN** ★

7. Research Contact your local solid waste disposal authority. Find out how solid waste is disposed of in your community. Note the location of any landfills.

Assessment & Activities

Review to Learn

Section 1
- Government leaders make public policy, which is a general agreement among leaders about how to deal with particular issues.

Section 2
- Local school leaders face funding issues, low test scores, high dropout rates, and crime and violence on school property.

- Federal, state, and local law enforcement agencies fight crime, although most of the daily work is done by uniformed police officers.

Section 3
- Environmentalism is the concern that our environment must be protected.
- Through the EPA, the government tries to reduce air and water pollution.

FOLDABLES™
Study Organizer

Using Your Foldables Study Organizer
Review your completed foldable and select one issue you have written about. Using that example, explain how a community would decide how to handle that issue. You may choose to complete this activity by creating a flowchart.

Reviewing Key Terms

Write the chapter key term that matches each clue below.

1. a document that describes community's goals and how it plans to accomplish them over time
2. a community's system of roads, bridges, water, and sewers
3. the careful preservation and protection of our natural resources
4. the goals a community considers most important or most urgent
5. a kind of government money order that can be used to pay private school costs
6. the money, people, and materials available to a community to accomplish its goals
7. a general agreement among government leaders about how to deal with issues or problems

Reviewing Main Ideas

8. What is the role of a planning commission?
9. What are the provisions of the education bill known as the "No Child Left Behind Act"?
10. Identify and explain two nonfinancial problems facing school systems today.
11. What have many states done to measure how students and school districts are doing?
12. What are three ways in which communities have tried to solve solid waste disposal problems?
13. How has the Temporary Assistance to Needy Families Act affected the welfare rolls in most states?
14. Why is there controversy over school vouchers?
15. What is community policing?

Critical Thinking

16. **Evaluating Information** Which of the environmental issues discussed in this chapter do you think is the most critical today? Explain your answer.

17. Identifying Point of View In a chart like the one below, list the pros and cons of alternatives to public school. Then explain why you favor public education or one of the alternatives.

Alternative to Public Education:	
Pro:	Con:

Analyzing Visuals

Read the "Crime Clock" below, that shows the relative frequency of occurrence of crimes based on annual reported crimes, and answer the following questions.

THE CRIME CLOCK

One murder every 33.9 minutes

One violent crime every 22.1 seconds

One robbery every 1.3 minutes

One property crime every 3.1 seconds

One motor vehicle theft every 27.1 seconds

Source: www.fbi.gov

18. About how often does an instance of violent crime take place in the United States? Why do you think Americans fear becoming the victims of violent crimes?

★ CITIZENSHIP COOPERATIVE ACTIVITY ★

19. What are the most important environmental problems in your community? Form a group of four students and research their causes; find out what local government and individuals are doing to solve the problems.

Practicing Skills

20. Recognizing Bias Find written material about a topic of interest in your community. Write a short report analyzing the material for evidence of bias.

Technology Activity

21. Use an Internet search engine to conduct a search on tuition vouchers. Find arguments both for and against tuition vouchers. Create a chart that summarizes arguments on both sides.

Economics Activity

22. Contact your state department of education. Find out what percentage of school funding dollars in your state comes from the state government and from local taxes. Report your findings to the class.

Standardized Test Practice

Directions: Choose the *best* answer to the question below.

Which of the following statements is FALSE?

F Individuals and interest groups help shape public policy.

G Changing a public policy requires an amendment to the Constitution.

H Elected officials write laws and take action in response to problems.

J Ideas for public policy come from government leaders, interest groups, and private citizens.

Test-Taking Tip

Read the question carefully before answering. You are looking for the statement above that is *not* true.

The Individual, the Law, and the Internet

Why It Matters

The United States is a nation of laws. Our laws bring order into our lives and protect our individual rights. As our nation gains technological knowledge, these laws must be reviewed against a new system that includes new technologies such as the Internet.

 Use the **American History Primary Source Document Library CD-ROM** to find primary sources about the law and technology.

★ BE AN ACTIVE CITIZEN ★

Organize the class into two groups. Pairs from one group should conduct a public opinion poll on crime in their community. Pairs from the other group should research the changing crime rate in the community over several years. Compare the findings of the groups.

An American archaeologist in Cairo, Egypt, accesses information through the Internet.

CHAPTER 15

Legal Rights and Responsibilities

★ CITIZENSHIP AND YOU ★

The Constitution and the Bill of Rights contain important provisions, or laws, safeguarding the rights of Americans. In return, our system of laws gives American citizens a number of responsibilities, including the duty to serve on a jury. Contact the court system at the county level to find out how it selects the names of people for jury duty and how it determines who actually serves. Summarize your findings in an informational chart or diagram.

To learn more about legal rights and responsibilities, view the **Democracy in Action** video lesson 15: The Law and You.

FOLDABLES™
Study Organizer

Summarizing Information Study Foldable *Make this foldable journal about our legal rights and responsibilities, and use it as a study guide.*

Step 1 *Fold a sheet of paper in half from top to bottom.*

Step 2 *Fold it in half again from side to side and label as shown.*

Law Journal

Reading and Writing *As you read the chapter, use your "law journal" to write what you learn about the types of laws, their sources, and their impact on Americans.*

Members of the New York City Police Department ▶

CIVICS Online

Chapter Overview Visit the *Civics Today* Web site at civ.glencoe.com and click on **Chapter Overviews—Chapter 15** to preview chapter information.

POLICE LIN

The Sources of Our Laws

GUIDE TO READING

Main Idea
Modern laws that help people in the United States live together peacefully can be traced back to early laws like the Code of Hammurabi, the Code of Justinian, and English common law.

Key Terms
jurisprudence, common law, precedent, statute

Reading Strategy
Organizing Information As you read, take notes on a web diagram like the one below of early laws upon which modern legal systems are based.

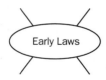

Early Laws

Read to Learn
- What are the functions of law?
- What early laws influenced modern legal systems?

Americans in Action

Read the following laws: "If any one is committing a robbery and is caught, then he shall be put to death." "If fire break out in a house, and some one who comes to put it out cast his eye upon the property of the owner of the house, and take the property of the master of the house, he shall be thrown into that self-same fire." These laws sound very harsh. However, they were a set of rules under which a people once lived.

Ancient tablet depicting King Hammurabi

Functions of Law

The laws mentioned above come from the Code of Hammurabi, the first known system of written law. The early leaders of our nation knew that it was important to establish a set of laws for the nation. In 1779 future president John Adams wrote in the original draft of the Massachusetts state constitution that the state should have "a government of laws, and not of men." He meant that government should operate according to established and dependable rules rather than the changeable and prejudiced feelings of officials. This principle, while not always fully realized, has guided the development of American society.

Laws are sets of rules that allow people to live peacefully in society. They are binding on everyone living in a particular community, state, or nation. They make it possible for all parties—people, organizations, and governments—to deal with one another because everyone knows which actions are permitted and which are not.

A major purpose of laws is to keep the peace and prevent violent acts. Laws set punishments that are meant to discourage potential criminals from such acts as murder, assault, or robbery. To help accomplish this, laws include the administration of justice, in the form of law-enforcement agencies (police) and courts. Laws also set the rules for resolving civil disputes, which are disagreements over money, property, contracts, and other noncriminal matters.

To be fully effective, laws must be fair and must treat all people equally. People in similar circumstances should be treated equally under the law. Good laws are reasonable, setting out punishments that fit the crime. Ordinary people must be able to understand laws, and the government must be able to enforce them. If most people understand the laws and believe they are reasonable and fair, then the laws will be obeyed, and enforcement will become much easier. When the writers of the Constitution created our government, they based the nation's system of laws on ideas, traditions, customs, and laws passed down from generation to generation.

Reading Check **Concluding** What are the purposes of laws?

Early Law

Legal scholars believe that some kind of law existed in even the earliest human societies. They trace its beginnings to prehistoric people, who used unwritten rules of behavior to help members avoid or cope with social conflict. These earliest laws were probably passed from one generation to the next by word of mouth. Then, after people learned to write, they began to write down their laws.

$ Economics and You

Underground Economy

Illegal activities that produce unreported income are part of the underground economy. It consists of people who violate tax laws by not reporting their earnings. The underground economy costs the nation billions of dollars in lost tax revenues. Research one of history's most famous tax evasion cases—the 1931 trial and conviction of Al Capone. Report your findings in the form of a mock radio report. Include a summary of the charges and penalties imposed on Capone.

Code of Hammurabi

As mentioned, the first known system of written law was the Code of Hammurabi. King Hammurabi of Babylonia, an ancient Middle Eastern empire, compiled his code in about 1760 B.C. The code was a collection of 282 laws regulating everyday behavior. By today's standards, the Code of Hammurabi prescribed harsh penalties. If someone stole property, for example, the thief had to pay back 10 times the value of what was taken. If he could not afford to pay, he was put to death.

Another set of early laws is the Ten Commandments found in the Bible. Hebrews living in ancient Palestine followed these laws. The Commandments

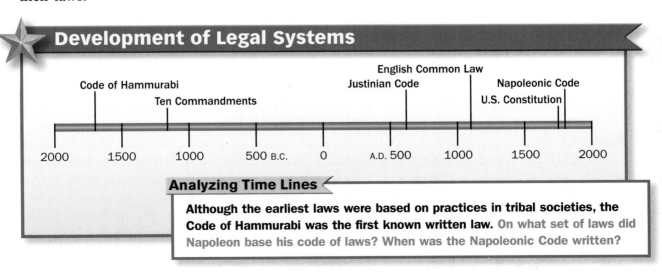

Development of Legal Systems

Code of Hammurabi
Ten Commandments
English Common Law
Justinian Code
Napoleonic Code
U.S. Constitution

2000   1500   1000   500 B.C.   0   A.D. 500   1000   1500   2000

Analyzing Time Lines
Although the earliest laws were based on practices in tribal societies, the Code of Hammurabi was the first known written law. On what set of laws did Napoleon base his code of laws? When was the Napoleonic Code written?

American Biographies

John Peter Zenger (1697–1746)

Freedom of the press owes its origins, in part, to German immigrant John Peter Zenger. In 1733 Zenger agreed to print the *New York Weekly Journal,* founded to expose New York's corrupt royal governor, William Cosby. Zenger, who had come to America at age 13, knew the risks. No government at the time, including Britain, granted newspapers such freedom.

Stories in the *Journal* infuriated Cosby, who ordered copies of the paper publicly burned. Cosby charged Zenger with libel and threw him into jail. Unable to meet the high bail, Zenger sat in a cell for eight months, while his wife Anna kept the paper alive.

When the case went to trial in 1735, Cosby tried to handpick the jurors but failed. Zenger's lawyer, Andrew Hamilton of Philadelphia, told jurors, "Nature and the laws of our country have given us a right to liberty . . . by speaking and writing the truth." Had Zenger printed the truth? Jurors thought so. It took them just 10 minutes to reach a verdict: "Not guilty."

include moral rules about how people should behave toward one another. Ideals of the Commandments, such as "thou shalt not steal" and "thou shalt not kill," are reflected in our laws today.

Roman Law

The Romans made a science of the law, which they called **jurisprudence,** a word we use today to mean the study of law. The first code of Roman law was published in 450 B.C. As in the Code of Hammurabi,

Roman penalties for offenses were drastic by later standards: "If any person has sung or composed against another person a song such as was causing slander or insult to another," said one of the laws, "he shall be clubbed to death."

Over several centuries the Roman senate adopted a great many laws, and Roman judges wrote commentaries on them, which often became part of the law. Later Roman emperors created law by issuing edicts—commands that were equivalent to laws. As the Roman Empire grew, these laws spread to Europe, Africa, and Asia. In A.D. 533 Emperor Justinian I, ruler of the Byzantine, or Eastern Roman, Empire, boiled down the confusing mass of Roman law into an orderly body of rules called the Code of Justinian. This code became the basis of law for the Byzantine Empire. Roman law also became part of the laws of the Roman Catholic Church, known as canon law.

More than twelve hundred years later, the French emperor Napoleon Bonaparte updated the Justinian Code and called it the Napoleonic Code. Napoleon went on to conquer much of Europe in the early nineteenth century, bringing his code with him. In turn, European colonists carried it to Asia and Africa later in the century. As a result, much of the world now lives under some form of Roman law as interpreted by the Napoleonic Code. Even the state of Louisiana, which was French-held territory that Napoleon sold to the United States in 1803, has a system of laws, unlike those of the other 49 states, based on the Napoleonic Code.

English Law

The most important source of American laws is English law. Perhaps the greatest contribution is the English system of **common law,** or law based on court decisions rather than on a legal code. After the Norman conquest of England in 1066, English kings sent judges into the countryside to administer justice. Over time, these judges began to compare the facts and rulings from earlier cases to new cases. When judges decided a new case, they looked in the books for a similar case and followed the earlier ruling, or precedent. **Precedents** are legal opinions that became part of the common law.

English judges were familiar with Roman law and canon law, and they blended these into the body of common law. The law came to include basic principles of citizens' rights such as trial by jury and the concept that people are considered innocent until proven guilty. Common law became the basis for the legal systems of many English colonies, including the lands that later became Canada, Australia, New Zealand, and the United States.

By the seventeenth century, as the English legislature, called Parliament, became stronger in relation to the monarchy, acts of Parliament—written **statutes**—came to dominate the English legal system. Still, common law continued to have a strong influence in legal matters. When English settlers came to the North American colonies in the 1600s and 1700s, they brought with them their traditions of

English Law By tradition, English lawyers, called barristers, wear wigs in court. Patricia Scotland, shown here, was Britain's first black female barrister. **What two principles of American law come from English law?**

common law and citizens' rights. Today these ideas are an important part of our legal system. The common law tradition of following precedents still survives in the interpretation of statutes by courts.

Reading Check **Concluding** Why was the Code of Hammurabi an important development?

SECTION 1 ASSESSMENT

Checking for Understanding

1. Key Terms Define the following terms and use them in sentences related to law and legal systems: jurisprudence, common law, precedent, statute.

Reviewing Main Ideas

2. Explain What did John Adams mean when he said that Massachusetts should have "a government of laws, not of men"?

3. Identify What three systems of law were based on Roman law?

Critical Thinking

4. Drawing Conclusions Why do you think common law predated statute law in the English system of law?

5. Making Comparisons Using a graphic organizer like the one below, compare early systems of law.

Early Systems of Law		

Analyzing Visuals

6. Interpret Read the time line on page 345. The Justinian Code was written about how many years after the Code of Hammurabi was written?

★**BE AN ACTIVE CITIZEN**★

7. Interview Invite a lawyer to your class to discuss how the system of laws in the United States differs from those of other nations.

Types of Laws

GUIDE TO READING

Main Idea
In addition to criminal law, there are other less well-known kinds of law, including civil law, public law, and international law.

Key Terms
plaintiff, defendant, felony, misdemeanor, lawsuit, torts

Reading Strategy
Summarizing Information As you read, define the different kinds of law on a graphic organizer like the one below.

Different Kinds of Law

Read to Learn
- What actions do various kinds of law govern?
- How do various kinds of law differ?

Americans in Action

"A Mercer County man was indicted today by a State Grand Jury on charges that he conned as much as $26,000 from six out-of-state victims by offering to sell them high-grade collectible sports cards over the Internet last year, Attorney John J. Farmer, Jr., and Division of Criminal Justice Director Kathyrn Flicker announced." This information from the Division of Criminal Justice of New Jersey shows Americans taking action in new ways. As society and technology change, so must the application of the law.

LOU GEHRIG

A collectible sports card

Criminal and Civil Law

Most people are familiar with criminal laws, such as prohibitions against fraud and drunk driving, robbing a store, selling drugs, physically attacking a person, and so on. Many other kinds of laws exist as well. Civil laws regulate noncriminal behavior that may end up in disputes between parties. Public law concerns alleged violations of constitutional rights and disputes involving the actions of government agencies. International law is the law of relations between countries. Two types of law affect Americans directly—criminal law and civil law. These laws help maintain a peaceful and orderly society. People who break these laws generally find themselves in the courtroom.

Criminal Law

Criminal laws are laws that seek to prevent people from deliberately or recklessly harming each other or each other's property. American courts operate on an adversary system of justice. Under this system, the courtroom serves as an arena in which lawyers for opposing sides try to present their strongest cases. The judge has an impartial role and should be fair to both sides. Critics of the adversary system argue that it encourages lawyers to ignore evidence that is not favorable to their side. Supporters, though, claim that it is the best system to bring out the facts of a case.

In criminal cases, the government is always the plaintiff—the party that brings the charges against the alleged criminal. This is because the American system of justice assumes that society—everyone—is the victim when a crime is committed. The individual or group being sued is the defendant. About 95 percent of criminal trials in the United States are for violations of state laws. Most criminal cases are titled in terms of the state against the defendant—for example, *State of California* v. *John Jones*. This shows that the government, rather than an individual crime victim, is bringing action against the defendant.

Crimes are graded as either felonies or misdemeanors, depending on their seriousness. Murder, rape, kidnapping, robbery and other serious crimes are felonies because they have very serious consequences. Misdemeanors are offenses such as vandalism, stealing inexpensive items, writing bad checks for low amounts, and so on. Typically, misdemeanors are punished with a fine or a jail sentence of less than one year.

Civil Law

Civil cases involve disputes between people or groups of people—individuals, organizations, or governments—in which no criminal laws have been broken. These disputes are not viewed as a threat to the social order, so the state will not take legal action. When a civil case goes to court, it is called a lawsuit. A lawsuit is a legal action in which a person or group sues to collect damages for some harm that is done. Individuals who think they have been wronged must take action themselves by filing a lawsuit. The person suing is the plaintiff.

In civil cases, individuals believe they have lost something of value or suffered some damage because of someone else's blameworthy actions. A case may be a dispute over

TIME Teens *in* Action

With its well-manicured lawns and upscale shopping malls, Mission Viejo, California, doesn't look like the kind of place gun violence would be an issue. Looks can be deceiving, say Lara and Alicia Miramontes, both 15. Tragedy can happen anywhere. "There are a lot of people who take things for granted," says Lara. "But with [gun violence] happening everywhere—why can't it happen here? We say, when it happens to you, that's when you're going to get involved. People should get involved before they're affected by it."

About two years ago, the Miramontes twins helped start a youth chapter of the Million Mom March, a grassroots organization that promotes gun registration and licensing. Among their activities: A victims' memorial dinner, get-out-the-vote rallies, petition signings, and educational programs. In 2000 the girls lobbied the California State legislature in support of a gun owner-licensing bill and were asked to appear on the floor of one of the houses! The bill was passed and was signed into law in the fall of 2001.

Now Alicia and Lara have started an anti-gun violence club at their school. They hope to educate others about firearm laws and statistics, paying special attention to gun-related suicides. For more information about gun violence or starting your own anti-gun violence group, contact the Million Mom March Web site at www.millionmommarch.org or the Brady Campaign to Prevent Gun Violence at www.bradycampaign.org

Lara and Alicia Miramontes from California

Patrolling U.S. Waters The Coast Guard patrols the waters using military vessels and Falcon planes. The Coast Guard is our nation's leading maritime, or sea, law enforcement agency. **Why would the Coast Guard need to know international laws?**

a contract in which one party believes that the other has not fulfilled the terms of an agreement. (A contract is an agreement between two or more parties.) Suppose, for example, that a supplier of raw materials signed a contract to deliver certain goods to a manufacturer by a given date. When the materials do not arrive on time, the manufacturer must shut down its production line. It loses money both because its factory is idle and because its sales drop due to lack of inventory. The terms of any contract are enforceable by law, so the manufacturer might sue the supplier for monetary damages.

Another type of dispute involves **torts,** or civil wrongs. In tort law a person may suffer an injury and claim that another party is responsible because of negligence. For example, if your neighbor fails to clear ice off her sidewalk and you fall and injure yourself, you might bring a tort action against her. You sue her to recover the costs of your medical treatment and other damages.

Another type of civil law is family law. Family law deals with family issues and problems. Typical cases involve divorce,

child custody, adoption, alimony, child support, and spouse and child abuse.

Reading Check **Comparing** What is the difference between a felony and a misdemeanor?

Public Law

As citizens, we are probably most familiar with criminal and civil law. There are, however, laws that affect us indirectly. Public law, or constitutional law, involves rights guaranteed under the Constitution or spelled out in congressional legislation. A constitutional law case would occur, for example, if a defendant in a criminal matter argued that he was the victim of an unreasonable search and seizure in violation of the Constitution's Eighth Amendment. Constitutional law is the guide for our courts and legislatures whenever they deal with punishments and fines. Constitutional laws are the highest laws in the land; they dictate how the government works.

Another element of public law is administrative law, which includes all the rules and regulations that government agencies of the executive branch must issue to carry out their jobs. In an administrative law case an individual might charge that an agency has acted wrongfully. For example, a plaintiff may claim that the Environmental Protection Agency acted contrary to the will of Congress in some of the regulations it issued on air or water pollution.

Statutory law is another type of public law. Recall from Section 1 that a statute is a law written by a legislative branch of government. The U.S. Congress, state legislatures, and local legislatures write thousands of these laws. Statutes regulate our behavior by, for example, setting speed limits, specifying rules for inspecting food products, and setting the minimum age to obtain a work permit. Statutes are also the source of many of the rights and benefits we take for granted, such as the right to get a Social Security check, to enter a veterans' hospital, to get a driver's license, and to return merchandise you bought at a store.

International Law

International law comprises treaties, customs, and agreements among nations. International law might involve military and diplomatic treaties, trade regulations, international agreements, and so on. Alleged violations of international law may be brought to the International Court of Justice, also called the World Court, which is located in The Hague, the Netherlands. The United Nations established the World Court in 1946 to hear and make rulings on disputes that nations have brought against other nations. The World Court, however, does not have enforcement powers and must rely on the willingness of the parties involved to accept its rulings. A typical international law case might involve a dispute over fishing rights, such as when one nation believes that fishing boats from another nation are operating in its territorial waters.

Reading Check **Identifying** What is an example of a case involving international law?

SECTION 2 ASSESSMENT

Checking for Understanding

1. **Key Terms** Define the following terms and use them in sentences related to different kinds of law: plaintiff, defendant, felony, misdemeanor, lawsuit, torts.

Reviewing Main Ideas

2. **Contrast** What is the difference between criminal and civil law? Who is the plaintiff and defendant in each case? How are the results of each type of case different?

3. **Identify** What does administrative law deal with? Why is administrative law considered part of public law?

Critical Thinking

4. **Making Judgments** In the event of a dispute with another nation, do you think the United States should abide by a ruling of the World Court, or should it maintain its independence and do what it thinks is right?

5. **Organizing Information** In a graphic organizer like the one below, write the four kinds of laws and give two examples of each.

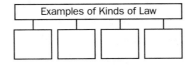

Examples of Kinds of Law

Analyzing Visuals

6. **Conclude** Reexamine the photographs on page 350. If a Coast Guard patrol should see another nation's ships violating U.S. territorial waters, what recourse can the United States take?

★**BE AN ACTIVE CITIZEN**★

7. **Research** Read your local newspaper for a week. List all the examples of criminal, civil, public, and international law that you find. Which kind of law was most often in the news? Report your findings to the class.

The American Legal System

GUIDE TO READING

Main Idea

The U.S. Constitution and the American legal system offer vital protections and rights to citizens of the United States, including those accused of a crime.

Key Terms

stare decisis, writ of habeas corpus, bill of attainder, ex post facto law, due process of law, search warrant, double jeopardy, grand jury, bail

Reading Strategy

Summarizing Information As you read, list on a web diagram like the one below the legal protections enjoyed by Americans that are included in Article I and the Bill of Rights of the U.S. Constitution.

Legal Protections Included in Article I and the Bill of Rights

Read to Learn

• What legal protections are guaranteed by the U.S. Constitution?

• What are the rights of people accused of a crime?

Americans in Action

Ernesto Miranda was only 23 years old when he was arrested by police for kidnapping and rape. At first, Miranda denied any involvement in the crime, but after two hours of questioning by the police, he confessed and signed a statement. At his trial Miranda was sentenced to 20 years in prison. He appealed, claiming that he had not realized that he had a right to have a lawyer present during the police questioning nor had he realized that he had the right to remain silent. Miranda's case went to the Supreme Court, and it changed the way police officers operate. Now, every person who is arrested hears the Miranda warnings.

Ernesto Miranda

Legal Protections in the U.S. Constitution

American colonists enjoyed a degree of liberty found in few countries in the eighteenth century. They owed their rights to legal principles that developed in England and were transferred to America with the colonists. Colonial lawyers studied from English law books, and judges used English common law as the basis for their decisions.

As in England, however, American law increasingly became a law of written statutes, which are the work of Congress and state legislatures. Although this legislation has replaced common law, courts still refer to common-law principles when no statutes exist to deal with a given legal issue.

The U.S. Constitution is the basic law of the land. It gives each branch of government a role in making, enforcing, and interpreting the law. The legislative branch of government makes most laws. The executive branch carries out these laws and, in doing so, makes laws as well. The judicial branch also sets laws by interpreting laws. Courts base their rulings on written laws and on the precedents of earlier cases. These rulings are then used to build decisions about similar cases in the future. This process is called **stare decisis,** which is Latin for "let the decision stand."

Article I of the Constitution includes several basic legal rights of Americans. One of the most important is the writ of habeas corpus. A writ is a written legal order; habeas corpus is a Latin phrase meaning "produce the body." The **writ of habeas corpus** requires an official who has arrested someone to bring that person to court and explain why he or she is being held. The officials holding the person must show good reasons for not releasing the person. This is a safeguard against being kept in jail unlawfully.

Article I also forbids enactment of bills of attainder and ex post facto laws. A **bill of attainder** is a law that punishes a person accused of a crime without a trial or a fair hearing in court. An **ex post facto law** is a law that would allow a person to be punished for an action that was not against the law when it was committed. For example, an ex post facto law making it a crime to buy lottery tickets could be applied to someone who bought tickets before the law was passed.

The Constitution's first 10 amendments—the Bill of Rights—further guarantee the freedoms of individuals. Several of these amendments spell out the rights of Americans in relation to law enforcement and the administration of justice. After the Civil War, Congress adopted the Fourteenth Amendment, extending these rights to formerly enslaved persons.

The Fifth and Fourteenth Amendments guarantee **due process of law.** This means, in part, that government may not take our lives, liberty, or property except according to the proper exercise of law. The law requires, for example, that accused people have the opportunity for a trial by jury and for questioning witnesses against them.

The equal protection of the law clause in the Fourteenth Amendment requires governments to treat all people equally. It

Constitutional Rights of the Accused

Article 1, Section 9
- ⭐ to be granted habeas corpus (released until trial)

Fifth Amendment
- ⭐ to have a grand jury hearing
- ⭐ to be protected from double jeopardy
- ⭐ to refuse to answer questions that may be incriminating

Sixth Amendment
- ⭐ to be informed of the accusation
- ⭐ to hear and question witnesses
- ⭐ to be able to subpoena witnesses
- ⭐ to be represented by an attorney
- ⭐ to have a speedy and public trial by an impartial jury
- ⭐ to be represented by a lawyer

Fourteenth Amendment
- ⭐ to have due process of law
- ⭐ to have equal protection of the laws

Evaluating Charts

The Constitution guarantees our basic legal rights. What protections does the Fourteenth Amendment guarantee?

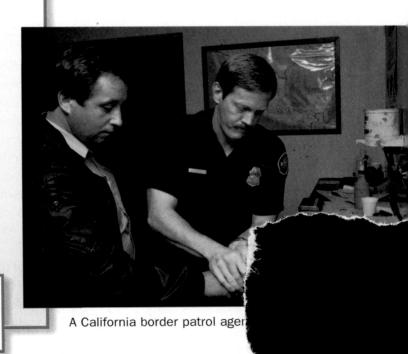

A California border patrol age[...]

House Arrest This man is under house arrest, which means that a person convicted of a crime is confined to the home instead of prison while serving out a sentence. Like most people under house arrest, this man wears a monitor around his ankle so law enforcement officials can monitor his activities. **If a convicted person felt that he was subjected to an unreasonable search of his home, what amendment might he cite in his appeal?**

forbids unfair or unequal treatment based on such factors as gender, race, or religion. Since the 1950s, this clause has been the major civil rights tool of minorities and women when challenging laws or government policies that discriminate against them.

The Constitution defines only one crime—the crime of treason. Article III states that people can be convicted of treason only if they wage war against the United States, join its enemies, or give aid and comfort to the enemy. No one can be convicted of treason without proof. Treason is defined so that the government cannot misuse the law to punish people for political acts. In some countries, criticizing the government is considered treason.

Reading Check **Inferring** Why is the writ of habeas corpus an important right?

Rights of People Accused of Crimes

Several parts of the Bill of Rights protect citizens accused of crimes. These rights ensure that accused people are treated fairly and receive every chance to defend themselves. Each of these rights is based on the idea that a person is presumed innocent until proven guilty in a court of law. The burden of proving an accusation against a defendant falls on the prosecution. The defendant does not have to prove his or her innocence.

Fourth Amendment: Search and Seizure

The Fourth Amendment protects citizens against "unreasonable searches and seizures." It gives Americans a fundamental

Fact Fiction Folklore

Do we protect criminals?

Critics of the exclusionary rule claim that it goes too far in protecting criminals because, as a result of it, many people who are known to have com... ...s go free. Following the ...cks of September 11, ...Americans have argued ...ed more authority, while ...want to change our ...s.

right to be secure in their homes and property. Police seeking to intrude on this security must first get a search warrant—a judge's authorization—specifying the exact place to be searched and describing what objects may be seized. A judge may issue a search warrant if the police can show that they have probable cause—a good reason to believe that a wanted person is hiding in that place or that goods or evidence are housed there.

In the 1961 case *Mapp* v. *Ohio,* the Supreme Court adopted what is called the exclusionary rule. This rule says that if the police gain evidence in a way that violates the Fourth Amendment, that evidence may not be used in a trial.

Fifth Amendment: Self-Incrimination, Double Jeopardy, and Grand Juries

The Fifth Amendment states that people may not be required to incriminate themselves—to say anything that might show them to be guilty of a crime. Sometimes when being questioned, a person may say, "I decline to answer on the grounds that it may tend to incriminate me." This is known as "taking the Fifth." Before the 1960s, police often questioned suspects, sometimes under great pressure, to push them to confess to a crime before they saw a lawyer or appeared in court. In 1966 the Supreme Court held, in *Miranda* v. *Arizona,* that police must inform suspects that they have the right to "remain silent"—to refuse to answer police questions. However, if this right is misused—for example, if a person is using it to protect another person—the judge may hold the person in contempt of court. This means that the judge believes the person is obstructing or interfering with the judicial process, and that person could be jailed.

The Fifth Amendment also bans double jeopardy. This means that a person who is tried for a crime and found not guilty may not be placed in jeopardy—put at risk of criminal penalty—a second time by being retried for the same crime.

The Fifth Amendment says, furthermore, that people accused of serious federal crimes must be brought before a grand jury to decide whether the government has

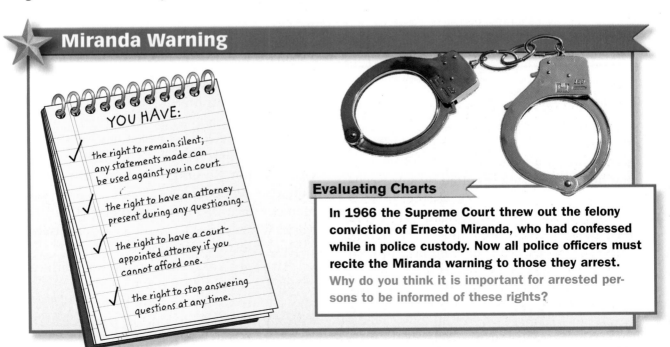

Miranda Warning

YOU HAVE:

✓ the right to remain silent; any statements made can be used against you in court.

✓ the right to have an attorney present during any questioning.

✓ the right to have a court-appointed attorney if you cannot afford one.

✓ the right to stop answering questions at any time.

Evaluating Charts

In 1966 the Supreme Court threw out the felony conviction of Ernesto Miranda, who had confessed while in police custody. Now all police officers must recite the Miranda warning to those they arrest. Why do you think it is important for arrested persons to be informed of these rights?

The Law and You

Should It Be a Crime?

Rank these 8 offenses from the most serious (1) to the least serious (8). Make your decision based on your opinion, not on what the law says.

- A factory knowingly dumps waste in a way that pollutes the water supply of a large city.
- A person sells crack cocaine to others.
- A person breaks through the firewall of a bank's computer system just to see if she can do it.
- A person with a gun robs a victim of $50. No physical harm occurs.
- A drunk driver kills a teen pedestrian by driving an automobile recklessly.
- A person downloads music from the Internet.
- A person releases a virus into the city's police and rescue squad computer system.
- A person intentionally sets fire to a business, causing damage worth $250,000.

★ BE AN ACTIVE CITIZEN ★

Meet with two classmates to compare rankings and discuss the reasons for your decisions. Follow up by researching federal and state laws relating to the actions above.

enough evidence to bring them to trial. (In some states, a preliminary hearing is used instead of a grand jury indictment.) A grand jury is a group of 12 to 23 citizens that hears evidence presented by a prosecutor. The grand jury decides whether there is enough evidence to indicate that the accused has committed the crime. If the grand jury finds sufficient evidence to proceed to trial, it indicts the accused person, or issues a formal charge that names the suspect and states the charges against him or her.

Sixth Amendment: Legal Counsel and Trials

The Sixth Amendment says that an accused person has the right to be defended by a lawyer. In 1963 the Supreme Court, in *Gideon* v. *Wainwright,* interpreted the amendment to mean that if a defendant cannot afford a lawyer, the state must provide one. Previously the federal government provided lawyers for poor defendants, but some states did not.

The Sixth Amendment also guarantees that accused people must be informed of the nature and cause of the accusations against them and have "the right to a speedy and public trial, by an impartial jury" and the right to confront, or question, witnesses against them. Most state and federal courts require the government to bring an accused person to trial within about 100 days. This protects defendants against being held in jail for an unreasonably long time. It also means that trials usually may not be closed to the public or the news media.

A person accused of a crime also has the right to a trial by an impartial jury. Impartial means that jury members will be people who do not know anyone involved in the case and have not already made up their minds about the case. Jury members usually must be drawn from the area where the crime was committed.

In federal courts, all trial juries, called petit juries, have 12 people, and they must reach a unanimous verdict in order to convict or acquit. Several states have juries with as few as six people. Some states allow 12-member juries to reach a verdict if 10 jurors agree. When juries as small as six are used, verdicts must be unanimous.

Although everyone charged with a crime has a right to a jury trial, defendants may choose to appear only before a judge, without a jury. This kind of trial is called a bench trial. A person might request a bench trial to avoid the long and drawn-out process and expense of a jury trial. Even so, many criminal prosecutions do not come to trial at all—with or without a jury—because of plea bargains. Plea bargaining is a negotiation between the defense attorney and the prosecutor, who is the government's attorney. In a plea bargain, the government offers the defendant a chance to plead guilty to a less serious crime in exchange for receiving a less severe penalty. A judge must agree to any bargain reached. People often agree to plea bargains to cut down on the expense and time of a trial or to get a lighter sentence if they fear conviction. Judges often agree to plea bargains as a way to handle the tremendous volume of criminal cases that courts must process every year.

Eighth Amendment: Punishment and Bail

This amendment outlaws "cruel and unusual punishments." Torture, for example, would be cruel. Also, a punishment may not be out of proportion to the crime, such as imposing the death penalty for robbery. There is controversy, however, over how this protection relates to the death penalty. In 1972 the Supreme Court ruled in *Furman* v. *Georgia* that the death penalty as then administered was not constitutional. The Court found that the death penalty was being imposed in unfair ways, for a wide variety of crimes, and mainly on African Americans and poor people. This decision, though, did not outlaw the death penalty. In response to the *Furman* decision, about three-fourths of the states revised their death penalty laws to comply with guidelines laid down by the Supreme Court. Some states have established a two-stage process to deal with death penalty cases. First, a

jury trial determines the guilt or innocence of the defendant. Then a separate hearing is held to determine the degree of punishment.

The Eighth Amendment also prohibits "excessive bail." **Bail** is a sum of money an arrested person pays to a court to win release from jail while awaiting trial. The purpose of requiring this payment is to guarantee that the person will voluntarily return for the trial. After the trial, the person gets back the money. Courts may not set bail so high that a person is unnecessarily and unfairly forced to stay in jail. For example, a judge cannot set bail at $100,000 for a motorist accused of running a red light.

TIME

Political Cartoons

"*You are entitled to one call, one fax, or one e-mail.*"

and it seems to be diverted toward money and time. Making the world a more convenient place to live was a collaboration among several

Schnei
ing

Analyzing Visuals The American legal process contains many provisions to safeguard the rights of those accused of committing crimes—including the right to make a phone call after being arrested. What is the setting of this cartoon? How would you summarize the cartoonist's point?

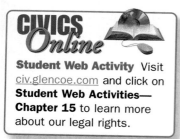
If a person is accused of a serious crime, however, the judge may set a very high bail. In case of an extremely serious criminal action such as murder, or if the arrested person seems highly likely to flee or to be a danger to the community, the judge may deny bail altogether, and the defendant is remanded—returned to custody until the trial. On the other hand, sometimes a judge will require no bail at all, releasing a person on his or her own recognizance, or simple promise to return.

 Reading Check **Concluding** Why must police be aware of the exclusionary rule when investigating crimes?

Our Legal Responsibilities

The Declaration of Independence stated, "all men are created equal." This does not mean that everyone is born with the same characteristics. Rather, this democratic ideal of equality means that all people are entitled to equal rights and treatment before the law. Americans have a number of legal responsibilities. By fulfilling them, we ensure that our legal system works as it should and that our legal rights are protected. Serving on a jury and testifying in court are both important responsibilities. The legal right to a jury trial can only be effective if people are willing to serve on juries and appear in court.

Other responsibilities include obeying laws and cooperating with law enforcement officials. A government's ability to enforce a law depends to a great extent on people's willingness to obey it. The effectiveness of law enforcement officials often depends on people's willingness to become involved and tell what they know about a crime.

Americans must work peacefully to change unfair, outdated laws. This might involve gathering voters' signatures on petitions to place an issue on a ballot for a vote or asking legislators to change the law.

 Reading Check **Summarizing** What are the legal responsibilities of Americans?

SECTION 3 ASSESSMENT

Checking for Understanding

1. Key Terms Define the following terms and use them in sentences related to constitutional legal protections and rights of the accused: writ of habeas corpus, bill of attainder, ex post facto law, double jeopardy, bail.

Reviewing Main Ideas

2. Identify What are three basic legal rights of all citizens, and what do these rights mean?

3. Explain What must police show a judge in order to obtain a search warrant?

Critical Thinking

4. Drawing Conclusions Which of the rights guaranteed to people accused of a crime do you think is the most important? Explain.

5. Organizing Information On a graphic organizer like the one below, explain the constitutional rights of the accused in the United States.

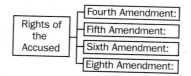

Rights of the Accused	Fourth Amendment:
	Fifth Amendment:
	Sixth Amendment:
	Eighth Amendment:

Analyzing Visuals

6. Identify Review the chart on page 353. Which part of the U.S. Constitution includes the guarantee that if you are arrested you must be informed of the charges against you?

★**BE AN ACTIVE CITIZEN**★
7. Interview Talk with a police officer. Find out what procedures police must follow to obtain a search warrant and what they must do at the time of an arrest. Share your findings with the class.

Citizenship
SKILLBUILDER

Making Decisions

Why Learn This Skill?

Making decisions is part of living. Deciding what to wear or what to have for lunch is just part of your daily routine. Many decisions, however, are more serious. Deciding what subjects to pursue in school, what career to plan for, or how to help a troubled friend can all have lasting consequences. You may have to make decisions as a leader in school or perhaps in government when you become an adult. These decisions could affect many other people.

Learning the Skill

Following the steps below will help you make more thoughtful decisions.

- State the situation or define the problem. Gather all the facts. Ask: Why do I have to make a decision on this matter? Whom will my decision affect? Then, define your objective. State as clearly as possible what you hope to accomplish.
- List your options. Think of all the different courses of action open to you. Ask: What are the alternatives? How can I deal with this situation in a different way?
- Consider the possible outcomes. Ask yourself what the likely results of each option would be.
- Compare the possible outcomes to your objective. Consider your values. Values are the beliefs and ideas that are important to you. Your values should serve as your guidelines in making all decisions.
- Decide and act. Having thought out the situation, you know you have made the best decision possible at the time.
- Evaluate your decision. Review the actual outcome and ask yourself if you would make the same decision again.

Practicing the Skill

On a separate sheet of paper, write out the decision-making steps for the fictional situation described below.

Maria sees her friends Beth and Amy drop some earrings from a store counter into their pockets. Beth and Amy do not know Maria is watching. What action will Maria take? Maria wants to keep Beth's and Amy's friendship. She thinks it's even more important that Beth and Amy do not break the law.

Maria's objective: _____
Maria's options:
a. Confront her friends   b. _____
c. _____   d. _____
Possible outcomes:
a. Friends don't listen   b. _____
c. _____   d. _____
Outcomes v. Objective
a. Friends shoplift again b. _____
c. _____   d. _____
Maria decides and acts: _____
Maria evaluates her decision: _____

Applying the Skill

Research a new law your local or state leaders are considering. Place yourself in their position. How would you decide to vote if it were up to you? Record the steps you took in making your decision.

Practice key skills with Glencoe's
Skillbuilder Interactive Workbook CD-ROM, Level 1.

Assessment & Activities

Review to Learn

Section 1

• Laws keep the peace and prevent violent acts. They set punishments and rules for resolving disputes.

• Early laws like the Code of Hammurabi, the Ten Commandments, Roman law, and English law have influenced our laws today.

Section 2

• Many types of law exist including public law, international law, and criminal and civil law.

• Whereas criminal law deals with criminal acts, civil law deals with disputes between people or groups.

Section 3

• Article I of the U.S. Constitution and the Bill of Rights include several protections for those Americans accused of a crime.

FOLDABLES™
Study Organizer

Using Your Foldables Study Organizer
Work with a partner and your completed foldable to review the chapter. Face each other. One person begins by reciting a fact from his or her completed foldable. Then the partner recites a related fact. Repeat the process as many times as you can.

Reviewing Key Terms

Choose the key term from the chapter that best matches each clue below.

1. guarantees a person's right to appear before a judge to determine whether he or she was being held legally

2. a person bringing suit against another party

3. less serious crimes or minor offenses such as traffic violations

4. protects people from being tried for the same crime a second time

5. laws written by a legislative branch

6. a sum of money an arrested person pays to win release from jail while awaiting the trial

7. legal opinions or court decisions upon which later decisions are based

8. serious crimes such as robbery or murder

Reviewing Main Ideas

9. Identify four characteristics of effective laws.

10. How did English law influence the development of American law?

11. How is common law different from statute law?

12. Name four types of laws.

13. Give at least two reasons a person might file a lawsuit.

14. Give two examples of a felony and two examples of a misdemeanor.

15. What does "taking the Fifth" mean?

16. How do grand juries and petit juries differ?

$ Economics Activity

17. The Supreme Court ruled in *Gideon* v. *Wainwright* that the government must provide a lawyer to anyone accused of a crime who cannot afford one. Contact the local bar association in your area or a lawyer in your community. Find out how much it would cost to hire a lawyer for different kinds of cases, for example, criminal, civil, and so on.

Practicing Skills

18. **Making Decisions** Use local newspaper archives to read about an event that has affected or that affects your community. Make an educated decision about how you would handle the event if you were a government official. Explain your decision and your reasoning.

Analyzing Visuals

Read the bar graph below. Then answer the following questions.

19. Which age group includes the most victims of violent crimes?

20. Summarize the information on the graph in a few sentences.

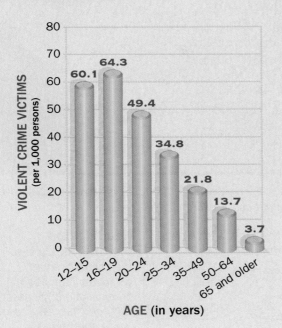

VIOLENT CRIME VICTIMS (per 1,000 persons)

Age	Value
12–15	60.1
16–19	64.3
20–24	49.4
25–34	34.8
35–49	21.8
50–64	13.7
65 and older	3.7

AGE (in years)

★ CITIZENSHIP COOPERATIVE ACTIVITY ★

21. Divide into three or four groups and find out about specialties of the lawyers in your community. As a group, focus on one area of law. Interview a lawyer practicing that area of law to find out about typical cases and report your findings to the class.

Critical Thinking

22. **Identifying Alternatives** Are there any other legal rights you think people should have? Explain.

23. **Organizing Information** In a chart like the one below, describe the U.S. Constitution's role in protecting the rights of U.S. citizens.

Part of Constitution	Role in Protecting Rights

Technology Activity

24. On the Internet go to the FindLaw Web site: http://news.findlaw.com/. Look for an article that relates to the legal protections described in this chapter. Read the article and summarize its main points.

The Princeton Review

Standardized Test Practice

Directions: Choose the *best* answer to the question below.

Which amendment to the U.S. Constitution guarantees the "equal protection of the laws"?

A Fourth Amendment
B Fifth Amendment
C Eighth Amendment
D Fourteenth Amendment

Test-Taking Tip

Find the best answer by eliminating answer choices that you know are incorrect, thereby narrowing the choices.

Civil and Criminal Law

★ CITIZENSHIP AND YOU ★

Each year millions of Americans are charged with crimes, while others are involved in civil lawsuits. We can help maintain law and order by obeying laws, respecting the rights of others, being aware of current laws, and supporting the police. Contact your local police department to find out about any new or altered laws. Prepare a pamphlet informing others of these laws.

To learn more about civil and criminal law, view the **Democracy in Action** video lesson 11: The Federal Court System at Work.

FOLDABLES™
Study Organizer

Organizing Information Study Foldable *Make the following foldable to help you organize what you learn about civil and criminal law.*

Step 1 *Fold a sheet of paper into thirds from top to bottom.*

This forms three rows.

Step 2 *Open the paper and refold it into thirds from side to side.*

Fold it into thirds.

This forms three columns.

Reading and Writing *As you read the chapter, record what you learn about criminal and civil cases and court procedures in the appropriate spaces on your foldable table.*

Step 3 *Unfold, turn the paper, and draw lines along the folds.*

Step 4 *Label your table as shown.*

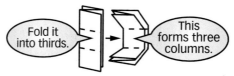

	Types of Cases	Court Procedures
Civil Law		
Criminal Law		

A courthouse in Waxahachie, Texas ▶

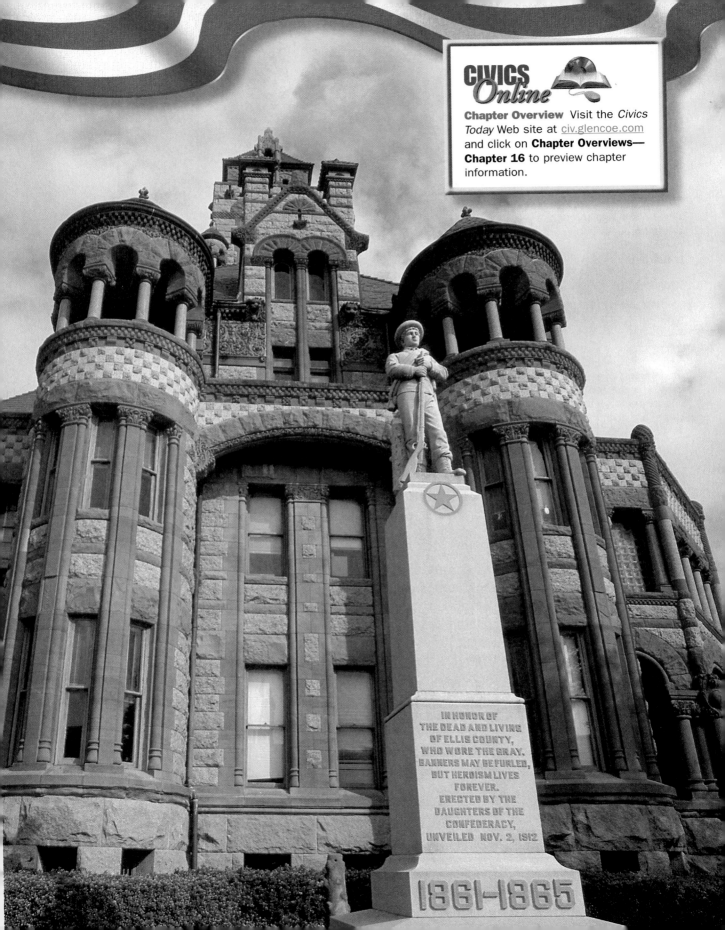

CIVICS Online

Chapter Overview Visit the *Civics Today* Web site at <u>civ.glencoe.com</u> and click on **Chapter Overviews— Chapter 16** to preview chapter information.

IN HONOR OF
THE DEAD AND LIVING
OF ELLIS COUNTY,
WHO WORE THE GRAY.
BANNERS MAY BE FURLED,
BUT HEROISM LIVES
FOREVER.
ERECTED BY THE
DAUGHTERS OF THE
CONFEDERACY,
UNVEILED NOV. 2, 1912

1861-1865

Civil Cases

GUIDE TO READING

Main Idea

Civil lawsuits go through a legal process before reaching trial or settlement.

Key Terms

plaintiff, defendant, injunction, complaint, summons

Reading Strategy

Sequencing Events Use a graphic organizer like the one below to show the steps in a civil lawsuit.

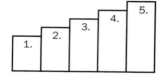

Reading to Learn

• What are the various types of civil law?
• What are the steps in a civil lawsuit?

Americans in Action

In November 2000, residents of Palm Beach County in Florida filed a civil lawsuit against the Palm Beach County Canvassing Board, claiming their civil rights had been violated. The suit sought damages totaling $250,000 for stripping the right to vote from several American citizens. The plaintiffs claimed that the ballot format was misleading and deceptive, causing them to cast votes for candidates other than the candidate for whom they intended to vote. This civil suit and others like it brought wide media attention because the outcome of the presidential election of 2000 was at stake.

A disputed election

Types of Civil Lawsuits

The civil cases filed over the election in Florida led to a recounting of votes and reached the Supreme Court. The Supreme Court's ruling eventually led to George W. Bush winning the presidency. In civil cases the plaintiff—the party bringing a lawsuit—claims to have suffered a loss and usually seeks damages, an award of money from the defendant. The defendant—the party being sued—argues either that the loss did not occur or that the defendant is not responsible for it. The court's job is to provide a place to resolve the differences between the plaintiff and the defendant. Lawsuits involving damages of a few thousand dollars or less are often handled in a small claims court, and the people involved may act as their own attorneys. Lawsuits involving more money, however, often require lawyers and juries in larger civil courts.

The American judicial system hears many different kinds of civil lawsuits. Lawsuits may involve property disputes, breach of contract, or family matters, such as divorce. Many lawsuits deal with negligence, or personal injury. A negligence suit is filed when a person has been injured or killed or when property has been destroyed because someone else has been careless or negligent.

Suits in Equity

A special type of lawsuit is a suit in equity. Equity is a system of rules by which disputes are resolved on the grounds of fairness. In this type of suit, a person or group seeks fair treatment in a situation where there is no existing law to help decide the matter. Often, people bring suits in equity to prevent a damaging action from taking place. An equity court could require an action to stop a wrong before it occurred. For instance, a group of Americans could file a suit in equity to try to prevent their state from building a highway through a local park.

A judge, not a jury, usually decides suits in equity. When deciding such a suit, the judge may issue an **injunction,** which is a court order commanding a person or group to stop a certain action. For example, in the case just mentioned, a judge might issue an injunction to stop construction of the highway.

✓ Reading Check **Identifying** What do civil lawsuits usually involve?

What Happens in a Civil Case?

We will use an imaginary case to follow the steps of a civil lawsuit. Imagine that you have slipped on a neighbor's icy sidewalk and suffered a broken wrist. You feel that your neighbor should have cleared the sidewalk of snow and ice to keep it safe, and in failing to do so, you believe he is responsible for your injury. You want your neighbor to pay you for the costs of your medical care and lost time at work, as well as to compensate you in cash for your pain and suffering. You decide to sue your neighbor.

Bringing Suit

You start the process by hiring a lawyer, who files a **complaint** with the proper court. The complaint is a formal statement naming the plaintiff and the defendant and describing the nature of the lawsuit. The court then sends the defendant a **summons,** a document telling him of the suit against him and ordering him to appear in court on a given date and time.

Civil Cases Lawsuits involving major sums of money often go to civil court where they are heard by a jury. **What is the first step in filing a civil lawsuit?**

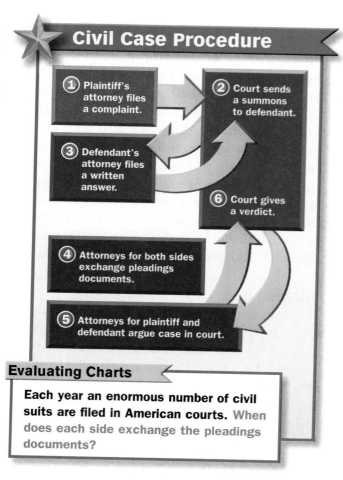

Civil Case Procedure

1. Plaintiff's attorney files a complaint.
2. Court sends a summons to defendant.
3. Defendant's attorney files a written answer.
4. Attorneys for both sides exchange pleadings documents.
5. Attorneys for plaintiff and defendant argue case in court.
6. Court gives a verdict.

Evaluating Charts

Each year an enormous number of civil suits are filed in American courts. When does each side exchange the pleadings documents?

The Defendant's Response

The defendant may respond to the charges by having his own attorney file an "answer" to the complaint. The answer will either admit to the charges or offer reasons why the defendant is not responsible for the injuries that the plaintiff is claiming. The complaint and the answer together are referred to as **pleadings.**

Before going to trial, the lawyers on each side have an opportunity to check facts and gather evidence by questioning the other party and possible witnesses. This process is called **discovery.** The purpose of the discovery phase is for each side to try to avoid any surprises at the trial.

Pretrial Discussions

The judge appointed to hear the case might call a pretrial conference with both parties to help clarify differences between the two sides and prepare for the trial. At this stage you and your lawyer might come to the conclusion that your case looks weak, and you may decide to drop the suit.

On the other hand, your neighbor and his lawyer may conclude that your case is very strong and that you are likely to win your suit. They may, therefore, offer you a settlement. This is similar to the plea bargaining process in criminal cases, except that the parties usually agree on an amount of money that the defendant will pay to the plaintiff.

Another way to resolve disputes is by a process called mediation, in which each side explains its side of the dispute and must listen to the other side. A trained mediator leads the discussions, acting as a neutral party to keep communications open. The mediator does not decide the issue; instead the two sides decide the issue with the mediator's help. The two sides may also agree to submit their dispute to arbitration. Arbitration is a process conducted by a professional arbitrator who acts somewhat like a judge by reviewing the case and resolving the dispute. The arbitrator's decision is usually binding on all parties.

Either party in a lawsuit may propose a settlement at any time. This often happens during the discovery phase as costs begin to build up and people become more willing to compromise. Most civil cases are settled before trial for several reasons. First, the outcomes of many trials are hard to predict, and parties prefer the certainty of a negotiated outcome. Also, most courts have a large backlog of waiting cases so it may be years before a new case finally comes to trial. Finally, because trials are time-consuming and expensive, all the major participants—the defendant, the insurer, the plaintiff, the judge, and the attorneys—are likely to prefer a settlement.

Trial

If the parties do not settle, the case goes to trial. There may be a jury of 6 to 12 members, or more likely, a judge will hear the case alone. The plaintiff presents its side first, followed by the defendant. Both sides then summarize their cases.

In criminal trials the prosecution must prove the defendant guilty "beyond a reasonable doubt." Civil cases have a lesser standard. The plaintiff in a civil case has to present only a "preponderance of evidence"—enough to persuade the judge or jury that the defendant, more likely than not, was responsible for the incident that caused the damages.

After all the evidence has been presented and the arguments made, the judge or jury will consider the case and then decide on a verdict, or decision, in favor of one of the parties. If the plaintiff wins, a remedy is set. In this case, the remedy might be for your neighbor to pay your medical costs, replace your lost earnings, and compensate you for your pain and suffering with a cash payment. If the defendant wins, the plaintiff gets nothing and must pay court costs.

Economics and You

Direct Expenditures

The moneys paid out by individuals, businesses, and governments to cover their expenses are known as direct expenditures. The direct dollars spent on civil and criminal justice by federal, state, and local governments total more than $135 billion per year. Expenses include the salaries of people who work within the justice system. Find out about public law–related jobs by contacting your local justice office or court.

Appeal

If the losing side believes that the judge made errors during the trial or some other type of injustice took place, it may appeal the verdict to a higher court. In cases in which the plaintiff wins a large cash award, the defendant or the defendant's insurance company will very often appeal to have the award reduced. As a result, a winning plaintiff may have to wait years before seeing any of the money the court awarded, and may even end up with nothing.

Reading Check **Summarizing** Why are most civil cases settled before they go to trial?

SECTION 1 ASSESSMENT

Checking for Understanding

1. **Key Terms** Use the following terms in complete sentences: plaintiff, defendant, injunction, complaint, summons.

Reviewing Main Ideas

2. **Compare** How do suits of equity differ from other civil lawsuits?

3. **Identify** What do the pleadings include? What is the purpose of the discovery phase of a civil trial? Describe what happens during this process.

Critical Thinking

4. **Drawing Conclusions** In your opinion, should mediation and arbitration be used to settle most civil suits to prevent overloading the court system?

5. **Sequencing Information** Use a graphic organizer similar to the one below to summarize the steps involved in mediation.

Steps in Mediation

☐ → ☐ → ☐ → ☐

Analyzing Visuals

6. **Identify** Review the procedures of civil courts on page 366. In civil court proceedings, what are the two main functions of the court?

★ **BE AN ACTIVE CITIZEN** ★

7. **Interview** Talk with a friend or relative who has been involved in a civil lawsuit. What was the nature of the case? How was the suit resolved?

Criminal Cases

Main Idea

Criminal cases follow a legal procedure from arrest to the verdict and sentencing.

Key Terms

crime, arraignment, testimony, cross-examine, acquittal, hung jury

Reading Strategy

Analyzing Information
Outline the procedures that take place in a criminal case after an arrest is made, using a graphic organizer similar to the one below.

Steps in Criminal Cases

Read to Learn

• What are the general types of criminal cases?

• What procedures do criminal cases follow?

Americans in Action

The Bill of Rights established that persons accused of committing a crime have the right to be represented by lawyers. The Supreme Court has interpreted that right to mean that if a defendant cannot afford a lawyer, the court will appoint one to represent him or her. Court-appointed attorneys are called public defenders. Connecticut's Division of Public Defender Services seeks to dispel some myths about public defenders. Public defenders are not inexperienced, rather they are skilled attorneys who specialize in criminal law and practice their profession every day in the courtroom by representing their clients.

A judge delivers a verdict.

Types of Cases

In criminal law cases the government charges someone with a crime and is always the prosecution—the party who starts the legal proceedings against another party for a violation of the law. The person accused of the crime is the defendant. A **crime** is an act that breaks a federal or state criminal law and causes harm to people or society in general. Crimes are defined in each state's written criminal laws, called the penal code. A state's penal code also spells out the punishments that go with each crime. Penal codes establish classifications, or degrees of seriousness, for certain crimes to set appropriate penalties. In general, the more serious the crime, the harsher the punishment will be.

In Chapter 15 we divided crimes into two main groups—serious law violations called felonies and minor violations called misdemeanors. Whereas persons convicted of misdemeanors may be fined or sentenced to one year or less in jail, persons convicted of felonies could be imprisoned for one year or more. In the case of murder, the punishment could be death. Felonies can, in turn, be classified in terms of who or what was harmed when a crime was committed.

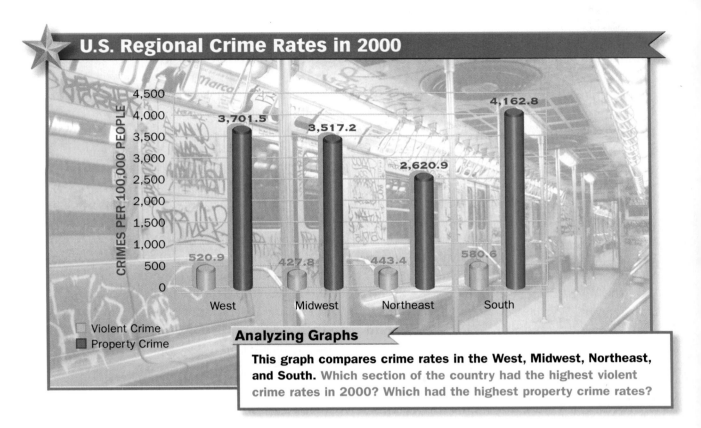

U.S. Regional Crime Rates in 2000

CRIMES PER 100,000 PEOPLE

West — 520.9 / 3,701.5
Midwest — 427.8 / 3,517.2
Northeast — 443.4 / 2,620.9
South — 580.6 / 4,162.8

Violent Crime
Property Crime

Analyzing Graphs

This graph compares crime rates in the West, Midwest, Northeast, and South. Which section of the country had the highest violent crime rates in 2000? Which had the highest property crime rates?

Penalties for Crimes

People who are accused and convicted of crimes are usually punished by fines and/or imprisonment, depending on the nature and severity of the crime. Criminal penalties serve several functions. They provide punishment so that a criminal pays for an offense against a victim or society. They help protect society by keeping dangerous criminals confined in prison. In this way, lawbreakers cannot continue to commit crimes and harm others. Criminal penalties can also keep other people from committing the same crimes by serving as warnings or examples to deter others. Finally, criminal penalties are intended to help prepare lawbreakers for reentering society after their prison terms have ended. Through counseling, education, and vocational training, some prisons help inmates learn skills that will help them lead productive lives after prison.

Some prisoners may be eligible for parole after serving part of their sentences. This means that a parole board reviews a request for parole and decides whether or not to grant a prisoner early release from prison. If parole is granted, the person must report to a parole officer until the sentence has expired.

Critics of the parole system claim that many sentences end up much shorter than intended because of it. In answer to this criticism, some states have established mandatory sentencing, which means that judges must impose whatever sentence the law directs. Opponents of mandatory sentencing, though, claim that in some cases, the judge must impose harsher sentences than the circumstances of the case justify. Other systems of sentencing include indeterminate sentences, in which a judge gives a minimum and maximum sentence. A set range of sentences applies to each kind of crime. Under any system, similar crimes should receive similar punishments, but judges have some leeway in considering the unique circumstances of each individual case.

Types of Felonies

The crimes that Americans tend to fear most are crimes against people. These are violent or potentially violent crimes such as murder, manslaughter (the accidental killing of a person), assault (physical injury or threat of injury), rape, and kidnapping.

Crimes against property are the most common types of crime. Burglary, robbery, and theft are all forms of larceny, the taking of property unlawfully. Vandalism (the deliberate destruction of property) and fraud (taking property by dishonest means or misrepresentation) are other common crimes against property.

Some crimes, such as unauthorized gambling or the use of illegal drugs, are considered victimless crimes or crimes against morality because there is no victim to bring a complaint. Because of this, laws regarding these crimes are very hard to enforce. Although some people argue that these acts should not be considered crimes because there are no victims, victimless crimes *can* in fact harm others. For instance, people frequently steal to get money to purchase illegal drugs, and victimless crimes could be committed by criminal gangs who commit other violent crimes against society.

Reading Check **Describing** What does it mean if a prisoner is granted parole?

TIME

Political Cartoons

ZOOLOGICAL GARDENS

"We had to let the animals go. No one informed them of their rights when they were arrested."

and it seems to be diverted toward money and time. Making the world a more convenient place to live was a collaboration among several

Analyzing Visuals Under the *Miranda* ruling of 1966, police officers must inform suspected criminals of their rights. In what ways does the *Miranda* ruling help protect the United States Constitution?

What Happens in a Criminal Case?

The criminal justice system is the system of state and federal courts, judges, lawyers, police, and prisons that have the responsibility for enforcing criminal law. As you will learn in Section 3 of this chapter, there is a separate juvenile justice system with special rules and procedures for handling cases dealing with young people, called juveniles, who in most states are people under the age of 18.

Criminal cases follow several steps. At each step defendants are entitled to the protections of due process guaranteed in the Bill of Rights. Criminal cases begin when police and other law enforcement officers arrest a person on suspicion of having committed a crime.

Arrest

Officers make arrests if they have witnessed a suspected crime, if a citizen has made a complaint or report of a crime, or if a judge has issued an arrest warrant. When the arrest is made, the officers will read the suspect his or her rights. As you recall from Chapter 15, as a result of the Supreme Court ruling in the case of *Miranda* v. *Arizona* in 1966, all police officers must inform anyone they arrest of the following four rights:

- The right to remain silent; any statement made can be used against you in court.
- The right to have an attorney present during any questioning.
- The right to have a court-appointed attorney if you cannot afford one.
- The right to stop answering questions at any time.

The suspect is taken to a local police station and booked, or charged with a crime. As part of the booking process, the police fingerprint and photograph the suspect. During that time he or she is allowed to call a lawyer. If the suspect cannot afford a lawyer, the state will provide one.

Hearing, Indictment, and Arraignment

A few hours after being booked, the suspect appears in court and is informed of the charges against him or her. At this time the prosecution must show the judge that there is probable cause—a good reason—for believing that the accused committed the crime with which he is charged. The judge then either sends the accused back to jail, sets bail for him, or releases him on his own recognizance, which means the accused is released without having to pay bail. Instead, the accused promises to appear in court when called.

As noted in Chapter 15, in federal courts and many state courts, grand juries are used to decide whether a person should be indicted—formally charged with a crime. In some states, a preliminary hearing is used instead of a grand jury

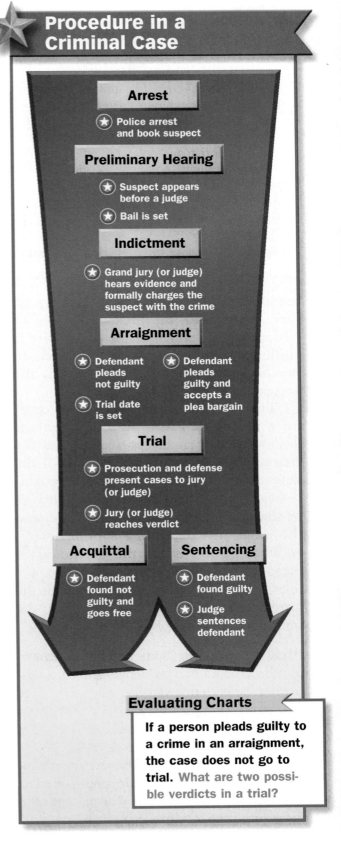

Procedure in a Criminal Case

Arrest
- ★ Police arrest and book suspect

Preliminary Hearing
- ★ Suspect appears before a judge
- ★ Bail is set

Indictment
- ★ Grand jury (or judge) hears evidence and formally charges the suspect with the crime

Arraignment
- ★ Defendant pleads not guilty
- ★ Defendant pleads guilty and accepts a plea bargain
- ★ Trial date is set

Trial
- ★ Prosecution and defense present cases to jury (or judge)
- ★ Jury (or judge) reaches verdict

Acquittal
- ★ Defendant found not guilty and goes free

Sentencing
- ★ Defendant found guilty
- ★ Judge sentences defendant

Evaluating Charts

If a person pleads guilty to a crime in an arraignment, the case does not go to trial. What are two possible verdicts in a trial?

indictment. In some cases, when a grand jury is not used, the prosecutor files an "information," which claims that there is sufficient evidence to bring the accused person to trial. If the judge agrees, the accused is indicted.

The defendant then appears in court for a procedure called an **arraignment.** He or she is formally presented with the charges and asked to enter a plea. If the defendant pleads not guilty, the case continues. If the defendant pleads guilty, he or she stands convicted of the crime, and the judge will determine a punishment. Another option is for the defendant to plead no contest. This means that he or she does not admit guilt but will not fight the prosecution's case. The effect is much the same as for a guilty plea.

Plea Bargaining Sometimes after reviewing the charges and evidence against a suspect, a defendant's lawyer may encourage him to accept a plea bargain. A plea bargain is an agreement in which the accused person agrees to plead guilty, but to a lesser charge. By accepting a plea bargain, the defendant avoids a time-consuming and lengthy trial. It also ensures that a person will be punished for committing a crime.

Trial

If the case goes to trial, the defense has much work to do. The lawyer interviews witnesses, studies the laws affecting the case, and gathers as much information as possible. Although criminal defendants have a constitutional right to a jury trial, many give up that right and have their cases tried before a judge alone in what is called a bench trial. If the defense does ask for a jury trial, the first step when the trial starts is to choose the jurors. Both sides select potential jurors from a large pool of residents within the court's jurisdiction. Both sides try to avoid jurors who might be unfavorable to their side. Either side can reject a certain number of jury candidates without having to give reasons and can ask the judge to dismiss others for various causes.

After the jury has been chosen, the lawyers for each side make an opening statement in which they outline the case they will present. The prosecution and defense then present their cases in turn. Each side calls witnesses who swear that their **testimony**—the answers they give while under oath—will be "the truth, the whole truth, and nothing but the truth."

After a witness testifies for one side, the other side is allowed to **cross-examine** him or her. The questions asked in cross-examination are often designed to make the witness's original testimony appear unreliable or untrue. Finally, each side makes a closing statement highlighting the testimony and evidence that support it and questioning the other side's testimony and evidence. The judge then "instructs" the jury, or explains the law that relates to the case.

The Verdict and Sentencing

The last part of a trial begins when the jury goes off to think over and discuss the case and reach a verdict. After choosing a foreman or forewoman to lead the discussion, the jurors review the evidence and legal arguments they have heard. Jury deliberations are secret and have no set time limit. Finally, they vote on whether the defendant is guilty or not guilty. To decide that a person is guilty, the jury must find the evidence convincing "beyond a reasonable doubt." Most states require a unanimous vote. If a jury feels that the prosecution has not proven its case, it can decide on acquittal. **Acquittal** is a vote of not guilty. The defendant is then immediately released.

Sometimes a jury cannot agree on a verdict, even after days of discussion and many votes. When that happens, the judge declares a **hung jury** and rules the trial a mistrial. With a mistrial, the prosecution must decide whether to drop the charges or ask for a retrial.

If a defendant is found guilty, the judge sets a court date for sentencing. In some cases, a jury recommends a sentence. More often, however, the judge decides on the sentence after considering the defendant's family situation, previous criminal record, employment status, and other information.

Sentences often specify a period of time to be spent in prison. Today victims of the crime are often allowed to make statements about the sentence, and judges may take those statements into account. Sentences may include fines or a set number of hours spent doing community service work.

If the defendant is found guilty, the defense may, and often does, appeal the verdict to a higher court. (If the case was a capital case, or one involving the death penalty, the appeal could go directly to the state supreme court.) Usually the appeal contends that the judge made errors or that the defendant's constitutional rights were violated. If the jury votes not guilty, however, the Fifth Amendment prohibition against double jeopardy bars the prosecution from appealing the verdict.

Student Web Activity Visit civ.glencoe.com and click on **Student Web Activities— Chapter 16** to learn more about court systems.

Reading Check **Explaining** What does the defendant do during the arraignment?

SECTION 2 ASSESSMENT

Checking for Understanding

1. Key Terms Use the following key terms in a paragraph that relates to criminal cases: crime, arraignment, testimony, cross-examine, acquittal, hung jury.

Reviewing Main Ideas

2. Identify What are four functions of penalties for crimes? How are those convicted of crimes usually punished?

3. Define What is the basic procedure of a criminal case? Outline and describe each step in a criminal case.

Critical Thinking

4. Drawing Conclusions Why do you think judges allow some suspects to be released on their own recognizance?

5. Summarizing Information What is the jury's job? Outline the functions of the jury on a chart similar to the one below.

Duties of Jury	Possible Jury Votes/Outcomes

Analyzing Visuals

6. Infer Review the procedures in criminal cases on page 371. What occurs if a defendant pleads guilty and accepts a plea bargain? What happens if a defendant pleads not guilty?

★ **BE AN ACTIVE CITIZEN** ★

7. Research Read a local or national newspaper to find an ongoing or recent criminal case. Describe the procedures of a criminal case using details from the particular case you've found.

Landmark Supreme Court
Case Studies

Gideon v. Wainwright

Background of the Case

In 1942 the Supreme Court, in *Betts* v. *Brady,* ruled that the Sixth Amendment did not require states to appoint attorneys for people who could not afford them. By way of the Fourteenth Amendment, however, it held that states were required to supply lawyers in cases that held the death penalty. In June 1961, Clarence Earl Gideon of Florida was accused of theft, a non-death penalty crime. Gideon mistakenly believed the Supreme Court had entitled him to court-appointed counsel, and so asked for a lawyer. His request was denied, so Gideon defended himself in an intelligent but inadequate manner. The judge sentenced him to five years in prison.

The Supreme Court agreed to hear the case after Gideon himself wrote and sent his own petition from his prison cell. Because only lawyers may speak before the Supreme Court, a Washington, D.C., attorney was appointed for Gideon. A Florida lawyer represented Louie Wainwright, head of the state's prisons.

The Decision

The Court's ruling came on March 18, 1963. Justice Hugo L. Black wrote the unanimous decision:

Clarence Earl Gideon

In the 1930s, the Supreme Court ruled that the Sixth Amendment requires the government to supply lawyers for those defendants who cannot afford one in all federal cases. How did poor defendants acquire Sixth Amendment rights in state courts?

> We accept Betts v. Brady's assumption . . . that a provision of the Bill of Rights which is "fundamental and essential to a fair trial" is made obligatory upon the States by the Fourteenth Amendment. We think the Court in Betts was wrong, however, in concluding that the Sixth Amendment's guarantee of counsel is not one of these fundamental rights. . . . any person hauled into court, who is too poor to hire a lawyer, cannot be assured a fair trial unless counsel is provided for him.

The Court thus overturned *Betts.* Under the "due process" clause of the Fourteenth Amendment, it found the Sixth Amendment guarantee of counsel binding on state as well as federal courts.

Why It Matters

Although some states by 1963 already provided court-appointed lawyers in non-death penalty cases, the *Gideon* decision assured this protection in all the states. Gideon was retried and found not guilty.

Analyzing the Court Decision

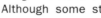

1. How did the *Gideon* ruling affect the earlier *Betts* decision?
2. How did the Court apply the Fourteenth Amendment in *Gideon?*

Young People and the Courts

GUIDE TO READING

Main Idea
When young people, or juveniles, commit crimes, the American judicial system treats them differently from adults. Juvenile criminal cases follow a general standard procedure.

Key Terms
juvenile, juvenile delinquent, rehabilitate

Reading Strategy
Contrasting Information
In a diagram similar to the one below, write how juveniles and adults are treated differently in the American criminal system.

Juvenile Offenders — Both — Adult Offenders

Read to Learn
- What are the stages in the juvenile justice system?
- What role does rehabilitation play in the juvenile justice system?

Americans in Action

In the eighteenth century, children as young as seven could be tried and sentenced in the same criminal courts as adults. Then, in 1825, the Society for the Prevention of Juvenile Delinquency founded a shelter that tried to correct the behavior of young criminals instead of simply punishing them. These earliest reformers were called "child savers." Cook County, Illinois, established the first juvenile court in 1899, and followed the doctrine of *parens patriae*—"the State as parent." This meant it was the state's duty to protect and guard the interests of the child.

A young girl hears the charges against her.

Causes of Juvenile Delinquency

Every state designates a certain age at which people become adults in the eyes of the criminal justice system. Anyone under that age—18 in most states—is considered a juvenile, someone who is not yet legally an adult. Our system treats young people who commit crimes—called juvenile delinquents—somewhat differently from adults. All states and the federal government, however, allow older juveniles who are charged with very serious crimes or already have criminal records to be tried as adults.

Children and teenagers commit many crimes each year. Some of these crimes are misdemeanors such as shoplifting. Others, however, are serious crimes such as armed robbery, rape, or murder. Studies have shown that children who are abused or neglected, or who suffer emotional or mental problems, are more likely than others to get into trouble with the law. They have also shown that children who grow up in poverty, in overcrowded and rundown neighborhoods where drug and alcohol abuse are common, are more likely to become delinquents.

Although these factors may contribute to juvenile delinquency, they do not explain why some young people commit crimes. Many children who suffer abuse and live amid poverty never have trouble with the law, while children from all backgrounds can become juvenile delinquents.

Marian Wright Edelman (1939–)

Marian Wright Edelman once told an interviewer that she "never for a moment lacked a purpose worth fighting, living, or dying for." At first, Edelman found her "purpose" in the civil rights movement of the 1950s and 1960s. Then, in 1973, she organized the Children's Defense Fund (CDF). The CDF's mission is to win programs to keep children healthy, in school, and out of trouble.

Edelman, the youngest of five children, credits her parents with teaching her to help other people. "Working for the community was as much a part of our existence as eating and sleeping," Edelman recalled. With their support, she obtained a law degree from Yale and went on to become the first African American woman to practice law in Mississippi. She also served as a leader in the NAACP Legal Defense and Education Fund.

By the 1980s, Edelman's work with the CDF had earned her the reputation as "the children's crusader." Today the CDF is the leading lobby on behalf of children, especially the some 14.3 million children who live in poverty.

Stages in the Juvenile Justice System

When juveniles are charged with committing crimes, their cases are handled in separate courts, called juvenile courts. The primary goal of juvenile courts is to try to rehabilitate, or correct a person's behavior, rather than punish the person. Nearly three-fourths of juvenile court cases begin when police arrest young people for crimes. The rest result from petitions to the courts that school administrators, store managers, or others in contact with children have filed. Parents who cannot control the behavior of their children also may petition a court for help. This means that children can be put into the juvenile justice system without having been accused of a crime—for example, if they have repeatedly run away from home.

The juvenile court system was set up in the late 1800s as a result of judicial system reforms. Before then, juvenile offenders, or lawbreakers, over age 14 were treated like adults. They received the same sentences and were sent to the same prisons as adults. Now the guiding principle of juvenile courts is to do whatever is in the best interest of the young people.

Juvenile courts handle basically two types of cases: neglect and delinquency. Cases of neglect involve juveniles who are neglected or abused by their caregivers. A juvenile court has the power to place these youths with other families in foster homes, where they will be protected and cared for. Delinquency cases involve juveniles who commit crimes. Juvenile courts also handle cases in which juveniles perform acts that are considered illegal for juveniles but not for adults, including running away from home, skipping school, or violating curfew laws.

Diversion or Detention

When a juvenile is arrested, the police notify his or her parents or caregivers. Depending on the crime, the young person may be sent home or kept in a juvenile detention center until it is time to appear in court.

Most police departments have officers who handle juvenile cases. These officers often have the authority, especially in nonviolent cases, to divert juveniles away from court and into special programs. Because the emphasis is on rehabilitation—improving the young person's behavior—rather than punishment, the system has counseling, job-training, and drug-treatment programs that juveniles can be diverted into.

Even if juveniles are eventually diverted from the system, they may be held in custody at first, while authorities decide how to proceed with the case. In such a case, a judge will hold a detention hearing to determine whether the juvenile might be dangerous to himself or others. Young people judged to be dangerous are candidates for further confinement.

The Trial

For juveniles who continue to be held, the next stage is a preliminary hearing. As in the adult system, the purpose of this procedure is to determine whether there is probable cause to believe that the young person committed the crime as charged.

The court procedure for juveniles is similar to adult trials, but with important differences. For example, at the court appearance, the juvenile and his or her caregivers meet with their lawyer, the judge, the police officer who made the arrest, and the probation officer who investigated the case. This meeting or hearing is similar to a trial, but it is less formal. Only the parties involved may attend the hearing. As in a trial, both sides are allowed to call and cross-examine witnesses. There is no jury, however. Juveniles do not have the right to a jury trial. In most cases the judge decides whether the juvenile is delinquent or nondelinquent.

The juvenile court system tries to protect juveniles by keeping the identity of offenders secret and not allowing the public to view their criminal records. In some cases, those criminal records can be erased when the offender becomes an adult. In addition, when juveniles are arrested, they are not fingerprinted or photographed.

Some states have been experimenting with peer juries made up of other juveniles. Jury members receive special training on the philosophy of the juvenile justice system. Typically, peer juries are used only for the sentencing stage, and the defendant must agree to the use of a peer jury.

If a juvenile has been found delinquent, or guilty, the court holds another hearing to decide the disposition of the case—the equivalent of sentencing.

Juvenile court judges can sentence juvenile offenders in different ways. They may simply send them home with a stern lecture, or they may place offenders with a previous history of delinquency in a special training school, reformatory, treatment

Peer Juries Peer juries are used to divert nonviolent juvenile offenders from formal court action. Jury members are usually volunteers selected by the chief of police or other officials, and the sentence usually includes community service. **Why do you think juvenile courts are using peer juries?**

center, or teen shelter. Often the juvenile formally agrees to attend school or obey his or her caregivers during a probationary period. If the young person successfully completes probation, the charges will be dropped and the matter will be removed from the record. Juveniles who are neglected or have poor home lives may become wards of the court. The court becomes their guardian and can supervise them until adulthood. Judges may place juveniles with serious mental or emotional problems in a hospital or institution. Because of the emphasis on rehabilitation, however, a judge can divert a juvenile from the system even after he or she has been found delinquent.

Reading Check **Describing** What does it mean to "divert" a juvenile from the court system?

Supreme Court Rules

In 1967 the Supreme Court established several rules for juvenile criminal cases. For instance, the parents or guardians of the juveniles must be notified of the arrest as soon as possible. Juveniles and their caregivers must be notified in writing of all the charges against them. Juveniles have the right to an attorney and the right to remain silent. Juveniles also have the right to confront witnesses against them.

These rights were established by the *In re Gault* Court case. In the 1967 case, 15-year-old Gerald Gault of Phoenix, Arizona, was charged with making indecent telephone calls to a neighbor. His parents were not informed of his arrest. During the hearing that followed, Gault did not have an attorney present and the neighbor was not questioned. The judge sentenced Gault to a reformatory until the age of 21—a period of six years. If Gault had been an adult, his sentence would have been a $50 fine and a few months in jail.

The Supreme Court overturned the judge's decision and established that juveniles have the right to counsel, the right to confront witnesses, and the right not to be forced to incriminate themselves. Justice Abe Fortas wrote the majority opinion stating, "Whatever may be their precise impact, neither the Fourteenth Amendment nor the Bill of Rights is for adults alone."

Reading Check **Concluding** Why was the *Gault* case important?

SECTION 3 ASSESSMENT

Checking for Understanding

1. **Key Terms** Contrast the following terms in a sentence: juvenile, juvenile delinquent. Explain the term rehabilitate by using it in a sentence related to the juvenile court system.

Reviewing Main Ideas

2. **Identify** What are two factors that contribute to juvenile delinquency?

3. **Describe** What is the primary goal of juvenile courts?

Critical Thinking

4. **Making Judgments** Do you agree with the use of peer juries? Why or why not?

5. **Summarizing Information** In a graphic organizer like the one below, list the options judges have when sentencing juvenile offenders.

Options for Juvenile Court Judges

Analyzing Visuals

6. **Infer** Review the photograph of a peer jury on page 377. Would you call the use of peer juries an innovative development? Explain your answer.

★ **BE AN ACTIVE CITIZEN** ★

7. **Interview** Visit a juvenile detention center in your community. Find out about the rehabilitation programs offered there and report your findings in a brief report.

SKILLBUILDER

Problem Solving

Why Learn This Skill?

Solving problems does not end with math class. Individuals and societies alike must sometimes resolve difficult issues. Whether the problem is serious or not, a solid approach to solving it can lead to a faster and more satisfactory end.

Learning the Skill

Follow these steps in a problem-solving situation:

- Define the problem. Recognize why you have the problem and what needs to change.
- Look at all sides of the issue. Are others involved? How are they affected?
- Keep your emotions in check. Anger, fear, or anxiety can stand in your way.
- Draw on past experience. What have you done or seen others do that could help?
- Consult an authority. You might do research to learn more facts or talk with an authority figure you trust.
- Take action. Face the problem directly and avoid delays that might make the problem grow worse.

Practicing the Skill

Read the passage on this page. Then on a separate sheet of paper, answer the following questions.

❶ How did Nick define his problem?
❷ What other people concerned him?
❸ When did he apply past experience?
❹ What actions did Nick take?

Nick slammed his book bag into the corner of his room. "Who would do something like that to me?" he yelled. When he opened the bag at school this morning, a packet of drugs fell out. Nick grabbed it up right away, but he knows several other kids around his locker saw it.

Nick's sure somebody slipped the drugs into his book bag at the party last Friday after school. Could it have been his friend Zach? Zach's been acting kind of weird lately. The next morning, Nick felt determined. Somehow he had to find out if Zach did it and make sure his own name was in the clear.

When Nick got to his locker that morning, he waited for some of the kids with lockers near his. Nick explained to them about the not-very-funny trick somebody had played on him. He was careful, though, not to bring Zach's name into it.

After the last bell rang in the afternoon, Nick headed into Coach's office. "You did the right thing by talking to me," Coach assured him. "If Zach is the culprit, he needs to know it's not funny. It's also important to know that he isn't thinking about doing drugs himself. Come back tomorrow and bring Zach with you. We'll talk."

Applying the Skill

Think of a problem that exists in your school or local community. Using the steps in problem solving, draw up a plan for a solution to the problem.

GO TO

Practice key skills with Glencoe's **Skillbuilder Interactive Workbook CD-ROM, Level 1.**

Assessment & Activities

Review to Learn

Section 1
- Civil law includes disputes over rights, property, or agreements.
- In a civil lawsuit, the plaintiff files a complaint against the defendant and the defendant responds.

Section 2

- Criminal cases are divided into two main groups—felonies and misdemeanors.
- Criminal cases follow certain steps.

Section 3
- When a juvenile is arrested, the police must notify his or her parents or caregivers. Then a preliminary hearing is held, followed by a court appearance. There is no jury in juvenile court cases.
- The primary goal of juvenile courts is to try to rehabilitate, or correct the behavior, of offenders.

Study Organizer

Using Your Foldables Study Organizer
Use the foldable you created during the study of this chapter to summarize the court procedures in civil and criminal cases into two flowcharts. Use only your completed foldable to create the civil and criminal case flowcharts.

Reviewing Key Terms

Write the key term that matches each definition below.

1. to correct a person's behavior rather than to punish him or her
2. an act that breaks a criminal law
3. the party bringing the lawsuit
4. a criminal procedure in which the accused is formally presented with charges and asked to enter a plea
5. the party being sued
6. a court order commanding a person or group to stop a certain action
7. a young person who commits a crime
8. a vote of not guilty
9. a formal statement naming the plaintiff and defendant and the nature of the civil lawsuit
10. a jury that cannot agree on a verdict

Reviewing Main Ideas

11. What are four types of lawsuits?
12. What are the two main types of crime? How do they differ?
13. What happens during the verdict and sentencing parts of a criminal trial?
14. What is plea bargaining and why is it an important part of the legal process in criminal cases?
15. What happens during the hearing phase of a criminal case?
16. Identify four rules the Supreme Court has established for juvenile cases.
17. What special protections do the juvenile courts provide for juveniles?
18. What is the purpose of a suit in equity?

Critical Thinking

19. **Analyzing Information** Do you think civil cases should be tried before a jury? Why or why not?

20. Drawing Conclusions How does the idea of "guilty beyond a reasonable doubt" protect the rights of defendants? Organize your answer by using a graphic organizer similar to the one below.

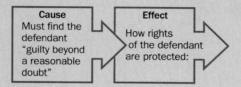

Cause	Effect
Must find the defendant "guilty beyond a reasonable doubt"	How rights of the defendant are protected:

Analyzing Visuals

Examine the graph on page 369 and answer the following questions.

21. In general, which types of crimes occur most often in the United States, violent crimes or property crimes?

22. Which region of the country experiences the least amount of crime overall?

Practicing Skills

23. Problem Solving Describe a decision you might face today or in the near future, such as the choice to go to college or get a job after high school. List the steps of the problem-solving process. At each step, write down questions and information you would consider and what your answers might be. Evaluate what you think would be your best option.

 Economics Activity

24. Individuals and businesses seek to protect themselves from civil lawsuits by purchasing liability insurance. Liability insurance helps cover legal fees and the damages claimed by the plaintiff. Damages may include physical injury, destroyed property, or violations of contracts. Contact a local insurance agent to collect information on the various types of liability policies, ranging from automobile insurance to malpractice insurance. Summarize your findings in an informational pamphlet.

Self-Check Quiz Visit the *Civics Today* Web site at civ.glencoe.com and click on **Self-Check Quizzes—Chapter 16** to prepare for the chapter test.

★ CITIZENSHIP COOPERATIVE ACTIVITY ★

25. In groups of four, prepare arguments, pro or con, for debating the following statement: The Miranda rule should be suspended so criminals can be prosecuted more easily. Support your arguments with opinions, information from the text, and other research. Debate this issue with the rest of the class by allowing each group to present its position to the class. Then hold a class vote to see what position is supported by most class members.

 Technology Activity

26. Search the Internet to find information on juvenile law in your state. Use the information you find to create a flowchart showing the process that juveniles accused of crimes must follow in your state.

The Princeton Review — Standardized Test Practice

Directions: Choose the *best* answer to complete the statement below.

In a civil case, a court

F settles a dispute between two parties.

G punishes a criminal offender.

H decides how best to rehabilitate a juvenile offender.

J all of the above

Test-Taking Tip

Find the best answer by carefully identifying the key words in the statement to be completed.

Citizenship and the Internet

★ CITIZENSHIP AND YOU ★

Democracy needs citizens who are willing to take part in civic life. The Internet is increasing opportunities to do just that. Before reading this chapter, find an example of how the Internet encourages democracy and how it presents challenges to democracy.

To learn more about citizenship and e-commerce, view the **Democracy in Action** video lesson 14: Citizenship in the United States and **Economics & You** video lesson 28: Technological Change and the Economy.

FOLDABLES™
Study Organizer

Summarizing Information Study Foldable *Make and use this foldable to record the main ideas and supporting facts found in Chapter 17.*

Step 1 *Collect two sheets of paper and place them about 1 inch apart.*

Keep the edges straight.

Step 2 *Fold up the bottom edges of the paper to form 4 tabs.*

This makes all tabs the same size.

Reading and Writing *As you read the chapter, write the key points of each section under the appropriate tab of your foldable.*

Step 3 *When all the tabs are the same size, crease the paper to hold the tabs in place and staple the sheets together. Label each tab as shown.*

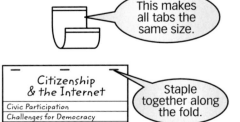

Citizenship & the Internet

Civic Participation
Challenges for Democracy
Regulating the Internet

Staple together along the fold.

The computer room at the New York City public library ▶

CIVICS
Online

Chapter Overview Visit the *Civics Today* Web site at <u>civ.glencoe.com</u> and click on **Chapter Overviews—Chapter 17** to preview chapter information.

Civic Participation

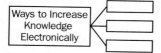

Ways to Increase Knowledge Electronically

Americans in Action

Ohio resident Frank Coffin grew up in rural Indiana and still owns property there in Owen County. A proposed extension of Interstate Highway 69 could cut Owen County in half. From his home in Columbus, Ohio, Coffin actively opposes the highway route by logging onto a Web site maintained by Citizens for Appropriate Rural Roads, Inc., a grassroots organization whose aim is to preserve the farms and woodlands of south-central Indiana. The site allows Coffin and other interested parties, whether they are local residents or not, to learn about the issues, keep up with developments, and voice their support.

A farm in Indiana

A Tool for Political Education and Action

The Internet and the World Wide Web present great opportunities and challenges for citizens in a democracy. The **Internet** is a mass communication system of millions of networked computers and databases all over the world. The **World Wide Web** operates within the Internet, allowing users to interact with the billions of documents stored on computers across the Net. Thanks to the Internet and the World Wide Web, we can now communicate with one another efficiently, share information conveniently, and even shop and bank online. Just a click of the computer mouse lets us send electronic mail (e-mail), transfer data, and explore the vast array of **Web sites**—"pages" on the World Wide Web that may contain text, images, audio, and video.

Currently the Net has about 100 million computers and 500 million users and is growing daily. In 1993 there were 130 Web sites. Today there are many millions, with the number doubling every few months. More than 40 percent of the U.S. population has access to the Web. Soon half the population of the world will access the Web, many through wireless devices.

The Internet is increasing opportunities for citizens to participate in democracy. Citizens cannot make thoughtful decisions about government and public policy unless they stay informed.

By searching the World Wide Web, you can find information on almost every topic imaginable. Not all of what is posted on the Internet is accurate, however. Before believing what you read, be sure to evaluate the credibility of the source (see the Skillbuilder lesson on page 388).

Gathering Information

More and more citizens today are using the Internet to keep informed about current events. Most national newspapers and newsmagazines, like *USA Today* and *TIME,* publish online every day and keep archives, or files of older stories. Your hometown newspaper may have a Web site as well. You can also log onto the sites of television and radio networks like Cable News Network (CNN) and National Public Radio (NPR) to read news accounts, watch video broadcasts, and listen to newscasts.

Research and educational have informative Web sites as well. Th. only present their findings on current to. ics and make policy recommendations but also often provide useful links to other sites. Be aware, though, that not all "think tanks" are nonpartisan; that is, they are not free from political party ties or bias. Many, like the Brookings Institution and the Heritage Foundation, have some ideological bias.

E-Government

Many parts of the federal government, along with state, county, and local governments, have created their own Web sites. At

Government Sites The Smithsonian National Air and Space Museum's Milestones of Flight exhibit presents the 1903 *Wright Flyer* and the Apollo 11 command module *Columbia.* Why do you think the federal government maintains Web sites, such as the Smithsonian's Web site (below)?

the national level, hundreds of sites exist for the branches of government, federal agencies, and resources like the Smithsonian Institution museums. These sites often offer documents, pictures, and electronic card catalogs from various libraries and searchable databases.

E-government is making it much easier for citizens to learn about public policy, check on elected officials, request services, and participate in government directly. Rick Perry, the governor of Texas, put it this way:

> 66 **By allowing citizens to interact with their government through one central Web site, we are making government more efficient . . . I look forward to the day when a citizen can do business with Texas government online, instead of standing in line.** 99

Government Web sites are helping people do everything from obtain marriage licenses to comment on the performances of public servants. North Carolina citizens, for example, can use their state government's Web site to register to vote, request an absentee ballot, learn how their representative voted on a certain issue, view the state constitution, see the state budget, and much, much more.

Group Action Online

As you read in Chapter 11, one good way to influence government is by supporting a special-interest group. The Internet can help you find groups with goals and values similar to your own. Most significant interest groups today have Web sites.

Newsgroups, or Internet discussion forums, provide another way to exchange information and ideas with people who share your concerns. Whether you want to protect the environment, curb TV violence, help homeless children, or get involved in any other cause, you can probably find a related newsgroup. When you join, you will get regular postings and the chance to contribute your own thoughts.

Reading Check **Explaining** What is the relationship between the Internet and the World Wide Web?

Election Campaigns

Although citizens can use the Internet routinely to stay politically aware and active, they may turn to it even more during election campaigns. The Internet is changing how citizens can participate in elections and how candidates run for office. One campaign manager recently said, "We see the Web as the best campaign tool since the phone and the television."

Both the Republican and Democratic Parties maintain Web sites with information about their activities, as do a number of minor parties. Nearly every candidate for higher political office will also have his or her own Web site.

Voters can visit sites to learn about the candidate's background, position on issues, schedule of appearances, recent speeches, and more. Many sites feature an electronic newsletter that gives subscribers weekly e-mail updates on the candidate's activities. Some candidates even list their campaign contributors online. During the 2000 presidential election, Al Gore, the Democratic nominee, and George W. Bush, the Republican candidate, maintained extensive Web sites.

When you visit these Web sites, though, you must use caution because political party and candidate Web sites do not present a diversity of opinions. The goal of these sites is to build support for their ideas and candidates, not to explain both sides of an issue. They usually have links only to other like-minded sites.

E-Mailing Candidates

In most campaigns, few voters have a chance to meet those running for office. The Internet, however, is creating a new avenue for direct, personal contact with candidates or their staff. During a recent election for California's attorney general, one citizen e-mailed each of the candidates and "asked them to address the top 10 questions I was concerned with." She then based her vote "on how they responded to my questions and the time it took them to answer."

Grassroots Web Sites

During the 2000 presidential campaign, citizens participated in a new way by setting up independent Web sites to support their favorite candidates. By the end of the election, more than 6,500 homegrown sites had appeared to support either Bush or Gore. These Web sites were the cyberspace version of people putting a sign in their front yard or a bumper sticker on their car.

Grassroots Web sites provide an inexpensive and convenient way for citizens to get directly involved in an election. The creator of one such site explained that "the Internet gave me the opportunity to be active . . . [on] my schedule." Another site developer believes "these sites will increase democracy. . . . You will have independent citizens voicing their opinions in a way they couldn't before."

Grassroots Web sites do raise some concerns for the major parties and their candidates, though. These sites may contain misinformation or have links to extremist groups that a candidate would not want to be associated with. Further, it can be hard to tell the difference between official and unofficial sites.

✓ **Reading Check** **Concluding** What role did grassroots Web sites play in the 2000 presidential election?

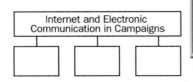

SECTION 1 ASSESSMENT

Checking for Understanding

1. Key Terms Define the following terms and use them in sentences related to electronic communication: Internet, World Wide Web, Web site, archives, nonpartisan, newsgroups.

Reviewing Main Ideas

2. Infer What danger do people face when using "think tank" Web sites? How might people prepare for that danger?

3. Explain What are grassroots Web sites? Why might major party candidates for office have concerns about grassroots Web sites that support them?

Critical Thinking

4. Drawing Conclusions The Internet offers many advantages for gathering information. What do you think is the biggest disadvantage or danger?

5. Analyzing Information In a graphic organizer like the one below, describe how the Internet and electronic communication have become part of political campaigning.

Internet and Electronic Communication in Campaigns

Analyzing Visuals

6. Infer Examine the photograph and Web page on page 385. Why do you think places like this maintain Web sites? How are the photograph and Web site related?

★ **BE AN ACTIVE CITIZEN** ★

7. Research Look up the Web site of your representative to Congress or one of your senators. What kind of information can you gather from the site? Share your findings with the class.

Evaluating a Web Site

Why Learn This Skill?

Going to the Internet for news and information can be quick and convenient. Knowing which Web sites to trust, however, can challenge any Web surfer. No one supervises Internet content. To get reliable information, you need to make a number of judgments about individual Web sites and the pages that they present.

Learning the Skill

To evaluate a Web site, follow these steps:

- Determine the source or authorship. The person or group sponsoring the site should be clearly identified. An author's credentials should be stated.
- Check for accuracy. Factual content should include sources that can be verified. A quality Web site will also be free of spelling and language errors.
- Determine the intent. An informational site meant to serve the public will be free of advertising. If advertising does appear, it will be clearly identified.

- Check to see how current a site is. A valid page will include information on when it was written and when it was placed on the Internet.

Use these questions as a guide to help you analyze the content of a Web site:

- Are the facts on the site documented?
- Is more than one source used for background information within the site?
- Are the links within the site appropriate and up-to-date?
- Is the author clearly identified?
- Does the site contain links to other useful resources?
- Is the information easy to access? Is it properly labeled?
- Is the design appealing and easy to navigate?

Practicing the Skill

On a separate sheet of paper, use the following questions to evaluate the Web site as shown on this page.

1. Who sponsors this Web site?
2. Briefly describe the language and presentation on this site.
3. Why might the page be termed a public-service piece?
4. What times and dates are indicated on the site?
5. Overall, how reliable do you think this Web site is?

Applying the Skill

Access the Web site www.glencoe.com/sec/socialstudies/. Write a paragraph to evaluate the site, addressing the four steps in this lesson.

Challenges for Democracy

GUIDE TO READING

Main Idea
Although the Internet offers an opportunity to spread democratic ideas worldwide, some people cannot afford computers or Internet access, and invasions of privacy are a constant threat.

Key Terms
authoritarian, dissident, propaganda

Reading Strategy
Summarizing Information
As you read, list some of the dangers posed by use of the Internet on a web diagram like the one below.

Internet Dangers

Read to Learn
• How does the Internet divide American society?
• What is the threat to privacy posed by the Internet?

Americans in Action

Don't be a victim—take action. "This nightmare began in March 1997 when we received a phone call from Nations Bank in Norfolk, Virginia. . . . They wanted to know why I was delinquent in making payments. . . ." This testimonial from a victim of identity theft is typical. Many victims of identity theft don't know about the problem until months or even years after the crime begins. According to the Federal Trade Commission, identity theft is the fastest-growing crime today. More than 700,000 people became victims in 2000 alone.

A crime in progress

Divisions in Society

When the Internet and the World Wide Web started, people thought these things would promote the global expansion of democracy. Information and opinions would flow freely across national borders. By spreading democratic ideas worldwide, the Internet would help undermine authoritarian regimes. An **authoritarian** regime is a government in which one leader or group of people holds absolute power.

Authoritarian governments, however, are finding ways to limit online political communications. They have begun building electronic borders similar to the "firewalls" that protect business networks from intruders.

China, for example, encourages its citizens to get on the Internet. However, the government strictly controls access to the Web sites of human rights groups, foreign newspapers, and similar organizations. Messages that Chinese users post online are closely watched. Furthermore, the government has shut down the Web sites of some dissident groups. A **dissident** group includes people who disagree with the established political or religious system.

For Americans, the Internet has been an aid to the free exchange of knowledge and ideas; yet the Internet may still pose challenges to our democracy. Some people fear that the Internet

Limiting Access Teens surf the Internet at the Feiyu Net Café in Beijing, China. The Chinese government, which strives for near-total control of the media, has closed thousands of Internet cafes, accusing them of promoting crime and corrupting the young. **Why do authoritarian regimes monitor Internet use?**

is widening the gap between the "haves" and "have-nots" and empowering intolerant extremist groups that seek to splinter society. Another concern is that the Internet leaves citizens vulnerable to invasions of privacy.

Democracy does not guarantee everyone equal wealth. It does aim to give all citizens an equal opportunity to develop their talents, though. It also emphasizes equal treatment for all Americans, regardless of their gender, race, or religion. How is the Internet affecting these two key ingredients of democratic community?

A Digital Divide

The ability to use the Internet is becoming a necessity in today's world. People who are not "wired" risk being shut out of a key method for gathering information, participating in civic life, and making money. A report released by the U.S. Census Bureau in September 2001 found striking differences in access by race and family income level. The wealthiest families were far more likely to have home computers and Internet access than were households at the lowest income level.

Schools and public libraries are helping equalize access to computers, however. In every ethnic and income group, at least 70 percent of schoolchildren now use computers at school. Business, community, and political leaders have also begun addressing the technology gap. Some have suggested creating nonprofit organizations to provide training and Internet access to millions of low-income Americans. Congress is considering legislation that would support a number of programs.

Extremist Groups

Just as the Internet can help advance democratic values, it can also aid the spread of ideas that may run counter to democracy. The Internet has become the host for many hate groups and extremist political organizations. (Extremist groups are those whose ideas are the farthest from the political center.) In the past, these people might have been isolated from one another. The Internet is allowing extremists to find one another, band together electronically, spread propaganda, and recruit new members to their causes. **Propaganda** is the spreading of certain ideas and may involve misleading messages designed to manipulate people. (See the descriptions of propaganda techniques in Chapter 11.)

To the extent that the Internet helps strengthen intolerant extremist movements, it may weaken our sense of national unity. Most Americans, however, still take pride in our country's diversity and believe in freedom of speech and expression and equal rights for all Americans.

Reading Check **Explaining** How do authoritarian regimes limit Internet communication?

Threats to Privacy

If intolerant extremist speech on the Internet leads to hate crimes, terrorism, or other illegal acts, the government can step in. Indeed, law enforcement officials are working hard to fight all kinds of cybercrime, including fraud, identity theft, and child pornography. Although most citizens understand the need for some government surveillance of the Internet, controversy surrounds the potential threat to citizens' privacy. Concerns also arise about online companies that invade consumers' privacy.

Internet Wiretapping

Law enforcement officials have a powerful new crime-fighting tool—wiretapping technology for the Internet. Known as "Carnivore" (but officially named DCS 1000), the system was developed by the Federal Bureau of Investigation (FBI) and is meant for use only in criminal investigations when authorized by a court.

Carnivore can watch for particular words and phrases in messages sent by anyone on a network. When a suspect sends or receives an e-mail, Carnivore can record the e-mail address without monitoring what is being written. However, Carnivore can also intercept the full content of all network traffic. In the process, it captures not only a suspect's messages but the unrelated messages of bystanders as well.

A leading member of Congress recently voiced "strong concerns" that Carnivore "is infringing on Americans' basic constitutional protection against unwarranted search[es]," guaranteed by the Fourth Amendment. (Recall that the Fourth Amendment protects people from unreasonable searches and seizures.) Other people think the government should have even more power to monitor information in cyberspace to stop and prevent crimes.

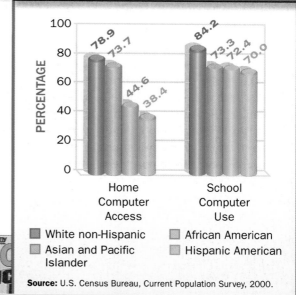

Computer Access Among School-Age Children, 2000

PERCENTAGE

Home Computer Access: 78.9, 73.7, 44.6, 38.4
School Computer Use: 84.2, 73.3, 72.4, 70.0

- White non-Hispanic
- Asian and Pacific Islander
- African American
- Hispanic American

Source: U.S. Census Bureau, Current Population Survey, 2000.

Analyzing Graphs

The number of public schools in the United States with Internet access has grown from 50 percent in 1995 to 95 percent in 1999. Such technology means that students today are learning in a different way than their parents or grandparents did. Which racial group has the highest percentage of computer access? What groups have almost equal or the closest access at school?

A class learns how to design Web pages.

Like most kids living in Delmar, New York, Emily Wistar hadn't given much thought to the child labor issue—the worldwide problem of children, some as young as six, working in factories. Then, three years ago, Wistar attended a Kids Can Free the Children (FTC) conference in Toronto, Ontario. This is an international organization that empowers young people to help eliminate exploitation of children around the world. The meeting changed the way she viewed the world. "Once I heard the issues," says Wistar, 17, "I couldn't step away from it. I know I'm not going to fix the child labor problem overnight, but I can do little things that can help people in the long run."

Wistar's "little things" led to bigger things. Wistar and other FTC volunteers helped the New York State Labor-Religious Coalition lobby for a "Sweat-Free Schools bill." The legislation, passed in October 2001, allows schools to consider a company's labor practices before purchasing clothing—school uniforms, hats, and jackets, for example. Before the bill, schools had to buy from the lowest bidder, regardless of whom the company employed or how workers were treated.

"[The sweat-free schools bill] was a big breakthrough," Wistar told TIME. "In an educational facility, we shouldn't be in any way encouraging other children to stay out of school. Children all over the world don't deserve to be working in factories—and we should support that." For more information about Kids Can Free the Children, go to www. freethechildren.com

Emily Wistar from New York

Invading Consumers' Privacy

Government surveillance is not the only threat to citizens' privacy online. Some employers keep tabs on how their workers use the Internet on company time. Criminals can intercept other people's files and e-mail unless they are encrypted (or specially coded). The most serious privacy risk, though, probably comes from simply "surfing" the Web. When a person surfs the Web, he or she is traveling from Web site to Web site. Most companies that operate sites on the World Wide Web gather information about visitors. For example, when you buy something on the Internet, join an online club like Disney's Blast, or register to access information from a site, you probably provide your name, e-mail address, home address, phone number, and perhaps a credit card number.

Web sites can also collect data about you without your knowledge. As you browse, the site may track the pages you visit, the links you click, the terms you search for, and so on. Before long, the business may have built a personal profile that includes your age, reading preferences, shopping tastes, favorite travel spots, and other details.

Many Web site operators not only collect data for their own use but also sell it to others. As a result, you might find yourself flooded with unwanted advertisements and junk mail. Even worse, information that you wanted to keep private might be passed on without your permission. Imagine that you consulted a medical Web site about a health problem. If insurance agents and drug companies then began contacting you, you would probably consider it an invasion of your privacy.

Promote Responsible Net Commerce: Help Stamp Out Spam!

Have you ever received "spam"? Spam is Internet junk mail.

Political Cartoons

and it seems to be diverted toward money and ... Making the world a more convenient | Schneider, two men with little hope, of regaining the company's ... While the wage was ... | to be diverted tim...

Analyzing Visuals As use of the Internet has increased, so too have Americans' concerns about the loss of privacy while they are online. In the cartoonist's opinion, how does traveling on the "Information Highway" affect citizens' privacy?

In 1998 Congress tried to prevent marketers from taking advantage of young Web users by passing the Children's Online Privacy Protection Act. This law requires Web site companies to establish a privacy policy describing the information they are collecting from children and how they will use it. According to the law, Web site companies must also get permission from parents to gather information from children younger than 13.

Reading Check **Inferring** How does surfing the Web endanger a person's privacy?

SECTION 2 ASSESSMENT

Checking for Understanding

1. Key Terms Define the following terms and use them in sentences related to the Internet and democracy: authoritarian, dissident, propaganda.

Reviewing Main Ideas

2. Define What is the purpose of the Children's Online Privacy Protection Act? What does the act require Web site companies to do?

3. Explain What is meant by the "digital divide"? How might it affect democracy in the United States?

Critical Thinking

4. Making Judgments Do you agree with the member of Congress who expressed "strong concerns" that Carnivore "is infringing on Americans' basic constitutional rights against unwarranted searches"? Why or why not?

5. Analyzing Information In a chart like the one below, describe the effects of threats to privacy posed by the Internet.

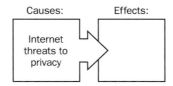

Causes: Effects:

Internet threats to privacy

Analyzing Visuals

6. Compare Review the bar graph on page 391. Which race had the greatest difference between computer access at home and school in 2000?

★**BE AN ACTIVE CITIZEN**★

7. Analyze Think about people in your community who cannot afford a home computer or online access. What other ways can they get access? Is there enough access in your community for people who cannot afford home computers and online access?

Issues to Debate

Should Americans Be Permitted to Vote Online?

Can a mouse run off with an election? Some people think so—especially if it is a computer mouse. Online voting, or e-voting, promises to be one of the hot topics of future elections. Your generation, in fact, may be the first to pick and click a president.

The states are taking the lead. In 2000, voters in the Arizona Democratic primary became the first to cast legally binding votes online. Several other states have held mock Internet elections, created task forces to study e-voting, or developed referendums on e-voting. However, there are pros and cons to "digital democracy." One of the biggest debates centers on this question: Is Internet voting fair?

A voter in Florida uses a touch-screen computer voting system during a mock election in 2001.

Yes

Internet voting provides a unique—and much needed—opportunity to increase voter participation by making the voting process more accessible, more convenient, and less time-consuming. Current U.S. voter turnout is so low that a minority of the eligible voters routinely elects our presidents. . . .

For those without direct Internet access, libraries, schools, and civic organizations will provide community access to the online voting booth.

—Eileen McGann, CEO of Vote.com

No

Internet voting initially presents itself . . . with the potential to reach voters not currently engaged in the process. But given the inequities of access to the Internet, . . . voting via the Internet . . . results in discrimination. . . .

The implications are profound [great]. Remote Internet voting could be used to manipulate election outcomes by structuring access to favor the most Internet-connected.

—Deborah Phillips, Chairman and President of the Voting Integrity Project

Debating the Issue

1. How does McGann think e-voting will affect elections?
2. Why does Phillips disagree with McGann?
3. Form groups of three or four. Your group will create a presentation supporting one side of this issue.
4. All groups should present their positions to the class. Hold a class vote to see what position is supported by a majority of your class members.
5. As a class, discuss the following issues: What central problem to e-voting is raised by this debate? What other problems do you think might be raised by e-voting? What, if any, steps would need to be taken for you to support e-voting?

Regulating the Internet

GUIDE TO READING

Main Idea

Many issues surround Internet usage, such as limits on free speech, protection of intellectual property, taxation of e-commerce, and regulation of the Internet in schools.

Key Terms

intellectual property, copyright, revenue

Reading Strategy

Summarizing Information The Internet raises many issues that the Framers of the Constitution could never have imagined. As you read, list issues that have arisen as a result of the Internet on a web diagram like the one below.

Internet Issues

Read to Learn

• What free speech issues are associated with the Internet?

• Why have issues like taxing e-commerce and regulating the Internet in schools arisen?

Americans in Action

On July 17, 1998, Senators Richard Bryan (D-NV) and John McCain (R-AZ) introduced to the 105th Congress the Children's Online Privacy Protection Act of 1998. In his introduction, Senator Bryan said this: "I was, frankly, surprised to learn the kinds of information these Web sites are collecting from our children. Some were asking where the child went to school, what sports he or she liked, what siblings they had, their pet's name, what kind of time they had after school alone without the supervision of parents." The bill became law on October 21, 1998.

Is her privacy protected?

Internet Speech

The Children's Online Privacy Protection Act is just one way in which governments, from the U.S. Congress to your local school board, are scrambling for some control over the Internet. In regulating the Internet, though, does the government infringe on the right of free speech?

Free speech is a key democratic right, spelled out in the First Amendment to the Constitution. The Internet has promoted free speech by giving anyone with a computer the chance to circulate his or her views across the world. Unfortunately, this has also enabled hate groups and others to infuse the Internet with offensive material.

Computer users can block objectionable Web sites by installing filtering software. However, lawmakers have also tried to enact laws censoring some online speech. In 1996 Congress passed the Communications Decency Act. This law made it a federal crime to send or display indecent or obscene material over the Internet "in a manner available" to those under the age of 18.

Numerous groups challenged the law in court. They argued that it violated the rights of adults, who can lawfully view graphic material considered inappropriate for children. In *Reno* v. *American Civil Liberties Union* (1997), the Supreme Court declared the indecency portions of the law unconstitutional. The Court held that speech on the Internet should have the highest level of First Amendment protection, similar to the protection given to books and newspapers. This decision was a strong endorsement of free speech on the Internet.

Limiting Free Speech in Schools

As you read earlier, the Supreme Court has ruled that Internet speech is protected by the First Amendment. However, restrictions may apply to school-sponsored newspapers on the World Wide Web.

In 1988 the Supreme Court ruled that school administrators can regulate the content of student print publications if doing so serves an educational purpose (see the *Hazelwood School District* v. *Kuhlmeier* case on page 263). The Court has not yet ruled on Internet student newspapers. Lower courts across the nation, however, are starting to hear cases. Several courts have found that students who produce online papers in school with school equipment may indeed be subject to regulation.

✓ **Reading Check** **Comparing** How do the First Amendment rights of students differ from those of adults?

Intellectual Property

Americans have always believed in the right of individuals to own property and to use it as they see fit. You can freely sell your old bike, loan your jacket to a friend, or trade away part of your baseball card collection if you so choose. However, special rules apply to **intellectual property**—things that people create, such as songs, movies, books, poetry, art, and software. When you purchase a CD by U2 or a book like *Harry Potter and the Sorcerer's Stone*, you do not gain ownership rights to the artistic product. Only the artist or author who created the work has a right to sell it or let others use it.

Over the years, many traditions, court decisions, and legal devices like copyrights have developed to protect the creators of intellectual property. A **copyright** is the owner's exclusive right to control, publish, and sell an original work. Copyrights are designed to prevent people from simply taking or copying someone else's creation without permission.

Computers and the Internet, however, make it easy to copy and widely distribute all kinds of intellectual property. As a result, the Internet has become a major battleground for intellectual property rights.

The Napster Battle Shawn Fanning, the creator of Napster (middle), listens as the Senate Judiciary Committee holds a hearing on online entertainment in 2001. Jack Valenti (left), president of the Motion Picture Association of America, and Don Henley (right), recording artist, look on. **Why did federal courts rule to shut down Napster?**

The Napster Battle

Napster began in 1999 as an online music service created by an 18-year-old college student, Shawn Fanning. The site made it possible for users to download copyrighted songs for free. Instead of buying new CDs, music lovers could simply swap files with others. Within two years, Napster became the global forum for the free exchange of music. It had 57 million registered users and was growing fast.

Songwriters, music publishers, and major record companies all sued Napster for breaking copyright laws. Court rulings against Napster forced it to shut down temporarily and stop providing copyrighted music free. Meanwhile, however, new music-swapping Web sites appeared. The battle will continue.

A Controversial Law

In 1998 Congress passed a law aimed at making intellectual property more secure in the Internet age. The Digital Millennium Copyright Act (DMCA) makes it a crime to develop or spread software that will bypass computer codes that protect copyrighted material.

The most high profile case involving the DMCA concerns Dmitri Sklyarov, a Russian software developer. Sklyarov created software that could break codes protecting electronic books. This was not illegal in Russia, where he lived. What's more, his company quickly stopped selling the software in the United States; yet when Sklyarov visited this country in July 2001, he was arrested for violating the DMCA. He was eventually released and the charges transferred to the corporation that produced the software.

The DMCA has been hotly debated. Major movie studios and recording companies strongly support the law. Jack Valenti, president of the Motion Picture Association of America, argues, "If you can't protect what you own, you don't own anything."

American Biographies

Philip Emeagwali (1954–)

Internet pioneer Philip Emeagwali stunned scientists in 1989 with the Connection Machine. While studying for his Ph.D. at the University of Michigan, Emeagwali used the Internet to link 65,000 computers, building the fastest computer on Earth. It performed 3.1 billion calculations per second.

Emeagwali thinks fast, too. At age 9, his father started daily math drills in which Emeagwali solved 100 math problems per hour, or one problem every 36 seconds. Soon Emeagwali could out-calculate his teachers, earning him the nickname "Calculus."

Born in Nigeria, Emeagwali faced an uncertain future as a teenager. A civil war forced him out of seventh grade and into refugee camps. Emeagwali studied on his own and, at age 17, won a full scholarship to Oregon State University. Since then, he has earned degrees in five subject areas, brought his family to the United States, and won a long list of awards. What are Emeagwali's plans for the future? He hopes to build the World Wide Brain—the "brain of brains" that will make the Internet faster and within reach of people all over the world.

★ ★ ★ ★

Critics of the law believe that it will punish computer scientists for exposing flaws in computer security systems, even if they do not steal copyrighted material. In addition, some civil liberties groups argue that software code is a form of speech. They claim the DMCA violates First Amendment guarantees of free speech.

 **Explaining** Why may people who hold copyrights be concerned about Internet use?

Online Businesses Boxes and boxes fill the floors of the Amazon.com Seattle warehouse as workers tackle the Christmas rush of orders in 1999. Amazon.com opened in 1995 and today offers millions of products to millions of customers. **How do virtual stores like Amazon.com affect state and local revenue?**

Taxing E-Commerce

Each year, consumers spend billions of dollars buying goods and services over the Internet. Online shopping is not only convenient, but it also allows customers to avoid paying sales tax. Although some states require online consumers to report purchase amounts on income tax forms, often state and local governments lose out on a prime source of revenue. **Revenue** is the income that a government or business collects.

Many state governors and other politicians favor taxation of e-commerce; so do traditional retail stores. After all, they lose business if you shop online instead of at your local mall. Many Internet merchants and policy analysts, however, believe that collecting sales taxes would unfairly burden online companies. Because sales taxes vary from state to state, online businesses would have to charge different rates depending on where customers live and

then send the funds back to different state governments. Collecting taxes would thus be unusually costly for Internet companies. Furthermore, unlike local merchants, they would share in none of the benefits those taxes pay for such as police and fire protection, roads, and other government services.

An advisory group created by Congress recently proposed that all state and local tax systems be simplified and made more uniform. Efforts could then be made to develop a fair Internet tax.

Reading Check **Defining** What is e-commerce?

The Internet at School

Millions of American students are spending classroom time online. Use of the Internet at school is creating new issues for lawmakers and educators.

School Filters

In 2000 Congress passed the Children's Internet Protection Act. This law requires nearly all schools in the United States to install technology that blocks student access to offensive or dangerous World Wide Web materials. Many schools are using filtering software that allows school officials to decide what material is harmful. The software also monitors the school's Internet traffic. It can identify anyone trying to use the Internet for prohibited activities like drug dealing. One school official reported that since his town installed the filtering software, "access of unauthorized Internet sites probably dropped by 98 percent."

Student Web Activity Visit civ.glencoe.com and click on **Student Web Activities— Chapter 17** to learn more about regulating the Internet.

Parental Review of Internet Records

Schools have begun keeping records of the Web sites visited by students and staff. Should parents be able to look at such records? James Knight, the father of a student in New Hampshire, sued his local school district to win that right. Knight said,

❝If we can find out what books are on the shelves of the school library or what textbooks are being used in the classroom, it seems consistent that we should be able to know where kids are going on the Internet.❞

School officials argued that releasing students' Internet records would violate their right to privacy. The judge, however, ruled that a parent could inspect the school district's Internet records as long as administrators removed any information that would identify individual students.

As the Internet becomes more fully integrated into American schools, policies and regulations for its use will continue to

Fact Fiction Folklore

How the Internet began

Although you may hear many explanations of how the Internet began, it really was created by the U.S. Department of Defense's Advanced Research Projects Agency in the 1960s. Called ARPANET, it was originally a network that could switch "packets" of information from computer to computer. Eventually the various networks were connected as the Internet.

evolve. School leaders must determine the level of disclosure of student information that is safe and appropriate, while maintaining their instructional goals. Parents must then approve or disapprove of the disclosure standards. School officials and lawmakers will keep trying to balance concerns about privacy, censorship, and the safety of young Internet users.

Reading Check **Explaining** Why do schools use filtering software?

SECTION 3 ASSESSMENT

Checking for Understanding

1. **Key Terms** Define the following terms and use them in sentences related to the Internet: intellectual property, copyright, revenue.

Reviewing Main Ideas

2. **Identify** What did the Supreme Court rule in *Reno* v. *American Civil Liberties Union* (1997)?

3. **Describe** What arguments do Internet merchants use to oppose taxing e-commerce? What arguments do those who support taxing e-commerce use?

Critical Thinking

4. **Making Judgments** Do you agree with the court ruling that shut down Napster as a source of free music? Why or why not?

5. **Evaluating Information** In a chart like the one below, summarize the arguments for each side. Then, state your opinion and reasons for it.

Parental Review of School Internet Records	
Pro	Con
My Opinion:	

Analyzing Visuals

6. **Infer** Reexamine the photograph of the Amazon.com warehouse on page 398. How might the physical site of an online business be different from that of a traditional business?

★**BE AN ACTIVE CITIZEN**★
7. **Research** Find out if your school system has an Internet policy for students. Does it keep track of Web sites visited by students? If so, are those records protected in any way? Share your information with the class.

Assessment & Activities

Review to Learn

Section 1

- The Internet allows people to communicate with one another efficiently, share information conveniently, and shop and bank online.

Section 2

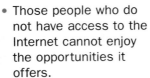

- Those people who do not have access to the Internet cannot enjoy the opportunities it offers.
- The privacy of Internet users is threatened by government and business surveillance.

Section 3

- Although the Internet promotes free speech by offering opportunities for expression, this free speech is restricted in schools.

FOLDABLES™
Study Organizer

Using Your Foldables Study Organizer
As a class or individually, create two columns on the board or on a sheet of paper labeled "Benefits" and "Dangers." Using the notes on your foldable, write information under each column concerning the Internet. Do the benefits of the Internet outweigh the dangers?

Reviewing Key Terms

Write key terms from the chapter to match each clue below.

1. income that the government collects for public use
2. this operates within the Internet, allowing users to interact with the billions of documents stored on computers across the Net
3. this is the owner's exclusive right to control, publish, and sell an original work
4. things that people create, like songs, books, poetry, art, and software
5. the mass communication system of millions of networked computers and databases all over the world
6. pages on the World Wide Web that may contain text, images, audio, and video
7. being free from party ties or bias

Reviewing Main Ideas

8. How does e-government allow citizens easier access to government services?
9. What caution should Internet users exercise when visiting the Web site of a politician?
10. How have some authoritarian regimes limited online political communication?
11. What is "Carnivore"?
12. What has the Supreme Court ruled regarding the regulation of content in student newspapers?
13. What is the purpose of the 1998 Digital Millennium Copyright Act (DMCA)?
14. How do schools narrow the digital divide?
15. What concerns might grassroots Web sites raise for major political parties?

Critical Thinking

16. **Constructing an Argument** Write a letter to the editor of a newspaper in which you support or oppose the Digital Millennium Copyright Act (DMCA).

17. Making Comparisons In a chart like the one below, list ways Americans use the Internet.

Internet Use
1.
2.

Practicing Skills

Evaluating a Web Site **Visit the Web site** http://www.whitehouse.gov/president/; **then answer the following questions.**

18. What information is presented on this Web site? What categories are used to organize the information?

19. What links does the site contain? Are they appropriate to the topic? Explain.

 Economics Activity

20. Companies that have traditional brick-and-mortar stores as well as online Web sites are known as "click-and-mortar" businesses. Look at advertisements in newspapers and magazines to identify popular click-and-mortar companies. Pick one and design a poster to show how it sells goods.

★ CITIZENSHIP COOPERATIVE ACTIVITY ★

21. Working in groups of four, do an Internet search for your congressional representatives. Find out if there is any information about their positions on whether e-commerce should be taxed. If there is no information, e-mail each one and ask them to explain their position.

 Technology Activity

22. Do an Internet search for your state's Web site. What services does your state offer to citizens through its site? What other information would make your state's Web site more useful to citizens?

Self-Check Quiz Visit the *Civics Today* Web site at civ.glencoe.com and click on **Self-Check Quizzes— Chapter 17** to prepare for the chapter test.

Analyzing Visuals

23. Study the table below. What do you think is the purpose of each of the sites listed on the table? Find another site for each of the four types of hosts.

> ★ org=an organization, profit or nonprofit; Mothers Against Drunk Driving= http://www.madd.org
>
> ★ gov=a government group; U.S. Senate= http://www.senate.gov
>
> ★ edu=educational institution; Vanderbilt University= http://www.vanderbilt.edu
>
> ★ com=a commercial group; Microsoft Corporation= http://microsoft.com

 Standardized Test Practice

Directions: Choose the *best* answer to the following question.

Why is the Internet a benefit for democracies?

A It allows dissident groups to communicate with one another.

B It allows citizens to take part in civic life.

C It creates a divide between those who have access and those who do not.

D All of the above

Test-Taking Tip

Read the directions carefully. Although all of the answer choices may be true, which one describes a *benefit* for democracies?

The
Economy
and the
Individual

Why It Matters

As American citizens, we live in a land of economic opportunity. Our economy provides us with a great variety of jobs, goods, and services. We can contribute to the nation's economic success by taking advantage of these opportunities. In Unit 6, you will study the American economic system and learn how it works and how it affects our lives.

 Use the **American History Primary Source Document Library CD-ROM** to find primary sources about the development and growth of the American economy.

 ★ *BE AN ACTIVE CITIZEN* ★

What do you think economics is? Describe how, in your opinion, economics affects you. After you complete your study of Unit 6, compare your initial ideas with the new information you learn.

Sacagawea, the Shoshone who assisted the Lewis and Clark expedition, is featured on this one-dollar coin.

What Is Economics?

 CITIZENSHIP AND YOU

The United States has a free enterprise system under which consumers and producers make the major economic decisions. As you study this chapter, think about how our economic system works and affects your daily life. Write your ideas in your civics journal.

To learn more about basic economic issues, view the **Economics & You** video lesson 2: What Is Economics?

 FOLDABLES™
Study Organizer

Organizing Information Study Foldable *Make the following foldable to help you organize your thoughts and information as you try to answer this question: What Is Economics?*

Step 1 *Fold a sheet of paper in half from side to side.*

Fold it so the left edge is about $\frac{1}{2}$ inch from the right edge.

Step 2 *Turn the paper and fold it into thirds.*

Reading and Writing *As you read the chapter, write what you learn about economics under the appropriate tab of your foldable. Write the main ideas and supporting facts of each main topic.*

Step 3 *Unfold and cut the top layer only along both folds.*

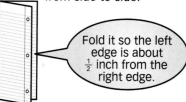

This will make three tabs.

Step 4 *Label as shown.*

The study of economics will help you make better decisions. ▶

CIVICS Online

Chapter Overview Visit the *Civics Today* Web site at civ.glencoe.com and click on **Chapter Overviews— Chapter 18** to preview chapter information.

The Fundamental Economic Problem

GUIDE TO READING

Main Idea
Economics is the study of how individuals and societies make choices about ways to use scarce resources to fulfill their needs and wants.

Key Terms
economics, needs, wants, scarcity, economic model

Reading Strategy
Organizing Information
As you read the section, complete a diagram like the one below by identifying the three economic choices every society must make.

Economic Choices

Read to Learn
- What is scarcity?
- How do wants and needs differ?

Americans in Action

A school library that couldn't afford books for a visually impaired second-grader sparked a remarkably effective economics lesson for his class and led to a prestigious award for the teacher. Bonnie Nyce, whose project was one of five top winners of America's National Awards for Teaching Economics, teaches second grade at the Plains Elementary School in Timberville, Virginia. When one student pointed out that classmate Zach Shifflett, blind since birth, could only stand around during the class's weekly visit to the library, she saw an opportunity. Through her Operation CARE program (Children Learning About Braille Reading and Economics), the class raised more than $2,000 for the purchase of Braille books. Ms. Nyce noted, "My hope is that the children who participated in Operation CARE will pursue further experiences in economics, assured that it is not a frightening topic but an interesting, relevant one that deserves attention at every level of learning."

Second-graders make a difference.

Economic Choices

In order to be a well-informed citizen, it is essential to have a good understanding of economics and the American economic system. Well-informed citizens do more than make choices in the voting booth, they also make rational economic choices, and they make these choices every day.

The choices we face are based on the fact that we do not have enough productive resources to satisfy all of our wants and needs. Even a seemingly plentiful resource such as water is considered scarce because it is not free; we pay to have it.

This is where economics comes in, because **economics** is the study of how we make decisions in a world where resources are limited. As you will discover, the study of economics will help us think about the process of making decisions—economics is sometimes called the science of decision making.

Scarcity

As individuals, we have many **needs** that are required for survival, such as food, clothing, and shelter. In addition, we also have an enormous number of **wants,** or things we would like to have, such as entertainment, vacations, and other items that make life more comfortable and enjoyable.

The fundamental economic problem is the issue of scarcity. **Scarcity** occurs whenever we do not have enough resources to produce all of the things we would like to have. In fact, even a country as rich as the United States does not have enough productive resources to produce all of our goods such as cars, houses, and clothing, and to provide all of our services such as public transportation, education, national defense, entertainment, and many other things we would like to have. Scarcity is the result, and because of scarcity, we have to make choices among alternatives. For example, a rational consumer compares prices and makes choices based on his or her limited resources. A rational consumer asks whether or not he or she can afford to buy a small car or a big car, own a home or rent, purchase brand name items or generic ones, and so on.

WHAT to Produce

One of the choices a society has to face is that of WHAT to produce. For example, if resources are limited, we may have to choose between making goods for defense or producing services for people who are retired or are too ill to work. Or, we may have to choose between improving our roads or schools or even a nearby stadium for athletic events. Any civic leader in any community in America could extend this list almost indefinitely given the wants and needs they have in their own communities.

Economic Choices Our society has needs and wants. We need to provide police and fire protection. We want to provide things like community pools. **What is the difference between wants and needs?**

HOW to Produce

A second choice that society has to make is that of HOW to produce. If we need more crude oil to satisfy our energy needs, should we allow drilling in an Alaskan wildlife sanctuary, or should we restrict oil recovery to more traditional areas? When it comes to manufacturing products in factories, how much pollution should we allow firms to generate? After all, businesses like to produce as cheaply as possible, and that sometimes means leaving waste behind that may pollute the environment. As you can see, the question of HOW to produce is faced by every producer of a good or service.

FOR WHOM to Produce

After goods and services are produced, a society must determine how the goods and services will be distributed among its members. Who receives the new cars? Who benefits from a new school? As you will read, most of the goods and services in the United States are distributed through a price system.

These questions concerning WHAT, HOW, and FOR WHOM to produce are not very easy for any society to answer. Nevertheless, they must be answered so long as there are not enough resources to satisfy people's unlimited wants.

Reading Check **Explaining** Because scarcity exists, we must make choices. Explain why this is so.

Using Economic Models

To economists, the word "economy" means all the activity in a nation that together affects the production, distribution, and use of goods and services. When studying a specific part of the economy—rising unemployment, for example—economists often formulate theories and gather data. The data that economists collect are called economic models. **Economic models** are simplified representations of the real world that are used to explain how the economy works, or to predict what would happen if something in the economy should change. For example, a model can be used to predict what will happen to the total production of goods and services if a new tax law is passed. Many of these models appear as graphs like the one shown on the top of page 413.

It is important to remember that models are based on assumptions, or things that we take for granted as true. We use them as facts even though we can't be sure that they are facts. For example, you might assume that a restaurant is out of your price range. You might not even try it because you assume you cannot afford it. However, you might be wrong—the prices at the restaurant might be quite reasonable. The quality

Choices All Societies Face

Unlimited Wants

Limited Resources

Scarcity

Choices All Societies Face

WHAT to produce

HOW to produce

FOR WHOM to produce

Evaluating Charts

In a world of scarcity, choices have to be made. What are the three basic economic questions?

Political Cartoons

and it seems to be diverted toward money and ... Making the world a more convenient

Schneider, two men with little hope, of regaining the company's ... While the wage was

to be divert... tim...

Analyzing Visuals Luxuries such as concert tickets often become necessities in the eyes of consumers. How do consumers satisfy their seemingly unlimited wants?

of a model is no better than the assumptions the model is based on.

It is also important to keep in mind that models can be revised. If an economic model results in a prediction that turns out to be right, the model can be used again. If the prediction is wrong, the model might be changed to make a better prediction the next time.

✓Reading Check **Identifying** What is an economic model?

SECTION 1 ASSESSMENT

Checking for Understanding

1. **Key Terms** Use each of the following terms in a sentence that will help explain its meaning: economics, needs, wants, scarcity, economic model.

Reviewing Main Ideas

2. **Identify** What is the basic economic problem that makes choices necessary?

3. **Describe** What is the purpose of an economic model? Do economic models always accurately predict economic behavior? Explain your answer.

Critical Thinking

4. **Evaluating Information** How do you think the study of economics can help you become a better decision maker?

5. **Classifying Information** On a diagram like the one below, provide at least three examples of items you have had to do without because limited resources could not keep up with your wants.

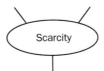

Analyzing Visuals

6. **Infer** Study the chart on page 408. If a company decides to use mass production methods that require more equipment and fewer workers, the company is addressing which question?

★**BE AN ACTIVE CITIZEN**★

7. **Record** Find an example in your local newspaper of one effect of scarcity. Your example may come from an article, editorial, or advertisement. Describe what economic choices were made.

Making Economic Decisions

GUIDE TO READING

Main Idea

Trade-offs are present whenever choices are made.

Key Terms

trade-off, opportunity cost, marginal cost, marginal benefit, cost-benefit analysis

Reading Strategy

Organizing Information As you read this section, complete a diagram like the one below by explaining what you need to know to become a good decision maker.

Making Decisions

Read to Learn

• How are trade-offs and opportunity costs related?

• What is the purpose of a cost-benefit analysis?

Americans in Action

"Beach replenishment was designed for the specific purpose of saving the federal government millions of dollars that would otherwise be spent in disaster assistance. More than 60 years ago, the U.S. Army Corps of Engineers . . . design[ed] a detailed cost-benefit analysis to determine which disaster-prone coastal areas could be protected through beach replenishment. . . . When this year's [major storm] hit, . . . the Army Corps of Engineers reported that replenished beaches prevented more than $2.9 million in damage along nine beaches in New York and New Jersey."

—USA TODAY, April 9, 2001

A family enjoys a day at the beach on the Jersey shore.

Trade-Offs

Economic decision making is surprisingly simple. It involves only a few terms and rules. In fact, you probably already think about many problems the same way that economists do.

The situation in the story above is a good example. In this case, preventive action was taken because the cost of doing something (the expense of beach restoration) was less than the benefit to be gained (the advantage of *not* having to pay for disaster assistance). Most economic decisions are made the same way—with common sense and careful analysis.

As you learned previously, scarcity forces people to make choices about how they will use their resources. Economic decision making requires that we take into account all the costs and all of the benefits of an action.

The economic choices people make involve exchanging one good or service for another. If you choose to buy a DVD player, you are exchanging your money for the right to own the DVD player rather than something else that might cost the same amount. A trade-off is the alternative you face if you decide to do one thing rather than another.

Economists identify many trade-offs in life. For example, more pollution-free air means less driving, and more driving means less pollution-free air. Taking more time to study for a test means having less time to talk on the telephone with friends, and talking for a long time on the telephone means spending less time studying for the test.

Think of a trade-off on a large scale. A country wants to put more money into education. This strategy may be a good one, but putting more money into education means having less money available for medical research or national defense. Individuals, families, businesses, and societies are forced to make trade-offs every time they choose to use their resources in one way and not in another.

Opportunity Cost

Suppose you decide to go to college after you graduate from high school. If you do, you will quickly discover that the cost of college is more than the cost of books, transportation, tuition, and other fees. One of the biggest costs is the full-time income that you will not be able to earn because of the time you will have to spend studying and going to classes.

Costs of Decisions If you have basketball practice while your friends are having a party, part of the opportunity cost of basketball practice is missing the party. **Why does every choice involve an opportunity cost?**

Economists have a term for this broad measure of cost. Opportunity cost is the cost of the next best use of your time or money when you choose to do one thing rather than another.

Note that opportunity cost includes more than just money. It also takes into account all the possible discomforts and inconveniences linked to the choice made. After all, the opportunity cost of cleaning the house is not just the price of cleaning products. It also includes the time you could spend doing other things, like listening to music or visiting with your friends.

Measures of Cost

Suppose you are in the business of producing bicycle helmets. Do you know how many helmets you would produce? Would

$ Economics and You

Rain Forest Trade-Offs

How do trade-offs of resources affect our future? The Amazon Basin in Brazil is the world's largest tropical rain forest and river system. Within the basin an area equal to 5,000 soccer fields is being destroyed every day, though. Farmers burn the forests to gain farmland for other profitable crops. Loggers cut and export the fine hardwoods for a profit. People have penetrated the forests to strip the Amazon of its curative and medicinal plants. Do research on the Amazon rain forest to find out what the trade-offs mean for the future.

it be 100, 500, or 10,000? You may have a feeling that you should not produce too few or too many, but how would you know what too few and too many were? To begin to answer these questions, we need to look more closely at costs and revenues.

Fixed Costs

All businesses have costs, but not all costs are the same. The first kind of cost is fixed costs—costs, or expenses, that are the same no matter how many units of a good are produced. Mortgage payments and property taxes are two examples of fixed costs. It makes no difference whether your company produces no bicycle helmets or a very large number, fixed costs remain the same.

Variable Costs

Another kind of cost is variable costs. Variable costs are expenses that change with the number of products produced. Wages and raw materials are examples of variable costs. These expenses will increase as production grows. Conversely, these expenses will decrease when production decreases.

Total Costs

If we add fixed costs to variable costs, we have total costs. Suppose you want to compute total costs for a month. If fixed costs are $1,000 for the month and variable costs are $500, then total costs are $1,500 for the month. Many businesses focus on average total cost. To arrive at average total cost, simply divide the total cost by the quantity produced. For example, if the total cost of making bicycle helmets is $1,500 and 50 are produced, then average total cost is $30 ($1,500 / 50 = $30).

Marginal Costs

One final and very crucial cost concept remains—marginal cost. **Marginal cost** is the extra, or additional, cost of producing one additional unit of output. Suppose total cost is $1,500 to produce 30 bicycle helmets, and $1,550 to produce 31 helmets. What is the marginal cost of the additional (31st) unit? The change in total cost is $50 and the change in the number of units is 1, so the marginal cost is $50.

Opportunity Cost Making decisions involves opportunity costs. What do you think is the opportunity cost of attending college?

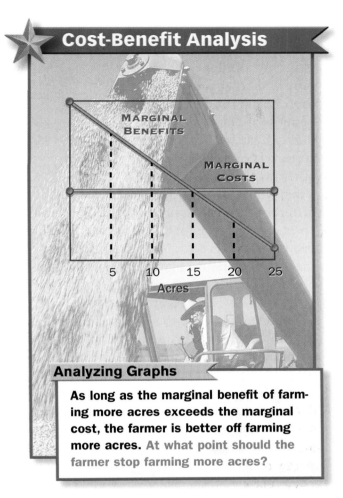

Cost-Benefit Analysis

MARGINAL
BENEFITS

MARGINAL
COSTS

5   10   15   20   25
Acres

Analyzing Graphs

As long as the marginal benefit of farming more acres exceeds the marginal cost, the farmer is better off farming more acres. At what point should the farmer stop farming more acres?

Businesses use two key measures of revenue to decide what amount of output will produce the greatest profits. The first is total revenue, and the second is marginal revenue.

Total revenue is the number of units sold multiplied by the average price per unit. If 42 units of a product are sold at $2 each, the total revenue is $84.

Marginal Revenue

When a business is thinking about a change in its output, it will consider how its revenue will change as a result of that change in output. What will be the additional revenue from selling another unit of output? Marginal revenue is the change in total revenue—the extra revenue—that results from selling one more unit of output.

Marginal Benefit

Finally, we usually do something because we expect to achieve some benefit. In other words, we are concerned with the **marginal benefit,** the additional or extra benefit associated with an action. When we define our costs and benefits in marginal terms, we can then proceed to our cost-benefit decisions.

✓ Reading Check **Identifying** What do economists call the next best alternative that had to be given up for the one chosen?

Cost-Benefit Analysis

Once we define the marginal costs and benefits of a decision, we can analyze the decision. To do this analysis, economists create an economic model called a **cost-benefit analysis.** This analysis requires you to compare the marginal costs and marginal benefits of a decision. Rational economic decision making tells us to choose an action when the benefits are greater than the costs. If the costs outweigh the benefits, we should reject the chosen option (or alternative).

Using Cost-Benefit Analysis

The graph on this page shows a sample cost-benefit analysis. Suppose you are a farmer trying to decide how much of your 25 acres to plant with wheat. Assume that the marginal (or extra) cost of planting and harvesting the wheat is the same for all 25 acres. As a result, the line showing marginal cost would be a horizontal line.

Let's assume, though, that some of the land is better than others. As a result, the size of the harvest that you can expect from each acre goes down as the number of acres increases. After all, you would plant the most fertile land first. As more land is planted, you must use land that is less productive. As the graph on page 413 shows, the line representing marginal benefit would be downward-sloping, indicating diminishing marginal benefits.

The information in the graph makes it easy to decide how much land you should plant. Clearly, you should plant the first 5 acres, because the marginal cost is low when compared with the marginal benefits to be gained. It would also be beneficial to plant 10 acres, even though the benefits are a bit lower. In fact, it would make sense to plant up to 15 acres because to that point the marginal benefit is greater than the marginal cost. However, you would not want to plant more than 15 acres. After 15 acres, the extra cost is greater than the extra benefit.

Answering the Basic Questions

The previous example shows how to use a cost-benefit analysis to answer the question of how much to produce. The same method can be used to answer other basic economic questions.

For instance, you could prepare a similar graph showing the costs and benefits of planting those 25 acres with crops other than wheat. Then you compare the results for all the different crops. Assuming the marginal costs are the same for all crops, the one that produces the greatest marginal benefits is the one you should plant. In this way, cost-benefit analysis can be used to answer the question of WHAT to produce.

You can also use this method to decide FOR WHOM to produce. Think of the costs and benefits of selling your wheat in a nearby town compared to selling it in a town 100 miles away. Shipping the wheat farther will probably cost more than trucking it locally, so that makes the marginal benefit of selling it nearby greater.

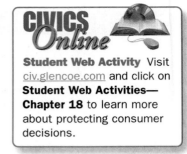

Student Web Activity Visit civ.glencoe.com and click on **Student Web Activities— Chapter 18** to learn more about protecting consumer decisions.

✓ **Reading Check** **Describing** What is the purpose of cost-benefit analysis?

SECTION 2 ASSESSMENT

Checking for Understanding

1. **Key Terms** Use each of the following terms in a sentence that will help explain its meaning: trade-off, opportunity cost, marginal cost, marginal benefit, cost-benefit analysis.

Reviewing Main Ideas

2. **Explain** What does making a trade-off require you to do?

3. **Describe** In what way is marginal benefit related to economic choice?

Critical Thinking

4. **Making Comparisons** How do fixed costs differ from variable costs?

5. **Categorizing Information** Identify a large purchase you would like to make. What are the trade-offs involved and what are the criteria you use to evaluate the alternatives? Illustrate your decision in the form of a grid like the one below.

Alternatives	Criteria 1	Criteria 2

Analyzing Visuals

6. **Infer** Study the graph on page 413. Should the farmer plant 16 or more acres? Why?

★ **BE AN ACTIVE CITIZEN** ★

7. **Compare** Because your time is limited, you are constantly facing trade-offs. Make a list of the trade-offs you have made in choosing how you used your time during a one-week period. What activities did you choose to do? What were the opportunity costs involved in your choices?

Critical Thinking
SKILLBUILDER

Reading a Circle Graph

Why Learn This Skill?

Today, we can gather a great many facts and figures. Presenting the facts and figures in organized ways makes them more understandable. A circle graph, sometimes called a pie chart, organizes data visually. Its circular shape represents a whole amount. The wedge-shaped sectors inside the circle represent particular parts of the whole. Reading circle graphs can help you see relationships and make comparisons.

Learning the Skill

To read a circle graph, follow these steps:

- Examine the title of the graph. The title tells you what the graph is about, or the kind of information the graph displays.
- Look at the sectors dividing the circle into parts. The size of each sector tells you its portion of the whole.

- Examine the labels for each sector. The name of a sector tells you the category of information it represents. The sector labels usually give mathematical data, or statistics, as well. The data may be shown as percentages or perhaps actual amounts.
- Study the sizes of the sectors. See how they relate to the whole. See how the size of each sector compares with the sizes of other sectors.

Practicing the Skill

On a separate sheet of paper, answer the following questions about the circle graph on this page.

1. What kind of information does the graph illustrate?
2. How many sectors are included?
3. What category takes up the largest sector?
4. How does the largest sector compare with the whole?
5. How does the amount spent on recreation compare with the amount spent on education?
6. What category represents the smallest amount of consumer spending?

Personal Consumer Spending in the United States, 1998

EDUCATION 2%
FOOD 15%
OTHER 12%
RECREATION 8%
CLOTHING AND PERSONAL ITEMS 8%
TRANSPORTATION 11%
HOUSING AND HOUSEHOLD ITEMS 26%
MEDICAL CARE 18%

Source: U.S. Department of Commerce.

Applying the Skill

Locate a circle graph in the news, library, or your school resources. Write three sentences based on the graph: one sentence describing the kind of information displayed, one relating a sector category with the whole, and another comparing two individual sectors.

GO TO

Practice key skills with Glencoe's **Skillbuilder Interactive Workbook CD-ROM, Level 1.**

Being an Economically Smart Citizen

GUIDE TO READING

Main Idea

In a market economy, people and businesses act in their own best interests to answer the WHAT, HOW, and FOR WHOM questions.

Key Terms

market economy, capitalism, free enterprise, incentive, rational choice

Reading Strategy

Organizing Information As you read this section, complete a diagram like the one below by describing your rights and responsibilities in a market economy.

My Role in the Economy

Read to Learn

• Why is it important to be informed about economic activity?

• What is rational choice?

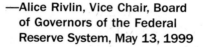

Americans in Action

"There are two senses in which increasing economic literacy contributes greatly to the functioning of our society. First, a free-market economy works well only when the participants—producers, consumers, savers, investors—have the information they need to make intelligent decisions. Second, democracy works well only when citizens participate, vote and make their views known to public officials. Without a basic understanding of how the economy works, what the essential terms and concepts are, the average citizen is likely to feel completely left out of any conversation, whether in the media or around the water cooler, about what is happening in the economy and what to do about it."

—Alice Rivlin, Vice Chair, Board of Governors of the Federal Reserve System, May 13, 1999

Making democracy work

Understanding Your Role in the Economy

To be good economic citizens, we must be informed. This means that we need to have an understanding of what part we play and how we affect the economy, and how the economy affects us. We have a **market economy.** This is an economic system in which supply, demand, and prices help people make decisions and allocate resources. Most economic decisions are made by individuals looking out for their own and their families' self- interests. A market economy is a participatory economy because the choices you make as a consumer affect the products that businesses make. Your choices also affect the prices that businesses receive for their products. Likewise, the products offered and their prices affect the choices you make. When people understand that they are a part of a larger process, their self-esteem rises.

A market economy is sometimes described as being based on **capitalism.** This is a system in which private citizens own most, if not all, of the means of production. A market economy is also based on **free enterprise,** because businesses are allowed to compete for profit with a minimum of government interference. Both "capitalism" and "free enterprise" describe the economy of the United States.

Keeping Informed

Keeping informed about how our economy works means developing an awareness of other features of the economy. You will learn about many aspects of our economy in later chapters. Keeping informed also means reading news stories, listening to news reports, and gathering information about the economic activities of business and government.

Understanding Incentives

Another important part of being economically smart citizens is understanding how economic incentives influence behavior. **Incentives** are rewards that are offered to try to persuade people to take certain economic actions. Price is one incentive, but there are many others. Businesses offer bonuses to salespersons who sell more of a product than expected. Credit-card companies offer low interest rates to try to convince consumers to choose their credit cards. Knowing how these incentives work can help individuals make wise choices about them.

Understanding the Role of Government

Understanding how our economy works also helps us understand the proper role of government in our economy. For example, if we understand how competitive markets establish prices, then we can see

why it is important for government to let this process work. As a result, economists argue that the role of government should be

to maintain competitive markets, not to intervene to establish prices for the benefit of one group or another.

At the same time, there are a number of services such as public education, national defense, justice, and even welfare that the private sector does not provide. A major role of government is to provide these services.

The government also plays important roles in the economy as a whole. For example, the government tries to make markets competitive. Competition forces firms or businesses to use the society's resources more efficiently to produce not only the goods and services that people prefer, but also to produce quality products at low costs. With low costs of production, consumers benefit by paying low prices for products.

Finally, the government influences the decisions of people and businesses by rewarding or punishing certain actions. It can offer "carrots"—incentives—to encourage people to take certain actions. For example, the government can encourage the consumption of services such as education by awarding scholarships and financial aid. The government can encourage the production of goods through subsidies (grants of money), for example, farm subsidies. The government can also use taxes as "sticks" to discourage other actions. For instance, tax laws can punish companies that cause pollution. The government can also discourage the consumption of goods by imposing high sales taxes on them. An example of such a tax is the cigarette tax.

 **Reading Check** **Describing** What are incentives?

Making Wise Choices

The ultimate goal of being an economically literate citizen is to be able to make wise choices. Good decision making leads to more satisfaction because we consider all the costs and benefits before making a decision.

American Biographies

Stephen Wozniak (1950–)
Steven Jobs (1955–)

Before the two Steves—Wozniak and Jobs—started tinkering with electronic gadgets, there was no such thing as a "personal" computer. "Woz" and Jobs had an idea, however. They wanted to figure out how to bring huge, complicated computers to ordinary people. Woz created the machine—a cross between a television and a typewriter—and the software to run it. Jobs planned the company to build and sell the computer.

To raise capital, the two entrepreneurs sold Jobs's van and Woz's calculator for a total of $1,350. Jobs was 21 and Woz was 26. On April 1, 1976, the company—Apple Computer—opened for business in Jobs's garage. That May, a local store owner bought 100 computers at $500 each. The two partners used the profits from the Apple I to develop the Apple II. It came with the first disk drive and floppy disk for a personal computer, which had been invented by Woz in two weeks. It was soon the top-selling computer in the world. Jobs and Woz became multimillionaires.

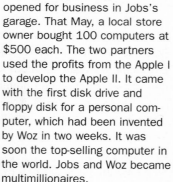

More inventions followed, including the highly successful Macintosh. The two friends eventually went their separate ways, but not before bringing a revolution to the whole computer industry—all for an investment of $1,350.

When you make consumer decisions based on opportunity cost, you are engaging in rational choice. **Rational choice** is choosing the alternative that has the greatest value from among comparable-quality products. As a consumer, you will make rational choices when you purchase the goods and services you believe can best satisfy your wants for the lowest possible costs.

Do not get the impression that wise consumers will all make the same choices. Remember the definition: A rational choice is one that generates the greatest *perceived* value for any given expenditure. Rational choices that are based on careful consumer decision making will still lead to billions of different consumer choices yearly.

Being an economically smart citizen will help you to use scarce resources wisely. Resources are scarce in the world today, and they are likely to become even more scarce in the future. If each of us uses those resources wisely, society as a whole benefits. In this way, wise decision making by individuals benefits society.

In a sense, the economic decisions we make are similar to the political decisions we make. A successful democracy is based

$ Economics and You

Microeconomics and Macroeconomics

As you read this textbook, keep in mind that economics is divided into two branches. In microeconomics, economists look at the small picture. They study the behavior and decision making by small units such as individuals and businesses. Macroeconomics looks at the big picture. It deals with the economy as a whole and decision making by large units such as government. Think of other terms you know that start with the prefixes *micro* and *macro*.

on an informed electorate. When we go to vote for political candidates, we are expected to understand the issues so that we can make the best possible choices. The same is true when we cast our dollar "votes" for goods and services. Being fully informed is the best way for all of us to make the best choices.

Reading Check **Explaining** Do all rational consumers think alike? Why or why not?

SECTION 3 ASSESSMENT

Checking for Understanding

1. **Key Terms** Use each of the following terms in a sentence that will help explain its meaning: market economy, capitalism, free enterprise, incentive, rational choice.

Reviewing Main Ideas

2. **Identify** What is an incentive? Provide an example of a government incentive.

3. **Explain** Why must we use our resources wisely?

Critical Thinking

4. **Analyzing Information** Explain the importance of the consumer in a market economy.

5. **Organizing Information** Complete a diagram like the one below, and list different types of incentives.

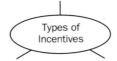

Types of Incentives

Analyzing Visuals

6. **Write** Look at the photograph on page 405. Write a caption for the photograph that includes the terms *incentive* and *rational choice*.

★ **BE AN ACTIVE CITIZEN** ★

7. **Record** For one week, keep track of all your economic decisions—the money you spend and the choices you make. Be aware of each decision and your reasons for making it.

Assessment & Activities

Review to Learn

Section 1
- The fundamental economic problem is scarcity.
- Economists define needs as those things that are necessary for survival.
- Wants are those things we desire but are not needed to survive.

Section 2
- Individuals face trade-offs among alternatives.
- The opportunity cost of an economic decision is the alternative given up when one course of action is chosen over another.
- Cost-benefit analysis is a process that involves comparing the costs of a course of action to its benefits.

Section 3
- In a market economy, people and businesses act in their own best interests to answer the WHAT, HOW, and FOR WHOM questions.
  - The economic system of the United States is based on capitalism and free enterprise.
  - The study of economics helps people make informed decisions.

FOLDABLES™
Study Organizer

Using Your Foldables Study Organizer
Use your completed foldable to make a list of ways in which people can be economically smart citizens. See who can create the longest list.

Reviewing Key Terms
Write the key term that matches each definition below.

1. a basic requirement for survival
2. the term for a market economy in which the productive resources are privately owned
3. the study of how people satisfy seemingly unlimited and competing wants with the careful use of scarce resources
4. the problem that results from a combination of limited resources and unlimited wants
5. an alternative that must be given up when one choice is made rather than another
6. the cost of the next best alternative use of money, time, or resources when one choice is made rather than another
7. when you choose the alternative that has the greatest value from among comparable-quality products
8. a reward offered to try to persuade people to take certain economic actions
9. a representation that describes how the economy works or is expected to perform
10. a good or service that makes life more comfortable but is not required for survival

Reviewing Main Ideas

11. What are the three basic economic questions?
12. Why is an economic model useful?
13. What do economists call exchanging one good or service for another?
14. What is marginal cost?
15. When we make an economic choice, we expect to gain something from it. What do economists call this gain?
16. What economic model helps you compare the marginal costs and marginal benefits of a decision?
17. What is capitalism?
18. Why can our economy be defined as a participatory economy?

Critical Thinking

19. **Categorizing Information** Your friend says, "I need some new clothes." Under what conditions would this be expressing a need? A want?

20. **Understanding Cause and Effect** Assume you want to make a model to describe the effects of hiring senior citizens into previously held teenage job markets. What factors would you analyze?

Effects of Hiring Senior Citizens

21. **Drawing Inferences** Nick is planning on attending college. The tuition is $10,000 per year. Assuming Nick goes to college for four years, is the opportunity cost of his attending college $40,000? Why or why not?

Practicing Skills

Reading a Circle Graph Study the circle graph on page 415. Then answer the following questions.

22. What are the top three categories of consumer spending?

23. Draw a circle graph like the one shown. Develop your own categories that reflect how you spend your income. Then calculate the amount you spend in each category.

Economics Activity

24. List your five favorite foods. Then visit five different food stores, or scan food advertisements in newspapers, and compare the prices of your listed items at each store. Explain why you think the stores had similar or different prices for each item.

★ CITIZENSHIP COOPERATIVE ACTIVITY ★

25. With a partner, locate a source of statistics on the United States in your library. One

Self-Check Quiz Visit the *Civics Today* Web site at civ.glencoe.com and click on **Self-Check Quizzes— Chapter 18** to prepare for the chapter test.

good source would be the *Statistical Abstract of the United States.* Select a topic that has a statistical table, such as the employment rate for different age groups. Study the table. Then write a summary of what the statistics show. Share your findings with the class.

Analyzing Visuals

26. Examine the figure from page 408. Select a specific good. Then list the three economic choices that were made to produce the good.

Technology Activity

27. Search the Internet for recent articles discussing scarcity. Summarize two articles and share your findings with the class.

Standardized Test Practice

Directions: Choose the *best* answer to complete the following statement.

Scarcity results from

F trade-offs and opportunity costs.

G limited wants and limited resources.

H limited resources and seemingly unlimited wants.

J the cost of the next best alternative use of resources.

Test-Taking Tip

As you read the stem of the multiple choice question, try to anticipate the answer before you look at the choices. If your answer is one of the choices, it is probably correct.

The American Economy

★ CITIZENSHIP AND YOU ★

As a consumer, your economic decisions can have far-reaching effects. Keep a list of the economic decisions you make each day. The list might include budgeting, purchasing items, and saving money. Compare your lists in class.

 To learn more about factors that affect production of goods and services, view the *Economics & You* video lesson 19: Financing and Producing Goods.

Summarizing Information Study Foldable *Make this foldable to help you organize and summarize what you learn about the American economy.*

Step 1 *Mark the midpoint of a side edge of one sheet of paper. Then fold the outside edges in to touch the midpoint.*

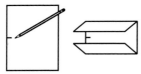

Step 2 *Fold the paper in half again from side to side.*

Step 3 *Open the paper and cut along the inside fold lines to form four tabs.*

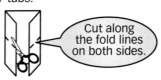

Cut along the fold lines on both sides.

Step 4 *Label as shown.*

Economic Resources | Circular Flow of Economic Activity | Characteristics of Capitalism | Economy & You

Reading and Writing *As you read the chapter, write information under each appropriate tab of your foldable. Be sure to summarize the information you find by writing only main ideas and supporting details on your foldable.*

An American worker inspects computer components. ▶

CIVICS Online

Chapter Overview Visit the *Civics Today* Web site at <u>civ.glencoe.com</u> and click on **Chapter Overviews— Chapter 19** to preview chapter information.

Economic Resources

GUIDE TO READING

Main Idea
Four factors of production are required to produce goods and services.

Key Terms
goods, services, factors of production, natural resources, labor, capital, entrepreneur, Gross Domestic Product (GDP), standard of living

Reading Strategy
Categorizing Information
As you read the section, complete a diagram like the one below by identifying the four factors of production.

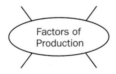

Read to Learn
• What are the four types of resources or factors of production?
• What is Gross Domestic Product and how is it measured?

Americans in Action

You are listening to the radio. The newscaster says that according to a new government report, the economy is growing and prices are rising only slightly. What exactly does it mean when someone says that the economy has been growing? One of the important measures of the economy's size is Gross Domestic Product, or GDP. U.S. Secretary of Commerce William M. Daley noted, "As we searched for our greatest achievement [of the 20th century, we decided that] it was the invention of . . . the gross domestic product, or GDP." Dr. Simon Kuznets developed the GDP in the early 1930s, and later won a Nobel Prize for his work. Ever since, the GDP accounts have been used by government and business officials to guide their economic policymaking.

An American production worker

Producing Goods and Services

At the beginning of this century, the United States's annual output, or amount produced, totaled about $10 trillion—nearly 30 percent of the world's total output. Some of this production is in the form of **goods,** or tangible products like books and automobiles that we use to satisfy our wants and needs. More of this production is in the form of **services,** or work that is performed for someone else. Services include haircuts, home repairs, and forms of entertainment such as concerts.

Factors of Production

There are four **factors of production,** or resources necessary to produce goods and services—natural resources, labor, capital, and entrepreneurs. These are broad categories that include many things that are already familiar to you.

Natural Resources

As an economic term, **natural resources** refers to all of the "gifts of nature" that make production possible. Natural resources include fertile fields, abundant rainfall, forests, mineral deposits and other resources that we use to make products.

For example, when your school was built, a certain amount of land was required for the building and grounds. Your school also consists of wood from forests, iron and steel extracted from ore, and bricks and mortar made from other natural materials. When these materials were in their natural state, before they were transformed into something else, they were part of the "natural resources" factor of production.

Labor

Labor is the nation's labor force or human resources. Labor refers to both physical and mental efforts that people contribute to the production of goods and services. The labor used to construct a building was supplied by carpenters, bricklayers, and electricians. The labor needed to produce the service of education is the effort put forth by your teachers and other support personnel.

Labor is a resource that may vary in size over time. Historically, such factors as population growth, immigration, education, war, and disease have had a dramatic impact on both the quantity and the quality of labor.

Capital

Another factor of production is capital, also called capital goods. These are the tools, machinery, and buildings used to make other products. The tools used to construct your school building included bulldozers, trucks, hammers, saws, drills, and any other human-made instruments of production that were used during its construction.

Capital goods are unique in that they are the *result* of production. For example, we can't find a hammer out in the forest like we can a tree—someone actually has to make a hammer for it to exist.

Economists differentiate capital goods from consumer goods. Consumer goods satisfy wants directly. Consumer goods are things like clothes, clocks, shoes, foods, bicycles, and radios. Capital goods satisfy wants indirectly by aiding production of consumer goods.

Capital Goods The trucking industry plays an important role in the nation's economy. **Why are trucks considered a capital good?**

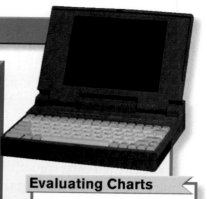

Final Goods and Services	Quantity (in thousands)	Average Price	Value (in millions)
Goods:			
Automobiles	6,000	$28,000	$168,000
Books	15,000	25	375
Computers	1,300	1,700	2,210
......			
Zippers	1,000	2	2
Services:			
Advertising (minutes of)	1,050,000	$1,000	$1,050,000
Babysitting (hours of)	50,000	5	250
Car Washes (number of)	15,000	10	150
......			
Zodiac Readings (number of)	400	10	4
Gross Domestic Product:			$10.2 trillion

Evaluating Charts

Gross Domestic Product is the dollar value of all final goods and services produced in the economy in one year. How do we calculate GDP?

Entrepreneurs

The fourth factor of production is the **entrepreneur.** These are individuals who start new businesses, introduce new products, and improve management techniques. Being an entrepreneur involves being innovative and willing to take risks in order to reap profits. Entrepreneurs are often thought of as the driving force in the American economy because they use the factors of production to produce new products.

✓**Reading Check** **Classifying** Under what factor of production would you classify a bulldozer? Oil deposits?

Gross Domestic Product

People can measure their economic success by the amount of their incomes and their ability to provide for themselves and their families. The success of the overall economy is measured in a similar way. One measure of the economy's size is **Gross Domestic Product (GDP).** This is the total value, in dollars, of all the *final* goods and services

produced in a country during a single year. The word *final* in the definition of GDP is important. A final good is a good, such as a loaf of bread, sold to its user. The intermediate goods that go into making a loaf of bread—flour or wheat, sugar, honey—are not counted in GDP. When computing GDP, economists count only final goods and services. If they counted both final and intermediate goods, they would be double-counting, or counting a good more than once.

In addition, secondhand sales—the sale of used goods—are not counted as part of GDP. When products already produced are transferred from one person or group to another, no new production is created. Although the sale of a used car, clothes, or compact disc player may give others cash that they can use on new purchases, only the original sale is included in GDP.

Measuring GDP

Remember that GDP is a monetary measure. A monetary measure is helpful if we are to compare the number of goods and services produced and get a meaningful idea of their relative worth. If the economy produces two computers and three dining room tables in year 1, and three computers and two tables in year 2, in which year is output greater? We cannot answer that question until prices are attached to these products as indicators of society's evaluation of their worth.

The chart on page 426 shows a simple version of GDP. In the first column, we list all of the final goods and services that are produced in the country. In the next column, we list the number of each that is produced, and in the third column we list the average price for each good or service. To compute GDP, first multiply the number of items produced by the average price of the item; then add up everything. What else does GDP tell us? If the new GDP is higher than the previous one, then the economy is expanding. If it is lower, the economy is declining. Economists study GDP figures regularly to analyze business cycle patterns.

GDP is an important measure of **standard of living,** the quality of life based on the possession of necessities and luxuries that make life easier. Whenever GDP grows faster than the population, there are more goods and services, on average, for

each of us to enjoy. GDP is a reasonably accurate and useful measure of economic performance. It is not a measure of society's overall well-being,

Student Web Activity Visit civ.glencoe.com and click on **Student Web Activities— Chapter 19** to learn more about measuring GDP.

though. Many things could make a country better off without necessarily raising GDP, such as a reduction of crime, greater equality of opportunity, and reductions of drug and alcohol abuse.

Quantity vs. Quality

Remember that GDP measures *quantity*. It does not accurately reflect improvements in the *quality* of products. There is a great difference between a $3,000 computer purchased today and a computer costing the same amount just a few years ago. Because of this, economists must take great care to account for quality improvement. Greater production of goods and services is only one of the many factors that contribute to raising the standard of living.

✓**Reading Check** **Describing** What does Gross Domestic Product measure?

SECTION 1 ASSESSMENT

Checking for Understanding

1. Key Terms Write a paragraph in which you use these key terms: goods, services, factors of production, natural resources, labor, capital, entrepreneur, Gross Domestic Product (GDP), standard of living.

Reviewing Main Ideas

2. Describe How do economists define natural resources?

3. Explain What are the major functions of the entrepreneur?

Critical Thinking

4. Making Comparisons Is a pizza oven a capital good or a consumer good? Explain.

5. Organizing Information Create a chart like the one below. Then list the four factors of production and provide two examples of each.

Factor of Production		
Example 1		
Example 2		

Analyzing Visuals

6. Interpret Study the table on page 426. What is the Gross Domestic Product for that particular economy?

★**BE AN ACTIVE CITIZEN**★

7. Organize Search your local newspaper to find a story about a business in your community. Organize the facts under the categories of *Natural Resources, Labor, Capital,* and *Entrepreneurs.*

Economic Activity and Productivity

GUIDE TO READING

Main Idea
The circular flow model provides an overview of the operation of the market economy.

Key Terms
factor market, product market, productivity, specialization, division of labor, economic interdependence

Reading Strategy
Categorizing Information As you read the section, complete a diagram like the one below by defining *specialization*. Then, identify at least two specialists in the categories.

Specialization is

Individuals who specialize:

Businesses that specialize:

Read to Learn
• What are factor markets and product markets?
• How does specialization increase production?

Americans in Action

High school and college students now have a new resource for finding jobs thanks to two students from Kansas City, Missouri. Michael and Ephren, both high school seniors, provide a service—a free online resource where students find employment opportunities. What kind of work will you do? What part do you play in the American market economy? You are a part of the system already. You buy things, so you are already a part of the consumer market. You might provide a service like Michael and Ephren. You might already have a part-time job. Part-time workers account for one of every five jobs in the U.S. economy. All of these activities are part of the market economy.

Part-time workers are part of a market economy.

Circular Flow of Economic Activity

To the economist, a market is a location or other situation that allows buyers and sellers to exchange a certain economic product. Markets may be local, regional, national, or global. In this section, you will learn about the major groups of decision makers and the major markets in the market system.

The Consumer Sector

Consumers make up one group of economic decision makers, but there are others—the business, government, and foreign sectors. The flow of resources, goods and services, and money in a market system between these groups is actually circular, as shown in the figure on page 429. Economists use this model, called a circular flow diagram, to illustrate how the market system works.

How does this circular flow operate? Consumers earn their income in **factor markets**—the markets where productive resources are bought and sold. Here, workers earn wages, salaries, and tips in exchange for their labor. People who own land may loan it in return for a type of income called rent. Finally, people who own capital exchange it for interest.

The Business Sector

When these individuals receive their incomes, they spend it in **product markets**—markets where producers offer goods and services for sale. The business sector receives payments in the product markets where they sell goods and services to consumers. Businesses use these payments to pay for natural resources, labor, and capital they use. These resources are then used to manufacture additional products that are sold in the product markets.

The diagram below shows that the business sector purchases some of the output it produces—primarily capital goods—so that it can continue to produce more goods and services. These purchases include things such as tools, factories, and other goods needed for current production. In actual practice, the business sector is much smaller than the consumer sector. While the consumer sector purchases about two-thirds of all output, the business sector usually consumes about 15 to 20 percent of our GDP.

The Government Sector

The government sector shown on the diagram below is made of all three levels of government—federal, state, and local. Because the government sector also produces goods and services, like national defense, health, education, transportation, and housing, the government sector purchases productive inputs in the factor markets. The government receives revenue from the services it sells. For example, public universities charge tuition, public hospitals charge fees, and city buses charge fares. However, because the total cost of government services is seldom covered by fees

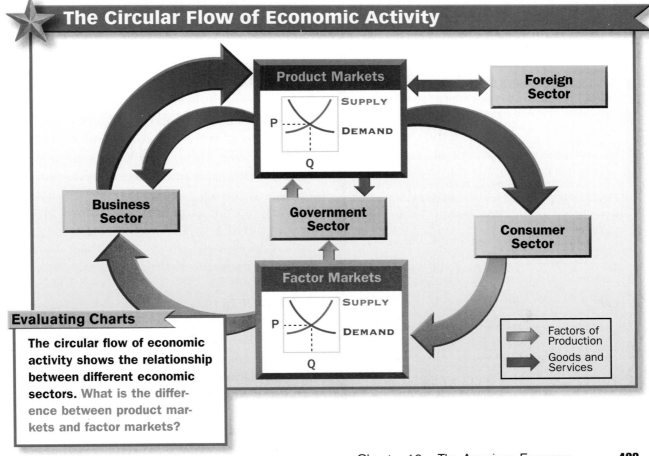

The Circular Flow of Economic Activity

Evaluating Charts

The circular flow of economic activity shows the relationship between different economic sectors. What is the difference between product markets and factor markets?

alone, the government sector receives most of its revenues from taxes on businesses and individuals.

Government also uses its revenue to purchase final goods and services in the product markets. School systems, for example, purchase books and buses, while the military purchases trucks, fighter planes, and ships. Historically, the government is the second-largest sector in our economy, purchasing approximately 20 percent of our GDP.

The Foreign Sector

The foreign sector in the diagram on page 429 represents all of the countries in the world. Notice that this sector is the only one with a line having an arrow at both ends. The reason for this is that we sell products to, as well as buy products from, other countries.

The value of the goods and services the United States purchases from other countries and the value of the goods and services it sells to other countries tend to offset one another. As a result, the foreign sector generally accounts for less than 4 percent of our nation's GDP.

Reading Check **Identifying** What is a product market?

Productivity and Economic Growth

Growth in the economy occurs when a nation's total output of goods and services increases over time. This means that the circular flow becomes larger, with more factors of production, goods, and services flowing in one direction, and more payments flowing in the opposite direction. Economic growth is important because it increases people's standard of living.

Productivity

Everyone benefits when resources that are scarce are used efficiently. This is described by the term **productivity,** which is a measure of the amount of output produced by a given amount of inputs in a specific period of time. Productivity goes up whenever more output can be produced

American Biographies

Milton Friedman (1912–)

Milton Friedman, a Nobel Prize–winning economist, thinks nothing regulates the economy better than free enterprise. He praises open competition and the ability of consumers, workers, and businesspeople to decide upon their own best interests. The pursuit of these interests, says Friedman, determines prices, wages, and profits.

The son of Jewish immigrants from eastern Europe, Friedman has seen nearly a century of economic ups and downs. He believes these swings are part of the natural workings of the marketplace. In his opinion, government should focus on one thing—balancing our purchasing power with our power to produce goods. Under this plan, known as monetarism, the government would increase the money supply each year based upon the expected growth in production.

Friedman has his share of critics, especially when he calls for an end to things like minimum wage laws, social welfare programs, and protective tariffs. He argues, however, that private enterprise can do almost anything more efficiently than governments. Friedman once remarked, "If a government were put in charge of the Sahara Desert, within five years, they'd have a shortage of sand."

Political Cartoons

Analyzing Visuals
Economists note that consumers' purchasing decisions are often motivated by impulse as opposed to hard logic. According to the cartoonist, what is "the story behind the statistics"?

with the same amount of inputs in the same amount of time or when the same output can be produced with less input.

Productivity is often discussed in terms of labor, but it applies to all factors of production. For this reason, business owners try to buy the most efficient capital goods, and farmers try to use the most fertile land for their crops.

Specialization

Specialization takes place when people, businesses, regions, and even countries concentrate on goods or services that they can produce better than anyone else. As a result, nearly everyone depends upon others to produce many of the things that he or she consumes. Specialization is important because it improves productivity.

We specialize because we can earn more by doing the things that we do well. We also specialize because it is efficient to do so. Few individuals or households seriously consider producing their own food, shelter, and clothing. When people specialize, they are usually far more productive than if they attempt to do many things. For example, Mary is a carpenter who wants to build a house. Even if Mary could build the entire house without any help, she could be better off hiring other workers who specialize in foundations, plumbing, and electrical wiring. Mary might even save money by first working for someone else and then using her earnings to hire specialized workers for her own project.

Division of Labor

The division of labor is the breaking down of a job into separate, smaller tasks, which are performed by different workers. The division of labor is a form of specialization that improves productivity.

Division of labor makes use of differences in skills and abilities. For example, you and your coworker each do the tasks you are best suited for. Even if your abilities are identical, specialization can be advantageous. By allocating all your time to a single task, you are more likely to discover improved techniques than by dividing your time among a number of different tasks.

Measuring Consumption

Every year, the United Nations Human Development Report looks for a new way to measure the lives of people. The report notes that the richest fifth of the world's population consumes 86% of all goods and services while the poorest fifth consumes just 1.3%. Indeed, the richest fifth consumes 58% of all energy used and owns 87% of all vehicles.

Human Capital

Productivity tends to increase when businesses invest in **human capital**—the sum of the skills, abilities, and motivation of people. Investments by government and businesses in training, health care, and employee motivation tend to increase the amount of production that takes place with a given amount of labor. Employers are usually rewarded with higher-quality products and increased profits. Workers often benefit from higher pay, better jobs, and more satisfaction with their work.

Economic Interdependence

Because of specialization, the American economy displays a remarkable degree of **economic interdependence.** This means that we rely on others, and others rely on us, to provide the goods and services that we consume.

Events in one part of the country or the world often have a dramatic impact elsewhere. For example, bad weather in a country where sugarcane is grown can affect sugar prices in the United States, which in turn can affect the price of snack foods and the demand for sugar substitutes elsewhere.

This does not mean that economic interdependence is necessarily bad. The gain in productivity and income that results from increased specialization usually offsets the cost associated with the loss of self-sufficiency. However, we need to understand how all the parts fit together, which is one of the many reasons we study economics.

Reading Check **Defining** What is specialization?

SECTION 2 ASSESSMENT

Checking for Understanding

1. **Key Terms** Write a paragraph in which you use the following terms: productivity, specialization, division of labor. Then, write a second paragraph using these terms: product market, factor market.

Reviewing Main Ideas

2. **Identify** Do consumers earn their income in the product market or the factor market?

3. **Summarize** Name three things that government produces.

Critical Thinking

4. **Drawing Inferences** In what industries or businesses does your community specialize? Why?

5. **Organizing Information** Describe three different transactions that could take place in the product market. Use a diagram like the one below to help you organize your answer.

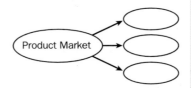

Analyzing Visuals

6. **Interpret** Study the chart on page 429. As a consumer, what role do you play in the circular flow of economic activity?

★ **BE AN ACTIVE CITIZEN** ★

7. **Research** Find out how either your local government or private groups protect consumer rights in your community. What ordinances protect consumers? How are complaints handled? What private organizations help consumers? Prepare a report for the class.

Landmark Supreme Court
Case Studies

Gibbons v. Ogden

The steamer *Hartford* by Joseph B. Smith

Background of the Case

In the early 1800s, the state of New York licensed Robert Fulton and his partner to operate a steamboat monopoly along its waterway. The partners then used their license to grant Aaron Ogden a monopoly on ferryboat travel between New York City and Elizabethtown, New Jersey. Thomas Gibbons, however, had a federal license to run boats between New York and New Jersey.

Ogden wanted to shut down his competition. He sued to close down Gibbons's operation. It was up to the Supreme Court to decide which would prevail, Ogden's state license or Gibbons's federal license.

The Decision

John Marshall delivered the unanimous opinion on March 4, 1824. His decision rested on the power of Congress to "regulate commerce," as granted in Article I, Section 8, of the U.S. Constitution. Marshall interpreted *commerce* to mean "every species of commercial [interaction]," including navigation.

This power [to regulate commerce], like all others vested in Congress, is complete in itself, may be exercised to its utmost extent, and

In the early years of the nation, each state jealously guarded its own commerce. Trade barriers among the states restricted commerce and stood in the way of a strong national economy. What changed this situation?

acknowledges no limitations other than are prescribed in the Constitution. . . . [However, this rule does not apply to] . . . that commerce, which is completely internal, which is carried on between man and man in a state, or between different parts of the same State, and which does not extend to or affect other States.

The decision gave the federal government sole power to regulate all possible forms of commerce between states. It also affirmed Congress's right to regulate trade with foreign nations. States retained the right to regulate trade entirely inside their borders, and Ogden lost his license.

Why It Matters

The *Gibbons* decision took on more significance in later years than it did at the time. Marshall's broad interpretation of the commerce clause, in fact, helped pave the way for today's strong national government. It allowed Congress to prevent companies from fixing prices in 1905. In 1964, Congress was able to prohibit racial discrimination in businesses serving the public because such discrimination was seen as affecting interstate commerce.

Analyzing the Court Decision

1. How did Marshall define the commerce clause?
2. How did this Supreme Court ruling affect states' control of economic activities?

Capitalism and Free Enterprise

GUIDE TO READING

Main Idea

The United States has a free enterprise, or capitalist, system.

Key Terms

capitalism, free enterprise, consumer sovereignty, private property rights, competition, profit, profit motive, voluntary exchange

Reading Strategy

Organizing Information As you read the section, complete a table like the one below by identifying the characteristics of a free enterprise economy. Then provide an example of each characteristic.

Characteristic	Example

Read to Learn

• What are the major features of free enterprise?

• What are some of the freedoms of free enterprise?

Americans in Action

Capitalism is an economic system in which individuals own most, if not all, resources and control their use. What are the benefits of capitalism and why has it spread to many countries? One writer noted that "capitalism has come to dominate the world's economies because no other system has been able to generate long-term economic growth in the 200 years since the onset of the industrial revolution. Many others have been tried, but they have all failed." In 1776 Adam Smith, a Scottish philosopher and economist, provided a philosophy for the capitalist system in his book, *The Wealth of Nations.* Smith wrote that individuals left on their own would work for their own self-interest. In doing so, they would be guided as if by an "invisible hand" to use resources efficiently and thus achieve the maximum good for society.

Economist Adam Smith

Features of Capitalism

The economy of the United States is built largely on free markets and private ownership. It is known as **capitalism,** an economic system in which private citizens own and use the factors of production in order to seek a profit. **Free enterprise** is another term used to describe the American economy. In a free enterprise economy, competition is allowed to flourish with a minimum of government interference.

In Americans in Action, you read about one of the most remarkable characteristics of our nation's economy: its ability to grow and accumulate wealth. No other economic system in the history of the world has been as successful. The unique features of this economic system combine to contribute to its success.

Markets

Markets are one important part of our economic system. Markets are the places where the prices of goods and services are determined as exchange takes place. However, markets do more than set prices; they are mechanisms that connect the different sectors of the economy. To illustrate, the chart on page 429 shows that consumers and businesses interact primarily in the product and factor markets.

When you go to work, your labor is being sold in the factor markets. When you go shopping, the goods and services you buy are being purchased in product markets. Markets, then, are the main places where buyers and sellers meet to negotiate product prices.

Under our economic system, the consumer is especially important because businesses usually try to produce the products that people want most. Because of this, we use the term **consumer sovereignty** to describe the consumer as the "king," or ruler, of the market, the one who determines what products will be produced.

Economic Freedom

In the United States, we place a high value on the freedom to make our own economic decisions. Choice is a key element of the free enterprise system. Specifically, each of us can choose the type of job or occupation we would like to have, and we can choose when and where we would like to work.

As consumers, we have the right to choose the products we will buy. Businesses have the right to choose the products they will produce and offer for sale. Along with this freedom come certain costs. In particular, individuals must normally accept the consequences of their decisions in our free enterprise system. If an entrepreneur starts a business that fails, the government usually won't help out.

Private Property Rights

Another major feature of capitalism is **private property rights.** This means that we have the freedom to own and use, or dispose of, our own property as we choose as long as we do not interfere with the rights of others.

Private property rights give us the incentive to work, save, and invest, because we know we can keep any gains that we might earn. In addition, we tend to take better care of things if we actually own them so they tend to last longer. For example, someone who owns his or her own home often takes better care of it than does the person who rents property from someone else.

Competition

Capitalism thrives on **competition**— the struggle that goes on between buyers and sellers to get the best products at the lowest prices. The competition between sellers keeps the cost of production low and the quality of the goods higher than they would be otherwise. Buyers likewise compete among themselves to find the best products at the lowest prices.

Because of this, competition rewards the most efficient producers. Competition also forces the least efficient producers out

Economic Freedom The freedom to own a business is one characteristic of a capitalist society. **What are other characteristics of capitalism?**

Consumer Sovereignty Consumers play an important role in the American free enterprise economy. **What is consumer sovereignty?**

of business or into other industries. The result is that competition makes for efficient production, higher-quality products, and more satisfied customers.

The Profit Motive

Under free enterprise and capitalism, people are free to risk their savings or any part of their wealth in a business venture. If the venture goes well, the people will earn rewards for their efforts. If things go poorly, they could lose part or even all of the investment. The possibility of financial gain, however, leads many to take risks in hopes of earning a profit.

Profit is the amount of money left over after all the costs of production have been paid. Profit, then, is the extent to which persons or organizations are better off economically at the end of a period than they were at the beginning. The **profit motive**—the driving force that encourages individuals and organizations to improve their material well-being—is largely responsible for the growth of a free enterprise system based on capitalism.

Voluntary Exchange

Voluntary exchange is the act of buyers and sellers freely and willingly engaging in market transactions. Who benefits when you buy something—you or the seller? As long as the transaction involves a voluntary exchange, both you and the seller benefit— or the exchange would not have happened in the first place.

The buyer gives up money to obtain a product. The seller gives up the product to obtain money. Unless both parties believe they will be better off afterward than before, neither will make the exchange. When exchange takes place, it does so only because both parties feel they will make a profit. Voluntary exchange, then, is both a characteristic of capitalism and a way for us to improve our economic well-being.

Reading Check **Summarizing** What incentives does private property give people?

The Spread of Capitalism

No one person invented the idea of capitalism. It developed gradually from the economic and political changes in medieval and early modern Europe over hundreds of years. Two important concepts laid the foundation for the market system that is at the heart of capitalism. First is the idea that people could work for economic gain. Second is the idea that government should have a very limited role in the economy.

Major changes in the economic organization of Europe began with the opening of trade routes to the East in the 1200s. As trade increased, people began to invest money to make profits. By the 1700s, Europe had nation-states, a wealthy middle class familiar with money and markets, and a new attitude toward work and wealth. Included in this new attitude were the ideas of progress, invention, and the free market. The free market meant that buyers and sellers were free to make virtually unlimited economic decisions in the marketplace.

Adam Smith and Capitalism

Adam Smith was a Scottish economist and philosopher. His best known work, *The Wealth of Nations,* was published in 1776. Smith's book offered a detailed description of life and trade in English society. It also scientifically described the basic principles of economics for the first time.

Smith believed that individuals, seeking profit, end up benefiting society as a whole. From the writings of Smith and others came the basic idea of laissez-faire economics. Laissez-faire, a French term, means "to let alone." According to this philosophy, government should not interfere in the marketplace. In laissez-faire economics, the government's role is strictly limited to those few actions needed to ensure free competition in the marketplace.

Many of America's Founders read *The Wealth of Nations* and were influenced by it. James Madison read it, and Alexander Hamilton borrowed heavily from it in his "Report on Manufactures." In a letter to Thomas Mann Randolph in 1790, Thomas Jefferson wrote, ". . . in political economy I think Smith's *Wealth of Nations* the best book extant [in existence] . . ."

Historically, communism and capitalism have been viewed as two opposing political and economic structures. The collapse of communism, however, did not mean that the transition to capitalism will be smooth. Despite problems, the rise of capitalism is one of the most remarkable phenomena of this era.

Reading Check **Explaining** What is laissez-faire economics?

SECTION 3 ASSESSMENT

Checking for Understanding

1. Key Terms Write a paragraph about free enterprise using all of the following terms: consumer sovereignty, private property rights, competition, profit, voluntary exchange.

Reviewing Main Ideas

2. Explain What is a free enterprise economy? How does consumer sovereignty affect the free enterprise system?

3. Explain What are the limits of private property rights?

Critical Thinking

4. Analyzing Information What economic choices will you be free to make upon graduating from high school?

5. Making Comparisons Create a diagram like the one below to list the advantages and disadvantages of competition to buyers and sellers.

Analyzing Visuals

6. Write Create a caption for the photo on page 436. In your caption, indicate how the photo illustrates the characteristic of voluntary exchange.

★ **BE AN ACTIVE CITIZEN** ★

7. Interview Survey five fellow students, friends, and neighbors to discover what the term "free enterprise" means to them. Review your findings and analyze why people might have different views of free enterprise.

The Economy and You

GUIDE TO READING

Main Idea
To make good economic decisions, we need to be aware of our rights and responsibilities as consumers.

Key Terms
consumerism, warranty, ethical behavior, disposable income, discretionary income, saving, interest

Reading Strategy
Organizing Information
As you read the section, complete a diagram like the one below to list your rights as a consumer.

Consumer Rights

Read to Learn
- What private and federal help can you receive as a consumer?
- What considerations should govern your decision making as a consumer?

Americans in Action

Richard Hecker and Ruchit Shah met online and soon discovered that they shared an interest in business. The two high school students ultimately formed a multimillion-dollar company, called ClickZen.com. It is an advertising network that sells and serves banner space on a variety of Web sites. According to a 2001 article from Rediff.com, Ruchit, a resident of Charlotte, North Carolina, from an early age "displayed an intense interest in the Internet and ways of doing business on the Net. Looking back, Shah credits his parents with his success: 'A person can only be as remarkable as the people around him, which are my parents, my friends and my little brother Rishi. I couldn't have done it without them. I really have to thank them and my teachers.'" For his part, Hecker discounts the idea that being so young is a liability in the business world. He says, "As long as we provide results, age doesn't matter."

Richard Hecker

Consumer Rights and Responsibilities

The American free enterprise system bestows numerous economic rights and protections on individuals like you, your teachers, your relatives, and your friends. You have the right to enter into just about any profession or enterprise you are interested in, just as Ruchit Shah and Richard Hecker did. You have the right to buy those products and brands that you like and to reject the others.

In earlier chapters, you discovered that with every right comes certain responsibilities. In the same way, our rights as consumers require some responsibility on our part. We should find out as much as we can about the products we buy so that we can recognize good quality. We should also find out where we can get the best value for our money. We cannot always rely on stores and businesses to protect us. We must take steps to protect ourselves.

Protecting Consumer Rights

Throughout much of history, consumer rights could be summed up in one Latin phrase: *caveat emptor,* or "let the buyer beware." In this section, you will learn how consumerism, a movement to educate buyers about the purchases they make and to demand better and safer products from manufacturers, affects you personally.

Congress has passed a number of laws over the years that protect consumer rights. Many of these laws involve labeling. For example, the Fair Packaging and Labeling Act requires that every package have a label identifying its contents and how much it weighs. Other laws protect consumers' health and safety. An early example is the Pure Food and Drug Act, passed in 1906. It requires manufacturers of foods, cosmetics, and drugs to prove their products are safe.

Many private groups and organizations have taken on the task of protecting individual consumers. One of the oldest of these consumer groups is the Better Business Bureau. There are about 145 better business bureaus in communities around the country. Surprisingly, business groups rather than consumers run these organizations. These businesspeople recognize that the key to success lies in earning the trust of their customers. They provide information about local businesses and warn consumers about dishonest business practices. They also investigate consumer complaints.

Consumer Bill of Rights

In the 1960s, a special effort was made to strengthen the consumers' voice. President John F. Kennedy and, later, President Richard Nixon emphasized five major rights of consumers.

- Consumers have the *right to a safe product*—one that will not harm their health or lives.

- Consumers have the *right to be informed* for protection against fraudulent, deceitful, or grossly misleading information and to be given the facts needed to make informed choices.
- Consumers have the *right to choose*—to have available a variety of products and services at competitive prices.
- Consumers have the *right to be heard*—the guarantee that consumer interests will be listened to when laws are being written.
- Consumers have the *right to redress*—the ability to obtain from the manufacturers adequate payment if their product causes financial or physical damage.

Rights and Responsibilities When you buy something, you have a right to expect quality and a responsibility to recognize it. **What are other consumer rights and responsibilities?**

The Law and You

An Appearance in Small Claims Court

Javier purchased a radio/CD player. Ten days later it stopped working. The store refused to exchange it for another one, so Javier brought his complaint to small claims court. Javier has the receipt and the broken radio/CD player as evidence. The law requires that all new items include an implied promise that they can do what they are supposed to do for a reasonable length of time. In small claims court, the proceedings went as follows:

The Radio Shop
415 Mudd Road
Octagon, Oregon

Date: November 14

1 Radio/CD Player $79.95
            tax   + 3.10
                   $83.05

This product is fully guaranteed for five days from the date of purchase. If defective, return it in the original box for credit toward another purchase.

Judge: "Both sides should be given an opportunity to present their case with the support of their witnesses. I will then make my decision."

Witness Statements

Javier: "I really wanted a radio/CD player and the salesperson talked me into this model. When it didn't work I went back to the store, but the salesperson would not take it back. I have the evidence and I want my money back!"

Ruby (Javier's mother): "Javier was excited about his purchase and upset when it didn't work. We thought the store would give us a credit so soon after the purchase. They must not have very good merchandise. Javier earned this money and deserves to have a good product."

Tyrone (Salesperson): "I sold the radio/CD player and, of course, I thought it worked. Why wouldn't it work if it was still in the original cardboard box—right from the factory? I think Javier broke it."

Hattie (Store manager): "We haven't had any complaints about this model. We accept returns within 5 days in the original box. Otherwise, we would have been happy to give him a credit—our customers are important to us."

★ BE AN ACTIVE CITIZEN ★

How should the judge decide the case? In a brief report, make a decision on this case and give your reasons for it.

Consumer Responsibilities

Just as consumers have rights, they also have responsibilities. If a product or service is faulty, it is the consumer's responsibility to begin the problem-solving process. If it happens to you, you should report the problem immediately. Do not try to fix a product yourself, because doing so may cancel the **warranty,** the promise made by a manufacturer or a seller to repair or replace a product within a certain time period if it is faulty. State the problem and suggest a fair solution. Keep an accurate record of your efforts to get the problem solved. If you need to contact the manufacturer in writing, type your letter or send an e-mail directly. Keep a copy of your letter.

Another responsibility of consumers is to exhibit **ethical behavior** by respecting the rights of producers and sellers. For example, a responsible consumer will not try to return a used item because it has been advertised elsewhere for a lower price.

✓ **Reading Check** **Summarizing** What is the purpose of better business bureaus?

Your Role as a Consumer

Your role as a consumer depends on your available income and how much of it you choose to spend or save. Income can be both disposable and discretionary.

Uses of Income

Disposable income is the money income a person has left after all the taxes on it have been paid. People spend their disposable income on many kinds of goods and services. First, they generally buy the necessities of living: food, clothing, and housing. **Discretionary income** is money left over after paying for these necessities that can be used for satisfying wants, including luxury items or savings accounts.

Regardless of the size of a person's income, spending that income requires constant decision making. As a consumer, each person has a series of choices to make.

Decision Making

Virtually all of the steps in decision making involve an opportunity cost. Remember that opportunity cost is the value of your highest alternative choice that you did not make. Suppose a friend recently purchased athletic shoes. You like them, and you want to buy a pair for yourself. Before you do, however, ask yourself, "What can't I buy or do, if I buy the shoes?" In other words, you have to decide if the shoes are worth what you would give up to buy them.

What Are Your Goals?

It is also important to consider your goals when you make buying decisions. Suppose you work on weekends to save money for a new computer. You see many things that you would like to buy now—new clothes, magazines and books, and so on. If you buy these things, you will find it harder to accomplish your long-term goal. What option do you choose?

You could buy what you want now and reduce, or postpone, the chances of buying the computer or buy less of what you want now and increase the chances of buying the computer. Long-term goals often conflict with short-range spending decisions.

Saving for the Future

One way to help you reach your long-term purchasing goals is to save. Saving is to set aside a portion of income for a period of time so that it can be used later. It is that part of your income that you don't spend.

Saving money can be a difficult habit to establish. Some people feel they should enjoy every penny they earn. As a result,

they spend their money as quickly as it comes in. There are, however, many good reasons for saving. Most people cannot make major purchases, such as a car or a house, without putting aside money to help pay for them. Saving also comes in handy in emergencies.

When an individual saves, the economy as a whole benefits. Saving provides money for others to invest or spend. Saving also allows businesses to expand, which provides increased income for consumers and raises the standard of living.

Saving Regularly

To make it easier for people to save, most employers withhold a fixed amount from employees' paychecks. This money is automatically deposited into participating employees' savings accounts. Many people, however, handle the responsibility

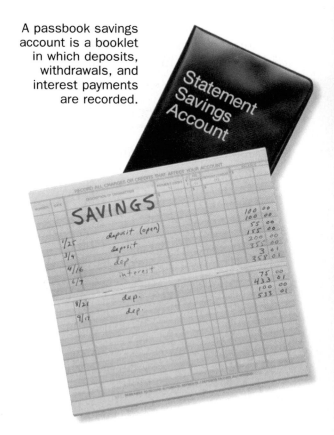

A passbook savings account is a booklet in which deposits, withdrawals, and interest payments are recorded.

Economics and You

Public Disclosure

The government helps citizens make informed purchases through the use of public disclosure—the requirement that businesses reveal certain information about their products or services to the public. The Food and Drug Administration, for example, requires food companies to put labels on cans and other containers. Pick a product that you use often. Report on any information or warnings on the labels or containers.

themselves. Each week or month, they budget a specific amount of money to put aside for savings.

Generally, when people think of saving they think of putting their funds in a savings bank or a similar financial institution where it will earn interest. Interest is the payment people receive when they lend money or allow someone else to use their money. A person receives interest at periodic intervals on his or her savings for as long as funds are in the account.

Deciding About Your Savings

Like every other activity, saving involves a trade-off. The more you save today, the more you can buy a year from now, 10 years from now, or 30 years from now. Saving increases a person's future purchasing power. You will, however, have less to spend today. Deciding how much to save depends on your answer to several questions: How much do you spend on your everyday expenses? What are your primary reasons for saving? How much interest can you earn on your savings and, therefore, how fast will your savings grow? How much income do you think you will be earning in the future?

If you expect to make a much higher income tomorrow, you have less reason to save a large percentage of today's income. When you are self-supporting and have more responsibilities, you will probably save for other reasons, such as having funds in case of emergencies and for your retirement. It is a good idea, however, to have some sort of savings plan.

✓ Reading Check **Defining** What is discretionary income?

SECTION 4 ASSESSMENT

Checking for Understanding

1. **Key Terms** Use each of the following terms in a sentence that will help explain its meaning: consumerism, warranty, ethical behavior, disposable income, discretionary income, saving, interest.

Reviewing Main Ideas

2. **Summarize** What private and federal help can you receive as a consumer?

3. **Explain** What kinds of products are purchased with disposable income?

Critical Thinking

4. **Making Generalizations** Why do some people buy brand-name products and other people buy generic products?

5. **Synthesizing Information** On a chart like the one below, develop a checklist of three rules for making an important purchase.

My Checklist
1.
2.
3.

Analyzing Visuals

6. **Interpret** Look at the cartoon on page 431. Are the goods being purchased necessities (needs) or are they discretionary (wants)? Explain.

★ **BE AN ACTIVE CITIZEN** ★

7. **Compare** Select a product you use every day: toothpaste or a hair dryer, for example. Do some comparison shopping by finding at least three separate locations that sell this product. What were the differences in price for the product?

Predicting Consequences

Why Learn This Skill?

What should I do? You answer this question every time you choose a course of action. Every time you act, you get results. These results are the consequences of your action. Of course, you want the consequences to be all that you had hoped for with no unpleasant surprises. The way to avoid unpleasant surprises is to predict the consequences before you act. Predicting consequences may prevent you from having to ask, "Why did I do that?"

Learning the Skill

To predict the consequences of an action, follow these steps:

- Clarify the issue or situation. Form a statement or a question that clearly states the decision that needs to be made.
- Identify the options and analyze patterns.
- Predict the possible consequences of each option.
- Make a prediction.

Practicing the Skill

On a separate sheet of paper, predict one or more possible consequences of the options listed below.

From his monthly job earnings of $150, Joseph has saved $575 toward the future purchase of a computer costing $850. He wants a computer now, however, to do online research for two lengthy reports due in three weeks. What is the most satisfactory way for Joseph to acquire the use of a computer?

Option 1. Work nighttime hours stocking groceries for two months to earn the additional $275 needed to buy the computer.

A job can help teens reach their goals.

Option 2. Use the $575 as a down payment and make monthly credit payments of $35 for the next 12 months.

Option 3. Spend $500 for a rebuilt computer that carries no warranty.

Based on the consequences you have listed, which action would you choose? Explain.

Applying the Skill

Suppose you receive a gift of $300 to save for your education after high school. How should you invest the money? List the options you might have. Beside each option, list the predicted consequences. Use your predictions to select the most suitable course of action.

Practice key skills with Glencoe's **Skillbuilder Interactive Workbook CD-ROM, Level 1.**

Assessment & Activities

Review to Learn

Section 1

- The four factors of production are natural resources, labor, capital, and entrepreneurs.
- The factors of production provide the means for a society to produce its goods and services.

Section 2

- Productivity relates to the efficient use of resources.
- Productivity tends to go up when workers specialize in the things they do best.

Section 3

- The economic system of the United States is based on capitalism and free enterprise.
- Important characteristics are markets, economic freedom, competition, private property rights, the profit motive, and voluntary exchange.

Section 4

- Consumer advocates promote the following consumer rights: the right to safety, to be informed, to choose, to be heard, and to redress.

Using Your Foldables Study Organizer
Use your completed foldable to explain, in a brief essay, how you fit into the circular flow of economic activity.

Reviewing Key Terms

Choose the key term from the chapter that best matches each clue below.

1. natural resources, labor, capital, and entrepreneurs used to produce goods and services
2. the amount of goods and services produced from a given level of inputs
3. a transaction in which a buyer and seller work out their own terms of exchange
4. role of consumer as ruler of the market when determining goods and services produced
5. the use of resources by an individual, a firm, a region, or a nation to produce one or a few goods and services

Reviewing Main Ideas

6. What factors of production are required to produce the things that people use?
7. What are goods?
8. What are services?
9. What is the difference between a final good and an intermediate good?
10. What is the term for breaking down a job into numerous, separate tasks?
11. What does the idea of consumer sovereignty express?
12. What is voluntary exchange?
13. What is the drive to improve your material well-being called?
14. What is a warranty?
15. What is the income after taxes used to buy the necessities of living called?
16. What is interest?

Critical Thinking

17. **Categorizing Information** Describe how either you or a relative of yours who has a job fits into the circular flow model. Be sure to discuss both the factor and product markets.

18. Understanding Cause and Effect Define the meaning of the division of labor and explain how it improves the efficiency of production.

19. Understanding Cause and Effect Copy the following diagram onto a separate sheet of paper. Use upward, downward, or horizontal arrows to show what would happen to the size of the boxes in situations A, B, and C.

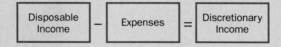

| Disposable Income | − | Expenses | = | Discretionary Income |

a. You receive a pay raise.

b. You cut energy expenses.

c. Wanting to graduate from college sooner rather than later, you leave your full-time job for a lower-paid, part-time position.

Practicing Skills

20. Predicting Consequences Suppose that your government wanted to make health care more affordable for everyone. To do this, state legislators put a series of price controls in place that cut the cost of medical services in half. What would happen to the demand for medical services at the new, lower price? What would happen to the supply of medical services that doctors would be willing to provide at the new, lower price? Where do you think new doctors would prefer to set up practice? Explain the reasons for your answers.

 Economics Activity

21. Choose a product that you use frequently. Research to find the answers to these questions regarding how the product is produced.

- What natural resources were used?
- What types of skills did the workers need?
- What types of tools were used?
- Is the firm that made the product large? What other products does it produce?

Self-Check Quiz Visit the *Civics Today* Web site at civ.glencoe.com and click on **Self-Check Quizzes— Chapter 19** to prepare for the chapter test.

★ CITIZENSHIP COOPERATIVE ACTIVITY ★

22. With a partner, find at least two examples of capital goods that are used in your school to provide the service of education. Would productivity go up or down if these capital goods were not available to your school? Explain why or why not.

Analyzing Visuals

23. Study the chart on page 426. What does the figure show? What two categories of economic products are shown?

 Technology Activity

24. Using a search engine on the Internet, find and research an entrepreneur. Explain what benefits were brought to society by this person's risk taking.

The Princeton Review **Standardized Test Practice**

Directions: Choose the *best* answer to the following question.

Which of the following statements about Gross Domestic Product is NOT true?

A It includes intermediate goods.

B It includes services as well as goods.

C It is based on dollar value.

D It includes final goods.

Test-Taking Tip

Read the question carefully. When a question uses the word *not* or *except*, you need to look for the answer that does not fit.

Demand

★ CITIZENSHIP AND YOU ★

When you buy something, do you ever wonder why it sells at that particular price? Few individual consumers feel they have any influence over the price of an item. In a market economy like ours, however, all consumers individually and collectively have an influence on the price of all goods and services. One way Americans influence prices in the marketplace is through demand. If you are interested in the prices you pay for goods and services, or why some people earn higher salaries than others, you will be interested in learning how demand works.

To learn more about demand, view the *Economics & You* video lesson 5: What Is Demand?

FOLDABLES
Study Organizer

Organizing Information Study Foldable *Make the following foldable to help you organize information about demand in a market economy.*

Step 1 *Fold a sheet of paper into thirds from top to bottom.*

Step 2 *Turn the paper horizontally, unfold, and label the three columns as shown.*

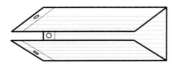

What Is Demand?	Factors Affecting Demand	Description of Factors

Reading and Writing *As you read the chapter, record your thoughts and the information you learn about demand in a market economy in the appropriate columns of your foldable.*

Demand—shown by these people waiting to buy tickets—is the willingness to buy ▶ a product at a particular price.

CIVICS Online

Chapter Overview Visit the *Civics Today* Web site at civ.glencoe.com and click on **Chapter Overviews— Chapter 20** to preview chapter information.

What Is Demand?

Main Idea

You express your "demand" for a product when you are willing and able to purchase it.

Key Terms

demand, demand schedule, demand curve, law of demand, market demand, utility, diminishing marginal utility

Reading Strategy

Analyzing Information As you read the section, complete the diagrams below to illustrate the law of demand.

Prices	Quantity Demanded
Rise →	
Fall →	

Read to Learn

• What does it mean when demand rises or falls?

• What does the law of demand state?

Americans in Action

Why do some CDs cost more than others? Why does the price of video rentals go down when another video store opens in the neighborhood? One of the factors that has an effect on price is demand. A November 2001 news story discussed how demand and other factors affected the price of gas: "Among early holiday gifts this season is the lowest-priced gasoline in three years. Memo to consumers: Don't get used to it. The falling prices are a matter of supply and demand. Supplies are plentiful because petroleum-exporting countries can't agree to cut production and refineries have been humming. But demand is down because of the economic downturn in this country and abroad. Moreover, fears about terrorism have curtailed the appetite for travel. . . . But . . . prices will not remain low. They will climb again when demand increases or if production is scaled back."

Enjoying low gas prices

An Introduction to Demand

The story above illustrates a key feature of the American economy. In the United States, prices are set by demand and supply. To understand prices, you have to understand these two forces. We will study demand in this chapter, seeing how it affects price and why it changes. In the next chapter, we will study supply more closely. Then we will see how supply and demand work together to set prices.

What is demand? The word **demand** has a specific meaning in economics. It refers to the desire, willingness, and ability to buy a good or service. For demand to exist, a consumer must *want* a good or service. Second, the consumer has to *be willing* to buy that good or service. Finally, the consumer must *have the resources* available to buy it.

The Individual Demand Schedule

A demand schedule is a table that lists the various quantities of a product or service that someone is willing to buy over a range of possible prices. Look at the demand schedule on this page. It shows how many video games George would be willing to buy at different prices. For example, George would not purchase any video games if they cost $50 each. If the price were only $20 per game, though, he would be willing to buy two.

The Individual Demand Curve

Demand can also be shown graphically. A demand curve is a graph that shows the amount of a product that would be bought at all possible prices in the market. The curve is drawn with prices on the vertical axis and quantities on the horizontal axis. Each point on the curve shows how many units of the product or service an individual will buy at a particular price.

Look at the demand curve on this page. Notice that each point matches the quantity listed in the demand schedule. George would buy five video games if the price were $5 each, three games at $10 each, and so on.

The Law of Demand

Look at the graph again. As you see, demand curves usually slope downward because people are normally willing to buy less of a product if the price is high and more of it if the price is low. According to the law of demand, quantity demanded and price move in opposite directions.

Of course, this is just common sense. Think about your own buying habits. Aren't you more interested in buying more of something when the price is lower than when the price is higher?

Reading Check **Comparing** Describe the relationship between the demand schedule and the demand curve.

Individual vs. Market Demand

So far we have been looking at only one person's demand for a product or service. Companies hope to sell to many, many people, though. They have to take into account the demand of all those people. They are interested in the market demand—the total demand of all consumers for their product or service.

An Individual Buyer's Demand

Demand Schedule

Price	Quantity
$50	0
$40	1
$30	1
$20	2
$10	3
$5	5

DEMAND CURVE

Analyzing Graphs and Charts

Demand is illustrated on a schedule or a curve.
How many video games would George be willing to purchase at a price of $10 each?

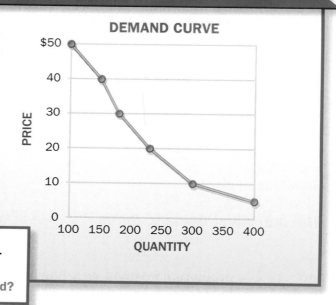

Demand Schedule	
Price	Total Quantity Demanded
$50	100
$40	150
$30	180
$20	230
$10	300
$5	400

Analyzing Graphs and Charts

The demand curve is the graphic representation of the law of demand. Why does the demand curve slope downward?

Market demand can also be shown as a demand schedule or as a demand curve. See the examples at the top of this page.

Demand Illustrated

A knowledge of demand is essential to understand how a market economy works. As you read in Chapter 18, in a market economy people and businesses act in their own best interests to answer the WHAT, HOW, and FOR WHOM questions of production. Knowledge of demand is also important for sound business planning.

To illustrate, imagine you are opening a bicycle repair shop. Before you begin, you need to know where the demand is. You will want to set up your shop in a neighborhood with many bicycle riders and few repair shops. After you identify an area in which to locate the shop, how do you measure the demand for your services? You may visit other shops and gauge the reactions of consumers to different prices. You may poll consumers about prices and determine demand from this data. You could study data compiled over past years, which would

show consumer reactions to higher and lower prices. All of these methods would give you a general idea as to the desire, willingness, and ability of people to pay.

Diminishing Marginal Utility

Almost everything that we buy provides utility, meaning the pleasure, usefulness, or satisfaction we get from using the product. The utility of a good or service may vary from one person to the next. For example, you may get a great deal of enjoyment from a home computer, but your friend may get very little. Your friend may love pepperoni pizza, but you may not. A good or service does not have to have utility for everyone, only utility for some.

The utility we get from consumption usually changes as we consume more of a particular product. For example, when eating pizza, you may be very hungry before you eat the first slice, and so it will give you the most satisfaction. Because you are not quite as hungry after consuming the first slice, you receive less *marginal utility,* or less *additional satisfaction,* from each additional slice that you eat. This illustrates **diminishing marginal utility**—the principle that our additional satisfaction, or our marginal utility, tends to go down as more and more units are consumed.

The concept of diminishing marginal utility helps explain why the demand curve in the figure on page 450 slopes downward. For example, when we buy something, we usually ask ourselves if the marginal utility we will get from a purchase is worth the money we have to give up to get it. This is exactly the type of cost-benefit analysis we examined in the last chapter. If the extra benefits (the marginal utility) to be gained are greater than the marginal cost (the money given up), then we make the purchase. If the additional benefits are less than the extra costs, we do not make the purchase and we keep the money instead.

Because our marginal utility diminishes when we consume more and more of a product, it stands to reason that we would not be as willing to pay as much for the second item as we did for the first. Likewise, we would not

be willing to pay as much for the third item as we did for the second. When the demand curve slopes downward, it simply tells us that we would be willing to pay the highest price for the first unit we consume, a slightly lower price for the next, and an even lower price for the third—and so on.

Reading Check **Comparing** What is the difference between individual demand and market demand?

SECTION 1 ASSESSMENT

Checking for Understanding

1. **Key Terms** Use each of these terms in a complete sentence that helps explain its meaning: demand, demand schedule, demand curve, law of demand, market demand, utility.

Reviewing Main Ideas

2. **Explain** What is the term for a line plotted on a graph showing the quantities demanded of a good or service at each possible price?

3. **Explain** According to the law of demand, what would happen in a situation in which the average price of concert tickets rose from $40 to $80?

Critical Thinking

4. **Making Predictions** You sell popcorn during your school's football games. Knowing that people usually buy more when the price is lower, how would you price your popcorn after halftime?

5. **Making Predictions** On a diagram like the one below, identify a relatively rare good or service today that you think will be in very high demand in 20 years. Provide at least two reasons for your prediction.

| Good or Service | Reason: |
| | Reason: |

Analyzing Visuals

6. **Interpret** Study the schedule and graph illustrating market demand on page 450. What is the quantity demanded at $30? What happens to total quantity demanded as the price increases?

★ **BE AN ACTIVE CITIZEN** ★

7. **Research** Interview a local merchant to determine the demand for a particular product over a specific period of time. Present your findings in graph form. Write a paragraph explaining what factors most affected demand for the product.

Factors Affecting Demand

MAIN IDEA
Several factors can cause demand to either increase or decrease.

Key Terms
substitute, complement, demand elasticity

Reading Strategy
Organizing Information As you read the section, complete a diagram like the one below by identifying six factors that affect demand.

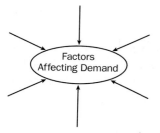

Factors Affecting Demand

Read to Learn
- **What does it mean when the demand curve shifts?**
- **What factors can cause a change in demand?**

Americans in Action

Many factors influence the demand for goods and services. One of these is changes in income. When your income goes up, you can afford to buy more goods and services. A TIME article described what happened in November 2001 when income fell: "Surveys find that households are planning to spend some $28 less than 2000's $490 average [on holiday presents]. . . . Retail Forward Inc. forecasts a drop of 1.5 percent in the season's sales of apparel, furniture, consumer electronics, and other general merchandise over last season's. . . . The reason for all the gloom and doom is obvious: Unemployment numbers are rising . . . and the current pop psychology says folks will be thinking more about spending time with friends and family than throwing a lot of money at them."

Buying fewer gifts
this year

Changes in Demand

The demand for any product or service is not the same over time. Sometimes people are willing to buy higher quantities of a product or service at a particular price. At other times they are less willing to do so. As a result, demand can go up or down.

Several factors cause market demand to change. Market demand can change when more consumers enter the market. Market demand can also change when the incomes, tastes, and expectations of the consumers in the market change. Finally, changes in the prices of related goods affect demand.

These changes can all be graphed using a market demand curve. When demand goes down, people are willing to buy fewer items at all possible prices (see the graph showing a decrease in demand on page 453). In this case, the demand curve shifts to the left. When demand goes up, people are willing to buy more of the same item at any given price. This pushes the entire demand curve to the right. Look at the graph on page 453 that shows an increase in demand.

Changes in the Number of Consumers

Demand for a good in a particular market area is related to the number of consumers in the area. The more consumers, the higher the demand; the fewer consumers, the lower the demand. Suppose a company puts up a new apartment building and the building is soon filled with families. These new residents begin to buy products and services from area businesses. As a result, demand for gasoline, food, and video rentals in this area will go up. In this case, the demand curve will shift to the right.

The same factor can cause a change in the opposite direction. When many people move out of an area, demand for goods and services goes down. Here the demand curve shifts to the left.

The number of consumers in a particular market area may change for a number of reasons. A higher birthrate, increased immigration, or the migration of people from one region to another increases the number of consumers. Factors such as a higher death rate or the migration of people out of a region can also cause the number of consumers to fall.

Changes in Consumers' Income

Demand also changes when consumers' income changes. When the economy is healthy, people receive raises or move to better-paying jobs. With more money to spend, they are willing to buy more of a product at any particular price.

Again, the opposite can happen, too. In economic hard times, people lose their jobs. They have less income to spend, and so demand goes down.

Changes in Consumers' Tastes

Changing tastes can affect demand as well. When a product becomes popular, perhaps through an advertising campaign, the demand curve shifts to the right. More people are willing to buy the product at a particular price. We often see this during the holiday shopping season when a new product becomes the "must-buy" of the year.

Many products, though, fade in popularity over time. When that happens, the demand curve shifts to the left. This shows that people are less willing to spend money on those products.

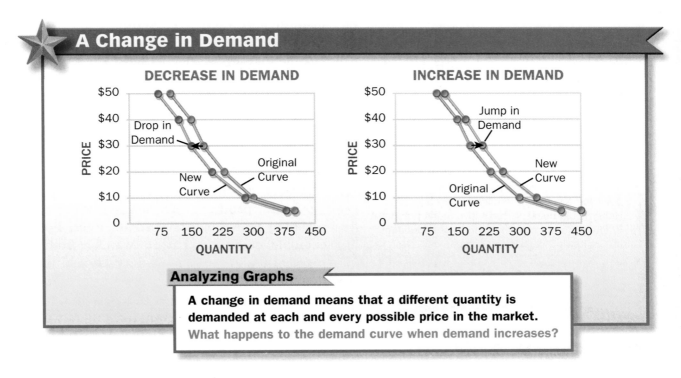

A Change in Demand

Analyzing Graphs

A change in demand means that a different quantity is demanded at each and every possible price in the market.
What happens to the demand curve when demand increases?

Changes in Consumers' Expectations

"Expectations" refers to the way people think about the future. For example, suppose that a leading maker of audio products announces a technological breakthrough that would allow more music to be recorded on a smaller disk at a lower cost than before. Even if the new product might not be available for another year, some consumers might decide to buy fewer music CDs today simply because they want to wait for the new product. Expectations also affected demand in the Americans in Action article that began this section. People were worried about hard times in late 2001. As a result, they were less willing to spend money on holiday gifts. The demand for goods was reduced.

Expectations can also force demand higher. If people expect a shortage of something, such as gasoline, demand increases. This shifts the demand curve to the right.

Changes in Substitutes

Demand can be influenced by changes in the price or quality of related products. The demand for older computers falls when new models with faster processors come out. The demand for a certain brand of tire may increase when another tire has safety problems.

Competing products are called substitutes because consumers can use one in place of the other. When two goods are substitutes, a change in the price of one good causes the demand for the other good to move in the *same* direction. For example, for many people, butter is a substitute for margarine. If the price of margarine increases, the demand for butter also increases (shifts to the right) as people substitute butter for the higher-priced margarine. Other examples of substitutes include coffee and tea, pens and pencils, and Ford cars and Chrysler cars.

Changes in Complements

Some products are **complements,** meaning that they are used together. For example, computers and software are complements. With complementary goods, the demand for one moves in the opposite direction as the price of the other. So if computer prices rise, fewer computers will

Beulah Louise Henry (1887–1973)

When asked why she designed so many new products, Beulah Henry declared, "I invent because I can't help it." Born in Memphis, Tennessee, in 1887, Henry came from a family of artists. However, instead of drawing landscapes or portraits, she sketched gadgets.

Henry went on to invent more than 100 items, earning 49 patents. For the home, she designed the first bobbinless sewing machine and a vacuum (sealed) ice cream maker. For the office, she created continuously attached envelopes for mass mailings and an early photocopier—a typewriter that made multiple copies without copier paper. For children, she invented the Kiddie Klock to teach time and a doll with a radio inside.

Henry became known as the "Lady Edison," after Thomas Alva Edison. Like Edison, Henry not only invented, she thought of innovative ways to market her products. If a new machine was needed to manufacture an item, she invented it. If she needed a company to produce the goods, she founded it. By age 37 Henry could boast, "I have inventions patented in four different countries, and I am president of two newly incorporated companies."

Elastic Demand A new car may be considered a luxury. Medicine is a necessity. **The demand for which of these two items is more likely to be elastic?**

be demanded, and the demand for computer software will go down. Because people are buying fewer new computers, they need less new software.

You can also see the same effect when the price goes down instead of up. When the price of DVD players goes down, more DVD players are demanded, which also results in an increase in the demand for DVDs. Other examples of complements (or complementary goods) include cars and gasoline, videotapes and VCRs, lightbulbs and lamps, and tennis rackets and tennis balls.

✓ Reading Check **Comparing** Are butter and margarine substitute goods? Why or why not?

Elasticity of Demand

The law of demand states that price and quantity demanded move in opposite directions. If price goes up, quantity demanded goes down; and if price goes down, quantity demanded goes up.

Now suppose price goes up from $1 to $1.25, a 25 percent rise. We know that quantity demanded will go down, but we don't know by how much. Quantity demanded could go down by 25 percent, by less than 25 percent, or by more than 25 percent.

All products and services are not affected by these factors in the same way. Economists call this phenomenon demand elasticity. **Demand elasticity** is the extent to which a change in price causes a change in the quantity demanded.

Elastic Demand

For some goods and services, demand is elastic. This means that each change in price causes a relatively larger percentage change in quantity demanded. For example, when automakers reduce car prices modestly, the quantity sold goes up greatly. When they raise the price of their cars, the quantity sold goes down a great deal.

When there are attractive substitutes for a good or service, demand tends to be elastic. That is because consumers can choose to buy the substitute. Expensive items generally have elastic demand. That is because consumers are less willing to pay even more for goods that are expensive in the first place. Finally, demand is usually elastic when a purchase can be postponed until later. In this case,

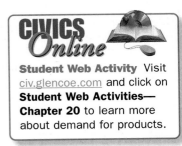

Student Web Activity Visit civ.glencoe.com and click on **Student Web Activities—Chapter 20** to learn more about demand for products.

Political Cartoons

"There's Only One Economic Indicator I Go By"

and it seems to be diverted toward money and time. Making the world a more convenient place to live was a collaboration among several

Analyzing Visuals To monitor the health of the economy, the government keeps track of a wide range of indicators. What is the cartoonist implying about the relationship between economic indicators and consumers' purchasing decisions?

consumers delay buying the good or service in the hopes that the price will go down.

Inelastic Demand

For other goods and services, demand is inelastic. This means that price changes have little effect on the quantity demanded. For example, the demand for turkey at Thanksgiving tends to be inelastic. Many people make turkey a central part of their Thanksgiving meal. If supermarkets slightly raise the price of turkey, they would probably not lose many customers. At another time of year, higher turkey prices might cause consumers to purchase other meat products instead.

The demand for goods with very few or no substitutes, like pepper, electricity, and some medicines, is likely to be inelastic. Heart medicine, for example, has relatively few substitutes; many people must have it to stay well. Even if the price of heart medicine doubled, quantity demanded probably would not fall by much.

Reading Check **Inferring** Why is the demand for insulin, a medicine for people with diabetes, inelastic?

SECTION 2 ASSESSMENT

Checking for Understanding

1. **Key Terms** Write a paragraph in which you use each of these terms correctly: substitute, complement, demand elasticity.

Reviewing Main Ideas

2. **Explain** How do we show on a demand curve an increase in the demand for a good?

3. **Describe** What is the term that describes the relationship between a change in price and the resulting change in the number sold?

Critical Thinking

4. **Making Generalizations** Will products that are very important to us and that have no close substitutes have elastic or inelastic demand?

5. **Understanding Cause and Effect** Create a chart like the one below to show how a change in the price of substitutes influences quantity demanded.

Price	Effect
Increases	
Decreases	

Analyzing Visuals

6. **Infer** Study the graphs showing change in demand on page 453. Would a decrease in income cause an increase or a decrease in demand? How would a decrease in the price of cameras affect the demand for film?

★ **BE AN ACTIVE CITIZEN** ★

7. **Research** Find an example of the law of demand or elasticity of demand in a newspaper or magazine article or advertisement. Share your findings with the class.

Reading a Line Graph

Why Learn This Skill?

What is the status of consumer demand for fuel-efficient automobiles? Is the labor market as strong this year as it was last year? Industries and governments routinely collect statistics that answer these kinds of questions. Such statistics are often arranged on line graphs. A line graph condenses a large amount of information into a visual format. Reading line graphs can help you make comparisons and trace trends.

Learning the Skill

To read a line graph, follow these steps:

- Read the title. The title of the graph tells you what kind of information the graph presents.
- Read the key. The key lists specific categories of data displayed. It also shows the symbol or device used to represent each category.
- Examine the labeling along the vertical and horizontal axes. Determine the area of information shown on each axis and determine how the graph grid is divided.
- Locate specific points where the line intersects with the grid. Identify the single fact indicated at that point.
- Look for relationships. Compare patterns among the different areas shown on the graph. Trace graph lines to identify trends over time.

Practicing the Skill

On a separate sheet of paper, answer the following questions about the line graph on this page.

1 What is the subject of this graph?
2 Into what three categories are the statistics grouped?
3 What information is shown along the vertical axis?

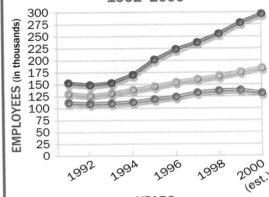

DEMAND FOR WORKERS IN MOTION PICTURE INDUSTRY, 1992–2000

- Production and Services
- Video Tape Rentals
- Theaters

4 In which sector of the motion picture industry was the demand for workers the lowest?
5 Did the overall demand for workers in the motion picture industry rise or fall in the 1990s?

Applying the Skill

Use newspapers or magazines to locate a line graph showing some current economic statistics. Record at least two specific points of information and one trend you note after reading the graph.

Practice key skills with Glencoe's **Skillbuilder Interactive Workbook CD-ROM, Level 1.**

Assessment & Activities

Review to Learn

Section 1

- You express demand for a product when you are both willing and able to purchase it.
- Demand can be summarized in a demand schedule.
- Demand can also be shown graphically in a downward-sloping demand curve.

Section 2

- A change in demand means that people have changed their minds about the amounts they would buy at each and every price.
- Change in consumer incomes, tastes, expectations, and the price of related goods causes a change in demand.
- Elasticity is a measure of responsiveness to an increase or a decrease in price.

Study Organizer

Using Your Foldables Study Organizer
After you have completed your foldable, pair up with a classmate. One person should name a factor that affects demand. The other person should describe how that factor affects demand. Take turns in the same manner until you have named all of the factors.

Reviewing Key Terms

Write the key term that best matches each definition below.

1. an economic rule stating that the quantity demanded and price move in opposite directions
2. the desire, willingness, and ability to buy a product
3. a product related to another product in such a way that an increase in the price of one reduces the demand for both
4. a downward-sloping graph that shows the quantities demanded at each possible price
5. a situation in which consumers demand different amounts at every price, causing the demand curve to shift to the left or right
6. a product that can be used in place of another product
7. a listing that shows the quantities demanded of a product at various prices
8. a situation in which the rise or fall in a product's price greatly affects the amount that people are willing to buy

Reviewing Main Ideas

9. What is the law of demand?
10. What does a demand curve show?
11. What happens to quantity demanded of a product when the price goes down?
12. How do we show in a graph an increase in the demand for a good?
13. What is the difference between elastic and inelastic demand?
14. What is the term for a good that is often used with another product?
15. Butter and margarine are substitutes. What happens to the demand for butter as the price of margarine rises?
16. What does it mean when a demand curve shifts to the right? To the left?

Critical Thinking

17. Summarizing Information Why is the demand for a product with many substitutes elastic?

18. Understanding Cause and Effect Recreate the diagram at right. Use arrows to indicate the direction of movement of the demand curve for the statements below.

- the demand curve for CDs if all wages increased by 20 percent
- the demand curve for chicken if the price of beef falls

Analyzing Visuals

Study the table below; then answer the following questions.

Price of Cassettes	Olivia	Gabriel	June	Market Demand
$1.00	9	6	1	16
$1.50	8	5	1	14
$2.00	7	4	0	11
$2.50	6	3	0	9
$3.00	5	2	0	7

19. At a price of $3, how many cassettes does each person demand?

20. Does the data suggest that, at lower prices, new demanders enter the market? Explain.

Practicing Skills

21. Reading a Line Graph Analyze the line graph on page 457. What are the three categories of workers shown? What category made up the largest number of motion picture workers in 2000? The smallest?

Self-Check Quiz Visit the *Civics Today* Web site at civ.glencoe.com and click on **Self-Check Quizzes— Chapter 20** to prepare for the chapter test.

$ Economics Activity

22. For each of the cases below, identify the factor that is causing demand to change.
- The demand for snow tires in Chicago increases when a weather forecast predicts a blizzard.
- The demand for tea decreases when the price of coffee falls.

★ CITIZENSHIP COOPERATIVE ACTIVITY ★

23. Working in a team of four, interview four students in the school, asking the following questions: Do any recent purchases represent a change in your buying habits? If so, what factors caused the change?

After completing the interviews, summarize your information and draw conclusions.

Standardized Test Practice

Directions: Choose the *best* answer to the following question.

When a demand curve shifts to the right, it means

F an increase in price will lower total revenue.

G the product has few substitutes.

H buyers are willing and able to buy more units of the good at all prices.

J buyers are willing and able to buy fewer units at all prices.

Test-Taking Tip
Read all the answer choices carefully before you select an answer.

Supply

★ CITIZENSHIP AND YOU ★

What roles do you play in the marketplace? You are a buyer, and you express your demand when you purchase a product. Do you have a part-time job? Do you do household chores for an allowance? By taking part in these activities, you are also a supplier. You are supplying an economic product—your labor—to buyers in the marketplace. Find three articles from newspapers that illustrate the concept of supply.

To learn more about the effect of supply and demand on prices, view the *Economics & You* video lesson 12: The Price System at Work.

Organizing Information Study Foldable *Make the following foldable to help you organize information about supply in a market economy.*

Step 1 *Fold a sheet of paper into thirds from top to bottom.*

Step 2 *Turn the paper horizontally, unfold, and label the three columns as shown.*

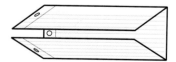

Reading and Writing *As you read the chapter, record your thoughts and the information you learn about supply in a market economy in the appropriate columns of your foldable.*

New technology in the auto industry helps workers produce more cars. ▶

CIVICS
Online

Chapter Overview Visit the *Civics Today* Web site at civ.glencoe.com and click on **Chapter Overviews—Chapter 21** to preview chapter information.

What Is Supply?

GUIDE TO READING

Main Idea
For almost any good or service, the higher the price, the larger the quantity that will be offered for sale.

Key Terms
supply, law of supply, supply schedule, supply curve, profit, market supply

Reading Strategy
Organizing Information Draw the diagrams shown below. As you read this section, complete the diagrams by adding arrows to indicate increase or decrease to the Quantity Supplied bar.

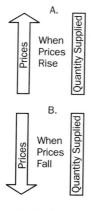

A.
Prices | When Prices Rise | Quantity Supplied

B.
Prices | When Prices Fall | Quantity Supplied

Read to Learn
• What does the law of supply state?
• What is the difference between a supply schedule and a supply curve?

Americans in Action

Just as a coin has two sides, so does a market. A coin has heads and tails; a market has a buying side and a selling side. The buying side is relevant to what is called demand, and the selling side is relevant to what is called supply. A *Philadelphia Inquirer* story discussed how supply affected price in the spring of 2001: "Retail beef prices are soaring—reaching a record $3.21 a pound for USDA-choice cuts . . . because of a harsh Plains winter that has been tough on cattle. Prices are likely to dip by the summer, but then rebound because of tight cattle supplies. Producers are only starting to rebuild herds that they had thinned because of drought and low prices in the late 1990s. The winter has been so cold and damp that cattle are taking several months longer than usual to fatten."

The supply of goods, like meat, affects prices.

An Introduction to Supply

In the previous chapter, you read about one of the major forces that contributes to setting prices in our economy. That force was consumers' demand for goods and services. There is another major force at work, called supply. As you can see from the Americans in Action feature above, a low supply of beef led to high prices in early 2001.

Exploring Supply and Demand

What is supply? Supply refers to the various quantities of a good or service that producers are willing to sell at all possible market prices. Supply normally refers to the output of a single business or producer. However, as in the case of demand, it is also possible to add the supply of all producers together to get the supply for the entire market.

Supply is the opposite of demand. Buyers demand different quantities of a good depending on the price that sellers ask. Suppliers offer different quantities of a product depending on the price that buyers are willing to pay.

462 Chapter 21 Supply

The Law of Supply

Remember that the law of demand states that the quantity demanded varies according to price. As the price rises for a good, the quantity demanded goes down. As the price of a good goes down, the quantity demanded rises.

The quantity supplied also varies according to price—but in the opposite direction. As the price rises for a good, the quantity supplied rises. As the price falls, the quantity supplied also falls. This is the law of supply, the principle that suppliers will normally offer more for sale at higher prices and less at lower prices. The higher the price of a good, the greater the incentive is for a producer to produce more. The producer will expect to make a higher profit because of the higher price. The profit incentive is one of the factors that motivates producers in a market economy.

We can represent the law of supply with numbers, just as we did with the law of demand. The table at the bottom of this page shows such a relationship. As the price goes up from $5 to $10 to $20 and to $50, the quantity supplied goes up from 1 to 10 to 30 and to 100. A numerical chart, like this one, that illustrates the law of supply is called a supply schedule.

The Individual Supply Curve

We can also illustrate the law of supply with a graph. A supply curve is a graph that shows the amount of a product that would be supplied at all possible prices in the market. Like the demand curve, the supply curve graph is drawn with prices on the vertical axis and quantities on the horizontal axis. In the supply curve on this page, the quantities are the amounts of the good or service that the business will supply. The supply curve tells us that the company is willing to sell 100 video games at a price of $50, 90 at $40, 70 at $30, and so on.

Unlike the demand curve, the supply curve slopes upward. This reflects the fact that suppliers are generally willing to offer more goods and services at a higher price and fewer at a lower price.

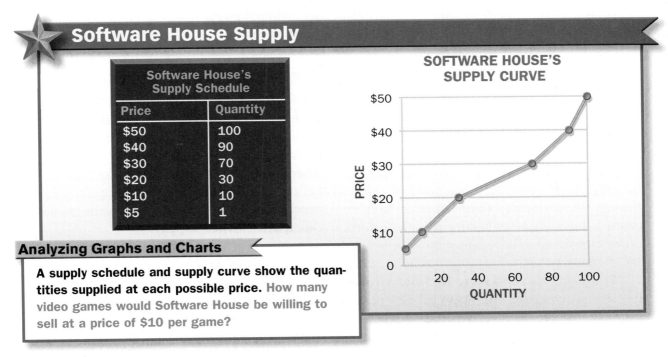

Software House Supply

Software House's Supply Schedule

Price	Quantity
$50	100
$40	90
$30	70
$20	30
$10	10
$5	1

SOFTWARE HOUSE'S SUPPLY CURVE

Analyzing Graphs and Charts

A supply schedule and supply curve show the quantities supplied at each possible price. How many video games would Software House be willing to sell at a price of $10 per game?

Market Supply

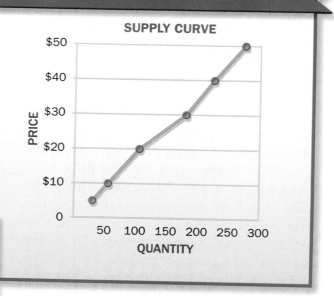

Supply Schedule	
Price	Total Quantity Supplied
$50	275
$40	225
$30	180
$20	105
$10	55
$5	30

SUPPLY CURVE

Analyzing Graphs and Charts

The market supply curve shows the quantities offered at various prices by all firms in a given market. What is the relationship between the price of a good and the quantity supplied?

The Profit Motive

Businesses invest time, money, and other capital resources in order to make money. The desire to cover costs and to earn profits explains why businesses wish to sell their goods and services at higher prices. Businesses try to set prices at a level that allows them to cover their costs. If they do not, they will lose money.

In our economy, businesses provide goods and services hoping to make a profit. Profit is the money a business receives for its products or services over and above its costs. If it costs Software House $40 to make a video game and it sells the game for $40, the company gains nothing from the sale. Like most people, though, the company wants to make some money. That requires selling the game for more than $40. The additional money is the owner's profit.

Producers can choose to use their profits in many different ways. They can increase wages they pay their workers. They can invest the money back into the

business to acquire more space, buy new equipment, or hire new workers. They can also keep the money for themselves. Whatever profits are used for, earning them is a primary goal for business owners in our economy.

Reading Check **Defining** What is supply?

Graphing Market Supply

Recall that when you studied demand in Chapter 20, you looked at the total of all consumers' demand. This concept is called the market demand. You will do the same thing when you study supply. If you combine the supply schedules of all the businesses that provide the same good or service, the total is called the market supply.

An Upward Slope

The figure on this page shows the market supply for video games in one community. Notice that the market supply for all producers is larger than the supply for Software

House alone. (Compare the graphs on pages 463 and 464.) Still, the market supply curve has the same shape as in the individual supply curve. The upward slope shows that all of the producers in the market would prefer to sell more video games at higher prices and fewer games at lower prices.

The Influence of Price

When constructing a supply curve, keep in mind that the price is the most significant influence on the quantity supplied of any product. For example, you are offering your services for sale when you look for a job. Your economic product is your labor, and you would probably be willing to supply more labor for a high wage, or price, than you would for a low one.

Other Factors

However, other factors can and do affect supply. The supply curve is drawn assuming that these and other things are fixed and do not change. If any of these factors does change, a change in supply will occur—the entire supply curve will shift. You will read more about change in supply in the next section.

TIME

Political Cartoons

and it seems to be diverted toward money and time. Making the world a more convenient place to live was a collaboration among several

Analyzing Visuals Business owners always need to be aware of the relationship between supply and demand. Why is the store holding a sale?

✓ Reading Check **Explaining** How is market supply determined?

SECTION 1 ASSESSMENT

Checking for Understanding

1. **Key Terms** Write a paragraph related to supply using these key terms: supply, law of supply, supply schedule, supply curve, profit, market supply.

Reviewing Main Ideas

2. **Explain** What does the law of supply state?

3. **Compare** Describe the difference between the supply curve and the supply schedule. What do the supply curve and the supply schedule show?

Critical Thinking

4. **Cause and Effect** How does the incentive of greater profits affect the quantity supplied?

5. **Organizing Information** Create a graph by plotting the information shown on the supply schedule below.

Price (dollars)	Quantity Supplied (units)
$1	10
2	20
3	30
4	40

Analyzing Visuals

6. **Interpret** Study the individual supply schedule and curve on page 463. How many video games will be supplied at a price of $30?

★ **BE AN ACTIVE CITIZEN** ★

7. **Research** Clip articles from newspapers or magazines that show the law of supply in operation. Discuss your clippings in class.

Factors Affecting Supply

GUIDE TO READING

Main Idea

Several factors can cause supply to either increase or decrease.

Key Terms

productivity, technology, subsidy, supply elasticity

Reading Strategy

Organizing Information
As you read the section, complete a diagram like the one below by identifying six factors that can lead to a change in market supply.

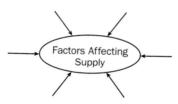

Factors Affecting Supply

Read to Learn

- What are the factors that can change supply?
- What is supply elasticity?

Americans in Action

As you've learned, consumers demand products and services at the lowest possible prices. In contrast, suppliers, like Wal-Mart, exist to make a profit. *U.S. News & World Report* discussed the actions other suppliers had to take to compete with Wal-Mart: "Retailers also have to keep prices low to compete against Wal-Mart, the world's biggest merchant. 'They make the supply chain so efficient that it cuts costs,' says [economist Frank Badillo]. Last week, for example, Wal-Mart said it wouldn't use a particular Visa debit-card system because transaction fees had been increased. Wal-Mart passes on such savings to consumers, who then expect the same from the competition. So the likes of Target, Kmart, Sears, Kohl's, and department stores duke it out to woo consumers."

Suppliers compete with one another for customers.

Changes in Supply

Remember that demand does not stay the same over time. When consumers' situations change—or as the economy changes—demand increases or decreases. It probably is not surprising to hear that the same is true with supply. Supply can increase or decrease, depending on many different factors.

In order for a change in supply to take place, producers must decide to offer a different quantity of output at each possible price in the market. This might happen for a number of reasons—changes in the cost of production, in government policies, in the number of producers, or in the expectations of businesses.

When supply goes down, the supply curve moves to the left. When supply goes up, the supply curve is pushed to the right. In this case, suppliers are willing to sell a larger quantity of goods and services at lower prices. You can see these changes in the figure on page 468. Now let us look at what can cause supply to change.

Changes in the Cost of Resources

Earlier, you learned how four resources, or factors of production, are used to produce goods and services. When these resource prices fall, sellers are willing and able to produce and offer to sell more of the good. The supply curve shifts to the right. The reason for this is that it is cheaper to produce the good.

When resource prices rise, sellers are less able to produce and sell the same quantities of the good. The supply curve shifts to the left, because it is more expensive to produce the good.

Productivity

One way businesses can cut costs—and increase profits—is by improving productivity. Productivity is the degree to which resources are being used efficiently to produce goods and services. Most of the news you will hear about productivity concerns labor. When workers are more efficient—when they produce more output in the same amount of time—a company's costs go down. The result is that more products are produced at every price, which shifts the supply curve to the right. When productivity falls, it costs more for a company to produce the same amount of goods and services. In this case, the supply curve will shift to the left.

Technology

Costs are also affected by technology. Technology refers to the methods or processes used to make goods and services. New technology can speed up ways of doing things. At many stores, cashiers use scanners to register the prices of goods that customers are buying. These scanners do more than speed up checkout. They also automatically track the number of units that the store has sold and how many are left on the shelf. As a result, store managers quickly know when they need to reorder a product. This is faster than having workers count all the goods on the store's shelves.

Technology often can cut a business's costs. This pushes the supply curve to the right, showing that the business is willing to supply more at the same price.

Technology New computer technology has greatly increased productivity. **What effect does improved technology usually have on supply?**

A Change in Supply

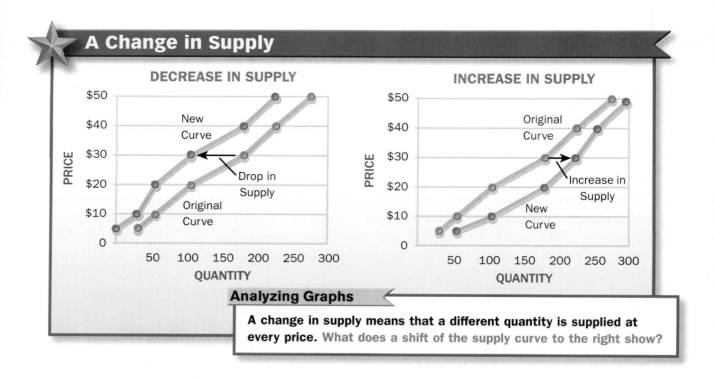

DECREASE IN SUPPLY

New Curve

Original Curve

Drop in Supply

PRICE — $50, $40, $30, $20, $10, 0

QUANTITY — 50 100 150 200 250 300

INCREASE IN SUPPLY

Original Curve

New Curve

Increase in Supply

PRICE — $50, $40, $30, $20, $10, 0

QUANTITY — 50 100 150 200 250 300

Analyzing Graphs

A change in supply means that a different quantity is supplied at every price. What does a shift of the supply curve to the right show?

Changes in Government Policies

Actions by the government can affect supply as well. Suppose that the government passes a law requiring that fast-food restaurants pay all workers $10 an hour. The restaurants—faced with higher labor costs—might then decide to lay off some workers. The fewer workers who remain would produce fewer hamburgers, resulting in a decrease in supply.

When the government establishes new regulations, the cost of production can be affected, causing a change in supply. For example, when the government orders new safety features for automobiles, such as air bags or emissions controls, autos cost more to produce. Auto manufacturers adjust to the higher production costs by producing fewer cars at each and every price in the market.

In general, increased—or tighter—government regulations restrict supply, causing the supply curve to shift to the left. Relaxed regulations allow producers to lower the cost of production, which results in a shift of the supply curve to the right.

Changes in Taxes and Subsidies

Tax laws also affect businesses. To businesses, taxes are a cost. Higher taxes mean higher costs, pushing the supply curve to the left. Lower taxes—lower costs—move the supply curve to the right. This increases the amount of a good or service supplied at each and every price.

A **subsidy** is a government payment to an individual, business, or other group for certain actions. Suppose the government subsidizes the production of corn by paying farmers $2 for every bushel of corn. The subsidy lowers the cost of production and encourages current producers to remain in the market and new producers to enter. When subsidies are repealed, costs go up, producers leave the market, and the supply curve shifts to the left.

Finally, the expectations of producers affect supply as well. If businesses believe that consumer demand will not be very high in the near future, they will produce less of their products. This cuts down on the supply. On the other hand, if they expect demand to go up, they will produce more at all possible prices. This is the reason that stores stock up on swimsuits as summer nears. They expect that consumers will want to buy more of these garments at that time of the year.

A change in the number of the suppliers causes a change in market supply. As more firms enter an industry, the supply curve shifts to the right. In other words, the larger the number of suppliers, the greater the market supply. If some suppliers leave the market, supply decreases, shifting the curve to the left.

Elasticity of Supply

Like demand, supply can be elastic or inelastic. **Supply elasticity** is a measure of how the quantity supplied of a good or service changes in response to changes in price. If the quantity changes a great deal when prices go up or down, the product is said to be supply elastic. If the quantity changes very little, the supply is inelastic.

Supply elasticity depends on how quickly a company can change the amount of a product it makes in response to price changes. Oil is supply inelastic. When oil prices go up, oil companies cannot quickly find a new site with oil, dig a new well, build a pipeline to move the oil, and build a refinery to turn it into gasoline. The same is true of other products that require producers to invest large sums of money in order to produce them.

The supply curve is likely to be elastic, however, for kites, candy, and other products that can be made quickly without huge amounts of capital and skilled labor. If consumers are willing to pay twice the price for any of these products, most producers will be able to gear up quickly to increase production.

✓**Reading Check** **Explaining** What is supply elasticity?

SECTION 2 ASSESSMENT

Checking for Understanding

1. **Key Terms** Write a paragraph about supply in which you use all of the following terms: productivity, technology, subsidy, supply elasticity.

Reviewing Main Ideas

2. **Explain** In which direction does the supply curve shift when supply decreases? In which direction does the supply curve shift when supply increases?

3. **Explain** What determines whether a business's supply curve is elastic or inelastic? Is supply elastic or inelastic in a situation in which the price of books rises 10 percent and the quantity supplied rises 15 percent?

Critical Thinking

4. **Making Generalizations** Why does new technology shift the supply curve to the right?

5. **Understanding Cause and Effect** Complete a table like the one below to explain how supply would be affected—would it increase or decrease in these situations?

Cause	Effect on Supply
The cost of a product's basic raw materials goes down.	
Government offers tax incentives to your company.	

Analyzing Visuals

6. **Identify** Describe what the two graphs on page 468 are showing. Which of the graphs more accurately illustrates a situation in which the number of firms in an industry increases?

★**BE AN ACTIVE CITIZEN**★

7. **Analyze** Contact the foreign language teachers in your school to see if they have any advertising material from other countries. Even without translating the language, can you understand the purpose of the advertisement? Write several paragraphs describing how marketing in other countries differs from our ads.

Using a Computerized Card Catalog

Why Learn This Skill?

Libraries contain an overwhelming amount of information. Going to the library to find information or to check out a certain book usually means using the card catalog to help you narrow your search. The card catalog lists all the book titles, periodicals, recordings, and other publications the library offers. Modern libraries store their card catalogs in computer databases.

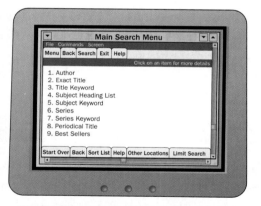

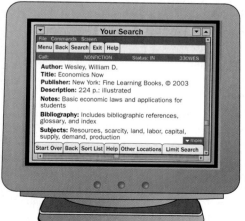

[book on call screen not an actual publication]

Learning the Skill

Using a computerized card catalog makes it easy to find any information you need for a term paper or a research project. The following guidelines will help you get started in your search for information.

- Type in a subject heading, or the name of an author, or the title of a book, videotape, audiocassette, or CD.
- The computer will list on screen the subject, author, or title you requested.
- The "card" that appears on screen also lists other important information. Use this information to determine if the material meets your needs.
- Check to see if the material is available. Find the classification and call number under which it is shelved.
- Ask a librarian for help if needed.

Practicing the Skill

Study the computerized card catalog screens to the left. Then answer the following questions.

1. Your research topic is "supply and demand." Which options might you select from the Main Search Menu?
2. You narrow your search to a book titled *Economics Now*. How do you know this title will be of help to you?
3. Why might you use the "Author" search option on the Main Search Menu?

Applying the Skill

Select a topic from this chapter. Search your topic on a computerized card catalog. Jot down two titles and explain why you think they would be useful.

Markets and Prices

GUIDE TO READING

Main Idea
Supply and demand work together to determine market price.

Key Terms
surplus, shortage, equilibrium price

Reading Strategy
Understanding Cause and Effect As you read the section, complete a diagram like the one below by describing three advantages of using prices to distribute goods and services.

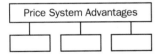

Price System Advantages

Read to Learn
- How do demand and supply work together to determine price?
- How do shortages and surpluses affect price?

Americans in Action

The profit incentive is one of the factors that motivates people in a market economy. In the case of supply, the higher the price of a good, the greater the incentive is for a producer to produce more. This ABC News story describes what actions oil-producing nations of the Middle East took when prices tumbled: "The Organization of Petroleum Exporting Countries [OPEC] is an 11-nation cartel of oil-producing countries. It once controlled 70 percent of the world's oil production. And OPEC is powerful—with enough clout to resist American pressure for a large increase in oil production that would lead to lower consumer prices for oil products. In addition, OPEC's refusal to produce as much as the U.S. wants is much about OPEC acting in its own self-interest, some Wall Street analysts say. . . . American motorists now pay an average of $1.59 per gallon for unleaded gasoline, an increase of nearly 60 cents since prices bottomed out at 99.8 cents per gallon in February 1999, according to a survey of 10,000 U.S. gas stations released Saturday. Industry analysts warn of possible shortages and gas prices at $2 a gallon during the peak driving season this summer."

Oil suppliers

Supply and Demand at Work

In 2001 the oil producers who made up OPEC felt that demand was too low and supply too high. As a result, their oil was selling for less than they wanted. Their action of cutting supply shows how supply and demand work together in the market to set price.

As you learned earlier, a market is any place or mechanism where buyers and sellers of a good or service can get together to exchange that good or service. For example, people who want to buy corn might go to a farmers' market or a supermarket. Someone who wants to buy stock might use a computer to purchase it from a stock market. In each case, markets bring buyers and sellers together.

★ The Price Adjustment Process

Price	Total Quantity Demanded	Total Quantity Supplied
$50	100	275
$40	150	225
$30	180	180
$20	230	105
$10	300	55
$5	400	30

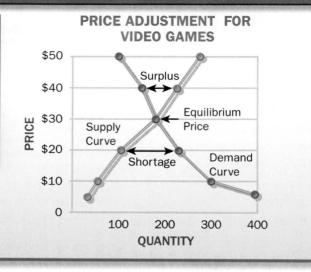

PRICE ADJUSTMENT FOR VIDEO GAMES

Analyzing Graphs and Charts

A supply curve can be combined with a demand curve to analyze the price adjustment process. At what price does quantity demanded equal quantity supplied?

The forces of supply and demand, as we saw in the feature, work together in markets to establish prices. In our economy, prices form the basis for economic decisions.

The Price Adjustment Process

Markets consist of all buyers and sellers of a product. To see how supply and demand work together, we need to combine the supply and demand curves. Look at the graph on this page. It shows the market demand curve for video games from Chapter 20 and the market supply curve for those games (from page 464).

Surplus

Suppose we start by watching how buyers and sellers react to a price of $40 in this market for video games. The graph shows that sellers will supply 225 video games to the market at this price. Buyers, however, are willing to buy only 150 games at $40 each. This leaves a surplus of 75 video games.

A **surplus** is the amount by which the quantity supplied is higher than the quantity demanded. The surplus also appears as the horizontal distance between the supply

and demand curves at any point above where the demand and supply curves intersect. A surplus signals that the price is too high. Consumers are unwilling to pay the price in large enough numbers to satisfy producers. If the market is competitive, this surplus will not exist for long. Sellers will have to lower their price if they want to sell their goods.

Shortage

What if the price had been $20? Look at the graph again. At this price, suppliers offer only 105 video games for sale. Consumers, though, are willing to buy 230 games. This difference is a shortage. A **shortage** is the amount by which the quantity demanded is higher than the quantity supplied. The shortage is shown as the horizontal distance between the two curves at any price below the point where demand and supply cross.

A shortage signals that the price is too low. In this situation, suppliers are unwilling to sell their goods or services in large enough numbers to meet all the demand. If the market is competitive, the shortage will not last. The price will have to rise.

Market Forces

One of the benefits of the market economy is that it eliminates shortages and surpluses when it operates without restriction. Over time, a surplus forces the price down and a shortage forces the price up. This goes on until supply and demand are balanced. The point where they achieve balance is the equilibrium price. At this price, there is neither a surplus nor a shortage. In the figure on page 472, the equilibrium price for video games is $30.

Once the market price reaches equilibrium, it will tend to stay there until either supply or demand changes. Once that happens, the market will have a temporary surplus or shortage. If there is a surplus, the price will be driven down. If there is a temporary shortage, the price will be driven up. The price will move in this way until the market establishes a new equilibrium price.

Price Controls

Occasionally the government sets the price of a product because it believes that the forces of supply and demand are unfair. When this happens, the new price may favor either consumers or producers.

A price ceiling is a government-set maximum price that can be charged for goods and services. For example, city officials might set a price ceiling on what landlords may charge for rent. A price floor is a government minimum price that can be charged for goods and services. Price floors—more common than price ceilings—prevent prices from dropping too low. The minimum wage, the lowest legal wage that can be paid to most workers, is a price floor.

Reading Check **Explaining** If the price of a product is above its equilibrium price, what is the result?

Jeffrey Bezos (1964–)

In 1994 Jeff Bezos left a secure job to jump into e-commerce—the buying and selling of goods over the Internet. With use of the Internet growing at 2,300 percent in a one-year period, he asked, "OK, what kind of business opportunity might there be here?"

Bezos decided to open the world's biggest online book-store—Amazon.com. Since 1995, he has added other products—CDs, videos, pots and pans, auctions, and more. As the 2000s opened, Amazon.com had become one of the leading e-tailers—online retailers or merchants.

People who know Bezos are not surprised by his success. Born in Albuquerque, New Mexico, Bezos learned to work hard on his grandfather's Texas cattle ranch. After moving to Florida, he graduated as valedictorian from a Miami high school. He then went on to Princeton University, where he majored in computer science.

Does Bezos think e-commerce will prosper? Yes, he says. Just like the Industrial Revolution reshaped the nineteenth century, he believes Internet commerce will reshape the century in which we now live.

Prices as Signals

The different parts of the economy need a system of signals so they can work smoothly together. In our economy, prices are signals. They help businesses and consumers make decisions. Prices also help answer the basic economic questions—WHAT to produce, HOW to produce, and FOR WHOM to produce.

For example, consumers' purchases help producers decide WHAT to produce. They focus on providing the goods and services that consumers are willing to buy at prices that allow the suppliers to earn profits. A company will make video games as long as consumers are willing to buy them at a price that generates profits. If consumers aren't willing to pay that price, the company won't be willing to make video games.

Prices also help businesses and consumers decide the question of HOW to produce. Suppose it costs a hair salon $20 in labor and supplies to provide a haircut. Consumers, though, are willing to pay only $15 for the haircut. To stay in business, the salon needs to find less costly ways of providing that haircut. That way, it can afford to meet the price consumers are willing to pay.

Finally, prices help businesses and consumers decide the question of FOR WHOM to produce. Some businesses aim their goods or services at the small number of consumers who are willing to pay higher prices. Other businesses aim their goods or services at the larger number of people who want to spend less.

Advantages of Prices

You know that consumers look for the best values for what they spend, while producers seek the best price and profit for what they have to sell. The information that prices provide allows people to work together to produce more of the things that people want.

Without prices, the economy would not run as smoothly, and decisions about allocating goods and services would have to be made some other way. Prices do a good job answering the questions of WHAT, HOW, and FOR WHOM to produce.

Prices Are Neutral First, prices in a competitive market economy are neutral because they favor neither the producer nor the consumer. Prices are the result of competition between buyers and sellers. In this way, prices represent compromises with which both sides can live. The more competitive the market is, the more efficient the price adjustment process.

Prices Are Flexible Second, prices in a market economy are flexible. Unforeseen events such as war and natural disasters affect the supply and demand for items. Buyers and sellers react to the new level of prices and adjust their consumption and production accordingly. Before long, the system functions as smoothly as it had before. The ability of the price system to absorb unexpected "shocks" is one of the strengths of a market economy.

Prices and Freedom of Choice Third, the price system provides for freedom of choice. Because a market economy typically provides a variety of products at a wide range of prices, consumers have many choices. If the price is too high, a lower-priced product can usually be found. Even if a suitable alternative cannot be found, no one forces the consumer to pay a certain price for a product in a competitive market economy.

In command economies, such as those found in Cuba and North Korea, consumers face limited choices. Government planners determine the total quantity of goods produced—the number of radios, cars, toasters, and so on. The government then limits the product's variety to keep production costs down. Items such as food, transportation, and housing are offered to citizens at artificially low prices, but seldom are enough produced to satisfy everyone. Many people go without.

Prices Are Familiar Finally, prices are something that we have known about all our lives—they are familiar and easily understood. There is no ambiguity over a price—if something costs $4.99, then we know exactly what we have to pay for it. This allows people to make decisions quickly and efficiently.

CIVICS Online

Student Web Activity Visit civ.glencoe.com and click on **Student Web Activities— Chapter 21** to learn more about supply of products.

✓**Reading Check** **Explaining** What signal does a high price send to buyers and sellers?

SECTION 3 ASSESSMENT

Checking for Understanding

1. Key Terms Write short paragraphs about price using these terms: surplus, shortage, equilibrium price.

Reviewing Main Ideas

2. Explain What is the point called at which the quantity demanded of a product and the quantity supplied meet?

3. Explain What causes prices to rise—a shortage or a surplus of a good or service?

Critical Thinking

4. Drawing Conclusions If a firm charges a price below the equilibrium price, will the price go up or down? Explain.

5. Understanding Cause and Effect Create a diagram like the one below to show how shortages and surpluses affect prices of goods and services.

Shortage: → Impact on Prices ← Surplus:

Analyzing Visuals

6. Infer Study the graph of the price adjustment process on page 472. Does a price of $40 result in a surplus or a shortage? What is the equilibrium price?

★**BE AN ACTIVE CITIZEN**★

7. Research Compare the prices of a product at three stores. What do the individual prices tell you about the equilibrium price for the product?

Assessment & Activities

Review to Learn

Section 1

- Supply is the willingness and ability to provide goods and services at different prices.
- As the price rises for a good, the quantity supplied also rises. As the price falls, the quantity supplied falls.

Section 2

- A change in supply is a change in the quantity that will be supplied at each and every price.
- Several factors can result in a change in market supply.

Section 3

- In free enterprise systems, prices serve as signals to consumers and producers. Prices help decide the WHAT, HOW, and FOR WHOM questions.

FOLDABLES™
Study Organizer

Using Your Foldables Study Organizer
After you have completed your foldable, pair up with a classmate. One person should name a factor that affects supply. The other person should describe how that factor affects supply. Take turns in the same manner until you have named all of the factors.

Reviewing Key Terms

Write the key term that best matches each definition below.

1. result when the quantity demanded is greater than the quantity supplied
2. price when the amount producers are willing to supply is equal to the amount consumers are willing to buy
3. result when the quantity supplied is greater than quantity demanded
4. a government payment to encourage or protect a certain economic activity
5. the amount of a good or service that producers are able and willing to sell at various prices
6. graph showing the quantities supplied at each possible price
7. table showing quantities supplied at different possible prices
8. a measure of how the quantity of a good or service produced changes in relation to changes in price

Reviewing Main Ideas

9. How does the price of a product affect the quantity offered for sale?
10. How does supply differ from demand?
11. Why does the supply curve slope upward and to the right?
12. List the factors that can cause an increase or decrease in supply.
13. How is the equilibrium price determined?
14. What effect does a shortage have on the price of goods and services?
15. What would an increase in taxes do to the position of the supply curve?
16. If the price of a product is above its equilibrium price, what is the result?
17. How does the price system provide for freedom of choice?

Critical Thinking

18. Making Generalizations Some people argue that an equilibrium price is not a fair price. Explain why you agree or disagree with this statement.

19. Categorizing Information Suppose that you own a store that sells shoes. On a diagram like the one below, identify three different things you could do to try to increase the demand for your product.

Increased Sales

Analyzing Visuals

20. Reproduce the diagram below. Draw arrows indicating the direction of movement of the supply curve—and the new supply curve—for each of the following:

- The supply curve for television sets if the price of raw materials used in making TVs falls.

- The supply curve for television sets after the government cuts taxes on sales of TVs.

Practicing Skills

21. Using a Computerized Card Catalog Reread the paragraphs under Learning the Skill on page 470. Then use a library computerized card catalog to research and produce a brochure on market demand. Select one product. Trace how the product was introduced and how the market reacted to it.

 Economics Activity

22. What do merchants usually do to move items that are overstocked? What does this tell you about the equilibrium price for the product?

★ CITIZENSHIP COOPERATIVE ACTIVITY ★

23. Working in teams of five, compare the prices of a single brand of one of these products at four different stores: orange juice, coffee, chicken soup, frozen pizza, and flour. Calculate the unit price of each brand, and choose the brand that is the better buy for each food product. Share your findings with your team and then with the class as a whole.

The Princeton Review

Standardized Test Practice

Directions: Choose the *best* answer to the following question.

What will happen to prices when the supply of a product increases and demand is inelastic?

A Prices will rise markedly.
B Prices will fall markedly.
C Prices rise slightly.
D There is no effect on prices.

Test-Taking Tip

This question requires you to understand the economic concepts of *supply, demand,* and *elasticity.* If you have trouble answering the question, review these concepts, then try again.

Business and Labor

★ CITIZENSHIP AND YOU ★

In the United States, many important decisions are made by economic institutions. Do you work at a business? Participate in a club? Chances are these businesses and economic institutions play a significant role in your life.

To learn more about how business organizations and economic institutions operate, view the *Economics & You* video lesson 4: Business Organizations.

FOLDABLES™
Study Organizer

Know-Want-Learn Study Foldable *Make this foldable to help you organize what you know, what you want to know, and what you learn about business and labor.*

Step 1 *Fold two sheets of paper in half from top to bottom. Cut the papers in half along the folds.*

Cut along the fold lines.

Step 2 *Fold each of the four papers in half from top to bottom.*

Step 3 *On each folded paper, make a cut 1 inch from the side on the top flap.*

1"

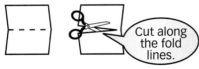

Cut 1 inch from the edge through the top flap only.

Step 4 *Place the folded papers one on top of the other. Staple the four sections together and label the top three tabs: Types of Businesses, Labor Unions, and Business in Our Economy.*

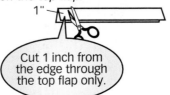

Staple here. *Types of Businesses*

Reading and Writing *Before reading the chapter, write what you already know about the types of businesses, labor unions, and businesses in our economy under the tabs of your foldable. Also write one question you have on each tab. As you read, summarize what you learn under each tab.*

Running a business involves risks as well as expectations. ▶

Civics Online

Chapter Overview Visit the *Civics Today* Web site at civ.glencoe.com and click on **Chapter Overviews— Chapter 22** to preview chapter information.

SECTION 1

Types of Businesses

GUIDE TO READING

Main Idea

Sole proprietorships, partnerships, and corporations are the three common forms of business organizations.

Key Terms

sole proprietorship, unlimited liability, financial capital, partnership, articles of partnership, corporation, charter, stock, stockholder, board of directors, limited liability, double taxation, cooperative

Reading Strategy

Classifying Information
As you read the section, complete a diagram like the one below by identifying at least two real-life examples in each of the categories.

Sole Proprietorship	⟶
Partnership	⟶
Corporation	⟶

Read to Learn

- What are the different ways in which businesses are organized?
- What are the advantages and disadvantages of each type of business organization?

★ ★ ★ ★

Americans in Action

Almost every day of your life you come into contact with some kind of business. Businesses can be organized in a number of ways. Some are corporations, while others are small companies, owned and operated by one individual or by a few people. The small business remains the main economic force in many American communities: "Small businesses employ the bulk of the workers in New Orleans and spell the future of the area economy, a local economist said. . . . In his latest study, Timothy Ryan, dean of the University of New Orleans College of Business, found that over the past decade, there had been a 36 percent increase in the number of businesses that employ fewer than 100 employees. The number of firms with more than 100 employees had declined by 6.4 percent. . . . But, the bulk of the growth has been in sole proprietorships, which are up 74.6 percent. . . ."

—The *Times-Picayune* (New Orleans), June 21, 2001

A small restaurant in New Orleans

Proprietorships

It is one thing to dream about running your own business, but it is something quite different to actually do it. Many people think of business ownership in terms of independence, freedom, and profits. They tend to overlook competition, responsibility, and the possibility of failure. In this section, you will study the different types of business organizations that are common in the American economy. You will discover that each type of business organization has advantages and disadvantages in different situations.

The most common form of business organization in the United States is the **sole proprietorship**, or proprietorship—a business owned and operated by a single person. You have seen such businesses in your neighborhood—beauty salons or cleaners or pizza restaurants. Though common, the proprietorship is only one of three ways of organizing a business.

Look at the graphs of business organizations on page 481. You'll see that there are more proprietorships than any other type of business.

Structure

A proprietorship is the easiest form of business to set up. Have you ever earned money mowing lawns or babysitting? If so, you were a sole proprietor. Generally, anyone can start a sole proprietorship whenever they want to.

Advantages

The biggest advantages of sole proprietorships are that the proprietor has full pride in owning the business and receives all the profits. In addition, the proprietor can make decisions quickly, without having to consult a co-owner, boss, or "higher-up." This flexibility means that the owner can make an immediate decision when problems arise.

Disadvantages

Sole proprietorships have several disadvantages, though. First, the owner is financially responsible for any and all problems related to the business. This is called **unlimited liability.** If the business has debts, the owner's personal assets, or items of value such as houses, cars, jewelry, and so on, may be seized to pay the debts.

Second, sole proprietors find it difficult to raise **financial capital**—the money needed to run a business or enable it to grow larger. Most sole proprietors use their own savings or credit cards or borrow from friends and family when they need money for their businesses.

Another disadvantage is the difficulty of attracting qualified employees. Many high school and college graduates are more likely to be attracted to positions with larger firms that can offer better fringe benefits—paid vacations, sick leave, and health and medical insurance—in addition to wages and salaries.

Reading Check **Identifying** Who makes the decisions in a sole proprietorship?

Partnerships

A **partnership** is a business owned by two or more people. As you see on the graph, there are fewer partnerships than any other form of business.

Structure

When they start the business, partners draw up a legal agreement called **articles of partnership.** This document identifies how much money each will contribute and what role each will play in the business. It clarifies how they will share profits or losses. Finally, the document describes how to add or remove partners, or even how to break up the business if they want to close it down.

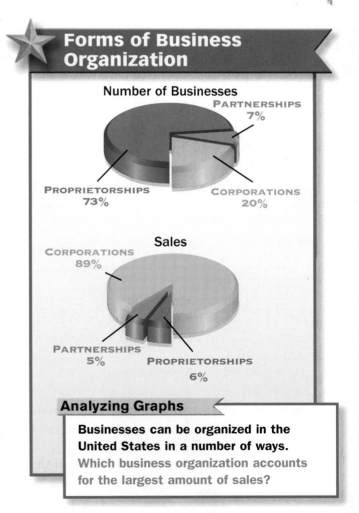

Forms of Business Organization

Number of Businesses

PARTNERSHIPS 7%

PROPRIETORSHIPS 73%

CORPORATIONS 20%

Sales

CORPORATIONS 89%

PARTNERSHIPS 5%

PROPRIETORSHIPS 6%

Analyzing Graphs

Businesses can be organized in the United States in a number of ways.

Which business organization accounts for the largest amount of sales?

Partnership When two or more people pool their resources, they may form a partnership. **Who assumes the risk in a partnership?**

Advantages

Partnerships overcome some disadvantages of a proprietorship. Because there are multiple owners, partnerships can usually raise more money. If money cannot be borrowed, the partners can always take in new partners to provide funds. Like proprietors, partners pay no corporate income tax. In addition, each owner often brings special talents to the business. As a result, each can oversee a particular part of the business, which helps the business succeed.

Disadvantages

One disadvantage of the partnership is that the legal structure is complex. When a partner is added or removed, a new agreement has to be made.

The main disadvantage, however, is that the owners have unlimited liability. This means that each owner is fully responsible for all the debts of the partnership. Suppose that you and four others form an equal partnership. You would own one-fifth of the business and have the right to one-fifth of its profits. Suppose, though, that someone

was hurt by the company and sued for damages. If you were the only owner who had any money, you could be required to pay 100 percent of the damages.

Reading Check **Describing** What is the main disadvantage of a partnership?

Corporations

The **corporation** is a business recognized by law that has many of the rights and responsibilities of an individual. In fact, a corporation can do anything a person can do—own property, pay taxes, sue or be sued—except vote. One-fifth of all businesses are corporations.

Structure

First, someone who wants to start a corporation must get a **charter**—a government document granting permission to organize. The charter includes the name, purpose, address, and other features of the business. The charter also specifies the amount of **stock,** or ownership shares of the corporation, that will be issued. The people who buy this stock—the **stockholders**—become the owners of the corporation. The corporation uses the money received from selling the stock to set up and run the business.

The stockholders elect a **board of directors** to act on their behalf. The board hires managers to run the corporation on a daily basis. The chart on page 484 shows the relationship of these groups. As you can see, the business owners and the managers of a corporation are different groups of people.

Advantages

The first advantage of the corporation is the ease of raising financial capital. If it needs additional money to expand, for example, the corporation can sell new shares of stock. Corporations also find it easier than the other types of businesses to borrow large sums of money.

The second advantage results from the ease of raising capital. This allows corporations to grow to be huge. Today's large corporations employ thousands of workers and carry out business around the world.

Many modern corporations are huge. A study conducted in the late 1990s found that some of these corporations are bigger than the economies of many countries. Many are automakers. Mitsubishi has the world's 18th largest economy, General Motors ranks 26th, and Ford Motor is 31st. Other U.S. corporations include Wal-Mart (43), General Electric (53), and Sears-Roebuck (65). All these giants had larger economies than Greece, Egypt, or the Philippines.

Third, the board of directors can hire professional managers to run the business. If those managers do not succeed, the board can replace them with a new team.

A fourth advantage is that ownership of the corporation can be easily transferred. For example, if you own shares in one

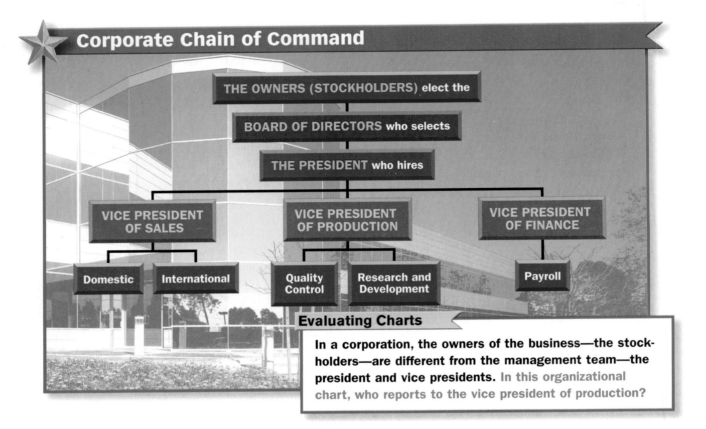

Corporate Chain of Command

THE OWNERS (STOCKHOLDERS) elect the

BOARD OF DIRECTORS who selects

THE PRESIDENT who hires

VICE PRESIDENT OF SALES

VICE PRESIDENT OF PRODUCTION

VICE PRESIDENT OF FINANCE

Domestic   International

Quality Control   Research and Development

Payroll

Evaluating Charts

In a corporation, the owners of the business—the stockholders—are different from the management team—the president and vice presidents. In this organizational chart, who reports to the vice president of production?

corporation and you would rather have shares in another, you simply sell the first stock and buy the second.

A final advantage of the corporation is limited liability. Only the corporation, not its owners, is responsible for the debts of the corporation. For instance, if you paid $1,000 for stock in a corporation that later went bankrupt, you would lose your $1,000 investment—but no more than that. Unlike the proprietorship or the partnership, you would not be liable for the company's debts.

These advantages have combined to make corporations very successful. As the graphs on page 481 show, they account for about 90 percent of all sales by all businesses.

Disadvantages

Corporations have their disadvantages as well. First, they often are expensive and complex to set up.

In addition, the business owners have very little say in the management of the business. Millions of people own the shares of major corporations, but it is difficult for them to unite to force the managers to act in a particular way.

Third, corporations are subject to more regulation by government than the other forms. They must release certain reports on a regular basis. These reports give detailed financial information about the company. The reports are designed to keep potential and current shareholders informed about the state of the business.

Finally, stockholders are subject to double taxation, or paying taxes twice on corporate profits. First, the corporation pays a tax on its profits. Then, when the profits are distributed to the stockholders, the stockholders have to pay income tax on those earnings. Sole proprietors and partners also must pay taxes on the profits they earn. However, proprietorships and partnerships do not pay a separate profit tax.

Other Business Organizations

Profit-seeking proprietorships, partnerships, and corporations are not the only types of business organizations. Other organizations operate on a "not-for-profit" basis. A nonprofit organization operates in a businesslike way to promote the interests of its members. Examples of nonprofit institutions include churches, hospitals, and social service agencies.

Another example of a nonprofit organization is the cooperative. A cooperative is a voluntary association of people formed to carry on some kind of economic activity that serves to benefit its members. Cooperatives provide a variety of services. Consumer cooperatives buy bulk amounts of goods on behalf of their members. Service cooperatives provide services such as insurance and credit to their members rather than goods.

Producers, like consumers, can also have cooperatives. A producer cooperative helps members promote or sell their products. For example, farmer cooperatives help members sell their crops directly to central markets or to companies that use the members' products.

Reading Check **Describing** Is it the duty of the board of directors to run the corporation's day-to-day operations? Explain.

SECTION 1 ASSESSMENT

Checking for Understanding

1. Key Terms Use the following terms in complete sentences that demonstrate each term's meaning: sole proprietorship, partnership, corporation.

Reviewing Main Ideas

2. Describe What are the advantages of a partnership over a sole proprietorship? What are the advantages of a sole proprietorship over a partnership?

3. Compare Name three kinds of cooperatives and describe what they do for their members.

Critical Thinking

4. Making Comparisons If you were planning to open your own business, which form of business organization would you prefer—sole proprietorship, partnership, or corporation? Justify your answer.

5. Organizing Information On a diagram similar to the one below, identify the advantages of the corporation.

Advantages

Analyzing Visuals

6. Interpret Study the circle graphs on page 481. Is any single form of business organization responsible for more than one-half of the nation's sales? What percentage of businesses are partnerships?

★**BE AN ACTIVE CITIZEN**★
7. Classify Keep a record of all the businesses you visit during a week. Classify each as a sole proprietorship, partnership, or corporation. Compare your lists in class.

Labor Unions

GUIDE TO READING

Main Idea
A labor union is an organization that seeks to increase the wages and improve the working conditions of its members.

Key Terms
labor union, closed shop, union shop, right-to-work laws, modified union shop, collective bargaining, mediation, arbitration, strike, lockout

Reading Strategy
Organizing Information As you read the section, complete a diagram like the one below by identifying three kinds of union arrangements.

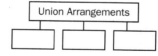

Read to Learn
• What are the different types of unions?
• How are negotiations between unions and management conducted?

Americans in Action

To have some control over the wages they receive as well as over other working conditions, American workers form labor unions. Unions are based on the idea that workers as a group will have more influence on management than will individual workers acting alone. "San Bernardino County and the union representing 11,600 workers agreed Thursday to [salary] and benefit increases costing $75 million over three years, negotiators said. . . . The San Bernardino Public Employees Association contract, if approved, will raise salaries 9.3 percent and increase employees' benefits allowances by 42 percent over three years. . . . Chris Prato, general manager of the Public Employees Association, said of the benefits increase, 'We had been campaigning on that publicly and privately for more than a year, and it worked.'"

—The *Press-Enterprise* (Riverside, California), December 21, 2001

Union workers

Organized Labor

Some workers choose to organize. They join together to form **labor unions,** groups of workers who band together to have a better chance to obtain higher pay and better working conditions. Only about 14 percent of American workers belong to unions. Still, unions play an important role in the nation's economy and political life.

Types of Unions

There are two types of unions. Workers who perform the same skills join together in a craft or trade union. Examples are the printers union or the plumbers union. Some unions bring together different types of workers who all belong to the same industry. These are called industrial unions. An example is the United Auto Workers, which includes many different kinds of workers in the auto industry.

In the past, unions were formed mainly by workers in heavy industry. Today, though, people in jobs as different as airline workers, teachers, and professional athletes belong to unions.

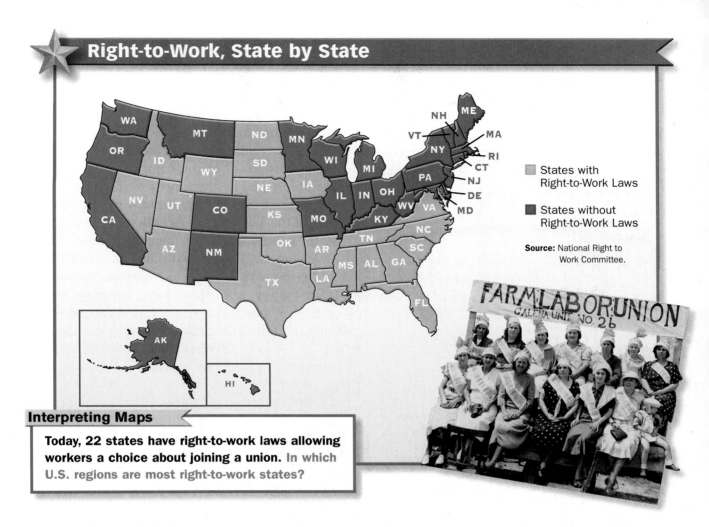

Right-to-Work, State by State

States with Right-to-Work Laws

States without Right-to-Work Laws

Source: National Right to Work Committee.

Interpreting Maps

Today, 22 states have right-to-work laws allowing workers a choice about joining a union. In which U.S. regions are most right-to-work states?

How Unions Are Organized

Organized labor operates at three levels; the local union, the national or international union, and the federation.

A local union is comprised of the members of a union in a factory, company, or geographic area. The local union deals with a company by negotiating a contract and monitoring the terms of the contract.

Above the local unions are the national unions. These organizations are the individual craft or industrial unions that represent local unions nationwide. Unions that also have members in Canada or Mexico are often called international unions.

National unions send organizers to help employees campaign to set up local unions. To help in negotiating a contract between a local union and a particular company, the national unions provide lawyers and other staff members. In certain industries such as steel and mining, the national union negotiates the contracts for the entire industry. After the majority of union members accepts the contract, all the local unions within the industry must work under that contract. Some of the largest unions are the United Automobile Workers (UAW) and the United Steelworkers of America (USWA).

At the federation level is the AFL-CIO, formed in 1955 by the merger of the American Federation of Labor and the Congress of Industrial Organizations. The federation represents more than 13 million working men and women nationwide.

Union Arrangements

Some people criticize labor unions for trying to control the supply of labor. In the past some unions supported the closed shop. This means that a worker had to belong to the union in order to be hired by a company. This arrangement was more common in the past than today. When the government passed the Taft-Hartley Act in 1947, closed shops became illegal for any company that makes goods that are sold in states other than the state in which the company is located. Since most businesses make goods for interstate sales, there are few closed shops today.

More common now is the union shop. Under this arrangement, companies can hire nonunion people, but those workers must join the union once they begin working. One part of the Taft-Hartley Act allows individual state governments to ban this kind of arrangement. Twenty-two states have passed right-to-work laws, which prevent unions from forcing workers to join. The map on page 487 shows the states that have union shops and those that have right-to-work laws.

In a modified union shop, workers do not have to join the union after they are hired but they can choose to do so. If they do, they must stay in the union as long as they work for that employer.

A union cannot be brought into a workplace unless a majority of the workers votes in favor of it. They might join an existing union or form a completely new one. A federal government agency, the National Labor Relations Board (NLRB), makes sure that these union elections are carried out fairly and honestly.

Reading Check **Summarizing** Is the union shop illegal in right-to-work states? Explain.

Negotiations

Once workers choose to be represented by a union, the union carries out collective bargaining for them. Under collective bargaining, officials from the union and from the company meet to discuss the terms of the workers' new contract. Each contract typically covers a few years. As the contract nears its end, labor and management meet to negotiate a new contract.

American Biographies

César Estrada Chávez (1927–1993)

César Chávez knew the suffering of farmworkers. He had labored in the fields since age 10, when his family lost their Arizona farm during the Great Depression. Like thousands of other farmers, the Chávez family became migrant workers. Chávez attended some 65 schools before dropping out at the end of 8th grade.

After serving in World War II, Chávez took a paid job to win greater rights for Mexican Americans. However, he could not forget the migrant workers. In 1962, with the support of his wife Helen Fabela Chávez, he returned to the fields and his dream of organizing farmworkers into a union.

In 1965, Chávez launched La Huelga— "the strike"—in which he battled the power of grape growers in the San Joaquin Valley. Chávez, who lived on a salary of $5 a week, asked Americans to boycott grapes until growers signed union contracts. Some 17 million Americans responded. "For the first time," Chávez said, "the farmworker got some power." The power came in the form of the United Farm Workers, the first successful farmworkers union in the nation's history.

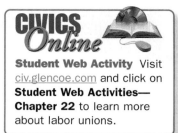
The negotiations focus on how much the workers will receive in wages and benefits. They also talk about how long the workday is and how many holidays the workers will have. The two sides discuss rules for working and procedures for changing those rules.

Getting Outside Help

At times the two parties cannot agree on the terms for the new contract. When that happens, they have different options.

They might try **mediation,** in which they bring in a third party who tries to help them reach an agreement. The mediator meets with both sides and tries to help labor and management reach a compromise.

In some cases, the two sides choose **arbitration.** In this situation, a third party listens to both sides and then decides how to settle the disagreement. Both parties agree in advance to accept whatever the arbitrator decides.

Labor-Management Conflict

Unions and management can also use different tools to try to pressure the other side to accept their positions. Workers can call a **strike,** in which all workers in the union refuse to go to work. Workers who choose to go on strike often picket the business, marching in front of company buildings while holding signs. The signs explain what the strike is about. The workers hope that the business will have to shut down without any employees to do the work, forcing the company to accept the union's contract terms. If striking and picketing do not settle the dispute, unions can encourage members and the public to boycott, or refuse to buy, the business's products. The strongest tool that management has is the lockout. In a **lockout,** the company blocks workers from entering its buildings until they agree to accept its contract terms. The business hopes that the loss of income will cause difficulties for the union members and convince them to accept the company's position.

Reading Check **Comparing** What is the difference between a strike and a lockout?

SECTION 2 ASSESSMENT

Checking for Understanding

1. Key Terms Write a true statement *and* a false statement for each of the following terms: closed shop, mediation, lockout. Indicate which statements are true and which are false. Below each false statement explain why it is false.

Reviewing Main Ideas

2. Identify What are the two kinds of labor unions?

3. Identify What is the process through which unions and management negotiate contracts called?

Critical Thinking

4. Summarizing Information How does a right-to-work law protect independent workers?

5. Analyzing Information Assume that you have been given the job of mediating a strike between the workers in a grocery store and its management. On a diagram, identify three things you would want to know before you suggested a solution.

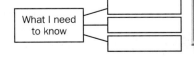

What I need to know

Analyzing Visuals

6. Identify Study the map on page 487. Does North Carolina have a right-to-work law in place? Does Colorado?

★ *BE AN ACTIVE CITIZEN* ★

7. Research Contact a firm in your community that has a union. Ask if all workers in the company are required to join or if only some are. Based on your information, determine if the union arrangement is a closed shop, a union shop, or a modified union shop.

Making Generalizations

Why Learn This Skill?

Every day you observe people and events or read facts and information. In the process you make generalizations. That is, you reach broader conclusions derived from a number of facts or details. Making valid generalizations can lead you to new facts and insights.

Learning the Skill

To make generalizations, follow these steps:

• Review the facts or particulars available to you, separating facts from opinions.
• Look for trends or patterns that could be applied to several points of information.
• Ask yourself if you have enough information to draw accurate conclusions. Incomplete or inaccurate data may cause incorrect conclusions.
• Formulate a general statement that makes a point and check your backup facts.

Practicing the Skill

Read the account of the Homestead Strike on this page. On a separate sheet of paper, copy the valid generalizations among the following statements. Then tell how you can support the generalizations you select.

❶ Americans of the 1800s generally supported union workers.
❷ Both Carnegie and Frick wanted to crush the union at the Homestead Mill.
❸ Labor disputes could turn violent in the early years of the labor movement.
❹ The Pinkerton Detective Agency opposed labor unions.

Homestead Strike, 1896

In 1896, iron and steel workers at the Homestead Mill, owned by Andrew Carnegie, near Pittsburgh, Pennsylvania, wanted to negotiate with the owners for higher wages and greater recognition.

Carnegie's partner, Henry Frick, responded to the union request by ordering a lockout and calling in strikebreakers. The company hired the Pinkerton Detective Agency to protect its factories. Several people were killed when violence broke out between the strikers and the guards.

At Frick's request, the governor sent in the Pennsylvania National Guard to subdue the workers and the townspeople. Frick reopened the mill with 1,700 nonunion workers. "I will never recognize the union, never, never!" he said.

Henry Frick

Applying the Skill

Research some recent data on women in the workforce, such as the kinds of jobs they hold, salaries and wages, number employed, and so on. Write two generalizations based on the facts.

Practice key skills with Glencoe's **Skillbuilder Interactive Workbook CD-ROM, Level 1.**

Businesses in Our Economy

GUIDE TO READING

Main Idea
In a free enterprise economy, businesses have responsibilities as well as rights.

Key Terms
transparency, discrimination, social responsibility

Reading Strategy
Organizing Information As you read the section, complete a diagram like the one below by identifying one or more responsibilities of businesses in each category.

Consumers:	Owners:
Responsibilities	
Employees:	Community:

Read to Learn
- What does social responsibility entail?
- What are the responsibilities of businesses to consumers, owners, employees, and their communities?

★ ★ ★ ★

 **Americans in Action**

Equality for women, educational opportunities for the disenfranchised, and corporate responsibility [of business] are not new concepts for the family behind the largest gift ever to the University of Colorado at Boulder. . . . On Wednesday, university officials hailed the New York–based Gerry and Lila Leeds family for giving Colorado University a record $35 million gift, the sixth-largest to a business school nationwide and the largest ever for the Boulder campus. . . . Michael Leeds (the Leeds's son) graduated from CU in 1974 with a degree in business administration. His brother, Richard, graduated from CU with a degree in computer science the following year. "I am very grateful to my professors for giving me the educational background to help me drive a business forward into great success," Richard, 49, said.
—*Rocky Mountain News*, October 4, 2001

Leeds family members

The Roles of Business

As the story about the Leeds's gift to the university reveals, businesspeople can be very generous. This generosity comes not only from major corporate givers like the Leedses. Local businesses, too, make similar efforts. They donate money or supplies to school fund-raisers. They give money to support children's athletic teams. This community involvement is just one way that business plays a role in society.

Businesses play many different roles in our economy. Sometimes businesses act as consumers—they buy goods and services from other businesses. Manufacturers buy energy and raw materials like steel, plastic, and glass. Insurance companies buy office furniture and supplies like paper. Stores purchase computers and software to track sales.

Businesses are also employers. They provide jobs—and pay wages—to millions of workers across the country.

Of course, businesses are also producers. Businesses produce a wide variety of goods and services for people with many

Effects Many economic activities may create unintended effects. **Do you think the nearby railroad line had positive or negative effects on people living in this neighborhood? Why?**

different tastes, levels of income, and locations. Businesses large and small produce the food, clothing, and shelter that meet people's basic needs. They also create the cars, movies, CDs, appliances, banking services, air conditioning, and amusement parks that make life more enjoyable and more comfortable.

Reading Check **Explaining** How do businesses act as consumers?

The Responsibilities of Business

As they carry out these roles, businesses have different responsibilities. Sometimes laws spell out those responsibilities. If so, business managers may suffer serious consequences if they do not act responsibly.

Responsibilities to Consumers

One set of responsibilities is to consumers. Businesses have the responsibility of selling products that are safe. Products and services should also work as they are promised to work. A new video game should be undamaged and run without flaws. An auto mechanic should change a car's oil correctly. Businesses also have the responsibility of being truthful in their advertising. Finally, businesses should treat all customers fairly.

Of course, it is good business to meet these responsibilities. Doing so makes customers happy, and happy customers are more likely to come back to the business again. Still, the government is sometimes forced to step in when a business does not meet one of these responsibilities. It might require a manufacturer to remove a product from the market because the product is unsafe. It might prosecute a business for violating customers' rights. These cases are infrequent, however.

Responsibilities to Owners

Another responsibility is to the owners of the business. This is especially important in corporations, in which the managers and owners are different groups of people.

To protect stockholders, corporations are required to release important financial information regularly. As a result, shareholders get income statements—reports on sales, expenses, and profits—several times a year along with reports from auditors to see that the information is accurate. Corporations even post this information on the World Wide Web for everyone to examine.

Revealing this information is called **transparency.** The purpose of publishing this information is to provide investors with full disclosure before they choose to invest, or continue to invest, in the company. With full disclosure, it becomes the responsibility of the investor to choose whether the cost of the investment is worth the risk. Sometimes the managers of a corporation are not completely honest in what they say about the business. When that happens, the government can prosecute them for breaking the law. The scandal involving bankrupt energy company Enron showed the damage that can be done to investors when critical financial information is not reported by auditors.

Responsibilities to Employees

Of course, businesses also have responsibilities to employees. They are required

$ Economics and You

Business Philanthropy

A desire to make reading material available to people at no cost led industrialist Andrew Carnegie to found libraries. In the late 1800s and early 1900s, Carnegie donated more than $55 million to build 2,500 libraries in the United States and many other countries. An immigrant from Scotland, Carnegie believed that people with the desire to learn should be able to educate themselves. Chances are you've been in a library founded by Carnegie.

to give their workers a safe workplace and to treat all workers fairly and without **discrimination.** This means that they cannot treat employees differently on the basis of race, religion, color, gender, or age. The 1990 Americans with Disabilities Act barred employers from treating workers unfairly who had mental or physical disabilities. Some companies are recognized for working hard to meet the needs of their employees. Johnson & Johnson, which

TIME

Political Cartoons

"*Your Majesty, my voyage will not only forge a new route to the spices of the East but also create over three thousand new jobs.*"

and it seems to be diverted toward money and ... Making the world a more convenient | Schneider, two men with little hope, of regaining the company's ... While the wage was | to be diverted ... tim

Analyzing Visuals State-sponsored activities, such as exploration of new territories and scientific research, not only yield exciting new discoveries, but also foster economic growth. What argument is the speaker making to win support for his voyage?

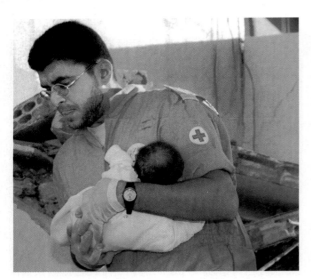

Social Responsibility Responsible companies provide help to organizations that help victims of disasters. *What is social responsibility?*

makes baby and health care products, takes an active role in fulfilling its responsibilities to its employees. *Latina* and *Working Mother* magazines cite Johnson & Johnson as one of the best U.S. companies in this area.

Workers at the retail company The Container Store are enthusiastic about good pay and first-rate benefits, and they believe they are a valued part of the company—in a survey 94 percent of the employees feel they make a difference.

Responsibilities to the Community

More and more businesses are emphasizing their **social responsibility**—the obligation they have to pursue goals that benefit society as well as themselves. Gifts to charities are one example of how businesses meet this social responsibility. Many businesses take an active role in meeting the needs of their communities.

The retail store Target, for example, promotes programs of community and national volunteering. These projects range from delivering food for Meals on Wheels to cleaning up playgrounds and shores. In 2000, Target donated more than $14 million to support education in the form of scholarships, grants, and other programs.

American Express has built a tradition of responding to emergencies and providing assistance to disaster victims through grants to relief agencies. Another significant company program involves raising public awareness of historical and environmental preservation. American Express also funds a variety of performing arts, including children's theaters.

✓ Reading Check **Defining** What is discrimination?

SECTION 3 ASSESSMENT

Checking for Understanding

1. Key Terms Write a paragraph relating to the social responsibility of businesses using the following terms: discrimination, transparency.

Reviewing Main Ideas

2. Describe What does the Americans with Disabilities Act state?

3. Explain Why is it important for corporations to publish their financial information regularly?

Critical Thinking

4. Making Judgments Do you think "truth-in-advertising" laws should be strengthened? Explain.

5. Organizing Information On a diagram like the one below, identify as many of the responsibilities of businesses to consumers as you can.

> Responsibilities to Consumers

Analyzing Visuals

6. Interpret Study the cartoon on page 493. Who are the figures in the cartoon?

★ **BE AN ACTIVE CITIZEN** ★
7. Analyze Contact a local business and ask how the business contributes to the community. Describe the actions of the business and what you think the effects are. Share your findings with the class.

Issues to Debate

Should the Government Create Personal Retirement Accounts?

The Social Security system works on a pay-as-you-go plan. Payroll taxes go into a trust fund, which is used to pay the benefits for current retirees. However, the number of retirees is growing faster than the number of people paying taxes to support them.

Many people predict that Social Security payments will exceed tax revenues by 2017. They also think the system will go broke by 2041.

In order to solve the problem, the federal government must increase the program's income (raise taxes), decrease its expenses (reduce benefits), or find a new source of funding to supplement the system. Some support the creation of personal retirement accounts (PRAs). This plan would allow workers to invest a percentage of their payroll taxes in stocks, bonds, or funds. Are PRAs a solution to the Social Security problems?

A Social Security card

Yes

People say fix Social Security, but don't reduce my benefits; fix Social Security, but don't increase my taxes; fix Social Security, but don't increase my age eligibility. That's a pretty big challenge.

One of the things a commission that I served on recommended was individual retirement accounts; carve out 2% of the payroll tax to allow people to invest. The stock market has never had a 20-year negative return. . . . The baby boomers are already in fact experienced in investing.

—*Louisiana Senator John Breaux, chairman, Special Committee on Aging, 2001*

No

Privatization would add huge costs to Social Security, because any scheme has to pay full benefits to boomers who are about to retire while also prefunding the private accounts of younger workers. To pay for these costs, any privatization plan would require deep cuts in benefits, increases in the retirement age and a dramatic increase in insecurity. . . .

In exchange, . . . what do we get? We get a chance to gamble on the stock market with money needed to create a secure floor under our families.

—*Jesse Jackson, founder, Rainbow Coalition and Operation PUSH, 2001*

Debating the Issue

1. Why does Breaux think PRAs are safe?
2. Why does Jackson oppose PRAs?

3. This issue will affect the taxes you'll be asked to pay. What questions would you need answered before deciding whether you are for or against PRAs?

Assessment & Activities

Review to Learn

Section 1

- Sole proprietorships are small, easy-to-manage enterprises owned by one person.
- Partnerships are owned by two or more persons.
- Corporations are owned by shareholders.

Section 2

- A labor union is an organization of workers formed to represent its members' interests.
- Unions participate in collective bargaining when they negotiate with management.

Section 3

- Businesses have a responsibility to their customers to provide safe, working products.
- Businesses have an obligation to pursue goals that benefit society as a whole, as well as themselves.

FOLDABLES
Study Organizer

Using Your Foldables Study Organizer
Your completed foldable should have three labeled tabs with information written under each tab. On the last tab of your foldable, write one question or concept that you would like to investigate further. Research and write the information you find under the tab.

Reviewing Key Terms

Write the key term that matches each definition below.

1. a business that is owned by one individual
2. the stage in contract negotiations in which a neutral person tries to get both sides to reach an agreement
3. union and management submit issues on which they cannot agree to a third party for a final decision
4. one of the owners of a corporation
5. a situation that occurs when management prevents workers from returning to work until they agree to a new contract
6. the legal responsibility of corporations to release financial information regularly
7. union arrangement that hires only union members
8. a nonprofit association that performs some economic activity for the benefit of its members
9. the deliberate refusal to work by workers
10. the process of negotiations between union and management representatives

Reviewing Main Ideas

11. What is the most common form of business organization?
12. What are the disadvantages of a sole proprietorship?
13. Which type of business organization accounts for the smallest proportion of sales?
14. What is unlimited liability?
15. What is the structure of every corporation?
16. Which group within a corporation chooses the board of directors?
17. Identify the purpose of cooperatives.
18. What are craft unions?
19. What kind of workers make up an industrial union?

Critical Thinking

20. **Drawing Conclusions** Why would a person decide to be part of a partnership rather than a sole proprietorship?

21. **Making Comparisons** Create a table like the one below and indicate the single most important advantage that you believe this form of business organization has.

Business Organization	Advantage
Sole Proprietorship	
Partnership	
Corporation	

Practicing Skills

22. **Making Generalizations** Read the following excerpt, then make a generalization based on the reading.

Henry Ford introduced the first moving assembly line in 1913 at his Model T plant in Highland Park, Michigan. Different conveyor systems carried subcomponents to the main assembly line in a finely orchestrated manner. Before the advent of the assembly line, a Model T took more than 12 hours to produce and cost $950. By 1927, after numerous refinements, Model Ts were being turned out in less than half that time, with a price tag of $290 apiece.

—*Business Week:* "100 Years of Innovation," Summer 1999

★ CITIZENSHIP COOPERATIVE ACTIVITY ★

23. Work in small groups to draw up a report on a sole proprietorship and a partnership in your community. Include in your reports such information as goods and services provided; number of factories, stores, or offices; number of employees; and so on. Conclude your report with observations on whether the businesses chose the most appropriate form of organization for their operations.

CIVICS Online

Self-Check Quiz Visit the *Civics Today* Web site at civ.glencoe.com and click on **Self-Check Quizzes— Chapter 22** to prepare for the chapter test.

Analyzing Visuals

24. In states that have right to-work laws, new workers have the choice to join or not to join a union. Study the map on page 487. Is the Northeast a stronger region for right-to-work laws than the Southeast? Explain.

Technology Activity

25. Congress set out to protect small businesses by passing the Small Business Act. This act set up the Small Business Administration. Visit the SBA at http://www.sba.gov/. How does the SBA help small businesses?

The Princeton Review Standardized Test Practice

Directions: Choose the *best* answer to the following question.

How do right-to-work laws affect workers who do not belong to unions?

F These laws force workers to join unions.

G They affect only workers who belong to craft unions.

H They are an essential part of collective bargaining.

J They protect the right of the worker to continue working at a job without joining a union.

Test-Taking Tip

This question requires you to know the definition of *right-to-work.* Even if you are unsure of the phrase's meaning, try to determine the definition. Which answer fits best with this information?

UNIT 7

The Free Enterprise System

Why It Matters

In this unit, you will find out how the major parts of our economy fit together into a system. Economists call this "macroeconomics," and it means you will be looking at the economy as a whole. What role does government play in the economy? How does our monetary system work? You will learn about the policies and factors that influence our economic stability in Unit 7.

Use the **American History Primary Source Document Library CD-ROM** to find primary sources about the federal government and the economy.

★ BE AN ACTIVE CITIZEN ★

Interview two local entrepreneurs about the health of the free enterprise system. Ask about the current business climate, the state of the economy, and government policies that affect their businesses. Write a summary of your findings for your portfolio.

Government expenditures are used to maintain transportation systems, like this system in Seattle, Washington.

499

Government and the Economy

★ CITIZENSHIP AND YOU ★

The government's economic policies are aimed at strengthening the economy, solving economic problems, and protecting the economic interests of citizens. Ask a local librarian for help in finding information on recent government economic policies.

To learn more about how statistical measures are used to monitor the economy's performance, view the **Economics & You** video lesson 20: Measuring the Economy's Performance.

FOLDABLES™
Study Organizer

Analyzing Information Study Foldable *Make this foldable to help you understand the role the government plays in maintaining economic stability, ways in which the economy is measured, and the impact these things have on your life.*

Step 1 *Mark the midpoint of the side edge of a sheet of paper.*

Draw a mark at the midpoint.

Step 2 *Fold the outside edges in to touch at the midpoint.*

Step 3 *Cut one of the large tabs in half to form two smaller tabs and label as shown.*

Reading and Writing *As you read the chapter, take notes by writing information under each appropriate tab.*

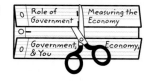

Role of Government | Measuring the Economy
Government & You | Economy

State Building in San Francisco ▶

CIVICS Online

Chapter Overview Visit the *Civics Today* Web site at civ.glencoe.com and click on **Chapter Overviews— Chapter 23** to preview chapter information.

The Role of Government

Main Idea

One of our nation's most important goals is to create an economic environment favorable to growth and stability.

Key Terms

private goods, public goods, externality, antitrust law, merger, natural monopoly, recall

Reading Strategy

Comparing and Contrasting As you read the section, complete a diagram like the one below by differentiating between public goods and private goods. Provide at least one example of each.

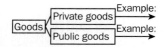

Read to Learn

- What public goods does government provide?
- What actions does government take to regulate economic activity?

★ ★ ★ ★

Americans in Action

The economic activities of government affect your well-being every day. When you receive a check for your part-time or summer job, you see deductions for income and Social Security taxes. Laws requiring seat belts and motorcycle helmets are government mandates. Another is airport security. In November 2001 *USA Today* reported: "Congress approved an overhaul of the nation's aviation security system yesterday to put the federal government firmly in control of airport safety operations. . . . The legislation would replace the private baggage-screening system with a 28,000-person federal workforce that will inspect passengers' luggage. The bill also would strengthen cockpit doors, put federal sky marshals on flights and grant wide authority to a transportation security chief who will implement the new measures."

Airport security

Providing Public Goods

Government plays several important roles in the economy. One role is providing goods and services—such as safer air travel—that private businesses do not provide.

Most goods and services that businesses produce are **private goods,** or goods that, when consumed by one individual, cannot be consumed by another. Consumption of private goods and services is subject to the **exclusion principle.** This means that a person is excluded from using that good or service unless he or she pays for it. Private goods are the items we normally buy, for example, clothes, shoes, food, and so on. Private services include such things as insurance, haircuts, medical services, auto care, and telephone services.

This is in contrast to **public goods,** or goods that can be consumed by one person without preventing the consumption of the good by another. Consumption of public goods is subject to the **nonexclusion principle.** This means that no one is excluded from consuming the benefits of a public good whether or not he or she pays. Examples of public goods include public parks, public libraries, museums, highways, and street lighting.

Because of the difficulty of charging for public goods, the government usually provides them. If government did not provide these public goods and services, then the private sector would not provide them in adequate amounts because it is so difficult to get people to pay for them.

As a result, the production of public goods is one of the responsibilities of government. The government still has to pay for them, of course, but it raises the money in the form of taxes and then provides the products to everyone.

✓Reading Check **Defining** What are public goods?

Dealing With Externalities

The government also plays a role in handling externalities. An **externality** is the unintended side effect of an action that affects someone not involved in the action. Suppose a company pays end-of-year bonuses to its workers. Restaurants and stores in the area will probably see their sales go up because the workers have more money to spend. These businesses experience externalities. They were not involved in the paying of bonuses, but they were affected by it.

One reason that governments provide public goods is that these goods produce positive externalities. Everyone—not just drivers—benefits from good roads. Good roads make it cheaper to transport goods. As a result, those transported goods can have lower prices, which benefits everybody.

Governments can also take actions that indirectly lead to positive externalities. In the 1960s, the government wanted to put a man on the moon. The space program needed someone to develop smaller computers to achieve this goal. The government provided money to researchers who developed tiny computer chips. Today, those chips are found in cars, household appliances, and pocket calculators, benefiting many people. Many government activities encourage positive externalities.

Some externalities can be negative. That happens when an action harms an uninvolved third party. Suppose a chemical

Private and Public Goods
A ticket to the theater is an example of a private good. Highways are one of the public goods the government provides.
How do private goods differ from public goods?

Federal Regulatory Agencies

AGENCY	RESPONSIBILITY
Consumer Product Safety Commission (CPSC)	Makes sure that products are safe
Environmental Protection Agency (EPA)	Prevents air and water pollution
Equal Employment Opportunity Commission (EEOC)	Makes sure that employers do not discriminate in hiring and treating workers on the job
Federal Aviation Administration (FAA)	Oversees the air travel industry
Federal Communications Commission (FCC)	Gives licenses to radio and television stations and oversees prices for interstate telephone and telegraph services
Federal Energy Regulatory Commission (FERC)	Oversees the transmission of energy
Federal Trade Commission (FTC)	Makes sure that businesses do not engage in unfair competition
Food and Drug Administration (FDA)	Makes sure that food, drugs, and cosmetics are pure, effective, and truthfully labeled
National Labor Relations Board (NLRB)	Oversees issues related to labor unions and labor-management relations
Occupational Health and Safety Administration (OSHA)	Makes sure that workplaces are safe and healthful
Securities and Exchange Commission (SEC)	Oversees the sale of stocks and bonds and the work of people who trade in them

Evaluating Charts

The federal government has created many agencies that regulate business. Some oversee businesses in a particular industry. Others oversee certain kinds of business activities. Which agency oversees buying and selling of stock?

company tried to cut costs by dumping poisonous waste into a river. People who relied on the river water would suffer a negative externality from this pollution. One of the roles of government is to prevent these and other kinds of negative externalities.

Reading Check Explaining Do externalities always have negative effects?

Maintaining Competition

Markets work best when there are large numbers of buyers and sellers. Sometimes, however, a market becomes controlled by a **monopoly,** a sole provider of a good or service. With no competition, a monopoly can charge any price it wants, and consumers may suffer.

Antitrust Laws

Historically, one of the goals of government in the United States has been to encourage competition in the economy. The government tries to meet this objective through its **antitrust laws,** or laws to control monopoly power and to preserve and promote competition. In 1890, the federal government passed the Sherman Antitrust Act. This law banned monopolies and other business combinations that prevented competition. In 1911, the government used this law to break up the Standard Oil Company, which had a monopoly on oil. More than 70 years later, the government used the act to break up American Telephone and Telegraph (AT&T). This action created more competition in telephone service.

Mergers

Whenever a **merger,** a combination of two or more companies to form a single business, threatens competition, government may step in to prevent it. For example, when the two leading office-supply stores, Staples and OfficeMax, wanted to merge, the federal government was able to prevent the merger. The government felt that a merger of these two giant firms would result in less competition and higher prices for consumers.

On the other hand, the 2001 proposed merger of Hewlett-Packard and Compaq Computer, two leading personal computer makers, attracted little resistance from the federal government. If the merger had presented a potential problem, either the Justice Department or the Federal Trade Commission would have been involved.

Regulating Market Activities

Recall that governments want to reduce negative externalities. To carry out this work, they regulate some activities by businesses. That is, government agencies make sure that businesses act fairly and follow the laws. Some of the federal agencies that regulate businesses are shown on the chart on page 504. Government regulation is needed in three important areas.

Natural Monopolies

Sometimes it makes sense to have a single firm produce all of a particular good or service for a market. For example, it would not make sense to have three or four telephone companies compete in a local community if each company had to put up its own set of telephone poles.

This often leads to a **natural monopoly,** a market situation in which the costs of production are minimized by having a single firm produce the product. In exchange for having the market all to itself, the firm agrees to be regulated by the government.

Natural Monopolies Some local utilities (electric, gas, water) are the sole providers of their services in an area. **What is a natural monopoly?**

Economics and You

Limited Role of Government

In *The Wealth of Nations,* economist Adam Smith, in 1776, argued against government interference in the marketplace. He said that individuals left on their own would work for their own self-interest. In doing so, they would be guided as if by an "invisible hand" to use their resources efficiently and thus achieve the maximum good for society. Smith's ideas still wield considerable influence among many economists and political leaders today.

This is why so many public services such as gas, electricity, and water are delivered by a single producer.

Advertising and Product Labels

Government is also involved when it comes to truth in advertising and product labeling information. For example, some sellers may be tempted to give misleading information about a product in order to sell it.

Even the content of food labels is important because some people are allergic to certain products like eggs, milk, and peanuts. Other people, such as diabetics, need to know the contents of food because they have to watch their sugar intake.

The Federal Trade Commission deals with problems of false advertising and product claims. The Food and Drug Administration (FDA) is the agency that deals with the purity, effectiveness, and labeling of food, drugs, and cosmetics.

Product Safety

Product safety is another important area of regulation. From time to time, the Consumer Product Safety Commission recalls products that pose a safety hazard. In a **recall,** a company pulls a product off the market or agrees to change it to make it safe. In August 2000, Firestone recalled more than 14.4 million tires that contained a safety-related defect. In 2001, the federal government recalled a variety of products, including a baby crib that fell apart, a brand of sunglasses with a substance that harmed a person's skin, and a minivan with dangerous windshield wipers.

Reading Check **Defining** What is a merger?

SECTION 1 ASSESSMENT

Checking for Understanding

1. Key Terms Write a paragraph related to government's role in the economy using the following terms: private goods, public goods, externality, antitrust law, merger, natural monopoly, recall.

Reviewing Main Ideas

2. Explain What does the Sherman Antitrust Act ban?

3. Identify What government agency deals with problems related to false advertising?

Critical Thinking

4. Making Generalizations Should all monopolies be banned? Why or why not? Explain.

5. Comparing On a diagram like the one below, give an example of a negative externality and a positive externality of having an airport built near your home.

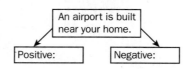

An airport is built near your home.

Positive: Negative:

Analyzing Visuals

6. Interpret Study the chart on page 504. Which agency might conduct tests on the safety of a new drug? Which agency might you contact if you have questions about the regulation of cable television?

★ **BE AN ACTIVE CITIZEN** ★

7. Survey Develop several questions to ask local businesspeople about their experiences with government regulation. Report your findings to the class.

Issues to Debate

Should Consumers Be Able to Download Internet Music?

Internet music struck a sour note when five major record companies and a group of recording artists charged Napster with hijacking the music industry. How can a whole industry be hijacked? Napster's founder, Shawn Fanning, invented new software that allows users to copy songs from each other's computers. The program creates a directory of songs available on the hard drives of other Napster users, then creates a computer-to-computer link via the Internet to transfer the chosen song or songs.

Napster provided the service, not the music. However, every song traded over the Internet belongs to someone. Court battles led Napster to switch from a "for free" to a "for fee" service so songwriters, musicians, and recording companies get paid when their songs are downloaded. However, file sharing is now widely available, both for fee and for free. Should free song sharing be permitted?

Teens listen to music they've downloaded from Napster.

Yes

The truth is that Hollywood secretly wants us to pay every time we listen to a song or watch a movie. . . . Once I buy a CD I should be able to do any noncommercial thing I want with it. . . . What's the real difference between swapping CDs with friends and swapping songs with people who you just met over the Web? Or having the Internet make this material available instead of the library?

Hollywood . . . fights any technology it thinks will dilute its profits. They failed with VCRs and MP3 players and Internet radio, and they deserve to fail here.

—Paul Somerson, staff writer
for ZDNET's Smart Business

No

Each time a Napster user downloads a copy of a song I have composed, I am deprived of the royalty that my work should have earned me. . . .

I fear for the 17-year-old songwriter looking forward to a career in the music business today. Napster and companies like it are threatening not only my retirement, but the future of music itself. In fact, by taking the incentive out of songwriting, Napster may be pushing itself closer to a time when there won't be any songs for its users to swap.

—Mike Stoller,
songwriter

Debating the Issue

1. What arguments does Somerson use to defend swapping music over the Internet?
2. On what grounds does Stoller object to free file-sharing services?

3. Work with a group of classmates to draw up a fair-use code for downloading music. Be prepared to defend your guidelines.

SECTION 2

Measuring the Economy

GUIDE TO READING

Main Idea

The business cycle refers to the ups and downs in economic activity.

Key Terms

real GDP, business cycle, expansion, peak, recession, civilian labor force, unemployment rate, fiscal policy, inflation, consumer price index (CPI)

Reading Strategy

Organizing Information
As you read the section, identify at least four ways that the economy can be measured by completing a diagram like the one below.

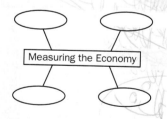

Read to Learn

• What is real GDP?
• What does the business cycle illustrate?

⭐ ⭐ ⭐ ⭐

Americans in Action

Much of the work of economists involves predicting how the economy will grow in the future. However, forecasts are often wrong. Why is this so? A *New York Times* columnist contended that "The economy has too many complicated moving parts, and despite all the sophisticated forecasting techniques, too little is known about how the parts interact. . . . Yet the great majority persist in their optimism, magnifying the positive data and minimizing the [negative] . . . . And now, optimistic forecasting is swamping a minority view that the current recession . . . could endure, dooming the economy to contraction or very sluggish growth for months or years."

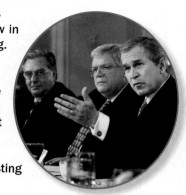

President Bush meets with congressional leaders about the economy.

Measuring Growth

As the Americans in Action feature makes clear, the economy is complex. Another fact becomes clear from this feature. The economy does not perform smoothly at all times. Sometimes it grows, but sometimes it falters. How do economists decide which period the economy is in? How do government leaders decide what to do about these changes in economic performance? In this section, you will learn the answers to these questions.

One measure of an economy's performance is whether or not it is growing. When the economy grows, businesses are producing more goods and services, and they hire more workers. As a result, people have more money and buy more.

The gross domestic product (GDP) is a measure of the economy's output. Remember that GDP is the dollar value of all final goods and services produced in a country in a year. All the dollars spent on cars, apples, CDs, haircuts, movies, and everything else bought and sold in the country go into the GDP.

Even if the country produces the same amount of goods and services from one year to the next, the gross domestic product could go up simply because prices increase. That would make it *seem* that the economy was growing even though it really did not. To avoid being misled in this way, another measure, real GDP, is used. **Real GDP** shows an economy's production after the distortions of price increases have been removed. This eliminates the false impression that output has gone up when prices go up.

✓ **Reading Check** **Explaining** Why do economists use real GDP to chart an economy's production?

Business Fluctuations

The economy tends to grow over time, but it does not grow at a constant rate. Instead, it goes through alternating periods of growth and decline that we call the **business cycle.** The graph on this page tracks the typical ups and downs in business activity. The line on the graph tracks real

GDP. When the line moves upward, real GDP is growing. A downward slope shows a decline in real GDP.

Expansions

An economic **expansion** takes place when real GDP goes up. It doesn't matter whether the economy is growing by a little or by a lot. As long as the real GDP is higher from one period to the next, the economy is expanding. At some point, real GDP reaches a **peak,** or the highest point in an expansion. Then it starts to decline.

Expansions are normally longer than recessions. The longest recent expansion lasted from March of 1991 until March of 2001, exactly 10 years.

Recessions

A **recession** takes place when real GDP goes down for six straight months, although most last longer than that. On the business cycle graph, the recessions

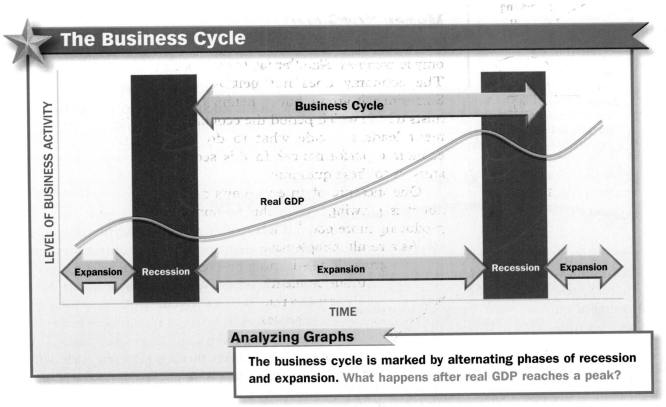

The Business Cycle

LEVEL OF BUSINESS ACTIVITY

Business Cycle

Real GDP

Expansion   Recession   Expansion   Recession   Expansion

TIME

Analyzing Graphs

The business cycle is marked by alternating phases of recession and expansion. What happens after real GDP reaches a peak?

American Biographies

Hector V. Barreto, Jr. (1961–)

"He's a natural," said friends when the Senate unanimously approved Hector V. Barreto, Jr., as head of the Small Business Association (SBA) in 2001. The son of a Mexican-born father and Mexican American mother, Barreto watched his parents turn a family-run restaurant into a string of businesses. They then helped other Latino business owners by founding the U.S. Hispanic Chamber of Commerce.

Barreto—a native of Kansas City, Missouri—followed in his parents' footsteps. Starting as a 9-year-old waiter in the family restaurant, he went on to launch his own California-based businesses. He also served on numerous small-business committees, including the U.S. Hispanic Chamber of Commerce. In 1999, *Hispanic Business Magazine* added Barreto to its list of "100 Most Influential U.S. Hispanics."

Today Barreto oversees an agency that promotes the growth of small businesses through loans, disaster insurance, and government contracts. "Small businesses create good jobs," explains the SBA chief, "jobs that enable people to invest for the future, to buy homes, to build up communities—and to achieve the American dream."

★ ★ ★ ★

are shown by a colored background. Fortunately, recessions tend to be shorter than expansions, with the average recession lasting about one year. Even so, recessions are painful times. When the economy declines, many people lose their jobs.

 **Reading Check** **Describing** How long do recessions usually last?

Unemployment

Another way of measuring the economy is to look at employment. Economists start by identifying the **civilian labor force,** which includes all civilians 16 years old or older who are either working or are looking for work. In the United States, about half of all people belong to the civilian labor force.

The **unemployment rate** is the percentage of people in the civilian labor force who are not working but are looking for jobs. As the graph on page 511 shows, the unemployment rate tends to rise sharply during recessions and then comes down slowly afterward.

Changes in the unemployment rate are important in terms of the economy as a whole. A 1 percent rise in the unemployment rate results in a 2 percent drop in total income in the economy. In 2001, total income in the American economy was about $10.2 trillion. As a result, a 1 percent rise in unemployment cuts total income by about $204 *billion*.

Of course, the personal impact of this lost income can be tremendous. Some people cut back on luxuries such as vacations and new cars. Others must cut back on basic needs such as insurance and health care. Some families go deeper into debt by buying more goods on credit.

Fiscal Policy

Times of high unemployment create stress for many people. High unemployment becomes a problem that requires some government action. When the government does step in, it uses **fiscal policy,** which is changes in government spending or tax policies. The government might cut taxes, for instance. It takes this action hoping that with more money in their pockets people will buy more goods and services. This increased demand will convince businesses to hire more workers, reducing unemployment. Sometimes the government increases spending. By buying more goods and services itself, it tries to convince businesses to hire more workers to boost production.

Unfortunately, political differences often prevent the effective use of fiscal policy. Specifically, it is usually difficult to implement effective fiscal policies when recessions are short and political leaders have different ideas about whether to cut taxes or increase spending.

✓ Reading Check **Cause and Effect** How might a decrease in taxes raise employment?

Price Stability

Another important indicator of an economy's performance is **inflation.** This is a sustained increase in the general level of prices. Inflation hurts the economy because it reduces the purchasing power of money and may alter the decisions people make.

To keep track of inflation, the government samples prices every month for about 400 products commonly used by consumers. The prices of these 400 items make up the **consumer price index (CPI),** which is a popular measure of the price level.

Typically, the prices of some items in the CPI go up every month, and the prices of others go down. However, the change in the average level of prices as measured by the CPI determines the rate of inflation.

Inflation and the Value of Money

Suppose that an ice cream cone that costs you a dollar doubles in price. This price increase causes the purchasing power of your dollar to fall because you have to use twice as many dollars to buy the same

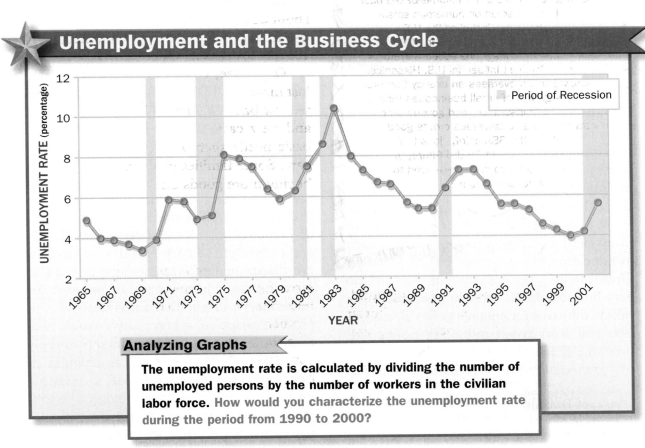

Unemployment and the Business Cycle

UNEMPLOYMENT RATE (percentage)

YEAR

Period of Recession

Analyzing Graphs

The unemployment rate is calculated by dividing the number of unemployed persons by the number of workers in the civilian labor force. How would you characterize the unemployment rate during the period from 1990 to 2000?

Analyzing Visuals The history of the stock market demonstrates that periods of upward movement are often followed by sharp drops. **How would you answer the question posed in the caption of this cartoon?**

item. Inflation is particularly hard on people who have fixed incomes—people who get a pension or other fixed amount of money. Inflation also reduces the value of money in a savings account because it will buy less after inflation than before.

Prices provide the signals that help individuals and businesses make the economic decisions that allocate the factors of production. High rates of inflation distort this process because people begin to speculate, or buy things like land, works of art, or other things they think will go up in value.

When speculation takes the place of investment in capital goods or services such as education, the economy begins to suffer. Unfortunately, the government itself can do very little to prevent inflation because inflation results from monetary policy decisions. You will read about monetary policy and how the Federal Reserve System implements monetary policy in the next chapter.

Reading Check **Identifying** What is a prolonged rise in the general price level of goods and services called?

Stocks and Stock Markets

You hear news about the stock market every day: "The Dow Jones Industrial Average rose 2 percent today," or "Standard & Poor's announced that the stock market fell following a rise in interest rates." What do these statements mean and what do they tell us about the state of the economy?

Why Stock Prices Change

Investors normally want to buy stock if they think they will make money on it. Profits from stock come in two ways—from dividends or from capital gains. **Dividends** are a share of the corporation's profits that are distributed to shareholders. A **capital gain** occurs when stock can be sold for more than it originally cost to buy.

The price of a company's stock, like most other things, is determined by supply and demand. Factors such as changes in sales or profits, rumors of a possible takeover, or news of a technological breakthrough can change the demand for a company's stock and, therefore, its price.

512 Chapter 23 Government and the Economy

Stock Market Indexes

Because most investors are concerned about the performance of their stocks, they often consult stock indexes—statistical measures that track stock prices over time. The Dow-Jones Industrial Average (DJIA) and Standard and Poor's (S&P) are the two most popular indexes. The DJIA tracks prices of 30 representative stocks, and the S&P 500 index tracks the prices of 500 stocks. Both measures give us an idea of the well-being of the stock market as a whole.

Stock Exchanges

Stocks in publicly traded companies are bought and sold at a stock market, or a **stock exchange,** a specific location where shares of stock are bought and sold. The exchange makes buying and selling easy, but you don't have to actually travel to a stock exchange in order to buy or sell stock. Instead, you can call a stockbroker, who can buy or sell the stocks for you.

The first stock exchanges started in parts of Western Europe, then spread to other parts of the world. Most stocks in the United States are traded on the New York Stock Exchange (NYSE), the American Stock Exchange, or an electronic stock market like the NASDAQ. The NYSE, located on Wall Street in New York City, is the oldest, largest, and most prestigious. Stock exchanges can also be found in Sydney, Tokyo, Singapore, Moscow, and most other major cities. Computer technology and electronic trading make it possible for investors to trade major stocks around the clock, anywhere in the world.

CIVICS Online

Student Web Activity Visit civ.glencoe.com and click on **Student Web Activities— Chapter 23** to learn more about measuring our economy.

The Stock Market and the Economy

Indexes like the DJIA and the S&P 500 do more than tell us about the general level of stock prices—they reveal investors' expectations about the future. If investors expect economic growth to be rapid, profits high, and unemployment relatively low, then stock prices tend to rise in what is referred to as a "bull market." If investors are pessimistic, stock prices could fall drastically in what is called a "bear market."

✓ **Reading Check** **Explaining** What are dividends?

SECTION 2 ASSESSMENT

Checking for Understanding

1. **Key Terms** Use each of these terms in a complete sentence that will help explain its meaning: real GDP, business cycle, civilian labor force, unemployment rate, fiscal policy, inflation, consumer price index (CPI).

Reviewing Main Ideas

2. **Identify** What are the two main phases of a business cycle?

3. **Describe** What does the consumer price index track?

Critical Thinking

4. **Analyzing Information** How is the unemployment rate computed?

5. **Drawing Conclusions** On a chart like the one below, evaluate how a sharp increase in inflation might affect these individuals.

Inflation Rises	Effect
A doctor on staff at a large hospital	
Retired autoworker on a fixed pension	

Analyzing Visuals

6. **Describe** Study the graph showing the phases of the business cycle on page 509. How are the recessionary periods in this graph illustrated?

★ **BE AN ACTIVE CITIZEN** ★

7. **Analyze** Try to analyze what you think occurs throughout the economy during a recession. Make a list of some of the things that business owners may do in reaction to a recession.

Developing Multimedia Presentations

Why Learn This Skill?

When you communicate with someone, you use a certain medium. The most common medium you use is your voice, an audio medium. When you make a formal presentation before the class, however, you may want a more vivid approach. You could use more than one medium. In other words, you could develop a multimedia presentation.

Learning the Skill

To develop a multimedia presentation, follow these steps:

- Select one or more partners to work with you. You may need help in preparing and assembling different components.
- Prepare still visuals such as posters. Your posters may show charts, time lines, tables, drawings, or photographs.
- Make sound recordings. Use an audio recorder to present speeches, interviews, and such. You might record background music and noises such as traffic, machinery, or crowds.

Making a presentation

- Use a still camera to make slides. Project the slides and use them as talking points in your presentation.
- Create a video with a camcorder. Your videotape may combine actions, scenes, and sounds related to your report. You might also record your whole report on video and play it as a taped presentation rather than a live one.

Practicing the Skill

Read the items numbered 1–4 below. They represent four events in the experience of Cameron and Celia as they open a new taco restaurant. Read the multimedia components lettered a–d. Copy the four events on a separate sheet of paper. Beside each event, write the letter of the component you would choose to illustrate it in a multimedia presentation of Cameron and Celia's business experience.

1. Planning stage
2. Influence of supply and demand
3. Opening of shop
4. Advertising for new business

   a. Video of small number of customers entering shop and enjoying the tacos
   b. Photo of crowded taco shop with menu showing increase in prices
   c. Poster chart of expected expenditures, receipts, and profits
   d. Audiotape of a radio commercial

Applying the Skill

With a partner, plan a multimedia presentation illustrating how the business cycle works and its effects on businesses and consumers. Then produce one of the media components in your plan.

Government, the Economy, and You

GUIDE TO READING

Main Idea
The number of years you are educated has a direct effect on your income.

Key Terms
food stamps; Women, Infants, and Children (WIC) program; workfare; progressive income tax; Earned Income Tax Credit (EITC)

Reading Strategy
Organizing Information
As you read the section, complete a diagram like the one below by identifying three major causes of income inequality.

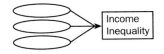

Read to Learn
• What are the reasons for income inequality?
• How do antipoverty programs work?

Americans in Action

The purposes of government in the United States are to protect individual rights, to promote a stable environment for economic activity, and to promote policies that support the general well-being of all citizens. To measure its progress, government agencies such as the Census Bureau compile statistics such as these: "Median household income in 2000 held steady at the all-time high level reached in 1999, at $42,100 (that is, half of all households had incomes above $42,100 and half below). The poverty rate fell for the fourth consecutive year, from 11.8 percent in 1999 to 11.3 percent in 2000, the lowest since 1979."

Median household income held steady in 2000.

Income Inequality

Though the United States is a wealthy country, not all Americans are personally wealthy. Income levels vary for many reasons. Some people—such as Tiger Woods, Jennifer Lopez, and Stephen King—have special talents that enable them to earn huge amounts of money. These people are rare, though. Education, family wealth, and discrimination are more common reasons for income differences.

Education

Level of education has a major impact on a person's income. As the chart on page 516 shows, the average income of a college graduate—someone with a bachelor's degree—is nearly twice the average income of a high school graduate. More advanced degrees increase income even more.

Because education contributes so much to income, the federal government tries to encourage people to improve their education. This is why there are many programs that encourage education, from free or subsidized lunches to college grants and low-interest loans. As you will see in Chapter 25, governments offer financial help to students at both state and private colleges and universities.

Education and Income

EDUCATION	AVERAGE INCOME FOR:	
	MALES	FEMALES
Less than 9th Grade	$25,555	$17,299
9th to 12th Grade (No diploma)	30,966	19,827
High School Graduate (or Equivalency)	38,225	25,796
Some College, No Degree	47,405	30,675
Associate Degree	47,418	32,357
Bachelor's Degree	70,329	43,831
Master's Degree	85,375	55,249
Professional Degree	120,632	72,452
Doctoral Degree	96,471	61,453

Source: U.S. Bureau of the Census.

Evaluating Charts

There is a strong relationship between income and level of education. What are the average incomes for men and for women who have a bachelor's degree?

Wealth

Some people are born into wealth. Having wealthy parents often gives them access to excellent colleges. In addition, wealthy parents can set up their children in a business or pass on their own business.

Discrimination

Discrimination is one of the reasons some people do not receive higher incomes. Women and members of minority groups may not be hired into jobs that pay well, or they may not receive promotions for which they are eligible. The chart on education and income illustrates that salaries for men are normally higher than those for women. This difference is partly a result of discrimination against women.

The government has passed several laws to reduce discrimination. The Equal Pay Act of 1963 requires equal pay for jobs that require equivalent skills and responsibilities. The Civil Rights Act of 1964 bans discrimination on the basis of gender, race, color, religion, and national origin. The Americans with Disabilities Act of 1990 extended this protection to people with physical and mental disabilities. People who suffer discrimination can use the courts to enforce these laws.

Reading Check **Explaining** What was the goal of the Civil Rights Act of 1964?

Poverty

People living in poverty, those who are at the very bottom of the income scale, receive special attention from government. Poverty is a major problem in America, and it is extremely difficult to solve.

Because of this, a number of different programs have been devised to help those in need. The most effective ones are those that have built-in incentives that encourage people to go back to work or to improve their employment situation.

The government uses the poverty guidelines shown on page 518 to determine whether someone is eligible for certain programs. These guidelines are revised annually and are based on conservative estimates of how much it costs to buy enough food, clothing, and shelter to survive.

For example, the $8,860 annual income for a single person works out to a little more than $24 a day. Today, there are more than 31 million Americans who fall *below* these income guidelines.

Welfare Programs

Most welfare programs are federal programs. The federal food stamp program serves millions of Americans. **Food stamps** are government coupons that can be used to purchase food. Low-income Americans can obtain a small number of stamps at little or no cost. They can then use them like money to buy food at authorized stores. Some states use electronic debit systems in place of coupons. These systems track a person's purchases and account electronically.

Another federal welfare program is the **Women, Infants, and Children (WIC) program.** It provides help with nutrition and health care to low-income women, infants, and children up to age 5.

Income Assistance

Other programs pay cash to certain people. Supplemental Security Income (SSI), for instance, gives payments to blind or disabled people and to persons age 65 and older. Temporary Assistance to Needy Families (TANF) is another direct cash program. TANF makes payments to families who need help because a parent is dead, disabled, or absent. TANF has incentives that encourage families to plan for a better life and even save while they receive benefits. The number of months that a recipient can receive benefits is limited. The intent of this limit is to make sure that people do not rely on the program but look for paying work.

Workfare Programs

Workfare is a term used to describe programs that require welfare recipients to exchange some of their labor in exchange for benefits. Most of the programs are run at the state level, and most are designed to

---

STREET LAW™
The Law and You

Minor's Contract

Dean, 16, a drummer in a popular local band, goes to a music store which advertises "easy credit" to purchase a set of drums. The drums cost $750. He offers to put down $150 and make monthly payments on the remaining amount. Because Dean is only 16, the salesclerk refuses to let him make payments on credit. Dean is upset and leaves the store.

If Dean buys an item on credit, he is entering into a contract. A contract is a promise between two or more people to exchange something of value. The right to enter into a contract is accompanied by the responsibility to live up to the promise.

Dean is considered a minor because he is under 18, which is the age of legal majority (in most states). Although he can make a contract, unless he is buying a "necessity" he usually cannot be forced to carry out his promises, and he may refuse to honor the contract. Dean could ask one of his parents to be a cosigner for the agreement. A cosigner agrees to be responsible for the debt if the minor cannot. Dean believes he can pay for the drums, as he earns about $75 per band engagement.

★ BE AN ACTIVE CITIZEN ★

Role-play a negotiation between Dean and the manager of the music store. Brainstorm the key points for Dean in negotiating with the manager.

Poverty Guidelines, 2002

FAMILY SIZE	POVERTY GUIDELINES
1	$8,860
2	11,940
3	15,020
4	18,100
5	21,180
6	24,260
7	27,340
8	30,420
for each additional person add	3,080

Source: *Federal Register*, 2002.

Evaluating Charts

Poverty guidelines help the government determine financial eligibility for certain federal programs. What was the measure of poverty in 2002 for a family of four?

teach people the skills they need to succeed in a job. Many states also require some form of workfare if families want to receive TANF benefits. People who are part of workfare often assist law enforcement officials or sanitation and highway crews, or they may perform other types of community service work.

Tax Policies

Another way the government helps poor people is with a **progressive income tax.** That means that the tax rate is lower at lower incomes and higher for higher incomes. This helps lower-income people by taking a smaller proportion of their income in taxes. The federal government provides additional help for low-income families and individuals. Many workers use the federal **Earned Income Tax Credit (EITC),** which gives tax credits and even cash payments to qualified workers. This program benefits about 20 million working families every year.

✓ **Reading Check** **Describing** How do workfare programs operate?

SECTION 3 ASSESSMENT

Checking for Understanding

1. **Key Terms** Use each of these terms in a sentence that will help explain its meaning: food stamps, workfare, progressive income tax, Earned Income Tax Credit (EITC).

Reviewing Main Ideas

2. **Identify** What law requires equal pay for jobs that require equivalent skills and responsibilities?

3. **Describe** What does Supplemental Security Income provide?

Critical Thinking

4. **Evaluating** Which of the antipoverty programs do you think is the most effective? Explain your answer.

5. **Organizing Information** On a diagram like the one below, identify four major programs or policies designed to alleviate the problem of poverty.

Programs to Relieve Poverty

Analyzing Visuals

6. **Compare** Study the chart that shows education and income on page 516. How much can you expect to make per year if you do not graduate from high school? If you graduate from college with a bachelor's degree?

★ **BE AN ACTIVE CITIZEN** ★
7. **Research** Scan a local newspaper for a short editorial or article about income. Take notes by writing down the main idea and supporting facts. Summarize the article using only your notes.

Landmark Supreme Court
Case Studies

McCulloch v. Maryland

The First Bank of the United States in Philadelphia

Background of the Case

Alexander Hamilton, the nation's first secretary of the Treasury, urged Congress to pass a law establishing a national bank. With the backing of President George Washington, Congress did so in 1791. The bank's funds were used to build roads, canals, and other projects that would help the nation grow. The first bank lasted until 1811; a second bank was chartered in 1816.

Many citizens withdrew deposits from state banks and reinvested them in the new national bank. Angry over the competition from the national bank, states worked to weaken it. Some states, including Maryland, taxed national bank branches operating inside their boundaries. James McCulloch of the Baltimore branch bank refused to pay the state's $15,000 tax. Maryland sued him and won in a state court. McCulloch appealed to the Supreme Court.

The Decision

The Court had to decide if the national bank was constitutional, even though it was not mentioned in the Constitution. Chief Justice John Marshall

How did the national government expand its financial powers to meet the needs of a growing nation?

delivered the unanimous decision on March 6, 1819:

> There is no phrase . . . [that] excludes incidental or implied powers; and which requires that everything granted shall be expressly and minutely described . . . the states have no power, by taxation or otherwise . . . to impede the operation of constitutional laws enacted by Congress.

Marshall based the ruling on Article I, Section 8, which gives Congress powers to "make all laws . . . necessary and proper" for carrying out its duties.

Why It Matters

The Court's unpopular decision upheld the national bank and denied states the power to tax it. The modern Federal Reserve System eventually grew out of the national bank concept.

The case established the implied powers doctrine, which meant Congress had, under the "necessary and proper" clause, a wide range of powers to carry out the powers that the Constitution *expressly* gave it. *McCulloch* v. *Maryland* also established the principle of national supremacy, which forbids the states from intruding into the constitutional operations of the national government.

Analyzing the Court Decision

1. How did Marshall justify the *McCulloch* decision?
2. Do you think the decision affected the ways Americans viewed our federal system?

Assessment & Activities

Review to Learn

Section 1
- One role of government is to provide economic stability.
- Government is able to influence economic conditions in many areas.

Section 2
- A business cycle is the repeated rise and fall of economic activity over time.
- Inflation erodes the purchasing power of the dollar.

Section 3
- Education, wealth, and discrimination may affect income level.

- It is important that we assure a minimum standard of living for all Americans, even if they are unable to work.

FOLDABLES™
Study Organizer

Using Your Foldables Study Organizer
Form a group with two other students. Each one of you should take two to three minutes to answer one of the following questions. What is the role of the government in the economy? How does the government measure the economy? How does the government's involvement in the economy affect me?

Reviewing Key Terms

Write the key term that matches each definition below.

1. the joining of two corporations
2. a tax rate that is lower for lower incomes and higher for higher incomes
3. provides federal tax credits to low-income workers
4. a law passed to prevent monopolies and promote competition
5. goods and services whose use by one person does not reduce use by another
6. a prolonged increase in the general level of prices
7. the total number of people 16 years old or older who are either employed or actively seeking work
8. the federal government's use of taxation and spending policies that affects overall business activity
9. GDP that has been adjusted for the distortions of price changes

Reviewing Main Ideas

10. Why do private producers fail to produce public goods?
11. What is an externality?
12. What antitrust act was used to break up American Telephone and Telegraph?
13. What is a product recall?
14. What is the business cycle?
15. How does inflation affect consumers?
16. What is the relationship between level of education and income?
17. What does the Americans with Disabilities Act provide?
18. How are food stamps used?
19. What program provides help for nutrition and health care to low-income families?

Critical Thinking

20. **Organizing Information** Use a chart like the one below to describe the purpose of three federal regulatory agencies.

Agency	Purpose

21. **Making Generalizations** Study the table showing the per capita GDP of eight nations below. What generalizations can you draw from this information?

Luxembourg	$36,400	Denmark	$25,500
United States	$36,200	Iceland	$24,800
Norway	$27,700	Japan	$24,900
Switzerland	$28,600	Canada	$24,800

22. **Making Comparisons** What are the fundamental differences between the goals of antitrust legislation and the goals of federal government regulatory agencies?

Practicing Skills

23. **Developing Multimedia Presentations** Plan and create a multimedia presentation on a topic found in the chapter. List three or four major ideas you would like to cover. Then think about how multimedia resources could enhance your presentation.

 Economics Activity

24. Examine the food ads in your local newspaper for one week. List those food items that are common to each ad. Compare the prices from the different food stores for the common items. What is the largest percentage difference between the highest and lowest prices?

Self-Check Quiz Visit the *Civics Today* Web site at civ.glencoe.com and click on **Self-Check Quizzes— Chapter 23** to prepare for the chapter test.

★ CITIZENSHIP COOPERATIVE ACTIVITY ★

25. Working with a partner, identify five public goods or services that you frequently use. For each, explain how you would be affected if the government did not provide these things. Summarize your ideas.

 Technology Activity

26. The consumer price index (CPI) is the measure of the change in price over time of a specific group of goods and services used by the average household. To find data on the CPI, go to the Bureau of Labor Statistics Web site at www.bls.gov/data/top20.html and find "Most Requested Statistics." Click on "CPI—Average Price Data." Select two products from the list and analyze the data. Write a paragraph describing the changes in prices for these products.

The Princeton Review — Standardized Test Practice

Directions: Choose the *best* answer to complete the following statement.

A period of business recovery when economic activity increases is called

A a recession.
B real GDP.
C the business cycle.
D an expansion.

Test-Taking Tip

This question requires you to understand what it means when economic activity increases. Which answer fits best with this information?

CHAPTER 24

Money and Banking

★ CITIZENSHIP AND YOU ★

The basis of the market economy is voluntary exchange. In the American economy, the exchange usually involves money in return for goods and services. Why do you accept money in exchange for goods or services? What gives money its value? Where do you keep your money? Answer the questions above in a brief essay.

To learn more about how our money and banking system works, view the *Economics & You* video lesson 18: Money and Banking.

FOLDABLES™
Study Organizer

Summarizing Information Study Foldable *Make this foldable and use it to record what you learn about money and banking.*

Step 1 *Collect two sheets of paper and place them about 1 inch apart.*

Keep the edges straight.

Step 2 *Fold up the bottom edges of the paper to form four tabs.*

This makes all tabs the same size.

Step 3 *When all the tabs are the same size, crease the paper to hold the tabs in place and staple the sheets together. Label each tab as shown.*

Staple together along the fold.

Money & Banking
What Is Money?
The Federal Reserve System
How Banks Operate

Reading and Writing *As you read, identify the key points of each section in the chapter and write these main ideas under the appropriate tabs of your foldable.*

Investing in the stock market is one way people use their money. ▶

CIVICS Online

Chapter Overview Visit the *Civics Today* Web site at civ.glencoe.com and click on **Chapter Overviews— Chapter 24** to preview chapter information.

What Is Money?

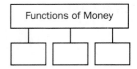

Americans in Action

The primary purpose of the U.S. Mint is to produce an adequate supply of circulating currency for the nation to conduct its trade and commerce. The U.S. Mint is also in charge of producing special commemorative coins. Shown here is the first coin that ever featured an African American—the Booker T. Washington Memorial half-dollar. It honors the famous educator who was born a slave in Virginia in 1856. Designed by Scott Hathaway, the sale of this commemorative coin raises money to pay for a memorial for Washington.

Booker T. Washington Memorial half-dollar

Money

All of us know what money looks like, and we know how to spend it. In this chapter, we'll look at how money makes our lives easier and allows the economy to function more smoothly.

Money is more interesting than you might think. It serves different functions, comes in several different forms, and has value for reasons that are not immediately obvious.

Three Functions of Money

Money has three functions. First, it serves as a medium of exchange. This means that we can trade money for goods and services. Second, money serves as a store of value. We can hold our wealth in the form of money until we are ready to use it.

Third, money serves as a measure of value. Money is like a measuring stick that can be used to assign value to a good or service. When somebody says that something costs $10, we know exactly what that means.

Types of Money

Anything that people are willing to accept in exchange for goods can serve as money. At various times in history, salt, animal hides, gems, and tobacco have been used as mediums of exchange. Each of these items has certain characteristics that make it better or worse than others for use as money.

Tobacco, for example, is easy to transport, but it is not durable. Gems are easy to carry but they are not easy to split into small pieces to use.

The most familiar types of money today are coins and currency. **Coins** are metallic forms of money such as pennies, nickels, dimes—and the Booker T. Washington half-dollar discussed in the feature that began this section. **Currency** includes both coins and paper money.

There are other forms of money as well. Some people keep their money in the form of checking accounts, and some is kept in savings accounts. You will learn more about these accounts later in the chapter.

Why Money Has Value

We value and accept money for a simple reason—we are absolutely sure that someone else will accept its value as well. If we did not have this confidence in money, we would not accept it from someone else for payment in the first place.

Money by itself generally has no other value. A $10 bill costs only a few cents to make and has no alternative use. Even coins contain small amounts of precious metal that are worth much less than the value of the coins. The same is true of checking and savings accounts—they have value only because we accept that they have value.

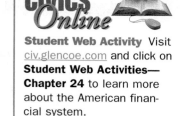

CIVICS Online

Student Web Activity Visit civ.glencoe.com and click on **Student Web Activities— Chapter 24** to learn more about the American financial system.

Reading Check **Describing** What are currency and coins?

The Financial System

People and businesses with money to save take it to financial institutions. These institutions do not simply put the money in a safe and leave it there. Instead, they put the money to work by lending it to other people or businesses that need funds. The financial institution covers its costs—and makes a profit—from the interest (fees) it charges for those loans.

Money Through the course of history, people have used many different materials—gold, copper, beads, and even feathers—as money. **What two types of money are most commonly used today?**

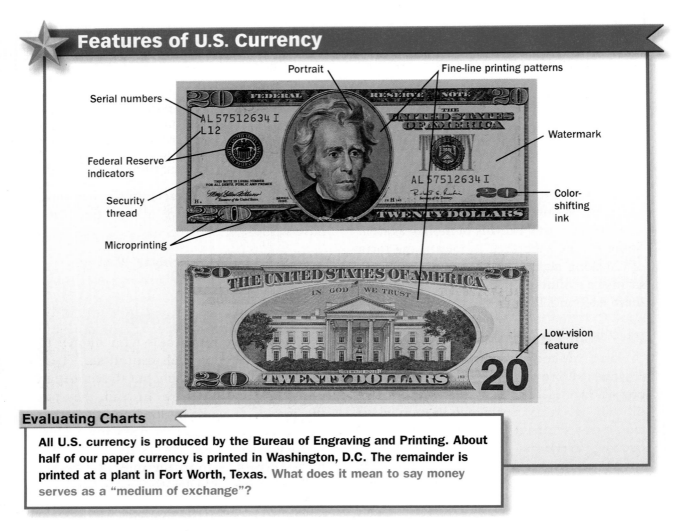

Portrait

Fine-line printing patterns

Serial numbers

Watermark

Federal Reserve indicators

Color-shifting ink

Security thread

Microprinting

Low-vision feature

Evaluating Charts

All U.S. currency is produced by the Bureau of Engraving and Printing. About half of our paper currency is printed in Washington, D.C. The remainder is printed at a plant in Fort Worth, Texas. What does it mean to say money serves as a "medium of exchange"?

Types of Financial Institutions

Commercial banks are financial institutions that offer full banking services to individuals and businesses. They are probably the most important part of our financial system because of their large areas of influence. Most people have their checking and savings accounts in commercial banks.

Savings and loan associations (S&Ls) are financial institutions that traditionally loaned money to people buying homes. They also take deposits and issue savings accounts in return. Today, S&Ls perform many of the activities that commercial banks do.

Credit unions work on a not-for-profit basis. They are often sponsored by large businesses, labor unions, or government institutions. They are open only to members of the group that sponsors them. Credit unions give these workers a financial institution that has low costs.

Although these three types of institutions have differences, each performs a similar function. They all act to bring savers and borrowers together. They give people a safe place to deposit their money when they want to save it and a source for borrowing when they need a loan.

Keeping Our Financial System Safe

The United States has one of the safest financial systems in the world. This high degree of safety results from two factors—regulation and insurance.

First, financial institutions are closely regulated. In fact, banking is one of the most regulated industries in the country. Most financial institutions have to report to one or more regulatory agencies on a regular basis. They are required to follow rules and accounting practices that minimize unnecessary risk.

Despite the best efforts of regulators, some financial institutions fail. When this happens, federal deposit insurance protects consumers' deposits. The most important insurance agency is the **Federal Deposit Insurance Corporation (FDIC),** a federal corporation that insures individual accounts in financial institutions for up to $100,000. This means that if a depositor's bank goes out of business, the person does not lose his or her savings. The FDIC will send the person a check for the amount that was on deposit at the bank—up to $100,000.

When the banking system collapsed in 1934, the resulting crisis wiped out people's entire savings. Congress passed, and President Franklin D. Roosevelt signed, legislation to protect deposits. This legislation created the FDIC.

Fact Fiction Folklore

Susan B. Anthony was the first woman whose portrait was used on U.S. money.

You might think that Susan B. Anthony or Sacagawea were the first women to be featured on money, but that isn't true. Martha Washington appeared on the one-dollar silver certificates in 1886, 1891, and again in 1896.

Because accounts in financial institutions have some type of government insurance, consumers feel safer wherever they deposit their money. As a result, they continue to make deposits—and those deposits give financial institutions the funds they need to make loans that help fuel economic growth.

Reading Check **Explaining** What is the purpose of the Federal Deposit Insurance Corporation?

SECTION 1 ASSESSMENT

Checking for Understanding

1. Key Terms Define the following terms and use them in sentences related to money and the American financial system: coin, savings and loan association (S&L), credit union, currency, commercial bank.

Reviewing Main Ideas

2. Explain In the American financial system, what gives money its value?

3. Describe Why is the American financial system one of the safest in the world?

Critical Thinking

4. Making Generalizations What advantage does a credit union offer its customers?

5. Organizing Information In a graphic organizer like the one below, describe the types of institutions in the American financial system.

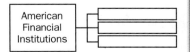

Analyzing Visuals

6. Infer Look at the features of U.S. currency on page 526. Why do you think currency is printed with special inks and includes a security thread?

★**BE AN ACTIVE CITIZEN**★

7. Compare Obtain brochures from several banks and savings and loans. Compare their services and fees. If you had $1,000, which institution would you choose? Explain your choice.

Reading a Time Zone Map

U.S. Time Zones

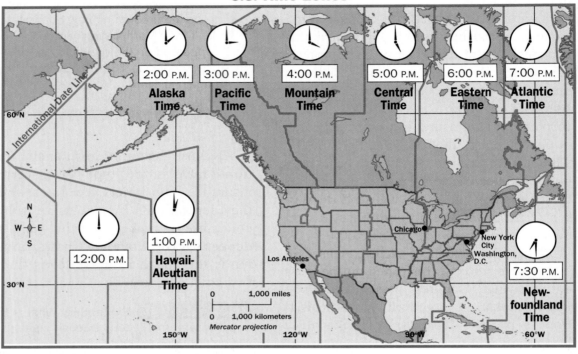

Why Learn This Skill?

The world is divided into 24 different time zones. Six of them divide the United States. Communicating or traveling between them requires making time adjustments.

Learning the Skill

To read a time zone map, follow these steps:

- Trace the vertical sections dividing the map. Each section represents a time zone.
- Observe the east-west progression of the zones across the map. The starting point is 0° longitude.
- Read the labels showing the time in different zones.
- Subtract or add hours among zones to determine time differences.

Practicing the Skill

Read the map above; then answer the following questions.

1. Which time zone is located farther west, the central or mountain time zone?
2. When it is 3 P.M. in Los Angeles, what time is it in New York City?

Applying the Skill

A banker in Chicago needs to attend a meeting in Washington, D.C., starting at 1 P.M. The total travel time is three hours. What time must the Chicago banker leave?

Practice key skills with Glencoe's **Skillbuilder Interactive Workbook CD-ROM, Level 1.**

The Federal Reserve System

GUIDE TO READING

Main Idea

As our nation's central bank, the Federal Reserve is a regulatory agency; it serves as the government's bank. It controls monetary policy in the United States.

Key Terms

central bank, Federal Open Market Committee (FOMC), monetary policy, discount rate, reserve, open market operations

Reading Strategy

Categorizing Information As you read, describe in a graphic organizer like the one below the various roles played by the Federal Reserve in the economy of the United States.

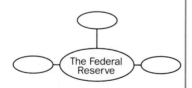

The Federal Reserve

Read to Learn

• How is the Federal Reserve System organized?

• What role does the Federal Reserve play in the economy?

Americans in Action

The Federal Reserve cannot put a dollar in anyone's pocket, provide jobs for very many people, or buy more than a tiny number of goods and services that the nation produces. But the Federal Reserve can have an enormous impact on how you spend, invest, or borrow money. This November 2001 news article from CNN/Money describes one of the government bank's actions: "The Federal Reserve cut interest rates by a half-percentage point Tuesday, its tenth cut of the year . . . , in an effort to keep American consumers spending and boost the economy. . . . [T]he central bank's goal is . . . to let consumers and U.S. stock markets know it's doing everything it can to keep the world's largest economy from slowing down too much."

The decisions of the Federal Reserve Board affect the nation's money supply.

Structure and Organization

The Federal Reserve System, known as the Fed, is the **central bank** of the United States. When people or corporations need money, they borrow from a bank. When banks need money, they borrow from the Fed. The Federal Reserve System is a banker's bank.

The United States is divided into 12 Federal Reserve districts. Each district has one main Federal Reserve Bank. In addition, most Federal Reserve Banks have branch banks within their districts.

Thousands of banks in the United States are members of the Federal Reserve System. Federally chartered commercial banks called national banks are required to be members of the Fed. State-chartered banks may also become members. Member banks are owners of the Fed because they buy stock in the Fed and earn dividends from it.

Board of Governors

When the Fed was established in 1913, the government did not have enough money to set up a new central bank. To raise that money, it required the largest banks to buy stock in the

Fed. To prevent these banks from having too great an influence over the Fed, the law required that the president appoint and the Senate ratify the seven members who make up the Board of Governors. The president selects one of the board members to chair the Board of Governors for a four-year term.

Board members and the chairperson are independent of the president. Even Congress exercises little control or influence over the board, because the board does not depend on Congress for an annual appropriation for operating expenses. This allows the Board of Governors to make economic decisions independent of political pressure.

Advisory Councils

To keep informed of developments in the economy, the Fed has several advisory councils. One council reports on the general condition of the economy in each district. Another reports on financial institutions. A third reports on issues related to consumer loans. Officials of the district banks serve on these councils.

The major policy-making group within the Fed is the **Federal Open Market Committee (FOMC).** The FOMC makes the decisions that affect the economy as a whole by manipulating the money supply. The FOMC has 12 members. Seven are permanent members of the Board. The other five come from the district banks, and their memberships are rotated.

✓ **Reading Check** **Describing** How is the Fed organized?

Federal Reserve Seal

Structure of the Federal Reserve System

PARTICIPATES

BOARD OF GOVERNORS
7 members appointed by the president and confirmed by Congress to serve 14-year terms

ADVISES

FEDERAL OPEN MARKET COMMITTEE
7 Board members
5 District bank presidents

FEDERAL ADVISORY COMMITTEES

12 District Banks

Boston New York City Philadelphia Cleveland Richmond Atlanta Chicago St. Louis Minneapolis Kansas City Dallas San Francisco

Evaluating Charts

The Federal Reserve System, including its 12 district banks, is our nation's central bank. Who owns the Fed?

Functions of the Fed

The Fed has two main regulatory functions: it deals with banking regulation and consumer credit.

The Fed oversees many large commercial banks. If two national banks wish to merge, the Fed will decide whether the action will lessen competition. If so, the Fed could block the merger. It also regulates connections between American and foreign banking. It oversees the international business of both American banks and foreign banks that operate in this country.

The Fed enforces many laws that deal with consumer borrowing. For example, laws require that lenders spell out the details of a loan before a consumer borrows money. The Fed specifies what information lenders must provide.

Acting as the Government's Bank

The Fed also acts as the government's bank in three ways. First, it holds the government's money. Government revenues are deposited in the Fed. When the government buys goods, it does so by drawing on these accounts.

Second, the Fed sells U.S. government bonds and Treasury bills, which the government uses to borrow money. When someone wants to buy a $10,000 Treasury bill, he or she does so at a Fed district bank. When the bill reaches maturity, he or she simply goes back to a district bank and exchanges the bill for a check drawn from the government's account.

Third, the Fed issues the nation's currency, including paper money and coins. This money is produced by government agencies, but the Fed controls its circulation. When coins and currency become damaged, banks send them to the Fed for replacement.

Reading Check **Identifying** What organization regulates foreign banks that do business in the United States?

American Biographies

Alan Greenspan (1926–)

Alan Greenspan, chairman of the Federal Reserve Board, knows how to spot a recession. The son of a stockbroker and a retail worker, the cautious economist lived through the Great Depression as a child. President Gerald Ford appointed him as an economic adviser when the economy plunged in the 1970s. Then, just three months after Greenspan was named chairman of the Federal Reserve Board in 1987, stock prices crashed. Since then, four presidents—Ronald Reagan, George H.W. Bush, Bill Clinton, and George W. Bush—have relied on Greenspan to balance the economy somewhere between boom and bust.

Many Americans consider Greenspan second only to the president in terms of power. Consumers and investors wait to see what he will do with interest rates—raise them or lower them. What many don't know is that Greenspan loves musical notes almost as much as banknotes. He studied at the Juilliard School of Music and traveled for a year as a clarinet and saxophone player with a swing band. Today Greenspan has a fan club—but it's for his ability to handle economic rhythms rather than musical rhythms.

Conducting Monetary Policy

One of the Fed's major responsibilities is to conduct **monetary policy.** Monetary policy involves controlling the supply of money and the cost of borrowing money—credit—according to the needs of the economy. The Fed can increase the supply of money or decrease the supply.

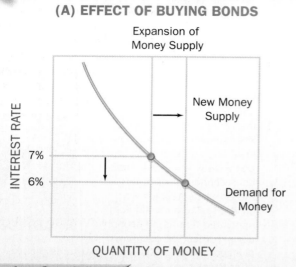

(A) EFFECT OF BUYING BONDS

Expansion of
Money Supply

(B) EFFECT OF SELLING BONDS

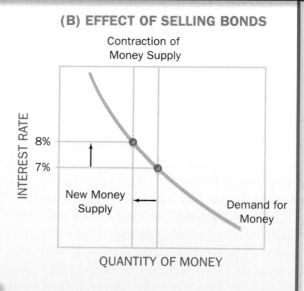

Contraction of
Money Supply

Analyzing Graphs

Buying and selling bonds affects the money supply and, then, interest rates. What happens to interest rates when the money supply contracts?

Changing the Supply of Money

The supply and demand diagrams on this page show how monetary policy works. Because the amount of money is fixed at any given time, the money supply is shown as a vertical line. In the diagrams, the point where supply of money and demand for money meet sets the interest rate—the rate that people and businesses must pay to borrow money. The Fed can change interest rates by changing the money supply. So, if the Fed wants a *lower* interest rate, it must expand the money supply by moving the supply curve to the right. This is shown in Panel A. If the Fed wants to *raise* the interest rate, it has to contract the money supply by shifting the supply curve to the left (see Panel B).

The Fed uses several tools to manipulate the money supply. First, the Fed can raise or lower the discount rate. The **discount rate** is the rate the Fed charges member banks for loans. If the Fed wants to stimulate the economy, it lowers the discount rate. Low discount rates encourage banks to borrow money from the Fed to make loans to their customers. If the Fed wants to slow down the economy's rate of growth, it raises the discount rate to discourage borrowing. This contracts the money supply and raises interest rates. High discount rates mean banks will borrow less money from the Fed.

Second, the Fed may raise or lower the **reserve** requirement for member banks. Member banks must keep a certain percentage of their money in Federal Reserve Banks as a reserve against their deposits. If the Fed raises the reserve requirement, banks must leave more money with the Fed, and they have less money to lend. When the Fed lowers the reserve requirement, member banks have more money to lend.

Third, the Fed can change the money supply through **open market operations.** These are the purchase or sale of U.S. government bonds and Treasury bills. Buying

TIME

Political Cartoons

Frank and Ernest

BANK

UH-OH, LOOKS LIKE THE FED IS TIGHTENING THE MONEY SUPPLY AGAIN.

THAVES

© 1999 Thaves / Reprinted with permission. Newspaper dist. by NEA, Inc.

and it seems to be diverted toward money and ... ne. Making the world a more convenient | Schneider, two men with little hope, of regaining the company's m......While the wage was | to be divert... tim...

Analyzing Visuals When too much money enters the economy too quickly, spending increases—and inflation results. To help prevent this situation from occurring, the Federal Reserve can order banks to increase the amount of funds they keep in reserve, thereby "tightening" the money supply. What visual clues does the cartoonist use to convey the concept of the Federal Reserve "tightening" the money supply?

bonds from investors puts more cash in investors' hands, increasing the money supply. This shifts the supply curve of money to the right, which lowers interest rates. Consumers and businesses borrow more money, which increases consumer demand and business production. As a result, the economy grows. If the Fed decides that interest rates are too low, the Fed can sell bonds.

Why Is Monetary Policy Effective?

Monetary policy can be implemented efficiently. Decisions made by politicians often take a long time because the views of many different people have to be taken into

account. The Fed, however, can move quickly. The Fed can also fine-tune its policy. Fed officials can watch the results of selling bonds or raising the discount rate. If the desired result has not occurred, they can act again, selling even more bonds or raising the discount rate slightly higher.

Interest rates influence business investment and consumer spending. The Fed can affect these activities by manipulating interest rates. Finally, Fed officials are largely free of the constraints faced by politicians.

✓ Reading Check **Describing** What happens when the Fed raises the reserve requirement?

SECTION 2 ASSESSMENT

Checking for Understanding

1. **Key Terms** Define the following terms and use them in sentences related to the Federal Reserve: central bank, discount rate, monetary policy, open market operations, Federal Open Market Committee (FOMC).

Reviewing Main Ideas

2. **Identify** What is the Federal Reserve System?

3. **Describe** What is the function of the Federal Open Market Committee (FOMC)?

Critical Thinking

4. **Drawing Conclusions** What would Fed officials likely do if prices rise too quickly?

5. **Cause and Effect** In a graphic organizer like the one below, explain the effects of the following causes.

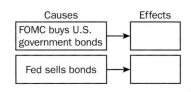

Causes	Effects
FOMC buys U.S. government bonds	
Fed sells bonds	

Analyzing Visuals

6. **Interpret** Study the two graphs on page 532. What happens to interest rates when the money supply expands?

★ **BE AN ACTIVE CITIZEN** ★

7. **Compare** Contact three banks in your community. Find out what interest rate they are charging on loans for a three-year loan on a new car. Compare this to the current Fed discount rate. Which is higher or lower?

How Banks Operate

GUIDE TO READING

Main Idea
After people deposit their money in a savings or checking account, banks make a profit by lending some of those deposits to other consumers.

Key Terms
checking account, savings account, certificate of deposit (CD)

Reading Strategy
Organizing Information
As you read, complete a graphic organizer like the one below to show the main activities of banks.

Activities of Banks

Read to Learn
• How are banks started?
• How do banks operate and make money?

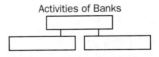**Americans in Action**

"Washington Elementary School is working with the Norco branch of the Arrowhead Credit Union on a program to get children used to saving money. Once a month, on Savings Day, a credit union employee visits the school to collect deposits from students adding to their savings accounts. . . . The accounts have no monthly fee and can be opened with a minimum of $1. Parents or guardians must sign an application for their child to participate. . . . Fifth-grader Sebastian Ruiz has been making deposits for months. . . . He says he has a special reason for adding more money each month. 'I've been saving up to buy my mom a birthday present,' he said."

—Nicole Buzzard, Riverside, California, *Press-Enterprise*, January 29, 2002

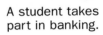
A student takes part in banking.

Banking Services

The students at Washington Elementary School are learning a valuable lesson. If they save their money, small amounts can grow larger—large enough to allow them to buy something special. Millions of Americans put their money in financial institutions, just like these students are doing. In this section you'll find out what banks and other financial institutions do with that money.

Banks are started by investors. They pool financial investments, money, property, and even certificates of deposit to provide banking services to people in their community. If 10 investors each put up $10,000, the new bank would have $100,000 in funds.

Some of this money, of course, would be needed to cover expenses, such as rent, furniture and supplies, and salaries for workers. A large portion, though, would be available to lend to consumers or businesses.

A bank that simply relied on the funds raised by its initial investors would not grow. It would have only a limited amount of money available for loans. Banks need to attract depositors in order to survive.

Accepting Deposits

Banks hope to attract customers who make deposits. They offer **checking accounts,** which allow customers to write checks or use check cards. Checks can be used to pay bills or to transfer money from one person to another quickly and efficiently.

People typically do not keep money in checking accounts for very long. They deposit the money and then use the funds to meet their regular expenses—buying food, paying for telephone service, and so on.

Sometimes people have some money that they can leave untouched for longer periods of time. They put these funds in a different kind of account. With **savings accounts,** banks pay interest to customers based on how much money they have deposited. Because the bank pays interest, the money in a savings account actually grows larger the longer it is left in the bank.

Banks also offer **certificates of deposit (CDs).** With these products, customers loan a certain sum to the bank for a specific period of time. In return, the bank pays interest during that time period. When the time period ends, the customers can turn in their certificates and regain control of their money. They cannot withdraw their money any sooner unless they pay a substantial penalty.

People who buy CDs lose control of their money for some time. On the other hand, banks tend to pay higher rates for CDs than for savings accounts.

Making Loans

One of the principal activities of banks is to lend money to businesses and consumers. Loans can actually increase the supply of money.

Suppose that Maria deposits $1,000 in the bank. The bank can use some of that money to make loans to other customers. Those people then deposit the money they have borrowed, and that money, too, can be loaned to new customers. In that way, the amount of money in circulation continues to grow.

Reading Check **Describing** What is a checking account?

Changes in the Banking Industry

The history of central banking in the United States does not begin with the Federal Reserve. The Bank of the United States received its charter in 1791 from the Congress and was signed by President Washington. Like state banks, the Bank was

Obtaining Loans Consumers often need a loan from a financial institution to make an expensive purchase. **From what sources do financial institutions obtain funds to make loans?**

Financial Services Financial institutions provide a variety of products and services to satisfy consumers' needs. **What are certificates of deposit?**

privately owned and operated. The Bank of the United States, however, was much larger than any of the state banks and had a federal, rather than a state, charter. The Bank acted much like the current Department of the Treasury in that it collected fees and made payments on behalf of the federal government. The charter of the Bank was allowed to lapse in 1811, in part because state banks opposed the Bank.

The Second Bank of the U.S. was chartered in 1816 with the same powers as the First Bank. After the lapse of the Second Bank's charter, the only banks in the nation were those chartered by the states. The federal government neither chartered banks nor regulated the state banks.

State banks issued their own currency by printing their notes at local printing shops. People who wanted loans borrowed these notes and paid them back with interest. Because the federal government did not print paper currency until the Civil War, most of the money supply was paper currency that privately owned, state-chartered banks issued.

The National Banking Act

In 1863, Congress passed the National Banking Act. This act created the system known as dual banking, in which banks could have either a state or federal charter. The federally chartered private banks issued national banknotes, or national currency, which were uniform in appearance and backed by U.S. government bonds.

The Federal Reserve

The National Banking Act corrected some of the weaknesses of the pre-Civil War banking system. Bank crises, however, did not disappear. Panics occurred in 1873, 1884, 1893, and 1907. The Panic of 1907 resulted in the passage of the Federal Reserve Act of 1913.

The Federal Reserve serves as the nation's central bank with power to regulate reserves in national banks, make loans to member banks, and control the growth of the money supply. In 1914 the system began issuing paper money called Federal Reserve notes. These notes soon became the major form of currency in circulation.

The Great Depression

The Great Depression of the 1930s dealt a severe blow to the banking industry. Stocks and other investments owned by banks lost much of their value. Bankrupt businesses and individuals were unable to repay their loans.

A financial panic forced thousands of banks to collapse. The number of commercial banks declined from 26,000 in 1928 to about 14,000 in 1933. When Franklin D. Roosevelt became president, he declared a "bank holiday," closing all banks. Each bank was allowed to reopen only after it proved it was financially sound. Congress passed the Glass-Steagall Banking Act, establishing the Federal Deposit Insurance Corporation (FDIC). The new agency helped restore public confidence in banks by insuring funds of individual depositors in case of a bank failure.

The Savings and Loan Crisis

Because of the many banking failures during the Great Depression, financial institutions had been closely regulated by the federal government. By the late 1970s almost all financial institutions were begging for relief from federal regulations. Congress began the process of deregulation—relaxing restrictions on their activities.

In 1982 Congress decided to allow the S&Ls to make higher-risk loans and investments. When these investments went bad, hundreds of S&Ls failed in the late 1980s and early 1990s. The federal government insured the assets of most savings and loan depositors; and as the banks failed, it found itself saddled with large debts. The full cost of bailing out these institutions cost taxpayers an estimated $200 billion. The FDIC took over regulation of the S&L industry.

The Gramm-Leach-Bliley Act

The Gramm-Leach-Bliley Act, passed in 1999, permits bank holding companies greater freedom to engage in a full range

Economics and You

Debit Cards

Debit cards look like credit cards, but they work a lot differently. Instead of purchasing goods on credit, the debit card transfers money directly from the cardholder's bank account to the seller's account. Debit cards work on the principle of "buy now, pay now." Talk with several people who have both a debit card and a credit card. Ask them to discuss the pros and cons of each type of card. Present your findings in the form of a chart.

of financial services, including banking, insurance, and securities. Some analysts believe that the act will lead to the formation of "universal banks" that offer a full range of financial services. Critics of the law warn that the act may in due course weaken competition for financial services in the United States. Others caution that the act will lead to more sharing of customer information among the affiliated companies, therefore damaging protection of privacy.

Reading Check **Explaining** Why did deposit insurance develop in the 1930s?

SECTION 3 ASSESSMENT

Checking for Understanding

1. Key Terms Define the following terms and use them in sentences related to the banking industry: checking account, savings account, certificate of deposit (CD).

Reviewing Main Ideas

2. Describe What advantage do savings accounts have over certificates of deposit?

3. Explain Why must banks keep a reserve?

Critical Thinking

4. Evaluating Information If your goal was to get the highest interest rate for your savings, what kind of account would be best?

5. Understanding Cause and Effect In a graphic organizer like the one below, show how banks make money.

What Banks Do:		Result:
	→	Profits

Analyzing Visuals

6. Explain Study the photograph that appears on page 535. Write a paragraph explaining what is happening in the picture.

★ **BE AN ACTIVE CITIZEN** ★

7. Compare Obtain brochures from at least three banks that explain the banks' services to customers. How are they alike? How are they different?

Assessment & Activities

Review to Learn

Section 1

- Money is a part of the broad financial system, and it serves three functions. It is a medium of exchange, a store of value, and a measure of value.

Section 2

- The Federal Reserve wields a great deal of power in our economy. It serves as the nation's central bank, it controls monetary policy, and it regulates commercial banks.

Section 3

- Banks provide services to consumers, such as savings and checking accounts, and they make a profit by lending money to consumers.

FOLDABLES™
Study Organizer

Using Your Foldables Study Organizer
Use your completed foldable to create a 10-question quiz. Prepare an answer key on a separate sheet of paper. Trade quizzes with a classmate and then grade each other's answers.

Reviewing Key Terms

Write the key term that best matches each definition below.

1. the policy that involves changing the rate of growth of the supply of money in circulation
2. a bank whose main functions are to accept deposits and lend money
3. a certain percentage of deposits that banks have to set aside as cash in their own vaults or as deposits in their Federal Reserve district bank
4. paper money issued by the Federal Reserve
5. the most powerful agency of the Federal Reserve System
6. financial institutions that traditionally loaned money to people buying houses
7. a federal corporation that insures individual accounts in financial institutions up to $100,000
8. a bank that can lend money to other banks in times of need
9. the interest rate the Federal Reserve charges on its loans
10. an account in which customers receive interest based on how much money they have deposited

Reviewing Main Ideas

11. Name two forms of money in addition to currency and coin.
12. What is the purpose of the Federal Deposit Insurance Corporation (FDIC)?
13. Who controls the Federal Reserve System?
14. What are the two main regulatory functions of the Fed?
15. What kind of account requires the deposit to remain in the bank for a certain period of time?
16. In what kind of account do savers have the most control over their money?

Critical Thinking

17. Drawing Conclusions If you read in the newspaper that the Federal Reserve had just lowered the discount rate, what might you conclude about the economy?

18. Organizing Information In a graphic organizer like the one below, explain the reasons for the Federal Reserve's effectiveness in using monetary policy.

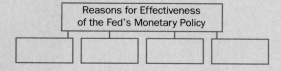

Reasons for Effectiveness of the Fed's Monetary Policy

Practicing Skills

19. Reading a Time Zone Map Study the map on page 528. It takes two hours to fly from Denver, Colorado, in the mountain time zone to Chicago, Illinois, in the central time zone. If you leave Denver at 2 A.M. Friday, what time will it be in Chicago when you arrive?

Analyzing Visuals

20. Look at the graphs on page 532. What effect does selling bonds have on interest rates?

$ Economics Activity

21. For two days, keep track of any time you use money, see money used, or see dollar values written out somewhere. Try to determine in each instance which of the functions the money is serving.

★ CITIZENSHIP COOPERATIVE ACTIVITY ★

22. During the 1930s, the United States underwent a tragic economic depression. Work in groups to research the following aspects of daily life.

- What happened to income and prices?
- What happened to savings accounts?
- What happened to the availability of jobs?

Each member of your group should research one of the three questions. Then summarize the group's notes to develop a presentation that describes what actually happened during the Great Depression.

Technology Activity

23. On the Internet, go to the Federal Reserve education Web site at www.federalreserve education.org/. From the "Choose a Category" drop-down menu, select "Resources and Research." Then click on "Economic Literacy Project." On the right side of the Web page under "Test Yourself," click on "Mpls. Fed's economic literacy quiz." Take the quiz and see how you do. What did you learn about the economy by taking the test?

The Princeton Review
Standardized Test Practice

Directions: Choose the *best* answer to the following question.

If the reserve requirement is 5 percent, how much of a $100 deposit may a bank lend?

F $5
G $95
H $100
J $50

Test-Taking Tip

Remember that a reserve requirement is the percentage of a deposit that a bank must put aside and not use for loans.

25

Government Finances

★ CITIZENSHIP AND YOU ★

If you borrow money because you spend more than you earn, you run a deficit. You have a responsibility to repay the sum you borrow. In this chapter, you will learn how federal deficits and surpluses influence the United States's economy.

 To learn more about government expenditures and revenues, view the *Economics & You* video lesson 4: How Government Spends, Collects, and Owes.

Organizing Information Study Foldable *Make the following foldable to help you organize what you learn about financing our government.*

Step 1 *Collect two sheets of paper and place them about 1 inch apart.*

Keep the edges straight.

Step 2 *Fold up the bottom edges of the paper to form four tabs.*

This makes all tabs the same size.

Reading and Writing *As you read the chapter, use your foldable to write what you learn about the revenues and expenditures of governments in the United States under each appropriate tab.*

Step 3 *When all the tabs are the same size, crease the paper to hold the tabs in place and staple the sheets together. Label each tab as shown. Then cut the three lower tabs in half, forming six tabs.*

Staple together along the fold.

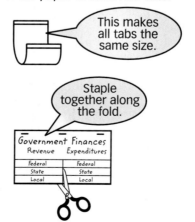

Government Finances	
Revenue	Expenditures
Federal	Federal
State	State
Local	Local

Government expenditures are used to build and maintain transportation systems such as "The Big Dig" in Boston. ▶

CIVICS Online

Chapter Overview Visit the *Civics Today* Web site at civ.glencoe.com and click on **Chapter Overviews— Chapter 25** to preview chapter information.

The Federal Government

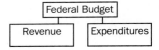

Americans in Action

Government plays a major role in most aspects of our lives. One measure of this role is government spending. The Citizen's Guide to the Federal Budget pointed out that in 2002 "your Federal Government will spend nearly $2.0 trillion." Needless to say, that's a lot of money. In fact, that's almost $7,000 for every man, woman, and child in the country; nearly $5.4 billion per day; and about $3.7 million per minute. George Washington was able to put all the figures for the national government's expenditures for one year on one large sheet of paper. Today the federal budget consists of more than 1,000 pages of small type.

The 2002 federal budget

Preparing the Budget

As the feature points out, the federal government spends a huge amount of money. In fact, purchases by the federal government equal about 18 percent of our GDP. Understanding the finances of the federal government is an important part of understanding how our economy works.

Each year, the federal government creates a **budget.** This budget is a blueprint of how the government will raise and spend money. Both the president and Congress help create it.

The government's budget year is actually not a calendar year. The government uses a **fiscal year (FY),** a 12-month period that may or may not match the calendar year. The federal government's budget year begins October 1 and ends on September 30 of the following year. Consequently, the budget that begins on October 1, 2004, is the fiscal year 2005 budget because 9 of the 12 months fall in that year.

The Budget Process

According to law, the president must present a proposed budget to Congress by the first Monday in February, although this deadline is sometimes missed when a new president assumes office. In this budget, the president outlines where he or she thinks the government should spend its money. The president then formally sends the proposed budget to Congress along with an annual budget message.

Congress then takes the next step by passing a **budget resolution.** This document totals revenues and spending for the year and sets targets for how much will be spent in various categories. Spending is divided into two types; mandatory and discretionary.

Mandatory spending is spending that does not need annual approval. Examples are Social Security benefit checks and interest payments on the government debt, which must be paid every year. **Discretionary spending** is government expenditures that must be approved each year. These include things like money for the Coast Guard, agriculture, space exploration, highway construction, and defense. Discretionary spending makes up only about one-third of the federal budget.

Appropriations Bills

Before the government can actually spend any money, Congress must pass an **appropriations bill.** This is a law that approves spending for a particular activity. Congress splits discretionary spending into 13 separate appropriations bills. These bills must go through the normal process for any bill. Each bill must be approved by both houses and acted upon by the president, either signed into law or vetoed.

The law requires all appropriations bills to be finalized by September 15. If that does not happen, Congress and the president can agree to a temporary, or "stop gap," appropriation. These continuing bills are passed until the appropriations bill for that category of spending finally becomes law.

Reading Check **Describing** What is the purpose of the federal budget?

Federal Revenues

The federal budget has two main parts—revenues and expenditures. The main sources of federal revenues are shown in the graph on the left on page 544.

Taxes on Income and Profits

The income tax paid by individual Americans supplies nearly half of all the federal government's revenue. A portion of the paychecks of workers is withheld each payday. At the end of the year, workers file a **tax return.** This is an annual report to the government that calculates the tax a worker must pay on his or her income. If more money has been withheld than the taxpayer owes in tax, the worker can receive a refund. If the amount withheld is less than the tax owed, the taxpayer must pay the difference.

Corporations also pay income tax on profits they earn. The corporate income tax provides the federal government with about 10 percent of its revenue.

Government Spending The federal government's budget supplies money for many services and programs. Is the space program an example of mandatory spending or discretionary spending?

Payroll Taxes

The second-largest source of federal income is **payroll taxes.** About one-third of federal revenues come from payroll taxes. These taxes are deducted from a worker's paycheck to fund Social Security and Medicare. **Social Security** is a government program that provides money to people who are retired or disabled. **Medicare** pays some health care costs of elderly people.

Other Revenues

Consumers pay an excise tax when they purchase such goods as gasoline, tobacco, alcohol, legal betting, and telephone services. These taxes contribute only 3.4¢ of every dollar collected.

When wealthy people die, the federal government collects an estate tax on the wealth passed on to the deceased person's heirs. The government also charges a tax on certain gifts. Together, these two taxes account for a tiny 1.3¢ of every federal revenue dollar. Miscellaneous sources account for about 2 percent of federal revenues. This category includes such sources as the entry fees for national parks and the fees paid by oil companies that drill for oil on public land.

Forms of Taxation

Actual taxes are classified according to the effect they have on those who are taxed. In the United States today, these classifications include proportional, progressive, and regressive taxes.

A proportional tax is the easiest type of tax to understand. A proportional tax takes the same percentage of income from everyone regardless of how much he or she earns. If there is a tax of 10 percent on all income and you earn $1,000, then you pay $100 in taxes. If you earn $10,000, you pay $1,000 in taxes, and so on.

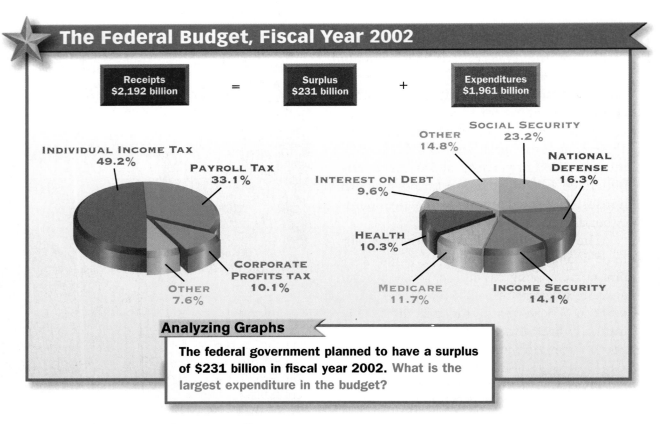

The Federal Budget, Fiscal Year 2002

Receipts $2,192 billion = Surplus $231 billion + Expenditures $1,961 billion

INDIVIDUAL INCOME TAX 49.2%
PAYROLL TAX 33.1%
CORPORATE PROFITS TAX 10.1%
OTHER 7.6%

OTHER 14.8%
SOCIAL SECURITY 23.2%
NATIONAL DEFENSE 16.3%
INTEREST ON DEBT 9.6%
HEALTH 10.3%
MEDICARE 11.7%
INCOME SECURITY 14.1%

Analyzing Graphs

The federal government planned to have a surplus of $231 billion in fiscal year 2002. What is the largest expenditure in the budget?

With a progressive tax, the tax rate (the proportion of earnings taken in taxes) increases as your income increases. Therefore, the higher the income, the larger the percentage of income paid as taxes. A good example of a progressive tax is our federal income tax system.

A regressive tax is the opposite of a progressive tax. The percentage that you pay actually goes down as you make more money income. Examples of regressive taxes are Social Security taxes, gasoline taxes, and sales taxes. For example, poorer families spend a larger proportion of their income on gasoline. Therefore, the sales tax they pay on gasoline takes up a larger proportion of their total income than a wealthier family pays.

Reading Check **Identifying** What percentage of the federal government's revenues comes from payroll taxes?

Federal Expenditures

The graph on the right on page 544 also shows where the federal government planned to spend its money. As you can see, expenditures for FY 2002 were estimated at $1.961 trillion.

Social Security, Medicare, Income Security, and Health

Social Security was the largest single spending category, accounting for about 23.2¢ of every federal dollar spent in FY 2002. Because the number of older people in the population is growing, this expense is expected to grow in the near future.

Medicare is also likely to rise as the population continues to age. This is the fourth-largest category of federal spending.

Income security includes retirement benefits paid to people who used to work in the government or who served in the military. It also includes retirement payments

American Biographies

Frances Perkins (1882–1965)

The Social Security tax owes its origins to Frances Perkins, the first female cabinet member. In 1934, President Franklin Roosevelt named Perkins—secretary of labor from 1933 to 1945—to chair the Committee on Economic Security. There she helped draft a new Social Security bill.

Perkins, a well-known social reformer, impressed people with her confidence. She had successfully waged battles for the rights of women, workers, and consumers. However, she worried about the fate of a broad Social Security program. Would the courts decide that the federal government had overstepped its power?

In late 1934, Perkins shared her concerns at a tea party hosted by Supreme Court Justice Harlan Stone and his wife. She wondered about the constitutional basis for a Social Security law. When nobody was looking, Justice Stone whispered: "The taxing power of the federal government, my dear."

Perkins heeded Stone's advice and based the program on the government's right to levy payroll taxes to pay for it. As Stone predicted, the Supreme Court indeed upheld the Social Security Act of 1935 by a 7–2 decision.

to railroad workers and disabled coal miners as well as payments to poorer Americans for housing and child nutrition.

Health includes payments for Medicaid, which pays for health care for people with low incomes. This category also includes spending on research to find cures for diseases.

Economics and You

Principles of Taxation

Taxes are usually classified according to two major principles. Under the *benefits-received principle,* those who use a particular government service should support it with taxes in proportion to the benefit they receive. Those who do not use a service do not pay taxes for it. Under the *ability-to-pay principle,* those with higher incomes pay more taxes than those with lower incomes, regardless of the number of government services they use. On which principle is a tax on gasoline to pay for highway construction and repair based?

National Defense

National defense is the second-largest category of federal expenditures. The original FY 2002 budget set defense spending at about 16.3¢ of every federal dollar spent. Because of the cost of the war on terrorism that began in late 2001, though, the amount actually spent was higher. President Bush requested $396.1 billion for defense

spending for fiscal year 2003. This figure represented $45.5 billion above the previous year's levels, an increase of 13 percent.

Interest on Debt

Each year, some portion of the federal budget goes to pay interest on the money the government has borrowed. The amount paid depends on how much money has been borrowed and the interest rates of that debt. While it is only the sixth-largest expenditure in FY 2002, interest payments have ranked as high as third largest in the past.

Other Expenditures

The federal government also spends on programs from education to highways to natural resources. These categories account for billions of dollars of spending. Still, the government spends less in these areas than most people think.

Reading Check **Identifying** What is the federal government's second-largest expenditure?

SECTION 1 ASSESSMENT

Checking for Understanding

1. Key Terms Define the following terms and use them in sentences related to federal budgeting: budget, fiscal year (FY), budget resolution, mandatory spending, discretionary spending, appropriations bill, tax return, payroll tax, Social Security, Medicare.

Reviewing Main Ideas

2. Explain What must Congress do before the government can actually spend any money?

3. Describe What are the two main categories that are part of the federal budget?

Critical Thinking

4. Evaluating If the government needed to increase government revenue, which kind of tax do you think should be increased?

5. Describing on a diagram like the one below, list in order of priority the most important federal expenditures.

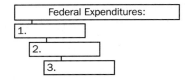

Federal Expenditures:
1.
2.
3.

Analyzing Visuals

6. Summarize Study the 2002 federal budget on page 544. What two major categories are represented? What percentage of expenditures was budgeted for health?

★ **BE AN ACTIVE CITIZEN** ★
7. Categorize List five ways that local, state, and federal governments are involved in your daily life. Provide specific examples in your list.

Writing a Journal

Why Learn This Skill?

A journal is a written day-to-day record of expenses, events, thoughts, and other accounts to which the journal keeper can refer at a later date. Governments and businesses keep journals of receipts and expenditures. Individuals, too, keep journals for business and personal reasons. Keeping a journal can help you keep track of school assignments, recall important information, and express your own thoughts.

Learning the Skill

To write a journal, follow these steps:

- Designate a notebook or other booklet with blank pages and reserve it for your journal entries.
- Start each entry with the date on which you record it.
- Write down any unique information or experience that you want to remember from that day. Use language that is brief and to the point. Short phrases are often adequate.
- Express any thoughts you may have about data you record.
- Stay up-to-date. Record events on the day they happen.
- Refer to your journal entries for accurate information tailored to your own needs and interests.

Practicing the Skill

On a separate sheet of paper, write numbers 1–7. Place a check mark beside each number to indicate which items from the following list would be useful journal entries.

1. Amounts added to your savings account
2. Correct answers to questions you missed on a civics quiz
3. Time school started each morning
4. Steps you took to log on to the Internet on your computer
5. Amount of federal spending for next year as announced on the news
6. Your opinion on how the federal government spends tax money
7. Points about local spending on schools you wish to discuss in class

Journal writing is personal writing with a casual style.

— Applying the Skill —

Examine the sales receipts from purchases you make in one week. Make a journal entry recording the amount you are taxed each day for your purchases. At the end of the week, add your own generalization or opinion relating to government taxation.

Practice key skills with Glencoe's **Skillbuilder Interactive Workbook CD-ROM, Level 1.**

State and Local Governments

GUIDE TO READING

Main Idea
Like the federal government, state and local governments must prepare yearly budgets to account for annual revenue and expenditures.

Key Terms
intergovernmental revenue, sales tax, property tax, entitlement program, subsidize

Reading Strategy
Categorizing Information
As you read, complete a graphic organizer like the one below to show categories of state and local expenditures.

Expenditure Categories (Largest to Smallest)	
State	Local

Read to Learn
• What are the sources of revenue for state and local governments?
• What are the major expenditures for state and local governments?

Americans in Action

Congress extended the ban on taxes on Internet sales until 2006. Congress also opened the door for states to collect sales tax after that. According to a news report from CNN/Money, "the deal also gives states . . . five years to write a simplified tax-collection plan. . . . If [the plan is] approved by Congress, taxes on almost all online and catalog purchases would be collected." Companies that sell over the Internet argue that there are too many sales tax rates imposed by as many as 7,600 state and local tax jurisdictions, the paper said. According to the new tax deal, states would have to agree on one national sales tax, or one rate per state.

Buying from an online shop

Sources of Revenue

State and local governments have their own budget approval processes, revenues, and expenditures. Of course, as shown by the Americans in Action feature, with 50 states and thousands of local government bodies, there are many differences among all these different governments.

State and local governments, like the federal government, have their own revenue sources. Each source is described on the following pages.

State Governments

The main sources of state government revenues are shown in the graph at the top of page 550. The most important are **intergovernmental revenues.** This is money that one level of government receives from another level. For states, most of this revenue comes from the federal government. The federal government gives states money for welfare, highway construction, hospitals, and other activities. As you can see from the figure, states receive 22¢ of every revenue dollar from intergovernmental revenues.

Sales Tax The second-largest source is the state sales tax. A **sales tax** is a general tax levied on consumer purchases of nearly all products. The tax is a percentage of the purchase price, which is added to the final price the consumer pays. The merchant turns over the taxes to the proper state government agency on a regular basis. Most states allow merchants to keep a small portion of what they collect to compensate for their time and bookkeeping costs. Sales taxes account for nearly 21¢ of each state revenue dollar, making them very important to state governments. That is why states are not pleased about the growth of shopping over the Internet, because most Internet sales are not subject to sales taxes. Five states—Alaska, Delaware, Montana, New Hampshire, and Oregon—do not have sales taxes. In the other states, rates range from 2.9 percent to 7 percent.

Contributions The third-largest source of state revenue, accounting for 17.5¢ of every revenue dollar, comes from the contributions that states and state government workers make to their own retirement plans. This money is invested until it is needed to pay retirement benefits.

Income Tax The last major category of revenue is state income taxes. As with sales tax rates, state income tax rates vary a great deal. Some states—such as Colorado and Rhode Island—tax a percentage of the federal income tax. A few states charge a single rate to all taxpayers. In the other states, the rate goes up as income goes up. Seven states—Alaska, Florida, Nevada, South Dakota, Texas, Washington, and Wyoming—have no state income tax at all.

Local Governments

For many local governments, intergovernmental revenues are even more important than they are for states. About 34.4¢ of every local revenue dollar comes from other levels of government. States provide most of this money.

Education Local governments' largest spending category is primary and secondary education. **Which level of government has the major responsibility for college and university education?**

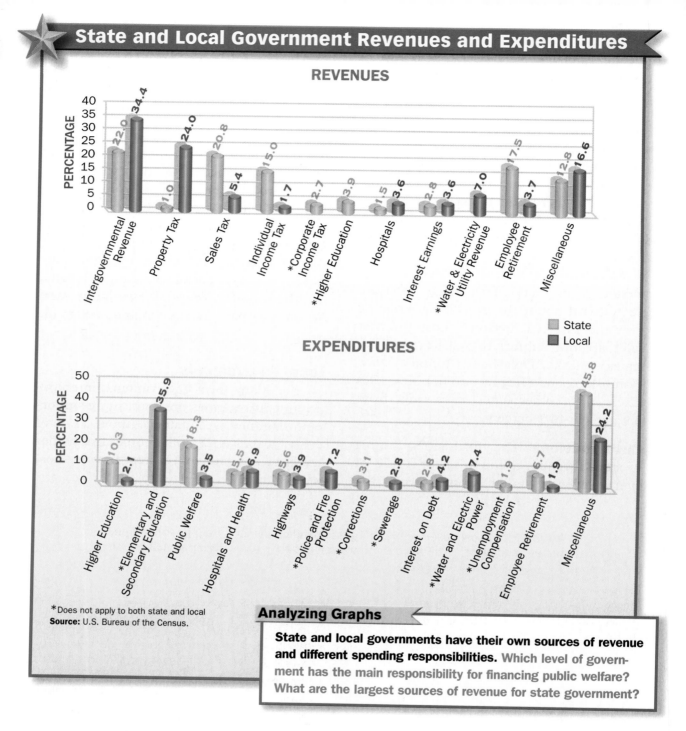

REVENUES

PERCENTAGE

Intergovernmental Revenue — 22.0 | 34.4
Property Tax — 1.0 | 24.0
Sales Tax — 20.8 | 5.4
*Individual Income Tax — 15.0 | 1.7
*Corporate Income Tax — 2.7
*Higher Education — 3.9
Hospitals — 1.5 | 3.6
Interest Earnings — 2.8 | 3.6
*Water & Electricity Utility Revenue — 7.0
Employee Retirement — 17.5 | 3.7
Miscellaneous — 12.8 | 16.6

■ State
■ Local

EXPENDITURES

PERCENTAGE

Higher Education — 10.3 | 2.1
*Elementary and Secondary Education — 35.9
Public Welfare — 18.3 | 3.5
Hospitals and Health — 5.5 | 6.9
Highways — 5.6 | 3.9
*Police and Fire Protection — 7.2
*Corrections — 3.1
*Sewerage — 2.8
Interest on Debt — 2.8 | 4.2
*Water and Electric Power — 7.4
*Unemployment Compensation — 1.9
Employee Retirement — 6.7 | 1.9
Miscellaneous — 45.8 | 24.2

*Does not apply to both state and local
Source: U.S. Bureau of the Census.

Analyzing Graphs

State and local governments have their own sources of revenue and different spending responsibilities. Which level of government has the main responsibility for financing public welfare? What are the largest sources of revenue for state government?

Property Tax The second-largest source of local revenue comes from local property taxes. These are taxes that people pay on the land and houses they own. Property taxes are collected on real property and personal property. Real property includes lands and buildings. Personal property consists of portable objects—things that can be moved. Personal property includes such things as stocks and bonds, jewelry, furniture, automobiles, and works of art.

Most local governments now tax only real property. Although it may vary from state to state, government taxes property based on its assessed value—the estimated value of each property used in the computation of the property tax.

Other Sources Revenue from water and electric utility systems is the third-largest source of revenue. The graph on page 550 shows that local governments receive 7 percent of revenue from these sources.

Local governments have other revenue sources as well. These include sales taxes, local income taxes, and fines and fees.

The local income tax is a tax on personal income. If the state and the local community both have an income tax, the taxpayer pays three income taxes: federal, state, and local.

The sales tax is a tax on the sale of goods or services, generally calculated as a percentage of the selling price. Many states allow their local governments to use this tax. In some places it is a selective sales tax that is applied to only a few items.

Fines paid for traffic and other violations, and fees for special services provide part of the income for local governments. Special assessments are fees that property owners must pay for local services that benefit them in some particular way. For example, a city may impose a special assessment when it improves a sidewalk.

Reading Check **Summarizing** Is the rate of the sales tax the same in every state?

Expenditures

State and local governments' direct expenditures are shown in the lower graph on page 550. Bear in mind that this graph shows the proportion of government spending in the various categories. The fact that the two bars are the same height does *not* mean that state and local governments spend the same number of dollars.

State Governments

Government efforts to maintain basic health and living conditions for people who have insufficient resources of their own are called public welfare, or human services.

Public welfare is an important state government expenditure. Most of these expenditures cover **entitlement programs.** These programs provide health, nutritional, or income payments to people meeting established eligibility requirements. Costs for these programs tend to go up during a recession and down when the economy expands.

Higher Education The second-largest category of state spending is colleges and universities. Note that this spending—10.3¢ of every dollar—is much higher than the 3.9¢ that states collect from fees they charge for higher education. This shows how states **subsidize,** or pay part of the costs, of a college education. Without this subsidy, college students at state schools would have to pay more in tuition and other fees.

Highway construction and road improvement represent 5.6 percent of state expenditures. The federal government pays for much of the interstate highway system, but states maintain those and other highways that link smaller communities with larger ones.

The remaining categories take up a relatively small percentage of expenditures. Employee retirement, hospitals and health, and corrections account for 15.3¢ of every dollar that state governments spend. State governments also fund public education.

Local Governments

Local governments provide education, fire and police protection, water, sewage and sanitation services, trash collection, libraries, and recreation.

Education Providing education is one of the most important functions of government. In many states a large share of local tax revenues goes to pay for public schools. Some states pay a large percentage of local public school costs, but local school districts generally provide most of the money and make the key decisions regarding the operation of the public schools. The largest category of expenditures for local governments is elementary and secondary education. These expenditures account for more than one-third of local government spending.

Police and Fire Protection Police and fire protection are important and make up a large part of the local budget. Fire protection is a local function that varies with the size of the community. In small towns, volunteers usually staff the fire department. In large cities, professional, full-time fire departments provide fire protection.

Water Supply Local governments make the vital decisions regarding water service. Smaller communities may contract with privately owned companies to supply water. The threat of pollution has prompted some local governments to create special water districts. In case of a water shortage, such districts or local governments may try to limit the amount of water used.

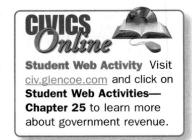

Student Web Activity Visit civ.glencoe.com and click on **Student Web Activities— Chapter 25** to learn more about government revenue.

Sewage and Sanitation Local governments are responsible for sewage disposal. Because many cities draw water from the same body into which they discharge sewage, proper sewage treatment is vital to the conservation of useful water supplies. Many local governments maintain sewage treatment plants to deal with this problem.

At one time, most trash and garbage was buried. Because of environmental concerns, these landfills are no longer the simple solution to sanitation that they once were. Some local governments use garbage-processing plants to dispose of the community's solid wastes.

Reading Check **Identifying** What is the largest expenditure for local government?

SECTION 2 ASSESSMENT

Checking for Understanding

1. **Key Terms** Define the following terms and use them in sentences related to state and local governments: intergovernmental revenue, sales tax, property tax, entitlement program, subsidize.

Reviewing Main Ideas

2. **Generalize** Why are many states not happy about the growth of Internet shopping?

3. **Summarize** What is the source of most intergovernmental revenue for state governments? For local governments?

Critical Thinking

4. **Evaluating Information** If you needed to raise local government revenues, which source of revenue would you target for an increase? Explain.

5. **Making Comparisons** Re-create a Venn diagram like the one shown below. Then, compare state revenue sources to local revenue sources.

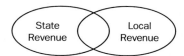

Analyzing Visuals

6. **Interpret** Study the two graphs that appear on page 550. What do they show? Are police and fire protection the responsibility of state or local governments?

★ **BE AN ACTIVE CITIZEN** ★

7. **Research** Contact your local government. Find out where it spends the greatest amount of money. What is its greatest source of revenue? Report your findings to the class.

Managing the Economy

GUIDE TO READING

Main Idea

Governmental budgeting is an uncertain process because governments sometimes collect more or spend more than anticipated. In an attempt to make budgeting more predictable, governments also try to influence the economy.

Key Terms

surplus, deficit, bond, debt, balanced budget, automatic stabilizer

Reading Strategy

Organizing Information
As you read, complete a graphic organizer like the one below to describe automatic stabilizers in the United States's economy.

Automatic Stabilizers	
Stabilizer:	What it does:
Stabilizer:	What it does:
Stabilizer:	What it does:

Read to Learn

• What are government surpluses and deficits?

• What is a balanced budget?

Americans in Action

To carry out all of their functions, governments spend huge sums of money. Because all resources are scarce, an increase in spending in one area will cause a decrease in spending in some other area. *U.S. News & World Report* noted that Texas lawmakers in early 2001 "had visions of an additional $1 billion [that could be spent on] favored programs. But their dreams were fleeting: They quickly discovered that the extra money was needed to pay off budget overruns from the past two years. Spiraling Medicaid costs and increased prison expenditures had put the state nearly $700 million over budget. . . . Texas isn't the only state in financial trouble. Many other governors, including those in Missouri, Kansas, and Virginia, who could once deliver generous tax cuts thanks to a robust economy are also facing fiscal restraints. Some even ace tax-cut rollbacks. Among the major reasons . . . : soaring Medicaid costs coupled with [lower tax receipts]."

Governor Rick Perry of Texas

Surpluses and Deficits

As the feature above reveals, governmental budgeting can be a difficult task. A budget, after all, is built on forecasts—predictions. If tax revenues are lower than expected, the budget is in trouble. The same is true if expenses are higher than anticipated because of some emergency. In this section, you will learn what happens when the government spends more—or collects more—than it planned. You will also see what steps government can take to try to influence the economy in certain ways.

A government enjoys a surplus when it spends less than it collects in revenues. Look at the proposed federal budget on page 544. As you can see, the federal government planned to end the fiscal year with a surplus of $231 billion.

A government runs a deficit when it spends more than it collects in revenues. Look at graph A on page 555. You will see that the federal government had deficits for almost all the years shown in the graph.

Debt

When the federal government runs a deficit, it must borrow money so it can pay its bills. The government does this by selling bonds. A bond is a contract to repay the borrowed money with interest at a specific time in the future. All the money that has been borrowed over the years and has not yet been paid back is the government's debt.

When the government has deficits, the total debt goes up. On the other hand, surpluses can be used to cut the debt. Suppose that the country had a deficit of $100 billion in one year, followed by a deficit of $75 billion the next. If the country had no earlier debt, it would have a total debt of $175 billion after two years. Suppose then it had a surplus of $50 billion in the third year. That money could be used to reduce the debt to $125 billion.

Because of huge budget deficits in the 1980s and early 1990s, the federal debt held by the public is now approximately $3.4 trillion. This equals about $11,800 for every man, woman, and child in America.

Balanced Budget

When spending equals revenues, the government has achieved a balanced budget. The federal government is not required by law to have a balanced budget, although many state and local governments are. In these cases, governments must cut their spending when revenues go down. This was the situation faced by some of the states in the Americans in Action feature.

Revenues often go down during bad economic times. Yet those are the times when states need to spend more on entitlements. This can make the budgeting process very difficult. Many state and local governments are prohibited from borrowing to pay operation expenses. For that reason, they try to maintain an emergency fund balance—a government savings account from which deficits can be paid.

Reading Check **Describing** What is the federal debt? How do surpluses and deficits affect the debt?

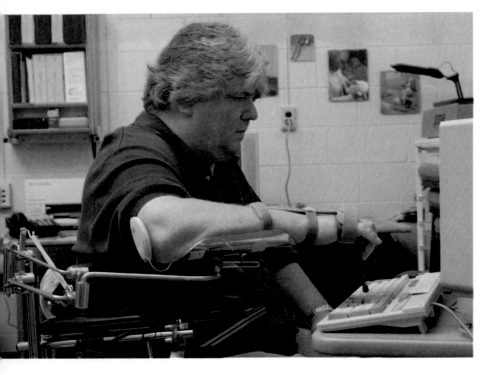

Government Spending
Social insurance programs pay benefits to retired and physically challenged people. What happens when government expenditures are greater than government revenues?

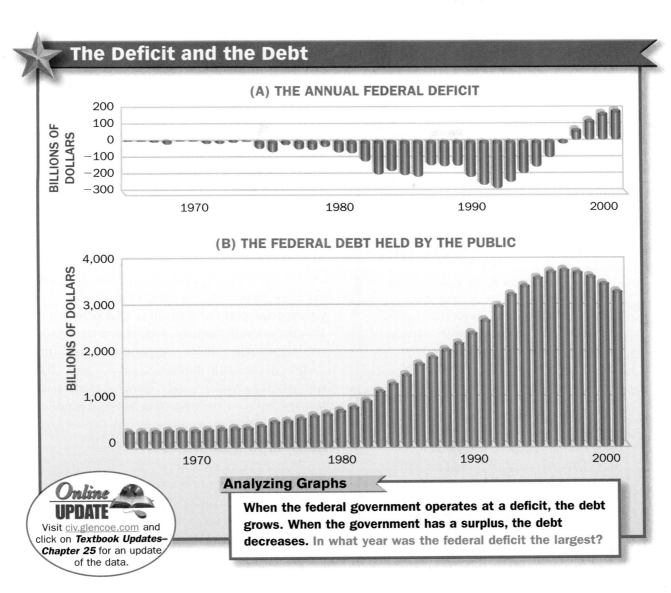

The Deficit and the Debt

(A) THE ANNUAL FEDERAL DEFICIT

BILLIONS OF DOLLARS

200
100
0
−100
−200
−300

1970   1980   1990   2000

(B) THE FEDERAL DEBT HELD BY THE PUBLIC

BILLIONS OF DOLLARS

4,000

3,000

2,000

1,000

0

1970   1980   1990   2000

Online UPDATE

Visit civ.glencoe.com and click on **Textbook Updates– Chapter 25** for an update of the data.

Analyzing Graphs

When the federal government operates at a deficit, the debt grows. When the government has a surplus, the debt decreases. In what year was the federal deficit the largest?

Fiscal Policy

You may recall from your reading of Chapter 23 that the federal government can try to use taxes and spending to help the economy grow. This practice is known as fiscal policy.

Fiscal Policy in Theory

In theory, the government can stimulate the economy during a recession by increasing spending and cutting taxes. Of course, these steps might also increase deficits. That would drive up the federal debt, creating problems for future generations.

When the economy begins to grow again, less stimulus is needed. In those times, the government can reduce spending and increase taxes. This would produce a surplus, which could lower government debt.

Fiscal Policy in Practice

In practice, these decisions are difficult to make. Many people want lower taxes regardless of the state of the economy. Many people also want government services, so the federal government has a difficult time cutting spending even when the economy is booming. As a result, the

Ruchit Shah has a favorite saying: "You live, you learn." It's a fitting philosophy, especially for a young man who has lived in three different countries and eight different towns and has started two successful businesses—all before his 18th birthday.

Born in India, the University of Texas freshman heads up ClickZen, a Web-based advertising agency he runs with his 17-year-old partner, Richard Hecker.

They pooled their resources—$280—and launched ClickZen in the spring of 2000. In 2001, the firm had 25 employees and earned $1.5 million in annual revenues.

"When I was a kid I always had the ambition to make a lot of money," Shah told TIME. Shah adds, "The biggest myth is that it takes money to make money. We started with 280 dollars. It doesn't take hard work, it takes smart work." (It also takes parental support: neither Shah nor Hecker were old enough to sign the initial partnership papers, so that was left to their parents.)

Shah and Hecker are now thinking about how to give something back. They plan to launch a new Web site that they hope will promote world unity through information and education.

Says Shah: "While we're looking to build our business, we're also looking to make a difference in the world."

Ruchit Shah from North Carolina

government sometimes stimulates the economy by spending large sums of money even when no stimulus is needed.

Further, some leaders might oppose increased spending or tax cuts on ideological grounds. Even when a majority of leaders can agree that a stimulus is needed, they often argue over where and how the money should be spent. As a result of these political issues, it is very difficult to get the government to act in a timely manner to stimulate the economy.

In addition, government action doesn't always have the desired effect. Sometimes it takes a long time for political leaders to agree on a plan to stimulate the economy. It takes even longer for them to pass the supporting laws—appropriations, for instance—to put that plan into effect. By then, many months may have passed, and the economic situation may have changed.

Automatic Stabilizers

For these reasons, it is very difficult for the federal government to use fiscal policy to effectively stabilize the economy. Fortunately, the economy has a number of **automatic stabilizers.** These are programs that begin working to stimulate the economy as soon as they are needed. The main advantage of these programs is that they are already in place and do not need further government action to begin.

Unemployment insurance programs are one example. When people lose their jobs—as in a recession—they collect unemployment payments. These payments are not very large. Still, they do give people some help until they can find a new job—or until the economy improves and they are hired back by their former employers.

Many welfare programs also provide automatic assistance. For example, people might begin to collect welfare or Medicaid when their income falls below a certain

TIME

Political Cartoons

Frank and Ernest

YOUR TAX DOLLARS
AND A WHOLE LOT
OF BORROWED
MONEY AT WORK

THAVES

© 1984 Thaves / Reprinted with permission. Newspaper dist. by NEA, Inc.

Analyzing Visuals
Revenues collected through taxes make it possible for the government to provide services such as schools, parks, and roads—but tax dollars are not always suffi-cient to finance ambitious public projects. Explain the argument the cartoonist is making about the financing of the construction project shown in this image.

level. These payments are maintained to provide a minimum standard of living for low-income Americans. These payments help prevent consumer demand from falling even lower—which would force businesses to lay off even more workers.

The fact that the federal income tax is progressive is another stabilizer. Remember from Chapter 23 that progressive tax rates are lower at lower income levels. When people lose their jobs, their income goes down. This pushes them to lower income levels—

and puts them in a lower tax bracket. This helps ease the impact of the cut in income.

When the economy recovers, the oppo-site happens. People make more money and, therefore, need and receive less help from entitlements. Generally, automatic sta-bilizers go into effect much more rapidly than **discretionary** fiscal policies—policies that government *chooses* to implement.

Reading Check **Identifying** What are automatic stabilizers?

SECTION 3 ASSESSMENT

Checking for Understanding

1. **Key Terms** Define the following terms and use them in sen-tences related to governmental management of the economy: surplus, deficit, balanced budget.

Reviewing Main Ideas

2. **Summarize** How does a govern-ment that runs a deficit raise the money necessary to pay its debts?

3. **Evaluate** What is the main advantage of automatic stabilizers?

Critical Thinking

4. **Drawing Conclusions** Do you think the federal government should be required, like many state governments, to balance the budget every year? Explain.

5. **Understanding Cause and Effect** In a graphic organizer like the one below, describe the possible effects of economic stimulus by the government.

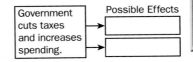

Government cuts taxes and increases spending.	Possible Effects

Analyzing Visuals

6. **Explain** Look at the graphs that show the deficit and the debt on page 555. In what year did the federal debt first surpass $1,000 billion?

★ **BE AN ACTIVE CITIZEN** ★

7. **Research** What is your share of the national debt today? Search the Internet under "national debt" for the debt total. Then divide that number by an esti-mate of the current population.

Assessment & Activities

Review to Learn

Section 1

- Just like private citizens, the government must develop a budget each year that predicts revenues and expenditures.
- The federal government's largest expenditures include Social Security, national defense, and income security.

Section 2

- State and local governments also have to prepare budgets every year that predict revenues and expenditures.
- The largest single category of spending for local governments is elementary and secondary education.

Section 3

- The federal government budgeting process tries to predict annual revenues and expenditures, and it tries to influence the economy through fiscal policy.
- Deficits add to the federal debt.

FOLDABLES™
Study Organizer

Using Your Foldables Study Organizer
Use your completed foldable to compare in an essay, table, or diagram either federal revenues to federal expenditures, state revenues to state expenditures, or local revenues to local expenditures. Share your comparison with the class.

Reviewing Key Terms

Write the key term that matches each definition below.

1. a 12-month financial planning period that may not coincide with the calendar year
2. the program that uses established eligibility requirements to provide health, nutritional, or income benefits to individuals
3. an act of Congress that approves government spending for particular purposes
4. government-funded health insurance for people age 65 and older
5. funds that one level of government receives from another level of government
6. an excess of government expenses over revenue
7. a tax based on the value of one's personal property and real property
8. a note from the government or a corporation promising to repay money with interest by a certain date
9. government spending that does not need the annual approval of the United States Congress
10. government expenditures that must be approved by Congress each year

Reviewing Main Ideas

11. What is the largest source of revenue for the federal government?
12. What was the largest single spending category in FY 2002 for the federal government?
13. What is the largest category of state government expenditures?
14. For which level of government does intergovernmental revenues comprise the largest percentage of revenue? Explain your answer.
15. Why is governmental budgeting such a difficult task?
16. Why is fiscal policy so difficult to enact in actual practice?

Critical Thinking

17. Identifying Alternatives What do you think the government's spending priorities should be? Give reasons for your answers.

18. Making Comparisons In a graphic organizer like the one below, compare the major categories of federal government expenditures to the major categories of state and local government expenditures. Are there similarities?

Major Categories of Government Expenditures		
Federal	State	Local

Practicing Skills

19. Writing a Journal List all the activities in which you take part during a three-day period in your journal. Next to each item on the list, indicate what role the government might have in that activity. Conclude with a summary on the pros and cons of government involvement in your life.

Analyzing Visuals

Study the federal budget on page 544. Then answer the following questions.

20. What were the federal government's three main sources of revenue?

21. What were its three largest categories of expenditures?

 Economics Activity

22. Many Americans are concerned over the future of the Social Security system. They fear that as the American population ages, more money will be withdrawn from the system than will be paid into it. Research the ideas put forward to secure the future of Social Security. Share your findings with the class.

 ★ **CITIZENSHIP COOPERATIVE ACTIVITY** ★

23. Work in groups representing at least three regions of the United States. Each member should choose one or more states in the group's region to research. Determine which states in the region have the highest tax rate. The information needed will be:

- Highest tax rate applied to personal income
- Highest tax rate applied to corporate income
- Sales tax rate

 Technology Activity

24. Go to the IRS Web site at www.irs.gov/. Find out the following: What is e-file? How can you get help with e-filing?

The Princeton Review **Standardized Test Practice**

Directions: Choose the *best* answer to the following question.

All of the following are ways to reduce a budget deficit EXCEPT

A cut government spending.

B increase tax revenues.

C cut tax revenues.

D raise tax revenues and decrease government spending.

Test-Taking Tip

When a question uses the word *except,* you need to look for the answer that does *not* fit.

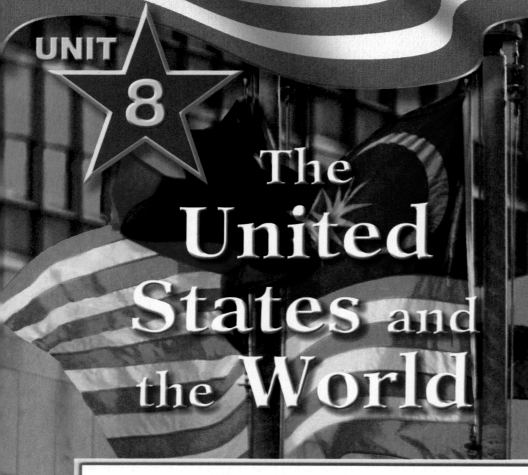

UNIT 8

The United States and the World

Why It Matters

Modern transportation and communication have brought people around the globe closer together. As a result, countries today are more dependent upon one another. As citizens of the United States and members of the global community, we have a responsibility to keep informed about developments in other nations and the world.

Use the **American History Primary Source Document Library CD-ROM** to find primary sources about the global economy.

 BE AN ACTIVE CITIZEN

As you study this unit, pay attention to world events. Make a list in your civics journal of the ways in which international developments can affect your life. Next to each entry, note what you, as an individual, can do about these developments.

The United Nations was created
after World War II to support global
cooperation and world peace.

Comparing Economic Systems

 CITIZENSHIP AND YOU

Each nation of the world has a unique history, its own cultural values, political interests, and economic needs. Contact the embassy or consulate of a country in which you are interested. Find out about the country's history, government, people, culture, and economy. Incorporate your information into a fact sheet.

To learn more about international trade, view the **Economics & You** video lesson 24: International Trade.

 **FOLDABLES** ™
Study Organizer

Explaining Vocabulary Study Foldable *Make the following foldable to help you identify and learn key vocabulary terms in Chapter 26.*

Step 1 *Fold a sheet of paper in half from side to side.*

Step 2 *On one side, cut along every third line.*

Tabs will form as you cut.

Step 3 *Label your foldable as shown.*

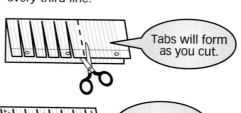

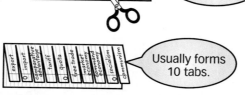

Usually forms 10 tabs.

Reading and Writing *As you read the chapter, note the terms written on the front of your foldable and write a definition for each term under the tab.*

A marketplace in Peru ▶

CIVICS Online

Chapter Overview Visit the *Civics Today* Web site at civ.glencoe.com and click on **Chapter Overviews—Chapter 26** to preview chapter information.

International Trade and Its Benefits

GUIDE TO READING

Main Idea

Trade is important because imports supply us with many goods and natural resources, and many American workers are employed in industries that export products abroad.

Key Terms

export, import, comparative advantage, tariff, quota, free trade, European Union (EU), North American Free Trade Agreement (NAFTA), World Trade Organization (WTO), exchange rate, balance of trade, trade deficit, trade surplus

Reading Strategy

Comparing and Contrasting On a Venn diagram like the one below, compare quotas and tariffs.

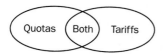

Read to Learn

• Why do nations trade?
• How do regional trade agreements work?

Americans in Action

Intense competition and economic cooperation characterize today's global, interdependent economy. Although the trend toward free trade continues to grow, every nation wants to ensure that it protects its own economy and its workers—sometimes by restricting trade: "The European Union [(EU)] has threatened to impose trade restrictions against the U.S. if President George W. Bush introduces steel tariffs. EU Trade Commissioner Pascal Lamy slammed possible U.S. tariffs on steel imports in a hard-hitting speech to the [United Kingdom] Steel Association on Thursday. Lamy said the EU would launch a World Trade Organization complaint if the Bush administration goes ahead and slaps tariffs of up to 40 percent on some products. The proposed U.S. tariffs are meant to force steel-exporting countries to cut . . . production. The U.S. steel industry contends lower-priced imports are being dumped in violation of U.S. trade laws."

—CNN.com Europe
(December 14, 2001)

American steelworker

Why Nations Trade

International trade is one of the major forces in the world today. Because of trade, Americans can eat fruit grown in Central and South America during the winter. Through trade, American computers are sold in Africa and Asia. In a recent year, about 10 percent of all the goods produced in the United States were **exported,** or sold to other countries. A slightly larger amount of goods were **imported,** or purchased from abroad. These purchases give Americans products they might not otherwise be able to enjoy.

The basic problem in economics, you recall, is scarcity. People do not have enough resources to meet all their wants and needs. The same is true of nations. Trade is one way that nations solve this problem of scarcity.

To Obtain Goods They Cannot Produce

Nations trade for some goods and services because they could not have them otherwise. The United States buys coffee and bananas from other countries because it does not have the soil and climate to grow these foods. It buys industrial diamonds from other countries because it has no deposits of these minerals.

In the same way, other nations trade for goods that they cannot produce but the United States can produce. Commercial aircraft built in Washington State are sold to other countries that do not have the factories or the skilled workers needed to build these vehicles.

To Reflect Comparative Advantage

Countries also trade with one another because of **comparative advantage.** This is the ability of a country to produce a good at a lower cost than another country can. The United States could make color televisions. Other countries, however, can make them more efficiently. That is, they can make televisions at a lower cost. As a result, the United States buys many color televisions made abroad.

Comparative advantage allows nations to specialize. They use their scarce resources to produce those things that they produce better than other countries. Specialization can result in overproduction. Countries produce more of a good than all the people in the country could consume. The answer to the problem is to sell the extra amount abroad.

Sometimes comparative advantage is based on natural resources. Saudi Arabia, for instance, has huge deposits of oil. Its comparative advantage allows it to export this oil. Sometimes comparative advantage is based on labor and capital. The United States has large supplies of wealth, many highly skilled workers, and advanced technology. As a result, it has a comparative advantage in making expensive products like airplanes and weapons.

To Create Jobs

Trade creates jobs. Suppose American airplane makers built planes for only American airline companies. If so, they would have a limited market because each airline needs only so many new planes each year. By exporting the planes, the companies have a chance to win more orders. Then they must hire more workers so they can fulfill those contracts to make more planes.

✓ **Reading Check** **Defining** What is comparative advantage?

Barriers to International Trade

International trade can cause problems for workers who make a product in a country that does not have a comparative advantage. Consumers are likely to buy foreign-produced goods because they are cheaper. When they do so, though, the companies in the consumers' own country that employ these workers lose sales. Those companies

Major U.S. imports are cars and raw petroleum products.

are likely to cut back on production and lay off workers. When this happens, the affected workers and industries often demand that the government step in to remedy the situation. The two most common kinds of barriers to trade are tariffs and quotas.

Tariffs

As you read in the Americans in Action feature, President Bush was considering putting tariffs on imported steel. A **tariff**, or customs duty, is a tax on an imported good. Suppose the United States wanted to protect American steel producers. The government could put a 20 percent tariff on all imported steel. This would add 20 percent to the price of every ton of steel brought into the country. A shipment of steel that costs $100,000 originally would then cost $120,000.

The goal of tariffs is to make the price of imported goods higher than the price of the same good that is produced domestically. As a result, consumers would be more likely to buy the domestic product.

Quotas

Sometimes people want a product so badly that higher prices have little effect. When this happens, countries can block trade by using **quotas,** or limits on the amount of foreign goods imported. No more than the amount of the good set by the quota can be brought into the country.

During most of the 1970s, for example, Japanese-made automobiles were very popular in the United States. Growing sales of these cars cut deeply into the sales of American-made cars. The jobs of American autoworkers were threatened. President Ronald Reagan then placed quotas on Japanese-made automobiles to protect automakers and autoworkers.

Problems With Trade Barriers

Trade barriers can cause problems, however. Sometimes barriers simply do not work. The Japanese responded to the quotas on autos by building factories in the United States. The cars they built still competed with American-made cars. American

Political Cartoons

and it seems to be diverted toward money and ... Making the world a more convenient | Schneider, two men with little hope, of regaining the company's ... While the wage was ... | to be diverted ... tim...

Analyzing Visuals The globalization of industry has brought about increased interdependence—as well as challenges—for the nations of the world. Whom do the two sets of figures in this image represent? What is the relationship among the figures?

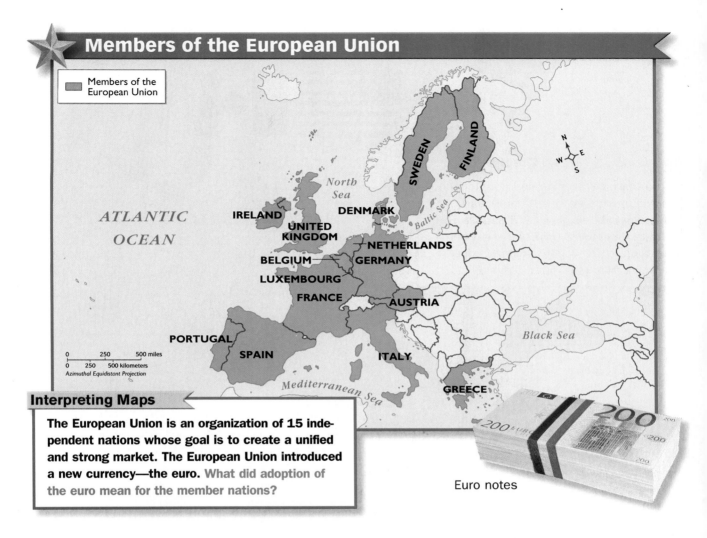

Members of the European Union

Members of the European Union

ATLANTIC OCEAN

North Sea

SWEDEN

FINLAND

IRELAND

DENMARK

Baltic Sea

UNITED KINGDOM

NETHERLANDS

BELGIUM

GERMANY

LUXEMBOURG

FRANCE

AUSTRIA

PORTUGAL

Black Sea

SPAIN

ITALY

GREECE

Mediterranean Sea

0 250 500 miles
0 250 500 kilometers
Azimuthal Equidistant Projection

Interpreting Maps

The European Union is an organization of 15 independent nations whose goal is to create a unified and strong market. The European Union introduced a new currency—the euro. What did adoption of the euro mean for the member nations?

Euro notes

automakers, then, were not helped—although the new factories did create more jobs for American workers.

A bigger problem with trade barriers is that they force consumers to pay higher prices. After all, tariffs raise prices. Quotas can increase prices, too. As a result, these barriers sometimes make consumers pay more than they should have to for the sake of protecting inefficient industries.

In general, most policymakers believe that the total costs of trade barriers are higher than the benefits gained. For this reason, most countries now try to reduce trade barriers. They aim to achieve **free trade.** That means convincing countries not to pass laws that block or limit trade.

Regional Trade Agreements

An important trend is for countries to join together to set up zones of free trade with a few key trading partners. This increases trade among those countries.

The European Union Fifteen European countries belong to the **European Union (EU).** Their combined GDP—total dollar value of all final goods and services produced—is almost as large as that of the United States. The population of these countries is nearly 380 million. The EU offers a huge market to many businesses.

There are no trade barriers among these nations. Goods, services, and even workers can move freely between them. Cheese made

The North American Free Trade Agreement (NAFTA)

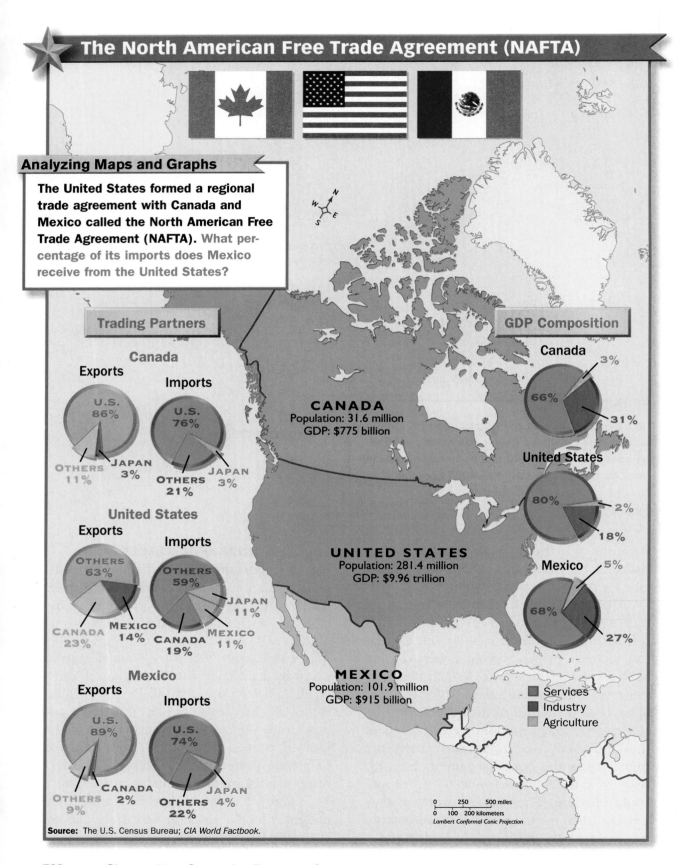

Analyzing Maps and Graphs

The United States formed a regional trade agreement with Canada and Mexico called the North American Free Trade Agreement (NAFTA). What percentage of its imports does Mexico receive from the United States?

Trading Partners

Canada

Exports
- U.S. 86%
- OTHERS 11%
- JAPAN 3%

Imports
- U.S. 76%
- OTHERS 21%
- JAPAN 3%

United States

Exports
- OTHERS 63%
- CANADA 23%
- MEXICO 14%

Imports
- OTHERS 59%
- JAPAN 11%
- MEXICO 11%
- CANADA 19%

Mexico

Exports
- U.S. 89%
- OTHERS 9%
- CANADA 2%

Imports
- U.S. 74%
- OTHERS 22%
- JAPAN 4%

GDP Composition

Canada
- 66%
- 3%
- 31%

United States
- 80%
- 2%
- 18%

Mexico
- 68%
- 5%
- 27%

Legend:
- Services
- Industry
- Agriculture

CANADA
Population: 31.6 million
GDP: $775 billion

UNITED STATES
Population: 281.4 million
GDP: $9.96 trillion

MEXICO
Population: 101.9 million
GDP: $915 billion

0   250   500 miles
0   100   200 kilometers
Lambert Conformal Conic Projection

Source: The U.S. Census Bureau; *CIA World Factbook*.

in France can be shipped to Germany just as easily as Vermont cheddar is shipped to New York. In January 2002, these countries became even more closely linked when most began using a common currency. No longer do the French use francs or do the Germans use marks. Instead, all sales in these countries are now made with euros. (The United Kingdom, Denmark, and Sweden chose not to take part in the common currency.)

The EU is an important part of the world economy. It will grow even larger in the future. The organization is considering adding other nations as members.

NAFTA The growing economic power of the EU encouraged other countries to lower trade barriers in order to increase trade. In the 1990s, the United States, Canada, and Mexico signed a pact called the North American Free Trade Agreement (NAFTA). This deal will eventually eliminate all barriers to trade among the three countries. Since NAFTA was enacted, trade among them has grown twice as fast as the economies themselves have grown. Opponents of NAFTA contended that American workers would lose their jobs because U.S. plants would move to Mexico to take advantage of cheaper wages and less stringent enforcement of environmental and workers' rights laws. NAFTA supporters argued that increased trade would stimulate growth and put more low-cost goods on the market.

The WTO An international body called the World Trade Organization (WTO) oversees trade among nations. It organizes negotiations about trade rules and provides help to countries trying to develop their economies. As you read in the Americans in Action feature, it also plays a role in settling trade disputes.

In recent years, the World Trade Organization and the growth of trade have been harshly criticized. Critics say that the WTO policies fav. the expense of work corporations at and poor countries. environment,

✓ **Reading Check** Explainin. sometimes place quotas on a do nations 'ed good?

Financing Trade

Different nations have different c cies. The United States uses the dollar a medium of exchange; Mexico, the pe Britain, the pound; and Japan, the yen. It you travel outside the United States or invest in foreign business, you will want to know the exchange rate—what the price of your nation's currency is in terms of another nation's currency. Most of the world's nations use a flexible exchange rate

Protesting WTO Policies At an anti-WTO demonstration, protesters criticize the organization for implementing policies that erode human rights and labor and environmental standards. **What is the World Trade Organization?**

...ne forces of system. Under this ...wed to set the supply and dema... ...es. Thus, a cur-price of various ... ...ge each day. rency's price ...

Trade

The Bala... exchange rate can have an A cu...ect on a nation's balance of import... balance of trade is the differ-trade... ...ween the value of a nation's exports enc... ...its imports. If a nation's currency ar... ...reciates, or becomes "weak," the nation ...ill likely export more goods because its products will become cheaper for other nations to buy. If a nation's currency appreciates in value, or becomes "strong," the amount of its exports will decline.

Trade Deficits and Surpluses

A country has a **trade deficit** whenever the value of the products it imports exceeds the value of the products it exports. It has a **trade surplus** whenever the value of its exports exceeds the value of its imports.

Effects of a Trade Deficit

What are the effects of a trade deficit? To illustrate, the large deficit in the United States's balance of payments in the late 1990s flooded the foreign exchange markets with dollars. The increase in the supply of dollars caused the dollar to lose some of its value. The weaker dollar caused unemployment in import industries as imports became more expensive, and it caused employment to rise in export industries as the prices of these goods became more competitive.

Eventually, under flexible exchange rates, trade deficits tend to automatically correct themselves through the price system. A strong currency generally leads to a deficit in the balance of payment and a subsequent decline in the value of the currency. A weak currency tends to cause trade surpluses, which eventually pull up the value of the currency.

✓ Reading Check **Describing** What is a trade deficit?

SECTION 1 ASSESSMENT

Checking for Understanding

1. **Key Terms** Write a paragraph related to international trade using the following key terms: export, import, comparative advantage, free trade.

Reviewing Main Ideas

2. **Explain** How can a nation restrict imports? Why would a nation wish to restrict its imports?

3. **Describe** What is the purpose of the North American Free Trade Agreement (NAFTA)? How is NAFTA different from the World Trade Organization?

Critical Thinking

4. **Evaluating Information** What do you think is the single most important reason nations trade with one another? Explain your answer.

5. **Cause and Effect** On a diagram like the one below, explain how a quota on a good or service produced in your community might affect the workers in a particular industry. Then explain how the same quota might affect consumers.

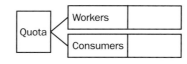

Analyzing Visuals

6. **Interpret** Study the map of the European Union on page 567. How many countries are part of the organization? Is Italy part of the EU? Is Russia?

★ **BE AN ACTIVE CITIZEN** ★

7. **Research** Find opinions about NAFTA on the Internet. Scan several articles to identify which groups support NAFTA and which groups oppose it. Provide the reasons each group gives for its position.

Building a Database

Why Learn This Skill?

A database is a collection of information, or data, stored in a computer or on diskette files. It runs on software that organizes large amounts of information in a manner that makes it easy to access, search, sort, and make additions or deletions. It often takes the form of a chart or table. Governments and businesses maintain databases containing information they need to store and update regularly, such as tax revenues. Families may use databases for budgeting purposes. You might build databases to store information related to a class at school, your weekly schedule, or friends' birthdays.

Learning the Skill

To create a database using word-processing software, follow these steps:

- Define the type of information your database will hold. Enter a title identifying the type of information in your document and file names.
- Determine the set of specific points of information you wish to include. For example, you might want to record data on the GDP, products, imports, and exports of countries in Asia.
- Enter the information categories along with country names as headings in a five-column chart. Each column makes up a field, the basic unit for information stored in a database.
- Enter data you have collected into the cells, or individual spaces, on your chart.
- Use your computer's sorting feature to organize the data. You might alphabetize by country name or arrange from highest to lowest GDP.
- Add, delete, or update information as needed in the future. Database software automatically adjusts the cells in the chart.

U.S. International Commerce

Country	Japan	United Kingdom	Canada
Exports to U.S.	Engines, rubber goods, cars, trucks, buses	Dairy products, beverages, petroleum products, art	Wheat, minerals, paper, mining machines
Value of Exports to U.S.	$128 billion	$35.2 billion	$232.6 billion
Imports from U.S.	Meat, fish, sugar, tobacco, coffee	Fruit, tobacco, electrical equipment	Fish, sugar, metals, clothing
Value of Imports from U.S.	$67.3 billion	$42.8 billion	$199.6 billion

You can organize information in a database.

Practicing the Skill

On a separate sheet of paper, answer the following questions referring to the database on this page.

1. What type of information does this database contain?
2. What related fields of information does it display?
3. If the author sorts the data alphabetically according to country names, how will the data in the third field read?
4. The author learns that Canada also exports clothing, beverages, and art to the United States. Is it necessary to create a new database? Explain.

Applying the Skill

Build a database to help you keep track of your school assignments. Work with four fields: Subject, Assignment Description, Due Date, and Completed Assignments. Be sure to keep your database up-to-date.

Economic Systems

GUIDE TO READING

Main Idea

To deal with the fundamental problem of scarcity, different types of economic systems exist.

Key Terms

market economy, per capita GDP, command economy, socialism, communism, mixed economy

Reading Strategy

Organizing Information
As you read the section, complete a diagram like the one below by describing three characteristics of a market economy.

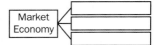

Read to Learn

• How does a market economy work?

• What are the characteristics of a command economy?

• What is a mixed economy?

Americans in Action

China and its 1.3 billion people joined the World Trade Organization in December 2001, ending a 15-year quest and ushering in a new era of reform expected to bring sweeping changes to the Communist-ruled nation. Reuters news agency reported that "foreign investors have waited eagerly for the world's largest potential market to become an integral part of the global economy. The Communist Party [newspaper] *People's Daily* urged officials to abide by WTO commitments and said entry would fundamentally change the way the government handled the economy."

U.S. trade negotiator Charlene Barshefsky meets with China's Minister of Foreign Trade Shi Guangsheng

Market Economies

Not all economic systems are alike. Some, like the one in the United States, are based on markets. Others, like China's, include far greater government control. These different economies deal with scarcity in different ways. All societies face the basic questions of WHAT to produce, HOW to produce it, and FOR WHOM to produce it. The way these questions are answered determines a society's economic system. In a pure market economy, these decisions are made in free markets based on the interaction of supply and demand. **Capitalism** is another name for this system.

One of the chief characteristics of a market economy is that private citizens—not the government—own the factors of production. As you recall, those factors are natural resources, capital, labor, and entrepreneurship.

Because the factors of production are in private hands, a market economy offers a high degree of individual freedom. Businesses make their own decisions regarding what to produce, how to produce it, and for whom to produce it. Driving those decisions is the business owner's desire to earn a profit. At the same time, consumers make their own decisions about what to buy.

In a market economy, these decisions take place in the market. Supply and demand interact to set prices, and producers and consumers base their decisions on prices.

A market economy is decentralized. That is, decisions are made by all the people in the economy and not by just a few. The economy seems to run by itself because no one coordinates these decisions.

There are no pure market economies in the world. In the United States, for example, government provides public goods such as defense and a system of justice.

Another government role is to make sure that markets stay competitive. Effective competition requires a large number of sellers. The U.S. government ensures this by regulating businesses. It also punishes businesses that break laws meant to ensure competition.

Finally, the government plays a role with externalities. These are the unintended side effects that have an influence on third parties. For example, the government works to reduce pollution, which is a negative externality. The government also takes steps to encourage activities that generate positive externalities. For instance, it provides money to fund basic science research. That research can be used by businesses to develop new products.

The majority of the largest economies in the world today are market economies. Look at the map on this page, which shows the **per capita GDP** for selected nations.

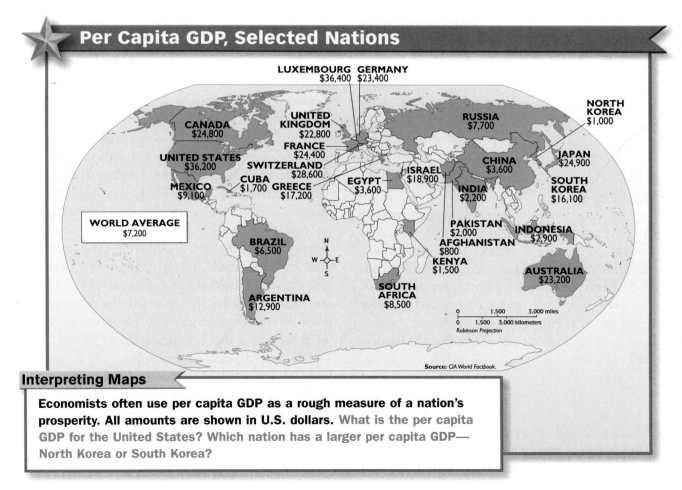

Per Capita GDP, Selected Nations

LUXEMBOURG $36,400
GERMANY $23,400
CANADA $24,800
UNITED KINGDOM $22,800
FRANCE $24,400
UNITED STATES $36,200
SWITZERLAND $28,600
CUBA $1,700
MEXICO $9,100
GREECE $17,200
EGYPT $3,600
ISRAEL $18,900
RUSSIA $7,700
CHINA $3,600
INDIA $2,200
NORTH KOREA $1,000
JAPAN $24,900
SOUTH KOREA $16,100
PAKISTAN $2,000
AFGHANISTAN $800
KENYA $1,500
INDONESIA $2,900
WORLD AVERAGE $7,200
BRAZIL $6,500
ARGENTINA $12,900
SOUTH AFRICA $8,500
AUSTRALIA $23,200

0   1,500   3,000 miles
0   1,500   3,000 kilometers
Robinson Projection

Source: CIA World Factbook.

Interpreting Maps

Economists often use per capita GDP as a rough measure of a nation's prosperity. All amounts are shown in U.S. dollars. What is the per capita GDP for the United States? Which nation has a larger per capita GDP— North Korea or South Korea?

Per capita GDP divides the total GDP by the country's population. By expressing GDP in terms of each person, we can compare one nation's economic success to another without regard to the size of the two economies. Look at the countries that have high per capita GDPs. Most of them, including the United States, have market economies.

Reading Check **Explaining** Why is economic freedom a characteristic of market economies?

Command Economies

The system that we know best in the United States is the market economy. The opposite of this system is the **command economy.** In a pure command economic system, the individual has little, if any, influence over how the basic economy functions. Under this system, the major economic decisions are made by the central government. The government tells producers what to do—it *commands* the actions they should take. This form of economic system is also called a controlled economy. The term "communism" applies to command economies.

In the early 1800s, some people believed that ending the misery of exploited workers required eliminating capitalism completely. They advocated **socialism,** the belief that the means of production should be owned and controlled by society, either directly or through the government. In this way, socialists felt that wealth would be distributed equally among all citizens.

Karl Marx, a German thinker and writer, was a socialist who advocated violent revolution. Marx believed that in industrialized nations, the population is divided into capitalists, or the bourgeoisie, who own the means of production, and

workers, or the proletariat, who work to produce the goods. Marx interpreted human history as a class struggle between the workers and the capitalists. Eventually, the workers would revolt and overthrow the capitalists in a revolution.

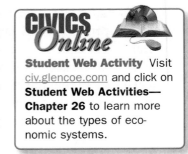

Student Web Activity Visit civ.glencoe.com and click on Student Web Activities—Chapter 26 to learn more about the types of economic systems.

Marx first called his own ideas "scientific socialism." He believed that in time, socialism would develop into full communism. Under **communism** one class would evolve, property would all be held in common, and there would be no need for government.

In a command economy, most productive resources—especially land and capital—are owned by government. They are not in the hands of private individuals. Because the government plays such a major role in these economies, people have less economic freedom. As a result, people in these systems generally have fewer choices than do those in market economies.

The government makes the three basic allocation decisions in a command economy. It decides WHAT to produce. For instance, it tells factory managers whether to make cars or buses or military vehicles. The government also regulates HOW goods will be produced. It tells managers where they should buy their raw materials, for example. Finally, the government decides FOR WHOM to produce. It fixes the wages of all workers and sets prices as well.

As you might expect, governments in command economies have planning agencies with a great deal of power. These organizations take control of different parts of the economy, such as agriculture, steel production, and shoe manufacturing. They make the important decisions in those industries.

Command economies can be very inefficient. As a result, they tend to grow more slowly and attain a lower per capita GDP than market economies. Cuba and North Korea are perhaps the two best current examples of command economies. Look at the map on page 573 to see how low their per capita GDPs are.

For many decades, the Soviet Union had a command economy. The Russian economy that survived it has been trying to convert to a market economy ever since. China is another command economy that is making the transition to a market economy. You will read how these two economies are changing in the next section.

Mixed Economies

A mixed economy combines basic elements of a pure market economy and a command economy. Most countries of the world have a mixed economy in which private ownership of property and individual

Command Economy North Korea's command economy has focused on producing weapons and not consumer goods. **Who owns most of North Korea's productive resources?**

decision making are combined with government intervention and regulations. In the United States, most decisions are made by individuals reacting to market phenomena—such as prices determined by supply and demand, competition, private property, and exchange. However, federal, state, and local governments make laws regulating certain areas of business.

Reading Check **Contrasting** What is the difference between a pure market economy and a mixed economy?

SECTION 2 ASSESSMENT

Checking for Understanding

1. **Key Terms** Write a true statement *and* a false statement for each of the following terms: market economy, command economy, mixed economy. Indicate which statements are true and which are false.

Reviewing Main Ideas

2. **Explain** What does it mean to say that a market economy is decentralized?

3. **Contrast** Does the government take a more active role in a market economy or in a command economy?

Critical Thinking

4. **Drawing Conclusions** Many nations are moving away from a command economic system and toward a market economic system. Why do you think this is so?

5. **Making Comparisons** On a chart like the one below, describe how the role of the individual differs under different economic systems.

Economic System	Role of Individual
Market	
Command	

Analyzing Visuals

6. **Interpret** Study the map on page 573. What is the per capita GDP for Argentina? For India? Does China's per capita GDP surpass the world average?

★**BE AN ACTIVE CITIZEN**★

7. **Research** Choose one familiar item that is imported to the United States. Collect information about the item, including where it comes from and how much it costs. Learn why the country it comes from produces this item. Present your information in class.

Economies in Transition

GUIDE TO READING

Main Idea

Developing nations are those with less industrial development and a relatively low standard of living.

Key Terms

developing country, traditional economy

Reading Strategy

Organizing Information As you read the section, complete a diagram like the one below by listing the main obstacles to economic growth in developing nations.

Obstacles to Growth

Read to Learn

• Why are some nations moving toward a market economic system?

• What are the obstacles to economic development that countries must face?

Americans in Action

Because the problems of developing nations are so great, economic development is a difficult task. Many approaches have been tried, and some, like the new policies instituted in Vietnam, have much promise: "During ten days in July, the Vietnamese government did more to promote economic growth . . . than it has done over the previous ten years. After three years of negotiations . . . , Vietnam signed a . . . trade agreement . . . with the United States. A few days later, . . . Vietnam opened its first post-war stock market. The decisions are of enormous . . . economic significance. . . . With economic growth at its lowest levels since 1990 and foreign investment down over 85% since its peak in 1996, [the country needed to act]. China's trade agreement with the U.S. added further pressure on Vietnam to access global markets or risk falling further behind its neighbors."

—*Vietnam Business Journal Archives,* December 12, 2001

Marketplace in Saigon, Vietnam

The Transition From a Command Economy

Today many nations in the world are making the transition from one type of economy to another. Some are moving from a traditional economy to a more developed system. Others are shifting from a command economy to a market-based system.

The main reason for the transition is the remarkable success of the major market economies in the world. Market economies have prospered, and many countries hope to be able to bring that prosperity to their own people.

Command economies became increasingly unattractive in the 1980s. They were unable to achieve the economic growth that market economies could. The Soviet Union, China, and the countries of Eastern Europe all had command economies. By 1991, however, they were all in the process of changing. In Eastern Europe, this economic change was accompanied by political changes. The countries moved toward greater democracy. The same transition took place in the Soviet Union, where change was accompanied by the actual breakup of the country. Russia emerged as the largest country to come out of the old Soviet Union.

Russia

The Soviet Union collapsed in 1991 because Communist leaders could no longer keep the economy going. Almost all major economic decisions during Soviet times were made by a central planning body called the Gosplan. Officials in this agency developed plans that answered basic production questions.

The Gosplan made the decisions to get millions of individual products made and shipped to stores. In the process, it frequently made mistakes. Supplies did not arrive on time, too much or too little of a good was produced, and goods were not always delivered to the places that needed them the most. The process became too complicated to work effectively.

After the Soviet Union broke up, Russia's leaders wanted to convert to a market-based economy. State-owned factories had to be put in the hands of private ownership. Stock markets had to be created so that people could own these factories. People had to learn how to let supply and demand set prices and how to make decisions based on market prices.

This transition has been a very difficult one. Russia is still in the midst of the changeover today, and the process will probably go on for many more years. In recent years, the economy has shown signs of improving.

China

China, like Russia, is moving away from a command economy and toward a market economy. The Chinese economy had been modeled on the Soviet system of central planning. By the 1980s, China was

Changing Economies Reforms in Russia and China gave individuals more decision-making power and the ability to sell part of their goods and services for a profit. **What role did the Gosplan play in the Soviet economy?**

falling far behind the market-based economies of its neighbors Taiwan, South Korea, Hong Kong, and Singapore. China began introducing market reforms to catch up. For example, it converted many state-owned factories to privately owned factories, and even set up a major stock exchange in Shanghai.

American Biographies

Daniel Katz (1961–)

Daniel Katz wanted to find some way to conserve the rain forests. In 1986, at the age of 24, he cofounded the Rainforest Alliance, a group aimed at getting environmentalists, business leaders, and the public to figure out new ways to stop deforestation, or destruction of forests.

With no money, office, or staff, everybody worked as volunteers at first. The alliance began with educational projects. Then, step-by-step, members developed two certification programs—SmartWood, the world's first program to certify tropical timber products, and ECO-O.K., the first program to certify tropical farm products, like bananas and cacao. The two programs set guidelines aimed at conserving the tropical forests while protecting workers and companies that depended upon the rain forests for income.

In the 1980s, Gibson Guitar signed on to make SmartWood guitars, while Chiquita Banana agreed to produce bananas on ECO-O.K. plantations. Other success stories followed. Under Katz's leadership, the alliance certified millions of acres of "well-managed" forests and plantations. "I think the alliance has had quite a few accomplishments," says Katz. "But we still need everybody's help while there's still time to save our tropical forests."

The reunification of Hong Kong with China in 1997 gave China even more incentive to change. Chinese leaders hoped to learn more about markets from Hong Kong.

The transition has had some success. China's economy has averaged 10 percent growth each year over the past 20 years—a very high level of growth. Many workers in China's cities can now buy goods they were never able to have in the old economy. Still, there are problems. Farmers are finding it hard to compete with cheaper food from abroad. About 160 million Chinese are unemployed. China's leaders need to find solutions to these problems.

Reading Check **Explaining** Why did China introduce market reforms?

Developing Countries

Many other countries are also trying to make the transition to a market-based economy. Most of these countries are called **developing countries,** or countries whose average per capita income is only a fraction of that in more industrialized countries.

Traditional Economies

Most of the countries trying to make this transition have **traditional economies.** In these systems, things are done "the way they have always been done." Economic decisions of what, how, and for whom to produce are based on custom or habit. For example, if your grandparents and parents fished for a living, you will fish for a living. Farmers grow the crops that have been grown in the area for many centuries. People make pottery or cloth using traditional methods and materials.

Problems Developing Countries Face

Developing countries are poor by western standards. They face several other obstacles that make economic growth difficult.

Social Statistics for Selected Nations

		LIFE EXPECTANCY AT BIRTH	INFANT MORTALITY (deaths per 1,000 live births)	LITERACY (% of people who can read and write)	POPULATION GROWTH (annual % 1980–2000)
Afghanistan		46	147	36	3.0
Canada		79	5	98	1.1
China		70	30	83	1.3
India		63	70	56	2.0
Japan		81	4	99	0.4
Kenya		48	76	81	3.0
Mexico		72	29	91	1.9
United States		77	7	97	1.1

Source: World Bank.

Evaluating Charts

A comparison of developing countries with industrialized countries shows a wide discrepancy in health and education. What nation's people have the shortest life expectancy? The longest?

The World Bank logo

One problem is a high rate of population growth. When population grows faster than GDP, per capita GDP declines. That is, each person has a smaller share of what the economy produces. Look at the table showing social statistics of selected countries on this page. You will see that countries with higher rates of population growth tend to have lower per capita GDPs (see the map on page 573). The countries with high per capita GDPs, on the other hand, have low rates of population growth.

Another problem is geography and natural resources. Many developing countries are landlocked and do not have access to ocean trade routes. Others might have ocean access but lack natural resources.

Many developing countries face severe problems left over from war. Countries such as Afghanistan, Ethiopia, Somalia, Cambodia, and Vietnam experienced wars in recent years. These wars destroyed roads, bridges, factories, and other resources. They also left many people dead. In addition, many unexploded land mines are still found in the countryside, making farming difficult—and even dangerous.

Some of these countries face the problem of severe debt. They borrowed large sums of money to spur economic growth. Now they owe more money than the GDP they produce in a year. This makes it difficult to pay off the loans. In fact, many cannot even pay the interest on their debt.

Finally, corruption delays the development of some economies. Nigeria, for example, is rich in oil but is still a relatively poor nation because of the chronic corruption of its government officials.

Helping Developing Countries

Countries can try to overcome some of these obstacles on their own, but they also need help. Two international organizations exist for this purpose. The **International Monetary Fund (IMF)** offers advice and financial assistance on monetary and fiscal policy. The IMF, for example, might help a government in a developing country keep the value of its currency stable. This can help the country build its economy.

The second is the International Bank for Reconstruction and Development, usually called the **World Bank.** This organization gives loans and advice to countries as they try to improve their economies. A recent World Bank program tried to control the desert locust in East Africa to help farmers there. Another worked to improve inland water transportation in Bangladesh.

Foreign aid agencies are uneasy, as many developing countries are unable to repay their foreign debts. About 40 percent of the countries most in debt owe more than $127 billion to the IMF and the World

Economics and You

Exchange Rates

Recall from Section 1 that an exchange rate is what the price of your nation's currency is in terms of another nation's currency. One way to see whether a currency is devalued or overvalued against the U.S. dollar is to use the "Big Mac Index" developed by *The Economist,* a newsmagazine. Economists compare the price of a Big Mac hamburger in the United States to what it costs in another country's local currency. Converting the foreign price to U.S. dollars shows whether the price of a Big Mac is undervalued or overvalued against the U.S. dollar.

Bank. Recently, leaders of several major industrialized nations took steps to ease this debt burden. They proposed a plan that would cancel about $70 billion in debt, leaving more funds for needed social programs and economic growth plans in developing nations.

Reading Check **Describing** What economic challenges do developing nations face?

SECTION 3 ASSESSMENT

Checking for Understanding

1. **Key Terms** Write a paragraph related to economies in transition using these key terms: developing country, traditional economy.

Reviewing Main Ideas

2. **Explain** What was the role of the Gosplan in the Soviet economy? Why was this body needed in the Soviet Union at the time?

3. **Explain** Why did China make changes toward a market-based economy? Has its move been successful? Explain your answer.

Critical Thinking

4. **Drawing Inferences** Governments in developing countries tend not to support a system of strong, well-defined property rights. Why is this a problem for farmers in these countries?

5. **Organizing Information** Create a diagram like the one below to identify four economic characteristics of developing nations.

Characteristics

Analyzing Visuals

6. **Identify** Study the chart on page 579. Which of the nations has the highest infant mortality rates? What countries have annual population growth rates 3 percent or more?

★ **BE AN ACTIVE CITIZEN** ★

7. **Research** Choose one of the nations profiled in this section. Go to the library to find information on the nation's move toward a market-based economy. Construct a collage of headlines about these developments.

Issues to Debate

Should the President Have Fast-Track Trade Power?

Opponents to fast-track trade might say it sidetracks Congress. The policy gives the president the power to negotiate trade agreements without formal input from Congress. Once negotiated, Congress has a limited time to debate the treaty. No amendments are permitted, and only a "yes" or "no" vote is accepted. Supporters argue that fast-track trade enables the president to act quickly and to show a commitment to free trade, something they say is important to ending world poverty. On December 6, 2001, the Trade Promotion Authority (TPA) bill passed by a razor-thin vote of 215–214. The vote cut across party lines as legislators asked: Should we allow the president to engage in fast-track trade?

President Bush could have the power for fast-track trade.

Yes

Sadly . . . the U.S. is party to only 3 of the estimated 133 free trade negotiations taking place around the globe today. . . . As a result, American workers and their families suffer.

The president must be granted the full authority to negotiate agreements on the behalf of the nation. The trade promotion bill . . . will give the president the ability to arrive at the best deal, and then have it either approved or disapproved by a vote of Congress. There will be no opportunity for special interest provisions to bog down the process.

—Dick Armey, Republican representative
from Texas, 2001

No

I . . . would support legislation granting [the] President . . . enhanced trade negotiating authority provided it addressed effectively the key issues of labor, the environment, and the role of the U.S. Congress. . . .

The current bill merely provides for more "consultations" with Congress. . . . When international trade directly affects the lives and livelihoods of an increasing number of Americans, Congress cannot be confined to the back bench.

The president is the one negotiator, but Congress must have meaningful input. Indeed the Constitution gives it the responsibility to "regulate commerce with foreign nations."

—Charles Rangel, Democratic representative
from New York, 2001

Debating the Issue

1. Why does Representative Armey support Trade Promotion Authority?
2. Why does Representative Rangel object to it?
3. List the pros and cons of fast-track trade. What trade-offs would you make if you supported the policy? What trade-offs would you make if you opposed it?

Assessment & Activities

Review to Learn

Section 1

- The United States is heavily involved in international trade.
- Nations trade according to the theory of comparative advantage.

Section 2

- A pure market economic system operates on the basis of price, profits, and private property.
- Under a command system, there is little private property and the government owns virtually all the factors of production.

Section 3

- Countries changing from command economies to market-based systems face severe challenges.
- Developing nations receive financing through foreign aid and technical and economic assistance.

FOLDABLES™
Study Organizer

Using Your Foldables Study Organizer
Pair up with a classmate and use your completed foldables to take turns asking each other to define a chapter term correctly without looking under the tab.

Reviewing Key Terms

Write the key term that matches each definition below.

1. a tax placed on an imported product
2. a system in which economic activity is the result of habit or custom
3. an economy that is neither pure market nor pure command
4. a country with a relatively low per capita GDP
5. goods sold to other countries
6. total GDP divided by the country's population
7. a system in which the government controls the factors of production
8. goods bought from other countries for domestic use
9. a system in which individuals own factors of production and make economic decisions
10. a legal limit on the number of units of a foreign-produced good that can enter a country

Reviewing Main Ideas

11. How do nations gain from importing products?
12. How can nations restrict imports?
13. Why do nations restrict imports?
14. Identify two major countries that are making the transition to a market economy.
15. What is the exchange rate?
16. How is per capita GDP calculated?
17. What does the World Bank do?

Critical Thinking

18. **Making Comparisons** State-run factories in the former Soviet Union could make products of extremely low quality and yet continue to exist. What do you think would happen to such a firm in the United States?
19. **Making Inferences** Is an abundance of natural resources required in order for a country to have economic growth and development? Explain your answer.

20. Cause and Effect Create a chart like the one below to explain how exchange rates affect the balance of trade.

	Effect on Exports	Effect on Balance of Trade
Weak Currency		
Strong Currency		

Analyzing Visuals

Study the chart on page 579; then answer the following questions.

21. What is the literacy rate? What nations have a literacy rate below 60 percent?

22. Define infant mortality. Which nation has the lowest infant mortality rate?

Practicing Skills

23. Building a Database Research and build a database that organizes information about U.S. trade with countries in South America. Explain why the database is organized the way it is and how it might be used in class.

 **Economics Activity**

24. Suppose the United States buys 1 million cars from Japan in the year 2010. If the dollar appreciates relative to the yen in 2011, will Americans buy more or fewer than 1 million cars from Japan? Explain your answer.

★ CITIZENSHIP COOPERATIVE ACTIVITY ★

25. Divide into at least five groups. Each group will study one part or region of the world, such as northern Africa, Central Africa, Southeast Asia, Central America, or western Europe. The goal of each group is to determine the percentage of the economy devoted to agriculture and the percentage devoted to industry. Each member of each group will obtain the relevant information for

Self-Check Quiz Visit the *Civics Today* Web site at civ.glencoe.com and click on **Self-Check Quizzes—Chapter 26** to prepare for the chapter test.

one or more countries in his or her chosen region. Compare the information obtained, selecting one person to prepare summary statistics for your group's region.

 Technology Activity

Use the Internet to find out more about international trade. Type "international trade" into your search engine. From the list of Web sites that appears on the monitor, select at least three to read. Answer each question below; then summarize your findings in a brief essay.

26. What types of Web sites did you find on your initial search?

27. List at least three trade organizations.

28. Select a country. What are three products that the United States trades with this country?

The Princeton Review

Standardized Test Practice

Directions: Choose the *best* answer to the following question.

If the value of a nation's exports is $100 and the value of its imports is $200, what does the balance of trade equal?

F a surplus of $100
G a deficit of $100
H a deficit of $200
J a surplus of $200

Test-Taking Tip

As you read the multiple-choice question, try to anticipate the answer before you look at the choices.

"THE MARKET," OBSERVED FORMER Soviet President Mikhail Gorbachev, "is not an invention of capitalism. It has existed for centuries. It is an invention of civilization." As Gorbachev pointed out, markets have flourished for thousands of years within a variety of economic systems. And though markets have taken many forms—ranging from the vast open-air gathering places of the ancient world to the computer-powered auction sites of the digital age—their essential function has remained the same. Through the ages, markets have served as forums that bring buyers and sellers together to exchange goods, services, or other commodities. On these pages, TIME presents a gallery of images that illustrate some remarkable continuities—and some striking contrasts—among markets of the past 2,500 years.

2 THE MIDDLE AGES (13th century) Medieval merchants offered their wares while entertainers performed at this outdoor market in a European village square.

3 WALL STREET (late 1700s) The first securities market in the U.S. was held outdoors. Brokers gathered near Wall Street in New York City to trade stocks.

4 BLACK MARKET (1944) In Bucharest, Romania, buyers inspected bottles of salad oil that were being sold despite a government order that citizens obtain food only through state-run markets.

BETTMANN/CORBIS (4)

1 ANCIENT GREECE (c. 500 B.C.) The agora, or marketplace, was the center of economic and political life in Athens. Citizens of Athens generally spent most of their day at the agora.

TRADING THROUGH THE AGES

WOLFGANG KAEHLER/CORBIS

PAUL ALMASY/CORBIS

BOB KRIST/CORBIS

REUTERS NEWMEDIA INC./CORBIS

CHARLES O'REAR/CORBIS

COPYRIGHT © EBAY INC.

5 FLOATING MARKET In Thailand, merchants travel by boat to seek out their customers.

6 PRODUCE MARKET Vendors offer chili peppers—an important crop in Nigeria—at a market in the city of Kano.

7 AUCTION Villagers bid for freshly baked bread at this auction in Portugal.

8 THE LANGUAGE OF TRADE Options traders convey their buy and sell orders via a complex system of hand signals.

9 POWERFUL TOOLS At the New York Stock Exchange, brokers use high-speed computers to aid in their trading.

10 A NEW ERA The Internet has brought the market-place into computer users' homes.

CHAPTER 27

Comparing Systems of Government

★ CITIZENSHIP AND YOU ★

By comparing political systems, we can develop an appreciation for those systems that provide a large degree of personal freedom and economic opportunity. Choose a foreign country to research. Look for significant historical events that influenced the country's government. Report your findings to the class.

 To learn more about comparative government, view the *Democracy in Action* video lesson 25: Parliamentary v. Presidential Systems.

FOLDABLES™
Study Organizer

Compare and Contrast Study Foldable *Make this foldable and use it to help you identify similarities and differences in governments around the world.*

Step 1 *Mark the midpoint of a side edge of one sheet of paper. Then fold the outside edges in to touch at the midpoint.*

Step 2 *Fold the paper in half from side to side.*

Step 3 *Open and cut along the inside fold lines to form four tabs.*

Cut along the fold lines on both sides.

Step 4 *Label as shown.*

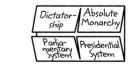

Dictatorship | Absolute Monarchy
Parliamentary System | Presidential System

Reading and Writing *As you read the chapter, write information under each tab to help you compare and contrast different types of governments and the countries where they are in place.*

A woman in Bizana, South Africa, encourages her fellow citizens to vote. ▶

Civics Online

Chapter Overview Visit the *Civics Today* Web site at civ.glencoe.com and click on **Chapter Overviews—Chapter 27** to preview chapter information.

Types of Government

Main Idea
Many countries are shifting toward a more democratic system of government.

Key Terms
authoritarian, absolute monarch, dictator, totalitarian, constitutional monarchy, parliamentary system, prime minister

Reading Strategy
Contrasting Information
Create a chart like the one below to explain the difference between authoritarian government and democratic government.

Government	
Authoritarian	Democratic

Read to Learn
- What types of government exist?
- Why are many nations changing from authoritarian rule to a more democratic form of government?

Americans in Action

As a teenager in World War II in Italy, Ginetta Sagan joined the underground resistance movement. During the war, the young girl helped publish an underground paper and carried information to the Allies in Switzerland. She escorted hundreds of fugitives—Jews, antifascists, soldiers who deserted, and many others—across a barbed wire fence that separated Italy from Switzerland. Ginetta immigrated to the United States in 1951 and over time helped found Amnesty International USA. Ginetta also worked to abolish torture practices in foreign prisons. For her efforts on behalf of the oppressed, she received the Presidential Medal of Freedom, the nation's highest civilian award.

Ginetta Sagan, proponent of amnesty and prisoners' rights

Authoritarian Government

Like snowflakes, no two governments are exactly alike. Each country is unique, shaped by its history, culture, political interests, and economic needs; yet for thousands of years, people have been studying and classifying governments.

Aristotle, for example, was a scholar who lived in ancient Greece. He identified three types of government: rule by a single person; rule by a small, elite group; and rule by the people. Many scholars prefer to describe governments by using two broad categories on a spectrum: those that are democratic (on one end of the spectrum) and those that are authoritarian (on the other end of the spectrum). In democratic regimes, as you know, the people rule. In authoritarian regimes, power is held by an individual or group not accountable to the people.

Winston Churchill, Great Britain's leader during World War II, said that "no one pretends that democracy is perfect or all-wise." Yet most people who live in democratic countries—and many who don't—would agree that democracy beats the alternatives. Nondemocratic, or authoritarian, governments take various forms. What they all have in common is that only a few people wield power, giving ordinary citizens little voice in government.

Absolute Monarchy

The word "monarchy" describes a government with a hereditary ruler—a king or queen (or czar, empress, sultan, or other royal figure) who inherits this position of power. Until about the 1600s, such rulers were mostly **absolute monarchs.** That is, they had unlimited authority to rule as they wished.

Many countries still have monarchs, but absolute monarchy is almost nonexistent. In the Middle East, however, the king of Saudi Arabia and the emir of Qatar might still be considered "absolute." Their power is technically unrestricted, although they do consult with advisers and are constrained by Islamic law.

Dictatorships

Dictators, like absolute monarchs, exercise complete control over the state. They usually take power by force, although sometimes, when a crisis situation demands a strong leader, authorities may place them in charge. To stay in power, most dictators rely on the police and military. They often tamper with elections or refuse to hold them. They also limit freedom of speech, assembly, and the press.

Scores of dictators have ruled throughout history. Those who only seek personal gain are often overthrown quickly. The ruler of Uganda, Idi Amin was deposed (removed from power) in 1979. His brutal regime led to hundreds of thousands of deaths and plunged the country into chaos and poverty. With the help of the United States, Panamanian dictator Manuel Noriega was deposed in 1989.

Others endure for decades. Fidel Castro has been in power in Cuba since 1959. Libya's leader, Muammar al-Qaddhafi, has governed as a military dictator since 1969.

Totalitarianism

Many dictators impose **totalitarian** rule on their people. In a totalitarian state, the government's control extends to almost all aspects of people's lives. Totalitarian leaders typically have a master plan for the economy and society. They ban political opposition. They regulate what industries

Forms of Government Democracies like Mexico and Japan endeavor to provide their citizens freedom and opportunities that Thomas Jefferson called "the pursuit of happiness." Vincente Fox (right) is Mexico's president. Junichiro Koizumi (below) is Japan's prime minister. **How do democracies and authoritarian regimes differ?**

Two Forms of Democracy

	Relationship Among Branches of Government	Method of Choosing Top Official	Role of Top Official
PRESIDENTIAL SYSTEM	Powers of executive, legislative, and judicial branches are separated	President is elected directly by popular vote	President acts as head of government *and* head of state
PARLIAMENTARY SYSTEM	Executive and legislative functions are united; judiciary operates independently	Prime minister is chosen by members of Parliament	Prime minister usually acts as head of government only (monarch or president is head of state)

Evaluating Charts

The branches of government have different responsibilities under the various forms of democratic government.
How does the method of choosing the top official differ?

and farms produce. They suppress individual freedom, dictating what people should believe and with whom they may associate. To enforce their ideology, totalitarian leaders control the media and use propaganda, scare tactics, and violence.

Three of the most notorious totalitarian regimes arose in the 1920s and 1930s. They were Nazi Germany under Adolf Hitler, Fascist Italy under Benito Mussolini, and the Soviet Union under Joseph Stalin. Today, China, Cuba, and North Korea are usually considered totalitarian states.

Reading Check **Describing** What is a totalitarian government?

Democratic Governments

Until the late 1600s, absolute monarchy was the dominant form of government. As early as the 1200s, however, the English began to place restrictions on their king. In most countries with monarchs, absolute monarchy has now given way to constitutional monarchy, in which the power of the hereditary ruler is limited by the country's constitution and laws.

Modern constitutional monarchies generally follow democratic practices. As you learned earlier, the characteristics of a democracy include individual liberty, majority rule with minority rights, and free elections with secret ballots.

The people participate in governing, and elected officials make laws and policies. The monarchs are heads of state only, presiding at ceremonies and serving as symbols of unity and continuity. The queen of Great Britain, the emperor of Japan, and the prince of Monaco are a few examples.

Another type of democracy is the republic—a representative government in which no leaders inherit office. As you learned, the voters hold sovereign power in a republic. The people elect representatives and give them the responsibility and power to make laws and conduct government. For most Americans today, the terms representative democracy, republic, and constitutional republic mean the same thing: a system of limited government in which the people are the ultimate source of governmental power. The United States, of course, was the first such democracy. From Argentina to Zimbabwe, there are now many more.

The Expansion of Democracy

The number of democratic states grew considerably in the mid-1900s, after World War II. Since the mid-1970s, a new wave of democratization has swept Latin America and parts of Europe, Asia, and Africa. Dozens of countries that were once authoritarian are now giving citizens more rights, letting opposition parties organize, holding fair elections, unshackling the press, and making other political reforms.

Democracy is more widespread today than ever before. Of the more than 190 countries in the world, nearly two-thirds have democratic governments elected by

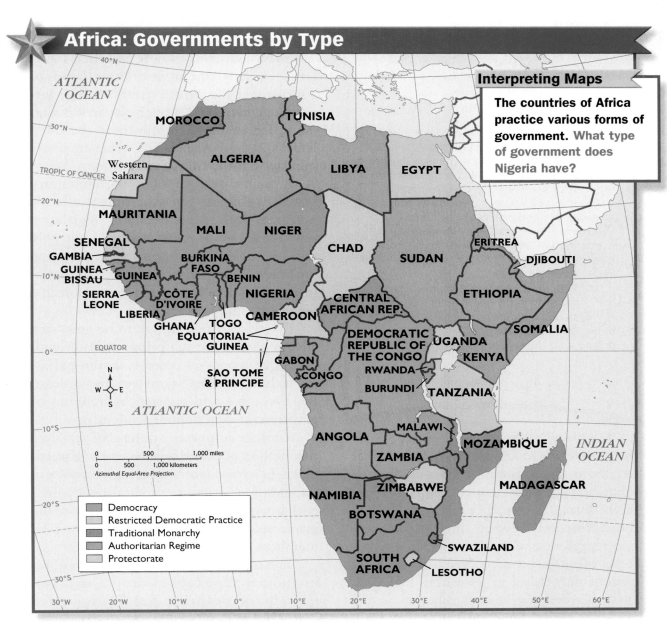

Africa: Governments by Type

Interpreting Maps

The countries of Africa practice various forms of government. What type of government does Nigeria have?

Democracy
Restricted Democratic Practice
Traditional Monarchy
Authoritarian Regime
Protectorate

American Biographies

Shirley Temple Black (1928–)

At the height of the Depression, President Franklin D. Roosevelt once remarked, "As long as our country has Shirley Temple, we will be all right." The child film star sang and danced her way through more than 40 movies before turning age 12. To a troubled world, Temple was America's best-loved "ambassador of goodwill."

At age 21, Temple retired, but only from films. After marrying Charles Black, she devoted her life to public service. She served as a delegate to the United Nations, the first female Chief of White House Protocol, teacher at the State Department, and ambassador to two countries—Ghana and Czechoslovakia.

Black arrived in Czechoslovakia as communism crumbled and the nation split into the Czech and Slovak republics. "My main job was human rights," Black later said, "trying to keep people like future [Czech] president Vaclav Havel out of jail."

In 1998, Black received a lifetime achievement medal at the Kennedy Center, but she still hasn't retired. She remains vice president of the American Academy of Diplomacy, an organization she cofounded.

the people. Democracy, of course, can be extensive or limited, stable or fragile. Democratic governments can also take different forms. You read in Chapter 1 about the distinction between direct democracy and representative democracy. No country today has a direct democracy, in which all citizens participate in governing firsthand. Instead, representative democracy is the norm, with citizens electing leaders to act for them. Individual countries, however, have various ways of choosing their representatives and organizing the government.

Presidential Versus Parliamentary Systems

The United States, Mexico, and the Philippines are among the handful of democracies with a presidential system of government. Most democratic countries in the world today, following the model of Great Britain, use the **parliamentary system** of government instead.

Such countries usually call their legislature a parliament and their head of government the **prime minister.** The terminology can vary, though. Japan's parliament, for example, is known as the Diet. Israel's is the Knesset. The German prime minister has the title of chancellor.

A major feature of a parliamentary system is that the top government officials perform both executive and legislative functions. The prime minister is not only the chief executive, responsible for carrying out the laws, but also a member of parliament, the arm of government responsible for making the laws.

Likewise, the cabinet ministers—the advisers who help the prime minister with executive work—also serve in the parliament. In a presidential system, by contrast, the executive and legislative branches of government operate independently.

Another important difference involves the method of choosing the head of government. In a presidential system, the voters of the nation elect the president directly. In a parliamentary system of government, the prime minister is elected or approved by members of the parliament.

The top office in each system can differ in another way, too. In presidential systems, the president acts not only as head of government (the country's political leader) but also as head of state (the country's ceremonial leader). In parliamentary systems, someone other than the prime minister may be the official head of state. In parliamentary monarchies like Great Britain, Spain, and Sweden, the head of state is the king or queen. In parliamentary republics like the Czech Republic, India, and Italy, the head of state is a president, chosen in most cases by the parliament.

Pros and Cons of the Parliamentary System

With a parliamentary system of government, as we have said, power is not strictly separated between the legislative and executive branches. This means there are fewer checks and balances on government leaders—a potential drawback. However, the unity among the legislative and executive branches does help the government run smoothly and act quickly.

Consider what happens in the United States when different political parties control the presidency and Congress. Disagreements along party lines often lead to "gridlock" that stalls political action. If Congress repeatedly rejects the president's budget proposals, for example, and the president frequently vetoes laws passed by Congress, little gets accomplished. Under a parliamentary system of government, however, the chief executive is typically from the majority party in the legislature. As a result, serious conflicts rarely erupt over laws, policies, or political appointees.

Changing With the Times

More than half of the countries in the world today didn't even exist in 1950. Many young countries, such as the republics that broke away from the Soviet Union in 1991, are still making the transition to democracy. However, even in well-established nations, systems of government evolve as times change and people with new agendas come to power.

In the next sections, we take a closer look at two countries that are centuries old: Great Britain and China. They have governments that differ markedly from ours—and from their own original form.

Reading Check **Explaining** What role does the prime minister have in Great Britain's system of government?

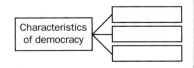

SECTION 1 ASSESSMENT

Checking for Understanding

1. **Key Terms** Write a one-sentence explanation of each of the following terms: authoritarian, absolute monarch, dictator, totalitarian, constitutional monarchy, parliamentary system.

Reviewing Main Ideas

2. **Identify** What totalitarian rulers took control in Germany and Italy in the 1920s and 1930s?

3. **Identify** Name a country that has a constitutional monarchy.

Critical Thinking

4. **Drawing Inferences** How does a republic provide a good government for diverse people?

5. **Organizing Information** On a diagram like the one below, identify three characteristics of democracy that distinguish it from other forms of government.

```
┌─────────────────┐        ┌──────────┐
│ Characteristics │───────▶│          │
│ of democracy    │───────▶│          │
│                 │───────▶│          │
└─────────────────┘        └──────────┘
```

Analyzing Visuals

6. **Interpret** Study the map of Africa on page 591. What types of government are depicted in the key? What African nations have traditional monarchies?

★ BE AN ACTIVE CITIZEN ★
7. **Write** Write a one-page paper describing how you think your life would have been different had you been reared in a country under authoritarian rule.

Landmark Supreme Court Case Studies

Scott v. Sandford

Dred Scott appeared with his wife and two daughters in an 1857 newspaper.

Background of the Case

Dred Scott, an enslaved African American, worked for a physician. A member of the military, the physician moved often, taking Scott with him. As a result, Scott lived for a time in the state of Illinois and in the territory of Wisconsin, both slave-free zones. Both zones were also north of the boundary set by Congress in the Missouri Compromise of 1820. The Missouri Compromise permitted slavery south of the line and prohibited slavery north of it.

By 1846, the physician had died, and Scott was again living in Missouri. There he continued to work for the physician's widow and her brother John Sandford, who was from New York. Scott sued for his freedom. He claimed that his earlier residence in a free state and a free territory made him free. Missouri's courts denied Scott, however. In order to claim federal court jurisdiction, Scott's lawyers then stated that Scott was a citizen of Missouri bringing suit against Sandford, a citizen of New York.

Before the Civil War, Americans were asking: Are African Americans citizens of the United States? May Congress prohibit the enslavement of African Americans in U.S. territories?

The Decision

The Supreme Court decided the case on March 6–7, 1857. Chief Justice Roger B. Taney spoke for the seven-justice majority. Taney first asserted his own view of the Framers' so-called original intent: "The only rights and privileges African Americans were meant to have were those granted by their so-called 'owners' or by the government. Therefore, Dred Scott could not be a citizen." He wrote further:

> [I]t is the opinion of the Court that the act of Congress which prohibited . . . [slaveholding] north of the line mentioned therein is . . . void; and that neither Dred Scott himself, nor any member of his family were made free by being carried into this territory, ...

The Court was saying that the suit of noncitizen Scott and the Missouri Compromise were unconstitutional. Therefore Scott was not free.

Why It Matters

The ruling added to the tensions that led to the Civil War. In 1868, three years after the end of the war, the Fourteenth Amendment to the United States Constitution overruled the *Dred Scott* decision.

Analyzing the Court Decision

1. Why was Dred Scott not freed as a result of the Supreme Court's decision?
2. What is your opinion of Taney's view of the Framers' "original intent"?

A Profile of Great Britain

GUIDE TO READING

Main Idea
Great Britain developed the parliamentary system of government.

Key Terms
unitary system, devolution

Reading Strategy
Organizing Information
As you read the section, create a table like the one below and identify the two houses of the British Parliament. Then explain the role each plays in the national government.

House	Role

Read to Learn
• What are the parts of the British constitution?
• How does Great Britain select its prime minister?

Americans in Action

Democratic ideals developed in Europe and were brought to the Americas by the English colonists who settled here. Today, the United States and the United Kingdom share a common heritage and belief in the values of democracy. President George W. Bush and Prime Minister Tony Blair reaffirmed the uniquely close relationship that exists between the United States and the United Kingdom by calling it ". . . a relationship rooted in common interests around the globe. We commit ourselves to the shared goals of a stronger transatlantic alliance and to helping build a Europe whole, free, and secure."

British Prime Minister Tony Blair

A Parliamentary Democracy

Great Britain, also known as the United Kingdom, includes England, Scotland, Wales, and Northern Ireland. This island nation, located just north of France, covers slightly less area than the state of Oregon. With a population of about 60 million, it is the third-largest country in Europe.

In terms of history, language, and culture, the United States has closer ties to Great Britain than to any other country. The 13 original states, after all, began as 13 English colonies. We owe many of our traditions to Britain, including our belief that citizens should have a voice in government and certain basic rights.

Nonetheless, the British and American systems of government are quite different. Britain is a constitutional monarchy, with a queen whose power is limited by the constitution. Britain's constitution is not a single document like ours but a collection of written and unwritten guides to the law.

These include several historical documents, such as the Magna Carta of 1215 and the Bill of Rights of 1689. Also included are the whole body of British laws, court decisions, and various traditions and customs. Until the constitution began to curb the monarch's authority, British kings and queens ruled as absolute monarchs, passing the crown from

Comparing Authoritarian and Democratic Systems

	Selection of Leaders	Extent of Government Power	Means of Ensuring Compliance	Political Parties
AUTHORITARIANISM (including absolute monarchy, dictatorships, and totalitarian)	Rulers inherit their positions or take power by force	Rulers have unlimited power; the government may impose an official ideology and control all aspects of political, economic, and civic life	The government relies on state control of the media, propaganda, military or police power, and terror	Power lies with a single party
DEMOCRACY	Leaders are chosen in fair elections with universal suffrage	The government is limited in power by the constitution and laws; citizens' rights and freedoms are protected	The government relies on the rule of law	Multiple parties exist

Evaluating Charts

All governments show behaviors ranging from democratic to authoritarian. How do the leaders gain their positions of power in each form of government?

one generation to the next. Today the royal family, led by Queen Elizabeth II, plays a largely ceremonial and symbolic role. Although the queen has the right "to be informed, to advise, and to warn" the government, real power rests with the elected legislature, Parliament.

How Britain's Government Works

Great Britain's great contribution to modern governments around the world was the development of the parliamentary system. Most former British colonies—Australia, Canada, India, and South Africa, to name just a few—have patterned their own governments after Britain's.

Parliament

The British Parliament is divided into the House of Commons and the House of Lords. The 650 members of the Commons are the main lawmakers. They represent particular districts and are elected directly by the voters.

Both houses of Parliament have a role in proposing and passing legislation, but the House of Commons has much greater power than the House of Lords. Any member of the House of Commons may introduce legislation, but most bills are introduced by the majority party. Members debate bills, then send them on to standing committees to work out the final details. The committees must report on every bill to the House of Commons for a vote. A majority vote is needed for passage.

The House of Lords, with about 700 members, is not an elected body and has relatively little power. Most members are "life peers" appointed by the prime minister as a reward for their achievements. A smaller number are nobles with inherited titles (dukes, baronesses, earls, and the like) or leading church officials. The House of Lords debates bills and can delay their passage, but it cannot stop measures that the House of Commons stands behind.

Political Parties and the Prime Minister

Two parties dominate politics in Great Britain: the Conservatives and Labour. The Conservative Party, like the Republican Party in the United States, supports private enterprise and minimal government intervention. The Labour Party, like our Democratic Party, favors a more active role for government. The Conservatives draw support from the upper classes, while Labour attracts working-class voters. Several minor parties are also active in Great Britain, notably the Liberal Democrats.

The political party that wins the most seats in the House of Commons selects the prime minister. If no party has a majority, then the strongest party typically forms an alliance with another party to secure backing for its candidate.

Tony Blair, the leader of the Labour Party, became Britain's prime minister in 1997. His election ended nearly 20 years of political control by the Conservatives.

No limits are set on how long a prime minister or member of Parliament may serve. In fact, no dates are fixed for parliamentary elections, but they must be held at least every five years. The prime minister usually calls for elections earlier, when his or her party has strong public support. This makes it possible for the party to gain even more seats in the House of Commons and use its majority to prolong its stay in office.

The Judiciary

England and Wales, Northern Ireland, and Scotland have their own separate legal systems. In each system civil cases are heard in certain courts, and criminal cases are heard in other courts. For most legal matters, a committee of the House of Lords is the highest court of appeal. Thus it acts as the equivalent of the United States Supreme Court.

British judges, like our federal judges, are appointed for life terms. This keeps them free from political pressure.

Reading Check **Identifying** What are Britain's two major political parties?

Regional Governments

As you know, the United States has a federal system of government in which power is shared by the states and the national government. Great Britain has a **unitary system** of government—one in which power is centralized. Most political decisions for all parts of the country are made in London, the capital. The role of local governments is chiefly to provide services paid for with central funds.

In the late 1990s, however, Britain began a policy of **devolution**—transferring power to local authorities. Elected assemblies were created in Scotland, Wales, and Northern Ireland. They now govern regional matters such as education and some taxes. However, the people in Scotland, Wales, and Northern Ireland still elect members to Parliament, too, and Parliament is still responsible for overall economic policy, national defense, and so forth.

The royal family logo as it appears on Buckingham Palace gate in London, England

The devolved government in Northern Ireland does not go far enough for some people there. Many Catholics, who are in the minority, oppose the Protestant majority and seek independence from Britain. Repeated violence between the two groups continues to plague Northern Ireland.

Economic Role

At one time, Great Britain ruled an immense empire that included nearly one-fifth of the world's land and population. Today it controls only a few small islands beyond its borders, but it remains a key player on the world stage.

Britain has the fourth-largest economy in the world, and London ranks with New York City as a leading financial center. The country is one of our closest allies and regularly consults with U.S. officials on foreign policy and global issues. Our two nations cooperated during both World Wars and in more recent conflicts, such as the 1991 Gulf War and the current campaign against terrorism.

Britain is also firmly tied to the rest of Europe as a member of the European Union (EU). Remember that the EU is an

Fact Fiction Folklore

"Are there any questions?"

This question signifies the start of Question Time. During Question Time, Parliament members ask one another questions; members explain things and are held accountable for their actions and votes. Although the U.S. Congress does not have Question Time, Americans can hold their representatives accountable at the voting booth.

organization of 15 countries that cooperate in matters of economics and trade, social and foreign policy, security, and justice. In 1999, the EU began to phase in a single currency, the euro, for its members. The idea is to make it easier for Europeans to do business with one another. So far, Britain has not switched to the euro, but it may do so in the future.

Reading Check **Describing** How often are parliamentary elections held?

SECTION 2 ASSESSMENT

Checking for Understanding

1. Key Terms Write a short paragraph about the government of Great Britain using these key terms: unitary system, devolution.

Reviewing Main Ideas

2. Describe What elements make up Great Britain's constitution? Identify two historical documents that are important parts of the constitution.

3. Identify What two houses make up Britain's Parliament?

Critical Thinking

4. Drawing Conclusions Why do you think Great Britain continues to have a monarchy, even though the monarch has limited power?

5. Making Comparisons On a diagram like the one below, describe the differences between the U.S. federal system and the British unitary system of government.

System of Government

Federal   Unitary

Analyzing Visuals

6. Interpret Study the chart on page 596. How do the powers of the government leaders differ under each system of government?

★ **BE AN ACTIVE CITIZEN** ★

7. Research For one week, find newspaper or magazine accounts about Great Britain. Find out what issues face the country today. Summarize the issues in a short, written report.

A Profile of China

GUIDE TO READING

Main Idea

China's moves toward free enterprise are opening the country to political change.

Key Terms

dynasty, collective farm, human rights

Reading Strategy

Sequencing Information
As you read the section, complete a time line like the one below by identifying important events in China.

Read to Learn

• How did the Chinese economic system develop following World War II?

• How is China's government structured?

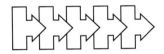

Americans in Action

Growing up in Los Angeles, Aaron Chung never lost sight of his Chinese heritage. Chung decided to visit Hong Kong and the village where his father was born to learn about his family's history. Chung noted, "I often used to see this label [Chinese American] as a handicap, with me not belonging fully to one group or the other. Through tracing my family ties to its origins in China, I was able to appreciate to a higher degree . . . what it meant to be Chinese. At the same time, being an American has presented many opportunities. . . . Now, instead of a hindrance, I see that being Chinese American allows me to have the best of both worlds."

A busy street in Shanghai, China

China in History

There is no ignoring the People's Republic of China. With a population of 1.3 billion, it is home to more people than any other country (nearly 20 percent of the world's population). China covers the third-largest land area, behind Russia and Canada. It boasts some of the world's largest cities, longest rivers, and highest mountains. The Great Wall of China, which stretches 4,500 miles, is the longest structure ever built. Even China's history is vast; with written records going back 3,500 years, the Chinese have the world's oldest continuous civilization.

Because of its size, China has great power. The country's enormous market potential and its exports of inexpensive clothing, toys, and other goods make it a valuable trading partner for us. At the same time, China's military strength and communist ideology keep us watchful.

The Soviet Union's collapse in 1991 left China as the last major Communist state. The Chinese Communist Party (CCP) has controlled the country since 1949. For centuries, however, China was ruled by a series of dynasties—families that hold power for many generations.

Asia: Governments by Type

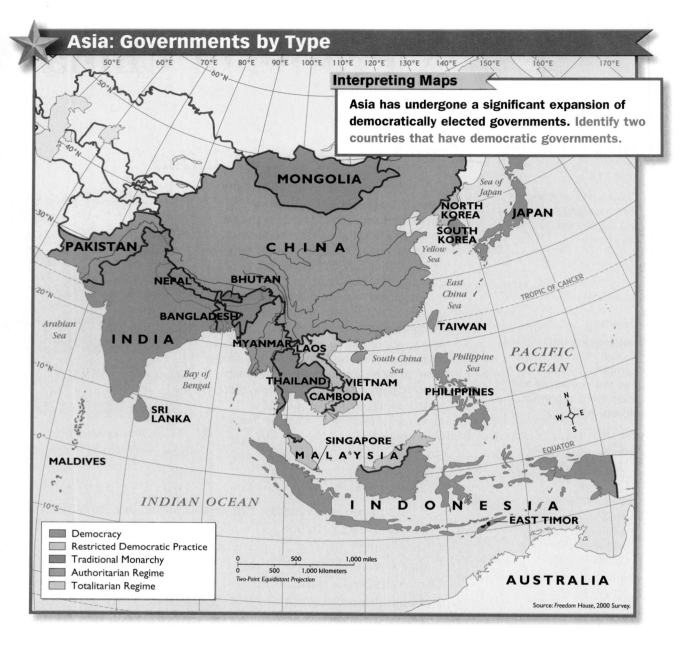

Interpreting Maps

Asia has undergone a significant expansion of democratically elected governments. Identify two countries that have democratic governments.

MONGOLIA

NORTH KOREA

SOUTH KOREA

JAPAN

PAKISTAN

CHINA

NEPAL

BHUTAN

BANGLADESH

INDIA

MYANMAR

LAOS

TAIWAN

THAILAND

VIETNAM

CAMBODIA

PHILIPPINES

SRI LANKA

SINGAPORE

MALAYSIA

MALDIVES

INDONESIA

EAST TIMOR

AUSTRALIA

Sea of Japan

Yellow Sea

East China Sea

TROPIC OF CANCER

Arabian Sea

Bay of Bengal

South China Sea

Philippine Sea

PACIFIC OCEAN

INDIAN OCEAN

EQUATOR

Democracy
Restricted Democratic Practice
Traditional Monarchy
Authoritarian Regime
Totalitarian Regime

0   500   1,000 miles
0   500   1,000 kilometers
Two-Point Equidistant Projection

Source: Freedom House, 2000 Survey.

The last dynasty began to crumble in the late 1800s, weakened by clashes with the West, economic problems, and social unrest. An uprising in 1911 overthrew the emperor, and China became a republic the next year. A stable government didn't emerge until the late 1920s, when the Kuomintang, or Nationalist Party, took power. Meanwhile, the rival CCP had formed, inspired by Soviet communism. Led by Mao Zedong, the Communists gained a strong following. By 1949, the CCP controlled most of the country, and the Kuomintang fled to Taiwan, an island about 100 miles east of the Chinese mainland. There they set up a separate government and a capitalist economy.

On October 1, 1949, Mao Zedong proclaimed the founding of the People's Republic of China, with its capital in Beijing. Mao led the country for nearly 30 years, setting it on a new political and economic path.

The Communist government wanted to turn China into a socialist state. The CCP quickly seized farmland and redistributed it among the peasants. To increase agricultural output, small holdings were combined into **collective farms,** worked jointly by groups of peasants under government supervision. The government also took control of all major industries, assigned jobs to workers, and developed five-year plans for economic growth.

Under Mao, the Chinese government took a hard line against individualism. More than 1 million political opponents were executed in the first year of Mao's rule. Strict controls were placed on freedom of expression, and organized religion was banned. Young people were taught unquestioning loyalty to the Communist Party and the state.

A Shift Toward Moderation

In the 1970s, with economic development lagging, the Chinese government began relaxing its iron grip on society. After Mao's death in 1976, the CCP expelled many of its more radical members, loosened central control over industry and agriculture, and permitted some degree of free enterprise.

A new Communist Party leader, Deng Xiaoping, dominated China during the 1980s. Deng welcomed foreign trade and investment, and China became more open to the rest of the world. At the same time, it resisted its own people's efforts to make the government more democratic. The most dramatic incident occurred in Beijing in 1989. Hundreds of unarmed, pro-democracy students who were demonstrating in Tiananmen Square were killed by Chinese military forces.

Economic reforms are continuing in China today. Private enterprise and foreign investment are expanding; yet political leaders remain heavily involved in directing the economy. The government sets the price of many goods, and it provides housing and food subsidies.

The government still regulates many aspects of private life. For example, policies designed to curb population growth try to limit families to one or two children. However, the government intrudes into people's personal affairs less than in the past. Religious freedom, for instance, is now officially protected, and many Chinese practice Buddhism, Daoism, Islam, or Christianity. As might be expected, China's massiveness makes strict social control difficult, especially in rural areas, where the majority of people live.

Political controls, meanwhile, remain tight. The government is quick to use intimidation and force to squelch criticism.

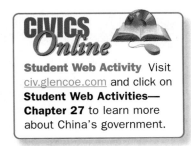

CIVICS Online

Student Web Activity Visit civ.glencoe.com and click on **Student Web Activities— Chapter 27** to learn more about China's government.

Tiananmen Square
In 1989, student-led demonstrators occupied Tiananmen Square in Beijing to demand reform. **What were the demonstrators supporting?**

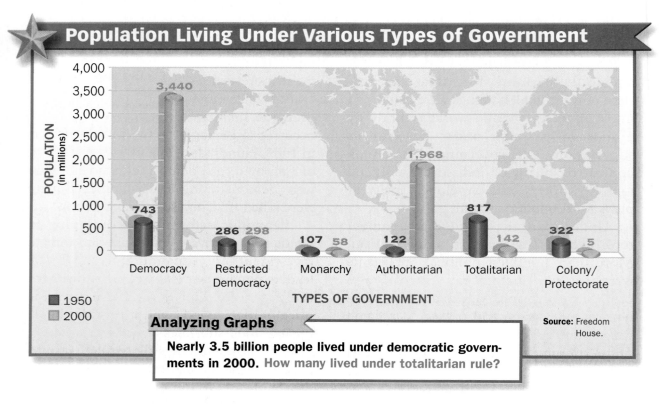

Population Living Under Various Types of Government

POPULATION (in millions)

Democracy: 743, 3,440
Restricted Democracy: 286, 298
Monarchy: 107, 58
Authoritarian: 122, 1,968
Totalitarian: 817, 142
Colony/Protectorate: 322, 5

TYPES OF GOVERNMENT

■ 1950
□ 2000

Source: Freedom House.

Analyzing Graphs

Nearly 3.5 billion people lived under democratic governments in 2000. How many lived under totalitarian rule?

China's constitution recognizes **human rights**—the fundamental rights that belong to every person on Earth. These include freedom from illegal imprisonment and torture, as well as basic civil liberties. Nonetheless, Chinese authorities frequently mistreat people. Anyone viewed as a threat may be beaten, locked away in prison or a mental institution, or shipped off to a labor camp.

Reading Check **Sequencing** When did the Communists take control of China's government?

The Structure of Government

The Chinese Communist Party, with 63 million members, is the dominant force in government. Its presence is felt at every level, in every aspect of policy. Several minor parties exist in China, but none have any real influence. At the center of government is the secretary-general of the CCP,

Jiang Zemin. He happens to hold the title of president of China as well, but that office is largely ceremonial.

Next to the secretary-general, the most important figure in the government is usually the premier, currently Zhu Rongji. The premier heads the State Council, which is China's executive body.

The Council implements party policies and handles the day-to-day running of the government. China's various ministries—for defense, education, health, and so forth—all fall under the authority of the State Council.

In theory, the highest governing body in China is the National People's Congress. The Congress includes about 3,000 members elected from different provinces. It meets for only about two weeks a year, however, and has little real power.

Instead, national policy is made by the Politburo, a group of about 20 top party leaders. Seven of these leaders, the "cream of the crop," serve on the Politburo Standing

Committee. This select group masterminds China's political, economic, and social policy. Both President Jiang and Premier Zhu are members.

A Vast Bureaucracy

China, like other Communist-led nations, has a unitary system of government. In other words, the central government in Beijing makes political decisions for the entire country. Still, given its huge size, China could not function without layers of local leadership. Each province has a governor, and power trickles on down to heads of counties, districts, townships, and towns. All together, about 10.5 million people work for the Chinese government.

An Improving Judicial System

China's judiciary, unlike ours, is not a completely independent branch of government. The courts bow to pressure from the Communist Party, and criminal proceedings leave much to be desired. Police can gather evidence with no search warrants. Lawyers cannot object to the opposing counsel's questions or cite legal precedents to support their case. Judges are often corrupt or inept; many came to the bench straight from law school or from careers in the military rather than law.

Recent reforms, however, now require legal training for judges. New rules are making trials fairer. For example, accused persons are allowed to see an attorney before trial and are assumed to be innocent until proven guilty. These are positive steps, but it is too early to know their effects.

Relations With the United States

After the People's Republic was proclaimed in 1949, the United States broke off diplomatic ties with the government in Beijing. For many years, our official contacts were with the Nationalist authorities in

Taiwan. In 1972, however, relations with Beijing warmed when President Richard Nixon made a historic visit to mainland China. In 1979, the United States recognized

TIME

Political Cartoons

...EYE TO EYE ON TRADE...

CHINA

HUMAN RIGHTS

and it seems to be diverted toward money and __me. Making the world a more convenient | Schneider, two men with little hope, of regaining the company's revenue. While the wage was | to be diverted time

Analyzing Visuals Human rights advocates urged the United States to deny most-favored-nation trading status to China because of concerns over China's record of human rights abuses. What comment is the cartoonist making about the U.S. decision to engage in trade with China?

Beijing as the sole legitimate government of China. Our two countries now trade briskly and engage in cultural, educational, and scientific exchanges.

Relations are still strained at times, especially over China's poor record of protecting human rights. The United States also criticized Chinese authorities for holding the crew of a U.S. surveillance plane in April 2001, which made an emergency landing after colliding with a Chinese fighter jet. (The 24 Americans were released after 11 days.) However, as a recent Chinese visitor told President Bush, maintaining "friendly relations and cooperation . . . is in the interest of Asia, the Pacific Region, and the world at large."

✓ **Reading Check** **Describing** What does the Politburo do?

SECTION 3 ASSESSMENT

Checking for Understanding

1. **Key Terms** Use each of the following terms in a sentence that will help explain its meaning: dynasty, collective farm, human rights.

Reviewing Main Ideas

2. **Identify** When was the People's Republic of China formed?

3. **Describe** How has China's economy become more moderate since the 1970s?

Critical Thinking

4. **Evaluating Information** Does China support human rights? Explain your answer.

5. **Organizing Information** On a diagram like the one below, describe the role each plays in China's government.

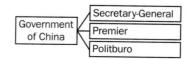

Government of China
- Secretary-General
- Premier
- Politburo

Analyzing Visuals

6. **Interpret** Study the map on page 600. What nations have governments that practice restricted democracy? What nations have totalitarian governments?

★ **BE AN ACTIVE CITIZEN** ★

7. **Write** Write an e-mail to an American company that conducts business in foreign countries to discover any cultural or business practices the company has incorporated into its operations.

Understanding Cause and Effect

Why Learn This Skill?

When you ask why an event occurred, you are looking for a cause-and-effect relationship. A cause is the action or situation that produces an event. What happens as a result of a cause is an effect. Tracing causes and effects as you read or study deepens your mental grasp of the topic.

Learning the Skill

To identify cause-and-effect relationships, follow these steps:

- Identify and focus on two or more events or developments.
- Decide if one event caused the other. Look for "clue words" such as *because, so, brought about, produced, as a result of,* or *therefore.*
- Look for logical relationships between events, such as "Vance's bike had a flat tire. He rode his scooter."
- Identify the outcomes of events. Remember that some effects have more than one cause, and some causes lead to more than one effect.

Practicing the Skill

On a separate sheet of paper, list the causes and effects in each statement that follows on diagrams similar to the sample on this page.

1 Although a member of the European Union, Great Britain has retained some of its traditional separation. It declined adoption of the euro in 2002.

2 Mexican and American governments have joined the Partnership for Prosperity to increase investment and job opportunities in Mexico's poorest regions. These places benefited little from the North American Free Trade Agreement.

3 Japan's constitution of 1889 allowed for no checks and balances among its legislative, executive, and judicial branches. As a result, military leaders were able to step in and seize power. After World War II, framers of the 1947 constitution corrected the earlier weaknesses.

4 Among the world pressures exerted against South Africa's apartheid government was its exclusion from international organizations. When apartheid ended, South Africa again participated in the United Nations and other world conferences.

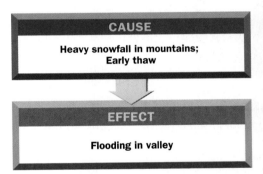

CAUSE

Heavy snowfall in mountains; Early thaw

EFFECT

Flooding in valley

Applying the Skill

In a current newsmagazine, read an account describing a government action or program. Identify at least one cause and one effect in the situation. Show the cause-and-effect relationship in a diagram like the one shown on this page.

Practice key skills with Glencoe's **Skillbuilder Interactive Workbook CD-ROM, Level 1.**

Assessment & Activities

Review to Learn

Section 1

- Democracy is a system of government in which the people rule.
- Authoritarian government is a system of government in which the power and authority to rule is held by an individual or a group not accountable to the people.

Section 2

- Great Britain has a parliamentary democracy. The monarch's power is limited.
- The national legislature, Parliament, holds almost all governmental authority in Great Britain.

Section 3

- Communists led by Mao Zedong seized power in China in 1949.
- China's leaders established a totalitarian government strictly controlled by the Communist Party.
- China has begun to allow some elements of free enterprise.

FOLDABLES™
Study Organizer

Using Your Foldables Study Organizer
Use your completed foldable to write four compare-and-contrast statements. For example, Great Britain's head of government is the _____, whereas China's government leader is the _____. Recite your statements to the class.

Reviewing Key Terms

Write the key term from the chapter that matches each definition below.

1. a system of government in which a king or a queen holds unlimited power
2. the form of government in which executive and legislative functions both reside in an elected assembly
3. the leader of the executive branch in a parliamentary system
4. fundamental rights that belong to all people
5. a government that exercises complete control of the state
6. the transfer of power to local authorities
7. a family that holds governing power over a long period of time
8. a government in which the power of the hereditary ruler is limited by the nation's constitution and laws

Reviewing Main Ideas

9. Who holds power under an authoritarian regime?
10. How do dictators usually gain control of a country?
11. What three totalitarian regimes emerged in the 1920s and 1930s?
12. What is another name for a representative democracy?
13. What group is the main lawmaker in Britain's Parliament?
14. What are the two major political parties in Great Britain?
15. When did the Communist Party take control of China?

Critical Thinking

16. **Making Comparisons** How does parliamentary government differ from presidential government?

17. Organizing Information On a diagram like the one below, explain why we expect to see numerous surpluses and shortages in an economy that is centrally planned and one in which government sets the prices.

| Government controls production and prices | → | Surpluses |
| | → | Shortages |

Technology Activity

18. Search for information on the Internet about China's economy. How is it changing? What are the economic problems it faces? Summarize your findings in a one-page paper.

Analyzing Visuals

Study the bar graph on page 602; then answer the following questions.

19. What comparison do the sets of graphs show?

20. How did the number of democratic governments change?

Economics Activity

21. Keep a log of items you use in one week. Include such items as your clothes, food, or sports equipment. Note whether each item is foreign-made or produced domestically. Then write a one-page paper in which you give your opinion on international trade and its effects on you.

★ CITIZENSHIP COOPERATIVE ACTIVITY ★

22. Working in small groups, research a nation whose government was not described in this chapter. Is it authoritarian or democratic? Presidential or parliamentary? Does it have legislative representatives? Do political parties compete for office? Compile your findings in a pamphlet.

Practicing Skills

23. Understanding Cause and Effect In your local newspaper, read an article describing a current event that took place in another country. Determine at least one cause and one effect of that event.

The Princeton Review

Standardized Test Practice

Directions: Read the excerpt from the writings of Adam Smith below. Then choose the *best* topic sentence for the selection.

"It is the highest impertinence and presumption, therefore, in kings and ministers, to pretend to watch over the economy of private people, and to restrain their expense. . . . They are themselves always, and without any exception, the greatest spendthrifts in the society. Let them look well after their own expense, and they may safely trust private people with theirs. If their own extravagance does not ruin the state, that of their subjects never will."

F Government should take every possible action to help the economy.

G Every nation progresses through six stages of economic development.

H Government should not be involved in the economic affairs of people.

J Economics provides a framework for decision making.

Test-Taking Tip

Read the excerpt carefully. Remember that Adam Smith supported the doctrine of laissez-faire. What does the doctrine say about government's role in the economy?

An Interdependent World

 CITIZENSHIP AND YOU

People today say the world is growing smaller. By this they mean that modern technological changes are bringing human beings all around the world into closer contact. As you study this chapter, pay attention to world events. In a journal, identify how international events may affect your life.

To learn more about the United Nations, view the **Democracy in Action** electronic field trip 9: The United Nations.

 FOLDABLES™
Study Organizer

Organizing Information Study Foldable *Make the following foldable to help you organize what you learn about the interdependent world.*

Step 1 *Fold one sheet of paper in half from side to side.*

Fold the sheet vertically.

Step 2 *Fold again, 1 inch from the top. (Tip: The middle knuckle of your index finger is about 1 inch long.)*

Step 3 *Open and label as shown.*

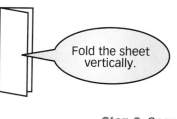

Draw lines along the fold lines.

Reading and Writing *As you read the chapter, take notes as you learn about international organizations and global issues in the appropriate columns of your foldable.*

1946 poster by American artist Ben Shahn, who was known for addressing social and political issues in his paintings and prints ▶

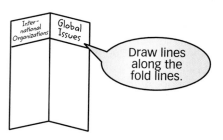

CIVICS Online

Chapter Overview Visit the *Civics Today* Web site at <u>civ.glencoe.com</u> and click on **Chapter Overviews—Chapter 28** to preview chapter information.

these rights
we've just begun

Global Developments

Americans in Action

Jimmy Carter served as president of the United States from 1977 to 1981. After leaving the White House, he and his wife Rosalyn founded the Carter Center in Atlanta, Georgia. The center focuses on global health, human rights, and democracy. Its many accomplishments include monitoring democratic elections in nations and a worldwide effort to eradicate Guinea worm disease that annually cripples more than 2 million Africans. The Carters are also involved in the Habitat for Humanity program. With thousands of other volunteers, they help build houses for the poor. Carter believes "To work for better understanding among people, one does not have to be a former president. . . . Peace can be made in the neighborhoods, the living rooms, the playing fields, and the classrooms of our country."

Two former presidents, Joseph Estrada of the Philippines and Jimmy Carter, build a wall.

Global Interdependence

Global interdependence means that people and nations all over the world now depend upon one another for many goods and services. It also means that what happens in one nation or region affects what happens in other places.

Today every country depends upon other countries for some of the products, services, and raw materials it needs to function. This relationship is called global economic interdependence.

The fuel to power our cars, planes, trains, trucks, and buses and to heat and light our homes and run our factories is an important example of growing interdependence. The United States must import about 50 percent of the oil it uses. An important goal of U.S. foreign policy, therefore, is to maintain good relations with oil-producing countries.

In addition, the United States imports many of the minerals its industries need in order to keep working. For instance, 98 percent of the manganese, 93 percent of the bauxite, 81 percent of the tin, and 62 percent of the mercury Americans use come from other countries.

Global interdependence also means that other countries depend upon us. The United States sells computers, telecommunications equipment, aircraft, medical equipment, farm machinery, and countless other high-technology products around the world. In addition, many smaller, poorer countries look to the United States for food, medicine, and arms.

Global Trade

The most important part of economic interdependence is trade. As you learned in Chapter 26, trade includes both competition and cooperation. Nations compete to sell their products. They also cooperate to make trade beneficial for everyone.

Global trade has many advantages. Businesses can make more profit, for example, by selling to a large world market. Increased competition may result in lower prices for consumers and a greater range of products from which to choose. However, global trade can also lead to problems. Competition may force weak companies

out of business, hurting some national economies and costing workers their jobs. Remember that nations often try to protect their industries from foreign competition by placing tariffs on imports. This policy, called **protectionism,** often harms the economies of other nations and the global economy. It may cause price increases and lead to trade wars, in which nations set up even greater trade barriers. Trade wars can create serious tensions between nations.

Hourly Compensation Costs, 2000

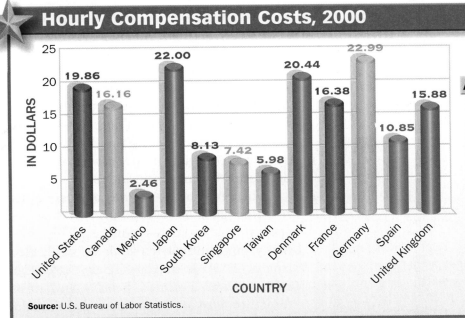

IN DOLLARS

United States 19.86, Canada 16.16, Mexico 2.46, Japan 22.00, South Korea 8.13, Singapore 7.42, Taiwan 5.98, Denmark 20.44, France 16.38, Germany 22.99, Spain 10.85, United Kingdom 15.88

COUNTRY

Source: U.S. Bureau of Labor Statistics.

Analyzing Graphs

This graph shows the compensation costs for production workers in manufacturing in 12 countries. Hourly compensation includes wages, bonuses, benefits, and other plans. All amounts are converted to U.S. dollars. What countries' production workers earn less than $10 per hour?

It all started with a vegetable patch. As a little boy, Everett Law used to love working in his backyard garden in Minneapolis, Minnesota. Every day, he would tend the soil, nurturing each plant. Eventually, the garden matured; so did Law, and so did his passion for protecting the earth.

In sixth grade, Law took his enthusiasm to middle school. He built a new garden in the central courtyard, using money he raised from several corporations. Two years later, in 1999, he organized the school's first Earth Day event. By the year 2000, Law's Earth Day program had 23 different groups taking part. In 2001, there were 50. The event was so popular, Law began organizing Earth Day programs in schools across Minnesota. He also started writing an Earth Day elementary school curriculum. "I guess it goes to show that youth are capable," Law told TIME. "Young people are able to do these kinds of things, even in an adult world."

Today, Law's group, Earth Day Operations, works with some 200 schools, environmental groups, corporations, colleges, and government agencies.

Want to find out more about Earth Day Operations? Go to www.webspawner.com/users/earthdayoperations/index.html. For information about Earth Day events worldwide, go to www.earthday.org

Everett Law from Minnesota

Trade Agreements

Many countries now support a policy of free trade that aims to eliminate tariffs and other economic barriers. The North American Free Trade Agreement (NAFTA) will gradually abolish all trade barriers between the United States, Mexico, and Canada. The World Trade Organization (WTO) will work to reduce tariffs among more than 150 nations and eliminate import quotas.

Reading Check **Explaining** What does free trade eliminate?

Global Problems and American Interests

Two of the biggest global problems are the growing economic inequality among nations and destruction of the environment.

Growing Economic Inequality

There is a growing split between the rich and poor nations of the world. An old saying describes what is happening: "The rich get richer and the poor get poorer." As this occurs, conflicts grow, and the United States faces difficult decisions.

On one side are the 25 or so rich, industrialized countries, including the United States, Japan, Germany, Canada, Great Britain, and France. These nations are called developed countries because they have built a way of life based on highly developed business and industry.

The developed countries possess natural resources such as coal and iron, or they have easy access to such resources. They have many large industries such as steel, electronics, and car making. Their citizens are relatively well educated, healthy, and accustomed to working in business and industry. They produce most of the manufactured goods sold around the world. They also consume much of the world's natural resources, enjoying a high standard of living.

On the other side are about 165 poorer and less developed nations. Many of their citizens live in the shadow of high death rates due to starvation or disease. Because most of the poor countries are trying to develop industrial economies, they are called developing countries.

Characteristics of Developing Nations

Some of these countries, such as Chad, Albania, Paraguay, and Uganda, are very poor. They have few natural resources and cannot produce enough food to feed their populations. They manufacture few products for export. They have high levels of unemployment, disease, and poverty. Their average life expectancy is less than 40 years.

Other developing countries have valuable natural resources. Countries such as Saudi Arabia and Venezuela have oil. Colombia grows coffee. The Democratic Republic of the Congo has copper. Some of these countries have little industry, though. Some do not have the health and educational facilities to develop their human resources. It generally takes scientists, engineers, bankers, and business leaders to develop industry.

For various reasons, most developed nations are located in the Northern Hemisphere, and most developing nations are in the Southern Hemisphere. As a result, policymakers and the news media often talk about the "North-South conflict" when discussing this global problem.

The Process of Economic Development

Developed and developing nations need each other. Rich nations sell their products to the poorer nations. In a recent year, for example, more than one-third of American exports went to developing countries. Developed nations also get much of the raw materials they need from developing countries. For their part, the developing nations badly need the food, technology, and money that the developed nations supply.

Many industrial nations try to help developing nations. The U.S. Agency for International Development, for example, distributes billions of dollars in financial and technical aid. American businesses help by investing money in poor countries to build factories, which provide jobs and training. U.S. citizens help by volunteering to teach important skills, such as modern methods of farming.

Foreign Aid

Americans and their government leaders face some difficult questions about foreign aid. Should the United States increase its aid to the poorer countries, or is it better to encourage them to get help from private investors? In giving aid, should we favor nations that support our policies, even if other nations might need that aid more? Should we distribute less foreign aid and spend more on problems at home?

$ Economics and You

Trademarks

With companies extending their reach around the world, trademarks have become increasingly important. A trademark is a name or symbol used to show that a product is made by a particular company. It is legally registered with a government so that no other manufacturer can use it. Use the most recent edition of *The Top Ten of Everything* to discover the nations with the most registered trademarks and with the best-selling registered brands.

Environmental Destruction

Another global problem today is destruction of the natural environment. Industries and motor vehicles have pumped poisonous metals such as mercury and lead into the air and water. Spills from tanker ships have spread millions of gallons of oil into the oceans and onto beaches, killing fish, sea birds, and food for marine life.

Coal-burning factories release sulfur dioxide gas into the air, where it mixes with water vapor and later falls to the earth as acid rain. Sulfur dioxide from factories in the American Midwest may fall as acid rain in Canada, damaging forests and raising the acid level in hundreds of Canadian lakes, killing many fish. The United States and Canada have formed a joint commission to explore solutions to the problem of acid rain.

To save the environment, countries around the world must work to end pollution both within their borders and internationally. An important way to reduce pollution is through conservation—limiting the use of polluting resources.

Conserving gasoline, for example, cuts back on the amount of gases that pollutes the atmosphere. Conserving forests protects wildlife habitats and leaves more trees to absorb carbon dioxide. Conservation will also help ensure that a variety of resources will be available when they are needed in the future.

Some people oppose conservation efforts, claiming that they slow economic growth. Others argue that a lack of conservation may produce short-term gains but long-term problems. Not dealing with air pollution, for example, may lead to dangerous changes in climate, destruction of

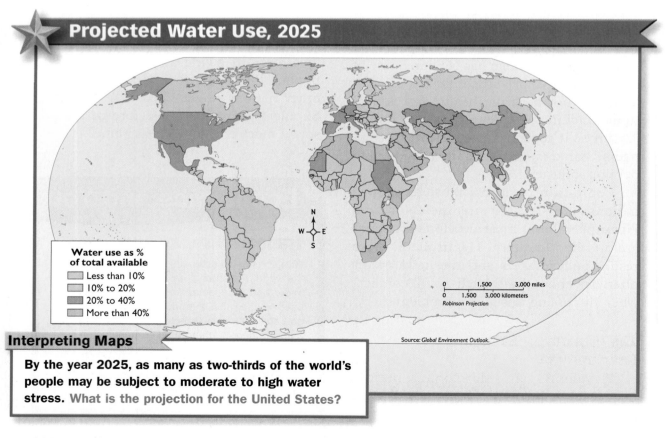

Projected Water Use, 2025

Water use as % of total available
- Less than 10%
- 10% to 20%
- 20% to 40%
- More than 40%

0   1,500   3,000 miles
0   1,500   3,000 kilometers
Robinson Projection

Source: Global Environment Outlook.

Interpreting Maps

By the year 2025, as many as two-thirds of the world's people may be subject to moderate to high water stress. What is the projection for the United States?

TIME

Political Cartoons

IF THAT'S NOT A SIGN I DON'T KNOW WHAT IS....

GLOBAL WARMING STUDY

Sack
STAR TRIBUNE

and it seems to be diverted toward money and me. Making the world a more convenient | Schneider, two men with little hope, of regaining the company's revenue. While the wage was | to be diverted time

Analyzing Visuals In recent years, experts have debated whether emissions from fossil fuels are gradually causing the earth's temperature to rise. What point is the cartoonist making about global warming? How does the cartoonist convey this argument?

forests and lakes, and severe health problems as people breathe polluted air.

Poor nations believe that antipollution regulations are unfair because such rules would make it more difficult for them to develop their own industries. They argue that the developed countries polluted freely while they were becoming rich, but now they do not want to let the poor countries do the same.

Should the United States push for the same pollution-control rules for everyone? Or, should the poorer countries be given the chance to develop their economies without worrying about pollution? These are questions that we and the leaders of our country must face.

Reading Check **Defining** What is conservation?

SECTION 1 ASSESSMENT

Checking for Understanding

1. **Key Terms** Define the following terms and use them in sentences related to environmental issues: acid rain, conservation.

Reviewing Main Ideas

2. **Explain** What is the purpose of protectionism?

3. **Identify** How are developing countries different from developed countries?

Critical Thinking

4. **Making Generalizations** What characteristics do industrialized nations share?

5. **Organizing Information** On a chart like the one below, describe the advantages and disadvantages of global trade.

Global Trade	
Advantages	Disadvantages

Analyzing Visuals

6. **Interpret** Study the graph on page 611. What countries' production workers' costs are between $16 and $20 per hour?

★ **BE AN ACTIVE CITIZEN** ★

7. **Research** Find out what opportunities your community offers for individual involvement in world issues. Find out how you might contribute to such efforts.

Critical Thinking
SKILLBUILDER

Reading a Time Line

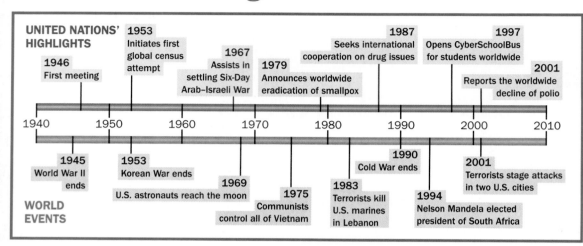

UNITED NATIONS' HIGHLIGHTS

1946 First meeting

1953 Initiates first global census attempt

1967 Assists in settling Six-Day Arab–Israeli War

1979 Announces worldwide eradication of smallpox

1987 Seeks international cooperation on drug issues

1997 Opens CyberSchoolBus for students worldwide

2001 Reports the worldwide decline of polio

1940   1950   1960   1970   1980   1990   2000   2010

1945 World War II ends

1953 Korean War ends

1969 U.S. astronauts reach the moon

1975 Communists control all of Vietnam

1983 Terrorists kill U.S. marines in Lebanon

1990 Cold War ends

1994 Nelson Mandela elected president of South Africa

2001 Terrorists stage attacks in two U.S. cities

WORLD EVENTS

Why Learn This Skill?
As you read or study, you learn of events occurring at different times. One way of organizing the events is to view them on a time line. A time line is a graphic that arranges events in the order in which they happened and shows the dates of their occurrences. Reading time lines helps you view an event in the context and sequence of other events.

Learning the Skill
To interpret a time line, follow these steps:
• Trace the time line from left to right. Note the dates at each end. This tells you the total span of time covered.
• Notice the shorter segments, or time intervals, marked off along the time line. The segments have a uniform length and may cover days, years, or other blocks of time.
• Read the title or label above the time line to determine the type of events displayed. There may be a title below the time line, indicating that a different category of events occurred during the same time span.
• Examine the events contained in the time line. Note which events occurred before or

after other events. Observe the length of time separating different events.

Practicing the Skill
Examine the time line on this page. Then answer the following questions.

❶ What span of time does this time line cover?
❷ What is the time interval between segments?
❸ In what year did the United Nations first attempt a global census?
❹ When did the Cold War end?
❺ Which happened first, the UN's announcement on smallpox or its introduction of CyberSchoolBus?

Applying the Skill

Make a list of important events that occurred in your school life this year. Construct a time line displaying those events.

Practice key skills with Glencoe's **Skillbuilder Interactive Workbook CD-ROM, Level 1.**

The United Nations

GUIDE TO READING

Main Idea
The United Nations was established to maintain peace by guaranteeing the security of member nations.

Key Terms
internationalism, veto, globalization, multinational

Reading Strategy
Organizing Information As you read the section, complete a chart like the one below by describing the functions of these units of the United Nations.

	Function
General Assembly	
Security Council	
Secretariat	

Read to Learn
- **What is the structure of the United Nations?**
- **How does the United Nations attempt to promote peace?**

Americans in Action

On September 11, 2001, the United Nations community in midtown Manhattan recoiled along with all other New Yorkers in the face of the terrorist attacks. Twenty-four hours later the Security Council, the General Assembly, and the secretary-general had raised their voices in condemnation of what they and the world had just seen. The U.S. ambassador to the United Nations, John D. Negroponte, noted, "This was no instance where the United States had to lobby for votes. Among all the issues and problems the UN confronts, global terrorism clearly was the new priority. Humanity was appalled; solidarity was complete."

Ambassador Negroponte

The Purpose of the United Nations

Internationalism is the idea that nations should cooperate to promote common aims, such as supporting economic development and fighting terrorism. They do this through membership in an organization made up of many nations. An example of such an organization was the League of Nations. It was formed after World War I, but the United States refused to join the League because many Americans feared that it would entangle their country in foreign conflicts. Without American participation, the League became a weaker organization and was unable to prevent World War II. When that war ended, the United States realized it must not make the same mistake again. It became a leader in forming a new organization, the United Nations (UN).

The United States and other nations started planning for the UN during World War II. In 1944 delegates from the United States, Great Britain, and the Soviet Union drafted a charter, or constitution, for the UN. In 1945 representatives from 50 countries—at that time, almost all the countries in the world—signed the charter at a meeting in San Francisco. The UN's main purposes are to maintain international peace, develop friendly relations among nations, promote justice and cooperation, and seek solutions to global problems.

On United Nations' Day, October 24, 2001, President George W. Bush praised the UN for its commitment to

> **promoting human rights, protecting the environment, fighting disease, fostering development, and reducing poverty.**

Structure of the UN

The UN now has 190 members. Its main headquarters is in New York City. The organization is divided into a variety of units.

The **General Assembly** is the only UN body to which all member nations belong. Each nation has a single vote. The assembly holds regular and special sessions to debate international issues and recommend courses of action. Decisions are made by majority vote.

The **Security Council** is the UN's peacekeeping arm. It has five permanent members—the United States, Great Britain, Russia, France, and China—the nations that led the fight to destroy the totalitarian regimes of Germany, Japan, and Italy in World War II. The Security Council also has 10 nonpermanent members. The General Assembly elects the nonpermanent members for two-year terms.

Each member has one vote, and all important decisions require nine "yes" votes. Any one of the five permanent members, however, can **veto,** or reject, a motion. This veto gives each of the permanent members a great deal of power to block actions it opposes.

Organization of the United Nations

UNITS	
International Court of Justice	Also known as the World Court, this is the main judicial agency of the UN. Consisting of 15 judges elected by the General Assembly and the Security Council, the Court decides disputes between countries.
Security Council	The Security Council is the UN's principal agency for maintaining international peace and security. Of the 15 Council members, 5 members—China, France, the Russian Federation, the United Kingdom, and the United States—are permanent members. The other 10 are elected by the General Assembly for two-year terms. Decisions of the Council require 9 yes votes.
General Assembly	All UN member states are represented in the General Assembly. It meets to consider important matters such as international peace and security, the UN budget, and admission of new members. Each member state has one vote.
Secretariat	The Secretariat carries out the administrative work of the United Nations as directed by the General Assembly, the Security Council, and the other agencies. Its head is the secretary-general.
Economic and Social Council	The Economic and Social Council recommends economic and social policies.
Trusteeship Council	The Trusteeship Council was established to ensure the rights of territories as they took the steps toward self-government or independence.

Evaluating Charts

The UN was established after World War II to preserve peace through international cooperation. Today, nearly 190 nations are UN members. What are the six principal units of the UN?

The Security Council meets throughout the year and also holds emergency sessions to cope with new crises in international affairs. It often tries to persuade quarreling nations to solve differences peacefully. It can also send UN troops, drawn from various nations, to try to prevent or stop a war.

The **Secretariat** carries out the day-to-day business of the United Nations. Under the direction of the UN secretary-general, a staff of more than 8,900 people provides administrative services to the General Assembly, the Security Council, and the various agencies of the organization.

The **secretary-general** is the chief executive officer of the UN. The General Assembly, after recommendations from the Security Council, appoints the secretary-general to a five-year term of office, with a two-term limit.

The **International Court of Justice,** also known as the World Court, is the judicial arm of the United Nations. Its headquarters is in The Hague, the Netherlands. The 15 justices that sit on the court hear disputes between nations and issue decisions based on international law. The court, however, has no power to enforce its rulings. It must rely on the cooperation of the parties to the disputes it hears.

Concern for bettering human living conditions is the main business of the **Economics and Social Council.** This agency tries to promote a higher standard of living around the world, including improvements in health, education, and human rights. The General Assembly elects the 54 countries that sit on the council, with one-third of them giving way to new members every three years.

The **Trusteeship Council** was responsible for helping 11 territories that were not colonial possessions but also did not enjoy self-government at the end of World War II. By 1994 the last of these territories had become either an independent nation or part of some other nation. The council ceased operations then, but it remains part of the UN structure.

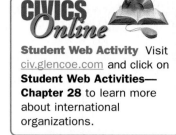

CIVICS Online

Student Web Activity Visit civ.glencoe.com and click on **Student Web Activities— Chapter 28** to learn more about international organizations.

UN Agencies

Special agencies do much of the work of the UN. These include the World Health Organization (WHO), the United Nations Children's Fund (UNICEF), the World Bank, and the International Monetary Fund (IMF).

The WHO strives to direct and coordinate international health work. Its goal is to bring the highest level of health to people across the globe.

The United Nations General Assembly created UNICEF in 1946 to help children in Europe after World War II had ended. First known as the United Nations International Children's Emergency Fund, it became a permanent part of the UN in 1953, seeking mainly to help children in need in developing countries. The goal of UNICEF is to help children all over the world get the care they need during the critical early years of life. It also seeks to encourage families to educate girls as well as boys, to reduce childhood death and illness, and to protect the children caught in the midst of wars and natural disasters. UNICEF accomplishes these goals by providing services and supplies to needy children, and by encouraging the world's leaders to implement policies that are in the best interest of children.

The World Bank is an agency of the UN set up in 1945 to make loans to developing countries at low interest rates. The IMF is an international organization of 183 member countries. It was established

VOTE FOR JOBS, PEACE AND FREEDOM.

ANC

UN Forces and Missions In 1963, the UN created the Special Committee against Apartheid to promote and monitor actions against apartheid, South Africa's segregation of blacks and whites. In April 1994, South Africans elected Nelson Mandela as president in its first nonracial national election. **Why did the UN send forces to Cambodia in the 1990s?**

to promote international financial and technical cooperation. The IMF also tries to encourage economic growth and provide financial assistance to countries, especially developing countries.

In general, these agencies try to combat hunger, disease, poverty, ignorance, and other problems by providing poor nations with money and expert assistance in health, industrial development, agriculture, education, and other fields.

Reading Check **Describing** How many nations are part of the UN?

Recent Activities of the United Nations

The UN has been successful in several ways. It has served as a meeting place where representatives from many nations can discuss mutual problems. It has been able to settle wars between several small nations. Some special agencies of the UN have done a great deal to fight sickness, poverty, and ignorance around the world. However, a

lack of cooperation among the Security Council's permanent members has made the UN less effective in settling disputes and preventing wars than many had hoped.

New Efforts to Promote Peace

Recently the UN has taken a greater role in peacekeeping efforts. For example, when Iraq invaded Kuwait in 1990, the Security Council voted to condemn Iraq and place trade sanctions on the country. It also set a deadline for Iraq to withdraw from Kuwait. When the deadline passed, a U.S.-led and UN-sanctioned coalition of nations attacked and defeated Iraq in the Persian Gulf War, liberating Kuwait.

In the 1990s the United Nations sent peacekeeping troops to oversee elections in Cambodia, provide humanitarian aid to starving people in Somalia, and monitor peace settlements in Bosnia-Herzegovina. In 1999, it carried out peacekeeping operations in Sierra Leone, the Democratic Republic of the Congo, Kosovo, and East Timor. The UN has also sent inspectors to Iraq to try to stop that country from developing weapons of mass destruction.

Responses to Global Problems

The United Nations was created to respond to global problems. By the start of the twenty-first century many of those problems were being treated under the umbrella of globalization, or individuals and nations working internationally across barriers of distance, culture, and technology. In 2001 Secretary-General Kofi A. Annan of Ghana wrote,

❝Globalization is transforming the world. . . . Our challenge today is to make globalization an engine that lifts people out of hardship and misery, not a force that holds them down.❞

In recent years many nations have become increasingly concerned about the environment. In 1992 a major conference on the environment was held in Rio de Janeiro, Brazil. This Earth Summit brought together representatives from 178 nations who discussed ways of protecting the environment. Leaders signed treaties pledging to safeguard the diversity of animal and plant life and limit pollution that causes global warming. In 1997 world leaders gathered at the United Nations for Earth Summit II. They agreed that while some progress had been made, much remained to be done.

In 1999 the United Nations responded to the global problem of economic inequality that divides the world into rich and poor nations. At the World Economic Forum in Davos, Switzerland, Secretary-General Annan proposed a "Global Compact" between the United Nations and the world's large multinational corporations, or multinationals. **Multinationals** are firms that do business or have offices or factories in many countries. The compact would call upon leaders of private enterprise to respect human rights and contribute to a fairer distribution of wealth throughout the world.

✓Reading Check **Identifying** What factor makes the UN less effective in settling disputes than many had hoped?

SECTION 2 ASSESSMENT

Checking for Understanding

1. Key Terms Write a short paragraph in which you use the following key terms: internationalism, veto, globalization, multinational.

Reviewing Main Ideas

2. Identify In what year was the United Nations formed? Name two recent activities of the United Nations.

3. Explain How many nations are permanent members of the Security Council? What do these nations have in common?

Critical Thinking

4. Analyzing Information What actions can the UN Security Council take to try to keep peace?

5. Organizing Information On a diagram like the one below, describe three purposes of the United Nations.

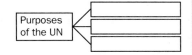

Analyzing Visuals

6. Interpret Study the chart on page 618. How many nations represent the Security Council? How are the judges to the World Court selected?

★BE AN ACTIVE CITIZEN★

7. Research Take a poll of adults you know in your community. Find out their opinions about the work of the United Nations. Also find out what they think about U.S. involvement in that organization.

Democracy and Human Rights

GUIDE TO READING

Main Idea

Throughout its history, the United States has worked to promote democracy and human rights.

Key Terms

international tribunal, genocide, apartheid, sanctions, satellite, Cold War

Reading Strategy

Classifying Information As you read the section, complete a chart like the one below by describing the characteristics of these types of governments and giving an example of each.

	Characteristics
Fully Free	
Partly Free	
Not Free	

Read to Learn

• Why are many nations turning to a more democratic form of government?
• What actions are being taken to safeguard human rights?

Americans in Action

On a visit to Guatemala in the late 1980s, Mark Richard saw a disabled woman crawling along a roadside. He made up his mind to bring the woman a wheelchair. When he returned to the United States, Mark contacted the local chapter of the Spinal Cord Injury Association. Together they began delivering wheelchairs. Mark and his brother, Richard, cofounded Wheels for Humanity. In a California warehouse, volunteers restore battered wheelchairs that are distributed to disabled children in Vietnam, Guatemala, Bosnia, Nicaragua, and many other countries. In four years, Wheels for Humanity distributed 4,000 wheelchairs in 26 countries. Monetary donations are important. "We have to raise $125 per chair," David Richard says. "That is what it costs to go out, pick up a chair, refurbish it, box it, and ship it to another country."

Amputee Tun Channareth of Cambodia won the Nobel Prize for a campaign to ban land mines.

Standards for Human Rights

Human rights are the basic freedoms and rights that all people should enjoy. Human rights include the right to safety, to food, and to shelter, among other things. In democracies like the United States, these rights lie at the heart of the U.S. political system and enable citizens and noncitizens to worship as they please, speak freely, and read and write what they choose.

In recent decades, the issue of human rights has captured world attention. According to human rights' groups, despite democratic advances many governments still imprison and abuse people for speaking their minds. Among the countries accused of human rights violations are China, Indonesia, and Myanmar. Other countries, such as Iran, Iraq, Cuba, and Sudan, have also been charged with sponsoring terrorist acts outside their borders.

The good news is that human rights abuses are more carefully monitored than they were. In South Africa, Haiti, and El Salvador, for example, national commissions have investigated abuses of past governments, and international groups have called individuals to account for their war crimes.

The Universal Declaration of Human Rights

In 1948 the United Nations adopted what has become the most important human rights document of the post–World War II years—the Universal Declaration of Human Rights. Addressing social and economic as well as political rights, the 30 articles of the Declaration form a statement not of the way things are but of the way they should be.

Articles 1 and 2 proclaim that "all human beings are born equal in dignity and rights." Articles 3 to 21 state the civil and political rights of all human beings, including many of the same liberties and protections of the U.S. Constitution. They also include other rights, such as freedom of movement, the right to seek asylum, the right to a nationality, the right to marry and found a family, and the right to own property.

Articles 22 to 27 spell out the economic, social, and cultural rights of all people, including the right to social security, the right to work, the right to receive equal pay for equal work, the right to form and join trade unions, the right to enjoy rest and leisure, the right to have a standard of living adequate for health and well being, the right to education, and the right to participate in the cultural life of the community. Articles 28 to 30 state that all people should be free to enjoy all the rights set forth in the Universal Declaration.

Protecting Human Rights

The UN High Commissioner for Human Rights directs the organization's human rights activities. The Commissioner oversees programs that promote and protect human rights. For example, the UN Commission on Human Rights monitors and reports rights violations in all parts of the world. By drawing attention to these abuses, the UN hopes to bring pressure to halt them.

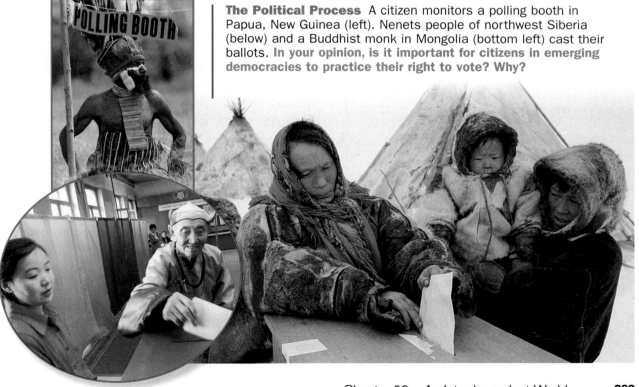

The Political Process A citizen monitors a polling booth in Papua, New Guinea (left). Nenets people of northwest Siberia (below) and a Buddhist monk in Mongolia (bottom left) cast their ballots. **In your opinion, is it important for citizens in emerging democracies to practice their right to vote? Why?**

The Law and You

Human Rights

Imagine you are on the staff of a member of the U.S. Congress. You have been asked to draft a memo providing information and recommending a position on some key points in the Universal Declaration of Human Rights (UNDHR). The focus of the memo is the right to shelter and the right to

health care. These rights are not currently found in the U.S. Constitution. While some people agree that it would be nice to have these rights, there is quite a lot of disagreement about these issues.

The UNDHR is an international document created in 1948. Its 30 articles were intended to be "a common standard of achievement for all peoples and all nations." Human rights are rights that universally belong to people regardless of their gender, race, language, national origin, age, class, religion, or political beliefs. A person has human rights simply because she or he is a human being.

★ BE AN ACTIVE CITIZEN ★

Draft the memo that addresses the following questions: Why are these rights important? How much do these rights need to be protected in the United States? How would we pay for protecting these rights? What would the impact be on taxpayers? What impact is felt right now by not having these rights protected? Do we have a moral responsibility to protect these rights?

In 1993 the UN held the Second World Conference on Human Rights in Vienna, Austria. The 171 participating nations proclaimed that human rights are the "concern of the international community" and that "all human rights are universal."

The Security Council has acted to punish human rights violators by establishing **international tribunals.** These are courts with authority from the UN to hear cases

and make judgments about violations of international human rights law. In 1993 a tribunal was set up to investigate and try cases related to the breakup of Yugoslavia. A number of military leaders and government officials, including Yugoslavia's former president, Slobodan Milosevic, have been tried. Many of them have been found guilty and punished.

During the 1990s, ethnic tensions in the East African nations of Rwanda and Burundi led to violent conflict. In 1994 the Hutu-led Rwandan government battled Tutsi-led guerrillas. In a **genocide,** or the deliberate killing of a racial or cultural group, Hutu forces killed more than 500,000 people. The International Criminal Tribunal Court for Rwanda began bringing to justice people accused of participating in the genocide.

✓ Reading Check **Describing** What do the UN's international tribunals do?

Spread of Democracy and Liberty

The United Nations has encouraged the spread of democracy and human rights throughout the world. So has the United States, which has made these causes an important part of its foreign policy.

Growth of Democracy

At the beginning of the twentieth century, only about 12 percent of the world's people lived in a democracy. By 1950 there were 22 democratic nations with 31 percent of the world's population.

Over the next 50 years, democracy grew rapidly, especially after 1980. By 2001 nearly 60 percent of the world's population in 120 countries lived under conditions of democracy. A publication called *Freedom in the World* provides an annual evaluation of political rights and civil liberties for more than 190 countries. At a minimum, "a democracy is a political system in which the people choose their authoritative leaders freely from among competing groups and individuals who were not chosen by the government."

Countries that go beyond this standard for democracy offer the broadest range of human rights, such as those stated in the UN Universal Declaration of Human Rights. These countries are "fully free" democracies. In 2001, there were 86 countries with free and democratic governments.

There were 58 "partly free" countries, 34 of which met the minimal standard for democracy by holding free and fair elections. None of these countries guaranteed a broad range of individual liberties beyond those political freedoms, however. Twenty-four of the "partly free" countries did not quite measure up to the minimal standard for democracy.

In 2001 about 35 percent of the world's population lived in 48 countries that were not free. These nondemocracies often practiced or permitted terrible violations of human rights.

Fight for Rights in South Africa and Afghanistan

White leaders of South Africa legalized and strengthened a policy of racial separation between blacks and whites called apartheid. Apartheid laws dictated where blacks could travel, eat, and go to school. Black people could not vote or own property, and they could be jailed indefinitely without cause.

For more than 40 years, people inside and outside South Africa protested against the practice of apartheid. Nelson Mandela, imprisoned in 1962 on charges of treason, became a symbol of the struggle for freedom in South Africa. Both the United States and the European Economic Community (now known as the European Union) ordered economic sanctions, or coercive measures, against South Africa, and U.S. businesses began to withdraw their investments. Mounting pressure from foreign countries and the anti-apartheid movement brought a gradual end to apartheid. In April 1994, South Africa held its first election open to all races, and elected Nelson Mandela as the first black president.

Conflict The cycle of violence, wars between nations, and civil wars within nations, have brought much suffering to the people of the Middle East. This poster, hanging in Jerusalem, expresses the wish of those tired of conflict. **What might make people who share a language and religion feel loyal to one another, wherever they live?**

American Biographies

Jody Williams (1950–)

In 1991 Jody Williams declared war on land mines—the deadly underground weapons that killed or crippled up to 26,000 people a year in more than 60 nations. The destruction usually fell on civilians. "The land mine cannot tell the difference between a solider and a civilian," declared Williams.

Williams, who comes from Vermont, gave up a career in teaching English as a second language to found the International Campaign to Ban Landmines (ICBL). Within six years, the ICBL had convinced more than 100 nations to sign the Mine Ban Treaty of 1997. That year, Williams and the ICBL were awarded the Nobel Peace Prize.

The anti-mine campaign continues today. As the 2000s opened, crises in Afghanistan—one of the most heavily mined nations on Earth—brought the issue home to the United States. While U.S. troops helped search for the terrorists who planned the attack on the World Trade Center, Williams asked American leaders to search for weapons of terror beneath Afghani soil. "USA don't look away," urged one ICBL poster, "Ban land mines now!"

After Afghanistan collapsed into civil war, many people turned to the Taliban, a group educated in impoverished religious primary schools in Pakistan and Afghanistan after decades of war. By 1996 the Taliban had taken control of about 80 percent of the country. They put in place harsh policies based on a strict interpretation of Islam. Thousands of women were physically assaulted, and severe restrictions were placed on their liberty and fundamental freedoms. In late 2001 the United States accused the Taliban of supporting terrorists and began bombing Taliban forces. After the collapse of the Taliban government, the United Nations began working with the nation's new leaders to create a climate that protected human rights.

Safeguarding Democracy

During most of the twentieth century, the global advancement of democracy and liberty was a main objective of the U.S. government. President Woodrow Wilson declared during and after World War I that the United States and its allies should "make the world safe for democracy." During World War II, President Franklin D. Roosevelt said that the United States and its allies were fighting for democracy and freedom in the world. He said,

> 66 Freedom means the supremacy of human rights everywhere. Our support goes to those who struggle to gain these rights or to keep them. 99

The Cold War After World War II, the Soviet Union dominated Eastern Europe, forcing countries there to become Soviet **satellites**—countries politically and economically dominated or controlled by another more powerful country. Soviet actions during these years convinced the United States and its allies that the Soviet goal was to expand its power and influence. Most of the world soon divided into two hostile camps—the free nations of the West and the Communist nations.

The bitter struggle between the two sides came to be known as the **Cold War** because it more often involved a clash of ideas than a clash of arms. The clash was between the American ideas of democracy and freedom and Soviet communism and totalitarianism.

Soviet Domination Ends From 1945 until the fall of the Soviet Union in 1991, American presidents consistently declared their commitment to the global spread of democracy and liberty. President Ronald Reagan, for example, said on June 8, 1982,

> ❝We must be staunch in our conviction that freedom is not the sole prerogative of a lucky few, but the inalienable and universal right of all human beings.❞

After the collapse of Soviet totalitarianism, American presidents promoted the advance of democracy in the former Soviet Union and in other countries in central and eastern Europe that had suffered under Soviet domination. The spread of democracy elsewhere in the world also continued to be a goal of U.S. foreign policy.

War Against Terror In response to the September 11, 2001, terrorist attacks on the United States, President George W. Bush repeated America's commitment to democracy and liberty around the world. He said in a speech to Congress,

> ❝The advance of human freedom— the great achievement of our time, and the hope of every time—now depends on us.❞

A world that is increasingly democratic and free means that the United States and other nations will have an easier time maintaining peace, prosperity, and national security. Thus, it is in the national interest of the United States to promote the global advancement of democracy and liberty.

Reading Check **Identifying** What was the Cold War?

SECTION 3 ASSESSMENT

Checking for Understanding

1. Key Terms Write a paragraph that summarizes key points of this section. Use all of the following terms: apartheid, sanction, satellite, Cold War.

Reviewing Main Ideas

2. Explain What is genocide? How might an international tribunal deal with a case of genocide?

3. Compare Are more countries following democratic practices today than in 1900? How is a "democracy" defined?

Critical Thinking

4. Analyzing Information How do you think the United States should deal with regional conflicts in other parts of the world?

5. Sequencing Information After reviewing the entire section, choose what you feel are five important events. Place those events and their dates on a time line like the one below.

Analyzing Visuals

6. Infer Review the photographs on page 623. What are the people doing in the pictures? How would you describe their moods?

★ **BE AN ACTIVE CITIZEN** ★

7. Write Choose a country discussed in this section. Research the country. Imagine that you are traveling to the country. Write a letter to a friend describing the country and the extent to which the government affects people's lives.

Assessment & Activities

Review to Learn

Section 1
- Trade among nations is a major part of global interdependence.
- Since World War II, industrialized democracies have promoted free trade or the removal of trade barriers through the formation of regional associations.

Section 2
- The United Nations was established to provide a forum for nations to settle their disputes by peaceful means.
- Three of the major bodies that help fulfill the UN's goals are the General Assembly, the Security Council, and the International Court of Justice.

Section 3
- A wide variety of political systems can be found in the world today.
- A growing number of democracies endeavor to uphold human rights and to provide their citizens freedom and opportunities.

FOLDABLES™
Study Organizer

Using Your Foldables Study Organizer
Use your completed foldable to focus on one issue you have written about on your foldable. Identify a cause and effect associated with that issue in a brief essay.

Reviewing Key Terms
Write the key term that matches each definition below.
1. care and protection of natural resources
2. the idea that nations should cooperate to promote common aims
3. precipitation containing high amounts of pollutants
4. firms that do business in many countries
5. a conflict characterized by competition for world influence without declared military action
6. a nation politically and economically dominated or controlled by another, more powerful nation
7. policy of guarding industries from foreign competition by placing tariffs on imports
8. court set up by the UN to hear cases about violations of human rights

Reviewing Main Ideas
9. Why do some countries follow a policy of protectionism?
10. What do industrialized nations have in common?
11. How does reducing the use of gasoline promote conservation?
12. When was the charter of the United Nations drafted?
13. To which UN body do all member nations belong?
14. What nations are permanent members of the UN Security Council?
15. Name two UN agencies.
16. How did the UN respond to the Iraqi invasion of Kuwait in 1990?

Critical Thinking
17. **Evaluating Information** What do you think is the most important role of the UN in the world today? Why?

18. **Categorizing Information** Use a diagram like the one below to identify challenges facing democratic nations and how they dealt with them.

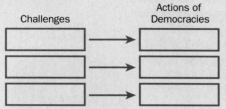

Challenges   Actions of Democracies

Technology Activity

19. Search the Internet for information about the latest technological innovations that are influencing our global culture. Create a bulletin board using the information retrieved from the Internet.

Practicing Skills

20. **Reading a Time Line** Research to find five key events that occurred in the United States and five key events that occurred in another country. Create a two-tiered time line displaying these events.

Economics Activity

21. Some people call the world a global village—a single community linked by electronic media, global trade, information technology, and more. Take an inventory of the things in your home that come from another nation. Don't forget to include raw materials or commodities that can't be found readily or in great abundance in the United States.

★ CITIZENSHIP COOPERATIVE ACTIVITY ★

22. With three other students, choose an environmental problem such as water pollution or forest destruction. Collect as many facts and figures as you can about this problem. Identify important sources of information and groups that are working to solve this particular problem.

CIVICS *Online*

Self-Check Quiz Visit the *Civics Today* Web site at civ.glencoe.com and click on **Self-Check Quizzes— Chapter 28** to prepare for the chapter test.

Analyzing Visuals

Study the map of projected water use on page 614; then answer the following questions.

23. In what category do most of the nations in South America fall? What is the outlook for China?

The Princeton Review

Standardized Test Practice

Directions: Read the paragraph below, and then answer the following question.

Foreign aid often goes to foreign governments that provide little relief for the poor. Aid may actually hinder foreign economic development. For example, food aid may depress the price of agricultural products, thus ruining the developing nation's farmers. Finally, the United States is no longer an economic giant that can afford foreign aid.

Which of the following statements *best* summarizes the paragraph?

F Foreign aid can help promote democracy.

G By contributing to the stability of developing nations, foreign aid protects the security of the United States.

H Foreign aid does not help promote economic growth and development.

J Most American foreign aid returns to the U.S. when foreign nations purchase American products.

Test-Taking Tip

Read through all of the answer choices before choosing the one that provides a general restatement of the information.

T HE AMBASSADORS FROM THE 15-NATION European Union got more than they bargained for when they invited National Security Adviser Condoleezza Rice to lunch two months after George W. Bush took office. With the United States still skeptical about the 1997 Kyoto Protocol to curb global warming by cutting emissions of carbon dioxide, the European Union was growing concerned that the pact might fall apart.

"We wanted to pass on the message that we take this issue seriously," one of the officials told Rice over lunch. Rice's reply stunned the ambassadors: she informed them that the Kyoto Protocol "is not acceptable to the Administration or Congress."

Did the White House agree that global warming is a looming crisis, the ambassadors asked. Yes, Rice answered. But, she explained, "we will have to find new ways to deal with the problem. Kyoto is dead."

Global reaction to this policy announcement was swift and furious. Governments condemned the president's stance as uninformed and even reckless, noting that the United States is home to 4% of the world's population but produces 25% of its greenhouse gases (*see graphic at right*). French President Jacques Chirac called on all countries to implement Kyoto; China's Foreign Ministry called U.S. actions "irresponsible."

President Bush stood firm, though. "Our economy has slowed down," he explained. "We also have an energy crisis, and the idea of placing caps on CO_2 does not make economic sense." Like Bush, members of Congress from both political parties see global warming as a long-term problem that carries little short-term political risk. The impact of policy decisions on global warming won't be felt for decades—and by then, today's legislators will be long gone. But if they foul up the economy, lawmakers know that they'll be sent home next Election Day.

❝The world community ... are all convinced of the seriousness of this issue. It is also an issue that is resonating here at home. We need to appear engaged.❞
— Christine Todd Whitman, Director of the Environmental Protection Agency, in a memo to President Bush

❝ We will work together [with other countries], but it's going to be what's in the interest of our country, first and foremost....❞
— President George W. Bush

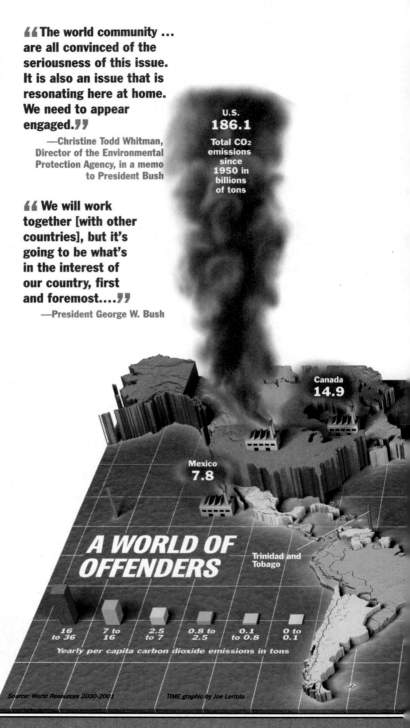

U.S.
186.1
Total CO_2 emissions since 1950 in billions of tons

Canada
14.9

Mexico
7.8

Trinidad and Tobago

A WORLD OF OFFENDERS

| 16 to 36 | 7 to 16 | 2.5 to 7 | 0.8 to 2.5 | 0.1 to 0.8 | 0 to 0.1 |

Yearly per capita carbon dioxide emissions in tons

Source: World Resources 2000-2001   TIME graphic by Joe Lertola

FORMULATING POLICY ON GLOBAL WARMING

TIME/CNN POLL
Citizens Weigh In

■ Would you be willing to pay an extra 25 cents per gallon of gas to reduce pollution and global warming?

Yes 48%
No 49%

■ Would you personally be willing to support tough government measures intended to help reduce global warming even if each of the following happened as a result:

	Yes	No
Your utility bills went up	47%	49%
Unemployment increased	38%	55%
A mild increase in inflation	54%	39%

■ When it comes to protecting the environment, does the government give in to business interests too often?

Yes 69%
No 26%

■ Should the government require improvements in fuel efficiency for cars and trucks even if this means higher prices and smaller vehicles?

Yes 55%
No 40%

■ Is global warming a very serious problem, a fairly serious problem, not a very serious problem, or not at all serious?

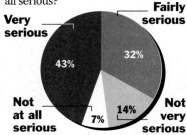

Very serious 43%
Fairly serious 32%
Not very serious 14%
Not at all serious 7%

From a telephone poll of 1,025 adult Americans taken for TIME/CNN on March 21-22, 2001, by Yankelovich Partners, Inc./Harris. Sampling error is ±3.1% "Not sures" omitted.

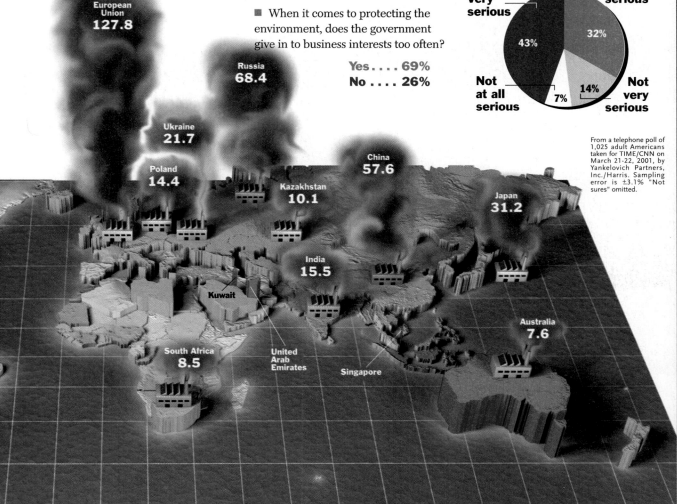

European Union 127.8
Russia 68.4
Ukraine 21.7
Poland 14.4
Kazakhstan 10.1
China 57.6
Japan 31.2
India 15.5
Kuwait
Australia 7.6
South Africa 8.5
United Arab Emirates
Singapore

Contents

Thomas Jefferson

In 1983 Fred Korematsu (center) won his case before the United States Supreme Court.

An intern at South Dakota's house of representatives sorts documents.

What Is an Appendix and How Do I Use One?

An appendix is the additional material you often find at the end of books. The following information will help you learn how to use the appendix in Civics Today: Citizenship, Economics, and You.

Careers Handbook

This will help you prepare for the future. The handbook contains practical information and tips that will help you find the right career.

Government and Economics Data Bank

A data bank is a collection of data organized for rapid search and retrieval. This data bank supplies information about the government and economy of the United States. It also includes information about state governments and economies.

United States Facts

This quick resource lists all the states and territories of the Union along with the year each was admitted and their populations, land areas, and number of representatives in Congress.

Presidents of the United States

The **presidents** have served as our nation's leaders. In this resource you will find information of interest on each of the nation's presidents, including their terms in office, political affiliations, and their occupations before they became president.

Documents of American History

This is a collection of some of the most important writings in American history. Each **document** begins with an introduction describing the author and placing the selection within its historical context.

Supreme Court Case Summaries

Supreme Court Case Summaries provide readable discussions of important Supreme Court cases. The summaries are listed in alphabetical order and include a summary of the facts of each case and its impact.

Glossary

A **glossary** is a list of important or difficult terms found in a textbook. Since words sometimes have other meanings, you may wish to consult a dictionary to find other uses for the terms. The glossary gives a definition of each term as it is used in the book. The glossary also includes page numbers telling you where in the textbook each term is used.

Spanish Glossary

A **Spanish glossary** does everything that an English glossary does, but it does it in Spanish. A Spanish glossary is especially important to bilingual students, or those Spanish-speaking students who are learning the English language.

Index

An **index** is an alphabetical listing that includes the subjects of the book and the page numbers where those subjects can be found. The index in this book also lets you know that certain pages contain maps, graphs, photos, or paintings about the subjects.

Acknowledgments

This section lists photo credits and/or literary credits for the book. You can look at this section to find out where the publisher obtained the permission to use a photograph or to use excerpts from other books.

TEST YOURSELF

Find the answers to these questions by using the Appendix on the following pages.

1. What are "intergovernmental revenues"?
2. Who was the sixth president of the United States and what term did he serve?
3. On what page can I find out about John Peter Zenger?
4. What year was Michigan admitted to the Union?
5. What was the Supreme Court's decision in *Marbury* v. *Madison*?

Honoring America

For Americans, the flag has always had a special meaning. It is a symbol of our nation's freedom and democracy.

Flag Etiquette

Over the years, Americans have developed rules and customs concerning the use and display of the flag. One of the most important things every American should remember is to treat the flag with respect.

- The flag should be raised and lowered by hand and displayed only from sunrise to sunset. On special occasions, the flag may be displayed at night, but it should be illuminated.

- The flag may be displayed on all days, weather permitting, particularly on national and state holidays and on historic and special occasions.

- No flag may be flown above the American flag or to the right of it at the same height.

- The flag should never touch the ground or floor beneath it.

- The flag may be flown at half-staff by order of the president, usually to mourn the death of a public official.

- The flag may be flown upside down only to signal distress.

- The flag should never be carried flat or horizontally, but always carried aloft and free.

- When the flag becomes old and tattered, it should be destroyed by burning. According to an approved custom, the Union (stars on blue field) is first cut from the flag; then the two pieces, which no longer form a flag, are burned.

★ ★ ★ ★ ★ ★ ★ ★

The Star-Spangled Banner

O! say can you see by the dawn's early light,
What so proudly we hailed at the twilight's last gleaming,
Whose broad stripes and bright stars through the perilous fight,
O'er the ramparts we watch'd, were so gallantly streaming?
And the Rockets' red glare, the Bombs bursting in air,
Gave proof through the night that our Flag was still there;
O! say does that star-spangled Banner yet wave,
O'er the Land of the free, and the home of the brave!

The Pledge of Allegiance

I pledge allegiance to the Flag of the United States of America and to the Republic for which it stands, one Nation under God, indivisible, with liberty and justice for all.

*I*t's official. Americans are among some of the hardest working people in the world. In 2000, the average American worked 1,978 hours per year—up from 1,942 in 1990. Only workers in South Korea and the Czech Republic logged more average annual working hours.

With so much time spent on the job, you naturally want to find work that interests you. However, with thousands of jobs to choose from, the task can be a bit overwhelming. The good news is that you don't have to stick with a job forever. You're likely to switch jobs almost 10 times during your lifetime. More than half of these job changes will occur between ages 18 to 24—years in which either you're working to help pay for college or you're fully employed for the first time.

It takes work to find work, especially full-time careers. You can get a head start by thinking about what you would like to do now. You can then begin to map out your career path—the steps needed to land the ideal job for you. The following information will help guide you through some of your future career decisions.

Inside Knowledge

You may already know something about the world of work. According to a recent study by the Department of Labor, about one-third of all teenagers work at some point during the year. The Fair Labor Standards Act regulates the type of work young people can do. For example, it prohibits the employment of those under age 14 and limits the hours and jobs open to those under age 16. However, many young people "free-lance" before these ages. They do one or more tasks for just a short period, usually a few hours, without a formal "boss." The top 10 free-lance jobs for 12- and 13-year-old youths include:

- **Baby-sitting**
- **Mowing lawns or other yardwork**
- **Delivering newspapers**
- **Shoveling snow**
- **Odd jobs or chores**
- **Farmwork**
- **Cleaning house**
- **Caring for pets**
- **Selling goods**
- **Carpentry, building, or painting**

Older teenagers also take "employee" jobs, or work in which they have an ongoing job with a specific employer. The tables on the next page show the most popular employee jobs among youths ages 15 to 17.

Although a teenager's early free-lance or employee jobs are not always like those of adults, the jobs raise some interesting questions for the future. Even if you haven't had a

Many young people work part-time jobs, like doing yardwork, while going to school.

Most Popular Jobs Among Youths, Ages 15–17

MALE	
Industry	**Percentage of total employed youths**
Stock handlers and baggers	13.4%
Cooks	12.0%
Cashiers	9.6%
Assistants to waiters and waitresses	5.2%
Miscellaneous food preparation jobs	5.1%
Farmworkers	4.7%
Janitors and cleaners	4.2%
Food counter and fountain jobs	3.5%
Groundskeepers and gardeners	3.3%
Sales workers, commodities	2.3%

FEMALE	
Industry	**Percentage of total employed youths**
Cashiers	24.3%
Food counter and fountain jobs	6.5%
Waitresses	6.4%
Sales workers, commodities	5.1%
Child care workers, private households	4.9%
Cooks	4.4%
Stock handlers and baggers	3.3%
Sales workers, clothing	3.2%
Supervisors, food preparation and service jobs	3.1%
Assistants to waiters and waitresses	2.9%

Source: U.S. Department of Labor, June 2000.

About 62 percent of employed teens ages 15 to 17 hold jobs in the retail industry. Within the retail industry, most teens work in the food services.

job yet, consider these questions or talk about them with working friends.

- Would you rather work for yourself or for a company?
- Do you like working with other people or alone?
- Are wage amounts or flexible hours more important to you?
- Does it matter if you work inside or outside an office?
- Is the job holding you back or helping you to get ahead in some way?
- Can you juggle the job and other activities, or must you give up something very important—perhaps too important to keep the job?

In addition to answering those questions, take a personal inventory. Ask yourself these questions: What are your strengths and weaknesses? What unique skills or talents do you possess? What are your favorite or least favorite subjects? Answer these questions, then ask yourself: What careers interest me the most? Pick at least three jobs, and keep them in mind as you read through the next sections.

The Real Deal

Now comes the time for a reality check. Suppose, for example, one of your top three jobs is "rock star." You may have the talent, but talent is no guarantee of success. In the year 2000 rock musicians accounted for only a small percentage of the 240,000 jobs held by musicians, singers, and related workers. More than 40 percent of all musicians only worked part-time, and more than 40 percent were self-employed.

Experts say the music industry will grow as fast as the average for all occupations, but most new jobs will not be for rock musicians. Nearly all new openings will be for music teachers, orchestra musicians, and other music-related jobs such as sound and audio technicians or music salespeople.

Does this mean you should hang up your guitar? Not necessarily. You might still follow your dream but with a backup plan in place. Some rock stars have earned college degrees in highly employable fields such as communications, finance, or molecular biology. Others have worked as disc jockeys, artists, dancers, or classical musicians. Such training or experience has helped protect them in an uncertain and competitive industry.

Before deciding on a career, whether it be as a rock musician or any other job, you must take into account job availability. That means looking at the job market, or the employment outlook for the future. This may sound like an impossible task, but the federal government supplies you with lots of help. Every two years, the Bureau of Labor Statistics (BLS) publishes its latest job projections. The data can be found in the Bureau's *Occupational Outlook Handbook,* the BLS Web site, and in almanacs or other statistical reference sources.

Help Wanted

The BLS has already put your generation into its computer. It predicts that more than 22 million new jobs will be added to the economy between 2000 and 2010, increasing the workforce from 146 million to more than 168 million. Young people ages 16 to 24 are expected to increase their share of the job market by 16.5 percent.

Bryan "Dexter" Holland, lead singer of The Offspring, was the valedictorian of his class in high school. He also has a pilot's license and is a Ph.D. candidate in molecular biology.

Most of the new jobs—a million more than were created in the 1990s—will result from changes in technology and in the United States's population itself. The population is not only getting larger but older and more diverse. Increasing or changing consumer demands will spur the need for more workers in a wide range of fields. Other job openings—some 58 million—will occur as the aging population edges its way into retirement.

If you do the math, roughly 80 million jobs must be filled between 2000 and 2010. Recall the jobs that you picked earlier. How will they fare in the job market of the future?

What's Hot, What's Not

Job openings depend on trends. Ten years ago, for example, the Internet was barely a flicker on the BLS computer screen. The BLS predicted that 5 of the 10 fastest-growing jobs—including 2 of the top 3—would be in health care. Health care jobs still rank high, but the explosive growth of the Internet and widespread use of personal computers (PCs) have rewritten job descriptions. Even everyday language has become computerized. Common words like "mouse," "click," "crash," "memory," or "virus" have new meanings.

Today the BLS says all of the top five fastest-growing jobs are in computer-related professions. Plus, most occupations from cashiers to automotive mechanics require some knowledge of the computer. Watch a cashier scan prices or an auto mechanic track down some outdated car part over the Internet.

While technology carves out new occupations, it also whittles others down. Imagine losing your job to a piece of computer software, a robot, or an innovation that boosts productivity and lowers labor costs. That's what has happened in many factories, such as automobile and textile plants.

Other occupations have suffered, too. Typists have been squeezed out of offices by PCs. Bank tellers have fallen victim to automated teller machines (ATMs). Small farmers have gone bankrupt competing with the commercial farms that use big machines.

FASTEST-GROWING JOBS, 2000–2010

Jobs	Percent Change
Computer software engineers, applications	100%
Computer support specialists	97%
Computer software engineers, systems software	90%
Network and computer systems administrators	82%
Network systems and data communications analysts	77%
Desktop publishers	67%
Database administrators	66%
Personal and home health care aides	62%
Computer systems analysts	60%
Medical assistants	57%

Source: U.S. Bureau of Labor Statistics, Office of Occupational Statistics and Employment Projections.

FASTEST-DECLINING JOBS, 1996–2008

Jobs	Percent Change
Private child care workers	–32%
Sewing machine operators	–30%
Textile machine operators	–26%
Computer operators, except for external hardware such as printers	–24%
Typists	–20%

Source: U.S. Bureau of Labor Statistics, Office of Occupational Statistics and Employment Projections.

Jobs related to information technology, or IT, are the fastest-growing jobs of the future. In addition to technological changes, competition with cheap overseas labor has forced the decline of many jobs.

There's still a future in these rapidly declining fields, though. After all, skilled workers are needed to run, repair, and improve the machines or software that do the work once done by people. Bank tellers may be declining, for example, but servicing or fixing ATMs is a hot job.

Speed or Need?

Fastest growth doesn't mean the same thing as largest growth. Before you decide to become a computer major, look at the occupations that the BLS predicts will need the most workers in the years ahead. You'll get a different picture of the job market. For example, you're in luck if you want to drive a truck. Truck driving—whether the rigs have 18 wheels or 4 wheels—is one of the top 10 jobs with the largest projected growth.

If you look beyond the tech world, the combination of changing consumer demands and retirement of workers has created some real labor shortages. The service industry— occupations that provide some type of personal service for the public—fall into this category. Retail, or selling, jobs and any form of transportation that moves goods and products also fall into this category.

If you want to go by the numbers, ask Uncle Sam (the federal government) for a job. With a workforce of more than 1.8 million, the federal government is the nation's biggest civilian employer. Plus, with some 53 percent of federal workers expected to retire between 2002 and 2007, Uncle Sam will be recruiting many workers.

Although the government hires more clerks and computer specialists than anything else, hundreds of other types of jobs will still be available. They range from astronaut to archaeologist, from chaplain to chemist, from forest ranger to firefighter, from chef to chauffeur. Don't forget about state and local governments either. They employ an additional 15 million workers in equally varied jobs.

Outside the Box

Before reading any further, take a few minutes to review your original career choices. Did you include only well-known jobs like doctor, lawyer, or teacher? In today's changing job market, many career counselors often advise people to "think outside the box," or go beyond the boundaries of familiar job categories. In other words, don't box yourself in by sticking with tradition.

There's a lot of work to be done in the United States, both now and in the future. Until recently, the Department of Labor (DOL) regularly updated a reference called the *Dictionary of Occupational Titles.* It lists more than 13,000 jobs, many of which probably never crossed your mind; yet apparently there are openings for such unusual jobs as door slingers, yeast washers, vein pumpers, or wrinkle chasers.

At the start of the 2000s, the DOL replaced the dictionary with a new online government reference known as O*NET (online.onetcenter.org), which lists much broader job categories. However, millions of Americans still work at odd—and creative—jobs. So remain open to new job ideas, or even create some new business or service of your own.

Do you think you're too young to climb out of the box? Then check teenage business accomplishments in magazines such as *Y&E: The Magazine for Teen Entrepreneurs, Young Biz,* or *Black Enterprise for Teens.* One teen, for example, wriggled his way out of the box by setting up a profitable earthworm industry, complete with a warehouse and a Web site.

Getting Into the Game

Even the most creative out-of-the-box thinker needs a game plan to succeed. As one career coach puts it: "When you fail to plan, you plan to fail." Just as landmarks guide you down a highway, job goals guide you down a career path. To reach your destination, you need to look at where you are today and where you want to be tomorrow. Kick off your career plan by looking at opportunities available in school. Lay some stepping stones to the future by picking courses and extracurricular activities that will help pave the way to the type of career that you hope to follow.

Suppose, despite limited openings, you still plan to become a rock musician. Then you'll need to grab every chance to perform in front of others—in school musicals, choirs, and bands. Because many successful rock musicians write their own music, you might want to take extra English classes, including poetry. Gymnastics and dance often go hand-in-hand, so don't slack off in physical education. Also remember to develop the computer skills needed to burn "demo" CDs and to set up a Web site for promoting your group.

Even if you only have a general idea of the type of career you want to follow, spend some time mapping out the courses, clubs, or extracurricular activities that will help you to enter this field. These learning experiences will form important signposts to the future.

JOBS GAINING THE MOST WORKERS, 1996–2008	
Jobs	**Projected Job Change (in thousands)**
Systems analysts	+577
Retail salespeople	+563
Cashiers	+556
General managers and top executives	+551
Truck drivers	+493
Office clerks	+463
Registered nurses	+451
Computer support specialists	+439
Personal care and home health aides	+433
Teacher assistants	+376

Source: U.S. Bureau of Labor Statistics, Office of Occupational Statistics and Employment Projections.

The fastest-growing jobs account for less than 20 percent of the projected employment between 1996 and 2008. The jobs with the most openings are in other fields, such as service and health-care industries.

SELECT GOVERNMENT OCCUPATIONS

Occupation	Job Description
Accountant	Keeps track of government finances
Census taker	Collects information about the American population, often in face-to-face interviews
Court reporter	Uses a special stenographic machine to record everything that is said during a legal proceeding
Customs inspector	Enforces laws that regulate the flow of goods in and out of the country
Economist	Evaluates, records, and advises governments on factors that influence the economy
Environmental Protection Agency (EPA) inspector	Inspects air, water, and soil for evidence of pollution
File clerk	Keeps records up-to-date and gets information for other workers
Immigration inspector	Interviews people who seek to enter, live in, or pass through the United States
Interior decorator	Designs government workplaces to promote employee productivity and health
Librarian	Catalogs government documents and publications, usually on a computer system
Paralegal aide	Performs much of the routine work involved in preparing lawsuits, contracts, and other legal documents
Pathologist	Identifies the nature, origin, and causes of disease, especially for the Centers for Disease Control and Prevention (CDC)
Police officer	Enforces government laws
Social worker	Helps people deal with social and personal problems, such as poverty, drug addiction, mental or physical illness, and criminal behavior
Statistician	Gathers and interprets data about trends in the economy, health care, employment, and much more
United States Department of Agriculture (USDA) inspector	Helps to maintain the quality and safety of meat and poultry

The government employs people in almost every field imaginable.

Self-Wealth

You can increase your self-wealth, or employment value, in other ways as well. More than three-fifths of all U.S. high schools offer school-to-work programs. The programs grew out of the 1994 School-to-Work Opportunities Act. The act provides federal funds to school districts and local businesses that form partnerships aimed at helping students to jump into the job market. Find out if your school offers such a program.

Even if your school does not have a school-to-work program, you can still gain career-related skills. Find a mentor or expert willing to advise you on the best way to travel along your career path. If possible, do some "job shadowing," or follow the person in the daily course of work.

You might also consider working as an intern—a trainee or lower-level assistant who works in an occupation in order to gain practical experience. Internships frequently go to college students, and many colleges give college credit for internships. However, some companies or organizations offer internships to high school students on either a paid or unpaid basis. To get an idea of the many kinds of internships available, visit the Web site for Rising Star Internships at www.rsinternships.com

You already know that a college degree provides the ticket into many occupations. However, if you are unsure of college, you might apply for an apprenticeship. As an apprentice, you'll receive paid work experience—usually 3 years—and on-the-job instruction—at least 144 hours. Apprenticeships open the door to skilled jobs such as the following:

- **Electrician**
- **Firefighter**
- **Chef**
- **Truck driver**
- **Child care specialist**
- **Printing press operator**
- **Carpenter**
- **Glassworker**
- **Machinist**

For more information on apprenticeships, contact the Bureau of Apprentice Training (BAT), maintained by the United States Department of Labor. The BAT registers apprenticeship programs in 23 states and oversees apprenticeship councils in 27 states. You might also talk to labor unions and employers in your area, or request information from your state's department of labor and industry. Some apprenticeships start when you are in high school, so you can begin right away.

Helping Hand

By lending a helping hand, you can help yourself into a job. Whether you read to a child or pitch in at a special event, you're adding to your resume—a summary of your work history. You're not only gaining new skills, you're getting a chance to try out career ideas. Do you want to be an actor? Volunteer with the community theater. Do you think you'd like to be a teacher? Volunteer as a tutor. Are you interested in police work? Join police officers in raising funds for the Police Benevolent Association (PBA).

Out of 13.3 million youth, more than 59 percent volunteer an average of 3.5 hours per week. By joining this army of volunteers, you can demonstrate leadership skills and personal responsibility. You can also obtain valuable letters of recommendation and perhaps even a scholarship for the service performed. Help somebody else and you'll also help yourself.

Dollars and Sense

Inventor Thomas Edison once remarked, "Opportunity is missed by most people because it is dressed in overalls and looks like work." Consider the example of Secretary of State Colin Powell. As a teenager, Powell

By volunteering, you add experience and skills to your resume.

washed factory floors during the summer to earn money for college. He worked so hard that the factory foreman noticed him. "Kid, you mop pretty good," said the foreman. "You gave me plenty of opportunity to learn," replied Powell. "Come back next summer," responded the foreman. "I'll have a job for you."

By the end of the following summer, Powell was a deputy shift leader. He had also learned a valuable lesson. "Always do your best," Powell tells teenagers, "because someone is watching."

Even a short-term or temporary job can be turned to your advantage. Learn from your experience and gain skills you can use for the future. From deputy shift leader, Powell eventually went on to become chairman of the Joint Chiefs of Staff—a job in which he oversaw more than 3 million military employees. Then he became secretary of state for the country. In this position he is the president's chief adviser on foreign affairs. Not bad for a kid who "mopped pretty good."

When it comes to careers, you have to weigh dollars and sense. As one career adviser puts it: "Don't let someone push you into a job that you're not going to be happy in." Two of the highest-paying jobs today are surgeons and dentists. However, the salaries won't make you happy if you dislike biology and hate the sight of blood.

Legwork and Paperwork

As you've read, you don't have to attend college to land a job. Because many companies or unions provide on-the-job training, a higher education is not always necessary. However, most people who continue their education earn more money in the long run than those who don't.

No matter when you start job hunting, track down as many potential leads as possible. Attend career fairs. Study classified ads and help-wanted signs. Contact the personnel offices of companies that interest you. Search the data banks kept by state employment services and online job sites like www.monster.com. Talk to "headhunters," the recruiters hired by companies to fill job openings.

To get an employer's attention, prepare a 1- to 2-page resume that highlights your talents and skills. Prevent it from landing in the recycle bin by keeping in mind the following resume do's and don'ts.

Resume Do's

Do include your contact information— name, address, telephone number, and, if you're on the Internet, an e-mail address.

Colin Powell is the secretary of state. He heads a major executive department of the United States.

HIGHEST-PAYING JOBS, 1998

Jobs	Annual Wages
Physicians and surgeons	$124,800 and over
Dentists	$110,200
Aircraft pilots and flight engineers	$91,800
Podiatrists	$79,000
Lawyers	$78,200
Engineering, mathematical, and natural sciences managers	$75,300
Petroleum engineers	$74,300
Physicists and astronomers	$73,200
Nuclear engineers	$71,300
Optometrists	$68,500

Source: "Occupational Employment Statistics Survey," Bureau of Labor Statistics.

Do make the layout easy to read.

Do highlight your special skills or training.

Do print your resume on high-quality paper.

Do use the spelling check feature on your computer, and ask a friend to review your resume for any grammar errors or other mistakes.

Resume Don'ts

Don't include any personal information such as your race, religion, family, or marital status.

Don't fudge dates or pad your resume with things you haven't actually done.

Don't use fancy binders or gaudy paper.

Don't include extra pieces of paper, like transcripts, letters of recommendation, or awards, unless you are asked to do so.

Don't write long paragraphs; use bulleted lists instead.

One final tip. When you send out your resume, include a cover letter. Just as you would never show up at an employer's door unannounced, your resume should never appear solo on someone's desk. Get right to the point. State your employment goal and highlight reasons why you are the best person for the job. Again, keep it brief and have someone check your letter.

The highest-paying jobs in the United States require a strong background in math and science. They also usually call for advanced degrees or schooling beyond college.

First Impression

If your resume opens the door to a job, keep it open by making a good first impression. Do your homework and research information about the company before you arrive. Have specific job goals in mind. Then practice interviewing with a friend or relative.

On the day of the interview, plan to arrive early. Dress to impress—nothing flashy, just well-groomed clothes suitable to the job. If you are carrying a cell phone, make sure it is turned off.

When you meet the interviewer, shake hands firmly. Address the person as Mr., Mrs., or Ms. unless told otherwise. Relax promptly and use good manners. Maintain eye contact throughout the interview, be enthusiastic, and answer questions clearly and honestly. Never talk poorly about previous employers. Focus instead on the training or experience you can bring to the job. Ask questions about the organization and the position. Thank the interviewer when you leave, and, as a follow-up, send a thank-you note.

Weighing the Offer

A job offer might come right on the spot or after other candidates are interviewed. In either case, take time to make your decision. Keep in mind the questions raised on page 636. In addition, consider the salary and benefits of the job. If you haven't already done so, research job turnover. High turnover might reveal employee dissatisfaction or a lack of job stability. Confirm the opportunities open to you—things like the chances for advancement or additional training.

You might create a balance sheet weighing the pros and cons of the job. If the pros outweigh the cons, take a deep breath and jump into the job market. You're on the way to building your career.

Contents

Online **UPDATE**
Visit civ.glencoe.com and click on **Textbook Updates** for an update of the data.

United States Population Growth, 1980–2000

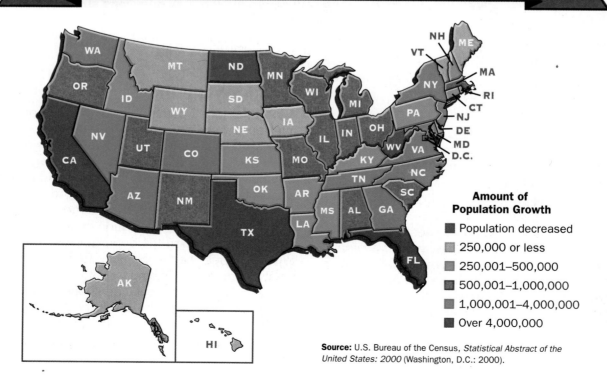

Amount of Population Growth

- Population decreased
- 250,000 or less
- 250,001–500,000
- 500,001–1,000,000
- 1,000,001–4,000,000
- Over 4,000,000

Source: U.S. Bureau of the Census, *Statistical Abstract of the United States: 2000* (Washington, D.C.: 2000).

Crime and the Justice System

Supreme Court Cases

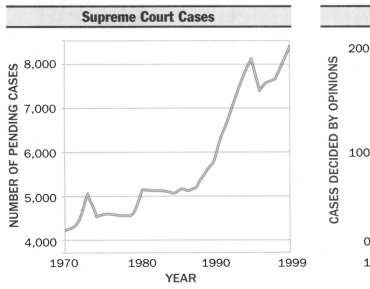

NUMBER OF PENDING CASES

YEAR

Supreme Court Decisions

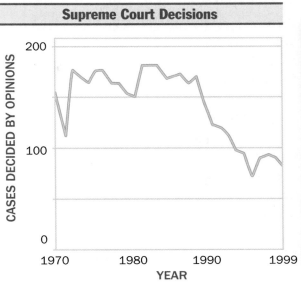

CASES DECIDED BY OPINIONS

YEAR

Types of Cases in Federal District Courts, 2000

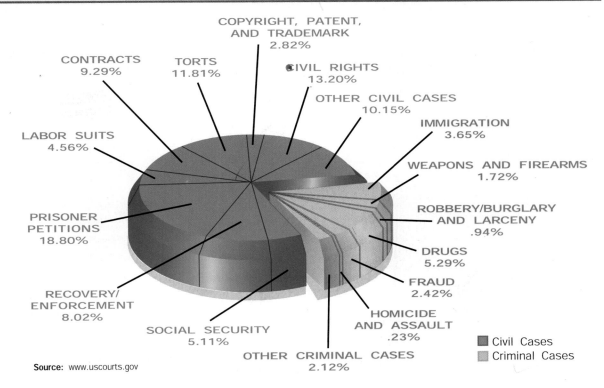

COPYRIGHT, PATENT, AND TRADEMARK 2.82%

CONTRACTS 9.29%

TORTS 11.81%

CIVIL RIGHTS 13.20%

OTHER CIVIL CASES 10.15%

IMMIGRATION 3.65%

LABOR SUITS 4.56%

WEAPONS AND FIREARMS 1.72%

ROBBERY/BURGLARY AND LARCENY .94%

PRISONER PETITIONS 18.80%

DRUGS 5.29%

FRAUD 2.42%

RECOVERY/ ENFORCEMENT 8.02%

HOMICIDE AND ASSAULT .23%

SOCIAL SECURITY 5.11%

OTHER CRIMINAL CASES 2.12%

■ Civil Cases
■ Criminal Cases

Source: www.uscourts.gov

Government and Economics Data Bank **645**

Bills Introduced, Passed, and Enacted by Congress, 1961–2001

CONGRESS (Years)	BILLS INTRODUCED* House	Senate	BILLS PASSED* House	Senate	BILLS ENACTED
87th (1961–62)	14,328	4,048	1,927	1,953	1,569
88th (1963–64)	14,022	3,457	1,267	1,341	1,026
89th (1965–66)	19,874	4,129	1,565	1,636	1,283
90th (1967–68)	22,060	4,400	1,213	1,376	1,002
91st (1969–70)	21,436	4,867	1,130	1,271	941
92nd (1971–72)	18,561	4,408	970	1,035	768
93rd (1973–74)	18,872	4,524	923	1,115	774
94th (1975–76)	16,982	4,114	968	1,038	729
95th (1977–78)	15,587	3,800	1,027	1,070	803
96th (1979–80)	9,103	3,480	929	977	736
97th (1981–82)	8,094	3,396	704	803	528
98th (1983–84)	7,105	3,454	978	936	677
99th (1985–86)	6,499	3,386	973	940	690
100th (1987–88)	6,263	3,325	1,061	1,002	758
101st (1989–90)	6,683	3,669	968	980	666
102nd (1991–92)	7,771	4,245	932	947	609
103rd (1993–94)	6,647	3,177	749	682	473
104th (1995–96)	4,542	2,266	611	518	337
105th (1997–98)	4,874	2,655	1,174	879	404
106th (1999–2000)	5,681	7,287	657	549	604
107th (2001, 1st session)	2,665	1,248	592	425	37

*Includes House and Senate resolutions, joint resolutions, and concurrent resolutions

Sources: Stanley and Niemi, *Vital Statistics on American Politics, 1997–1998* (Washington, D.C.: CQ Inc., 1997); U.S. Congress, Office of Legislative Information; Ornstein, Mann and Malbin, *Vital Statistics on Congress, 1997–1998* (Washington, D.C.: CQ Inc., 1998), thomas.loc.gov

Federal Revenue by Source, 2000

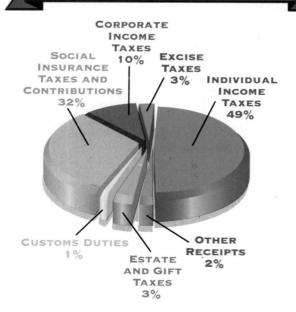

CORPORATE INCOME TAXES 10%

SOCIAL INSURANCE TAXES AND CONTRIBUTIONS 32%

EXCISE TAXES 3%

INDIVIDUAL INCOME TAXES 49%

CUSTOMS DUTIES 1%

ESTATE AND GIFT TAXES 3%

OTHER RECEIPTS 2%

Federal Expenditures by Category, 2000

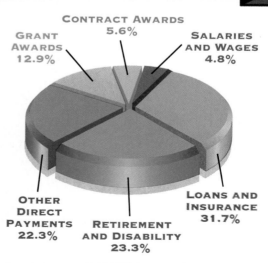

CONTRACT AWARDS 5.6%

GRANT AWARDS 12.9%

SALARIES AND WAGES 4.8%

OTHER DIRECT PAYMENTS 22.3%

RETIREMENT AND DISABILITY 23.3%

LOANS AND INSURANCE 31.7%

Percentages may not total 100% due to rounding.
Source: U.S. Congressional Budget Office, U.S. Congress, www.cbo.gov

Federal Government Revenues and Expenditures, 1960–2001

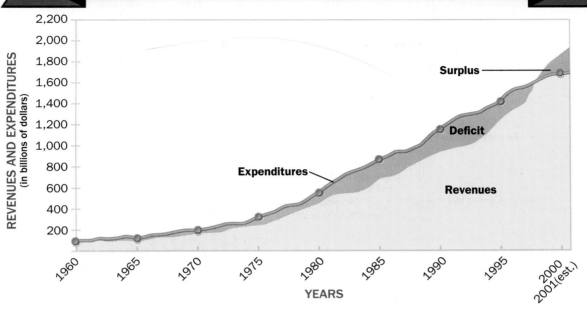

Surplus

Deficit

Expenditures

Revenues

REVENUES AND EXPENDITURES (in billions of dollars)

YEARS

Gross Federal Debt, 1960–2001*

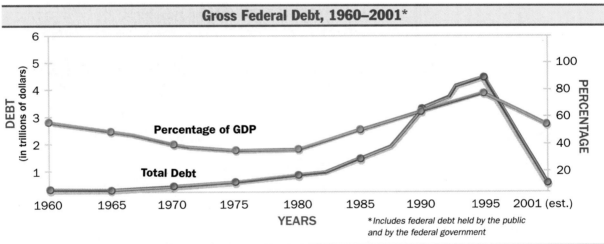

DEBT (in trillions of dollars)

Percentage of GDP

Total Debt

PERCENTAGE

YEARS

*Includes federal debt held by the public and by the federal government

National Debt per Capita, 1960–2001*

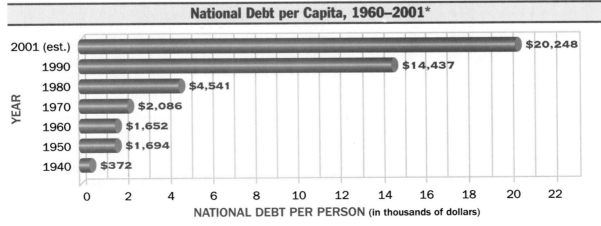

YEAR	
2001 (est.)	$20,248
1990	$14,437
1980	$4,541
1970	$2,086
1960	$1,652
1950	$1,694
1940	$372

NATIONAL DEBT PER PERSON (in thousands of dollars)

Sources: U.S. Bureau of the Census; U.S. Bureau of Public Debt; *Statistical Abstract of the United States: 2001*, (Washington, D.C.: 2001). *Includes federal debt held by the public and by the federal government

Executive Department Civilian Employees*

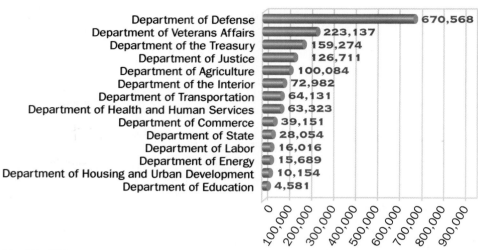

Department	Number of Employees
Department of Defense	670,568
Department of Veterans Affairs	223,137
Department of the Treasury	159,274
Department of Justice	126,711
Department of Agriculture	100,084
Department of the Interior	72,982
Department of Transportation	64,131
Department of Health and Human Services	63,323
Department of Commerce	39,151
Department of State	28,054
Department of Labor	16,016
Department of Energy	15,689
Department of Housing and Urban Development	10,154
Department of Education	4,581

NUMBER OF EMPLOYEES

*As of May 2001
Source: *World Almanac and Book of Facts, 2002.*

Major United States Treaties

YEAR	TREATY	MAJOR PROVISIONS
1783	Treaty of Paris	Great Britain recognized U.S. independence
1795	Pinckney's Treaty	Spain granted U.S. navigation rights on Mississippi River
1803	Louisiana Purchase	U.S. gained Louisiana Territory from France
1817	Rush-Bagot Agreement	Signed with Britain to demilitarize Great Lakes
1818	Convention of 1818	Set border with Canada west from Great Lakes as the 49th parallel
1819	Adams-Onís Treaty	Spain ceded Florida; U.S. border set with Spanish territory in West
1846	Oregon Treaty	Signed with Great Britain to settle claims to Oregon Country
1848	Treaty of Guadalupe Hidalgo	Ended Mexican War; U.S. gained Southwest and California
1867	Alaska Purchase	U.S. gained Alaska from Russia
1898	Treaty of Paris	Ended Spanish-American War; U.S. gained Puerto Rico and Philippines
1903	Hay-Buneau-Varilla Treaty	Signed with Panama to give U.S. right to build Panama Canal
1947	Rio Pact	Inter-American agreement for security of Western Hemisphere
1947	General Agreement on Tariffs and Trade	Multinational agreement to promote world trade
1949	North Atlantic Treaty	Multinational agreement for defense of Western Europe; created NATO
1968	Nonproliferation Treaty	International agreement to prevent spread of nuclear weapons
1972	SALT I	Agreements between U.S. and Soviet Union to limit nuclear weapons
1973	Paris Peace Agreement	Signed with North Vietnam to end U.S. involvement in Vietnam War
1977	Panama Canal Treaties	Transferred Panama Canal to Panama effective in 1999
1985	Vienna Convention	International agreement to protect Earth's ozone layer
1993	North American Free Trade Agreement	Established duty-free trade with Canada and Mexico
1996	Comprehensive Nuclear Test Ban Treaty	156 countries agreed to halt nuclear testing; U.S. Senate did not ratify
1996	Counterterrorism Accord	Israel and the U.S. agree to cooperate in the investigation and deterrence of terrorist acts
1997	Mutual Recognition Agreement	Reduces trade barriers between the U.S. and European Community

Source: U.S. State Department, *Treaties in Force;* Findling, *Dictionary of American Diplomatic History,* 2nd ed. (New York: Greenwood Press, 1989); Axelrod, *American Treaties and Alliances* (Washington, D.C.: CQ, Inc., 2000).

State Facts

State*	Year Admitted	Population 2000	Land Area sq. mile	Capital	Largest City	House Rep. 2000**
1. Delaware	1787	783,600	1,955	Dover	Wilmington	1
2. Pennsylvania	1787	12,281,054	44,820	Harrisburg	Philadelphia	19
3. New Jersey	1787	8,414,350	7,419	Trenton	Newark	13
4. Georgia	1788	8,186,453	57,919	Atlanta	Atlanta	13
5. Connecticut	1788	3,405,565	4,845	Hartford	Bridgeport	5
6. Massachusetts	1788	6,349,097	7,838	Boston	Boston	10
7. Maryland	1788	5,296,486	9,775	Annapolis	Baltimore	8
8. South Carolina	1788	4,012,012	30,111	Columbia	Columbia	6
9. New Hampshire	1788	1,235,786	8,969	Concord	Manchester	2
10. Virginia	1788	7,078,515	39,598	Richmond	Virginia Beach	11
11. New York	1788	18,976,457	47,224	Albany	New York City	29
12. North Carolina	1789	8,049,313	48,718	Raleigh	Charlotte	13
13. Rhode Island	1790	1,048,319	1,045	Providence	Providence	2
14. Vermont	1791	608,827	9,249	Montpelier	Burlington	1
15. Kentucky	1792	4,041,769	39,732	Frankfort	Louisville	6
16. Tennessee	1796	5,689,283	41,220	Nashville	Memphis	9
17. Ohio	1803	11,353,140	40,953	Columbus	Columbus	18
18. Louisiana	1812	4,468,976	43,566	Baton Rouge	New Orleans	7
19. Indiana	1816	6,080,485	35,870	Indianapolis	Indianapolis	9
20. Mississippi	1817	2,844,658	46,914	Jackson	Jackson	4
21. Illinois	1818	12,419,293	55,593	Springfield	Chicago	19
22. Alabama	1819	4,447,100	50,750	Montgomery	Birmingham	7
23. Maine	1820	1,274,923	30,865	Augusta	Portland	2
24. Missouri	1821	5,595,211	68,898	Jefferson City	Kansas City	9
25. Arkansas	1836	2,673,400	52,075	Little Rock	Little Rock	4
26. Michigan	1837	9,938,444	56,809	Lansing	Detroit	15
27. Florida	1845	15,982,378	53,997	Tallahassee	Jacksonville	25
28. Texas	1845	20,851,820	261,914	Austin	Houston	32
29. Iowa	1846	2,926,324	55,875	Des Moines	Des Moines	5
30. Wisconsin	1848	5,363,675	54,314	Madison	Milwaukee	8
31. California	1850	33,871,648	155,973	Sacramento	Los Angeles	53
32. Minnesota	1858	4,919,479	79,617	St. Paul	Minneapolis	8
33. Oregon	1859	3,421,399	96,003	Salem	Portland	5
34. Kansas	1861	2,688,418	81,823	Topeka	Wichita	4
35. West Virginia	1863	1,808,344	24,087	Charleston	Charleston	3
36. Nevada	1864	1,998,257	109,806	Carson City	Las Vegas	3
37. Nebraska	1867	1,711,263	76,878	Lincoln	Omaha	3
38. Colorado	1876	4,301,261	103,730	Denver	Denver	7
39. North Dakota	1889	642,200	68,994	Bismarck	Fargo	1
40. South Dakota	1889	754,844	75,898	Pierre	Sioux Falls	1
41. Montana	1889	902,195	145,556	Helena	Billings	1
42. Washington	1889	5,894,121	66,582	Olympia	Seattle	9
43. Idaho	1890	1,293,953	82,751	Boise	Boise	2
44. Wyoming	1890	493,782	97,105	Cheyenne	Cheyenne	1
45. Utah	1896	2,233,169	82,168	Salt Lake City	Salt Lake City	3
46. Oklahoma	1907	3,450,654	68,679	Oklahoma City	Oklahoma City	5
47. New Mexico	1912	1,819,046	121,365	Sante Fe	Albuquerque	3
48. Arizona	1912	5,130,632	113,642	Phoenix	Phoenix	8
49. Alaska	1959	626,932	570,374	Juneau	Anchorage	1
50. Hawaii	1959	1,211,537	6,423	Honolulu	Honolulu	2
District of Columbia	—	572,059	61	—	—	—
Puerto Rico	—	3,808,610	3,425	San Juan	San Juan	—
United States***	—	285,230,516	3,539,703	Washington, D.C.	New York City	—

*Numbers denote the order in which states were admitted
***Including Puerto Rico

**Number of members in U.S. House of Representatives based on the 2000 U.S. Census

Source: *World Almanac and Book of Facts,* 2002; *TIME Almanac,* 2002.

Government and Economics Data Bank   **649**

State Revenues and Expenditures

Total State Revenue by Category, 1998

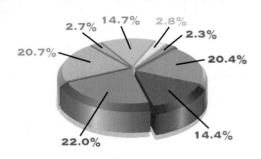

14.7% 2.8%
2.7% 2.3%
20.7% 20.4%
22.0% 14.4%

- ◼ Intergovernmental
- ◻ Sales Taxes
- ◻ Licenses
- ◻ Individual Income Taxes
- ◻ Corporate Income Taxes
- ◼ Other Taxes
- ◼ Public Employees Pension Contributions
- ◼ Miscellaneous Revenue

Source: U.S. Bureau of the Census.

Total State Expenditures by Category, 1998

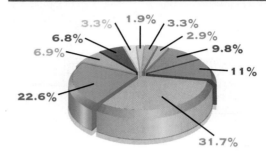

3.3% 1.9% 3.3%
6.8% 2.9%
6.9% 9.8%
22.6% 11%
31.7%

- ◻ Education
- ◻ Public Welfare
- ◻ Hospitals and Health
- ◼ Highways
- ◻ Police and Corrections
- ◻ Natural Resources, Parks and Recreation
- ◼ Government Administration
- ◻ Interest on Debt
- ◻ Public Employees Retirement Benefits
- ◼ All Other Expenditures

*Percentages may not total 100% due to rounding.

State Expenditures for Public Education, 1998

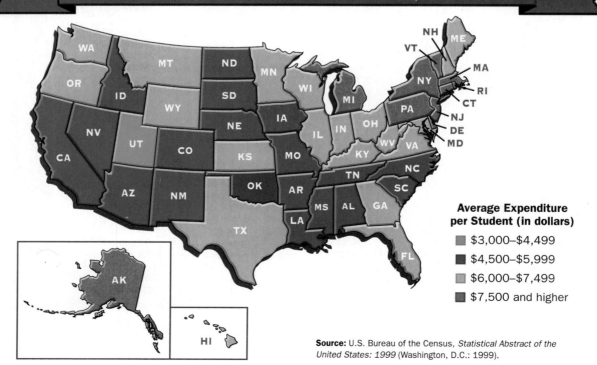

Average Expenditure per Student (in dollars)

- ◼ $3,000–$4,499
- ◼ $4,500–$5,999
- ◻ $6,000–$7,499
- ◼ $7,500 and higher

Source: U.S. Bureau of the Census, *Statistical Abstract of the United States: 1999* (Washington, D.C.: 1999).

Size of State Legislatures

State	House Members	Senate Members
Alabama	105	35
Alaska	40	20
Arizona	60	30
Arkansas	100	35
California	80	40
Colorado	65	35
Connecticut	151	36
Delaware	41	21
Florida	120	40
Georgia	180	56
Hawaii	51	25
Idaho	70	35
Illinois	118	59
Indiana	100	50
Iowa	100	50
Kansas	125	40
Kentucky	100	38
Louisiana	105	39
Maine	151	35
Maryland	141	47
Massachusetts	160	40
Michigan	110	38
Minnesota	134	67
Mississippi	122	52
Missouri	163	34
Montana	100	50
Nebraska	N/A	49
Nevada	42	21
New Hampshire	400	24
New Jersey	80	40
New Mexico	70	42
New York	150	61
North Carolina	120	50
North Dakota	98	49
Ohio	99	33
Oklahoma	101	48
Oregon	60	30
Pennsylvania	203	50
Rhode Island	100	50
South Carolina	124	46
South Dakota	70	35
Tennessee	99	33
Texas	150	31
Utah	75	29
Vermont	150	30
Virginia	100	40
Washington	98	49
West Virginia	100	34
Wisconsin	99	33
Wyoming	60	30

Source: Hovey and Hovey, *State Fact Finder, 2000* (Washington, D.C.: CQ Inc., 2000).

State Governors' Compensation

State	Annual Salary (2001)
Alabama	$94,655
Alaska	$83,280
Arizona	$95,000
Arkansas	$71,738
California	$175,000
Colorado	$90,000
Connecticut	$78,000
Delaware	$107,000
Florida	$123,175
Georgia	$122,998
Hawaii	$94,780
Idaho	$95,500
Illinois	$150,691
Indiana	$77,200
Iowa	$107,482
Kansas	$94,446
Kentucky	$103,018
Louisiana	$95,000
Maine	$70,000
Maryland	$120,000
Massachusetts	$135,000
Michigan	$177,000
Minnesota	$120,303
Mississippi	$101,800
Missouri	$119,982
Montana	$83,672
Nebraska	$65,000
Nevada	$117,000
New Hampshire	$96,060
New Jersey	$83,333
New Mexico	$90,000
New York	$179,000
North Carolina	$118,430
North Dakota	$85,506
Ohio	$126,496
Oklahoma	$101,140
Oregon	$88,300
Pennsylvania	$105,035
Rhode Island	$95,000
South Carolina	$106,078
South Dakota	$95,389
Tennessee	$85,000
Texas	$115,345
Utah	$100,600
Vermont	$115,763
Virginia	$124,855
Washington	$135,960
West Virginia	$95,000
Wisconsin	$122,406
Wyoming	$95,000

Source: *The World Almanac and Book of Facts, 2002.*

DATA BANK

Washington, D.C.
Population: 572,059
Land area: 61 sq. mi.

U.S. Territories

Puerto Rico
Population: 3,808,610
Land area: 3,425 sq. mi.

Guam
Population: 155,000 (est.)
Land area: 209 sq. mi.

U.S. Virgin Islands
Population: 121,000 (est.)
Land area: 134 sq. mi.

American Samoa
Population: 65,000 (est.)
Land area: 77 sq. mi.

The states are listed in the order they were admitted to the Union.

Population figures are based on U.S. Bureau of the Census for 2000. House of Representatives figures are from the Clerk of the House of Representatives. States are not drawn to scale.

1 Delaware
Year Admitted: 1787
Population: 783,600
Land area: 1,955 sq. mi.
Representatives: 1

Dover

2 Pennsylvania
Year Admitted: 1787
Population: 12,281,054
Land area: 44,820 sq. mi.
Representatives: 19
Harrisburg

3 New Jersey
Year Admitted: 1787
Population: 8,414,350
Land area: 7,419 sq. mi.
Representatives: 13
Trenton

9 New Hampshire
Year Admitted: 1788
Population: 1,235,786
Land area: 8,969 sq. mi.
Representatives: 2

Concord

10 Virginia
Year Admitted: 1788
Population: 7,078,515
Land area: 39,598 sq. mi.
Representatives: 11

Richmond

11 New York
Year Admitted: 1788
Population: 18,976,457
Land area: 47,224 sq. mi.
Representatives: 29

Albany

17 Ohio
Year Admitted: 1803
Population: 11,353,140
Land area: 40,953 sq. mi.
Representatives: 18

Columbus

18 Louisiana
Year Admitted: 1812
Population: 4,468,976
Land area: 43,566 sq. mi.
Representatives: 7

Baton Rouge

19 Indiana
Year Admitted: 1816
Population: 6,080,485
Land area: 35,870 sq. mi.
Representatives: 9
Indianapolis

24 Missouri
Year Admitted: 1821
Population: 5,595,211
Land area: 68,898 sq. mi.
Representatives: 9

Jefferson City

25 Arkansas
Year Admitted: 1836
Population: 2,673,400
Land area: 52,075 sq. mi.
Representatives: 4

Little Rock

26 Michigan
Year Admitted: 1837
Population: 9,938,444
Land area: 56,809 sq. mi.
Representatives: 15
Lansing

27 Florida
Year Admitted: 1845
Population: 15,982,378
Land area: 53,997 sq. mi.
Representatives: 25
Tallahassee

28 Texas
Year Admitted: 1845
Population: 20,851,820
Land area: 261,914 sq. mi.
Representatives: 32

Austin

33 Oregon
Year Admitted: 1859
Population: 3,421,399
Land area: 96,003 sq. mi.
Representatives: 5

Salem

34 Kansas
Year Admitted: 1861
Population: 2,688,418
Land area: 81,823 sq. mi.
Representatives: 4
Topeka

35 West Virginia
Year Admitted: 1863
Population: 1,808,344
Land area: 24,087 sq. mi.
Representatives: 3

Charleston

36 Nevada
Year Admitted: 1864
Population: 1,998,257
Land area: 109,806 sq. mi.
Representatives: 3

Carson City

37 Nebraska
Year Admitted: 1867
Population: 1,711,263
Land area: 76,878 sq. mi.
Representatives: 3
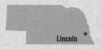
Lincoln

42 Washington
Year Admitted: 1889
Population: 5,894,121
Land area: 66,582 sq. mi.
Representatives: 9
Olympia

43 Idaho
Year Admitted: 1890
Population: 1,293,953
Land area: 82,751 sq. mi.
Representatives: 2

Boise

44 Wyoming
Year Admitted: 1890
Population: 493,782
Land area: 97,105 sq. mi.
Representatives: 1

Cheyenne

45 Utah
Year Admitted: 1896
Population: 2,233,169
Land area: 82,168 sq. mi.
Representatives: 3

Salt Lake City

46 Oklahoma
Year Admitted: 1907
Population: 3,450,654
Land area: 68,679 sq. mi.
Representatives: 5

Oklahoma City

4 Georgia
Year Admitted: 1788
Population: 8,186,453
Land area: 57,919 sq. mi.
Representatives: 13

5 Connecticut
Year Admitted: 1788
Population: 3,405,565
Land area: 4,845 sq. mi.
Representatives: 5

6 Massachusetts
Year Admitted: 1788
Population: 6,349,097
Land area: 7,838 sq. mi.
Representatives: 10

7 Maryland
Year Admitted: 1788
Population: 5,296,486
Land area: 9,775 sq. mi.
Representatives: 8

8 South Carolina
Year Admitted: 1788
Population: 4,012,012
Land area: 30,111 sq. mi.
Representatives: 6

12 North Carolina
Year Admitted: 1789
Population: 8,049,313
Land area: 48,718 sq. mi.
Representatives: 13

13 Rhode Island
Year Admitted: 1790
Population: 1,048,319
Land area: 1,045 sq. mi.
Representatives: 2

14 Vermont
Year Admitted: 1791
Population: 608,827
Land area: 9,249 sq. mi.
Representatives: 1

15 Kentucky
Year Admitted: 1792
Population: 4,041,769
Land area: 39,732 sq. mi.
Representatives: 6

16 Tennessee
Year Admitted: 1796
Population: 5,689,283
Land area: 41,220 sq. mi.
Representatives: 9

20 Mississippi
Year Admitted: 1817
Population: 2,844,658
Land area: 46,914 sq. mi.
Representatives: 4

21 Illinois
Year Admitted: 1818
Population: 12,419,293
Land area: 55,593 sq. mi.
Representatives: 19

22 Alabama
Year Admitted: 1819
Population: 4,447,100
Land area: 50,750 sq. mi.
Representatives: 7

23 Maine
Year Admitted: 1820
Population: 1,274,923
Land area: 30,865 sq. mi.
Representatives: 2

29 Iowa
Year Admitted: 1846
Population: 2,926,324
Land area: 55,875 sq. mi.
Representatives: 5

30 Wisconsin
Year Admitted: 1848
Population: 5,363,675
Land area: 54,314 sq. mi.
Representatives: 8

31 California
Year Admitted: 1850
Population: 33,871,648
Land area: 155,973 sq. mi.
Representatives: 53

32 Minnesota
Year Admitted: 1858
Population: 4,919,479
Land area: 79,617 sq. mi.
Representatives: 8

38 Colorado
Year Admitted: 1876
Population: 4,301,261
Land area: 103,730 sq. mi.
Representatives: 7

39 North Dakota
Year Admitted: 1889
Population: 642,200
Land area: 68,994 sq. mi.
Representatives: 1

40 South Dakota
Year Admitted: 1889
Population: 754,844
Land area: 75,898 sq. mi.
Representatives: 1

41 Montana
Year Admitted: 1889
Population: 902,195
! and area: 145,556 sq. mi.
Representatives: 1

47 New Mexico
Year Admitted: 1912
Population: 1,819,046
Land area: 121,365 sq. mi.
Representatives: 3

48 Arizona
Year Admitted: 1912
Population: 5,130,632
Land area: 113,642 sq. mi.
Representatives: 8

49 Alaska
Year Admitted: 1959
Population: 626,932
Land area: 570,374 sq. mi.
Representatives: 1

50 Hawaii
Year Admitted: 1959
Population: 1,211,537
Land area: 6,432 sq. mi.
Representatives: 2

In this resource you will find portraits of the individuals who served as presidents of the United States, along with their occupations, political party affiliations, and other interesting facts.

**The Republican Party during this period developed into today's Democratic Party. Today's Republican Party originated in 1854.

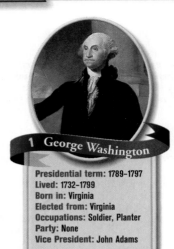

1 George Washington

Presidential term: 1789–1797
Lived: 1732–1799
Born in: Virginia
Elected from: Virginia
Occupations: Soldier, Planter
Party: None
Vice President: John Adams

2 John Adams

Presidential term: 1797–1801
Lived: 1735–1826
Born in: Massachusetts
Elected from: Massachusetts
Occupations: Teacher, Lawyer
Party: Federalist
Vice President: Thomas Jefferson

3 Thomas Jefferson

Presidential term: 1801–1809
Lived: 1743–1826
Born in: Virginia
Elected from: Virginia
Occupations: Planter, Lawyer
Party: Republican**
Vice Presidents: Aaron Burr, George Clinton

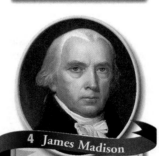

4 James Madison

Presidential term: 1809–1817
Lived: 1751–1836
Born in: Virginia
Elected from: Virginia
Occupation: Planter
Party: Republican**
Vice Presidents: George Clinton, Elbridge Gerry

5 James Monroe

Presidential term: 1817–1825
Lived: 1758–1831
Born in: Virginia
Elected from: Virginia
Occupation: Lawyer
Party: Republican**
Vice President: Daniel D. Tompkins

6 John Quincy Adams

Presidential term: 1825–1829
Lived: 1767–1848
Born in: Massachusetts
Elected from: Massachusetts
Occupation: Lawyer
Party: Republican**
Vice President: John C. Calhoun

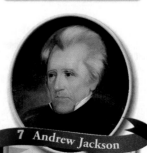

7 Andrew Jackson

Presidential term: 1829–1837
Lived: 1767–1845
Born in: South Carolina
Elected from: Tennessee
Occupations: Lawyer, Soldier
Party: Democratic
Vice Presidents: John C. Calhoun, Martin Van Buren

8 Martin Van Buren

Presidential term: 1837–1841
Lived: 1782–1862
Born in: New York
Elected from: New York
Occupation: Lawyer
Party: Democratic
Vice President: Richard M.
    Johnson

9 William H. Harrison

Presidential term: 1841
Lived: 1773–1841
Born in: Virginia
Elected from: Ohio
Occupations: Soldier, Planter
Party: Whig
Vice President: John Tyler

10 John Tyler

Presidential term: 1841–1845
Lived: 1790–1862
Born in: Virginia
Elected as V.P. from: Virginia
Succeeded Harrison
Occupation: Lawyer
Party: Whig
Vice President: None

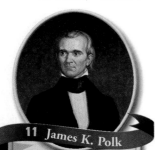

11 James K. Polk

Presidential term: 1845–1849
Lived: 1795–1849
Born in: North Carolina
Elected from: Tennessee
Occupation: Lawyer
Party: Democratic
Vice President: George M.
    Dallas

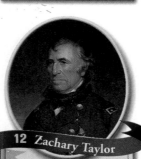

12 Zachary Taylor

Presidential term: 1849–1850
Lived: 1784–1850
Born in: Virginia
Elected from: Louisiana
Occupation: Soldier
Party: Whig
Vice President: Millard
    Fillmore

13 Millard Fillmore

Presidential term: 1850–1853
Lived: 1800–1874
Born in: New York
Elected as V.P. from: New York
Succeeded Taylor
Occupation: Lawyer
Party: Whig
Vice President: None

14 Franklin Pierce

Presidential term: 1853–1857
Lived: 1804–1869
Born in: New Hampshire
Elected from: New Hampshire
Occupation: Lawyer
Party: Democratic
Vice President: William R.
    King

15 James Buchanan

Presidential term: 1857–1861
Lived: 1791–1868
Born in: Pennsylvania
Elected from: Pennsylvania
Occupation: Lawyer
Party: Democratic
Vice President: John C.
    Breckinridge

16 Abraham Lincoln

Presidential term: 1861–1865
Lived: 1809–1865
Born in: Kentucky
Elected from: Illinois
Occupation: Lawyer
Party: Republican
Vice Presidents: Hannibal
    Hamlin, Andrew Johnson

U.S. PRESIDENTS

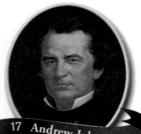

17 Andrew Johnson

Presidential term: 1865–1869
Lived: 1808–1875
Born in: North Carolina
Elected as V.P. from:
   Tennessee
Succeeded Lincoln
Occupation: Tailor
Party: Republican
Vice President: None

18 Ulysses S. Grant

Presidential term: 1869–1877
Lived: 1822–1885
Born in: Ohio
Elected from: Illinois
Occupations: Farmer, Soldier
Party: Republican
Vice Presidents: Schuyler
   Colfax, Henry Wilson

19 Rutherford B. Hayes

Presidential term: 1877–1881
Lived: 1822–1893
Born in: Ohio
Elected from: Ohio
Occupation: Lawyer
Party: Republican
Vice President: William A.
   Wheeler

20 James A. Garfield

Presidential term: 1881
Lived: 1831–1881
Born in: Ohio
Elected from: Ohio
Occupations: Laborer, Professor
Party: Republican
Vice President: Chester A.
   Arthur

21 Chester A. Arthur

Presidential term: 1881–1885
Lived: 1830–1886
Born in: Vermont
Elected as V.P. from: New York
   Succeeded Garfield
Occupations: Teacher, Lawyer
Party: Republican
Vice President: None

22 Grover Cleveland

Presidential term: 1885–1889
Lived: 1837–1908
Born in: New Jersey
Elected from: New York
Occupation: Lawyer
Party: Democratic
Vice President: Thomas A.
   Hendricks

23 Benjamin Harrison

Presidential term: 1889–1893
Lived: 1833–1901
Born in: Ohio
Elected from: Indiana
Occupation: Lawyer
Party: Republican
Vice President: Levi P. Morton

24 Grover Cleveland

Presidential term: 1893–1897
Lived: 1837–1908
Born in: New Jersey
Elected from: New York
Occupation: Lawyer
Party: Democratic
Vice President: Adlai E.
   Stevenson

25 William McKinley

Presidential term: 1897–1901
Lived: 1843–1901
Born in: Ohio
Elected from: Ohio
Occupations: Teacher, Lawyer
Party: Republican
Vice Presidents: Garret Hobart,
   Theodore Roosevelt

26 Theodore Roosevelt

Presidential term: 1901–1909
Lived: 1858–1919
Born in: New York
Elected as V.P. from: New York
   Succeeded McKinley
Occupations: Historian, Rancher
Party: Republican
Vice President: Charles W.
   Fairbanks

27 William H. Taft

Presidential term: 1909–1913
Lived: 1857–1930
Born in: Ohio
Elected from: Ohio
Occupation: Lawyer
Party: Republican
Vice President: James S.
   Sherman

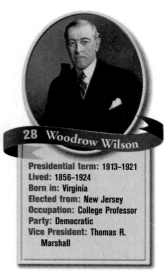

28 Woodrow Wilson

Presidential term: 1913–1921
Lived: 1856–1924
Born in: Virginia
Elected from: New Jersey
Occupation: College Professor
Party: Democratic
Vice President: Thomas R.
   Marshall

29 Warren G. Harding

Presidential term: 1921–1923
Lived: 1865–1923
Born in: Ohio
Elected from: Ohio
Occupations: Newspaper Editor,
   Publisher
Party: Republican
Vice President: Calvin Coolidge

30 Calvin Coolidge

Presidential term: 1923–1929
Lived: 1872–1933
Born in: Vermont
Elected as V.P. from:
   Massachusetts
Succeeded Harding
Occupation: Lawyer
Party: Republican
Vice President: Charles G. Dawes

31 Herbert C. Hoover

Presidential term: 1929–1933
Lived: 1874–1964
Born in: Iowa
Elected from: California
Occupation: Engineer
Party: Republican
Vice President: Charles Curtis

32 Franklin D. Roosevelt

Presidential term: 1933–1945
Lived: 1882–1945
Born in: New York
Elected from: New York
Occupation: Lawyer
Party: Democratic
Vice Presidents: John N.
   Garner, Henry A. Wallace,
   Harry S Truman

33 Harry S Truman

Presidential term: 1945–1953
Lived: 1884–1972
Born in: Missouri
Elected as V.P. from: Missouri
Succeeded Roosevelt
Occupations: Clerk, Farmer
Party: Democratic
Vice President: Alben W.
   Barkley

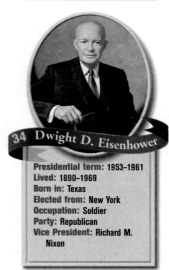

34 Dwight D. Eisenhower

Presidential term: 1953–1961
Lived: 1890–1969
Born in: Texas
Elected from: New York
Occupation: Soldier
Party: Republican
Vice President: Richard M.
   Nixon

U.S. PRESIDENTS

35 John F. Kennedy

Presidential term: 1961–1963
Lived: 1917–1963
Born in: Massachusetts
Elected from: Massachusetts
Occupations: Author, Reporter
Party: Democratic
Vice President: Lyndon B. Johnson

36 Lyndon B. Johnson

Presidential term: 1963–1969
Lived: 1908–1973
Born in: Texas
Elected as V.P. from: Texas
Succeeded Kennedy
Occupation: Teacher
Party: Democratic
Vice President: Hubert H. Humphrey

37 Richard M. Nixon

Presidential term: 1969–1974
Lived: 1913–1994
Born in: California
Elected from: New York
Occupation: Lawyer
Party: Republican
Vice Presidents: Spiro T. Agnew, Gerald R. Ford

38 Gerald R. Ford

Presidential term: 1974–1977
Lived: 1913–
Born in: Nebraska
Appointed as V.P. upon Agnew's resignation; succeeded Nixon
Occupation: Lawyer
Party: Republican
Vice President: Nelson A. Rockefeller

39 James E. Carter, Jr.

Presidential term: 1977–1981
Lived: 1924–
Born in: Georgia
Elected from: Georgia
Occupations: Business, Farmer
Party: Democratic
Vice President: Walter F. Mondale

40 Ronald W. Reagan

Presidential term: 1981–1989
Lived: 1911–
Born in: Illinois
Elected from: California
Occupations: Actor, Lecturer
Party: Republican
Vice President: George H.W. Bush

41 George H.W. Bush

Presidential term: 1989–1993
Lived: 1924–
Born in: Massachusetts
Elected from: Texas
Occupation: Business
Party: Republican
Vice President: J. Danforth Quayle

42 William J. Clinton

Presidential term: 1993–2001
Lived: 1946–
Born in: Arkansas
Elected from: Arkansas
Occupation: Lawyer
Party: Democratic
Vice President: Albert Gore, Jr.

43 George W. Bush

Presidential term: 2001–
Lived: 1946–
Born in: Connecticut
Elected from: Texas
Occupation: Business
Party: Republican
Vice President: Richard B. Cheney

The Magna Carta

The Magna Carta, signed by King John in 1215, marked a decisive step forward in the development of constitutional government in England. Later, it became a model for colonists who carried the Magna Carta's guarantees of legal and political rights to America.

1. . . . [T]hat the English Church shall be free, and shall have its rights entire, and its liberties unimpaired. . . . we have also granted for us and our heirs forever, all the liberties written out below, to have and to keep for them and their heirs, of us and our heirs:

39. No free man shall be seized or imprisoned, or stripped of his rights or possessions, or outlawed or exiled, or deprived of his standing in any other way, nor will we proceed with force against him, or send others to do so, except by the lawful judgment of his equals, or by the law of the land.

40. To no one will we sell, to no one deny or delay right or justice.

41. All merchants may enter or leave England unharmed and without fear, and may stay or travel within it, by land or water, for purposes of trade, free from all illegal exactions, in accordance with ancient and lawful customs. This, however, does not apply in time of war to merchants from a country that is at war with us. . . .

42. In future it shall be lawful for any man to leave and return to our kingdom unharmed and without fear, by land or water, preserving his allegiance to us, except in time of war, for some short period, for the common benefit of the realm. . . .

60. All these customs and liberties that we have granted shall be observed in our kingdom in so far as concerns our own relations with our subjects. Let all men of our kingdom, whether clergy or laymen, observe them similarly in their relations with their own men. . . .

63. . . . Both we and the barons have sworn that all this shall be observed in good faith and without deceit. Witness the abovementioned people and many others. Given by our hand in the meadow that is called Runnymede, between Windsor and Staines, on the fifteenth day of June in the seventeenth year of our reign.

Illuminated manuscript, Middle Ages

See the **American History Primary Source Document Library**
CD-ROM for the complete text of many of these documents.

The Mayflower Compact

On November 21, 1620, 41 colonists aboard the Mayflower *drafted this agreement. The Mayflower Compact was the first plan of self-government ever put in force in the English colonies.*

In the Name of God, Amen. We, whose names are underwritten, the Loyal Subjects of our dread Sovereign Lord King James, by the Grace of God, of Great Britain, France, and Ireland, King, Defender of the Faith, etc. Having undertaken for the Glory of God, and Advancement of the Christian Faith, and the Honour of our King and Country, a Voyage to plant the first Colony in the northern Parts of Virginia; Do by these Presents, solemnly and mutually, in the Presence of God and one another, covenant and combine ourselves together into a civil Body Politick, for our better Ordering and Preservation, and Furtherance of the Ends aforesaid: And by Virtue hereof do enact, constitute, and frame, such just and equal Laws, Ordinances, Acts, Constitutions, and Officers, from time to time, as shall be thought most meet and convenient for the general Good of the Colony; unto which we promise all due Submission and Obedience. In Witness whereof we have hereunto subscribed our names at Cape-Cod the eleventh of November, in the Reign of our Sovereign Lord King James, of England, France, and Ireland, the eighteenth, and of Scotland, the fifty-fourth, Anno Domini, 1620.

The Federalist, No. 10

James Madison wrote several articles supporting ratification of the Constitution for a New York newspaper. In the excerpt below, Madison argues for the idea of a federal republic.

By a faction, I understand a number of citizens . . . who are united and actuated by some common impulse . . . adverse to the rights of other citizens. . . .

The inference to which we are brought is that the causes of faction cannot be removed and that relief is only to be sought in the means of controlling its *effects*. . . .

James Madison

A republic, by which I mean a government in which the scheme of representation takes place . . . promises the cure for which we are seeking. . . .

The two great points of difference between a democracy and a republic are: first, the delegation of the government, in the latter, to a small number of citizens elected by the rest; secondly, the greater number of citizens, and greater sphere of country, over which the latter may be extended.

The effect of the first difference is . . . to refine and enlarge the public views, by passing them through the medium of a chosen body of citizens, whose wisdom may best discern the true interest of their country, and whose patriotism and love of justice will be least likely to sacrifice it to temporary or partial considerations. . . .

Washington's Farewell Address

At the end of his second term as president, George Washington spoke of the dangers facing the young nation. He warned against the dangers of political parties and sectionalism, and he advised the nation against permanent alliances with other nations.

. . . Citizens by birth or choice of a common country, that country has a right to concentrate your affections. The name of American, which belongs to you in your national capacity, must always exalt the just pride of patriotism more than any appellation derived from local discriminations. With slight shades of difference, you have the same religion, manners, habits, and political principles. You have in a common cause fought and triumphed together. . . .

In contemplating the causes which may disturb our union it occurs as matter of serious concern that any ground should have been furnished for characterizing parties by geographical discriminations. . . .

No alliances, however strict, between the parts can be an adequate substitute. They must inevitably experience the infractions and interruptions which all alliances in all times have experienced. . . .

George Washington

The great rule of conduct for us in regard to foreign nations is, in extending our commercial relations to have with them as little political connection as possible. . . .

. . . I anticipate with pleasing expectation that retreat in which I promise myself to realize . . . the sweet enjoyment of partaking in the midst of my fellow citizens the benign influence of good laws under a free government—the ever-favorite object of my heart, and the happy reward, as I trust, of our mutual cares, labors, and dangers.

HISTORICAL DOCUMENTS

The Star-Spangled Banner

During the British bombardment of Fort McHenry during the War of 1812, a young Baltimore lawyer named Francis Scott Key was inspired to write the words to "The Star-Spangled Banner." Although it became popular immediately, it was not until 1931 that Congress officially declared "The Star-Spangled Banner" as our national anthem.

O! say can you see by the dawn's early light,

What so proudly we hailed at the twilight's last gleaming,

Whose broad stripes and bright stars through the perilous fight,

O'er the ramparts we watch'd, were so gallantly streaming?

And the Rockets' red glare, the Bombs bursting in air,

Gave proof through the night that our Flag was still there;

O! say does that star-spangled Banner yet wave,

O'er the Land of the free, and the home of the brave!

The Monroe Doctrine

In 1823 President James Monroe proclaimed the Monroe Doctrine. Designed to end European influence in the Western Hemisphere, it became a cornerstone of United States foreign policy.

. . . With the existing colonies or dependencies of any European power we have not interfered and shall not interfere. But with the Governments who have declared their independence and maintained it, and whose independence we have, on great consideration and on just principles, acknowledged, we could not view any interposition for the purpose of oppressing them, or controlling in any other manner their destiny, by any European power in any other light than as the manifestation of any unfriendly disposition toward the United States. . . .

Our policy in regard to Europe, which was adopted at an early stage of the wars which have so long agitated that quarter of the globe, nevertheless remains the same, which is, not to interfere in the internal concerns of any of its powers; to consider the government *de facto* as the legitimate government for us; to cultivate friendly relations with it, and to preserve those relations by a frank, firm, and manly policy, meeting in all instances the just claims of every power, submitting to injuries from none. . . .

James Monroe

Memorial of the Cherokee Nation

Beaded shoulder bag, Cherokee people

The Indian Removal Act of 1830 called for the relocation of Native Americans to territory west of the Mississippi River. Cherokee leaders protested the policy.

We are aware that some persons suppose it will be for our advantage to remove beyond the Mississippi. We think otherwise. Our people universally think otherwise. . . .

We wish to remain on the land of our fathers. We have a perfect and original right to remain without interruption or molestation. The treaties with us, and laws of the United States made in pursuance of treaties, guaranty our residence and our privileges, and secure us against intruders. Our only request is, that these treaties may be fulfilled, and these laws executed. . . .

. . . We have been called a poor, ignorant, and degraded people. We certainly are not rich; nor have we ever boasted of our knowledge, or our moral or intellectual elevation. But there is not a man within our limits so ignorant as not to know that he has a right to live on the land of his fathers, in the possession of his immemorial privileges, and that this right has been acknowledged by the United States; nor is there a man so degraded as not to feel a keen sense of injury, on being deprived of his right and driven into exile. . . .

The Seneca Falls Declaration

One of the first documents to express the desire for equal rights for women is the Declaration of Sentiments and Resolutions, issued in 1848 at the Seneca Falls Convention in Seneca Falls, New York. Led by Lucretia Mott and Elizabeth Cady Stanton, the delegates adopted a set of resolutions that called for woman suffrage and opportunities for women in employment and education. Excerpts from the Declaration follow.

When, in the course of human events, it becomes necessary for one portion of the family of man to assume among the people of the earth a position different from that which they have hitherto occupied, but one to which the laws of nature and of nature's God entitle them, a decent respect to the opinions of mankind requires that they should declare the causes that impel them to such a course.

We hold these truths to be self-evident: that all men and women are created equal; that they are endowed by their Creator with certain inalienable rights; that among these are life, liberty, and the pursuit of happiness; that to secure these rights governments are instituted, deriving their just powers from the consent of the governed. Whenever any form of government becomes destructive of these ends, it is the right of those who suffer from it to refuse allegiance to it, and to insist upon the institution of a new government, laying its foundation on such principles, and organizing its powers in such form as to them shall seem most likely to effect their safety and happiness. Prudence, indeed, will dictate that governments long established should not be changed for light and transient causes; . . . But when a long train of abuses and usurpations, pursuing invariably the same object, evinces a design to reduce them under absolute despotism, it is their duty to throw off such government, and to provide new guards for their future security. . . .

The history of mankind is a history of repeated injuries and usurpations on the part of man toward woman, having in direct object the establishment of an absolute tyranny over her. To prove this, let facts be submitted to a candid world. . . .

Now, in view of the entire disfranchisement of one-half the people of this country, their social and religious degradation—in view of the unjust laws above mentioned, and because women do feel themselves aggrieved, oppressed, and fraudulently deprived of their most sacred rights, we insist that they have immediate admission to all the rights and privileges which belong to them as citizens of these United States. . . .

Elizabeth Cady Stanton

The Emancipation Proclamation

On January 1, 1863, President Abraham Lincoln issued the Emancipation Proclamation, which freed all enslaved people in states under Confederate control. The Proclamation was a step toward the Thirteenth Amendment (1865), which ended slavery in all of the United States.

. . . That on the 1st day of January, in the year of our Lord 1863, all persons held as slaves within any state or designated part of a state, the people whereof shall then be in rebellion against the United States, shall be then, thenceforward, and forever free; and the Executive Government of the United States, including the military and naval authority thereof, will recognize and maintain the freedom of such persons, and will do no act or acts to repress such persons, or any of them, in any efforts they may make for their actual freedom.

That the Executive will, on the 1st day of January aforesaid, by proclamation, designate the states and parts of states, if any, in which the people thereof, respectively, shall then be in rebellion against the United States; and the fact that any state, or the people thereof, shall on that day be in good faith represented in the Congress of the United States, by members chosen thereto at elections wherein a majority of the qualified voters of such states shall have participated, shall, in the absence of strong countervailing testimony, be deemed conclusive evidence that such state, and the people thereof, are not then in rebellion against the United States. . . .

And, by virtue of the power and for the purpose aforesaid, I do order and declare that all persons held as slaves within said designated states and parts of states are, and henceforward shall be, free; and that the Executive Government of the United States, including the military and naval authorities thereof, will recognize and maintain the freedom of said persons.

And I hereby enjoin upon the people so declared to be free to abstain from all violence, unless in necessary self-defense; and I recommend to them that, all cases when allowed, they labor faithfully for reasonable wages.

And I further declare and make known that such persons, of suitable condition, will be received into the armed service of the United States. . . .

And upon this act, sincerely believed to be an act of justice, warranted by the Constitution upon military necessity, I invoke the considerate judgement of mankind and the gracious favor of Almighty God. . . .

Abraham Lincoln

Members of the 4th Infantry

The Gettysburg Address

On November 19, 1863, President Abraham Lincoln gave a short speech at the dedication of a national cemetery on the battlefield of Gettysburg. His simple yet eloquent words expressed his hopes for a nation divided by civil war.

Four score and seven years ago our fathers brought forth on this continent a new nation, conceived in liberty, and dedicated to the proposition that all men are created equal.

Now we are engaged in a great civil war, testing whether that nation, or any nation so conceived and so dedicated, can long endure. We are met on a great battlefield of that war. We have come to dedicate a portion of that field as a final resting place for those who here gave their lives that that nation might live. It is altogether fitting and proper that we should do this.

But, in a larger sense, we can not dedicate—we can not consecrate—we can not hallow—this ground. The brave men, living and dead, who struggled here, have consecrated it far above our poor power to add or detract. The world will little note nor long remember what we say here, but it can never forget what they did here. It is for us, the living, rather, to be dedicated here to the unfinished work which they who fought here have thus far so nobly advanced. It is rather for us to be here dedicated to the great task remaining before us—that from these honored dead we take increased devotion to that cause for which they gave the last full measure of devotion; that we here highly resolve that these dead shall not have died in vain; that this nation, under God, shall have a new birth of freedom; and that government of the people, by the people, for the people, shall not perish from the earth.

Soldier's kit, Civil War

Gettysburg Memorial

I Will Fight No More

Shield made of buffalo hide

In 1877 the Nez Perce fought the government's attempt to move them to a smaller reservation. After a remarkable attempt to escape to Canada, Chief Joseph realized that resistance was hopeless and advised his people to surrender.

Tell General Howard I know his heart. What he told me before I have in my heart.

I am tired of fighting. . . . The old men are all dead. It is the young men who say yes or no. He who led the young men is dead. It is cold and we have no blankets. The little children are freezing to death. My people, some of them have run away to the hills, and have no blankets, no food; no one knows where they are—perhaps freezing to death. I want to have time to look for my children and see how many of them I can find. Maybe I shall find them among the dead. Hear me, my chiefs. I am tired; my heart is sick and sad. From where the sun now stands I will fight no more forever.

The Pledge of Allegiance

In 1892 the nation celebrated the 400th anniversary of Columbus's landing in America. In connection with this celebration, Francis Bellamy, a magazine editor, wrote and published the Pledge of Allegiance. The words "under God" were added by Congress in 1954 at the urging of President Dwight D. Eisenhower.

I pledge allegiance to the Flag of the United States of America and to the Republic for which it stands, one Nation under God, indivisible, with liberty and justice for all.

Students in a New York City school recite the Pledge of Allegiance

The American's Creed

William Tyler Page of Friendship Heights, Maryland, wrote The American's Creed. This statement of political faith summarizes the true meaning of freedom available to all Americans. The U.S. House of Representatives adopted the creed on behalf of the American people on April 3, 1918.

I believe in the United States of America as a Government of the people, by the people, for the people; whose just powers are derived from the consent of the governed; a democracy in a republic; a sovereign Nation of many sovereign States; a perfect union, one and inseparable; established upon those principles of freedom, equality, justice, and humanity for which American patriots sacrificed their lives and fortunes.

I therefore believe it is my duty to my Country to love it, to support its Constitution, to obey its laws, to respect its flag, and to defend it against all enemies.

The Fourteen Points

On January 8, 1918, President Woodrow Wilson went before Congress to offer a statement of aims called the Fourteen Points. Wilson's plan called for freedom of the seas in peace and war, an end to secret alliances, and equal trading rights for all countries. The excerpt that follows is taken from the president's message.

. . . We entered this war because violations of right had occurred which touched us to the quick and made the life of our own people impossible unless they were corrected and the world secured once for all against their recurrence. What we demand in this war, therefore, is nothing peculiar to ourselves. It is that the world be made fit and safe to live in; and particularly that it be made safe for every peace-loving nation which, like our own, wishes to live its own life, determine its own institutions, be assured of justice and fair dealing by the other peoples of the world as against force and selfish aggression. All the peoples of the world are in effect partners in this interest, and for our own part we see very clearly that unless justice be done to others it will not be done to us. The program of the world's peace, therefore, is our program; and that program, the only possible program, as we see it, is this:

I. Open covenants of peace, openly arrived at, after which there shall be no private international understandings of any kind but diplomacy shall proceed always frankly and in the public view.

II. Absolute freedom of navigation upon the seas, outside territorial waters, alike in peace and in war, except as the seas may be closed in whole or in part by international action for the enforcement of international covenants.

XIV. A general association of nations must be formed under specific covenants for the purpose of affording mutual guarantees of political independence and territorial integrity to great and small states alike. . . .

Brown v. Board of Education

On May 17, 1954, the Supreme Court ruled in Brown *v.* Board of Education of Topeka, Kansas, *that racial segregation in public schools was unconstitutional. This decision provided the legal basis for court challenges to segregation in every aspect of American life.*

. . . The plaintiffs contend that segregated public schools are not "equal" and cannot be made "equal" and that hence they are deprived of the equal protection of the laws. Because of the obvious importance of the question presented, the Court took jurisdiction. . . .

Our decision, therefore, cannot turn on merely a comparison of these tangible factors in the Negro and white schools involved in each of the cases. We must look instead to the effect of segregation itself on public education.

In approaching this problem, we cannot turn the clock back to 1868 when the Amendment was adopted, or even to 1896 when *Plessy* v. *Ferguson* was written. We must consider public education in the light of its full development and its present place in American life throughout the Nation. Only in this way can it be determined if segregation in public schools deprives these plaintiffs of the equal protection of the laws.

Today, education is perhaps the most important function of state and local governments. Compulsory school attendance laws and the great expenditures for education both demonstrate our recognition of the importance of education to our democratic society. . . . In these days, it is doubtful that any child may reasonably be expected to succeed in life if he is denied the opportunity of an education. Such an opportunity, where the state has undertaken to provide it, is a right which must be made available to all on equal terms.

We come then to the question presented: Does segregation of children in public schools solely on the basis of race, even though the physical facilities and other "tangible" factors may be equal, deprive the children of the minority group of equal educational opportunities?

We believe that it does.

. . . We conclude that in the field of public education the doctrine of "separate but equal" has no place. Separate educational facilities are inherently unequal. Therefore, we hold that the plaintiffs and others similarly situated for whom the actions have been brought are, by reason of the segregation complained of, deprived of the equal protection of the laws guaranteed by the Fourteenth Amendment. . . .

Troops escort students to newly integrated school

John F. Kennedy's Inaugural Address

President Kennedy's Inaugural Address on January 20, 1961, set the tone for his administration. In his address Kennedy stirred the nation by calling for "a grand and global alliance" to fight tyranny, poverty, disease, and war.

We observe today not a victory of party but a celebration of freedom—symbolizing an end as well as a beginning—signifying renewal as well as change. For I have sworn before you and Almighty God the same solemn oath our forebears prescribed nearly a century and three-quarters ago.

The world is very different now. For man holds in his mortal hands the power to abolish all forms of human poverty and all forms of human life. And yet the same revolutionary beliefs for which our forebears fought are still at issue around the globe—the belief that the rights of man come not from the generosity of the state but from the hand of God.

We dare not forget today that we are the heirs of that first revolution. Let the word go forth from this time and place, to friend and foe alike, that the torch has been passed to a new generation of Americans—born in this century, tempered by war, disciplined by a hard and bitter peace, proud of our ancient heritage—and unwilling to witness or permit the slow undoing of those human rights to which this nation has always been committed, and to which we are committed today at home and around the world.

Let every nation know, whether it wishes us well or ill,
that we shall pay any price, bear any burden, meet any hardship, support any friend, oppose any foe to assure the survival and the success of liberty.

This much we pledge—and more.

To those old allies whose cultural and spiritual origins we share, we pledge the loyalty of faithful friends. United, there is little we cannot do in a host of cooperative ventures. Divided, there is little we can do. . . .

Let us never negotiate out of fear. But let us never fear to negotiate.

Let both sides explore what problems unite us instead of belaboring those problems which divide us. . . .

Let both sides seek to invoke the wonders of science instead of its terrors. Together let us explore the stars, conquer the deserts, eradicate disease, tap the ocean depths, and encourage the arts and commerce. . . .

And so, my fellow Americans: ask not what your country can do for you—ask what you can do for your country.

My fellow citizens of the world: ask not what America will do for you, but what together we can do for the freedom of man. . . .

President Kennedy speaking at his inauguration

I Have a Dream

On August 28, 1963, while Congress debated wide-ranging civil rights legislation, Dr. Martin Luther King, Jr., led more than 200,000 people in a march on Washington, D.C. On the steps of the Lincoln Memorial he gave a stirring speech in which he eloquently spoke of his dreams for African Americans and for the United States. Excerpts of the speech follow.

. . . There are those who are asking the devotees of civil rights, "When will you be satisfied?"

We can never be satisfied as long as the Negro is the victim of the unspeakable horrors of police brutality. . . .

We cannot be satisfied as long as the Negro's basic mobility is from a smaller ghetto to a larger one.

We can never be satisfied as long as a Negro in Mississippi cannot vote and a Negro in New York believes he has nothing for which to vote. . . .

I say to you today, my friends, that in spite of the difficulties and frustrations of the moment I still have a dream. It is a dream deeply rooted in the American dream. I have a dream that one day this nation will rise up and live out the true meaning of its creed: "We hold these truths to be self-evident, that all men are created equal."

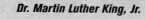

Dr. Martin Luther King, Jr.

I have a dream that one day on the red hills of Georgia the sons of former slaves and the sons of former slaveowners will be able to sit down together at the table of brotherhood.

I have a dream that one day even the state of Mississippi, a desert state sweltering with the heat of injustice and oppression, will be transformed into an oasis of freedom and justice.

I have a dream that my four little children will one day live in a nation where they will not be judged by the color of their skin but by the content of their character. . . .

. . . When we let freedom ring, when we let it ring from every village and every hamlet, from every state and every city, we will be able to speed up that day when all of God's children, black men and white men, Jews and Gentiles, Protestants and Catholics, will be able to join hands and sing in the words of the old Negro spiritual: "Free at last! Free at last! Thank God Almighty, we are free at last!"

The March on Washington

SUPREME COURT CASE SUMMARIES

The following summaries give details about important Supreme Court cases.

Brown v. Board of Education (1954)

In *Brown* v. *Board of Education of Topeka, Kansas,* the Supreme Court overruled *Plessy* v. *Ferguson* (1896) [see p. 209] making the separate-but-equal doctrine in public schools unconstitutional. The Supreme Court rejected the idea that truly equal but separate schools for African American and white students would be constitutional. The Court explained that the Fourteenth Amendment's requirement that all persons be guaranteed equal protection of the law is not met simply by ensuring that African American and white schools "have been equalized . . . with respect to buildings, curricula, qualifications and salaries, and other tangible factors."

The Court then ruled that racial segregation in public schools violates the Equal Protection Clause of the Constitution because it is inherently unequal. In other words, nothing can make racially segregated public schools equal under the Constitution because the very fact of separation marks the separated race as inferior. In practical terms, the Court's decision in this case has been extended beyond public education to virtually all public accommodations and activities.

Dred Scott v. Sandford (1857)

Dred Scott was taken by slaveholder John Sandford to the free state of Illinois and to the Wisconsin Territory, which had also banned slavery. Later they returned to Missouri, a slave state. Several years later, Scott sued for his freedom under the Missouri legal principle of "once free, always free." In other words, under Missouri law enslaved people were entitled to freedom if they had lived in a free state at any time. Missouri courts ruled against Scott, but he appealed the case all the way to the United States Supreme Court.

Dred Scott

The Supreme Court decided this case before the Fourteenth Amendment was added to the Constitution. (The Fourteenth Amendment provides that anyone born or naturalized in the United States is a citizen of the nation and of his or her state of residence.) The Court held that enslaved African Americans were property, not citizens, and thus had no rights under the Constitution. The decision also overturned the Missouri Compromise of 1820, which had outlawed slavery in territories north of 36° 30' latitude. Many people in the North were outraged by the decision, which moved the nation closer to civil war.

Furman v. Georgia (1972)

This decision put a halt to the application of the death penalty under state laws then in effect. For the first time, the Supreme Court ruled that the death penalty amounted to cruel and unusual punishment, which is outlawed in the Constitution. The Court explained that existing death penalty laws did not give juries enough guidance in deciding whether or not to impose the death penalty. As a result, the death penalty in many cases was imposed arbitrarily, that is, without a reasonable basis in the facts and circumstances of the offender or the crime.

The *Furman* decision halted all executions in the 39 states that had death penalty laws at that time. Since the decision, 38 states have rewritten death penalty laws to meet the requirements established in the *Furman* case.

Gibbons v. Ogden (1824)

Thomas Gibbons had a federal license to operate a steamboat along the coast, but he did not have a license from the state of New York to travel on New York waters. He wanted to run a steamboat line between Manhattan and New Jersey that would compete with Aaron Ogden's company. Ogden had a New York license. Gibbons sued for the freedom to use his federal license to compete against Ogden on New York waters.

Gibbons won the case. The Supreme Court made it clear that the authority of Congress to regulate interstate commerce (among states) includes the authority to regulate intrastate commerce (within a single state) that bears on, or relates to, interstate commerce.

Before this decision, it was thought that the Constitution would permit a state to close its borders to interstate commercial activity—which, in effect, would stop such activity in its tracks. This case says that a state can regulate purely internal commercial activity, but only Congress can regulate commercial activity that has both intrastate and interstate dimensions.

Gideon v. Wainwright (1963)

After being accused of robbery, Clarence Gideon defended himself in a Florida court because the judge in the case refused to appoint a free lawyer. The jury found Gideon guilty. Eventually, Gideon appealed his conviction to the United States Supreme Court, claiming that by failing to appoint a lawyer the lower court had violated his rights under the Sixth and Fourteenth Amendments.

The Supreme Court agreed with Gideon. In *Gideon* v. *Wainwright* the Supreme Court held for the first time that poor defendants in criminal cases have the right to a state-paid attorney under the Sixth Amendment. The rule announced in this case has been refined to apply whenever the defendant, if convicted, can be sentenced to more than six months in jail or prison.

Korematsu v. United States (1944)

After the Japanese bombing of Pearl Harbor in 1941, thousands of Japanese Americans on the West Coast were forced to abandon their homes and businesses, and they were moved to internment camps in California, Idaho, Utah, Arizona, Wyoming, Colorado, and Arkansas. The prison-like camps offered poor food and cramped quarters.

In 1983 Fred Korematsu (center) won a reversal of his conviction.

The Supreme Court's decision in *Korematsu* v. *United States* upheld the authority of the federal government to move Japanese Americans, many of whom were citizens, from designated military areas that included almost the entire West Coast. The government defended the so-called exclusion orders as a necessary response to Japan's attack on Pearl Harbor. Only after his reelection in 1944 did President Franklin Roosevelt rescind the evacuation orders, and by the end of 1945 the camps were closed.

Marbury v. Madison (1803)

During his last days in office, President John Adams commissioned William Marbury and several other men as judges. This action by Federalist president Adams angered the incoming Democratic-Republican president Thomas Jefferson. Jefferson then ordered James Madison, his secretary of state, not to deliver the commissions, thus blocking the appointments. William Marbury sued, asking the Supreme Court to order Madison to deliver the commission that would make him a judge.

The Court ruled against Marbury, but more importantly, the decision in this case established one of the most significant principles of American constitutional law. The Supreme Court held that it is the Court itself that has the final say on what the Constitution means. This is known as judicial review. It is also the Supreme Court that has the final say in whether or not an act of government—legislative or executive at the federal, state, or local level—violates the Constitution.

McCulloch v. Maryland (1819)

Following the War of 1812, the United States experienced years of high inflation and general economic turmoil. In an attempt to stabilize the economy, the United States Congress chartered a Second Bank of the United States in 1816. Maryland and several other states, however, opposed the competition that the new national bank created and passed laws taxing its branches. In 1818, James McCulloch, head of the Baltimore branch of the Second Bank of the United States, refused to pay the tax to the state of Maryland. The case worked its way through the Maryland state courts all the way to the United States Supreme Court.

The Supreme Court declared the Maryland tax unconstitutional and void. More importantly, the decision established the foundation for expanded congressional authority. The Court held that the necessary and proper clause of the Constitution allows Congress to do more than the Constitution expressly authorizes it to do. The decision allows Congress to enact nearly any law that will help it achieve any of its duties as set forth in the Constitution. For example, Congress has the express authority to regulate interstate commerce. The necessary and proper clause permits Congress to do so in ways not actually specified in the Constitution.

Miranda v. Arizona (1966)

In 1963, police in Arizona arrested Ernesto Miranda for kidnapping. The court found Miranda guilty on the basis of a signed confession. The police admitted that neither before nor during the questioning had Miranda been advised of his right to consult with an attorney before answering any questions or of his right to have an attorney present during the interrogation. Miranda appealed his conviction, claiming that police had violated his right against self-incrimination under the Fifth Amendment by not informing him of his legal rights during questioning.

Miranda won the case. The Supreme Court held that a person in police custody cannot be questioned unless told that he or she has: 1) the right to remain silent, 2) the right to an attorney (at government expense if the accused is unable to pay), and 3) that anything the person says after stating that he or she understands these rights can be used as evidence of guilt at trial. These rights have come to be called the Miranda warning. They are intended to ensure that an accused person in custody will not unknowingly give up the Fifth Amendment's protection against self-incrimination.

The New York Times Company v. United States (1971)

In June 1971, the *New York Times* published its first installment of the "Pentagon Papers," a classified document about government actions in the Vietnam War era. The secret document had been leaked to the *Times* by antiwar activist Daniel Ellsberg, who had previously worked in national

In 1963, the arrest of Ernesto Miranda (left) led to a landmark decision.

security for the government. President Richard Nixon went to court to block further publication of the Pentagon Papers. The *New York Times* appealed to the Supreme Court to allow it to continue publishing without government interference.

The Supreme Court's ruling in this case upheld earlier decisions that established the doctrine of prior restraint. This doctrine protects the press (broadly defined to include newspapers, television and radio, filmmakers and distributors, etc.) from government attempts to block publication. Except in extraordinary circumstances, the press must be allowed to publish.

Plessy v. Ferguson (1896)

In the late 1800s railroad companies in Louisiana were required by state law to provide "separate-but-equal" cars for white and African American passengers. In 1890 a group of citizens in New Orleans selected Homer Plessy to challenge that law. In 1892, Plessy boarded a whites-only car and refused to move. He was arrested. Plessy appealed to the Supreme Court, arguing that the Louisiana separate-but-equal law violated his right to equal protection under the Fourteenth Amendment.

Homer Plessy lost the case. The *Plessy* decision upheld the separate-but-equal doctrine used by Southern states to perpetuate segregation following the Civil War. The court ruled that the Fourteenth Amendment's equal protection clause required only equal public facilities for the two races, not equal access to the same facilities. This decision was overruled in 1954 by *Brown* v. *Board of Education of Topeka, Kansas* (discussed previously).

Roe v. Wade (1973)

Roe v. *Wade* challenged restrictive abortion laws in both Texas and Georgia. The suit was brought in the name of Jane Roe, an alias used to protect the privacy of the plaintiff.

In this decision, the Supreme Court ruled that females have a constitutional right under various provisions of the Constitution—most notably, the due process clause—to decide whether or not to terminate a pregnancy. The Supreme Court's decision in this case was the most significant in a long line of decisions over a period of 50 years that recognized a constitutional right of privacy, even though the word "privacy" is not found in the Constitution.

Tinker v. Des Moines School District (1969)

During the Vietnam War, some students in Des Moines, Iowa, wore black armbands to school to protest American involvement in the conflict. Two days earlier, school officials had adopted a policy banning the wearing of armbands to school. When the students arrived at school wearing armbands, they were suspended and sent home. The students argued that school officials violated their First Amendment right to free speech.

The Supreme Court sided with the students. In a now-famous statement the Court said that "it can hardly be argued that either students or teachers shed their constitutional rights of freedom of speech or expression at the schoolhouse gate." The Supreme Court went on to rule that a public school could not suspend students who wore black armbands to school to symbolize their opposition to the Vietnam War. In so holding, the Court likened the students' conduct to pure speech and decided it on that basis.

United States v. Nixon (1974)

In the early 1970s, President Nixon was named an unindicted co-conspirator in the criminal investigation that arose in the aftermath of a break-in at the offices of the Democratic Party in Washington, D.C. A federal judge had ordered President Nixon to turn over tapes of conversations he had with his advisers about the break-in. Nixon resisted the order, claiming that the conversations were entitled to absolute confidentiality by Article II of the Constitution.

The decision in this case made it clear that the president is not above the law. The Supreme Court held that only those presidential conversations and communications that relate to performing the duties of the office of president are confidential and protected from a judicial order of disclosure. The Court ordered Nixon to give up the tapes, which revealed evidence linking the president to the conspiracy to obstruct justice. He resigned from office shortly thereafter.

Worcester v. Georgia (1832)

State officials in Georgia wanted to remove the Cherokees from land that had been guaranteed to them in earlier treaties. Samuel Worcester was a congregational missionary who worked with the Cherokee people. He was arrested for failure to have a license that the state required to live in Cherokee country and for refusing to obey an order from the Georgia militia to leave Cherokee lands. Worcester then sued the state of Georgia. He claimed that Georgia had no legal authority on Cherokee land because the United States government recognized the Cherokee in Georgia as a separate nation.

The Supreme Court agreed with Worcester by a vote of 5 to 1. Chief Justice John Marshall wrote the majority opinion, which said that Native American nations were a distinct people with the right to have independent political communities and that only the federal government had authority over matters that involved the Cherokee.

President Andrew Jackson supported Georgia's efforts to remove the Cherokee to Indian Territory and refused to enforce the Court's ruling. After the ruling Jackson remarked, "John Marshall has made his decision. Now let him enforce it." As a result of Jackson's refusal to enforce the Court's order, thousands of Cherokees died on the long, forced trek to Indian Territory, known as the "Trail of Tears."

SUPREME COURT CASES

A

absentee ballot one that allows a person to vote without going to the polls on Election Day (p. 238)

absolute monarch a monarch that has complete and unlimited power to rule his or her people (p. 589)

acid rain rain containing high amounts of chemical pollutants (p. 614)

acquittal a vote of not guilty (p. 373)

affirmative action programs intended to make up for past discrimination by helping minority groups and women gain access to jobs and opportunities (p. 115)

alien a noncitizen (p. 15)

ambassador an official representative of a country's government (p. 177)

amend to change (p. 41)

amendment any change in the Constitution (p. 85)

amnesty a pardon to a group of people (p. 172)

Anti-Federalists those who opposed ratification of the Constitution (p. 59)

antitrust law legislation to prevent new monopolies from forming and police those that already exist (p. 505)

apartheid system of laws that separated racial and ethnic groups and limited the rights of blacks in South Africa (p. 625)

apathy a lack of interest (p. 240)

appeals court a court that reviews decisions made in lower district courts (p. 197)

appellate jurisdiction the authority of a court to hear a case appealed from a lower court (p. 197)

apportion divide among districts (p. 289)

appropriations bill legislation earmarking funds for certain purposes (p. 543)

arbitration situation in which union and company officials submit the issues they cannot agree on to a third party for a final decision (p. 489)

archives files of older stories (p. 385)

arraignment a hearing in which a suspect is charged and pleads guilty or not guilty (p. 372)

articles of partnership formal legal papers specifying the arrangement between partners (p. 481)

at-large election an election for an area as a whole; for example, statewide (p. 309)

authoritarian a government in which one leader or group of people holds absolute power (pp. 389, 588)

automatic stabilizer program that automatically provides benefits to offset a change in people's incomes (p. 556)

B

bail a sum of money used as a security deposit to ensure that an accused person returns for his or her trial (pp. 105, 357)

balance of trade the difference between the value of a nation's exports and its imports (p. 570)

balanced budget annual budget in which expenditures equal revenues (p. 554)

ballot the list of candidates on which you cast your vote (p. 237)

bicameral a legislature consisting of two parts, or houses (pp. 39, 139)

bill of attainder a law that punishes a person accused of a crime without a trial or a fair hearing in court (pp. 150, 353)

Bill of Rights the first 10 amendments to the Constitution (p. 85)

board of directors people elected by the shareholders of a corporation to act on their behalf (p. 483)

bond contract to repay borrowed money with interest at a specific time in the future (p. 554)

boycott the refusal to purchase certain goods (p. 34)

brief a written document explaining the position of one side or the other in a case (p. 208)

budget a plan for making and spending money (pp. 9, 542)

budget resolution congressional document that shows total spending and revenues for a year and how much will be spent in various categories (p. 543)

bureaucracy complex systems with many departments, many rules, and many people in the chain of command (p. 126)

business cycle alternating periods of growth and decline that the economy goes through (p. 509)

C

cabinet a group of advisers to the president that includes the heads of 14 top-level executive departments (p. 181)

capital previously manufactured goods used to make other goods and services (p. 425)

capitalism a system in which private citizens own most, if not all, of the means of production and decide how to use them within legislated limits (pp. 417, 434)

casework the work that a lawmaker does to help constituents with a problem (p. 154)

caucus a meeting of political party members to conduct party business (p. 224)

censorship the banning of printed materials or films due to alarming or offensive ideas (p. 99)

census a population count taken by the Census Bureau (p. 139)

central bank an institution that lends money to other banks; also, the place where the government does its banking business (p. 529)

certificate of deposit timed deposit that states the amount of the deposit, maturity, and rate of interest being paid (p. 535)

charter a written document granting land and the authority to set up colonial governments; or a government document granting permission to organize a corporation (pp. 30, 482)

charter schools schools that receive state funding, but are excused from meeting many public school regulations (p. 330)

checking account an account in which deposited money can be withdrawn at any time by writing a check (p. 535)

checks and balances a system in which each branch of government is able to check, or restrain, the power of the others (p. 91)

circuit the area of jurisdiction of a federal court of appeals (p. 197)

citizens community members who owe loyalty to the government and are entitled to protection from it (p. 6)

city charter a document granting power to a local government (p. 306)

civics the study of the rights and duties of citizens (p. 6)

civil liberties freedoms to think and act without government interference or fear of unfair legal treatment (p. 98)

civil rights the rights of full citizenship and equality under the law (p. 113)

civil service system the practice of hiring government workers on the basis of open, competitive examinations and merit (p. 185)

civil service worker person hired into a federal position (p. 185)

civilian labor force all civilians 16 years old or older who are either working or are looking for work (p. 510)

closed primary an election in which only the declared members of a party are allowed to vote for that party's nominees (p. 228)

closed shop company in which only union members can be hired (p. 488)

cloture a procedure used in the Senate to limit debate on a bill (p. 159)

coin metallic form of money such as pennies, nickels, and dimes (p. 525)

Cold War conflict between the United States and the Soviet Union dating from the later 1940s to the late 1980s, when the two countries competed for world influence without declared military action (p. 626)

collective bargaining process by which unions and employers negotiate the conditions of employment (p. 488)

collective farm a farm in which the land is owned by the government but rented to a family (p. 601)

colony a group of people in one place who are ruled by a parent country elsewhere (p. 30)

command economy an economic system in which the major economic decisions are made by the central government (p. 574)

commercial bank a financial institution that offers full banking services to individuals and businesses (p. 526)

common law a system of law based on precedent and customs (pp. 30, 346)

communism economic system in which the central government directs all major economic decisions (p. 574)

community a group of people who share the same interests and concerns (p. 125)

commute to reduce a criminal's sentence (p. 294)

compact an agreement, or contract, among a group of people (p. 31)

comparative advantage the ability of a country to produce a good at a lower opportunity cost than another country can (p. 565)

competition the struggle that goes on between buyers and sellers to get the best products at the lowest prices (p. 435)

complaint a formal notice that a lawsuit is being brought (p. 365)

complement product often used with another product (p. 454)

concurrent jurisdiction authority for both state and federal courts to hear and decide cases (p. 195)

concurrent powers powers shared by the state and federal governments (pp. 93, 284)

concurring opinion a statement written by a justice who votes with the majority, but for different reasons (p. 208)

confederation a group of individuals or state governments (p. 40)

conservation the careful preservation and protection of natural resources (pp. 335, 614)

constituent a person from a legislator's district (p. 139)

constitution a detailed, written plan for government (p. 39)

constitutional in accordance with the Constitution (p. 202)

Constitutional Convention meeting of state delegates in 1787 leading to adoption of new Constitution (p. 54)

constitutional monarchy a system in which the power of the hereditary ruler is limited by the country's constitution and laws (p. 590)

consumer price index measure of the change in price over time of a specific group of goods and services (p. 511)

consumer sovereignty the role of consumer as the ruler of the market, determining what products will be produced (p. 435)

consumerism a movement to educate buyers about the purchases they make and to demand better and safer products from manufacturers (p. 439)

cooperative a voluntary association of people formed to carry on some kind of economic activity that will benefit its members (p. 485)

copyright the owner's exclusive right to control, publish, and sell an original work (p. 396)

corporation type of business organization owned by many people but treated by law as though it were a person (p. 482)

cost-benefit analysis economic model that compares the marginal costs and marginal benefits of a decision (p. 413)

county normally the largest territorial and political subdivision of a state (p. 312)

county chairperson a person who runs a county committee, often having a great deal of political power in the county (p. 225)

county seat a town where the county courthouse is located (p. 312)

credit union nonprofit service cooperative that accepts deposits, makes loans, and provides other financial services (p. 526)

crime an act that breaks a law and causes harm to people or society in general (p. 368)

cross-examine to question a witness at a trial or a hearing to check or discredit the testimony (p. 372)

currency both coins and paper money (p. 525)

debt money borrowed and not yet paid back (p. 554)

defendant an individual or group being sued or charged with a crime (pp. 298, 349, 364)

deficit situation in which government spends more than it collects in revenues (p. 553)

delegate a representative to a meeting (pp. 35, 224)

demand the desire, willingness, and ability to buy a good or service (p. 448)

demand curve downward-sloping line that graphically shows the quantities demanded at each possible price (p. 449)

demand elasticity measure of responsiveness relating change in quantity demanded to a change in price (p. 455)

demand schedule table showing quantities demanded at different possible prices (p. 449)

democracy a government in which citizens hold the power to rule (p. 10)

deport to send an alien or immigrant back to his or her own country (p. 17)

developing country a country whose average per capita income is only a fraction of that in more industrialized countries (p. 578)

devolution the surrender of powers to local authorities by a central government (p. 597)

dictator a ruler who exercises complete control over a state (p. 589)

dictatorship a government controlled by one person or a small group of people (p. 10)

diminishing marginal utility decreasing satisfaction or usefulness as additional units of a product are acquired (p. 451)

direct democracy a form of democracy in which the people vote firsthand (p. 10)

direct primary an election in which voters choose candidates to represent each party in a general election (p. 227)

discount rate the interest rate the Fed charges on its loans (p. 532)

discretionary income money income left after necessities have been bought and paid for (p. 440)

discretionary spending spending for federal programs that must receive annual approval (p. 543)

discrimination unfair treatment based on prejudice against a certain group (pp. 113, 493)

disposable income money income left after all taxes on it have been paid (p. 440)

dissenting opinion a statement written by a justice who disagrees with the majority opinion, presenting his or her opinion (p. 208)

dissident group people who disagree with the established political or religious system (p. 389)

district courts federal courts where trials are held and lawsuits are begun (p. 196)

division of labor the breaking down of a job into separate, smaller tasks to be performed individually (p. 431)

docket a court's calendar, showing the schedule of cases it is to hear (p. 206)

double jeopardy putting someone on trial for a crime of which he or she was previously acquitted (pp. 104, 355)

double taxation the payment of taxes twice on corporate profits (p. 484)

draft to call up people for military service (p. 121)

due process following established legal procedures (p. 104)

due process of law procedures established by law and guaranteed by the Constitution (p. 353)

duty things we are required to do (p. 120)

dynasty line of rulers from the same family (p. 599)

Earned Income Tax Credit (EITC) a program that gives tax credits and even cash payments to qualified workers (p. 518)

economic interdependence a reliance on others, as they rely on you, to provide goods and services to be consumed (p. 432)

economic model simplified representation of the real world that economists develop to describe how the economy behaves and is expected to perform in the future (p. 408)

economics the study of how individuals and nations make choices about ways to use scarce resources to fulfill their needs and wants (p. 406)

elastic clause clause in Article I, Section 8 of the Constitution that gives Congress the right to make all laws "necessary and proper" to carry out its expressed powers (p. 146)

elector person appointed to vote in presidential elections for the major candidates (pp. 167, 243)

Electoral College a group of people named by each state legislature to select the president and vice president (pp. 58, 167, 243)

electorate all the people who are eligible to vote (p. 240)

electronic media radio, television, and the Internet (p. 264)

embargo an agreement among a group of nations that prohibits them all from trading with a target nation (p. 177)

eminent domain the right of government to take private property for public use (p. 105)

entitlement program a program using eligibility requirements to provide health, nutritional, or income supplements to individuals (p. 551)

entrepreneurs individuals who start new businesses, introduce new products, and improve management techniques (p. 426)

equilibrium price the price at which the amount producers are willing to supply is equal to the amount consumers are willing to buy (p. 473)

ethical behavior the responsibility of consumers to respect the rights of producers and sellers (p. 440)

European Union organization of European nations whose goal is to encourage economic integration into a single market in Europe (p. 567)

ex post facto law a law that would allow a person to be punished for an action that was not against the law when it was committed (pp. 150, 353)

exchange rate the price of one nation's currency in terms of another nation's currency (p. 569)

exclusive jurisdiction authority of only federal courts to hear and decide cases (p. 195)

executive agreement an agreement between the president and the leader of another country (p. 177)

executive branch the branch of government that carries out laws (p. 55)

executive order a rule or command that has the force of law (p. 172)

exit poll a survey taken at polling places of how people voted (p. 239)

expansion part of the business cycle in which economic activity increases (p. 509)

export to sell goods to other countries; or a good produced in one country, then sold to another (p. 564)

expressed powers powers that Congress has that are specifically listed in the Constitution (pp. 92, 146)

externality the unintended side effect of an action that affects someone not involved in the action (p. 503)

factor market a market where productive resources are bought and sold (p. 428)

factors of production resources necessary to produce goods and services (p. 424)

federal bureaucracy the collective agencies and employees of the executive branch (p. 183)

Federal Deposit Insurance Corporation (FDIC) federal agency that insures individual accounts in financial institutions for up to $100,000 (p. 527)

Federal Open Market Committee (FOMC) the most powerful committee of the Fed, because it makes the decisions that affect the economy as a whole by manipulating the money supply (p. 530)

federal system the sharing of power between the central and state governments (p. 282)

federalism a form of government in which power is divided between the federal, or national, government and the states (p. 58)

Federalists supporters of the Constitution (p. 58)

felony a serious crime such as murder, rape, kidnapping, or robbery (pp. 298, 349)

filibuster a tactic for defeating a bill in the Senate by talking until the bill's sponsor withdraws it (p. 159)

financial capital money used to buy the tools and equipment used in production (p. 481)

fiscal policy the federal government's use of spending and taxation policies to affect overall business activity (p. 510)

fiscal year 12-month planning period that may not coincide with the calendar year (p. 542)

food stamps government coupons that can be used to purchase food (p. 517)

foreign policy a nation's overall plan for dealing with other nations (p. 175)

franking privilege the right of senators and representatives to send job-related mail without paying postage (p. 152)

free enterprise economic system in which individuals and businesses are allowed to compete for profit with a minimum of government interference (pp. 417, 434)

free trade policy of reduced trade barriers (p. 567)

genocide mass murder of a people because of their race, religion, ethnicity, politics, or culture (p. 624)

gerrymander an oddly shaped district designed to increase the voting strength of a particular group (p. 139)

globalization individuals and nations working across barriers of distance, culture, and technology (p. 621)

goods tangible products that we use to satisfy our wants and needs (p. 424)

government the ruling authority for a community (p. 7)

government corporation a business owned and operated by the federal government (p. 184)

grand jury a group of citizens that decides whether there is sufficient evidence to accuse someone of a crime (pp. 104, 355)

grants-in-aid money awarded to the states by the federal government (p. 285)

Great Compromise agreement providing a dual system of congressional representation (p. 57)

Gross Domestic Product (GDP) total dollar value of all final goods and services produced in a country during a single year (p. 426)

home rule allows cities to write their own charters, choose their own type of government, and manage their own affairs (p. 307)

human rights fundamental freedoms of individuals (p. 602)

hung jury a jury that cannot agree on a verdict (p. 373)

immigrant a person who moves permanently to a new country (p. 15)

impeach to accuse government officials of misconduct in office (p. 148)

implied powers powers that Congress has that are not stated explicitly in the Constitution (p. 146)

import a good purchased from one country by another (p. 564)

GLOSSARY

incentive reward offered to try to persuade people to take certain economic actions (p. 417)

income tax a tax on people's earnings (p. 85)

incorporate to receive a state charter, officially recognizing the government of a locality (p. 306)

incumbent a politician who has already been elected to office (p. 250)

independence self-reliance and freedom from outside control (p. 36)

independent agency federal board or commission that is not part of any cabinet department (p. 184)

indictment a formal charge by a grand jury (p. 104)

inflation sustained increase in the general level of prices (p. 511)

infrastructure a community's system of roads, bridges, water, and sewers (p. 326)

initiative a procedure by which citizens can propose new laws or state constitutional amendments (p. 242)

injunction a court order commanding a person or group to stop a certain action (p. 365)

intellectual property things that people create, such as songs, movies, books, poetry, art, and software (p. 396)

interest the payment people receive when they lend money or allow someone else to use their money (p. 442)

interest group a group of people who share a point of view about an issue and unite to promote their beliefs (p. 259)

intergovernmental revenues funds one level of government receives from another level of government (p. 548)

International Monetary Fund (IMF) agency that offers monetary advice and provides loans to developing nations (p. 580)

international tribunal court with authority to hear cases about human rights violations (p. 624)

internationalism involvement in world affairs (p. 617)

Internet a mass communication system of millions of networked computers and databases all over the world (p. 384)

joint resolution a resolution that is passed by both houses of Congress (p. 157)

judicial branch the branch of government that interprets laws (p. 56)

judicial review the power of the Supreme Court to say whether any federal, state, or local law or government action goes against the Constitution (p. 202)

jurisdiction a court's authority to hear and decide cases (p. 194)

jurisprudence the study of law (p. 346)

justice of the peace the judge of a small, local court (p. 297)

juvenile a person not yet legally an adult (p. 375)

juvenile delinquent a child or teenager who commits a serious crime or repeatedly breaks the law (p. 375)

labor human effort directed toward producing goods and services (p. 425)

labor union association of workers organized to improve wages and working conditions (p. 486)

law of demand the concept that people are normally willing to buy less of a product if the price is high and more of it if the price is low (p. 449)

law of supply the principle that suppliers will normally offer more for sale at higher prices and less at lower prices (p. 463)

lawsuit a legal action in which a person or group sues to collect damages for some harm that is done (p. 349)

leak the release of secret government information by anonymous government officials to the media (p. 266)

legislative branch the lawmaking branch of government (p. 55)

legislature a group of people that makes laws (p. 29)

libel written untruths that are harmful to someone's reputation (pp. 101, 268)

limited liability when a business owner's responsibility for a company's debts is limited (p. 484)

line-item veto to veto only a specific part of a bill (p. 293)

lobbyist representative of an interest group who contacts lawmakers or other government officials directly to influence their policy making (pp. 152, 272)

lockout situation that occurs when management prevents workers from returning to work until they agree to a new contract (p. 489)

magistrate courts police courts generally located in larger towns, may handle traffic violations, civil cases involving small amounts of money, etc. (p. 297)

majority opinion a statement that presents the views of the majority of Supreme Court justices regarding a case (p. 208)

majority party in both the House of Representatives and the Senate, the political party to which more than half the members belong (p. 140)

majority rule political principle providing that a majority of the members of a community has the power to make laws binding upon all the people (p. 11)

mandatory spending federal spending required by law that continues without the need for annual approvals by Congress (p. 543)

marginal benefit the additional or extra benefit associated with an action (p. 413)

marginal cost the additional or extra opportunity cost associated with an action (p. 412)

market demand the total demand of all consumers for a product or service (p. 449)

GLOSSARY

market economy system in which individuals own the factors of production and make economic decisions through free interaction (pp. 416, 572)

market supply the total of all the supply schedules of all the businesses that provide the same good or service (p. 464)

mass media a mechanism of mass communication, including television, radio, newspapers, magazines, recordings, movies, and books (p. 259)

master plan a plan that states a set of goals and explains how the government will carry them out to meet changing needs over time (p. 327)

mediation situation in which union and company officials bring in a third party to try to help them reach an agreement (p. 489)

Medicare government program that provides health care for the aged (p. 544)

mercantilism the theory that a country should sell more goods to other countries than it buys (p. 33)

merger a combination of two or more companies to form a single business (p. 505)

merit system hiring people into government jobs on the basis of their qualifications (p. 185)

metropolitan area a large city and its surrounding suburbs (p. 311)

migration a mass movement of people from one area to another (p. 22)

minority party in both the House of Representatives and the Senate, the political party to which fewer than half the members belong (p. 140)

misdemeanor a relatively minor offense such as vandalism or stealing inexpensive items (pp. 297, 349)

mixed economy system combining characteristics of more than one type of economy (p. 575)

modified union shop an arrangement in which workers have the option to join a union after being hired (p. 488)

monarch king or queen (p. 28)

monetary policy policy that involves changing the rate of growth of the money supply in circulation in order to affect the cost and availability of credit (p. 531)

multinational firm that does business or has offices in many countries (p. 621)

national committee representatives from the 50 state party organizations who run a political party (p. 223)

national party chairperson individual elected by the national committee who manages the daily operations of the national party (p. 223)

national security the ability to keep the country safe from attack or harm (p. 175)

natural monopoly a market situation in which the costs of production are minimized by having a single firm produce the product (p. 505)

natural resources gifts of nature that make production possible (p. 424)

naturalization a legal process to obtain citizenship (p. 14)

needs requirements for survival, such as food, clothing, and shelter (p. 407)

newsgroups Internet discussion forums (p. 386)

nomination a process by which political parties select and offer candidates for public office (p. 227)

nonpartisan free from party ties or bias (p. 385)

North American Free Trade Agreement (NAFTA) trade agreement designed to reduce tariff barriers between Mexico, Canada, and the United States (p. 569)

open market operations purchase or sale of U.S. government bonds and Treasury bills (p. 532)

open primary an election in which voters need not declare their party preference to vote for the party's nominees (p. 228)

opinion a detailed explanation of the legal thinking behind a court's decision in a case (p. 197)

opportunity cost the cost of the next best alternative use of time and money when choosing to do one thing rather than another (p. 411)

ordinance a law, usually of a city or county (p. 308)

original jurisdiction the authority to hear cases for the first time (p. 196)

pardon a declaration of forgiveness and freedom from punishment (p. 172)

Parliament the British legislature (p. 29)

parliamentary system a system of government in which both executive and legislative functions reside in an elected assembly (p. 592)

parole to grant a prisoner an early release from prison, with certain restrictions (p. 294)

partnership a business owned by two or more people (p. 481)

patriotism the love for one's country (p. 23)

payroll tax tax on wages and salaries to finance Social Security and Medicare costs (p. 544)

peak period of prosperity in a business cycle in which economic activity is at its highest point (p. 509)

per capita GDP Gross Domestic Product per person (p. 573)

petition a formal request for government action; or, a process by which candidates who are not affiliated with one of the two major parties can get on the ballot for the general election in most states (pp. 100, 229)

plaintiff a person or party filing a lawsuit (pp. 298, 349, 364)

plank each individual part of a political party's platform (p. 222)

platform a series of statements expressing the party's principles, beliefs, and positions on election issues (p. 222)

plurality the most votes among all those running for a political office (p. 228)

GLOSSARY

pocket veto president's power to kill a bill, if Congress is not in session, by not signing it for 10 days (p. 161)

political action committee (PAC) political organization established by a corporation, labor union, or other special-interest group designed to support candidates by contributing money (pp. 250, 272)

political appointee a person appointed to a federal position by the president (p. 185)

political machine a strong party organization that can control political appointments and deliver votes (p. 226)

political party an association of voters with broad common interests who want to influence or control decision making in government by electing the party's candidates to public office (p. 218)

poll tax a sum of money required of voters before they are permitted to cast a ballot (p. 112)

polling place the location where voting is carried out (p. 237)

pollster a specialist whose job is to conduct polls regularly (p. 261)

popular sovereignty the notion that power lies with the people (p. 89)

pork-barrel projects government projects and grants that primarily benefit the home district or state (p. 155)

Preamble the opening section of the Constitution (p. 83)

precedent a ruling that is used as the basis for a judicial decision in a later, similar case (pp. 29, 197, 347)

precinct a geographic area that contains a specific number of voters (pp. 225, 237)

prime minister the leader of the executive branch of a parliamentary government (p. 592)

print media newspapers, magazines, newsletters, and books (p. 264)

prior restraint government censorship of material before it is published (p. 268)

priorities the goals a community considers most important or most urgent (p. 326)

private goods goods that, when consumed by one individual, cannot be consumed by another (p. 502)

private property rights the freedom to own and use our own property as we choose as long as we do not interfere with the rights of others (p. 435)

product market a market where producers offer goods and services for sale (p. 429)

productivity the degree to which resources are being used efficiently to produce goods and services (pp. 430, 467)

profit the money a business receives for its products or services over and above its costs (pp. 436, 464)

profit motive the driving force that encourages individuals and organizations to improve their material well-being (p. 436)

progressive income tax a tax that takes a larger percentage of higher incomes than lower incomes (p. 518)

propaganda certain ideas that may involve misleading messages designed to manipulate people (pp. 247, 390)

property tax tax on land and property (p. 550)

proposition a petition asking for a new law (p. 242)

protectionism policy of trade restrictions to protect domestic industries (p. 611)

public agenda issues considered most significant by government officials (p. 265)

public goods economic goods that are consumed collectively, such as highways and national defense (p. 502)

public interest group an organization that supports causes that affect the lives of Americans in general (p. 271)

public opinion the ideas and attitudes that most people hold about elected officials, candidates, government, and political issues (p. 258)

public opinion poll a survey in which individuals are asked to answer questions about a particular issue or person (p. 261)

public policy the course of action the government takes in response to an issue or problem (pp. 9, 272, 324)

quota a limit on the amount of foreign goods imported into a country (p. 566)

racial profiling singling out an individual as a suspect due to appearance of ethnicity (p. 115)

ratify to vote approval of (p. 41)

rational choice choosing the alternative that has the greatest value from among comparable-quality products (p. 419)

real GDP GDP after adjustments for inflation (p. 509)

recall a special election in which citizens can vote to remove a public official from office; situation in which a company pulls a product off the market or agrees to change it to make it safe (pp. 242, 506)

recession part of the business cycle in which the nation's output does not grow for at least six months (p. 509)

recycling reusing old materials to make new ones (p. 335)

referendum a way for citizens to vote on state or local laws (p. 242)

rehabilitate to correct a person's behavior (p. 376)

remand to send a case back to a lower court to be tried again (p. 197)

repeal to cancel a law (p. 34)

representative democracy a government in which citizens choose a smaller group to govern on their behalf (p. 10)

reprieve an order to delay a person's punishment until a higher court can hear the case (p. 172)

reserve a certain percentage of deposits that banks have to set aside as cash in their own vaults or as deposits in their Federal Reserve district bank (p. 532)

reserved powers powers that the Constitution does not give to the national government that are kept by the states (pp. 92, 283)

GLOSSARY

resources the money, people, and materials available to accomplish a community's goals (p. 326)

responsibility an obligation that we fulfill voluntarily (p. 120)

returns ballots and results of an election (p. 238)

revenue the income that a government collects for public use (p. 398)

rider a completely unrelated amendment tacked on to a bill (p. 159)

right-to-work laws state laws forbidding unions from forcing workers to join (p. 488)

roll-call vote a voting method in the Senate in which members voice their votes in turn (p. 161)

rule of law principle that the law applies to everyone, even those who govern (p. 90)

runoff primary second primary election between the two candidates who received the most votes in the first primary election (p. 228)

sales tax tax levied on a product at the time of sale (p. 549)

sanction measure such as withholding economic aid used to influence a foreign government's actions (p. 625)

satellite nation politically and economically dominated or controlled by another, more powerful country (p. 626)

saving to set aside income for a period of time so that it can be used later (p. 441)

savings account an account in which customers receive interest based on how much money they have deposited (p. 535)

savings and loan association (S&L) financial institutions that traditionally loaned money to people buying homes (p. 526)

scarcity not having enough resources to produce all of the things we would like to have (p. 407)

search warrant a court order allowing law enforcement officers to search a suspect's home or business and take specific items as evidence (pp. 103, 355)

segregation the social separation of the races (p. 113)

seniority years of service, which is used as a consideration for assigning committee members (p. 144)

separation of powers the split of authority among the legislative, executive, and judicial branches (p. 91)

services work performed by a person for someone else (p. 424)

shortage situation in which quantity demanded is greater than quantity supplied (p. 472)

slander spoken untruths that are harmful to someone's reputation (p. 101)

social responsibility the obligation a business has to pursue goals that benefit society as well as themselves (p. 494)

Social Security federal program that provides monthly payments to people who are retired or unable to work (p. 544)

socialism economic system in which government owns some factors of production and distributes the products and wages (p. 574)

soft money donations given to political parties and not designated for a particular candidate's election campaign (p. 249)

sole proprietorship a business owned and operated by a single person (p. 480)

solid waste the technical name for garbage (p. 334)

special district a unit of government that deals with a specific function, such as education, water supply, or transportation (p. 310)

special-interest group an organization of people with some common interest who try to influence government decisions (p. 158)

specialization when people, businesses, regions, and/or nations concentrate on goods and services that they can produce better than anyone else (p. 431)

spoils system rewarding people with government jobs on the basis of their political support (p. 185)

standard of living the material well-being of an individual, group, or nation measured by how well their necessities and luxuries are satisfied (p. 427)

standing committees permanent committees that continue their work from session to session in Congress (p. 143)

stare decisis the practice of using earlier judicial rulings as a basis for deciding cases (pp. 209, 352)

statute a law written by a legislative branch (p. 347)

stock ownership share of a corporation (p. 482)

stockholder an individual who has invested in a corporation and owns some of its stock (p. 483)

strike when workers deliberately stop working in order to force an employer to give in to their demands (p. 489)

strong-mayor system a type of government, usually in large cities, under which the mayor has strong executive powers (p. 308)

subsidize to aid or promote with money (p. 551)

subsidy a government payment to an individual, business, or group in exchange for certain actions (p. 468)

substitute a competing product that consumers can use in place of another (p. 454)

suffrage the right to vote (p. 111)

summons a notice directing someone to appear in court to answer a complaint or a charge (p. 365)

supply the amount of goods and services that producers are able and willing to sell at various prices during a specified time period (p. 462)

supply curve upward-sloping line that graphically shows the quantities supplied at each possible price (p. 463)

supply elasticity responsiveness of quantity supplied to a change in price (p. 469)

supply schedule table showing quantities supplied at different possible prices (p. 463)

surplus situation in which quantity supplied is greater than quantity demanded; situation in which government spends less than it collects in revenues (pp. 472, 553)

tariff a customs duty; a tax on an imported good (p. 566)

tax return annual report filed with local, state, or federal government detailing income earned and taxes owed (p. 543)

technology the methods or processes used to make goods and services (p. 467)

terrorism the use of violence by groups against civilians to achieve a political goal (p. 23)

testimony the statement a witness makes under oath (p. 372)

third party a party that challenges the two major parties (p. 219)

Three-fifths Compromise agreement providing that enslaved persons would count as three-fifths of other persons in determining representation in Congress (p. 57)

tolerance respecting and accepting others, regardless of their beliefs, practices, or differences (p. 123)

torts wrongful acts for which an injured party has the right to sue (p. 350)

totalitarian a system in which government control extends to almost all aspects of people's lives (p. 589)

town political unit that is larger than a village and smaller than a city (p. 315)

town meeting a gathering of local citizens to discuss and vote on important issues (p. 316)

township a subdivision of a county that has its own government (p. 317)

trade deficit situation in which the value of the products imported by a country exceeds the value of its exports (p. 570)

trade sanction an effort to punish another nation by imposing trade barriers (p. 177)

trade surplus situation in which the value of the products exported by a country exceeds the value of its imports (p. 570)

trade-off the alternative you face if you decide to do one thing rather than another (p. 410)

traditional economy an economic system in which the decisions of what, how, and for whom to produce are based on custom or habit (p. 578)

transparency process of making business deals more visible to everyone (p. 493)

treaty a formal agreement between the governments of two or more countries (p. 177)

tuition vouchers program providing subsidies for education payments, allowing families the option of sending students to private schools (p. 331)

two-party system a system of government in which two parties compete for power (p. 218)

unemployment rate the percentage of people in the civilian labor force who are not working but are looking for jobs (p. 510)

unicameral one-house legislature (p. 287)

union shop company that requires new employees to join a union after a specific period of time (p. 488)

unitary system government that gives all key powers to the national or central government (p. 597)

unlimited liability when a business owner is personally and fully responsible for all losses and debts of the business (p. 481)

utility the amount of satisfaction one gets from a good or service (p. 450)

veto refusal to sign a bill or resolution (pp. 161, 618)

voice vote a voting method in which those in favor say "Yea" and those against say "No" (p. 161)

voluntary exchange the act of buyers and sellers freely and willingly engaging in market transactions (p. 436)

volunteerism the practice of offering your time and services to others without payment (p. 126)

wants things we would like to have, such as entertainment, vacations, and items that make life comfortable and enjoyable (p. 407)

ward several adjoining precincts making up a larger election unit (p. 225)

warranty the promise made by a manufacturer or a seller to repair or replace a product within a certain time period if it is faulty (p. 440)

weak-mayor system a type of government under which the mayor has limited executive powers (p. 308)

Web site a "page" on the World Wide Web that may contain text, images, audio, and video (p. 384)

welfare the health, prosperity, and happiness of the members of a community (p. 126)

winner-take-all system a system in which the candidate who wins the popular vote in a state usually receives all of the state's electoral votes (p. 243)

Women, Infants, and Children (WIC) program a program that provides help for nutrition and health care to low-income women, infants, and children up to age 5 (p. 517)

workfare programs that require welfare recipients to exchange some of their labor in return for benefits (p. 517)

World Bank international agency that makes loans to developing nations (p. 580)

World Trade Organization (WTO) an international body that oversees trade among nations (p. 569)

World Wide Web operating within the Internet, it allows users to interact with the billions of documents stored on computers across the Net (p. 384)

writ of habeas corpus a court order that requires police to bring a prisoner to court to explain why they are holding the person (pp. 150, 353)

GLOSSARY

absentee ballot/voto por correspondencia–censorship/censura

A

absentee ballot/voto por correspondencia papeleta de votación que permite a una persona votar sin estar en el centro electoral en el día de las elecciones (pág. 238)

absolute monarch/monarca absoluto un monarca que tiene poder completo e ilimitado para regir a su pueblo (pág. 589)

acid rain/lluvia ácida lluvia que contiene grandes cantidades de contaminación química (pág. 614)

acquittal/absolución voto de no culpable (pág. 373)

affirmative action/acción afirmativa programas intencionados para compensar la discriminación anterior ayudando a grupos minoritarios y a mujeres a conseguir acceso a trabajos y oportunidades (pág. 115)

alien/extranjero persona viviendo en un país del cual no es ciudadana (pág. 15)

ambassador/embajador representante oficial del gobierno de un país (pág. 177)

amend/enmendar cambiar (pág. 41)

amendment/enmienda cambio a la Constitución (pág. 85)

amnesty/amnistía indulto a un grupo de individuos por una ofensa en contra del gobierno (pág. 172)

Anti-Federalists/antifederalistas los que se oponen a la Constitución (pág. 59)

antitrust law/ley antimonopolista legislación para prevenir la formación de nuevos monopolios y controlar los que ya existen (pág. 505)

apartheid/segregación racial sistema de leyes que separaban a grupos raciales y étnicos y limitaban los derechos de los negros en África del Sur (pág. 625)

apathy/apatía falta de interés (pág. 240)

appeals court/tribunal de apelación una corte que revisa las decisiones tomadas por las cortes federales menores (pág. 197)

appellate jurisdiction/jurisdicción de apelación la autoridad de una corte para ver un caso apelado de una corte menor (pág. 197)

apportion/asignar dividir entre distritos (pág. 289)

appropriations bill/ley de apropiación legislación asignando reservas para ciertos propósitos (pág. 543)

arbitration/arbitraje situación que oficiales del sindicato y la compañía entregan a un tercer partido asuntos en los que ellos no están de acuerdo para que éste tome una decisión final (pág. 489)

archives/archivos expedientes de historias antiguas (pág. 385)

arraignment/acusación audiencia en la cual un sospechoso es acusado y éste se declara inocente o culpable (pág. 372)

articles of partnership/artículos de asociación papeles legales formales especificando el arreglo entre socios (pág. 481)

at-large election/elecciones generales votación para toda un área, por ejemplo votación estatal (pág. 309)

authoritarian/autoritario gobierno en que un líder o grupo de personas lleva poder absoluto (págs. 389, 588)

automatic stabilizer/estabilizador automático programa que automáticamente proporciona beneficios para compensar un cambio en el ingreso de la gente (pág. 556)

B

bail/fianza cantidad de dinero usado como depósito para asegurar que una persona acusada regrese para su juicio (págs. 105, 357)

balance of trade/balance de comercio la diferencia entre el valor de las exportaciones y las importaciones de una nación (pág. 570)

balanced budget/presupuesto balanceado presupuesto anual en que los gastos igualan las rentas (pág. 554)

ballot/boleta para votar papel que se usa para votar (pág. 237)

bicameral/bicameral legislatura que consiste de dos partes o cámaras (págs. 39, 139)

bill of attainder/pena de ejecución ley que castiga a una persona acusada de un crimen sin juicio o audiencia imparcial en una corte (págs. 150, 353)

Bill of Rights/Declaración de Derechos las primeras diez enmiendas (pág. 85)

board of directors/mesa directiva personas elegidas por los accionistas para tomar decisiones en su nombre (pág. 483)

bond/bono contrato para pagar dinero prestado con intereses en una fecha especificada en el futuro (pág. 554)

boycott/boicoteo rechazo para comprar ciertos bienes (pág. 34)

brief/expediente documento escrito explicando la postura de un partido u otro en un caso (pág. 208)

budget/presupuesto plan para ganar y gastar dinero (págs. 9, 542)

budget resolution/resolución presupuestaria documento emitido por el congreso que indica los gastos e ingresos totales de un año y cuánto será gastado en varias categorías (pág. 543)

bureaucracy/burocracia sistemas complejos con muchos departamentos, muchas reglas y muchas personas en la serie del mando (pág. 126)

business cycle/ciclo de negocios períodos que experimenta la economía alternando entre incremento y decremento (pág. 509)

C

cabinet/gabinete grupo de asesores al presidente que incluye los directores de 14 departamentos ejecutivos al nivel superior (pág. 181)

capital/capital productos anteriormente manufacturados usados para producir otros bienes y servicios (pág. 424)

capitalism/capitalismo sistema en que ciudadanos privados son propietarios de la mayoría o todos de los medios de producción y deciden cómo usarlos entre límites legislados (págs. 417, 434)

casework/proyecto particular trabajo que hace un legislador para ayudar a sus constituyentes con un problema (pág. 154)

caucus/junta electoral junta de los miembros de un partido político para conducir el negocio del partido (pág. 224)

censorship/censura prohibir impresos o películas debido a ideas ofensivas (pág. 99)

census/censo cuenta de la población tomada por el Departamento del Censo (pág. 139)

central bank/banco central institución que presta dinero a otros bancos y el lugar donde el gobierno conduce su negocio bancario (pág. 529)

certificate of deposit/certificado de depósito depósito que indica la cantidad del depósito, fecha de vencimiento, y la taza de interés que será pagada (pág. 535)

charter/carta de privilegio documento escrito otorgando tierra y la autoridad para establecer gobiernos coloniales; o un documento gubernamental otorgando permiso para organizar una sociedad anónima (pág. 482)

charter schools/escuelas a carta de privilegio escuelas que reciben fondos estatales pero que no tienen que cumplir con muchos de los reglamentos de las escuelas públicas (pág. 330)

checking account/cuenta de cheques cuenta de la cual el dinero depositado puede ser sacado en cualquier tiempo escribiendo un cheque (pág. 535)

checks and balances/control y balances sistema en el cual cada ramo del gobierno puede controlar o restringir los poderes de los demás (pág. 91)

circuit/circuito el área de jurisdicción de un tribunal federal de apelación (pág. 197)

citizens/ciudadanos miembros de la comunidad que deben lealtad al gobierno y merecen su protección (pág. 6)

city charter/carta municipal documento otorgando el poder a un gobierno local (pág. 306)

civics/civismo el estudio de los derechos y deberes de ciudadanos (pág. 6)

civil liberties/libertades civiles libertad para pensar y actuar sin la interferencia gubernamental o temor de trato injusto bajo la ley (pág. 98)

civil rights/derechos civiles los derechos de plena ciudadanía e igualdad bajo la ley (pág. 113)

civil service system/sistema de servicio civil la práctica de emplear a trabajadores gubernamentales basada en examinaciones abiertas y competitivas y en el mérito (pág. 185)

civil service worker/trabajador de servicio civil personas empleadas para puestos federales (pág. 185)

civilian labor force/fuerza laboral civil civiles de 16 años de edad o mayores que trabajan o buscan trabajo (pág. 510)

closed primary/elección primaria cerrada una elección en la cual solamente los miembros declarados de un partido son permitidos a votar por los candidatos de este partido (pág. 228)

closed shop/taller cerrado empresa en la cual solamente los miembros del sindicato pueden ser empleados (pág. 488)

cloture/clausura procedimiento usado en el Senado para limitar debate en un proyecto de ley (pág. 159)

coin/moneda forma metálica de dinero, en EEUU *penny, nickel,* y *dime* (pág. 525)

Cold War/Guerra Fría conflicto entre Estados Unidos y la Unión Soviética desde fines de los años 1940 hasta fines de los años 1980 cuando los dos países competían por influencia mundial sin acción militar declarada (pág. 626)

collective bargaining/negociación colectiva proceso por el cual los sindicatos y empleadores negocian las condiciones del empleo (pág. 488)

collective farm/granja colectiva granja en la cual la tierra es propiedad del gobierno pero que está alquilada a una familia (pág. 601)

colony/colonia grupo de gente en un lugar regida por un país patrocinador en otra parte (pág. 30)

command economy/economía de mando sistema económico en que las decisiones económicas más importantes son tomadas por el gobierno central (pág. 574)

commercial bank/banco comercial instituciones financieras que ofrecen servicios bancarios completos a individuos y negocios (pág. 526)

common law/derecho consuetudinario sistema de leyes basado en precedente y costumbre (pág. 346)

communism/comunismo sistema económico en que el gobierno central dirige todas las decisiones económicas más importantes (pág. 574)

community/comunidad grupo de personas que comparten los mismos intereses y preocupaciones (pág. 125)

commute/conmutar reducir la sentencia de un criminal (pág. 294)

compact/convenio acuerdo o contrato entre un grupo de personas (pág. 31)

comparative advantage/ventaja comparativa la habilidad de un país para producir un bien a un costo de oportunidad más baja a la que otro país lo puede producir (pág. 565)

competition/competencia lucha entre compradores y vende-dores para conseguir los mejores productos a precios más bajos (pág. 435)

complaint/queja noticia formal de que se está llevando una demanda (pág. 365)

complement/complemento producto usado a menudo con otro producto (pág. 454)

concurrent jurisdiction/jurisdicción concurrente casos en que las cortes estatales y federales comparten la jurisdicción (pág. 195)

concurrent powers/poderes concurrentes poderes compartidos por los gobiernos estatales y federales (pág. 284)

concurring opinion/acuerdo de opiniones declaración escrita por un juez que vota con la mayoría pero por diferentes razones (pág. 208)

confederation/confederación grupo de individuos o gobiernos estatales (pág. 40)

conservation/conservación cuidado de la preservación y protección de los recursos naturales (págs. 335, 614)

constituent/constituyente residente de un distrito electoral (pág. 139)

constitution/constitución plan escrito detallado para el gobierno (pág. 39)

constitutional/constitucional leyes o acciones por los fun-cionarios de gobierno permitidas por la Constitución (pág. 202)

Constitutional Convention/Convención Constitucional reunión de delegados estatales en 1787 impulsando la adopción de una nueva Constitución (pág. 54)

constitutional monarchy/monarquía constitucional sistema en el cual el poder del gobernante hereditario está limitado por la constitución y las leyes de un país (pág. 590)

consumer price index/índice de precios de consumo medida del cambio del precio tras el tiempo de un grupo específico de servicios y bienes (pág. 511)

consumer sovereignty/soberanía del consumidor papel del consumidor como gobernante del mercado, determinando cuáles productos serán producidos (pág. 435)

consumerism/protección al consumidor movimiento para educar a los compradores sobre las compras que hacen y para demandar de los manufactureros productos mejores y más seguros (pág. 439)

cooperative/cooperativa asociación voluntaria de personas formada para llevar a cabo algún tipo de actividad económica que beneficiará a sus miembros (pág. 485)

copyright/derecho de autor derecho exclusivo del autor para controlar, publicar, y vender una obra original (pág. 396)

corporation/sociedad anónima tipo de organización de negocio propiedad de un grupo de personas pero tratada por la ley como si fuera una persona (pág. 482)

cost-benefit analysis/análisis de costos y ganancias modelo económico que requiere la comparación entre los costos y los beneficios marginales de una decisión (pág. 413)

county/condado normalmente el territorio y subdivisión política más grande de un estado (pág. 312)

county chairperson/presidente del condado persona que dirige el comité del condado, a menudo llevando mucho poder político en el condado (pág. 225)

county seat/capital del condado un pueblo donde está localizada la corte del condado (pág. 312)

credit union/asociación de crédito servicio cooperativo sin fin lucrativo que acepta depósitos, hace préstamos, y proporciona otros servicios financieros (pág. 526)

crime/crimen acto criminal que rompe con las leyes y perjudica a gente o a la sociedad en general (pág. 368)

cross-examine/interrogar proceso de cuestionamiento a un testigo en una audiencia o juicio para afirmar o desacreditar el testimonio (pág. 372)

currency/dinero corriente monedas y dinero en papel (pág. 525)

debt/deuda dinero prestado y aún no pagado (pág. 554)

defendant/defensor individuo o grupo siendo demandado o acusado de un crímen (págs. 298, 349, 364)

deficit/déficit situación en la cual el gobierno gasta más que lo que colecta en ingresos (pág. 553)

delegate/delegado representante para una junta (págs. 35, 224)

demand/demanda el deseo, buena voluntad, y capacidad para comprar un bien o servicio (pág. 448)

demand curve/curva de demanda línea inclinada hacia abajo que gráficamente demuestra las cantidades demandadas de cada precio posible (pág. 449)

demand elasticity/elasticidad de demanda medida de interés relacionando cambios en las cantidades demandadas a cambios del precio (pág. 455)

demand schedule/tabla de demanda gráfica demostrando las cantidades demandadas a los diferentes precios posibles (pág. 449)

democracy/democracia gobierno en que los ciudadanos mantienen el poder para gobernar (pág. 10)

deport/deportar mandar a un extranjero o inmigrante de regreso a su país (pág. 17)

developing country/país en desarrollo un país cuyo el ingreso promedio por cápita es solamente una fracción del de países más industrializados (pág. 578)

devolution/devolución renuncia de poderes a las autoridades locales por un gobierno central (pág. 597)

dictator/dictador gobernante que ejerce el control completo sobre un estado (pág. 589)

dictatorship/dictadura gobierno controlado por una persona o un pequeño grupo de personas (pág. 10)

diminishing marginal utility/decremento de utilidad marginal principio de que la satisfacción adicional, o utilidad marginal, del consumidor tiende a decrementar mientras consume más unidades (pág. 451)

direct democracy/democracia directa forma de democracia en la cual las personas votan directamente (pág. 10)

direct primary/elección primaria directa elección en la cual los votantes eligen candidatos para representar cada partido en una elección general (pág. 227)

discount rate/tipo reducido tipo de interés que el Banco Federal cobra en sus préstamos (pág. 532)

discretionary income/ingresos discrecionales ingreso que sobra después de que las necesidades han sido compradas y pagadas (pág. 440)

discretionary spending/gasto discrecional gastos para los programas federales que deben recibir autorización anual (pág. 543)

discrimination/discriminación trato injusto basado en prejuicio en contra de cierto grupo (págs. 113, 493)

disposable income/ingreso disponible ingreso que sobra después de que todos los impuestos han sido pagados (pág. 440)

dissenting opinion/opinión disidente declaración escrita que presenta la opinión de un juez que está en desacuerdo con la opinión mayoritaria (pág. 208)

dissident group/grupo disidente personas en desacuerdo con el sistema político o religioso establecido (pág. 389)

district courts/tribunal federal cortes federales donde los juicios se llevan a cabo y las demandas se inician (pág. 196)

division of labor/división de trabajo desglose de un rabajo en distintas tareas más pequeñas que se harán individualmente (pág. 431)

docket/registro calendario de la corte demostrando el horario de los casos que se verán (pág. 207)

double jeopardy/riesgo doble exponiendo a alguien en un juicio por un crimen del cual estuvo anteriormente absuelto (págs. 104, 355)

double taxation/impuesto doble pagando dos veces impuestos sobre las ganancias de una empresa (pág. 484)

draft/destacamento llamar a personas al servicio militar (pág. 121)

due process/proceso correspondiente siguiendo procedimientos legales establecidos (pág. 104)

due process of law/proceso legal correspondiente procedimientos establecidos por ley y garantizados por la Constitución (pág. 353)

duty/deberes cosas que estamos requeridos a hacer (pág. 120)

dynasty/dinastía línea de gobernantes de la misma familia (pág. 599)

Earned Income Tax Credit (EITC)/crédito del impuesto sobre ingreso ganado programa que les da créditos del impuesto y hasta pagos al contado a trabajadores elegibles (pág. 518)

economic interdependence/interdependencia económica depender de otros, así como ellos dependen de ti, para proveer bienes y servicios para ser consumidos (pág. 432)

economic model/modelo económico representación simplificada del mundo real desarrollada por economistas para describir cómo la economía funciona y debe de funcionar en el futuro (pág. 408)

economics/economía estudio de cómo los individuos y las naciones toman decisiones sobre la manera de usar recursos escasos para satisfacer sus necesidades y deseos (pág. 406)

elastic clause/cláusula elástica cláusula en Artículo I, Sección 8 de la Constitución que da al Congreso el derecho de hacer todas las leyes "propias y necesarias" para llevar sus poderes explícitos (pág. 146)

elector/elector personas designadas para votar en las elecciones presidenciales por los candidatos principales (págs. 167, 243)

Electoral College/Colegio Electoral grupo de personas nombradas por la legislatura de cada estado para elegir al presidente y vicepresidente (págs. 58, 167, 243)

electorate/electorado todas las personas que son elegibles para votar (pág. 240)

electronic media/medios de comunicación electrónicos radio, televisión e Internet (pág. 264)

embargo/embargo acuerdo entre un grupo de naciones que les prohibe comerciar con una nación señalada (pág. 177)

eminent domain/dominio eminente derecho del gobierno de tomar propiedad privada para el uso público (pág. 105)

entitlement program/programa de derechos programa utilizando requerimientos de elegibilidad para proporcionar reservas para salud, nutrición o ingresos a individuos (pág. 551)

entrepreneurs/empresarios individuos que forman negocios nuevos, introducen productos nuevos, y mejoran técnicas de manejo (pág. 426)

equilibrium price/precio de equilibrio precio en que la cantidad que los productores están dispuestos a ofrecer es igual a la cantidad que los consumidores están dispuestos a comprar (pág. 473)

ethical behavior/conducta ética la responsabilidad de los consumidores para respetar los derechos de los productores y vendedores (pág. 440)

European Union/Unión Europea organización de las naciones europeas cuyo el objetivo es para dirigir la integración económica como un solo mercado (pág. 567)

ex post facto law/ley con efecto retroactivo ley que permitiría a una persona ser castigada por una acción que no estaba en contra de la ley cuando fue cometida (págs. 150, 353)

exchange rate/tipo de cambio el precio de la moneda de una nación en términos de la moneda de otra nación (pág. 569)

exclusive jurisdiction/jurisdicción exclusiva casos en los cuales solo las cortes federales tienen jurisdicción (pág. 195)

executive agreement/acuerdo ejecutivo un acuerdo entre el presidente y el líder de otro país (pág. 177)

executive branch/ramo ejecutivo el ramo del gobierno que lleva las leyes (pág. 55)

executive order/órden ejecutiva un mandato que tiene la fuerza de la ley (pág. 172)

exit poll/encuesta de votación una encuesta llevada en los centros electorales de cómo la gente votó (pág. 239)

expansion/expansión parte del ciclo comercial en que la actividad económica aumenta (pág. 509)

export/exportación vender bienes a otros países; o bienes producidos en un país y después vendidos a otro (pág. 564)

expressed powers/poderes explícitos poderes que el Congreso tiene que están específicamente nombrados en la Constitución (págs. 92, 146)

externality/exterioridad el efecto no intencionado de una acción que afecta a una persona no involucrada en una acción (pág. 503)

factor market/mercado de factores mercado donde los recursos productivos son comprados y vendidos (pág. 428)

factors of production/factores de producción recursos necesarios para producir bienes y servicios (pág. 424)

federal bureaucracy/burocracia federal todos los empleados y las agencias del ramo ejecutivo (pág. 183)

Federal Deposit Insurance Corporation (FDIC)/Corporación Federal de Seguros de Depósitos agencia federal que asegura cuentas individuales en instituciones financieras hasta $100,000 (pág. 527)

Federal Open Market Committee (FOMC)/Comité Federal del Mercado Abierto el comité más poderoso del Fed porque toma las decisiones que afectan la economía como un todo manipulando el abasto de dinero (pág. 530)

federal system/sistema federal la participación del poder entre los gobiernos central y estatales (pág. 282)

federalism/federalismo forma de gobierno en que el poder es dividido entre el gobierno federal, o nacional, y los gobiernos estatales (pág. 58)

Federalists/federalistas los que apoyan la Constitución (pág. 58)

felony/felonía un delito mayor tal como asesinato, violación, rapto o robo (págs. 298, 349)

filibuster/filibustero un atentado para derrotar un proyecto de ley en el Senado hablando continuamente hasta que el patrocinador del proyecto lo retira (pág. 159)

financial capital/capital financiero dinero utilizado para comprar las herramientas y equipos usados en producción (pág. 481)

fiscal policy/política fiscal el uso por el gobierno federal de políticas de gastos e impuestos para afectar a la actividad empresarial (pág. 510)

fiscal year/año fiscal período de planeación de 12 meses que puede no coincidir con el año del calendario (pág. 542)

food stamps/estampillas para alimentos cupones emitidos por el gobierno que pueden ser usados para comprar alimentos (pág. 517)

foreign policy/política extranjera el plan de una nación para tratar con otras naciones (pág. 175)

franking privilege/privilegio de franqueo el derecho de senadores y representantes de enviar cartas relacionadas con el trabajo sin el pago de estampillas de correo (pág. 152)

free enterprise/empresa libre sistema económico en que individuos y empresas están permitidos a competir para beneficiarse con una mínima interferencia del gobierno (págs. 417, 434)

SPANISH GLOSSARY

free trade/libre comercio política de reducción de barreras al intercambio comercial (pág. 567)

genocide/genocidio asesinatos masivos de personas por causa de su raza, religión, etnia, política o cultura (pág. 624)

gerrymander/*gerrymander* un distrito electoral con forma irregular formado para aumentar la fuerza de votación de un grupo en particular (pág. 139)

globalization/globalización individuos y naciones trabajando a través de las barreras de la distancia, cultura y tecnología (pág. 621)

goods/bienes productos tangibles que usamos para satisfacer nuestras necesidades y deseos (pág. 424)

government/gobierno la autoridad reglamentaria para una comunidad (pág. 7)

government corporation/corporación gubernamental empresas propias y operadas por el gobierno federal (pág. 184)

grand jury/jurado de acusación grupo de ciudadanos que deciden si hay evidencia suficiente para acusar a alguien de un crimen (págs. 104, 355)

grants-in-aid/otorgaciones federales concesión de dinero para los estados por el gobierno federal (pág. 285)

Great Compromise/Gran Compromiso acuerdo proporcionando un sistema dual de representación en el Congreso (pág. 56)

Gross Domestic Product (GDP)/producto doméstico bruto valor total en dólares de todos los bienes y servicios al consumidor producidos en un país durante un solo año (pág. 426)

home rule/gobierno autónomo permitir a las ciudades desarrollar sus documentos de incorporación, escoger su tipo de gobierno y manejar sus asuntos (pág. 307)

human rights/derechos humanos libertades fundamentales (pág. 602)

hung jury/deber incumplido un jurado que no puede acordarse en un veredicto (pág. 373)

immigrant/inmigrante una persona que se traslada permanentemente a un nuevo país (pág. 15)

impeach/acusar acusar a oficiales del gobierno de mala conducta en su oficina (pág. 148)

implied powers/poderes implícitos poderes que tiene el Congreso pero que no están nombrados específicamente en la Constitución (pág. 146)

import/importación bienes comprados de un país por otro (pág. 564)

incentive/incentivo gratificación ofrecida para persuadir a la gente de tomar ciertas acciones económicas (pág. 417)

income tax/impuesto sobre utilidades impuesto en el ingreso neto de la gente (pág. 85)

incorporate/incorporada recibir una carta estatal, reconociendo oficialmente el gobierno de una localidad (pág. 306)

incumbent/actual un político que ya ha sido elegido para un puesto (pág. 250)

independence/independencia auto-dependencia y libertad de control exterior (pág. 36)

independent agency/agencia independiente comités y mesas directivas federales que no son parte de ningún departamento del gabinete (pág. 184)

indictment/acusación cargo formal por un jurado de acusación (pág. 104)

inflation/inflación incremento sostenido del nivel general de precios (pág. 511)

infrastructure/infraestructura el sistema de caminos, puentes, alcantarillados y agua de una comunidad (pág. 326)

initiative/iniciativa procedimieto por el cual los ciudadanos pueden proponer nuevas leyes o enmiendas a la constitución estatal (pág. 242)

injunction/entredicho una orden de la corte que manda que una persona o un grupo detenga cierta acción (pág. 365)

intellectual property/propiedad intelectual cosas que las personas crean, tales como canciones, libros, poesía, arte y software (pág. 396)

interest/interés el pago que la gente recibe cuando presta dinero o permite a otra persona usar su dinero (pág. 442)

interest group/grupo de interés grupo de personas que comparten sus puntos de vista sobre un tema, unidas para promover sus creencias (pág. 259)

intergovernmental revenues/ingresos intergubernamentales fondos que recibe el gobierno de un nivel del gobierno de otro nivel (pág. 548)

International Monetary Fund (IMF)/Fondo Monetario Internacional agencia que ofrece consejo monetario y provee préstamos a naciones en desarrollo (pág. 580)

international tribunal/tribunal internacional corte con autoridad para ver casos sobre violaciones de derechos humanos (pág. 624)

internationalism/internacionalismo participación en asuntos mundiales (pág. 617)

Internet/Internet sistema de comunicación masiva de millones de redes computacionales e informativa por todo el mundo (pág. 384)

joint resolution/resolución colectiva resolución es aprobada por ambas cámaras del Congreso (pág. 157)

judicial branch/ramo judicial ramo del gobierno que interpreta las leyes (pág. 56)

judicial review/revisión judicial poder de la Suprema Corte para determinar para determinar si una ley federal, estatal o local o acción de gobierno viola la Constitución (pág. 202)

jurisdiction/jurisdicción autoridad de una corte para ver y decidir casos (pág. 194)

jurisprudence/jurisprudencia estudio del derecho (pág. 346)

justice of the peace/juez de paz juez de una corte local y pequeña (pág. 297)

juvenile/juvenil una persona que todavía no es adulta legalmente (pág. 375)

juvenile delinquent/delincuente juvenil joven que comete un crimen grave o infringe la ley frecuentemente (pág. 375)

labor/trabajo esfuerzo humano dirigido hacia producir bienes y servicios (pág. 425)

labor union/sindicato asociación de trabajadores organizados para mejorar salarios y condiciones laborales (pág. 486)

law of demand/ley de demanda concepto que la gente normalmente está dispuesta a comprar menos de un producto si el precio es alto y más si el precio es bajo (pág. 449)

law of supply/ley de oferta principio que productores normalmente ofrecerán más para vender a precios altos y menos para vender a precios bajos (pág. 463)

lawsuit/juicio acción legal en que una persona o grupo demanda para cobrar por un daño (pág. 349)

leak/filtración comunicación de información gubernamental secreta por oficiales anónimos de gobierno a los medios informativos (pág. 266)

legislative branch/ramo legislativo ramo del gobierno que hace las leyes (pág. 55)

legislature/legislatura grupo de personas que hacen las leyes (pág. 29)

libel/difamación escritos falsos que son dañinos para la reputación de una persona (págs. 101, 268)

limited liability/responsabilidad limitada requerimiento en que la responsabilidad de un propietario por las deudas de una empresa es limitada (pág. 484)

line-item veto/veto particular vetar solamente una parte específica de una ley (pág. 293)

lobbyist/agenta de presión representantes de grupos de interés que comunican directamente con legisladores u otros oficiales de gobierno para influenciar su política (págs. 152, 272)

lockout/cierre patronal situación que ocurre cuando la dirección previene a los trabajadores de regresar a su trabajo mientras llegan a un acuerdo para el nuevo contrato (pág. 489)

magistrate courts/cortes magistrales corte policiaca generalmente localizada en ciudades grandes que pueden manejar violaciones de tráfico, casos civiles involucrando pequeñas cantidades de dinero, etc. (pág. 297)

majority opinion/opinión mayoritaria declaración que presenta la opinión general de la mayoría de los jueces de la Suprema Corte sobre un caso (pág. 208)

majority party/partido mayoritario en el Senado y la Cámara de Representantes el partido político al que pertenecen más de la mitad de los miembros (pág. 140)

majority rule/reglamento mayoritario principio político que estipula que la mayoría de una comunidad tiene el poder para hacer leyes obligatorias para toda la gente (pág. 12)

mandatory spending/gastos obligatorios gastos federales requeridos por ley que continúan sin la necesidad de aprobaciones anuales del Congreso (pág. 543)

marginal benefit/beneficio marginal beneficio adicional o extra asociado con una acción (pág. 413)

marginal cost/gasto marginal costo adicional o extra de oportunidad asociado con una acción (pág. 413)

market demand/demanda de mercado demanda total de todos los consumidores por su producto o servicio (pág. 449)

market economy/economía de mercado sistema en que los individuos son dueños de los factores de producción y tomas decisiones económicas a través de libre interacción (págs. 416, 572)

market supply/oferta de mercado total de todas las tablas de oferta de todas las empresas que proveen el mismo bien o servicio (pág. 464)

mass media/medios masivos informativos mecanismo de comunicación masiva, incluyendo televisión, radio, periódicos, revistas, grabaciones, películas y libros (pág. 259)

master plan/plan maestro plan que establece una serie de metas y explica cómo el gobierno las llevará para satisfacer necesidades mientras cambian tras el tiempo (pág. 327)

mediation/mediación situación en que los oficiales del sindicato y de las empresas traen a un tercer partido para tratar de llegar a un acuerdo (pág. 489)

Medicare/Medicare programa gubernamental que proporciona el cuidado de la salud para los ancianos (pág. 544)

mercantilism/mercantilismo teoría que un país debería de vender más bienes a otros países que los que compra (pág. 33)

merger/fusión empresarial combinación de dos o más compañías para formar un solo negocio (pág. 505)

merit system/sistema meritorio empleo de personas para trabajos de gobierno basado en sus calificaciones (pág. 185)

metropolitan area/área metropolitana ciudad grande y sus alrededores (pág. 311)

migration/migración movimiento masivo de personas de un lugar a otro (pág. 22)

minority party/partido minoritario en el Senado y la Cámara de Representantes, el partido político al que pertenecen menos de la mitad de los miembros (pág. 140)

misdemeanor/delito menor ofensas menores como el vandalismo o el robo de artículos de poco valor (págs. 297, 349)

mixed economy/economía mixta sistema en el cual se combinan características de más de un tipo de economía (pág. 575)

modified union shop/taller sindical modificado convenio donde los trabajadores tienen la opción de unirse a un sindicato después de haber sido contratados (pág. 488)

monarch/monarca rey o reina (pág. 28)

monetary policy/política monetaria política que involucra cambiando el tipo del aumento del abasto de dinero en circulación con el fin de afectar el costo y la disponibilidad de créditos (pág. 531)

multinational/multinacional empresa que conducta negocios o tiene sucursales en muchos países (pág. 621)

national committee/comité nacional representantes de las 50 organizaciones partidarias estatales que conducen un partido político (pág. 223)

SPANISH GLOSSARY

national party chairperson/líder de partido nacional individuo elegido por el comité nacional que dirige las operaciones diarias de un partido nacional (pág. 223)

national security/seguridad nacional habilidad de mantener el país seguro contra ataques o daños (pág. 175)

natural monopoly/monopolio natural situación del mercado donde los costos de producción son minimizados teniendo a una sola empresa produciendo el producto (pág. 505)

natural resources/recursos naturales regalos de la naturaleza que hacen posible la producción (pág. 424)

naturalization/naturalización proceso legal para obtener la ciudadanía (pág. 14)

needs/necesidades requerimientos para supervivencia, tales como alimento, ropa y hogar (pág. 407)

newsgroups/grupos noticiarios foros de discusión en Internet (pág. 386)

nomination/nominación proceso por el cual partidos políticos eligen y ofrecen candidatos para puestos públicos (pág. 227)

nonpartisan/no partidario sin alianza o tendencia partidaria (pág. 385)

North American Free Trade Agreement (NAFTA)/Tratado de Libre Comercio de Norte América convenio de comercio diseñado para reducir las barreras arancelarias entre México, Estados Unidos y Canadá (pág. 569)

open market operations/operaciones de mercado libre compra o venta de obligaciones del gobierno de Estados Unidos y bonos del tesoro (pág. 532)

open primary/elección primaria abierta elección en que los votantes deben declarar su preferencia partidaria para votar por los candidatos de un partido (pág. 228)

opinion/opinión explicación detallada de la razón legal bajo la decisión de una corte en un caso (pág. 197)

opportunity cost/costo de oportunidad costo del mejor uso alternativo de tiempo y dinero eligiendo hacer una cosa en lugar de otra (pág. 411)

ordinance/ordenanza una ley, usualmente de una ciudad o país (pág. 308)

original jurisdiction/jurisdicción original la autoridad para ver casos por primera vez (pág. 196)

pardon/indulto declaración de perdón o de libertad de castigo (pág. 172)

Parliament/Parlamento legislatura británica (pág. 29)

parliamentary system/sistema parlamentario sistema de gobierno en que una asamblea elegida lleva las funciones legislativa y ejecutiva (pág. 592)

parole/libertad condicional garantizar a un prisionero su liberación temprana de prisión con ciertas restricciones (pág. 294)

partnership/asociación un negocio propiedad de dos o más personas (pág. 481)

patriotism/patriotismo el amor de una persona por su país (pág. 23)

payroll tax/nómina de impuesto impuesto en sueldos y salarios para financiar los costos del Seguro Social y Medicare (pág. 544)

peak/auge período de prosperidad en el ciclo comercial en el cual la actividad económica está en el punto más alto (pág. 509)

per capita GDP/percapita PDB producto doméstico bruto por persona (pág. 573)

petition/petición pedida formal para acción gubernamental; o un proceso por el cual los candidatos que no están afiliados con uno de los dos grandes partidos pueden postularse en la boleta de votación para la elección general en la mayoría de los estados (págs. 98, 229)

plaintiff/demandante una persona o partido llevando una demanda (págs. 298, 349, 364)

plank/punto cada declaración de la plataforma de un partido (pág. 222)

platform/plataforma una serie de declaraciones expresando los principios, creencias y posiciones en asuntos de elección de un partido (pág. 222)

plurality/pluralidad la mayor cantidad de los votos entre todos aquellos que son candidatos para un puesto político (pág. 228)

pocket veto/veto indirecto poder del presidente de derrotar un proyecto de ley si el Congreso no está en sesión dejando de firmárlo por diez días (pág. 161)

political action committee (PAC)/comité de acción política organizaciones políticas establecidas por corporaciones, sindicatos laborales y otros grupos de interés diseñados para apoyar a los candidatos contribuyendo con dinero (págs. 250, 272)

political appointee/nombrado político personas designadas por el presidente para puestos federales (pág. 185)

political machine/maquinaria política poderosa organización partidario que puede controlar las designaciones políticas y entregar votos (pág. 226)

political party/partido político una asociación de votantes con amplios intereses comunes que quieren influenciar o controlar decisiones en el gobierno eligiendo a los candidatos del partido a cargos públicos (pág. 218)

poll tax/capitación suma de dinero requerida de votantes antes de emitir su voto (pág. 112)

polling place/urna electoral lugar de votación (pág. 237)

pollster/encuestador especialista de quien el trabajo es conducir encuestas (pág. 261)

popular sovereignty/soberanía popular la noción de que el poder está entre la gente (pág. 89)

pork-barrel projects/*proyectos pork-barrel* proyectos y otorgaciones gubernamentales que benefician el distrito o estado natal (pág. 155)

Preamble/Preámbulo la primera sección de la Constitución (pág. 83)

precedent/precedente una opinión usada como la base para otra decisión judicial en un caso similar (págs. 28, 197, 347)

precinct/recinto un área geográfica que contiene un número específico de votantes (págs. 225, 237)

prime minister/primer ministro líder del ramo ejecutivo de un gobierno parlamentario (pág. 592)

print media/medios de comunicación impresos periódicos, revistas, cartas y libros (pág. 264)

prior restraint/restricción anterior censura gubernamental de material antes de ser publicada (pág. 268)

priorities/prioridades las metas que una comunidad considera más importantes o más urgentes (pág. 326)

private goods/bienes privados bienes que siendo consumidos por un individuo no pueden ser consumidos por otro (pág. 502)

private property rights/derecho de propiedad privada la libertad de poseer y usar nuestra propiedad como lo queramos sin interferir con los derechos de otros (pág. 435)

product market/mercado de productos mercado donde los productores ofrecen bienes y servicios en venta (pág. 429)

productivity/productividad el grado en que los recursos se usan eficientemente para producir bienes y servicios (págs. 430, 467)

profit/ganancia el dinero que recibe una empresa por sus productos o servicios que es más del costo (págs. 436, 464)

profit motive/motivo lucrativo la fuerza directiva que anima a los individuos y organizaciones a mejorar su buenestar material (pág. 436)

progressive income tax/impuesto progresivo sobre la renta impuestos que toman un porcentaje más grande de ingresos altos que de ingresos bajos (pág. 518)

propaganda/propaganda diseminación de ciertas ideas que puede involucrar mensajes engañosos diseñados para manipular la gente (págs. 247, 389)

property tax/impuesto de propiedad el impuesto sobre tierra y propiedad (pág. 550)

proposition/proposición petición pidiendo una nueva ley (pág. 242)

protectionism/proteccionismo política de restricciones comerciales para proteger industrias domésticas (pág. 611)

public agenda/agenda pública asuntos considerados más significativos por oficiales de gobierno (pág. 265)

public goods/bienes públicos bienes económicos que son consumidos colectivamente, tales como carreteras y la defensa nacional (pág. 502)

public interest group/grupo de interés público organización que apoya las causas que afectan las vidas de americanos en general (pág. 271)

public opinion/opinión pública las ideas y actitudes que la mayoría de la gente mantiene sobre oficiales electos, candidatos, gobierno y asuntos políticos (pág. 258)

public opinion poll/encuesta de opinión pública encuesta en que los individuos contestan preguntas sobre un asunto o persona particular (pág. 261)

public policy/política pública curso de acción que el gobierno conduce en respuesta a un asunto o problema (págs. 272, 324)

quota/cuota límite en la cantidad de bienes extranjeros importados (pág. 566)

racial profiling/perfil racial separar a un individuo como sospechoso dado a la apariencia de etnia (pág. 115)

ratify/ratificar votar aprobación (pág. 41)

rational choice/selección racional elegir la alternativa que tiene el mayor valor entre productos de calidad comparable (pág. 419)

real GDP/PDB real PDB después de los ajustes por la inflación (pág. 509)

recall/revocación elección especial en que los ciudadanos pueden votar para sacar a un oficial público de su cargo; situación en que una compañía saca su producto del mercado o acuerda cambiarlo para hacerlo seguro (págs. 242, 506)

recession/recesión parte del ciclo comercial cuando el producto de una nación no aumenta por seis meses por lo menos (pág. 509)

recycling/reciclar volver a usar materiales viejos para hacerlos nuevos (pág. 335)

referendum/referéndum una manera para que los ciudadanos voten para leyes locales y estatales (pág. 242)

rehabilitate/rehabilitar corregir el comportamiento de una persona (pág. 376)

remand/remisión mandar un caso de regreso a una corte menor para ser tratado nuevamente (pág. 197)

repeal/revocar cancelar una ley (pág. 34)

representative democracy/democracia representativa un gobierno en que los ciudadanos escogen un grupo pequeño para gobernar en su representación (pág. 10)

reprieve/suspensión orden para retardar el castigo de una persona hasta que una corte mayor pueda ver el caso (pág. 172)

reserve/reserva cierto porcentaje de depósitos que los bancos tienen que apartar en sus propias cajas fuertes o como depósitos en su distrito del Banco de la Reserva Federal (pág. 532)

reserved powers/poderes reservados poderes que la Constitución no da al gobierno federal que son retenidos por los estados (pág. 283)

resources/recursos dinero, gente, y materiales disponibles para cumplir con las metas de una comunidad (pág. 326)

responsibility/responsabilidad obligación que llenamos voluntariamente (pág. 120)

returns/resultados votaciones y resultados de una elección (pág. 238)

revenue/ingreso la renta que el gobierno cobra por el uso público (pág. 398)

rider/cláusula adicional enmienda poco relacionada asumida al proyecto de ley (pág. 159)

right-to-work laws/leyes del derecho de trabajo leyes estatales prohibiendo a los sindicatos de forzar a los trabajadores a unirse (pág. 488)

roll-call vote/votación por nómina método de votar en el Senado en el cual los miembros expresan sus votos en turno (pág. 161)

rule of law/reglamento de ley la ley aplica a cada uno aún a aquellos que gobiernan (pág. 90)

runoff primary/elección primaria de desempate segunda elección primaria entre los dos candidatos que reciben la mayor cantidad de votos en la primera elección primaria (pág. 228)

sales tax/impuesto de ventas recaudación de impuesto en un producto al momento de su venta (pág. 549)

SPANISH GLOSSARY

sanction/sanción medida tal como la retención de asistencia económica para influenciar las acciones de un gobierno extranjero (pág. 625)

satellite/satélite nación política y económicamente dominada por otro país más poderoso (pág. 626)

saving/ahorros apartar el ingreso por un período de tiempo para que pueda ser usado después (pág. 441)

savings account/cuenta de ahorros cuenta en que los clientes reciben intereses basados en la cantidad de dinero que han depositado (pág. 535)

savings and loan association (S&L)/asociación de ahorros y préstamos instituciones financieras que tradicionalmente prestaban dinero a personas comprando casas (pág. 526)

scarcity/escacez no tener suficientes recursos para producir todas las cosas que quisiéramos tener (pág. 407)

search warrant/orden de búsqueda orden de la corte permitiendo a la policía buscar en la casa o negocio del sospechoso y tomar artículos específicos como evidencia (págs. 103, 355)

segregation/segregación separación social de las razas (pág. 113)

seniority/antigüedad años de servicio (pág. 144)

separation of powers/separación de poderes división de autoridad entre los ramos legislativo, ejecutivo y judicial (pág. 91)

services/servicios trabajo hecho por una persona para otra persona (pág. 424)

shortage/déficit situación en que la cantidad demandada es mayor a la cantidad oferta (pág. 472)

slander/difamación mentiras que perjudican la reputación de una persona (pág. 101)

social responsibility/responsabilidad social obligación de las empresas para perseguir metas que benefician a la sociedad tanto como a ellos mismos (pág. 494)

Social Security/seguro social programa federal que proporciona pagos mensuales a personas jubiladas o que están incapacitadas para trabajar (pág. 544)

socialism/socialismo sistema económico en que el gobierno es propietario de algunos factores de producción y distribuye los productos y salarios (pág. 574)

soft money/*soft money* donaciones dadas a partidos políticos y no designados para la campaña de elección de un candidato en particular (pág. 249)

sole proprietorship/propiedad exclusiva negocio propio y operado por una sola persona (pág. 480)

solid waste/deshecho sólido nombre técnico de basura (pág. 334)

special district/distrito especial unidad de gobierno que trata una función específica, tal como educación, suministro de agua o transportación (pág. 310)

special-interest group/grupo de interés especial organización de gente con algún interés en común que trata de influenciar decisiones del gobierno (pág. 158)

specialization/especialización cuando personas, negocios, regiones, o naciones se enfocan en bienes y servicios que ellos pueden producir mejor que nadie (pág. 431)

spoils system/sistema de despojos gratificando a gente con puestos gubernamentales por su apoyo político (pág. 185)

standard of living/norma de vida el bienestar material de un individuo, grupo o nación según el grado de satisfacción de sus necesidades y lujos (pág. 427)

standing committees/comité permanente comité permanente que continúa su trabajo de una sesión a otra (pág. 143)

stare decisis/stare decisis la práctica de utilizar opiniones judiciales anteriores como base para decidir casos (págs. 209, 352)

statute/estatuto ley escrita por un ramo legislativo (pág. 347)

stock/acciones compartición de propiedad de una corporación (pág. 482)

stockholder/accionista individuo que ha invertido en una corporación y posee algunas de sus acciones (pág. 483)

strike/huelga paro intencionado de trabajo por los trabajadores para forzar al empresario a satisfacer sus demandas (pág. 489)

strong-mayor system/sistema de presidente municipal fuerte tipo de gobierno, usualmente para ciudades grandes, en que el presidente municipal tiene fuertes poderes ejecutivos (pág. 308)

subsidize/subvencionar ayudar o promover con dinero (pág. 551)

subsidy/subvención pago gubernamental a un individuo, negocio, o grupo por ciertas acciones (pág. 468)

substitute/substituto productos competitivos que los consumidores pueden usar en lugar de otro (pág. 454)

suffrage/sufragio derecho a votar (pág. 111)

summons/requerimiento judicial noticia dirigiendo a alguien para presentarse en la corte para responder a una queja o un cargo (pág. 365)

supply/oferta cantidad de bienes y servicios que los productores pueden y están dispuestos a vender a varios precios durante un período específico (pág. 462)

supply curve/curva de oferta línea inclinada hacia arriba que gráficamente demuestra las cantidades ofertas a cada precio posible (pág. 463)

supply elasticity/elasticidad de oferta sensibilidad de la cantidad oferta a un cambio en el precio (pág. 469)

supply schedule/tabla de oferta gráfica demostrando cantidades ofertas a diferentes precios posibles (pág. 463)

surplus/excedente situación en que la cantidad oferta es mayor que la cantidad demandada; situación en que el gobierno gasta menos que lo que colecta en ingresos (págs. 472, 553)

tariff/tarifa derecho de aduana; impuesto sobre un artículo importado (pág. 566)

tax return/reporte de impuestos reporte anual entregado al gobierno local, estatal o federal detallando el ingreso ganado y los impuestos debidos (pág. 543)

technology/tecnología método o proceso utilizado para hacer bienes y servicios (pág. 467)

terrorism/terrorismo el uso de la violencia contra ciudadanos para lograr un gol político (pág. 23)

SPANISH GLOSSARY

testimony/testimonio la declaración que un testigo hace bajo juramento (pág. 372)

third party/tercer partido un partido que reta a los dos grandes partidos (pág. 219)

Three-fifths Compromise/Compromiso de tres quintos acuerdo estipulando que personas esclavizadas valdrían tres quintos de una persona para determinar la representación en el Congreso (pág. 57)

tolerance/tolerancia respetando y aceptando a otros a pesar de sus creencias, prácticas, o diferencias (pág. 123)

torts/agravios actos equivocados por los cuales un partido perjudicado tiene el derecho de demandar (pág. 350)

totalitarian/totalitario sistema en que el control del gobierno se extiende a casi todos los aspectos de la vida de la gente (pág. 589)

town/pueblo unidad política que es más grande que una villa y más pequeña que una ciudad (pág. 315)

town meeting/junta municipal asamblea de ciudadanos locales para discutir y votar en asuntos importantes (pág. 316)

township/municipio subdivisión de un condado que tiene su propio gobierno (pág. 317)

trade déficit/déficit comercial situación donde el valor de los productos importados por un país excede el valor de su exportación (pág. 570)

trade sanction/sanción comercial esfuerzo para castigar a otra nación imponiendo las barreras comerciales (pág. 177)

trade surplus/comercio excedente situación donde el valor de los productos importados por un país excede el valor de su importación (pág. 570)

trade-off/sustitución cambiando una cosa por el uso de otra (pág. 410)

traditional economy/economía tradicional sistema económico donde las decisiones de qué producir, cómo, y para quién están basadas en costumbres o hábitos (pág. 578)

transparency/transparencia proceso de hacer más visibles para todos los tratos comerciales (pág. 493)

treaty/tratado acuerdos formales entre los gobiernos de dos o más países (pág. 177)

tuition vouchers/vale educativo programa proporcionando subvenciones para pagos educativos permitiendo a las familias la opción de mandar a estudiantes a escuelas privadas (pág. 331)

two-party system/sistema bipartita sistema de gobierno en que dos partidos compiten por el poder (pág. 218)

unemployment rate/taza de desempleo porcentaje de gente en la fuerza laboral civil que no están trabajando pero están buscando trabajo (pág. 510)

unicameral/unicameral legislatura de una cámara (pág. 287)

union shop/taller sindicalizado compañía que requiere que los nuevos empleados se unen al sindicato después de un período específico de tiempo (pág. 488)

unitary system/sistema unitario gobierno que da todos los poderes claves al gobierno central (pág. 597)

unlimited liability/responsabilidad ilimitada requerimiento que un propietario que es personalmente y enteramente responsable por todas las pérdidas y deudas de un negocio (pág. 481)

utility/utilidad el placer, utilidad, o satisfacción de un producto para el consumidor (pág. 450)

veto/veto rehusar a firmar un proyecto de ley o resolución (págs. 161, 618)

voice vote/voto en voz alta método de votar en que aquellos a favor dicen "Sí" y aquellos en contra dicen "No" (pág. 161)

voluntary exchange/intercambio voluntario acto en que compradores y vendedores libre y voluntariamente se comprometen en transacciones comerciales (pág. 436)

volunteerism/voluntarismo práctica de ofrecer tiempo y servicios a otros sin sueldo (pág. 126)

wants/deseos cosas que nos gustaría tener tales como entretenimiento, vacaciones, y otros artículos que hacen la vida cómoda y agradable (pág. 407)

ward/distrito varios recintos juntos que forman una unidad electoral más grande (pág. 225)

warranty/garantía promesa hecha por un manufacturero o vendedor para reparar o remplazar un producto dentro de cierto período si está defectuoso (pág. 440)

weak-mayor system/sistema de presidente municipal poco poderoso tipo de gobierno en que el presidente municipal tiene poderes ejecutivos limitados (pág. 308)

Web site/página de web "hojas" en la Malla Mundial que pueden contener textos, fotos, sonido y video (pág. 384)

welfare/bienestar salud, prosperidad, y felicidad de los miembros de una comunidad (pág. 126)

winner-take-all system/sistema ganador-toma-todo sistema en que el candidato que gana el voto popular en un estado generalmente recibe todos los votos electorales del estado (pág. 243)

Women, Infants, and Children (WIC) program/programa para mujeres, infantes y niños programa que proporciona asistencia para la nutrición y cuidado de la salud para mujeres de bajos recursos, infantes y niños hasta la edad de 5 (pág. 517)

workfare/trabajo requerido programas que requieren que los que reciben asistencia pública contribuyan con algo de su trabajo a cambio de beneficios (pág. 517)

World Bank/Banco Mundial agencia internacional que hace préstamos a países en desarrollo (pág. 580)

World Trade Organization (WTO)/Organización Mundial del Intercambio organización internacional que supervisa el intercambio entre naciones (pág. 569)

World Wide Web/Malla Mundial operando a través del Internet, ésta permite a los usuarios interactuar con los billones de documentos almacenados en computadoras a través de la red (pág. 384)

writ of habeas corpus/escrito de hábeas corpus orden de la corte requiriendo que la policía traiga a un prisionero a la corte para explicar por qué tienen detenida a la persona (págs. 150, 353)

SPANISH GLOSSARY

INDEX

INDEX

INDEX

INDEX

INDEX

Acknowledgments

Glencoe would like to acknowledge the artists and agencies who participated in illustrating this program: Morgan Cain & Associates; MapQuest.

Photo Credits

Cover PhotoDisc; **iv–v** Joseph Sohm/CORBIS; **ix** (l)A. Ramey/Woodfin Camp & Assoc., (r)Bettmann/CORBIS; **vi–vii** Joseph Sohm, ChromoSohm Inc./CORBIS; **x** Bob Daemmrich/Stock Boston/PictureQuest; **xi** (l)North Wind Picture Archives, (r)Bettmann/CORBIS; **xxiv** AP/Wide World Photos; **xxv** (l)Marilyn Humphries/The Image Works, (r)AP/Wide World Photos; **2–3** Joseph Sohm, Visions of America/CORBIS; **4–5** Paul A. Souders/CORBIS; **6** Bridgeman Art Library; **7** AP/Wide World Photos; **8** Tony Freeman/PhotoEdit; **9** ©Tribune Media Services; **10** AP/Wide World Photos; **11** Peter Miller/Photo Researchers; **12** Joseph Sohm, ChromoSohm, Inc./CORBIS; **13** AP/Wide World Photos; **14** AP/Wide World Photos; **16** Bettmann/CORBIS; **18** AP/Wide World Photos; **19** Bettmann/CORBIS; **20** (t)Bettmann/CORBIS, (l)John Lei/OmniPhoto Communication, (r)John Lei/OmniPhotoCommunication; **21** Courtesy family of Mai Payia Vang; **22** (l)Thomas E. Franklin/Bergen Record/SABA/CORBIS, (r)AP/Wide World Photos; **24** (t)Kevin Fleming/CORBIS, (c)AFP/CORBIS, (b)Joseph Sohm, ChromoSohm, Inc./CORBIS; **25** Culver Pictures, Inc.; **26–27** Paul A. Souders/CORBIS; **28** North Wind Picture Archives; **29** (t)Stock Montage, (b)Bettmann/CORBIS; **31** House of the Delegates, State Capitol, Richmond VA; **32** (t)Private Collection, (b)Jeff Albertson/Stock Boston; **33** (l)Culver Pictures, (r)North Wind Picture Archives; **35** (l)The Library of Congress, (r)Peabody-Essex Museum, Salem MA; **36** (l)Bettmann/CORBIS, (r)Michael Nicholson/CORBIS; **37** The Library of Virginia; **38** The Library of Congress; **39** Mark Burnett; **40** Eric P. Newman; **41** Picture Research Consultants; **42** Mark Burnett; **43** file photo; **44** CORBIS; **46** (t)CORBIS, (b)Bettmann/CORBIS; **48** file photo; **49** Boltin Picture Library; **50–51** Bettmann/CORBIS; **52** Culver Pictures; **53** Hulton Archive/Getty Images; **54** Art Resource, NY; **55** North Wind Picture Archives; **56** CORBIS; **57** National Archives; **58** North Wind Picture Archives; **59** ©The New Yorker Collection 1994 J.B. Handelsman from cartoonbank.com. All rights reserved; **61** (l)Library of Congress, (r)Wes Thompson/The Stock Market; **62** White House Historical Assoc.; **63** PhotoDisc; **64** CORBIS; **66** Boltin Picture Library; **68** file photo; **76** IRS; **78** White House Historical Assoc.; **79** CORBIS; **80** Time, Inc.; **81** Sandy Schaeffer/TimePix; **82** North Wind Picture Archives; **83** (l)New York Historical Society, (r)Reuters/Kevin Lamarque/Archive Photos; **84** Joseph Sohm, Visions of America/CORBIS; **89** North Wind Picture Archives; **90** PhotoDisc; **91** Reuters, (r)Joseph Sohm/CORBIS; **92** Dave Bartruff/CORBIS; **94** (t)North Wind Picture Archives, (b)Joseph Sohm/ Chromosohm, Inc.; **96–97** Bettmann/CORBIS; **98** PhotoDisc; **100** (l)AP/ Wide World Photos, (r)David H. Wells/CORBIS; **102** Rachel Epstein/ PhotoEdit; **103** CORBIS; **104** FPG International; **105** Bettmann/CORBIS; **106** Carl Hubenthal; **108** Bettmann/CORBIS; **109** CORBIS; **113** Flip Schulke/CORBIS; **114** Collection of David J. & Janice L. Frent; **116** (t)Jonathan Nourok/PhotoEdit, (c)Penelope Breese/Liaison, (b)Bruce Roberts/Photo Researchers; **118–119** Joseph Sohm, ChromoSohm, Inc./ CORBIS; **120** Kim Kulish/CORBIS/SABA; **123** Courtesy family of Travis Gregory; **124** AP/Wide World Photos; **125** Reuters NewMedia Inc./CORBIS; **126** Edwards/Whig-Standard/Rothco; **127** AFP/CORBIS; **128** (l)AFP/CORBIS, (r)Reuters NewMedia Inc./CORBIS; **131** (t l)file photo, (r)D. Frazier, (b)Courtesy ALCOA; **132** The Library of Congress; **134–135** Joseph Sohm/CORBIS; **136–137** Joseph Sohm, Visions of America/CORBIS; **138** AP/Wide World Photos; **139** Bettmann/CORBIS; **143** (l)Mark Ransom, (r)AP/Wide World Photos; **144** AP/Wide World Photos; **146** Najlah Feanny/Stock Boston; **147** (l)The Military Picture Library/CORBIS, (r)AP/Wide World Photos; **148** (l)Official Senate Photo/CNP/Getty Images, (r)Bettmann/CORBIS; **150** Getty Images; **151** CORBIS; **152** Rex Banner/Getty Images; **153** AFP/CORBIS; **154** Courtesy family of Diana Bhaktul; **156** AFP/CORBIS; **157** Win McNamee/Reuters; **158** US Capitol; **159** Getty Images; **160** (l)Courtesy House of Representatives, (r)PhotoDisc, (b)AFP/CORBIS; **162** Dennis Brack/Black Star Publishing/PictureQuest; **164–165** Reuters NewMedia Inc./CORBIS; **166** AP/Wide World Photos; **167** David J. & Janice L. Frent Collection/CORBIS; **171** Hulton Archive/Getty Images; **174** The Library of Congress; **175** John Elk III/Stock Boston; **176** (l)Reuters NewMedia Inc./CORBIS, (r)AP/Wide World Photos; **177** AP/Wide World Photos; **178** AP/Wide World Photos; **179** Getty Images; **180** AP/Wide World Photos; **182** Getty Images; **183** AP/Wide World Photos; **184** Courtesy family of Haamid Johnson; **186** (t)Hulton/Archive, (c)Reuters NewMedia Inc./CORBIS, (b)AP/Wide World Photos; **188–189** Steven P. Widoff for TIME; **190–191** PhotoDisc; **192** Seattle Post-Intelligencer Collection, Museum of History & Industry/CORBIS; **194** Reuters NewMedia Inc./CORBIS; **196** AP/Wide World Photos; **197** Mark Burnett/Stock Boston; **198** AP/Wide World Photos; **199** (l)Fabian Falcon/Stock Boston, (r)Bettmann/CORBIS; **200** Crandall/The Image Works; **201** Steve Breen/Copley News Service; **202** Bettmann/CORBIS; **203** The Supreme Court Historical Society; **207** Paul Conklin/PhotoEdit; **209** (l)Bettmann/ CORBIS, (r)Getty Images; **210** Cartoonist & Writers Syndicate; **211** Liza Biganzoli, NGIC; **212** (l)Bob Daemmrich/Stock Boston, (r)Kelly-Mooney Photography/CORBIS; **214–215** Joseph Sohm/Photo Researchers; **216–217** AFP/CORBIS; **218** Bridgeman Art Library; **219** Bettmann/CORBIS; **220** AP/Wide World Photos; **221** Jacques M. Chenet/CORBIS; **223** Brooks Kraft/CORBIS Sygma; **224** Courtesy family of Sandra Valasquez; **225** (t)Democratic National Committee. All rights reserved, (b)Republican National Committee. All rights reserved; **227** AP/Wide World Photos; **228** Collection of David J. & Janice L. Frent; **229** Michael Newman/PhotoEdit; **230** ©Tribune Media Services, Inc. All rights reserved. Reprinted with permission; **231** Ed Frascino/The Cartoon Bank; **232** (t)Najlah Feanny/Stock Boston, (b)JonathanNourok/PhotoEdit; **233** Hulton/Archive/Getty Images; **234–235** Reuters NewMedia Inc./CORBIS; **236** Bob Daemmrich; **238** Courtesy family of Carl Jaramillo; **239** (l)Bob Daemmrich, (r)AP/Wide World Photos; **241** Getty Images; **242** Dave Granlund ©2000 *Metrowest Daily News;* **245** AP/Wide World Photos; **246** CORBIS; **247** Doug Martin; **248** Bettmann/CORBIS; **251** Rod Joslin; **252** (t)Bob Daemmrich/Stock Boston, (c)D. Young-Wolff/PhotoEdit, (b)AP/Wide World Photos; **253** Bernard Schoenbaum/ The New Yorker Collection; **254** (t)Charles Bennett/AP, (bl)Steve Kelley/Copley News Service, (br)Courtesy TIME; **255** (t)Stuart Ramson, (c)Carlos Puma/*The Press-Enterprise,* (bl)Vincent Lerz/AP, (br)Courtesy TIME; **256–257** Todd Gipstein/CORBIS; **258** Bettmann/CORBIS; **259** (l)A. Ramey/PhotoEdit, (r)James Nubile/The Image Works; **261 263** AP/Wide World Photos; **264** David Young-Wolff/PhotoEdit; **265** (t)AP/Wide World Photos, (b)NBC Photo; **266** (l)Hulton Archive/Getty Images, (r)Najlah Feanny/Stock Boston; **267** Federal Communications Commission; **270** Frank Siteman/Omni-Photo Communications; **271** Reuters NewMedia Inc./CORBIS; **272** Chester Commodore, courtesy *Chicago Defender;* **273** Bettmann/CORBIS; **276** AP/Wide World Photos; **278–279** Carl & Ann Purcell/CORBIS; **280–281** Zane Williams/Getty Images; **282** Steven Sutton/Duomo/ CORBIS; **283** (l)Uniphoto, (r)Staff Sgt. Jack Holt/Getty Images; **287** AP/Wide World Photos; **288** Neal Graham/Omni-Photo Communications; **289** AP/Wide World Photos; **290** Philip Gould/ CORBIS; **291** Bob Daemmrich/Stock Boston/PictureQuest; **292** AP/Wide World Photos; **293** Darren McCollester/Getty Images; **295** Steve Greenberg, courtesy *Seattle Post-Intelligencer;* **296** Robert C. Shafer/Folio; **297** www.fccourts.org; **299** (t)Courtesy Montana Governor's Office, (b)Courtesy Ruth Ann Minner; **300** (l)P. Vadnai/CORBIS Stock Market, (r)Richard Cummins/CORBIS; **301** John Chiasson/Getty Images; **302** (l)John Elk III/Stock Boston, (r)Joseph Sohm/Stock Boston; **304–305** Joseph Sohm, ChromoSohm, Inc./CORBIS; **306** Courtesy Mayor Jeffrey Dunkel; **307** Courtesy John C. Liu; **310** Steve Breen/Copley News Service; **312** Courtesy Commissioner Tom Bayla; **313** Mark Burnett; **314** AP/Wide World Photos; **315** CORBIS; **316** (l)CORBIS, (r)AP/Wide World Photos; **317** Courtesy family of Mary Rao; **318** AP/Wide World Photos; **320** (t)AP/Wide World Photos, (b)Joseph Sohm, ChromoSohm, Inc./CORBIS; **322–323** Billy Hustace/Getty Images; **324** Robert Dowling/CORBIS; **325** AP/Wide World Photos; **326** Juana Gutierrez; **327** (l)Per-Anders Pettersson/Getty Images, (r)Alexander Lowry/Photo Researchers; **328** file photo; **329** Columbus Committee for UNICEF; **330** A. Ramey/Stock Boston; **331** Jerry Barnett; **332** A. Ramey/Stock Boston; **334** Kevin R. Morris/CORBIS; **335** (l)James Prince/Photo Researchers, (r)Simon Fraser/Northumbrian Environmental Management Ltd./Science Photo Library/Photo Researchers; **336** Courtesy family of Brooke Crowther; **337** AFP/CORBIS; **340–341** YBSHY/CORBIS; **342–343** Joseph Sohm, ChromoSohm, Inc./CORBIS; **344** Photri; **346** Bettmann/CORBIS; **347** The Image Works; **348** Mark Burnett; **349** Courtesy family of Alicia & Lara Miramontes; **350** (l)Keith Chapman/Check Six/PictureQuest, (r)John De Waele/Stock Boston; **352** Bettmann/CORBIS; **353** Vince Streano/CORBIS; **354** A. Ramey/PhotoEdit; **355** Michael Newman/PhotoEdit; **356** A. Ramey/ Woodfin Camp & Assoc.; **357** © The New Yorker Collection 1995 Arnie Levin from cartoonbank.com. All rights reserved; **360** (t)Doug Martin/Photo Researchers, (c)Jeff Cadge/Getty Images, (b)AP/Wide World Photos; **362–363** Lindsay Hebberd/CORBIS; **364** Mark Burnett; **365 368** John Neubauer/PhotoEdit; **369** Gerd Ludwig/Woodfin Camp & Assoc.; **370** ©The New Yorker Collection 1996 J.B. Handelsman from cartoonbank.com. All rights reserved; **374** Bettmann/CORBIS; **375** John Neubauer/PhotoEdit; **376** AP/Wide World Photos; **377** Bob Daemmrich; **379** PhotoDisc; **380** (t)Richard Lord/PhotoEdit, (b)Spencer Grant/ PhotoEdit; **382–383** Rudi VonBriel; **384** Joseph Sohm/CORBIS; **385** Photo Researchers; **389** Tony Freeman/PhotoEdit; **390** AP/Wide World Photos; **391** Bob Daemmrich; **392** Courtesy family of Emily Wistar; **393** © Tribune Media Services, Inc. All rights reserved. Reprinted with permission; **394–396** AP/Wide World Photos; **397** Courtesy emeagwali.com; **398** AP/Wide World Photos; **400** Sion Touhig/Getty Images;

402–403 Bettmann/CORBIS; 403 file photo; 404–405 Bob Torrez/Getty Images; 406 David R. Frazier; 407 (l)Chris Anderson/Aurora, (r)Herb Snitzer/Stock Boston; 409 Reprinted with special permission of King Features Syndicate; 410 Richard Gilbert/Unicorn Stock Photography; 411 Aaron Haupt/Stock Boston; 412 Catrina Genovese/Omni-Photo Communications; 413 Les & Viola Van/Unicorn Stock Photography; 416 Joe Raedle/Newsmakers; 417 Courtesy family of Barbara Brown; 418 (t)AP/Wide World Photos, (b)AP/Wide World Photos; 420 (t)Aneal V. Vohra/Unicorn Stock Photography, (b)AP/Wide World Photos; 422–423 Joel Satore/NGIC; 424 AP/Wide World Photos; 425 Mark E. Gibson/Unicorn Stock Photography; 426 PhotoDisc; 428 AP/Wide World Photos; 430 Ed Kashi/CORBIS; 431 Mickey Siporin, courtesy *Newark Star-Ledger;* 433 Museum of the City of New York/CORBIS; 434 Hulton Deutsch/Woodfin Camp & Assoc.; 435 AP/Wide World Photos; 436 Tomas del Amo/Index Stock; 438 Courtesy family of Richard Hecker; 439 Spencer Grant/Stock Boston; 441 Aaron Haupt/Stock Boston/Picturequest; 443 Frank Siteman/PhotoEdit; 444 (t)Eric R. Berndt/Unicorn Stock Photography, (b)Tony Page/Getty Images; 446–447 Michele Burgess/Stock Boston; 448 Aaron Haupt; 452 John Eastcott/Yva Momatiuk/Woodfin Camp & Assoc.; 454 Illustrator: H. Mitchell; 455 (l)Peter Southwick/Stock Boston, (r)Joan Slatkin/Omni-Photo Communications; 456 Tom Engelhardt; 458 (t)Jonathan Nourok/PhotoEdit, (b)Mike Yamashita/Woodfin Camp & Assoc.; 460–461 Vladimir Pcholkin/Getty Images; 462 Susan Lapides/Woodfin Camp & Assoc.; 465 Courtesy Sidney Harris; 466 AP/Wide World Photos; 467 Fabian Falcon/Stock Boston; 471 Sam C. Pierson Jr./Photo Researchers; 473 Courtesy family of Dan & Betsy Nally; 474 AP/Wide World Photos; 476 (t)Matthew McVay/Stock Boston, (r)Jeff Greenberg/Omni-Photo Communications, (b)Pictor; 478–479 Catherine Karnow/Woodfin Camp & Assoc.; 480 Hazel Hankin/Stock Boston; 482 Pictor; 483 Courtesy family of Michael Chait; 486 Michael A. Dwyer/Stock Boston; 487 Arthur Rothstein/CORBIS; 488 Bettmann/CORBIS; 490 Bettmann/CORBIS; 491 Courtesy University of Colorado at Boulder; 492 James L. Amos/CORBIS; 493 ©The New Yorker Collection 1992 Dana Fradon from cartoonbank.com. All rights reserved; 494 Reuters NewMedia Inc./CORBIS; 495 Bettmann/CORBIS; 496 (t)James P. Dwyer/Stock Boston; (b)Stephen Frisch/Stock Boston; 498–499 CORBIS; 500–501 John Elk III/Stock Boston; 502 AP/Wide World Photos; 503 (l)Jacques M. Chenet/CORBIS, (r)AP/Wide World Photos; 504 Felicia Martinez/PhotoEdit; 505–510 AP/Wide World Photos; 512 Dick Locher ©Tribune Media Services, Inc.; 514 Mark Burnett/Stock Boston; 515 Lawrence Migdale/Stock Boston; 516 PhotoDisc; 517 CORBIS/PictureQuest; 519 CORBIS; 520 (t)Reuters NewMedia Inc./CORBIS, (b)Gary Conner/PhotoEdit; 522–523 Gail Mooney/CORBIS; 524 www.commem.com; 525 Brooks/Brown/Photo Researchers; 526 Aaron Haupt; 529 Rob Crandall/Stock Boston; 530 Louis Psihoyos/Matrix; 531 AP/Wide World Photos; 533 Thaves/*The Cincinnati Post;* 534 Laura Dwight/CORBIS; 535 Bob Daemmrich/Stock Boston; 536 AP/Wide World Photos; 538 (t)Russell D. Curtis/Photo Researchers, (c)Mark Burnett/Stock Boston, (b)AP/Wide World Photos; 540–541 Michael Dwyer/Stock Boston; 542 CORBIS; 543 NASA/Science Photo Library/Photo Researchers; 545 CORBIS; 547 *Jacksonville Journal Courier*/The Image Works; 548 Bob Daemmrich/Stock Boston; 549 Barrie Fanton/Omni-Photo; 553 Reuters NewMedia Inc./CORBIS; 554 Owen Franken/CORBIS; 556 Courtesy family of Ruchit Shah; 557 Bob Thaves; 558 (t)James L. Amos/CORBIS, (b)Larry Mulvehill/Photo Researchers; 560–561 Robert Holmes/CORBIS; 562–563 National Geographic Society; 564 Kevin Fleming/CORBIS; 565 Martyn Goddard/CORBIS; 566 Steve McBride; 567 Jean-Claude N'Diaye/Imapress/The Image Works; 569 Reuters NewMedia Inc./CORBIS; 572 575 AFP/CORBIS; 576 Dave G. Houser/CORBIS; 577 (l)Amelia Kunhardt/The Image Works, (r)Michael S. Yamashita/CORBIS; 578 Maggie Lear; 579 581 Reuters NewMedia Inc./CORBIS; 582 (t)Gary Conner/PhotoEdit, (b)AP/Wide World Photos; 584 Bettmann/CORBIS; 585 (t)Wolfgang Kaehler/CORBIS, (cl)Paul Almasy/CORBIS, (cr)Bob Krist/CORBIS, (bl)Reuters NewMedia Inc./CORBIS, (bc)Charles O'Rear/CORBIS, (br)©EBAY INC.; 586–587 AFP/CORBIS; 588 AP/Wide World Photos; 589 (l)AP/Wide World Photos, (r)AFP/CORBIS; 592 AP/Wide World Photos; 594 The Library of Congress; 595 Reuters NewMedia Inc./CORBIS; 597 Cleve Bryant/PhotoEdit; 599 M.E. Newman/Woodfin Camp & Assoc.; 601 Bohemian Nomad Picturemakers/CORBIS; 603 Courtesy family of Suzie Greenman; 604 Walt Handelsman; 606 (t)David & Peter Turnley/CORBIS, (b)Brian Yarvin/Photo Researchers, Inc.; 608–609 Burstein Collection/CORBIS; 610 AFP/CORBIS; 612 Courtesy family of Everett Law; 615 Steve Sack/Courtesy *Minneapolis Star-Tribune;* 617 AFP/CORBIS; 618 file photo; 620 A. Ramey/Stock Boston; 622 David & Peter Turnley/CORBIS; 623 (t l)AP/Wide World Photos, (r)Reuters NewMedia Inc./CORBIS; 624 AP/Wide World Photos; 625 Reuters NewMedia Inc./CORBIS; 626 AP/Wide World Photos; 628 (t)Reuters NewMedia Inc./CORBIS, (b)Michael A. Dwyer/Stock Boston; 632 Burstein Collection/CORBIS; 635 Mark Burnett; 637 Anthony Saint James/Retna Ltd, USA; 640–642 AP/Wide World Photos; 654–658 White House Historical Association; 659 North Wind Picture Archives; 660–662 Bettmann/CORBIS; 663 National Portrait Gallery/Smithsonian Institution, Art Resource; 664 (l)Mark Burnett, (r)Smithsonian Institution; 665 (l)file photo, (r)Mark Burnett; 666 (t)The Museum of the American Indian, NY, (b)CORBIS; 668 669 CORBIS; 670 Flip Schulke/Black Star; 671 Missouri State Historical Society; 672 CORBIS; 673 Bettmann/CORBIS.